THE POLITICAL COMMUNITY

A Comparative Introduction to Political Systems and Society

HARMON ZEIGLER

Philip M. Phibbs Distinguished Professor
of American Politics

University of Puget Sound

Longman

New York & London

The Political Community

Copyright © 1990 by Longman
All rights reserved.
No part of this publication may be reproduced,
stored in a retrieval system, or transmitted
in any form or by any means, electronic, mechanical,
photocopying, recording, or otherwise,
without the prior permission of the publisher.

Longman, 95 Church Street, White Plains, N.Y. 10601

Associated companies:
Longman Group Ltd., London
Longman Cheshire Pty., Melbourne
Longman Paul Pty., Auckland
Copp Clark Pitman, Toronto

Senior editor: David J. Estrin
Development editor: Elsa van Bergen
Production editor: Marie-Josée A. Schorp
Cover design: José L. Almaguer
Text art: Vantage Art, Inc.
Production supervisor: Priscilla Taguer

Library of Congress Cataloging-in-Publication Data

Zeigler, L. Harmon, 1936–
    The political community : a comparative introduction to political
    systems and society/Harmon Zeigler.
        p.   cm.
    Bibliography: p.
    Includes index.
    ISBN 0-582-28499-6
    1. Comparative government.   I. Title.
JF51.Z45   1990
320.3—dc20   89-12518
                                                              CIP

ABCDEFGHIJ-HA-99 98 97 96 95 94 93 92 91 90

To Pat, who locked one door,
and Irving who did not lock another.

Contents

Preface

In the Epilogue I write, "We are living at a propitious moment." Indeed, we are. Without telegraphing too much of the plot, I urge you to consider some evidence of change in political lives and institutions. In March, 1989, Soviet voters—for the first time not facing a completely rigged choice—voted against several dozen Communist Party leaders; a month later, Mikhail Gorbachev sacked 100 members of the Central Committee—including Andrei Gromyko, a legendary symbol of the Cold War. The Central Committee endured more "involuntary" turnover in a couple of months than has the American Democratic Party in the House of Representatives in three decades! The Communist party, also known as the "vanguard of the proletariat," was obviously less esteemed than its leaders assumed. Leadership isolation is not a unique problem. Generally elites are far more apt to believe life is satisfactory than are masses.

What *is* remarkable is that once totalitarian parties, admittedly with fits and starts and with the outcome very much in doubt, are giving up *some* of their power. Westerners easily apply the term "democratic" to any process which seems superficially so. In the case of the USSR, the intent is to keep the Communist Party in its leadership role, but with *intra*-party competition enhanced. Far less democratic than a genuinely competitive electoral system, the USSR experiment was intended to channel dissatisfaction and hence avoid the tragedy that befell China.

In China, simultaneously with the Soviet election, students, mourning the death of a prominent reformer, demanded—in massive demonstrations—more "democracy" (most admitted that they had no idea what the word meant, merely that it was not what the party espoused). The brutal suppression of these demonstrations in the summer of 1989 by the presumably pragmatic factions of the party showed the futility of the search for stability without legitimacy. Even so, China may not be able to return completely to its totalitarian past. One cannot demonstrate—a political act—but one can still listen to Beethoven, which was not the case a few years ago. Yet there is not now, nor has there ever been, much enthusiasm for the accoutrements of democracy, even among non-Marxists.[1]

In Poland at the same time, the party leadership agreed to face up to the possibility of defeat by sanctioning relatively open elections. Although Poland's rulers had crushed a revolt in 1981, they ultimately gave in to the trade union Solidarity. But surely the party did not anticipate humiliating defeat. Solidarity candidates won all but nine of the parliamentary seats they contested; seats automatically allocated to the Communist went unfilled in 294 out of 299 cases, since the majority of voters scratched their names off the ballot (thus denying them the required 50 percent). In the summer of 1989, Solidarity entered the Polish parliament as the first elected opposition in a Communist country.

In the latter part of 1989, the world witnessed Czechoslovakians engaged in unprecedented street demonstrations, nationwide strikes, and refusal to compromise on their demands for the radical diminution of the role of the Communist Party. The prelude to all this was the fall, or at least the fissure of, the wall that had separated the Germans. The dust has not settled, but one of the ideas explored in the following chapters emerges: The integration of culture and political institutions is a powerful drive. Decades of superimposed ideology are ultimately a poor substitute.

While other less ideologically committed autocracies—Chile, for instance—also gave every indication of accepting a more open system, it is to the citadel of Marxism, the Soviet Union, where totalitarianism began, that the eyes of the academic world have turned. For there (where Lenin once proclaimed that "National wars against the imperial powers are not only possible and probable; they are inevitable, progressive, and revolutionary"), socialism's end was declared by Gorbachev, who defined the once rigid ideology as a belief in "dignity among men." Truly we are all socialists now.

Those of us, most I assume, who were not there when the totalitarian revolution began are fortunate to be here when it ends. To political scientists such rare events, the beginnings and endings of revolutions, are like Halley's comet. They do not come along, as do elections, almost every day. The upheavals in the USSR and its European allies have the additional advantage (to scholars, not politicians) of rekindling interest in federalism, a subject almost forgotten except among Americanists. The surge of nationalism in Ukraine, Latvia, Lithuania, Estonia, and Georgia reminds us again of its potency.

Less apparent changes, ignored by the ubiquitous television, add yet more excitement: the United States slipped, virtually unnoticed, into economic decline, becoming a borrower rather than a lender, fueling its addiction to the "world's highest standard of living," with an ever increasing foreign debt. Its political process disabled by excessive fragmentation, the United States' model of the political and economic process seems as isolated as does, say, Cuba's. The United States' grand experiment—separation of powers, checks and balances, federalism (combined with more recent innovations such as presidential primary elections, political action committees, or "iron triangles")—is as outmoded as is Marxism.

None of these changes happened "overnight." But the opportunity presented by them seemed too good to pass up. Be warned that "change," "flux," and "transformation" are to the political scientist what "root canal" is to a dentist: gold. When I speak of change I do *not* mean utopia. The switch in the USSR from a command to a mixed economy will make that country less impoverished and less belligerent. The deterioration of the American political process will make *that* country less internationally competitive, economically. But human nature does not change and the fundamental *structure* of the political process is stable. Elites rule masses; the rationale, not the process, changes. The original totalitarian revolutions—and those that followed—did not substitute community for individuality, equality for oppression. The current changes will be equally *incremental* but equally significant.

Walking the corridors at conventions, schmoozing with editors and colleagues had convinced me that (1) the time was right for an introductory book that was "ironic;" and (2) that I could write it, having coauthored *The Irony of Democracy* through eight or so editions. Irving Rockwood, then editor at Longman, and later private consultant (who probably figured I owed him one for the couple of dogs with which I saddled him), originally enticed me. Irving deserves the annual Nerves of Steel Award for not expiring (and for not bouncing me) at an early meeting in New York which I—for reasons too complex to recount here—was neither intellectually, physically, nor emotionally in any shape to attend. By lunch (at the *Algonquin* . . . excellent soft-shelled crabs), Jerry Manheim (a friend and colleague who was advising Longman on the project) had managed to—discreetly—tell me just how bad my first efforts were (as if I needed to know!) and to slip me an outline to guide me in a new start. I often wonder if Irving's decision to, as they say, "pursue other opportunities," was somehow related to this experience.

Shortly thereafter, David Estrin became editor and—in 1985 at *Antoine's* in New Orleans—reaffirmed his and Longman's commitment. A year or so later, lunching at *Place Pigalle* in Seattle (where David tasted Washington's superb "microbeers" and declared them to be superior to those of England), he found one of the strengths of the manuscript to be its propensity for providing "new data for old questions." This, it seemed to me, was what I had intended. So I finished it. Upon receiving the final draft, my editor and friend (still!) wrote, "It has been a long road . . ." And how! It seemed like a good idea at the time.

These days, publishers are wont to talk about "market segmentation" and "product differentiation." "Market segmentation" means that there is no "market leader." The market for introductory texts is said to be segmented. Maybe, but so is political science, judging from the extant introductory texts. "Product differentiation" means, as one might surmise, making your "product" different (but not *too* different, since publishers always have one eye cocked toward the curriculum).

I am pleased to report that, at no time during the writing of this book, did anybody at Longman use these loathsome phrases. Presumably Longman does not believe that only books which match up with the exact needs of a market survey should be published; either that, or the company has poor judgment. Let me tell why I think the former explanation makes more sense. Here is what I set out to do:

1. To lay out the differences between individualist and collectivist theories, cultures, and politics;
2. To write as much about "the view from the streets" as about the view from the top (that is, to describe everyday life as well as elite decisions);
3. To be eclectic, using sources and ideas often overlooked (Eastern ideologies such as Confucianism, fiction and music to encapsulate culture);
4. To describe the *consequences* of theories as well as their *intent;*
5. To ask questions for which there is no ready answer;

6. To impose new data on old questions;
7. To teach skepticism.

Although these ambitions appear to be straightforward, they conceal the internecine warfare of our discipline. The first point requires that I use "the t-word" (totalitarianism). I do so unself-consciously not because of any silly ideological dispute but because (1) totalitarian governments are becoming scarce and hence, need to be understood in the event they enjoy a resurgence of elite support, and (2) that they existed at all, however briefly, is testimony to man's irrational bent. One might study the Chinese custom of binding women's feet or the Muslim tradition of female circumcision with the same combination of fascination and horror.

Of the remaining points, teaching skepticism might strike many of you as wanting an explanation. Simply put, in politics as in life, things are rarely as they seem. People yearn for, and politicians (joined on occasion by gullible academics) supply simple answers to complex questions. This book, whatever else it might do, does not lend credence to the American addiction to easy conspiracy theories or to single-cause explanations. It interweaves two themes, point and counterpoint: the conflict between *individualism* and *collectivism* and the tension between the *public* and the *private*. The two are, of course, inextricably intertwined. In 1989, when a woman was brutally beaten and raped in New York's Central Park by a group of teenagers who did it for fun ("wilding," as they said), explanations abounded. But one comment seemed unusually captivating to the student of political theory and behavior: "Something has gone wrong in our balance of individualism and community—our obligations to one another are being attacked by exaggerated devotion to self."[2] Does life imitate art? Among the comments about this act of harsh—even for New York—brutality, comparisons with the Anthony Burgess novel and movie, *A Clockwork Orange* (discussed in Chapter 1), abounded. Those who watched Malcolm MacDowell humming "Singin' in the Rain" while he performed his acts of "ultraviolence" find "wilding" an apt phrase. The balance between individualism and collectivism is a recurrent theme in this book. The "wilding" episode's explanations ranged from those who follow Rousseau and Marx (socialization, alienation) to modern Hobbesians ("Call them savages, black savages.")[3]

As a *leitmotif,* the book suggests that much of what appears to be change is illusion, that there are *constants:* elites rule masses and resources are unequally distributed. No government has ever altered these fundamental "laws" and none ever will. This view is against empty rhetoric and sloganeering; it is against ideology. David Mamet, American playwright, has a character in Speed the Plow say, "Why are nickels bigger than dimes? Because that's the way it is."

The structure of the book is as follows:

1. Chapter 1. Here the main themes of the book are set forth: individualism versus collectivism and public politics in contrast with private politics.
2. Chapter 2. This chapter addresses one of political science's most elusive problems: the interaction of culture and political life.
3. Chapters 3, 4, 5, and 6 cover the origins, structure, and performance of polyarchies (or democracies).

4. Chapter 7 describes that most pervasive of forms of government, authoritarianism. A fundamental distinction is made between authoritarian government and

5. Totalitarian government, the subject of Chapters 8 and 9. As the name indicates, totalitarian governments seek total control, an improbable aspiration but one which has wreaked havoc in our century.

    The themes, individualism and collectivism, public and private, are carried through from the *least* to the *most* intrusive types of polities.

6. In Chapter 10, revolution and its consequences (how polities are changed and for what) leads into the two last empirical chapters.

7. Chapters 11 and 12 are about public policy, political economy, and the seeming inability of governments to accomplish their goals.

8. I conclude with the obligatory Epilogue in which I argue that ideologies, especially inclusive and deeply felt ones, are serious impediments to our ability to understand—and hence presumably accept or try to change—our personal and public political arenas.

The structure and certainly the tone of the book are less conventional than many publishers or editors would have preferred. As noted above, I have used a more heterogenous collection of sources than is usual. I want to suggest a *unity* of knowledge. When C. P. Snow, English scientist and novelist, wrote of ''the two cultures'' (science and literature, art, and music, and so on), his own career belied his lament that cultures were too disparate to connect. The fusion should borrow from both cultures. Scientists need the insecurity imposed upon them by philosophy, the social sciences, and the humanities. Social scientists need the neutrality and rigor required of natural scientists. One obvious example of this is Thomas Hobbes's oft-quoted assertion that without the Leviathan (a powerful, autocratic central government) life is ''solitary, poor, nasty, brutish, and short.'' What a golden opportunity for empirical theory! One can ''operationalize'' these terms and actually *find out*. Thus, my wish to impose new data upon old questions is associated with my respect for *both* cultures. Two old friends, Heinz Eulau and John Orbell, fathered and nourished my commitment to theory and data; Orbell on Hobbes, and Eulau on Edmund Burke, stand as models of scholarship.

David Estrin, who encouraged my inclinations, is, miracle of miracles, an editor because he loves books; he *reads* them; he *read* my manuscript. We talk about ideas (and about baseball and wine). He is, in the truest sense, an intellectual, and thus keeps me from adding ''intellectual editor'' to my growing list of oxymorons (bottled beer, decaffeinated coffee, short-sleeved dress shirts, and so on). Surely, his colleagues in the ''biz'' regard him as an antediluvian throwback and scorn him as they head for the latest seminar on ''making a thin market fat'' or some such (today books, tomorrow condos). The operative appellation for such folk is ''belly editor'' (since they spend most of their time paying for—and eating—food). Don't misunderstand me. Estrin and I share an interest in food (one glance at either of us dispels any contradictory notion).

But there is more. Others at Longman associated with this project picked up the boss' perverse habits: they too read. Elsa van Bergen gave each revision a *microscopic* read, not just for style, but also for content and logic. Her exhaustive reviews were, simply, among the finest editorial work I have encountered in about three decades of writing. Is she the best? There are none better (there is one, Ellen Brownstein at ''another publisher,'' who ties her first place). Jerry Manheim did the same. I know it sounds trite, but I could not have written the book if Jerry had not gotten me on track, eliminating several dead ends, and keeping me pointed in the approximately right direction. There is more here than meets the eye, since the first drafts were truly awful. During the last stages of the project, Marie-Josée Schorp applied her sense of humor and mediated between me and copy editors. Anybody who can plow through this much that often is either dedicated or driven. My debt to these fine people is immense.

At the University of Puget Sound, my colleague Arpad Kadarkay acquainted me with the Marx–Shakespeare connection (Marx could quote Shakespeare's major tragedies from memory). David Berg proved to be sufficiently compulsive, running down the errant note, and—most importantly—working up the questions which end each chapter (he, with a student's eye, seemed a logical choice). It is a tribute to the quality of the University of Puget Sound's students that Berg wrote questions considered by Longman to be ''too complex for the average student.'' True enough: UPS students are *not* average. Among the students here who read and evaluated the manuscript, Kelley Dock, Kathy Dragoo, and David Quast earn my gratitude. Al DeMarco collected and organized much of the statistical information with admirable tenacity. Dan Hansen worked up much of the data for Chapter 10. Elin and Charlie, two good friends, kept the level of discourse affable. In retrospect, I enjoyed writing the book; I learned a lot about politics and about myself. I learned that some publishers do indeed care about ideas, and that some colleagues are remarkably generous with their time.

Harmon Zeigler
Philip M. Phibbs Distinguished Professor
Department of Politics and Government
University of Puget Sound
Tacoma, WA 98416

NOTES

1. See Andrew J. Nathan, *Chinese Democracy* (New York: Alfred A. Knopf, 1985), pp. 225–232.
2. Richard Reeves, ''Not Just Drugs, Race or Poverty, but America,'' *Seattle Post Intelligencer*, May 5, 1989, p. 11.
3. Ibid.

CHAPTER 1

The Idea of the Polity

Ed Marcus; reprinted with permission of the Marcus family.

GOVERNMENT IN THE FAMILY OF ORGANIZATIONS

"Who gets what, when, how." That's a definition of politics by one of the most distinguished practitioners of political analysis, Harold Lasswell. Politics is no more than an effort to achieve goals or interests. When, as is usually the case, our interests are seemingly in conflict with someone else's, those who impede our progress must be made to stop.

This sounds like a primal drive. But consider the results of a survey from 1988:[1]

How Important Is Politics in Our Lives?

Very important	12%
Somewhat important	41%
Not very important	30%
Not at all important	16%
Don't know	1%

Another recent questionnaire revealed that most Americans do not know what a deficit is, do not know where Nicaragua is, and do not have even primitive levels of information about politics:[2]

Know majority party in the House of Representatives	51%
Know representative from own legislative district	32%
Know name *and* party of representative from own district	25%

Do you find this lack of information shocking? Before recoiling in horror, answer a few questions yourself:

To which part of the paper do you turn first? Sports? Comics? Horoscope?
Do you *read* a paper regularly?
Rank the following in order of your concern:
    Making good grades
    Achieving peace in Nicaragua
    Pledging the right fraternity/sorority
    Getting a good job
    Passing trade legislation that encourages international competition
    Reducing the federal deficit
    Housing the homeless
    Improving your appearance
    Combating drug use

If you are like most students, you now realize how little you care about "politics," although you care very much about achieving personal goals. Success and failure in the private sector can be the cause of major changes in individual lives. A person may care very much about the outcome of a presidential election, but probably not as much as about the outcome of a custody hearing. A person may worry about Soviet influence in Latin America, but surely this would pale beside concern about overextended personal indebtedness.

Often students of politics forget how involved our lives are with everyday matters. Consider the Western response to Mikhail Gorbachev's dramatic efforts to move the Soviet Union away from a centrally planned, closed society toward a more individualistic one—the *glasnost* ("openness") and *perestroika* ("restructuring") efforts that made Gorbachev an international media star. Proposals for reform—the release of political prisoners, the cessation of the jamming of Western radio programs (Voice of America, Radio Free Europe), the efforts to introduce market forces into the economy, the dramatic declaration that the USSR no longer wished to impose its system on other nations—were justifiably proclaimed as major changes in Soviet policy. But the average Soviet citizen is not a political dissident: very few Soviet citizens have seen a gulag (labor camp) or given much thought to the exile of Alexander Solzhenitsyn (anti-Communist author whose works were prohibited in the USSR until 1990). What has changed for the average person? As the tumultuous year 1988 drew to a close, extreme food shortages were still common, and lines were longer than ever. Because the glasnost is indeed what it claims, we can read a letter from a man in a village in the Ural Mountains. "Recently, all you hear is perestroika, glasnost. But what has changed? Why is sugar rationed? Why are school uniforms rationed, shoes expensive and wages low?"[3] What has changed is that even the Soviet press, accustomed to intoning the glories of socialism and the evils of capitalism, complains: "By turns or in combinations, towels, toothpaste, toilet paper, lotion, sugar, and electric bulbs have disappeared from the shelves. Now, you cannot buy detergent and cheap soap. What will it be tomorrow?"[4]

Soviet citizens, like their counterparts elsewhere, paid scant attention to the rise and fall of various factions in the Gorbachev surge for power; they paid much more attention to the absence of soap and the price of vodka. As the 17th-century philosopher Thomas Hobbes wrote, "A plain husband-man is more Prudent in the affaires of his own house, than is a Privy Counselor in the affaires of other men."[5] People pay attention to matters that they can influence to some degree. Commenting on growing apathy among voters in France, an executive of the Gallup research firm saw this as normal distancing of the people from the political: "There is a big difference between the state of mind of the politicians and [that] of the citizens."[6]

What the surveys and observations reveal is that most people do not rank *public* politics, which is what they generally mean by the term *politics,* among their primary interests. All politics (the who using the how to get the what, when) involves power and decision making (even if the decision is ultimately not to decide); the thing that sets public politics apart is that it hinges on decisions that are applicable universally—they are authoritative, not dependent on personal compliance. In our example of life in Russia, two political systems are at work: the public politics of openness, of reform, and the private politics of lines and shortages. Ignorant of public politics, and feeling they wouldn't make a difference in policymaking, Soviet citizens are wise to the ways of private politics (Whom do you bribe to get a better cut of meat? What does the butcher at the state store need that you have? How can you get hard currency from tourists who do not know that the official exchange rate is vastly inflated?). The focus of this book is public politics, and we need to understand governmental power and relate to it; one place to start is in the realm of the private.

Political Power in Our Lives

Virtually every aspect of our lives is centered around an organization. We work, usually for an organization, and may belong to unions or occupational groups. Much of our recreation is organizational, whether we play in or support a club, team, or league. If we are active in "politics," it is within the framework of a formal association. An individual may have many associations, each competing for a piece of the total available loyalty, time, and money. Most of these organizations are voluntary; a few are compulsory.

To some degree, each organization constrains behavior as a condition of participation. Smaller "primary" groups, such as families, usually are more constraining than larger "secondary" organizations; that is, we feel more intimately involved with and indeed interrelated to family members and can see immediately the effects of our behavior. Large organizations that capture an essential portion of individual life, such as the company where one works to bring home the bacon, are more constraining, have more control over us than peripheral or optional groups, such as bowling teams. The most overarching and compulsory and powerful of all organizations is government.

All the associations in our lives are political in that they provide settings for the struggle for power: they are arenas of cooperation, compromise, demand, response, threat. Power is the capacity to affect people's conduct through the real or threatened use of rewards or punishments. Individuals, groups, private associations, and governments all exercise power by offering people things they want (or threatening to remove them): these things are the *power base*. Power bases may be physical safety and health, wealth, jobs, means to a livelihood, prestige, love, self-respect, food. Later in this chapter we will survey what governments offer when a man in the street asks, "What's in it for me?"

Power can rest on various bases, but these tend to be interdependent. People who control certain power bases have a leg up in controlling others. Wealth and political influence, in the United States and other developed countries, are not unrelated. In industrial societies, power is exercised by large institutions—governments, corporations, schools, the military, churches, newspapers, television networks, and so on. C. Wright Mills, an American student of power, wrote: "No one can be truly powerful unless he has access to the command of major institutions, for it is over these institutional means of power that the truly powerful are . . . powerful."[7]

Power is never distributed equally. Even though formal rules may insist on equal distribution of power ("one man, one vote"), political life—public and private—produces winners and losers. Power is thus a relationship, not an entity. A hermit has no political power.

Power is the resource of politics. It is finite, and it is scarce. In economic markets, the resource—money—is quite different, in that you and I can both get more simultaneously. Put another way, in economics, not all games are zero-sum games; in politics, most are.

Distinctions between Public and Private

When we think of politics—meaning public politics and government action—we tend to think in terms of ''we'' and ''they.'' But how private is the ''we''? The politics of everyday life may be easier to focus on and master, but that does not mean that public politics is disconnected from everyday life. In fact, the distinction between public and private is not very clear—not in individualistic societies like ours, and certainly not in collective ones, where the good of all is put above the good of each. Matters once assumed to be private are less so under conditions of crowding, scarcity, and international tension. The brutality with which families have been limited and separated in mainland China is *public* policy made necessary by a high rate of population growth. The personal consequences of a public decision may be tragic, but the public consequences may be a rising standard of living.

The personal decision to abandon the traditional family (male breadwinner and female homemaker) for more equitable divisions of labor is a choice with substantial public consequences, such as demand for day-care centers and comparable worth (equal pay for equal work regardless of gender). European countries provide for child care and pregnancy leave, and some have legislated against corporal punishment. Thus the family may be a primary group in our lives, but it is no longer private, as its structure has political consequences. State control over family is one example of governmental response to change, and the decline of the traditional family is a moderate example of the blurring of public and private. Various nations have responded in ways appropriate for their governmental structure, and the result has been a politicization of family life.

Even in the most benign of circumstances, therefore, ''public'' and ''private'' can be meaningless categories. Virtually every private act can have public consequences; the greater the will and ability of the state to intervene, the more totalitarian or all-controlling it becomes. The differences between governments are matters of *degree*. The difference between public and private is often determined not by the subject matter of an issue but by the manner in which it is resolved.

The mechanisms of public and private politics—the effort to gain and assert power—may be marginally similar, but, as we noted, the authoritative nature of public choices makes them fundamentally different. For example, if you violate the rules of a private organization, you may be expelled, but you will not be imprisoned. If you become disenchanted with your family, you can move away or get a divorce. Private politics allows compliance to be a matter of personal choice; public politics imposes compliance indiscriminately. Governments possess a legal monopoly on the use of force and are the only organizations that can impose decisions on other organizations. The American government can require the American Medical Association to cease excluding chiropractors from hospitals. The American Medical Association may try to influence this decision—by pressure, campaign contributions, public relations, and the like—but it must comply with the government's decision.

THE ORIGINS AND PURPOSES
OF GOVERNMENT: TWO VIEWS

Governments are institutions that possess the ultimate political authority. Although most governments consist of formal institutions, such as legislatures, political parties, and executives, they need not. Institutions are the legitimation, or formalization, of ways of interacting. Modern governments are formally organized because of their complexity. However, when such governments ''break down,'' they are replaced by less formal institutions. In Lebanon, no formally constituted government is able to command allegiance, but the residents of Beirut are nevertheless governed by gangs of militia. Ultimately, these informal arrangements give way to formal authority. Governments exist because there is no alternative. Anarchists (people who believe that all governmental authority is oppressive and illegitimate) have themselves formed organizations to further their belief (as in Russia prior to the revolution). The debate as to whether governments are indispensable evils or engines of self- and social improvement is central to political theory.

Self-interest and Individualism:
The Genesis of Hobbes's Theory

People who believe that human beings are basically selfish also argue that governments exist to prevent violence and destruction. Without governmental authority, we would resort to endless and deadly struggles for power, and the strongest, the most clever, and the most ruthless would tyrannize the weak. The inhabitants of this ''state of nature'' would find life so unbearable that they would welcome a stable government, no matter how authoritarian. Thomas Hobbes (1588–1679), an early promulgator of this pessimistic assessment of human nature, used the idea of a state of nature as a deliberate fiction (such as the Garden of Eden), a speculation about humanity before (or after) society. People, according to this view, are governed by passion more than reason. They seek self-aggrandizement above all, are incurably selfish, and are relentless in the pursuit of their own self-interest. People are not by nature political (in the public sense) or social.

Hobbes's theories were a profound break with the traditions of Western political theory. ''Man is a political animal,'' wrote Aristotle (384–322 B.C.), a notion that went unchallenged until Hobbes 1,800 years later. As we will see in Chapter 3, the tradition of the ancients argues that the *polis* (the Greek word for political community, for which no accurate English translation exists) was the perfect, the *only* mode of life. The notion of *individualism,* the idea that there is a sphere of life that is not the business of the state, came from Hobbes. The tradition is explained by Harry Jaffa:

> It makes no more sense to say that the *polis* exists for the citizen, or the citizen for the *polis,* than to say that the mind exists for the man or the man for the mind. . . . The means-end relationship we predicate of state and individual does not subsist between man and *polis,* and all inferences which assume such a relationship are false.[8]

This is not to say that governments before the 20th century actually paid much attention to ''private'' matters, for they did not; rather, people were left alone (as long as they were obedient) because it rarely occurred to rulers that there was any good reason not to do so. We must wait for modern collectivism to encounter the belief that man exists for the state.

Hobbes, the modern pessimist, believed that in the state of nature,

> men live without other security, than what is their own strength, and their own invention shall furnish them withal. In such condition there is no place for industry; because the fruit thereof is uncertain: and consequently no culture of the earth, no navigation, no use of the commodities that may be imported by sea; no commodious building; no instruments of moving and removing such things as require much force; no knowledge of the face of the earth; no account of time; no arts; no letters; no society; and which is worst of all, continual fear, and danger of violent death; and the life of man solitary, poor, nasty, brutish, and short.[9]

Hobbes was born a few years before the death of Queen Elizabeth I, at a time when English military power became paramount. His was one of the ghastliest periods of English history, dominated by the struggle between parliament and the Stuart kings, culminating in the bloody civil war of 1642–1649 (with the beheading of Charles I), the establishment of a republic under Puritan Oliver Cromwell, the restoration of the monarchy in 1660, and the reassertion of parliamentary supremacy during the so-called Glorious Revolution of 1688. Hobbes was of an abstract and scientific bent; he believed in the neutral analysis of information and behavior rather than in ideology. But he nevertheless asserted that the fundamental purpose of political theory was the avoidance of "calamities," the most serious of which was civil war.

In the context of the aberrant events of his time, Hobbes developed his notion of an *exchange* between the individual and the government. In exchange for security, subjects yield to the absolute power of the government. Hobbes assumed that the job of the government was to provide safety, order, and protection against invasion. If the government did these things, any resistance to or subversion of its authority could justifiably be repressed. If the government did not keep its part of the bargain, its citizens could replace it with one that would.

Although Hobbes argued for obedience, the most memorable portion of his theory is the idea of the exchange, the *social contract*. Sometimes regarded as a legitimator of totalitarian rule, Hobbes's ideas got him into trouble with both sides in the civil war. Neither king, Lord Protector (Cromwell), nor Parliament had any *unchallengeable* right to rule, according to these theories. The right to rule lasted as long as the social contract was kept; neither the divine right of kings nor any other legitimating doctrine other than the contract interested Hobbes. When it became apparent that the monarchy was going to lose, Hobbes, fearing for his life, fled to Paris; published his most remarkable work, *Leviathan* (in London); and presented a copy to the fugitive Charles II of England whom Hobbes tutored in mathematics. Charles was so outraged by the idea of the social contract that Hobbes felt it prudent to return to London and live as inconspicuously as he could. With the restoration of the monarchy, Charles II returned to England, forgave Hobbes and put him on retainer (making him one of the world's first consultants). The essence of his thought—that the state exists for the individual—would be developed into the central concept of modern democratic governments.

Modern scholars use the term *Hobbesian* to describe the belief that humans are "naturally" violent and driven to satisfy primitive longings. For example, Erich Fromm, attacking the German "instinctivist" Konrad Lorenz, calls his work a "Hobbesian cliché." [10] Hobbes believed that people are neither "good" nor "bad" but are simply prisoners of their urges. Hobbes, who was raised in sheep country, portrayed man as a "wolf" in regard to his fellow competitors; the wolf in the tale "Little Red Riding Hood" is a good embodiment of the Hobbesian view of humanity.

Hobbes's grim view of people moved by "appetites and aversions" led him to support powerful governmental authority as the only alternative to chaos. Modern authoritarian governments do not cite this in their defense, although Hobbes himself thought democracy a very bad idea. (Before discovering geometry, he studied the classics at Oxford and attributed his distrust of democracy to Thucydides, the historian of the Peloponnesian War and the end of Athenian democracy). Hobbes's followers seized on his idea of the social contract, that governments that failed to protect their subjects had broken the contract and hence lost their legitimacy. By stressing the contractual nature of the relationship between citizens and government, John Locke (1632–1704) influenced the authors of the American Declaration of Independence. Adopting Hobbes's argument that only the honoring of the contract made a government legitimate, Locke challenged the prevalent values of the time that monarchies ruled by divine right. Like Locke, Spinoza (1632–1677), Montesquieu (1689–1755), and David Hume (1711–1776) developed and expanded Hobbes's ideas.

Hobbes and his followers were thorough rationalists. Hobbes himself was more attracted to Francis Bacon and Galileo than to historians; his bent was toward *empiricism* (the belief that knowledge is derived from experience), even though his state of nature was a philosophical trick (the even more radically empirical Hume attacked the social contract on the grounds that people are in fact constrained by culture and habit to stay where they are, irrespective of the ability of an existing government to comply with the contract). Government—the contract—was based purely on *rational self-interest*.

The Nature of the State: A Collectivist View from Rousseau

The reaction to this cold logic came with romanticism in literature, music, and art. Its apogee in political theory was reached by Swiss-born Jean-Jacques Rousseau (1712–1778). His view of the state of nature was one of an idyllic paradise populated by cooperative people, naturally good, who were seduced into giving up their innocence by civilization and its attendant institutions of corruption, including government. "Man was born free, but everywhere he is in chains," Rousseau lamented. No government, no matter how benevolent, was preferable to the natural community in the state of nature. In Hobbes's state of nature one imagines endless violence, but Rousseau believed that "men are not naturally enemies." [11] The two views could not be more opposite.

In Rousseau's scheme of things, the government itself could make life "solitary, poor, nasty, brutish, and short." His view of 18th-century European government was consistent with his view of human nature: European monarchies were repressive and should be discarded—not because they had failed to protect their subjects but because they had corrupted them. Certainly no more repugnant example of the corruption of monarchies could be found than in the reign of Louis XV, who governed France during most of Rousseau's life. His predecessor, Louis XIV, had exhausted a once prosperous country with wars whose only purpose was the acquisition of more thrones and more territory. Louis XV had no territorial ambitions, merely a desire to continue the tradition of absolutist exploitation. His favorite courtesans, Mesdames du Barry and de Pompadour, were quite influential in the decadent politics of the day. His successor, Louis XVI, was beheaded during the French Revolution, in 1793.

Not surprisingly, Rousseau preferred his romantic state of nature, where naturally good people frolicked happily, to the insidious court politics and total disregard for mass welfare that characterized 18th-century France. His writing, like his life, was incoherent and poorly organized. He suffered from a common form of schizophrenia, which caused him to assume that his friends (for example, David Hume, who, despite their differences, respected Rousseau's genius) were his enemies. However, one does not need to be schizophrenic to resent the injury that broke forever the rhythm of his life. Walking in Paris, which lacked sidewalks, people were occasionally trampled by horses pulling royal carriages. Initially, (human) runners were engaged to shoo people out of the way, but Great Danes were found to be more effective at clearing men and women out of the path of the onrushing carriage. Rousseau was set upon by just such a Great Dane—engaged in its task of clearing a path for its master's carriage—and knocked to the ground by the beast. He remained unconscious for several minutes. He never recovered from the shock. No wonder he judged civil society to be aberrant! Could a humane civilization regard human life as so superfluous?

Rousseau's most influential work was *The Social Contract,* and he has occasionally been lumped together with the English social contract theorists. However, Rousseau's theories on the origin of the state and on the initial contract posited a far less rational and far less revocable contract than did the theories of Locke or Hobbes. He regarded people in a state of nature more as happy, lazy children than as shrewd, self-maximizing strategists.

Rousseau made no distinction between the state and the "community." Communities are groups to which individuals feel a sense of belonging, commitment, or obligation. Communities are more *inclusive* than mere groups, whose attraction for an individual is *particularistic.* We may join an occupational, recreational, or political group in anticipation of an explicit benefit, but commitment to a community is accompanied by the expectation that *all* needs (even those of which we are unaware) will be honored. For the individual, the antithesis of community is *alienation,* a sense of rootlessness. Thus the state as community does far more than protect life or property; it provides for the achievement of true individual happiness.

It does so, Rousseau contended, by means of the *general will.* This general will was not like "decision rules" that aggregate individual preference, such as majority rule (see Chapter 3). The general will was not the sum of all individual wills and hence could not be observed through devices to solicit individual preferences, such as elections. (Rousseau called opinions obtained in that way the "will of all.") The general will need not be legitimated by the number of people who share an opinion. The will of all could be wrong, no matter how many people share the opinion; by contrast, the general will may be right, even if but a single (enlightened) person ascertains it. People frequently do not know what is in their true best interest, and the good state is not beholden to expressions of popular will.

Ideology and the People

In our discussion of the distinction between public and private politics, we noted that most people know and care little about public politics. Would it not be strange if the common folk nevertheless had clear, consistent views of the good political life? Are those Rousseaus and Hobbeses among the people? Surprisingly, many scholars believe that there are. Accustomed to reading political theory and to organizing their thoughts along logically consistent lines, they assume that those with other interests are nevertheless sophisticated. But mass ideology is largely the response to *symbols*. For example, George Bush is said to have won the American presidency in 1988 because he exposed his opponent, Michael Dukakis, as a "liberal." The strategy was thought to be clever because only about one-fourth of the electorate identifies itself as "liberal." But majorities of the electorate cannot provide a definition of the term, and during a one-hour interview, 40 percent of them switched (that is, when asked later on in the interview they were conservative or liberal, they gave a response opposite to their initial one).[12]

One American government text states, "The least educated people are most likely to hold the Marxist ruling class view." *This is sheer poppycock.* How can the authors deduce it? If you argue that Marxism is a belief that political power follows economic power, you have no problem. Uneducated people are more likely to believe in the "economic dominance" model than the "pluralist" model.

Certainly majorities in the United States believe that "they" (that is, corporations and "the rich") "really run the country."[13] Is this Marxism? In fact, all the systematic research concludes that Marxism—even in a surrogate form—is far removed from the symbolic values of the common man in America. Even larger majorities believe that the free enterprise system is fair and does not lead to poverty; that economic competition leads to better performance, and that private ownership of property is crucial to the good of society.[14]

You definitely have to pick and choose to call these respondents Marxists. Further, the apparent inconsistency between believing that "the rich" *really* run the show and a notwithstanding commitment to "the system" is typical of mass attitudes. Fully three-fourths of those who had unfavorable attitudes toward the profit system had *favorable* attitudes toward property rights![15]

As McClosky and Zaller explain:

> no strictly logical considerations can explain why someone who believes in the sanctity of private property should also believe in business competition, unlimited private profits, and sharply stratified pay differentials. *These ideas, however, have been linked for at least two centuries as part of the capitalist creed. Hence insofar as an individual organizes his beliefs with respect to the principals of capitalism, he ought to exhibit fairly consistent support for (or opposition to) such values as private property, competition, and the profit system.*[16]

But "the less sophisticated members of the general public obviously exhibit little consistency in their response."

The "people" are

> more likely to make sweeping antidemocratic or anticapitalist statements . . . , but given the inconsistencies reflected in the attitudes they express, it is difficult to believe they are consciously rejecting capitalism and democracy out of conviction or principle. . . . It is highly unlikely that their views . . . are tied together as part of a well-developed and historically sanctioned belief system."[17]

Appropriately, the people know their limitations better than enthusiastic minorities do (see Table 1.1). To carry the logic to the extreme, the people can be said to be followers of Rousseau and the collectivists, since there is agreement that they are poor judges of what is best in public politics. No will of all can be found among the people. Here, then, is the collectivist answer to Hobbes: there can be no social contract because people do not know what is good for them. If they do not know what is good for them, how can they hold rulers accountable?

How the State Meets Its Obligations

Despite numerous variations, Hobbes's and Rousseau's starkly contrasting views of human nature and the purpose of government remain largely intact. The Hobbesian view leads to limited government, with a stress on the value of the individual, while the view linked to Rousseau's idea leads to an argument in favor of the value of the community. Rousseau's followers relied on the portion of his thought that stressed the goodness of communal living to argue that government could educate, could teach the virtues of collective life. The individualist tradition asks, "How can we channel natural self-interest into public good?" The collectivist tradition asks, "How can we eliminate self-interest?"

Modern Marxist governments (such as those in Cuba, China, and the Soviet Union) find much in Rousseau to applaud. Such governments believe, like Rousseau, that factional conflict is destructive of the common will, and rather than channel it, they seek to suppress it. Instead of two or more political parties, there is one. Instead of competitive elections, the general will is determined by an enlightened, or politically correct,

TABLE 1.1 Statements about Popular Wisdom

	General Public		Active Influentials	
	Agree	Disagree	Agree	Disagree
The main trouble with democracy is that most people don't really know what's best for them.	52%	48%	41%	59%
Most people don't have enough sense to pick their own leaders wisely.	48%	52%	28%	72%
"Issues" and "arguments" are beyond the understanding of most voters.	62%	38%	38%	62%

SOURCE: Herbert McClosky and Joe Zaller, *The American Ethos* (Cambridge, Mass.: Harvard University Press, 1984), p. 73. Reprinted with permission.

elite that knows what is really in the people's best interest. Such governments use phrases like "false consciousness" to describe the ill-informed desires of individuals and use the instruments of government to try to change human nature or, if necessary, eliminate intransigents. This comment by a Hungarian Communist leader during the Russian suppression of the 1956 revolt could have been written by Rousseau:

> The task of the leaders is not to put into effect the wishes and will of the masses . . . [but] to accomplish the interests of the masses. Why do I differentiate between the will and the interest of the masses? In the recent past we have encountered the phenomenon of certain categories of workers acting against their interests.[18]

Hobbes, Locke, and Rousseau saw the obligations of the state in varying degrees of *inclusiveness*. For Hobbes, the sole obligation was the preservation of life. For Locke, the state not only preserved life but also protected private property and provided order by the promulgation of laws. The state was to regulate, to referee, social conflict. For Rousseau, the state was to do all of these things but also create a mystic sense of belonging. Since each theorist's image of the state involved a progressively more complex set of obligations, each described an increasingly elaborate mechanism for finding out what the citizen expected.

For Hobbes, citizen expectations were a minor consideration. Either the state was guaranteeing life, or it was not. For Locke, government had to be better than life in the state of nature. His view of the state of nature stressed inconvenience more than chaos: "Men living together according to reason, without a common superior on earth with authority to judge between them, is properly the state of nature."[19] People could survive, even prosper, without a government. The government, regulating conflict, made life more rewarding. Thus its laws should be just, they should be fairly arrived at, and they should not infringe on individual freedom or the enjoyment of personal property. For Rousseau, none of these procedural guarantees were of any consequence. States were to act according to the general will. Without the determination of the general will, contracts are merely scraps of paper.

FORMS OF GOVERNMENT: MODERN INTERPRETATION OF THEORIES

Polity means either a society with an organized government or a group of people who have political (that is, power) relationships. Used in the first and more usual sense, polities run the gamut from individualistic to collectivist, and the forms of government that run them are so numerous as to defy precise ordering. But their underlying patterns are not difficult to grasp.

The State as the Guarantor of Individual Liberty

Theorists who draw on the tradition of Hobbes and, especially, Locke argue for substantial, explicit constraints to be imposed on governments. Locke had written that civil society, in contrast to the state of nature, consists of people "who are united into one body and have a common established law and judicature to appeal to, with authority to decide controversies between them and punish offenders."[20] Generally, advocates of this view believe that written constitutions or established traditions are required in order that individuals might be free of governmental tyranny. The individual's freedom is always weighed against the need for governmental coercion.

Theorists known as *conservatives* stress individual rights. At the heart of conservatism is the belief that man cannot be perfected, that human nature is flawed, that original sin is indeed sin, that we must make the best of a bad situation, that *"plus ça change, plus c'est la même chose."* Conservatives eschew global ideologies and avoid grand schemes. Writing about the French Revolution, perhaps the greatest conservative, Edmund Burke (1729–1797), suggested that human nature includes elements of irrationality, intolerance, extremism, ignorance, prejudice, hatred, and violence. Like the Hobbesians, Burke believed that people could easily degenerate into perpetual violence, a jungle. But what is needed is not the leviathan but rather laws, tradition, and respect for the past; such things as commitment to the fabric of time, maintenance of the social order, and conservation of and respect for institutions to keep us from behaving like animals. Therefore, change *only at peril.* Never change what can be left alone. Do not assume that government planning and scheming can eliminate poverty or eradicate disease; instead, assume that it cannot.

Conservatives routinely argue about the proper balance between individual needs and governmental obligation, and the decision rule is generally this: unless there is a clear and apparent public good to be obtained from the curtailment of individual liberty, such curtailment ought to be avoided. People will seek to maximize their own position vis-à-vis others, but this private competition is not destructive, it is in fact healthy. The government can establish conflict rules but ought not seek to eliminate the conflict. The job of the government is to channel conflict into healthy avenues of expression. The concept of individual "natural rights" means that governmental action (1) cannot abridge those rights, (2) cannot confiscate private property, and (3) cannot abridge individual freedom unless the social gain clearly outweighs the individual cost. Governments organized according to these prescriptions are the modern industrial democracies.

The U.S. Constitution, especially its defense by James Madison, Alexander Hamilton, and John Jay in *The Federalist Papers,* illustrates these beliefs. Madison, in *Federalist No. 10,* sets forth a position that is the exact reversal of the community theories of Rousseau. He writes that because property and personal wealth are unequally distributed, conflict among *factions* is unavoidable. Conflict is imbedded in human nature; thus attempts to eradicate its causes would be worse than the disease. Madison lamented the fact that inequality leads to conflict, but eradication would require the destruction of liberty by the elimination of inequality. The only alternative is to structure a government so as to allow conflict to flourish without destroying the fabric of community. The U.S. Constitution explicitly applies this theory. Separation of powers between branches of the national government (the legislature, the executive, and the judiciary) and division of authority between the nation and the states (federalism) are devices to diffuse conflict, to balance power, and to limit government. Limits on governmental action are even more clearly articulated in the Bill of Rights, the first ten amendments to the Constitution. Here the contract is precise: the government shall not establish a religion; abridge freedom of speech, press, assembly, and petition; or infringe on the right to "keep and bear arms." Inhabitants are protected against unreasonable searches and seizures, double jeopardy, and excessive bail.

To the Founding Fathers, the will of all was more legitimate than a vague general will: Madison called government "the greatest of all reflections of human nature. If men were angels, no government would be necessary."[21] Government cannot make people angels, as Rousseau believed, nor can it uncover a will more general than the sum of all expressed factional opinions. Rather than transforming humankind, government is content merely to contain conflict. Limits on governmental authority, the provision for the routine replacement of leaders by elections, the free flow of information, and freedom to form and join organizations are typical characteristics of individualistic governments.

Charles Lindblom calls such governments *polyarchies,* by which he means countries that meet the minimum requirements for real-world democracies rather than pure, abstract notions of the ideal democracy.[22] Such governments are not simply arbiters of factional conflict. They are providers of a variety of tangible and intangible commodities, such as these:

Goods and services that are poorly attended by the private economic market
Basic protection
Welfare
Education
Transportation
Regulation of economic competition
Rules of personal conduct

In some such countries, such as the Netherlands, a major portion of the gross national product (the sum of all goods and services produced in a country in a year) is attributable to central government spending. In others, such as the United States, Switzerland, and Japan, a much smaller proportion of GNP is traceable to the central government:[23]

Netherlands	59%	Norway	38%
Ireland	58%	Finland	32%
Belgium	57%	Spain	32%
Italy	53%	West Germany	31%
Denmark	47%	Australia	27%
Sweden	47%	Canada	26%
France	45%	United States	25%
New Zealand	42%	Japan	19%
United Kingdom	41%	Switzerland	19%
Austria	40%		

Yet whatever these governments do, they do for the presumed benefit of individuals. When individuals lack private incentives for cooperative behavior, polyarchies impose cooperative behavior on them, but a preferred solution is to structure behavior rather than to control it.[24]

The balance is a delicate one. In the United States, it is illegal to kill somebody; you cannot pay a "death tax" and pull the trigger (although it is not illegal to own a gun; in most countries, private ownership of firearms is outlawed). The curious American ambivalence about guns and violence has lead to some laws that would be unnecessary if firearms were prohibited. In several southern states, for example, *flagrante delicto* laws allow a person to shoot to kill a spouse's lover if—and the legal debate on this issue can get rather intense—"caught in the act." (Depending on the jury, "the act" has been narrowly construed to mean, well, the act itself, not the cigarette afterward. Some inept lovers have used impotence as a defense, but this is only appropriate if the wronged partner is male.)

It is not illegal to drive a car that gets 8 miles to the gallon, but you pay a "gas guzzler" tax as a penalty for your self-indulgence. It is not illegal to read or view pornography, but even the most ardent proponents of freedom of speech would agree that if it could be clearly demonstrated that otherwise normal people, after exposure to pornography, committed sexual violence as a consequence, a ban would be justified.

The individualist response to social or economic change involves a debate about the appropriate role of the state in enhancing the welfare of the individual. The "welfare state" may reduce individual freedom, but it invariably does so because of a commitment to improve *individual* life. Its goals are generally rather mundane: to provide education, health care, and housing "from the cradle to the grave"—in short, to cushion the unfortunate against the shock of adverse economic circumstances. For example, Norway, Denmark, and Sweden provide unemployment compensation to more than two-thirds of the unemployed; the United States extends such benefits to about 40 percent.[25] Fully 99 percent of all housing in the United States is privately constructed, compared with 67 percent in Sweden.[26] Irrespective of the consequences of welfare policies, no one doubts the benevolence of the authors of various welfare schemes, nor do we believe that welfare states necessarily compress the sphere of the "private"; in fact, much of the thrust of welfare policies is to make private life less stressful.

Modern *liberals,* like the conservatives, also believe in individual dignity but believe that strong government action is necessary to strengthen it; one cannot be dignified if one is poor. Government is not a threat, it is a tool to be used to correct social problems: eliminate discrimination, abolish poverty, furnish medical care, provide good education, and use the power of government to "do good." Liberals do not want to replace capitalism's private ownership of the means of production (as socialists do). Rather they want to reform the capitalistic system, much as the Democrats did in the 1930s through the New Deal. Liberals generally support government bureaucracies and regulations designed to oversee business and financial practices, guarantee minimum wages, promote affirmative action, safeguard occupational health, and otherwise care for citizens. Like socialists, liberals contend that true equality of opportunity and individual dignity cannot be achieved if there are significant numbers of people suffering from hunger, remediable illness, or extreme hardship. They want to transfer income, goods, and services from the affluent to the poor. The so-called *neoliberals* are a little bit different; they believe that unless the economy is healthy, redistribution is a lost cause. Unlike old liberals, neoliberals are pro-business; they are great admirers of the Japanese.

The Japanese mode of governance, consisting of tight cooperation between government and business, is often compared favorably with the American style of confrontation, and the undeniable truth—that Japan has displaced the United States as the world's most competitive nation in business—rankles neoliberals more than liberals.

> Japan has replaced the United States as the world's most competitive nation in business, the Geneva-based European Management Forum said in a report comparing 31 industrialized countries. The United States was in second place, followed by Switzerland, West Germany, and Denmark. The report cited a ''growing and efficient research and development effort'' and political stability as among Japan's strengths.[27]

The Collective Solution

Leaders who believe that they can identify and act on the general will do so, even if that general will and transitory private wills are in conflict. Ironically, the foundation for collectivism—ownership and control by the people for the benefit of the people—is superior elite knowledge. Modern collectivist governments have established varying criteria for elite dictatorship (ideological purity, religious orthodoxy, and so on), but all agree that a *responsive* polyarchy is a cruel injustice: responding to what people say they want is cruel to the very people who make the demands because, in many cases, they do not know what is best for them.

The irresponsibility of responsiveness is a key canon of narrowly constrained political and religious ideologies. Objective truth exists; to deviate from its pursuit is wrong, no matter how many people wish otherwise. In Iran, where religious orthodoxy is the power base, blasphemy is punishable by death, and to yield to popular revulsion or to tolerate unseemly criticism of Islam is irresponsible. In Cuba, where orthodox Marxism holds sway, Jesuit-educated dictator Fidel Castro intoned, ''We must watch over the ideological purity of the revolution, the ideological integrity of the revolution. That is why we cannot use any methods that reek of capitalism.''[28] Castro did not care whether or not Cubans wanted more economic freedom. If governments do not ignore ill-thought-out demands, they do the people long-run harm at the cost of short-run happiness.

Collectivist governments are future-oriented, generally with a clear vision of the good society. They focus more on ends than means, and they justify coercion in the name of the community. Not all collectivist governments try to enlighten their subjects; many are just brutal. Fascist governments command loyalty to the leader but do not encourage or tolerate suggestions that their regime is a transition to a better life. Fascist governments require blind obedience: ''everything for the state, nothing against the state, no one outside the state.'' In exchange for obedience, citizens are offered community. Communist governments, temporarily authoritarian, promise a future in which the state, having enlightened all, will wither away. The distinction may appear minor, as communist governments delay indefinitely the arrival of the utopia, but at least they invoke a higher good while imposing coercive rule.

Marxism.   Karl Marx (1818–1883) assumed that the basic nature of human beings can be changed from hostile, competitive, and conflict-ridden to cooperative and public-spirited through a process of evolution by changing the social and economic environment.[29] Marx believed not only that human nature responds by adjusting temporarily to stimuli but also that new and permanent preferred characteristics could be generally transmitted.[30] Capitalism "causes" greed and selfishness. Abolish capitalism and people become selfless. And when they reproduce, their genetic maps will contain no greed, and hence their children will need no conditioning.

Pathology (alienation) is caused by capitalism, and thus "industrial man" could not help himself. Greed is caused by the profit motive; crime, by poverty and ignorance. But just as millennarian religions promise relief from life's angst once the ways of the flesh are renounced, so does Marxism assure believers that they can be "born again." By renouncing the devilry of capitalism, a new life can begin. Writing of the allure of communism, Richard Crossman holds:

> If despair and loneliness were the main motives for converting to communism, they were greatly strengthened by the Christian conscience. . . . The intellectual, though he may have abandoned orthodox Christianity, felt its prickings more acutely than many of his unreflective churchgoing neighbors. He at least was aware of the unfairness of the status and privileges which he enjoyed. . . . The emotional appeal of communism lay precisely in the sacrifices—both material and spiritual—which it demanded of the convert. . . . The idea of an active comradeship of struggle—involving personal sacrifice and abolishing differences of class and race—has had a compulsive power in every Western democracy.[31]

A change in human nature was essential for Marx's utopian future. Institutional change was not enough. The doctrine remains part of the appeal of Marxism as a religion. It promises a utopia in which a reborn humanity, living in a classless state and hence without conflict, has no need for government. Hobbes proposed government as the solution to the harshness of life in a state of nature; the leviathan would constrain or moderate the deadly conflict of the state of nature. Marx believed in the possibility of the abolition of government by *altering* the state of nature.[32]

Here are the essential Marxist theories:

1. *Economic Determinism.* Communism believes that the nature of the economy, or "modes of production," is basic to all the rest of society. The mode of production determines the class structure, the political system, religion, education, family life, law, art, and literature. For example, the economic structure of feudalism creates a class structure of a privileged aristocracy and a suffering serfdom. The economic structure of capitalism creates a class structure of wealthy bourgeoisie (property-owning capitalists) who control the government and exercise power over the *proletariat* (propertyless workers).

2. *Class Struggle.* The first sentence of Marx's *Communist Manifesto* exclaims, "The history of all hitherto existing society is the history of class struggles." These class struggles are created by the modes of production; the class that owns the modes of production is in the dominant position and exploits the other classes. Such exploitation creates antagonism, which gradually increases until it bursts into revolution. The means of production in the Middle Ages was land, and the aristocracy that owned the land controlled government and

society. The industrial revolution created a new class, the bourgeoisie, which rose to importance because it owned the modes of production—money, machines, and factories. But just as the aristocracy was supplanted by the bourgeoisie, so the bourgeoisie will in the course of time be superseded by the proletariat. The capitalist exploits workers to the point at which the workers are forced to revolt against their oppressors and overthrow the capitalist state.

3. *Theory of Surplus Value.* Labor is the only source of value. Labor is the one thing common to all commodities and gives each commodity its value. As Marx put it, "All wealth is due to labor, and therefore, to the laborer, all wealth is due." Although laborers deserve the full value of the commodities they make, under capitalism, they receive only a small part of it, just enough to pay for their subsistence. The rest, which Marx called surplus, is taken by capitalists for their own enrichment. Thus capitalism is a gigantic scheme for exploiting the workers by confiscating the surplus value they have created. The solution is to make it impossible for capitalists to exploit workers by establishing "collective ownership of all means of production, distribution, and exchange." The proletariat must eliminate the capitalist and take over all the tools of production, distribution, and exchange so that the surplus value will not flow away from labor to capitalists.

4. *Inevitability of Revolution.* Not only did Marx predict the coming of the proletarian revolution, but he also sought to show that it was inevitable. "What the bourgeoisie produces above all is its own grave diggers. Its fall and the victory of the proletariat are equally inevitable." As capitalists become more greedy, the rich become richer and the poor become poorer; moreover, competition squeezes out small capitalists, and ownership is gradually concentrated in the hands of fewer and fewer capitalists. As exploitation increases and as more small capitalists are forced into the ranks of the proletariat, the strength and the antagonism of the proletariat increase. The proletariat develops a class consciousness and ultimately rises up against the exploiters. As capitalists drive down wages to maximize profits, capitalism becomes plagued by a series of crises—depressions—each worse than before (the "crisis of advanced capitalism"). As wages are forced ever lower, capitalists soon cannot sell their products because of the lower purchasing power of the proletariat, and depression follows. Further, as capitalists introduce more machinery, the demand for labor declines, and unemployment rises. The result of these internal contradictions in capitalism is a great deal of human misery, which eventually explodes in revolution. Thus in their drive for profit, capitalists dig their own graves by bringing the inevitable revolution closer.

5. *Dictatorship of the Proletariat.* Although the revolution is inevitable, Marx nonetheless urged workers to organize for revolutionary action. Picking up on Rousseau's "Man was born free, but everywhere he is in chains," Marx said, "The proletarians have nothing to lose but their chains. They have a world to win. Working men of all countries, unite." The capitalists will never peacefully surrender their ruling position, and thus a violent revolution is needed to displace them. The proletariat will set up a state of its own—the "dictatorship of the proletariat"—to protect its own class interests. Unlike the governments

of the past, however, which served oppressive minorities, the dictatorship of the proletariat will be a government by and for the working class. The bourgeoisie will be eliminated as a class.

6. *The Withering Away of the State.* Since class differences depend on ownership of the modes of production, the result of common ownership will be a one-class, or classless, society. Since the purpose of government is to assist the ruling class in exploiting and oppressing other classes, once a classless society is established, the government will have no purpose and will gradually "wither away." In the early stages of the revolution, the rule of distribution will be "from each according to his ability, to each according to his work." But after the victory of communism and the establishment of the classless society, the distribution rule will be "from each according to his ability, to each according to his need." After the elimination of classes, society will be peaceful and cooperative, and coercion will no longer be needed. Government will disappear forever.

Many modern collectivist governments are "preceptorial" meaning that they seek to educate, enlighten, and change their subjects. Coercion is undertaken with the expectation, at least initially, that it will become unnecessary when all have learned their lessons well.[33] Lindblom describes the ideal preceptorial method as "massive highly unilateral persuasion in which a small enlightened governmental elite instructs the masses in much the same way that Rousseau advised teacher to educate child and imagined a 'superior intelligence' transforming each individual."[34]

The Soviet Union, China, Cuba, and Nicaragua have spoken of, and tried to develop, the "new man." The new man will be selfless rather than self-aggrandizing, not because he is afraid, not because he is induced to cooperate, but because he *wants* to serve the collectivity. Ultimately, preceptorial governments will find it unnecessary to coerce. In *Nineteen Eighty-four,* George Orwell's fictional account of a totalitarian government, the central character, Winston, finally (by means of unbearable torture) learns that he must "love Big Brother" and does so. His individuality is annihilated, and he conforms to collective demands voluntarily. In so doing, he discovers that true freedom, as distinguished from false consciousness, is achieved only by the elimination of the individual self. As Rousseau explained, "Man must be forced to be free."[35]

Socialism.   The modern collectivist governments are largely socialist, and Rousseau was essential to their development. As Kenneth Hoover explains, "Rousseau had a major influence on the style and development of socialist thought. He focused on the fundamental question: how to get people to look beyond their immediate self-interest to the interest of the whole community.[36]

Collective ownership is the core of socialism, which is public ownership of the means of production, distribution, and service. Like Marxism, socialism condemns capitalism as exploitative, but, unlike Marxism, it rejects the inevitability of revolution; moreover, socialists reject the notion of a proletarian dictatorship and are committed to peaceful, constitutional, "political" methods of achieving their goal. Their ideal is a free society, the democratic society. They believe that true political democracy cannot be achieved until there is economic democracy, wealth is widely and equitably distributed, and the means of production are commonly owned. Wealth must be redistributed so that all will reap the benefits. Socialist parties in Europe are nowadays rather meek, having accepted evolution rather than revolution and having pretty much given up on massive public ownership.

Totalitarian and Authoritarian Variants

A distinction can be made between *totalitarian* governments and merely *authoritarian* ones.[37] The distinction is not between the goals or policies of governments, nor is it between members of friendly or hostile alliances. The distinction is solely on the degree of intervention into personal life. As the name implies, totalitarian governments view the entire range of human behaviors as appropriate for intervention.[38]

Cuba and Nicaragua.   Both Nicaragua and Cuba espouse the symbols of Marxism, of international communism (Cuba more consistently). The speeches of Cuban and Nicaraguan elites are laden with the standard Marxist references to the "international class struggle," the "war against imperialism," and so on. They speak of "strategic ties with the Soviet Union and other socialist states" and are in fact economically dependent on them. Economically, Cuba is a Soviet colony. Nicaraguan leaders have borrowed substantially from the Cuban model—especially rhetorically—and Nicaraguan and Cuban delegations regularly fly back and forth, demonstrating their solidarity. But although American leaders have occasionally lumped Cuba and Nicaragua together as totalitarian, they are not equally so:

> [The Nicaraguan] regime shows no tolerance for individuals engaged in political activity that even remotely questions its authority. There are disturbing accounts of large numbers of political prisoners and of the practice of the less grim forms of torture. Still, if Nicaraguans stay clear of politics, they are afforded considerable liberty. Sloths, for example, are not arrested—as they are in Cuba—for "social parasitism."[39]

If you stay out of politics, you enjoy considerable liberty: this statement encapsulates the authoritarian state. Such states have in common with totalitarian ones only that they are both nondemocratic.[40]

In totalitarian governments, no distinction between public life and private life is acknowledged, as everything one does is supposed to "serve the state." Marriage, childbirth, art, music, work, clothing, and recreation are regarded as legitimate areas of government control. What is more, the boundary, such as it is, is unstable. One can never know when an aspect of life has become "politicized." Mainland Chinese block committees became obsessed with personal hygiene during the late 1970s and subjected their charges to unremitting and humiliating inspections. Failure to brush one's teeth, to floss, and so on became acts of political subversion. Of course, rotten teeth are socially expensive in a collectivist society. Contrast the assumptions of Chinese block committees with the widespread aversion to compulsory helmet laws for motorcyclists in the United States.

China.   In mainland China, during the Cultural Revolution (1966–1976), an elaborate system of interlocking surveillance was created: the *danwei* (''workplace''), the street committee, and political study groups. The *danwei* generally provided housing, education, ration cards, and medical help. Marriages and divorces required *danwei* approval. The *danwei* maintained a dossier, including a three-generation class analysis (children of peasants were given an advantage over children of ''capitalists''), and job transfers had to be accompanied by a *danwei*-approved dossier. Overnight travel also required *danwei* approval, and travelers had to present a permission slip from their *danwei* to register at a hotel. Street committees took up the surveillance after work. In addition to seeing that all citizens cleaned their living quarters, and their bodies, before sleeping, street committees also decided who could become pregnant and who must have an abortion: ''We assign a person to keep track of each woman's menstrual cycle. If someone misses her period and isn't scheduled to have a baby, we tell her to have an abortion.''[41] The small groups were explicitly designed for political indoctrination. All of these instruments of surveillance were managed by the Public Security Ministry.

With the economic liberalization of the Chinese economy after Mao's death, Westerners naturally assumed that these forms of control were a thing of the past. But the average Chinese is, if anything, less free in 1989 than in 1979.[42] Political and social controls are ''pervasive.''[43] At the local level, family planning has not been relaxed appreciably, for example. Permission to have more than one child is still required, and, when local quotas have been filled, permission for *any* pregnancy is required. In 1985, well into the liberalization programs,

> women were required to have intrauterine birth control devices inserted after their first child and were strictly forbidden to remove them. . . . In some city hospitals, doctors automatically implant IUDs immediately after a woman gives birth, often without informing the woman or seeking her prior consent. Moreover, intrauterine devices are often inserted in assembly-line fashion without concern for sizing. . . . One partner of every Chinese couple with two or more children is required by law to be sterilized. . . . Women who manage to elude sterilization and become pregnant without receiving official authorization, after already having had one child, are required by law to abort the fetus.[44]

In 1981, the Chinese legalized infanticide. Killing of female children by parents had become common and was ignored; however, state-sanctioned infanticide, performed in hospitals, was a new wrinkle. Now, if a second child lived, the doctor could lose his or her job. The infanticide was performed by several methods:

> Doctors routinely smash the baby's head with forceps as it emerges from the womb. . . . Newborns are killed by injecting formaldehyde into the soft spot of the cranium. . . . All babies born of women without a ''birth authorization card'' are suffocated in a large can or drowned in water. . . . Some village clinics due to lack of experience even used boiling water to kill the newborns.[45]

China has been less concerned about population growth in rural areas and among ethnic minorities.

Totalitarian governments are rare because they are so costly. As we shall see, only a handful of countries have been able to sustain totalitarian rule. Many more can keep authoritarian rule intact. In totalitarian regimes, extreme surveillance is likely to result in more "illegal" behavior, much of which is not discovered. Of course, the very fact that much of normal life is illegal gives the totalitarian government an advantage in controlling individual behavior. As Robert Nisbet explains, "Whereas in authoritarian society everything is permitted that is not explicitly forbidden, nothing is permitted in totalitarian society that is not explicitly authorized."[46]

Yet even in aspiring totalitarian political systems, the theory and practice of surveillance and control are frequently at odds. No totalitarian state has been able to impose complete subservience. Perhaps North Korea is as close to the perfect totalitarian state as we can come. Even listening to a foreign radio station is a crime. Yet on a scale devised to measure adherence to human rights, with 0 representing total repression and 100 representing maximum freedom, North Korea earns a 17—not much, but not *totally* oppressive. It is not "perfect" because even though the official political ideology, *juche sasang*, is hammered into everybody's brain, repression of religion is "severe but not total."[47]

A Continuum of the World's Regimes

We need, then, to think less in terms of clearly defined types of regimes. It is more fruitful to imagine a *continuum*, ranging from countries with the strongest commitment to individualism to those with the strongest commitment to collectivism. In later chapters, each of these types will be explored in greater detail.

The continuum starts with the nations most committed to individualism, the *polyarchies* (polyarchy can be used interchangeably with *democracy*). They have meaningful and fair elections, political organization and expression are unrestricted, and official views get no preferential treatment. Australia, Austria, the United Kingdom, and the United States are polyarchies. Human rights ratings here are in the high 90s.

Next are the *near polyarchies*, countries in which meaningful and fair elections are held but some dissent is suppressed. An excellent example is India, where, since peaceful assemblies often turn into riots, the 1980 National Security Act allows for the banning of all public meetings and for the censorship of the media. India's human rights rating is 60.

The *authoritarian* governments, the most numerous and heterogeneous of all, range from those in which elections are marred by fraud and corruption and some independent political organizations are banned (Singapore, Nicaragua, Egypt) to those that hold no meaningful elections, have established an official party, and suppress some dissent (Algeria, Zaire). But even in the worst of them, say Zaire, the human rights rating is 30 because freedom of religion—and freedom from compulsory ideology—is respected.

Near totalitarian governments hold no meaningful elections, ban or control all organizations, suppress all dissent, provide no alternative sources of information, yet have not sought true totalism. Cuba, which is a brutal dictatorship by any standard, does not require *internal* travel permits.

At the end of the continuum, the *totalitarian* regimes seek control of every aspect of life, even, as in North Korea, of *thoughts* (thinking "individual" thoughts is prohibited).

WHAT GOVERNMENTS HAVE IN COMMON

The Monopoly of Force and the Development of Compliance

All governments, whether individualist or collectivist, perform certain fundamental tasks, the most important of which is monopolizing force in order to make authoritative decisions. Major differences arise in the degree to which this imposition of authority is accomplished.

Individualist governments are usually less arbitrary and more bound by procedural requirements. But no collectivist government, even without limitations, could survive indefinitely by exercising its monopoly on force. If the residents of Albania or North Korea were willing, en masse, to resist and to die, they could force the state to change its policy. In Romania, a Marxist dictatorship with a frightening reputation for ruthlessness, a scheme to uproot residents of small rural communities and relocate them in urban areas was moderated when it became obvious that they simply would not go.

Compliance in all governments is based on the acceptance of legitimacy (although there are various routes to acceptance), a belief that laws should be obeyed, and a sense of loyalty to the government as an organization (compliance is explored in detail in Chapter 2). The payment of income taxes is an excellent example of the mixture of coercion and voluntary compliance. Taxes are painful because the cost to the individual is direct and substantial, whereas the benefits are diffuse. Further, the benefits to individuals will not decrease if they pay less than their share or pay no taxes at all. Governments will therefore spend a substantial amount of money to make examples of cheaters, far more than they will collect in taxes by forcing the cheaters to pay.[48] Yet any rational taxpayer can figure out that the odds of prosecution are remote. Governments must rely on voluntary compliance, and a clear indicator of the decline of legitimacy of a government is an increase in tax fraud.

Conflict Resolution

As governments impose authoritative decisions, they also resolve conflict. When private organizations are unable to resolve disputes, they turn to governments. Deprived populations seek governmental redress of inequality and discrimination; business associations seek relief from destructive economic competition; religious groups seek official sanction for their beliefs. Governments do not consciously set themselves to the task of conflict resolution. They defeat dreaded enemies, preserve treasured customs, protect their citizens from the ravages of ill health and poverty, and teach them how to earn a living. In doing these primary tasks, they also resolve conflict. Public politics transforms private politics into institutionalized modes of conflict resolution. It provides rules of the game. Since no government, even the most collectivist, has ever achieved the perfect unity of purpose envisioned in Rousseau's theories of community, the rules of combat must be specified.

Especially in collectivist political systems, governments frequently engage in the rhetoric of unity, even while refereeing disputes. Hu Yaobang, an influential Chinese Communist party leader, proposed reunification with Taiwan. When asked if such reunification would allow the Nationalist party, which controlled Taiwan, to compete with the Communist party, Hu replied that the Nationalist party was not a legitimate representative of the aspirations of the Chinese people, whereas the Communist party was. As Hu explained, "Ours is not a one-party dictatorship but a people's democratic dictatorship under the leadership of the Communist Party."[49] The language is silly, but the reasoning is not: if politics is the resolution of conflict, no conflict means no politics and hence no need for an opposition party. Collectivist systems claim to have eliminated the cause of conflict and inequality and thus assert the legitimacy of a single party as keeper of the collectivist faith. The rules of the game include the operative decision rules: is a state determining policy by consensus, unanimity, or majority?

Consensus enjoys the advantage of avoiding bruised feelings, a constant problem with close majorities. Consensus also reduces the need to address the same issues year after year. When a close majority vote is lost, the losers will try again, creating the image of a never-ending process. Recurring consideration of the same or similar issues is common in majority-rule settings. In the U.S. Congress, the issue of aid to the *contras* (opponents of the Sandinista government in Nicaragua) was voted on four times in two years, with the final outcome quite different from the initial vote.

Persistence on the part of losers is frequently rewarded by victory even in the face of initial opposition because *intensity* is a more valuable political resource than numerical superiority. Except during elections, policy is more easily influenced by a small group of zealots, dug in to defend the status quo. People with strongly held beliefs are willing to devote more time and money to a political fight than people whose interests are peripheral. When Congress threatens to pass legislation requiring used car dealers to inspect a car and to display a list of defects, consumers benefit marginally, but dealers suffer potentially ruinous consequences. So even though there are more consumers than dealers, consumers' feelings are less intense and are therefore of less consequence than dealers'.

When the United States Supreme Court declared in 1973 that women had a right to obtain an abortion, most people either approved or disapproved with only marginal commitment, but the "right to lifers" saw the issue as one of good versus evil and prepared for the battle of Armageddon. An antiabortion activist recalls her reaction to a newspaper account of the decision:

> I sat down, I was very upset. . . . I wanted to cry in a way. . . . All of these things in my personal life—things that were no concern of mine, so to speak, you say, "That's somebody else's business"—all came together in one. . . . almost like seeing Providence. God was saying, "Lookit, sister, you better see what's going on there."[50]

People guided by God do not quit a fight when the going gets rough. Their intensity is, if anything, enhanced by political setbacks.

But consensus means less attention to collective needs and more cognizance of individuals demands, any one of which can delay a decision as long as necessary to prevent an unacceptable result. The notion of consensus is solidly nestled in the center of the argument between individualist and collectivist images of the good society. Consensus is ill suited for the sort of rough-and-tumble, individualist democracies that assume individual self-interest to be more reliable than the community as a stimulant to political behavior. If the social contract is necessary only because people lack the will to regulate individual interaction and if the engine of politics is self-interest, consensus is unlikely. This unsuitability is ironic, for consensus or unanimity decision rules elevate the individual to a more exalted status than majority rule.

In practical terms, political bodies that operate under a consensual decision rule are likely to produce compromises that suit nobody completely but everybody just enough to secure support. Although it uses a majority rule, the U.S. Supreme Court sometimes feels that unanimity is essential when an especially controversial decision is reached. The need for a unanimous decision was apparent in the first desegregation decision, *Brown v. Board of Education of Topeka*. The eventual ruling, while declaring segregation of schools unconstitutional, allowed compliance to proceed ''with all deliberate speed'' (in practice allowing resistance to continue for two decades after the decision), in order to secure the votes of southerners on the court. In the years to come, the threat of nonunanimous decisions gave potential dissenters added leverage:

> [Justice Hugo] Black sent a memo to his colleagues. He would not go along with any opinions that explicitly approved compulsory busing. . . . It had been bad enough the year before, when Black had threatened to dissent in the Mississippi desegregation case unless he got his way. Now he was doing it again. These continuing blackmail attempts were outrageous. Faced with recalcitrant school board members willing to seize any difference, unanimity in school cases was an important tradition. To hold it hostage . . . demeaned both Black and the Court.[51]

Justice Black's leverage came from his being a southerner whose nomination to the Court had been scarred by accusations of racism (Black had once been a member of the Ku Klux Klan). His acquiescence, while symbolic, was judged crucial for mass acceptance of the bitterly contested busing decisions.

With consensus as the decision rule, a *coalition* strategy is unlikely to be successful. If alliances do not include the single dissenter, they are of no value. The currency of coalition politics is therefore persuasion, intimidation, or an exchange of valued commodities. Pressure on the dissenter is greatest when a decision must be reached, as in the deliberations of juries, where the threat of an unending process is well established and feared. Pressure is less apparent when the opposite is true—when a veto simply means moving on to other items on the agenda, as in the United Nations Security Council.

Because of these dilemmas, *majority rule* generally replaces the demand for unanimity. As a defector from a small religious commune put it: ''When you have a leaderless group and try to be egalitarian, it's hard. We got so tired of meeting, of communicating feelings and achieving consensus.''[52] Majority rule lets people worry only about achieving 51 percent and enables them to ignore the opposition unless a member of the winning coalition plans to defect. Majorities are therefore less costly to achieve and maintain.

But is the rule of the majority used because it is ''right'' or merely because it is expedient? If majority rule is employed merely because the polity has grown too large for the exhaustive process of reaching a consensus, its defense is that it is a reasonable and less costly alternative to an unfeasible but desirable option. The answer to this question reflects the now familiar argument between collectivists and individualists.

Individualists believe that majority rule is a just means of ascertaining "the greatest good for the greatest number," Jeremy Bentham's formula for judging the merits of a policy. There are no absolute standards of right or wrong, merely the mathematical calculus of whether the policy does deliver the best available solution to a problem in the opinion of 51 percent of the people. Right is what the majority wants. The anguish of the minority that fails to prevail by one vote does not diminish the claims of individualists: the majority is "right" and the minority "wrong." You can assuage your anguish by persuading the swing votes of the merits of your case and, if you succeed, your position will be "right."

Collectivist thinking, you will recall, believes in the objective existence of the public interest. The collectivists' romantic notions of the community and the mystique of the group do not obviate the need to discover the public interest and to propose policies consistent with it. Public interests are not invariably discovered by discussion and voting. The more authoritarian of the romantic collectivists became contemptuous of democracy; the more populist did not. But unless an enlightened and universally admired benevolent despot has flawless judgment, the democratic collectivists accept the rule of consensus and, failing to achieve unanimity, endure the rule of the majority as the best solution.

Political Socialization

Political socialization is the process whereby we acquire our political values and our view of the political world. Governments seek to influence (in individualist systems) or control (in collectivist systems) this process. Since no government can rule indefinitely by force, all governments seek to develop loyalty. The institutions of socialization are the family, the school, the media, and occupational associations. Individualist nations do not attempt to monopolize all sources of socialization, as is customary in collectivist systems. Families in individualist societies pass down political values from generation to generation—less so as traditional families recede in importance, but still without intervention by the government. In collectivist societies, families may be monitored in order to assure their orthodoxy. The various block committees of mainland China, Cuba, and Nicaragua are especially active in monitoring family discussions.

Schools in individualist societies generally socialize to compliance, tradition, and patriotism, not because they are forced to do so, but because educational systems are conservators of tradition. In collectivist systems, schools are overt instruments of ruling party hegemony. Their goal is to instill loyalty, and their methods are blunt. There are the regular political education classes, of course, compulsory and detested. But political examples pervade the entire curriculum. Soviet medical students spend about one-fourth of their time studying Marxism. Mathematics lessons in the Soviet Union frequently use examples from American ghettos ("If the murder rate in Harlem is 1,000 per year, and this rate is four times the murder rate in Westchester County, what is the murder rate in Westchester County?").

Generally, forms of expression that are taken to be self-actualizing in individualist societies are viewed as instruments of socialization in collectivist ones. The mass media—especially television—are forms of entertainment and information in individualist societies. Art, music, and literature may be politically inspired, but rarely at the behest of the government. In collectivist societies, these media are sanctioned only insofar as they serve the state as agents of socialization. Of course, dissidents protest, but the state is usually able to channel a major portion of artistic efforts into approved modes of expression. Soviet composers such as Shostakovich and Prokofiev drifted in and out of official favor depending on arcane interpretations of their work by Soviet writers' and composers' unions. Some have said that these composers achieved greatness precisely because they had to learn subtle and indirect methods of expression in order to circumvent the censors. Soviet art depicts brawny workers and looks remarkably similar to Nazi art in the 1930s:

> The National Socialists were the first to make this battle for art a focal point of political conflict and to define an individual's position in it as evidence of his approval or rejection of National Socialist political goals and principles. [A leading German critic wrote,] "A life and death struggle is taking place in art, just as it is in the realm of politics. And the battle for art has to be fought with the same seriousness and determination as the battle for political power."[53]

Blond-haired, blue-eyed supermen adorned Nazi art, and Nazi music was dominated by the heroic, mythical operas of the virulently anti-Semitic Richard Wagner. So is Soviet art, which at its worst resembles caricatures of itself: bulging biceps, dams, tractors, and so on. The KGB at one point administered electrical shocks to young artists while forcing them to view reproductions of Picasso! In 1988, however, some Soviet painters, long banned because their style clashed with the officially approved socialist realism (counted on to "inspire people to support their new political and economic system")[54] were exhibited for the first time. Kazimir Malevich's *Black Supremacist Square* (1914) had been last displayed in 1929.

Television, unfettered in individualist societies, is the instrument of torture of American presidents, for example, most of whom become deeply suspicious of the media and some of whom (such as Richard Nixon) become persuaded that the media destroyed them. Entertainment on television is unconnected to regime support, even though television stations depend on the government for their licenses.

In collectivist societies, the mass media do not entertain, they indoctrinate. Following the theories of Joseph Goebbels, Nazi propaganda chief, Soviet television, for example, consists almost solely of Russian-made World War II movies, films of sports spectaculars with heavy political overtones, addresses by party leaders, and occasional self-help shows. Nothing remotely approaching entertainment in the American sense appears on Soviet television, since entertainment for its own sake is not considered a legitimate objective in broadcasting. In 1986, on prime time in Moscow, "Looking for Tomorrow: The Work of the Dnepropetrovsk Combine Factory" was followed by "Jubilee Night for the People's Artists of the USSR," neither of which was broadcast to capture ratings, which are unknown in Soviet television.[55]

Glasnost relaxed the preceptorial role of television somewhat. However, rather than opening mass communication to a variety of ideas, glasnost has substituted one set of heroes for another. Since the flaws of Soviet society have now been "officially" blamed on Stalin and Brezhnev (1964–1982), these two unfortunate souls are lambasted daily (Brezhnev's works have been removed from public and school libraries, as have the biographies that routinely praise Soviet leaders—*Leonid Brezhnev, Crusader for Justice and Revolution* and the like). But Lenin, whose ideas were said to be distorted by Stalin and Brezhnev, cannot be criticized. And Gorbachev himself cannot be attacked or condemned. Soviet comedy shows poking even gentle fun at leaders is still a long way off.

Lenin, the ideological and spiritual leader of the Russian Revolution, set forth the political uses of the media:

1. Agitation and propaganda to serve the purposes of the state-strengthening loyalty, improving worker output, and encouraging obedience to the regime
2. Education in Marxism-increasing mass solidarity, to improve support for the party, and to encourage hostility toward bourgeois (Western democratic) ideas
3. Spread of proletarian (communist) cultural values through art, music, theater, ballet, sports, and so on to extol the virtues of communism.

Recent Soviet and East German performances in the Olympics dramatize the politicization of popular culture.

In 1988, in the midst of glasnost, the USSR reasserted its control over publishing, removing publishing from the list of "cooperative" (that is, private) ventures. This was done to eliminate production of items of "doubtful aesthetic taste" (such as a calendar featuring a nude woman). Cinema and video production were banned to private business, as was the "publishing of works of science, literature, and art." The USSR rejected Western entreaties to intervene with Iran on behalf of Salman Rushdie, given a "death sentence" for *The Satanic Verses,* a novel blaspheming Islam. Other business activities (editing, printing, copying, the organization of concerts or discotheque, and the production or sale of recorded music) are allowed only if the cooperative works under contract from the state.

Maintaining the Common Defense

A few countries maintain no defense or military capabilities (Costa Rica and Iceland are perhaps the most celebrated), but it is fair to say that a military establishment, even a weak or symbolic one, is part of the normal spending of modern governments. The level of commitment is, of course, quite another matter, as Table 1.2 suggests. Generally, collectivist governments have a larger military budget than individualist ones. A philosophy of collective responsibility naturally suggests a major investment in defense. Look at the pairs in Table 1.2. Except for China, the collectivist government in each pair spends more than the individualist one. There are more military tasks under collective governments, including the exporting of the national ideology and surveillance of the population. Individualist countries may indulge in these activities too, but apparently with less financial commitment. When Gorbachev in 1988 renounced his intention to export revolution, he also announced his intention to reduce military expenditures.

Securing Domestic Tranquillity

The protection of citizens from physical or mental harm involves more governmental judgment than defense does. We may argue about the level of expenditures required for defense, but few of us would question its necessity. Yet protection from internal harm

TABLE 1.2 Militarism: Regional Comparisons

	Military Personnel (per 1,000 population)	Military Spending (percent of GNP)
North Korea	38.5	22.2
South Korea	14.6	5.5
China	3.7	6.7
Taiwan	22.8	7.6
Nicaragua	23.4	16.8
Central America (average)	4.9	2.5
Cuba	29.5	5.4
Other Caribbean (average)	2.0	1.5
Warsaw Pact (excluding Soviet Union)	15.2	10.7
NATO (excluding United States)	10.0	3.8
Soviet Union	16.1	12.5
United States	9.6	6.6

SOURCES: U.S. Arms Control and Disarmament Agency, *World Military Expenditures and Arms Transfers* (Washington, D.C.: GPO, 1986, 1987); International Institute for Strategic Studies, *The Military Balance, 1987–1988* (London: IISS, 1988).

gets to the heart of Hobbes's ideology. What are dangers? When is the cure worse than the illness?

As in other areas, collectivist and individualist societies approach the government's obligation to safeguard citizens from physical danger differently. The deprivation of life is a state monopoly, and murder is a crime in all societies; so are violent physical assault, robbery, burglary, rape, and other crimes against persons. But governments are not equally successful in protecting against all of these. Most theorists believe that violent crime is related to the pressures of modern industrial life, overcrowding, anonymity, loss of individuality, and alienation. Undoubtedly such a relationship exists but it is far from simple to delineate (see Table 1.3). The most violent society in the world is Lesotho, a former British protectorate in southern Africa. Its murder rate (140.8 per 1,000) is explained by unending tribal conflicts and a government too frail to stop the killing.

Among the developed nations, the United States is far and away in first place. Does the high murder rate in the United States reflect governmental anemia, as in Lesotho? The United States is not exceptional in suicide, only murder. Why do Americans kill each other at eight times the rate of Japanese? Is our culture violent because we can buy guns like the Japanese and Europeans buy detergent? Is it because of our glorification of individualism and violence, as exemplified in our continued fascination with the western frontier? Is it because we are not sure and swift in administering capital punishment? Is it because we are a heterogeneous, loosely woven society, unlike the homogeneous Japanese? Is it because our families are less cohesive than Japanese ones? One rarely explored idea is that public acts beget private violence—that war, an act of public violence, predisposes a population to become more aggressive because it seems to legitimate violence. Homicides increased in Belgium, Bulgaria, Germany, the Netherlands, and Portugal after World War I and in England, France, New Zealand, Norway, and South Africa after World War II; in Italy and Japan, they increased after both wars. Homicide rates either decreased or were unchanged in England, France, and Hungary

TABLE 1.3 Suicides and Homicides per 100,000 Population

Country (Year)	Suicides		Homicides	
	Men	Women	Men	Women
Totalitarian or Near-Totalitarian				
Bulgaria (1985)	23.3	9.4	4.6	1.8
Czechoslovakia (1985)	29.2	9.2	1.3	1.2
Repressive Authoritarian				
Argentina (1982)	10.5	3.4	6.7	1.7
Chile (1984)	10.7	1.8	5.9	—
Hungary (1986)	66.1	25.9	3.5	2.2
Poland (1986)	22.0	4.4	2.1	1.1
Yugoslavia (1983)	22.8	9.7	2.8	1.1
Democratic				
Australia (1985)	18.2	5.1	2.5	1.5
Austria (1986)	42.1	15.8	1.1	—
Canada (1985)	20.5	5.4	2.7	1.5
Costa Rica (1984)	7.4	1.5	7.3	1.7
Denmark (1985)	35.1	20.6	1.8	1.1
Finland (1985)	43.0	11.3	4.7	1.9
Iceland (1985)	20.6	5.8	—	—
Israel (1985)	7.5	3.5	2.9	1.4
Italy (1983)	11.0	4.3	3.3	—
Japan (1986)	27.8	14.9	1.0	—
Luxembourg (1986)	20.7	7.4	1.7	2.1
Netherlands (1985)	14.6	8.1	1.2	—
New Zealand (1985)	15.7	5.0	2.5	1.6
Norway (1985)	20.8	7.4	1.2	—
Spain (1981)	6.8	2.3	1.7	—
Switzerland (1986)	33.0	13.2	—	—
United Kingdom (1985)	12.1	5.7	—	—
United States (1984)	19.7	5.4	12.8	3.9
West Germany (1986)	26.2	12.0	1.3	1.1

SOURCE: Dane Archer and Rosemary Gartner, *Violence and Crime in Cross-national Perspective* (New Haven: Yale University Press), 1984, p. 126 and INTERPOL, *International Crime Statistics*, 1983–1984.

after World War I and in Canada, Finland, and the United States after World War II.[56] Where they increased, they increased among all segments of the population, noncombatants and soldiers alike.

Dane Archer and Rosemary Gartner conclude:

> The *public* acts of governments can influence the *private* acts of individuals. . . . War involves homicide legitimated by the highest auspices of the state. . . . The powerful influence of *governments* on *private behavior* seems to be what Justice Louis Brandeis had in mind when he wrote in 1928: "Our government is the potent, the omnipresent teacher. For good or ill, it teaches whole people by its example. Crime is contagious. If the government becomes a lawbreaker, it breeds contempt for law."[57]

Crime is a major issue in the United States. Socially conservative candidates for various public offices have, in times of domestic unrest, wooed voters with cries for "law and order" and the use of the death penalty as a deterrent to crime. If the Hobbesian view of human nature is accurate, the fear of death, if death were a certain consequence, *should* operate to deter potential murderers. Hard-line criminologists and politicians believe that the government, obligated to honor Hobbes's prescription, should have the means to accomplish the task. But it is not clear whether the death penalty is a deterrent; in any case, the certainty of punishment seems unlikely to forestall a murder committed without forethought, as is often the case.

There is no clear evidence that the deterrence that *should* happen *does* happen. Observe the homicide rates of eight nations that have abolished capital punishment:[58]

Change in Homicide Rate Five Years after the Abolition of Capital Punishment

Austria	+32%
Canada	+63%
England	+18%
Finland	−40%
Israel	−53%
Italy	−5%
New Zealand	+117%
Switzerland	−36%

Does the death penalty deter homicide? Apparently it does in Austria, Canada, England, and New Zealand, which suffered increases in homicide after abolition. But in Finland, Israel, Italy, and Switzerland, abolition was followed by a *decrease* in homicide!

Hobbes is also influential among practitioners of behavior modification, the assumption that the manipulation of rewards and punishments can eliminate undesirable behavior and encourage desired behavior. Families routinely do this; so do schools. But the degree of intervention required for a government to employ these techniques is generally viewed as too costly. Anthony Burgess's novel *A Clockwork Orange* realistically describes the degree of effort required for behavior modification: by constantly associating aggressive urges with extreme suffering, the protagonist was cured—at least temporarily—of his previously unabated urge to rape and kill. Similar techniques are tried in the Soviet Union, generally on political criminals and without conspicuous success.[59]

But governments can also heed the dictates of Rousseau in seeking to abate violent crime. If such crime is a response to intolerable economic and social conditions, governments can try to improve citizens' lives—either because they want to or because they believe that crime and poverty are linked. The Rousseauistic hero—the victim of oppression who kills without regard for the consequences—is Raskalnikov, the central character in Dostoyevsky's depressing novel, *Crime and Punishment*.

The Quality of Life: Who Is Responsible?

Whereas crime reduction is universally regarded as a public obligation and seemingly intractable, life extension and life enhancement appear to be less so. If deaths in childbirth are exceptionally high and average life span is exceptionally low, what is the theoretical distinction between such misery and a high death rate? Just as the murder rate varies enormously, so do life spans (see Table 1.4.) and infant mortality. The most

TABLE 1.4 Average Life Span in Various Countries

	1978	1981	1984	1988
Socialist				
Asia				
China	70	67	69	69
North Korea	63	66	68	70
Latin America				
Cuba	72	73	75	73
Europe				
Albania	69	70	70	71*
Bulgaria	72	73	71	71
Czechoslovakia	70	72	70	72
East Germany	72	73	71	73
Hungary	70	71	70	69
Poland	71	73	71	70
Romania	70	71	71	70
Soviet Union	70	72	67	69
Capitalist				
Asia				
Hong Kong	72	75	76	78
Japan	76	77	77	78
Singapore	70	72	72	73*
South Korea	63	66	68	69
Taiwan	64	72	74	73
Europe				
Austria	72	73	73	76
Belgium	72	73	75	75
France	73	76	77	76
Italy	73	74	77	77
Netherlands	74	76	77	77
Switzerland	74	76	77	78
United Kingdom	73	74	74	75
West Germany	72	73	75	76
North America				
Canada	74	75	76	77
United States	74	75	75	75

SOURCE: Data compiled from annual editions of the World Bank, *World Development Report* (New York: Oxford University Press), *Statistical Abstract of the United States* (Washington, DC: U.S. Bureau of the Census), and *The World Almanach and Book of Facts* (New York: St. Martin's Press).
*Data available for 1986 only.

obvious explanation is wealth: rich countries provide an environment for low infant mortality and long life spans while poor countries do not. Poor diet, poor sanitation, and poor medical facilities are just about as lethal as murder. The male life span in Gabon, a central African country with a relatively high average income, is 25 years. The problem is in the inequity of income. If wealth is concentrated in the pockets of a few, it can do little to increase the life chances of the masses of people. The oil-rich Middle Eastern countries have high incomes but relatively low qualities of life for precisely this reason.[60]

	Quality of Life (0–100)	Economic Performance (0–100)
Australia	63	34
Canada	64	38
United Kingdom	58	43
Brunei	28	37
Qatar	28	42
United Arab Emirates	25	37

The wealth of Brunei, Qatar, and the United Arab Emirates is not appreciably different from that of Australia, Canada, and the United Kingdom, but the quality of life (health, medicine, recreation, education) is significantly inferior. The United Arab Emirates has the highest recorded gross national product per capita in the world (estimated at between $22,000 and $32,000), significantly higher than that of Switzerland ($17,000), generally (and rightly) regarded as possessing the world's highest standard of living.

Consider the seemingly intractable problem of life spans. The individualists (as in Hobbes) and the collectivists (as in Rousseau) surely agree that keeping subjects alive is a reasonable measure of efficiency. Most countries are extending lives; some, such as Taiwan, quite spectacularly. But in others, notably the USSR, lives are getting *shorter*, and the crude death rate (deaths from any cause per 100,000) has increased. Among the many reasons are alcoholism (about 10 percent of the population is addicted, and most of this addiction is to the more dangerous forms of alcohol),[61] industrial pollution, increased infant mortality, and—possibly most important—poor diet. The Institute of USA and Canada Studies estimates that the diet of the average Soviet citizen is less nutritious now than it was in 1913, before the revolution. Soviet demographers attribute most of the increased mortality in the USSR to "factors relating to the quality of life."[62] Hobbes could argue that the Soviet government has not fulfilled the terms of the social contract.

Possibly the most precipitous *decline* in standard of living has occurred in the USSR (although the decline has been somewhat attenuated since 1988):

Although average worldwide life expectancy figures keep increasing, Soviet males are actually dying younger these days. Their life expectancy at birth has declined from 66.2 years in 1965 to 61.9 years today.

There are several factors in this unusual trend. One is rampant alcoholism. More hard stuff, vodka mostly, is put away in the USSR than in any other nation—an average of

8 liters a year per person. In fact, the typical family spends 25 to 50 percent of its monthly budget on alcohol. It should come as no surprise, then, that heart disease is epidemic among men or that 40,000 fatal cases of acute alcohol poisoning were reported in 1976 (when the United States reported 400).

Another culprit is the inadequacy of Soviet health services, even though the country boasts free medical treatment for all its citizens. In fact, health care improvements are routinely sacrificed in favor of increased defense expenditures. As a result, it has the lowest life expectancy among men in Europe as well as the highest infant mortality rate (44 deaths per 1,000 live births).

The Soviets' incredible shrinking life expectancy "has no historic parallel in time of peace." says French demographer Jean-Claude Chesnais.[63]

Blame cannot be placed with any confidence on the failure of the soviet economic system—other centrally planned economies have held their own (Poland), improved (Cuba), or declined slightly (East Germany). If the best measure of the standard of living is the quantity of goods and services consumed by the population, the USSR stands out for poor performance even among other centrally planned economies (see Table 1.5.) Clearly, the USSR is an example of a government that must "do something." But what? Soviet agriculture is only a generation away from the infamous collectivization period of Stalin, which, because of the eradication of millions of farmers, has deprived Soviet farmers of any memory of an open market, as opposed to a planned agricultural policy (in China, by contrast, farmers are only one generation away from capitalist agriculture, and central control was never as efficient as in the USSR). Soviet surveys indicate that only 1 or 2 percent of farmers would prefer the risks and opportunities of free agriculture to what they have now. Yet the Soviet Union cannot feed itself unless it develops a firm agriculture infrastructure.

But what about the United States? Once the world's richest country, its standard of living has now slipped below Switzerland's. In the face of massive public and private debt, its industrial productivity is declining. In 1967, one-third of the world's gross national product came from the United States. Today, that percentage has been *halved*. Unless these processes are reversed, the standard of living for individuals will decline. The United States, too, must "do something." And what about crime? Why should American streets be so dangerous, among the most threatening in the world? Even if

TABLE 1.5 Consumption in the USSR as a Percentage of Consumption in Other Countries

	United States	West Germany	Japan	Hungary	Poland
Total	34	46	59	74	80
Food, beverages, tobacco	58	65	69	70	77
Health	33	33	39	46	53

SOURCE: Gertrude E.. Schroeder, "Soviet Living Standards," in *Quality of Life in the Soviet Union,* ed. Horst Herlemann (Boulder, Colo.: Westview Press, 1987), pp. 14–19. Reprinted with permission.

murder is a rarity, satistically, robbery is not. You are *200* times more likely to be robbed in New York than in Tokyo.

Can "something" be done? The cases here—representing Rousseau, Marx, and collectivism on the one hand, and Hobbes, Locke, and individualism on the other— symbolize two traditions. In both cases we may conclude that the "something" may not be much. What difference, then, does the form of government make?

A Ugandan journalist remarks: "The average person doesn't mind who rules him. All he wants is for a daily meal, his kids to go to school, [and] to be able to sell his crops."[64] That astute analysis is made more vivid by the grimness of life in the writer's country, but the underlying message is generalizable to all political systems. As we will be discovering, all societies are governed by a small minority, by elites who are by definition apart from the people. There is actually little disagreement about this, since most people are not sufficiently interested in politics to participate or to argue. In developed countries, elites are frequently more competitive than in poorer countries, and the rules of political conflict are less violent, but *all* government is government by the few. Differences in government are not based on any evidence that mass participation is likely to change a system to government by the people.

Differences between governments, to repeat our earlier observation, are of *degree:* of competition among elites, of governmental responsiveness, of legal constraints. How strong a consensus is there on the fundamental values of society? What are the valued resources, the possession of which ensures entry into the elite? Is elite status earned by wealth, education, political loyalty, religious orthodoxy, representative legitimacy, or military prowess?

So as eventually to formulate a notion of what a government can do for and to us and to see what life is like under a variety of political systems, we now turn to studying the various factors—cultural, historical, theoretical, and circumstantial—that have contributed to the world's polities. This will let us see how and when power and people interact, how the view from the capital compares with the view from the street, how things change, and how they remain the same.

FOR FURTHER CONSIDERATION

1. What are "public politics?" Contrast that to "private politics."
2. What is the basic premise behind Hobbes's version of the social contract? Behind Rousseau's?
3. Define *liberal* and *conservative* according to political theory. Compare your definitions to their everyday usage.
4. List several characteristics of liberalism, conservatism, socialism, and Marxism. Could some characteristics define more than one ideology?
5. Briefly outline the roles modern governments are expected to fulfill.
6. What is meant by the phrase: "The quality of life?"

For the More Adventurous

1. Does the social contract discussed by Hobbes, Locke, and Rousseau purport to governments today? How? In his syndicated column of April 7, 1989, George Will wrote of public housing in America

[it] has become recrudescence [from the verb *to recrudesce,* meaning to reoccur after lying dormant] of the worst of the American frontier—Dodge City without a marshall. So, you modern-day Jeffersonians who think that government is best which governs least, welcome to your world. It is Hobbes' world, where life is always poor, nasty, brutish, and often short. Public housing . . . is anarchy tempered by juvenocracy—power wielded by adolescents.[65]

What would Hobbes say? How about Rousseau?

2. Justify an authoritarian government, then justify a polyarchic government. Which rationalization do you find more persuasive? Assume the following conclusion to be correct: ". . . exposure to television is . . . etiologically related to a major proportion—perhaps one half—of the rapes, assaults, and other forms of interpersonal violence in the United States."[66] Apply your arguments to this problem.

NOTES

1. "Importance of Politics in Our Lives," *USA Today,* April 18, 1988, p. 2.
2. Ibid.
3. Bill Keller, "For Grim Soviet Consumers, the New Year of Discontent," *New York Times,* January 1, 1989, p. 1.
4. Ibid.
5. Thomas Hobbes, *Leviathan* (New York: Collier, 1961), p. 133. (Originally published 1651.)
6. Christopher Wren, "Voter Apathy Becoming Universal," *New York Times,* December 1, 1988, p. 22.
7. C. Wright Mills, quoted in Thomas R. Dye, *Power and Society* (Monterey, Calif.: Brooks/Cole, 1986.), p. 68.
8. Harry Jaffa, "Aristotle," in *History of Political Philosophy,* ed. Leo Strauss and Joseph Cropsey (Skokie, Ill.: Rand McNally, 1963), p. 67.
9. Hobbes, *Leviathan,* p. 100. In the Bible, the leviathan was a sea monster, possibly a whale; Hobbes used the term to mean anything huge and powerful.
10. Erich Fromm, *The Anatomy of Human Destructiveness* (New York: Fawcett, 1973), p. 50.
11. Jean-Jacques Rousseau, *The Social Contract* (New York: Dutton, 1950), p. 55. (Originally published 1762.)
12. Warren Miller and the National Election Studies. Washington, D.C. Center for Political Studies: American National Election Study, 1984 (Mimeograph).
13. Herbert McClosky and John Zaller, *The American Ethos* (Cambridge, Mass.: Harvard University Press, 1984), p. 176.
14. Ibid.
15. Ibid., p. 269.
16. Ibid., p. 266.
17. Ibid.
18. János Kádár, Address to the Hungarian National Assembly, May 11, 1957, cited in Fred H. Willhoite, *Power and Governments* (Pacific Grove, Calif.: Brooks/Cole, 1988), p. 105.
19. John Locke, *An Essay Concerning Human Understanding* (Oxford, England: Clarendon Press, 1975), p. 89. (Originally published 1690.)
20. John Locke, *Second Treatise on Civil Government* (Chicago: Regnery, 1966), p. 102. (Originally published 1690.)
21. James Madison, *Federalist No. 51.* (Originally published 1788.)
22. Charles Lindblom, *Politics and Markets* (New York: Basic Books, 1977), p. 133.
23. *World Bank World Development Report 1988* (New York: Oxford University Press, 1988), p. 224.

24. Robert Axelrod, *The Evolution of Cooperation* (New York: Basic Books, 1985), p. 133.

25. Arnold J. Heidenheimer, Hugh Heclo, and Carolyn Adams-Teich, *Comparative Public Policy* (New York: St. Martin's Press, 1983), p. 203.

26. Ibid.

27. *The Economist,* April 18, 1988, p. 14.

28. Fidel Castro, quoted in Bill Keller, "Gorbachev Begins His Visit to Cuba," *New York Times,* April 4, 1989, p. 6.

29. Although some prominent American psychologists believe that the idea of personalities adjusting to external conditions of life is reasonable, Soviet psychology has been unable to explore this line of thought because the conclusions are already worked out in the official literature. Both the character traits (strength of will, fervor in building socialism, love of country, high moral standards) and the conditions under which they develop (socialism) are defined in advance. See Raymond A. Bauer, *The New Man in Soviet Psychology* (Cambridge, Mass.: Harvard University Press, 1952), p. 169.

30. Trofim Lysenko, an agronomist held in high repute during the Stalin era in the Soviet Union, claimed that he could change organisms by altering the environment and that the changes could be transmitted genetically. Hence human beings could induce evolutionary changes in human nature by changing institutions. The "new Soviet man" could be created by altering the environment, and once the desired characteristics were in place, they could be transmitted to the next generation. (Lysenko claimed that wheat that had been hardened in the cold north kept these characteristics when moved to warmer climes.) Lysenkoism was repudiated after World War II but was rehabilitated as a serious scientific mode of inquiry by Nikita Khrushchev in 1964. Though Lysenkoism is undeniably nonsense, there is some evidence that what we once assumed to be learned behavior (such as aggression and even the willingness to accept authority) may be inherited. No one believes that these characteristics can be modified and then retransmitted, however.

31. Richard Crossman, ed., *The God That Failed* (London: Hamish Hamilton, 1950), p. 11.

32. The role model for the new Soviet man was Alexander Stakhanov, a coal miner aroused to superhuman efforts by one of Stalin's speeches. Stakhanovites were workers honored by the Communist party for their commitment.

33. Lindblom, *Politics and Markets,* pp. 55–56.

34. Ibid., pp. 544–545.

35. Rousseau, *Social Contract,* p. 18.

36. Kenneth R. Hoover, *Ideology and Political Life* (Pacific Grove, Calif.: Brooks/Cole, 1987), p. 111.

37. Lindblom, *Politics and Markets,* p. 133.

38. Ibid.

39. Forrest D. Colburn, "Embattled Nicaragua," *Current History,* December 1987, p. 405.

40. See Giovanni Sartori, *The Theory of Democracy Revisited* (Chatham, N.J.: Chatham House, 1987), pp. 185–213.

41. Quoted in Fox Butterfield, *Alive in the Bitter Sea* (New York: Times Books, 1982), pp. 326–327.

42. Nicholas D. Kristof, "China Celebrates 10 Years along the Capitalist Road," *New York Times,* January 1, 1989, p. E3.

43. Raymond D. Gastil, *Freedom in the World* (New York: Freedom House, 1988), p. 292.

44. Maria Chang, "Women," in *Human Rights in the People's Republic of China,* ed. Yuan-Li Wu et al. (Boulder, Colo.: Westview Press, 1988), pp. 258–259.

45. Ibid.

46. Robert Nisbet, *Prejudice* (Cambridge, Mass.: Harvard University Press, 1982), p. 19.

47. Charles Hauptman, *World Human Rights Guide* (New York: Facts on File, 1986), p. 17.

48. See Axelrod, *Evolution of Cooperation*, p. 115.

49. Quoted in R. W. Apple, "Political Shifts Steel Economic Reform in China," *New York Times,* February 21, 1983, p. 4.

50. Quoted in Kristin Luker, *Abortion and the Politics of Motherhood* (Berkeley: University of California Press, 1984), pp. 137–138.

51. Bob Woodward, *The Brethren: Inside the Supreme Court* (New York: Avon, 1981), pp. 126–127.

52. Jane Mansbridge, *Beyond Adversary Democracy* (New York: Basic Books, 1980), p. 126.

53. Berthold Hinz, *Art in the Third Reich* (New York: Pantheon, 1974), p. 45.

54. Mark J. Porubcansky, "Soviets No Longer Brush Aside the Works of Kazimir Malevich," *New York Times,* January 7, 1989, p. 4.

55. Thomas R. Dye and Harmon Zeigler, *American Politics in the Media Age,* 2d ed. (Pacific Grove, Calif.: Brooks/Cole, 1986), p. 42.

56. Dana Archer and Rosemary Gartner, *Violence and Crime in Cross-national Perspective* (Berkeley: University of California Press, 1984), p. 88.

57. Ibid, pp. 92–94.

58. Ibid., p. 134.

59. For a discussion of theories of deterrence, see James Q. Wilson and Charles Herrnstein, *Crime and Human Nature* (New York: Simon & Schuster, 1985), pp. 516ff.

60. *International Living,* January 1987, p. 7.

61. The USSR ranks fourth in alcohol consumption per capita when beer and wine are included, first when they are excluded.

62. Vladimir G. Treml, "Alcohol Abuse in the Soviet Union," in *Quality of Life in the Soviet Union,* ed. Horst Herlemann (Boulder, Colo.: Westview Press, 1987), p. 159.

63. Lyn Crawford, "The Red Decline," *Science,* January 1986, p. 58.

64. Quoted in Edward A. Gargan, "Uganda Tries to Awaken from Its Nightmarish Past," *New York Times,* December 22, 1985, p. E3.

65. George Will, syndicated column, April 7, 1989.

66. Brandon S. Centerwall, "Exposure to Television as a Risk Factor for Violence," *American Journal of Epidemiology 129,* (April 1989): 651.

FOR FURTHER READING

Axelrod, Robert. *The Evolution of Cooperation.* New York: Basic Books, 1985. A very readable analysis of prisoners' dilemmas and an excellent essay on cooperation in the trenches of World War I.

Berger, Thomas. *The Capitalist Revolution.* New York: Basic Books, 1986. Berger argues that capitalism works and socialism does not.

Berman, Marshall. *All That Is Solid Melts into Air.* New York: Simon & Schuster, 1982. In the seemingly unending competition for inane titles (see *The Time Falling Bodies Take to Light,* by William Thompson), Berman rises above such shenanigans to write a fine account of writers, philosophers, urban developers, and the like in investigating response to the "modernist revolution."

Boyd, William. *The New Confessions.* New York: Morrow, 1988. A film director, obsessed by Rousseau's *Confessions,* devotes his life to the improbable task of making them into a movie.

Burns, James MacGregor. *Leadership.* New York: Harper & Row, 1978. A modern classic of organization and lucidity making a complex topic accessible.

Crossman, Richard, ed. *The God That Failed.* London: Hamish Hamilton, 1950. A moving personal testimony of ex-communists, especially strong on the religious nature of ideology.

Elms, Alan C. *Personality in Politics.* Orlando, Fla.: Harcourt Brace Jovanovich, 1976. Features a strong section on psychobiography.

Elster, John. *Karl Marx: A Reader.* Cambridge: Cambridge University Press, 1986. Marx in your pocket.

Gastil, Raymond D. *Freedom in the World.* New York: Freedom House, 1988. An annual review of freedom, featuring a country-by-country analysis.

Greenstein, Fred. *Personality and Politics.* Chicago: Markham, 1969. Greenstein is very strong in explaining the conditions that allow personality to affect public behavior and those that constrain its effect.

Hampton, Jean. *Hobbes and the Social Contract Tradition.* New York: Cambridge University Press, 1986.

Hauptman, Charles. *World Human Rights Guide.* New York: Facts or File, 1986. Assembled by *The Economist* of London, the best weekly newsmagazine in the world.

Hobbes, Thomas. *Leviathan.* New York: Collier, 1961. (Originally published 1651.)

Hsu, Leonard. *The Political Philosophy of Confucianism.* London: Curzon, 1975.

Jaffa, Harry. "Aristotle," *History of Political Philosophy,* ed. Leo Strauss and Joseph Cropsey. Skokie, Ill.: Rand McNally, 1963.

Kelly, Christopher. *Rousseau's Exemplary Life: The "Confessions" as Political Philosophy.* Ithaca, N.Y.: Cornell University Press, 1987. The stages of Rousseau's life and the ideology of the *Confessions* are brilliantly interwoven.

Lefort, Claude. *The Political Forms of Modern Society.* Cambridge, Mass.: MIT Press, 1986. Lefort teaches at L'École des Hautes Études en Sciences Sociales in Paris. This anthology, edited by John Thompson of Cambridge, introduces non-French readers to an important voice of the European left. Lefort does for "bourgeois ideology" what the right did to Marxism: reveals its bloody-mindedness.

Lindblom, Charles. *Politics and Markets.* New York: Basic Books, 1977.

Mazlish, Bruce. *The Meaning of Karl Marx.* New York: Oxford University Press, 1984. A "psychobiography" of Marx, showing his passion for Shakespeare. Mazlish argues that the father of modern alienation theory was "very much alienated from his own earthly father."

McClellan, David, ed. *Marxism: Essential Writings.* New York: Oxford University Press, 1988. Writings by modern Marxists, Mao and Marcuse among them.

McClosky, Herbert, and John Zaller. *The American Ethos.* Cambridge, Mass.: Harvard University Press, 1984. An exhaustive account of the ideology of the "common man."

Nisbet, Robert. *History of the Idea of Progress.* New York: Basic Books, 1980. One of the finest, most engaging histories of ideas extant.

Rogow, Arnold, and Harold D. Lasswell. *Power, Corruption, and Rectitude.* Englewood Cliffs, N.Y.: Prentice-Hall, 1963. Power may not corrupt but may *ennoble,* depending on personality and circumstance.

Rousseau, Jean-Jacques. *The Social Contract.* New York, Dutton, 1950. (Originally published 1762.)

Sennet, Richard. *Authority.* New York: Knopf, 1980. The act of rebellion creates a yet stronger need for authority—a paradox of revolution but a fundamental of human nature.

Taylor, Michael. *The Possibility of Cooperation.* Cambridge: Cambridge University Press, 1987. A more pessimistic, Hobbesian view than Axelrod's.

Wildavsky, Aaron. *Moses.* Tuscaloosa: University of Alabama Press, 1984.

Wilson, James Q., and Charles Herrnstein. *Crime and Human Nature.* New York: Simon & Schuster, 1985. Rousseau and Hobbes put to modern empirical testing. Rousseau does not come out very well!

CHAPTER 2

The Framework
of the Polity: Culture

The modern *nation-state* is a product of the Renaissance of the 16th and 17th centuries, and the identification of self with nation—nationalism—is even more recent. Earlier political entities—Rome, Athens, Sparta—were *city-states,* although they evoked loyalties similar to those of nation-states. Nationalism, although recent, can be a powerful, compelling, and even psychologically uplifting state of mind.

Its appeal is especially apparent when nationalism involves race and ethnicity, when culture assists as an organizing idea. When nation builders base their appeal on the creation of racial or ethnic homogeneity, they enlist a subnational identification into the quest for national identity. If nations can also arrange to have their boundaries roughly congruent with the natural borders of a homogeneous group, their chances of actually forging a durable nation are enhanced. Indeed, the pursuit of such congruence is in itself a powerful stimulus to nationalism.

No better example of the pursuit of congruence can be found than in today's Soviet Union and eastern Europe. Encouraged by a relaxation of central party control, three Baltic republics, Latvia, Estonia, and Lithuania, annexed by the USSR at the end of World War II, tried to achieve some measure of independence. These republics, independent between the world wars, are ethnically, linguistically, and culturally dissimilar to Russia. They were capitalist democracies during the period when the USSR was becoming a Marxist totalitarian state. In the 1930s, they became substantially more authoritarian. Occupied by German armies during the last years of World War I, the Baltic states were abandoned by the Soviets in the Brest-Litovsk peace treaty ending German-Soviet hostilities. When the German war effort collapsed in the west, the Soviet armies reinvaded the Baltic states but were successfully resisted by Latvians, Estonians, Lithuanians, remnants of the German armies, White Russians, and Finns.

Even as these nations' liberal democratic traditions deteriorated, their brand of authoritarianism was far milder than the totalitarianism then sweeping the USSR. During the darkest days of Stalin's purges and the collectivization of agriculture, in the Baltic states, "Literary, artistic, and musical life flourished. The increase in the number of schools was phenomenal. Each of the three countries maintained a national university, where higher education in the native language became available for the first time." [1]

Independence ended with the Molotov-Ribbentrop Pact of 1939, with a secret protocol assigning Estonia and Latvia to the USSR and Lithuania to Germany. After the collapse of Poland, Lithuania was placed within the Soviet sphere. Soon thereafter, the Red Army occupied the Baltic states and installed Russian-dominated Communist governments. When the Germans invaded in 1941, they once again occupied the Baltic republics. After the Germans were defeated, the Communist governments returned. Thus these small nations have suffered the ignoble fate of having been occupied by the 20th century's most brutal dictatorships. Small wonder they want to be left alone!

Since the end of World War II, underground independence movements have operated in the Baltic republics. During the initial Sovietization, living standards had plummeted. During the Stalin years, life got even worse, as independence movements were brutally repressed. But after Stalin's death, the nationalist organizations built up to full strength. Under Gorbachev, many nationalists—some of whom had spent most of their adult lives in labor camps—reemerged, demanding their own currency (convertible on world markets), national language, and (market-driven) economies.

The Baltic states are symbolically important and intellectually vibrant; the Ukraine—

the populous breadbasket of the USSR—is another matter entirely. Ukrainian nationalism, taking its cue from the Baltics, emerged as a serious problem in 1989. Ukrainian-language poetry flourishes in Kiev, where 10,000 people joined a Ukrainian-language society. As in the Baltics, the Ukrainian nationalists call for a halt to Russification, to the "raising of little Ivans who don't remember who their kin are."

Although Gorbachev speaks, optimistically, of "one family" with a "common home," he is inaccurate. Lithuania, the last of the Baltic states to nurture a political independence movement, in 1989 allowed Sajudis, an independence movement, to proclaim, "Our goal is a free Lithuania." In the March 1989 elections, Sajudis won a strong majority in the Lithuanian national congress. It declared that Lithuania had been "occupied against its will." The Soviet Union may be more artificial than anyone imagined.

This chapter will examine the ties that bind a people and lead individuals to relinquish power to a superior authority. A sense of the culture of a nation is needed to judge the appropriateness of governmental form and function.

THE COMPONENTS OF CULTURE

Nationalism stresses the legitimacy of a unique culture, a way of looking at life that is peculiar to a nation. A culture is simply the collected customs, habits, ideas, values, and traditions of a group of people. Cultures are blueprints or maps for life. They are "historically created *designs for living,* explicit and implicit, rational, irrational, and nonrational, which may exist . . . as potential guides for the behavior of man."[2] Cultures take many forms, some of them overlapping. In the United States, we speak of the culture of blacks, WASP (white, Anglo-Saxon Protestants), and southerners. We learn of the "culture of poverty," said to enfeeble the chronically poor and to impede upward economic mobility. Corporations, especially those with high levels of employee morale, have their own cultures; they instill "a system of informal rules that spells out how people are to behave most of the time."[3]

Informal rules of behavior—cultures—are both a cause and a consequence of variation in political systems. When informal rules become institutionalized, cultural expectations take on the role of laws and are enforced by the authority of the state. When laws do not embody the potency of culture, they are often of little consequence. During Prohibition, people drank; today people use drugs. The choice of addiction is culturally dictated, and the expectations of the *subculture* (variations in ways of life within a society, such as families, ethnic groups, or religions) outweigh the ability of the state enforce the law.

Do cultures and institutions (governments) develop simultaneously? Do institutions "institutionalize" ways of life? Or do institutions *create* ways of life that subsequently become incorporated in the culture? These questions are not easily answered. We can say, however, that efforts to *impose* culturally incompatible rules of behavior on a people stand a low chance of success. Americans in Vietnam, seeking to import democracy, floundered; Russians in Afghanistan, seeking to impose communism, failed. These failures are usually explained by the *interrelated nature* of culture. Linkages between the components of culture help explain why differences in child rearing, family structure, and economics may have psychological consequences that until now have been regarded as culture-free. Agoraphobia (fear of leaving home) and anorexia (an obsession with body weight) occur only in Western countries.

Culture is a consequence of five factors:

1. *Technology:* the ways in which people create and use tools and other material artifacts
2. *Economics:* the patterns of behaving relative to the production, distribution, and consumption of goods and services
3. *Social organizations:* characteristic relations among individuals in a society, including the division of labor and the social and political organization, and the relationships between societies
4. *Religion:* ways of life relative to the human concern for the unknown
5. *Symbolism:* the system of symbols (language, art, music, literature, folklore) used to acquire, comprehend, and perpetuate knowledge

How governments view the interrelatedness of these factors is a question of degree.

Collectivist ideologies attempt to encapsulate all the components of culture into a single, cohesive scheme; religion, art, the family, and so on, all serve the collectivity and cannot contradict it. Individualist societies are more patient with cultural diversity. Cultural biases and governmental preferences may be at odds over relatively humorous or quite serious matters. The 1988 Summer Olympics in South Korea brought much of the world face to face with the Oriental fondness for dog meat. Although the government required that restaurants alter their menus during the few months of Western invasion, the ban on dog meat was ignored. Dogs are raised and slaughtered like cows in Korea, and centuries of tradition could not be disrupted by government edict. Equally silly was the Cuban effort to move Christmas to July 26. The reasons for the decree were sensible: the best months for raising and harvesting sugar are November through May. Hence from 1970 onward, the annual extra quota of Christmas pork has been sold on July 16, distribution of the (two) children's toys occurs during the same month, and the three Magi from the East are portrayed as revolutionaries dressed in olive drab![4] With the exception of Premier Castro and a few trusted supporters, Cuban government officials continue tacitly to limit work during Christmas.

A Case of State versus Culture: Homosexuality.   Although its causes are unclear, homosexual behavior is ageless. Some societies—Oman, Aden, Afghanistan—do not regard homosexuality as an aberration. Others—ours, for example—routinely debate the morality, legality, and political legitimacy of homosexuality. But rarely have nations sought to abolish it or "cure" it, for what is the purpose?

One purpose for outlawing homosexual behavior is a declining birthrate. For instance, the Nazis became especially disturbed by Germany's declining birthrate during the 1930s. Hence as part of a glorification of the family (and thereby to win the "battle of the birthrate"), homosexuals were harassed unmercifully. Charges of homosexuality were filed in 30,000 instances in 1936, a 900 percent increase over three years earlier.[5] Interestingly, the birthrate did soar—from 14.7 in 1930 to 20.3 in 1939—but not necessarily within the family. The divorce rate climbed even more steeply, and premarital sexual intercourse, rampant in the Reich (an estimated 90 percent of the unmarried population of Munich, for example, engaged in frequent sex), naturally produced many a baby. The Nazi view of homosexuality was thus not ideological but instrumental.

But how does one explain the Communist abhorrence of homosexuality today, when there is no apparent "rational" justification for opposition? Surely in China, where birth control is so harsh that infanticide is rarely prosecuted, homosexuality should be ignored, but it is instead outlawed—a victim of the clash of cultures that makes life difficult in collectivist societies. Initially, in the first modern Communist society, the USSR, sexual preference was not considered worthy of much attention, as there were other more severe problems. However, Stalin came to regard homosexuality as a bourgeois vice and sought to eradicate it like the Nazis had. Although homosexuality is outlawed by the Soviet criminal code, Russian consenting adults can now, with the advent of *glasnost,* do what they please. But this is not so in Cuba, one of the few remaining hard-line Communist nations. Declared to be suffering from a "social disease," Cuba's homosexuals were rounded up and shipped off to labor camps (actually, the Cubans were less tolerant than the Nazis, as they rounded up anybody who "looked like" a homosexual).[6] Later, Cuban physicians found Marxism to be a proper cure: "There is only one medicine . . . and we have it in hand. It is Marxist philosophy, accompanied by hard labor that will force them into manly consciousness and gestures."[7]

Although these examples generate smirks, do not misunderstand the government's problem. The government sought to change cultural traditions, to produce a cultural patina more in harmony with state goals. The example of homosexuality makes the point clear, but there are other areas. Pity the poor Jehovah's Witnesses, whose unwillingness to accept allegiance to an "earthly power" led to their incarceration in Nazi Germany and in modern Cuba (Jehovah's Witnesses in Cuba had their genitals tortured with caustic chemicals). In the United States, the Witnesses needed judicial protection of their refusal to salute the American flag.

When cultural imperatives tug in different directions, nations, irrespective of ideology, are generally willing to use force to preserve the integrity of the state. Iraqis exterminate Kurds, and the U.S. North would not allow the South to secede; different motives, different times, different methods, but similar objectives.

TWO DIMENSIONS OF CULTURE: ACQUIESCENCE AND OBEDIENCE

Analyses of the components of culture suggest several of importance for political systems.

Cultures may encourage individuals to be passive, to accept their destiny without complaint, to ascribe good or bad fortune to "God's will" or to some impersonal, immutable force. This is typically part of the religion component of culture. Since people fear the unknown, religion reduces this fear by providing answers, by setting forth ways of behavior, by assuring individuals that it is permissible to leave matters to a higher authority.

Cultures that refuse to interrupt the process of death—watching a child drown in some Latin American Indian cultures or allowing a child to die for lack of a blood transfusion or other lifesaving devices among American fundamentalist—subscribe to *fatalism*. Such cultures are ideally suited for authoritarian or totalitarian political systems and for rigidly structured economic or social systems based on class (as in England) or caste (as in India). People who believe that their individual destiny is not only beyond their control but also in better hands than theirs are not likely to demand much, if anything, of government. Indeed, they may be accustomed to having major personal decisions made for them. When Russian immigrants arrive in the West, they frequently ask for a housing assignment, a job assignment, and so on. They are befuddled when they learn that no such authorities exist and occasionally develop symptoms of extreme anxiety or depression.

Conservative Religious Ideologies and Their Political Consequences

Among traditional, conservative religious and social doctrines that encourage a passive view of life, Confucian-based ideologies in Asia and some of the older, more tradition-ally ordered European countries stress a natural order, a hierarchy of positions, and obedience. But there are significant differences in the cultures of these two regions and corresponding variations in political attitudes, as we shall see.

Respect or scorn for authority is the most "political" of cultural attributes, for compliance with governmental authority cannot be maintained indefinitely without sub-stantial subject support or at least the absence of active hostility. Few cultures are as obsessed as ours with autonomy and defiance.

Confucian ethics preaches hierarchy and consensus. Relations between people are structured by their status, and individuals filling a given status are due respect and expect obedience, regardless of the circumstances of the individual exchange. This is not to say that absolute tyrants were not deplored in Confucian principles, but there was certainly no assumption of a contract. Despots who rule with a "mandate from heaven" are hardly disposed to temper their rule. Like all absolute rulers, Chinese emperors were checked by competition from the bureaucracy, the military, and fledgling regionally powerful lords. But they ruled a society in which every relationship was specified as between subordinate and superior: child to father, wife to husband, subject to ruler.

To be disobedient in any of these relationships was to violate mutually reinforcing rules. Decisions made in the upper echelons of the hierarchy are implemented at lower levels; obedience learned in primary relationships is transferred to more abstract levels. Loyalty lay at the heart of personal relations: no tenet of Confucian thought was more emphasized than filial piety. *The Twenty-four Examples of Filial Piety*, widely read until recently on the mainland and still read on Taiwan, indulges the Chinese penchant for parable with stories of sacrifice for parental well-being so grisly as to repel Western readers.

In Western cultures—especially that of the United States—books, workshops, ser-mons, and pop psychology jargon accent "parenting." In Asian cultures, the emphasis is quite the opposite. The goal of offspring is to gladden parents; parents are pleased by achievement; ergo, children work hard. The consequence is predictable:

> I was constantly struck by the almost universal good behavior of Chinese children. . . .
> They are quiet, obedient, quick to follow their teachers' instructions, and they seldom
> exhibit the boisterous aggressiveness or selfishness of American children. Nor do they
> cry, whine, throw tantrums, or suck their thumbs, some of the typical signs of anxiety
> and tension to which Western kids are prone.[8]

Asian children routinely outperform European and American ones on the various quantitative tests of achievement. Asian children achieve because their parents want them to. Asian culture—Confucianism—values learning and respect for authority. The Scholastic Aptitude Test results in Table 2.1 clearly illustrate one possible consequence. The Asian-American performance is the best among minority groups. In math, the Asian-Americans *outperform* whites; in verbal skills, they are a strong second. The superior performance of Asian-Americans raises new issues on the subject of cultural bias in the SAT, a point stressed by black leaders. In 1989, the cultural bias hypothesis was given added dimension by John Thompson, basketball coach of powerful Georgetown University, who walked off the court during a game to protest new requirements that black athletes score 700 on the SAT tests. Thompson claimed "proven cultural bias" (note that 700 is below the average for blacks taking the exam).

Perhaps there is a cultural bias, for something works for the Asians. Family cohesion may be a key: 61 percent of all black children are born out of wedlock (compared with 15 percent of whites), and the American divorce rate, highest among industrial nations, is about six times greater than that of Japan, South Korea, or Taiwan—the cultures of the Asian-Americans. The divorce rate among blacks is twice that of whites, which is four times that of Asian-Americans.

It would be silly to argue that Asian-Americans do better entirely because they are obedient, but a clear line of research does show that "time on task" (educational jargon for hard work) is strongly linked to achievement. As an Asian explained:

> Some American kids are really smart, but they just don't work as hard as Asians. . . .
> Asians pay more attention to their teachers, then go home and spend more hours doing
> their homework instead of watching TV or going on dates. . . . I promised my father
> to do good and to uphold our family honor. My father spent so much to send me here,
> and I am determined to repay him.[9]

TABLE 2.1 Scholastic Aptitude Test (SAT) Scores, 1984–1985

	Verbal	Math	Total
White	449	491	940
Asian-American	404	518	922
American Indian	392	428	820
Mexican-American	382	426	808
Puerto Rican	368	409	777
Black	346	376	772

SOURCE: Congress of the United States, Budget Office, *Trends in Educational Achievement* (April, 1986), p. 44.

One jarring cultural difference between the Americans and the Asians, a manifestation of our lack of interest in familial authority, is the treatment of old people. In the United States, the elderly are relegated to nursing homes, their infirmities mocked. In Asian countries, extended families take care of the elderly, who are honored.

During the first five years of life in most Asian cultures, children sleep with their mothers; American children are typically out in their own bedrooms and encouraged to establish autonomy. Around the age of 5, Asian children experience the trauma of a "crackdown," in which they are forcibly molded into the strict hierarchy of the culture:

> Compared to Americans, there's much less a sense of individual self among Asians. They experience themselves as far more embedded in a net of extremely close emotional relationships. They have a family self, one that includes close relationships in their own sense of who they are. This kind of self simply does not exist in the West to nearly the same degree. The child's "family self" promotes the feeling that what shames the child shames the family.[10]

Since the United States leads the world in divorce and out-of-wedlock births and since its students routinely trail those of Europe and Asia in standard tests of achievement, we should applaud the stellar performance of the Asians and note that blacks, while still lowest, have improved the most since 1978. American students, compared internationally, tend to come up boneheads. Consider these international math test scores:[11]

Score	Country
65	Japan
61	Finland
60	Hungary
59	Sweden
58	Canada
57	New Zealand
55	Belgium
55	United Kingdom
52	United States
50	Israel
57	**International average**

Transferring Loyalties: China

The translation of loyalty to parents into loyalty to the state is not difficult to imagine. It is, for one thing, not inappropriate to speak of the Chinese family: almost 95 percent of the populace is of one ethnic group. Further, since China traditionally has had a culture that honors absolutism, it does not tolerate unrest, which is perceived as a sign of weakness, over a long period. Until the momentous demonstrations in Tiananmen Square in May 1989, Chinese students would stop a protest as soon as they were told to; more often than not they were mobilized by a faction within the ruling elite in order to reveal mass support. Possibly the 1989 tragedy began in just this way and got out of hand.

Chinese history—of which the Chinese are immensely proud—has gone through periods of governmental decay until a new mandate of heaven is claimed. The fall of the Ching dynasty in 1911 introduced just such a period, which ended with the establishment of the People's Republic in 1949. The Mandarin dynasties were absolutist, and the 1911 revolution aspired to some lessening of the reach of the state. But nothing much along these lines was achieved, as the country was rendered helpless by continued resistance of warlords, Communist-Nationalist clashes, Japanese invasion, and finally civil war. Mao Tse-Tung (Mao Zedong, 1893–1975), leader of the People's Liberation Army and theoretician of the Chinese revolution, like his imperial predecessors, claimed the mandate and the deference that came with it.

Mao's death ushered in a brief period of uncertainty until Deng Xiaoping consolidated power. Clear evidence of absolutism can be seen in the swiftness with which Deng dismantled and replaced Mao's ideology. In 1989, Deng, in repressing the student–worker riots, reassembled Mao's police network in a matter of weeks.

In greater or lesser degrees, the same culture can be found in all Asian countries, even those that are nominally democratic. European communist governments, such as those in the USSR, Poland, and Hungary, have moved much more rapidly toward more open political systems than has China.

Loyalty in a Japanese Setting

Japanese schools, like Chinese ones, teach obedience and achievement. Respect for authority is buttressed by intense competition and nationally established examinations; loyalty is keyed to the large corporations that dominate the economy, and politics displays nearly as much consensus as in the People's Republic of China. All political parties were abolished by the military in 1940, but with defeat and occupation, two of the more conservative prewar parties reappeared, merged in 1955 to form the Liberal Democratic party and Japan is a more open society than most of its Asian counterparts, but its adaptation of imposed democracy to Japanese culture has certainly ensured continuity and consensus. The Liberal Democratic Party survived the implication of its leaders in bribery scandals on two occasions, and faced the possibility of defeat only after a reoccurrence of bribery charges took place in 1989, coupled with an unpopular sales tax, and the additional embarrassment of the entanglement of its leaders with the sordid Tokyo geisha scene. Governments in the United Kingdom (the Profumo affair, documented in the 1989 movie *Scandal*), the United States (Watergate, which interrupted Republican dominance of Presidential elections), and Greece (where the Prime Minister conducted an affair with a woman half his age) fell for less.

The Impact of Stoicism

In the West, Catholicism gradually allotted to church officials the authority as God's vicars to pardon sins, limiting, if not eliminating, individual responsibility. Religions that encourage stoic resolve in this life in exchange for benediction in the next also encourage submissive acceptance of hardship. To the extent that political authorities reinforce passive behavior, they and the church reinforce this dimension of culture. The Russian Orthodox church of czarist Russia gave religious sanction to authoritarian government, as did the Roman Catholic church in Europe, with clerics achieving notoriety as the confidants of monarchs.

In the American South, impoverished sharecroppers were attracted to fundamentalist sects that promised their followers that the poor and rich would exchange places in the hereafter; indeed, the Christian edict that the meek shall inherit the earth had similar origins in poverty. The Spanish-American culture of the American Southwest is regarded by anthropologists as classically acquiescent. As late as the 1930s, Spanish shepherds took no steps to protect land or flocks from storms, since such catastrophes were God's will and doctors' services were frequently refused for the same reason, reflecting a fatalistic attitude toward life or death.[12]

Fatalism can be carried to gruesome extremes, as in the Indian practice of *suttee* (or *sati*), the Hindu rite of widow burning. Banned by the British in 1829, the most recent case occurred in 1987, when 3,000 watched Roop Kunwar burn on the funeral pyre of her husband of six months. Suttee, dramatizing the "degeneracy of religion into cruel superstition and prejudice,"[13] nevertheless persisted, supported by cultural norms. In India, a widow is entitled to no support or even sympathy; her life is over, so why not finish the job? Economic necessity found cultural and religious justification.

Equally cruel is the Arab concept of honor. Westerners were shocked when in 1989 the Iranian Imam Ruhollah Khomeini declared a "death sentence" for Salman Rushdie, and Indian-born British subject whose novel *The Satanic Verses* was held to blaspheme the Prophet Muhammad. How could a culture exact so ruthless a price for a work of fiction? In Jaba, on the occupied West Bank of the Jordan, Israeli administrators have come to accept the Arab concept of honor. In March 1989, a 36-year-old woman, pregnant and unmarried, was strangled in a ritual slaying by her father. The father, surrendering to Israeli authorities, was tried in an Arab court that gives special dispensation for matters of family honor. Had the execution not been carried out, the father would have been ostracized. Israeli crime reports tell gruesome stories of Arab fathers showing up at police stations with the heads of their daughters in plastic bags.[14]

Thus Khomeini, in calling for Rushdie's death, did no more than lay bare to the West the Arab concept of honor and revenge. Moshe Sharon of Hebrew University maintains that Western and Jewish culture is "guilt-oriented." When a crime is committed, an individual, feeling guilt, is punished. But Arab culture is "shame-oriented":

> Anything an individual does is in relation to the group. If an individual dishonors himself, he dishonors the group, he brings shame on the group, and the only way to erase this shame is to carry out some kind of revenge.[15]

The *jihad*, or holy war against nonbelievers, is waged partially out of the shame of Arab defeat by Israeli armies in four wars. One must ask if these cultural necessities make hope for peace realistic.

Obedience in a European Context: Germany

Excluding the Eastern European one-party states, which have a streak of Asian-style authoritarianism in their cultures, the Western nation that is said to have developed the most obedient culture is Germany.

A relatively new country, it had only a brief and unsuccessful flirtation with democracy between defeat in World War I and the rise of the Nazi party. Whereas Asian obedience is a product of thousands of years of cultivation, the origins of German obedience are more recent—and more direct. Serving as the battleground for the Thirty Years' War, which began in 1618, reduced Germany's population by one-third:

> The daily presence of death . . . made the survivors willing to submit to any authority that seemed strong enough to prevent a recurrence of these terrors. They accepted the swollen presences of their princes uncritically and with an atavistic fear of the likely consequences of any dissolution of existing social relationships; and in time this acceptance came to appear normal and acquired the weight of tradition.[16]

We will trace the development of nationalism from this point later in this chapter. German obedience also appears more peripheral than Asian obedience. Although German children are popularly believed to be more tractable than American ones, German families are a far cry from the Asian model; it is unlikely that obedient German children grow into obedient citizens automatically. German children's stories are less likely to preach obedience and more likely to paint the world as a fearful place; children are brutalized by adults, placed into ovens, kidnapped, betrayed, held captive. The Grimms' tales, so beloved in their expurgated versions, are in German genuinely frightening. *Hänsel und Gretel* and *Die Königskinder,* made into popular operas by Humperdinck, are erroneously staged as delightful romps. Beneath the surface of German romanticism lurks the sinister: forests contain delightful elves but also evil hunters. In Weber's opera *Der Freischütz,* the Black Ranger easily ensnares and dominates his guileless foes. When darkness falls, forests become dreaded, frightening, and oppressive. Joseph Eichendorf muses on this sense of doom:

> *Twilight begins to spread its wings*
> *The trees bestir themselves with a shudder*
> *Clouds gather like oppressive dreams*
> *What does this dread signify?*[17]

The brothers Grimm, Weber, and especially E. T. A. Hoffmann, whose often misconstrued *Tales* became the libretto for an equally misunderstood opera (Offenbach's *Tales of Hoffmann*), were fascinated by terror and death. In their stories, death comes almost as a welcome resolution to the angst of life.

Just as the roots of German obedience lay in the devastation of the Thirty Years' War, German fairy tales portray life as threatening presumably because, in the years during and after the war, it was. Some cities lost as much as 80 percent of their population to the war; the plague, which stalked the various combatants; or cannibalism, which became the only means of survival. But German obedience was clearly more a natural response to adversity than a tradition, as it was in China and Japan.

The German political system is more competitive than the systems in the more pervasively obedient cultures. Politics is clearly less consensual in Germany than in the Far East. For example, after World War II, political mergers occurred in both Germany and Japan. In West Germany in 1966, the Christian Democratic party and the principal opposition, the Social Democrats, agreed to an informal coalition, but it lasted only three years and resulted in surges of popular enthusiasm for the Social Democrats, who were able to form a majority coalition and send their former partners into opposition. The Christian Democrats returned to power in 1983.

Two countries, both with strong to moderate obedient cultures, both defeated in

World War II, both without a strong democratic tradition, went their separate ways: the Japanese toward consensus politics and the Germans toward two-party competition. Japan experienced some moderate protests from students during the turbulent 1960s and 1970s, but Germany suffered from terrorism to a degree unequaled even in the United States—hardly the mark of a pervasively obedient culture. The universities became the centers of left-wing movements, the more peaceful variant evolving into today's Green party and the more virulent strain turning into the violence of the Baader-Meinhof gang and the Red Army Faction. About 15 percent of the university population was active in the "anarchist subculture" of the period, surely one of the largest of such subcultures in Europe.[18]

Acquiescence and the Social Class Structure: England

Rigid divisions between social classes can encourage acquiescence. No society, of course, is truly classless, but the value cultures place on class and family background varies considerably. England is a clear example of the durability of deference.

In England, there are distinct class accents and patterns of speech, with the London Cockneys speaking almost a different language from the private-school graduates who go on to Oxford or Cambridge. George Bernard Shaw's *Pygmalion* is based on the premise that it is impossible to teach the lower classes to be civil and to be understood. But the point of the play is that such a premise is taken on as a challenge, much in the same way that one would bet on a long shot in an athletic contest. The story was later successfully translated into the idiom of the American musical theater as *My Fair Lady*. The more charitable musical version accentuates speech patterns more than the original, which struck at the heart of the English class system.

Grammar schools, called "public" schools in England in spite of the fact that they are private, have traditionally preserved class distinctions, although they have always been open to the more ambitious members of the working class:

> The privileged classes [of the 19th century] were not stupid. They warmly welcomed the better-educated and more amusing members of the rising rich—and these graces could be obtained from the schools. . . . The upper classes had already gone far to evolve distinctive ways of speaking, dressing, ways of holding their knives and forks, styles of writing letters and so on.[19]

The public schools created a subculture that lasts a lifetime. In *The Old Boys*, by Irish novelist William Trevor, the protagonist dedicates his life to revenge against an upper classman who tormented him.

> Every day Nox blacked Jaraby's boots, tidied his books and help to wash up the dishes from which Jaraby had eaten. At the end of the period, when the new fags were allocated to new masters, Jaraby kept Nox on as his own particular servant. It was not that he had taken a fancy to him; it was that he had not yet trained him to his satisfaction.[20]

He is *consumed* by his public school experiences in a way simply impossible in the open environment of American education. A. N. Wilson's *Incline Our Hearts*, a semiautobiographical novel, has a character make those claims:

> The deprivations and hardships of an English school may be worse than a Soviet labor camp. What counts is that the inner torment is identical—the sharing of insanitary con-

ditions with too many uncongenial people, the strange friendships and distrusts which grow up among fellow prisoners, the same fear of the system which never quite leaves you. The only major difference is that *their* Gulag is something of which the Soviet government is ashamed, denying its very existence, whereas the English system of private schools is openly boasted about, one of the glories of the world.[21]

Traditional wealth in England—the upper classes—viewed the *nouveau riche* with amusement. The upper classes did not work; the middle classes, no matter how wealthy, did. In *Chariots of Fire,* the popular motion picture about the 1924 Olympics, upper-class aspirants to the English team were appalled because one of the competitors hired a professional coach. The spirit of the British class system is amateurism, devotion to good works, *never* winning at any cost. The lower classes know that certain pursuits are "not for the likes of me"; so do the upper classes, which eschew commercial activity. In *The Ice Age,* by the popular English novelist Margaret Drabble, the hero, having matriculated at Cambridge, does not read job announcements either in newspapers or on various bulletin boards because it "never crossed his mind":

> So deeply conditioned are some sections of the British nation that some thoughts are deeply inaccessible to them. Despite the fact that the national press was full of seductive offers, the college notice boards plastered with them, Anthony Keating, child of the professional middle classes, reared in an anachronism as an anachronism, did not even see the offers; he walked past them daily, turned over pages daily with as much indifference as if they had been written in Turkish or Hungarian.[22]

Irrespective of efforts to become more egalitarian, British universities are overpopulated by scions of traditional wealth. British political parties, left or right, are dominated by the same types of families. When Margaret Thatcher became prime minister in 1973, the shock was not so much that she was a woman but that her father was a shopkeeper (she did, however, go to Oxford).

Classes acquiesce in their status. The disdain for commercial achievement still persists, contributing to England's seemingly permanent status as a weak economy. Canadians, Americans, and Australians living in England (with the same ethnic and class origins) have routinely outdueled the British in trade.

> A Canadian or Australian who comes to England is outside the class system, doesn't have to be classified, and therefore can get on with everybody; whereas in England even today the class system still has an influence, and is a constrainer of energy.[23]

Former British colonies, settled largely by English émigrés (as distinguished from former British colonies in undeveloped areas), have consistently higher gross national product growth rates than the mother country (the sole exception is New Zealand).[24]

The English example shows both the strengths and the weaknesses of culture as an organizing idea. One might just as easily argue that as the British Empire and the industrial revolution developed together, the British relied more on their colonies for commercial and industrial development than other, less imperialistic countries did. After all, England was the first industrial nation; why then did it decline? If culture was at fault, why did it initially *encourage* economic development?

This is precisely the point of culture. It develops as economies progress. As the world's first industrial nation and its greatest colonial empire, Britain developed unique economic characteristics. Since British expansion occurred during an era when textiles dominated the market, start-up costs were low. Banks made short-term loans and did not involve themselves in the orchestration of commerce or the management of individual companies. Countries that industrialized later, in an era of heavy and light industry, relied more on central financing, with more participation by banks in the regulation of the economy. Britain, by comparison, was a nation of small businesses. Banks, not involved in industrialization, were major participants in colonization. They sent large amounts of capital out of the country, at a crucial point—around the turn of the 20th century—when the money was needed at home to allow British industry to meet the challenge of the United States, Germany, and Japan. Furthermore, the empire inhibited the growth of industrial technology, as British firms continued to sell to their semi-industrial colonies while the Americans and Germans were competing in the more developed European market and were thus producing more technologically sophisticated products. Finally, as trade unions were as fragmented as industry, shop floor opposition to innovations and resistance to work reorganization became widespread.[25]

So British economic decline and its cultural justification began at about the time that the empire was ending, the 1870s: "Britain seems to have suffered from a cruel historical paradox. Her very success at industrializing first, building an overseas empire, and achieving full employment in the three decades after the war sowed the seeds of industrial decline."[26] Cultures are hard to change precisely because their components are so interconnected.

THE ACHIEVING SOCIETY

The opposite of acquiescence is achievement. Cultures that stress this value approach life as a series of problems to be solved, obstacles to be overcome. The "can do" spirit of the early American republic, the spirit of the frontier, of expansion, of "manifest destiny," of the adoration of the entrepreneurial spirit have little in common with cultures that stress constraints or limits. The American culture is aggressive. It also incorporates variants of the achievement culture in a way that suggests that there are "bunches" of cultural characteristics.

American Individualism

The American culture is individualistic and aggressive. Sociologists call this form *utilitarian individualism*. It is a cultural artifact remarkably similar to the philosophical tenets of the theorists who justified government in terms of a social contract:

> [It is] a form of individualism that takes as given certain basic human appetites and fears—for Hobbes, the desire for power over others and the fear of sudden violent death at the hands of another—and sees human life as an effort by individuals to maximize their self-interest relative to these given ends. Utilitarian individualism views society as arising from a contract that individuals enter into only in order to advance their self-interest.[27]

Even though utilitarian individualism is rooted in fear ("Let's do it to them before they do it to us," said the sergeant at the beginning of each episode of *Hill Street Blues*), it is a culture of optimism. Americans tend to think that the only limits to individual achievement are individual commitment and ability. They emphatically reject Rousseau (not, of course, explicitly, since they have never heard of him).

American egalitarianism is expressed both in a disdain for titles, class distinctions, or rankings not based on ability and in a condemnation of people who explain failure in terms of unavoidable impediments, such as those proposed by Rousseau to explain crime. The American dream—wealth—is said to be within the grasp of anyone willing to work, to delay gratification, to innovate, to "take the bull by the horns." One seemingly unalterable belief on the part of whites is that discrimination is not a cause of black poverty, whereas blacks believe it to be the major cause.[28] American egalitarianism is therefore a far cry from collective egalitarianism and has nothing to do with equality of results or outcomes.

Most emphatically, American individualism need not be "conservative," or "right-wing" in the sense that these terms imply a commitment to established order or authority; indeed, the reverse is true. American culture, judging by attitudes toward change, is comparatively radical, as we see in the following list, which shows the percentage of the citizenry of various countries in favor of radical change in 1981.[29]

Northern Ireland	1%	Luxembourg	5%
Norway	2%	United States	5%
West Germany	3%	Belgium	7%
Denmark	3%	Italy	8%
Japan	3%	Spain	8%
Netherlands	3%	France	9%
Sweden	4%	Greece	9%
Ireland	4%	Mexico	12%
Canada	5%	Portugal	14%
England	5%	South Africa	25%

Reagan and Rambo: The Dream Lives.   These characteristics, including radicalism, bubble to the surface in a variety of ways. Popular culture is replete with examples of the lonely hero, bucking tradition to follow conscience. James Fennimore Cooper's Deerslayer became, in various incarnations, Shane, Rooster Cogburn, and Rambo. Along with popular gunslingers, we also honor the lonely life of the "private eye," whose strength is not only in individualism but also in moral purity. Right is not decided by laws, by majority vote, or the customs of impersonal bureaucracies. Right is decided by the instincts of the loner. Sam Spade, Lew Archer, Serpico, and Dirty Harry represent the strong *antiauthoritarian* component of individualism.

When Ronald Reagan was threatened with a budget, prepared by congressional Democrats, that exceeded the amounts he wished to spend on domestic welfare and other entitlement programs, he announced his intention to veto by saying, "Go ahead—make my day," a line made famous by Clint Eastwood, as Dirty Harry in *Sudden Impact,* urging a hoodlum to give him an excuse for killing him. Reagan's blending of popular culture and politics was unique, but the inferences he drew from this culture were not: they are pure Americana. Reagan likes Dirty Harry and Rambo (" 'Boy, I saw *Rambo* last night,' the President said in July 1985 after 39 hostages held in Lebanon had been released. 'Now I know what to do the next time this happens.' '')[30]

While most Americans were chuckling at Reagan, he was implementing a scheme in the grand tradition of the lonely hero. When he was denied congressional authorization and funding for his beloved *contras* (anti-Sandinista rebels in Nicaragua), he encouraged, at least through the tacit approval provided by the atmosphere pervading the executive office, an intrigue to fund them by raising money privately and by selling arms to Iran to raise more money.

The men who actually negotiated the series of complex exchanges, led by Marine Colonel Oliver North, viewed themselves as Rambos, intolerant of "the system" and deeply suspicious of the bureaucracy and Congress:

> Those involved were completely alienated from the rest of official Washington, including the rest of the Reagan Administration. They hated "the libs," as they called the liberal Democrats in Washington; they despised the career C.I.A. and they suspected all the N.S.C. [National Security Council] principals who were not involved.[31]

But they believed passionately in their cause. On the one hand were the "freedom fighters," on the other, the "terrorists." Obviously, freedom fighters believed in freedom. Most explicitly, they believed that free market economies are preferable to centrally planned ones, an ideology that fits well with the optimistic individualism of our culture. Our nation's mission is to spread the gospel of the market and thus to alleviate world poverty. So the Reagan administration broke the law but for a higher cause (like the civil rights activists of the 1960s who followed Dr. Martin Luther King, Jr., to jail? Like Henry David Thoreau who refused to pay taxes to support the Mexican War?) Reagan had found his Rambo, in the obscure but obsessed Oliver North (whom Reagan regarded as a "national hero").

The parallels between the Reagan administration's shenanigans and Rambo's equally implausible heroics is compelling:

> The Rambo story could stand for both the Iran arms deal and the *contra* operation. Rambo, after all, bucked the United States government to go rescue his buddies from prison camps and torturers; the lone warrior then came back from the jungle to take revenge on the bureaucrats who had so cynically left American soldiers to die. The Rambo story is the same story of justifiable, violent revenge against evildoers and "the system" that runs through so many American movies.[32]

These were the movies the president watched; they were his fantasy, the fantasy of the loner breaking the chains twisted around him by repressive governmental institutions. Most of us are content with living our fantasies out in private, but most of us are not president of the United States.

Shades of Collectivism

Interpersonal relations and relations between individuals and organizations lack structure, which fact makes the culture of the United States deeply suspicious of authority, especially organized authority. As we shall see in subsequent chapters, our instincts against organized authority have destroyed political party organizations. But this is merely the most obvious consequence of our suspicions. As Herbert Gans writes:

> People hope [that organizations] will pursue the relevant values as if they were individuals, although few are surprised when this is not the case. As a consequence people distinguish between immoral organizations and moral individuals in them. . . . Whenever possible . . . they search for moral individuals in organizations with which they must deal.[33]

A good example of Gans's point is Ronald Reagan, who believed that even though the Soviet government was an "evil empire," Gorbachev was a good guy. Like Gans's Middle Americans, Reagan believed people to be more trustworthy than organizations.

European and Asian democracies and authoritarian regimes and even Canada are much more collectivist and much less individualist than the United States. However, their mild form of collectivism is a far cry from the passionate collectivism of the totalitarian governments. At least 40 percent of Europeans, compared to about 25 percent of Americans, agree that "the individual owes his first duty to the state and only secondarily to his personal welfare."[34] We alone among industrial democracies regard government as the enemy of freedom.[35] In political terms, there is far less commitment in the United States than elsewhere to the idea of the state as an object of veneration, loyalty, or even obedience.

There is no political equivalent to Ronald Reagan among European nations—even in the English Conservative party's Margaret Thatcher, a leading proponent of a denationalized economy. Not only do European democratic cultures stress collective solutions, but their governments have always been more active in regulating the economy and providing social welfare. The British Conservative party has never proposed the abolition of nationalized medicine, and its proposal to reduce the government's commitment to welfare met with such opposition that it was quietly shelved. England, like the other Western industrialized democracies, requires pregnancy leaves for working mothers and provides tax-supported day care and preschool education. Sweden specifies an equal division of household chores and proscribes corporal punishment. West Germany provides for mandatory worker participation in plant governance. As a partial consequence of a more collectivist culture, about 48 percent of gross domestic product in the Western industrialized democracies is attributable to public spending, compared with 35 percent in the United States. In these same countries, tax revenue as a percentage of gross national product is 42 percent, compared with 31 percent in the United States.[36]

Cultures and Budgets

Another indicator of an achieving culture is the way it spends its money. Evidence of cultural variations can be seen in comparative expenditures for education, public health, and defense. Among the Western industrialized democracies, the United States ranks seventh out of 11 on per capita expenditures for education, eighth on per capita expenditures for health, but first on defense expenditures:

TABLE 2.2 Policy Contrasts in the Welfare State

	United Kingdom	Netherlands	United States	West Germany
Education	4.4	4.5	4.1	4.2
Health care	4.6	4.3	3.9	4.4
Housing	4.3	4.2	3.3	3.7
Old-age security	4.3	4.0	3.9	4.3
Employment	4.2	4.1	3.6	4.3

SOURCE: Copyright © 1983 by St. Martin's Press, Inc. From *Comparative Public Policy* by Arnold Heidenheimer, Hugh Heclo and Carolyn Teich Adams. Reprinted by permission of St. Martin's Press Incorporated.

In any international comparison, the United States stands out for its individualism, mistrust of public authority, fragmentation of political institutions, and emphasis on equal opportunity. Compared with European nations, key national social welfare programs arrived late (old age and unemployment insurance in the 1930's, disability insurance in the 1950's, Medicare and Medicaid in the 1960's) or not at all (cash allowances for families with children, comprehensive health insurance).[37]

Citizen support for various social welfare programs is lower in the United States than in other Western industrialized democracies. A national survey that measured public support for governmental responsibility in education, health care, housing, and employment found the Americans in last place. Table 2.2 is based on surveys of national populations, with respondents asked to indicate support of or opposition to government responsibility in a variety of policy areas. The higher the score, the greater the public support for governmental participation. In each of the policy areas, Americans ranked last in preference. Thus American budget priorities are in harmony with public preferences, or preferences are in harmony with policy (either explanation will do); see Table 2.3. Not only do the Americans reject the abstract notion of socialism, but they are also

TABLE 2.3 Public Expenses per Capita, 1984 (in U.S. dollars)

	Education	Health	Military
Canada	789	460	174
Denmark	789	823	287
France	560	654	424
Italy	259	262	136
Netherlands	850	691	359
Norway	857	721	357
Sweden	1,164	924	408
Switzerland	789	625	324
United Kingdom	360	343	342
United States	676	383	543
West Germany	566	676	404

SOURCE: Copyright © 1983 by St. Martin's Press, Inc. From *Comparative Public Policy* by Arnold Heidenheimer, Hugh Heclo and Carolyn Teich Adams. Reprinted by permission of St. Martin's Press Incorporated.

loath to accept governmental responsibility for "areas where the norms of free enterprise support for private initiative come into play most directly."[38]

Achieving, individualistic cultures are likely to be more internationally aggressive. So too are committed collectivist ones, such as the USSR. But among the industrialized democracies, the United States has no peer in military spending. The competitive "survival of the fittest" ethos is well suited to a strong military posture.

Now that we have seen how various nations reflect cultural traits, we should look more closely at the process of nation building.

NATIONALISM

Nation building requires the development—even the imposition—of a consciousness of place. When asked to tell someone who you are, where do you start? Among the most obvious aspects of self-identification are occupation, racial or ethnic origin, and place of birth. At what point in your self-definition do you say, "I am an American [Pole, Russian, German]"? The quicker your nation jumps into your consciousness, the stronger your sense of nationalism.

Nationalism is a state of mind in which an individual's primary loyalty is not to a region, a social class, a religion, or a tribe but to the nation. A Nicaraguan youth exclaims:

> Suddenly we were all talking about our nation, our Revolution, our new government. Suddenly the word *Nicaragua* was on our lips—not a story about Somoza, or some new gossip everyone heard, or the latest deal between one of Somoza's friends and some foreign company. We became more patriotic: I mean, we became more aware—how do you say, more *conscious*—of our country.[39]

For the moment, at least, nation had replaced class. Since all these aspects of our lives exert competing demands for our loyalty, nation building requires that subnational identification become either complementary or insignificant.

Nationalism is the essential ingredient in the integration of a people under the jurisdiction of a government. As we have seen, feelings of nationalism need not supplant other loyalties such as class allegiance or religious conviction. Indeed, *transference*—the replacing of affect toward one object with affect toward another—may occur. Robert Coles, asserting that "nationalism works its way into just about every corner of the mind's life" illustrates transference by this remark from a young boy: "I love my mother, my father, and my country."[40]

German Nationalism

The most obvious example of this sort of nationalism is that of Germany. We have learned of the reduction of the German territory to rubble during the Thirty Years' War. In the 19th century, Napoleon conquered Germany and virtually annexed Austria, Bavaria, and Prussia. Recognition that humiliation in battle would be their fate as long as Germany remained divided into independent states, German intellectuals turned to xenophobic nationalism, mystic racism, and glorification of the state. Nationalism derives not from children's stories but from intellectuals, writers, poets, philosophers, and composers. Nationalism ultimately becomes at least a partial mass movement, but its origins are with the elite.

The German intellectual elite was strongly romantic, mystically collectivist, almost irrational. Its theoretical defenses of authoritarian government were in the tradition of Rousseau, rather than Hobbes and Locke. The rationalism of the contract theorists was scorned as being too concerned with individual self-aggrandizement or self-actualization; the notion of states merely refereeing the process whereby individuals indulge their greed was abhorrent. Hegel and Nietzsche preached the glory of the state as a corporate personality that had a mission, a destiny of the use of power for war, conquest, and the unification of Germany. Nationalism blended well with anti-Semitism in the operas of Richard Wagner, perhaps the most celebrated composer of the last half of the 19th century. An irrational anti-Semite, Wagner in his operas spoke of mysticism, romantic disregard of self-interest, sacrifice, and death. He also preached a rejection of middle-class concern with material well-being and the irrelevance of the individual. Minus the anti-Semitism, the student radicals of the 1960s and 1970s were in the grand tradition of German romanticism: postwar Germany had become obsessed with consumerism and profit and needed to be returned to the collectivism of the last century.

World War I—yet another defeat for Germany—quickened the pace with which the abstract ideas of intellectuals were translated into political programs. Hitler's National Socialist party became the instrument of the translation, grabbing bits of theory hither and yon—some from the 19th-century romantics, other from cranks at the margins of respectability—and made German nationalism for the first time the dominant elite ideology. Hitler himself relied on obscure crackpots, almost all of whom are long forgotten. The pamphlets that attracted him were about as rational as the ravings of the American Ku Klux Klan. He adored Wagner's music and accepted Wagner's writings as the centerpiece of his Nazi party program. But Wagner's writings were as deranged as those of the other pamphleteers Hitler admired.

University faculties and to their students nevertheless found Hitler attractive. In the 1930s, German unemployment was acute: 30 percent of college graduates were unemployed. So even though the Nazis relied on a distorted and bizarre ideology, Nazism found acceptance among the very classes for which classic German romanticism has the most meaning—the university population, which had read Hegel, Nietzsche, Fichte, and the other nationalists. In the last two elections before the Nazis seized absolute power, they received about one-third of the vote—not a majority, but more than any of the other parties. There is a strong correlation between social class and support for Hitler's party: the higher classes—the university-educated population—were among the strongest proponents of Nazi nationalism.[41]

Once the Nazis had consolidated their control, their campaign for nationalism was well coordinated through command of the media. Initially based on the argument that Germany must regain territories lost in World War I and with them the ethnic Germans under the authority of Czechloslovakia and Poland (in the Sudetenland and Danzig, now Gdansk), Hitler appealed to the same sentiment that had contributed to the election in 1925 of a leading symbol of German nationalism, Field Marshal Paul von Hindenburg. Clearly, Germany was ready for nationalism, and its acceptance of a commitment to

Hitler's promised "thousand-year Reich" reduced hitherto strong regional and class identifications substantially.

The introduction of racial purity as a component of nationalism, while it reached extremes in Germany, is not a uniquely German component of nationalism. Ethnic homogeneity is a vital factor in the development of nationalism; in Germany, the long tradition of anti-Semitism made Jews a convenient target.[42]

Interactive Nationalism

Nationalism is rarely as virulent as in Germany, but the pressure of nationalism is seldom absent in the modern nation-state. We have seen it in the United States' belief in "manifest destiny," a doctrine of national supremacy that required that we spread democracy and Christianity to countries manifestly uninterested in either. Our Christian impulses have been muted by the continued growth of a heterogeneous population. However, the lesson of past excesses should not be forgotten. President McKinley was reported to have been given a message from God to colonize the Philippines.

The American Mission. The United States, less obsessed with spreading religious nationalism, has traditionally sought to export free market democracy. Americans take it for granted that democracy is a noble ideal. We believe that democracy is a universally superior form of government (ergo, all people want democracy, and failures to achieve it are diagnosed as illness in the body politic). Much of American foreign policy can be understood as an effort to export democracy. We believe that the failure of a country to establish the routine instruments of democracy, such as free elections, is due to the unwillingness of oppressive elites to risk the loss of their power. Writing of Latin America, political scientist Glen Dealy observes:

> Liberals have urged Central American governments to guarantee human rights, hold free elections. . . . Conservatives have provided arms in hopes of literally beating Marxist opposition into submission to give democratic forces a chance. Liberals and conservatives may differ substantially over methods, but they agree on the desirability of pluralist democracy and the belief that self-determination and democratic freedom are ultimately synonymous.[43]

The United States' enthusiasm for carving out a successful society at home has as a natural consequence a desire to export capitalism, democracy, and individual achievement. We plunged into adventures in the Philippines in the 19th century, in Mexico, Nicaragua, and Vietnam in the 20th. Not until our swords were blunted in Vietnam did we question the desirability of exporting the "American way of life." Our missionary spirit, fueled by the evangelism of our achievement creed, fostered a sense of responsibility for the entire world. Our message rarely varies, irrespective of the target culture: we preach private enterprise, limited government, and individual freedom. Whether the target culture is individualistic or collectivist is of no matter. After World War II, we wrote constitutions for vanquished nations, and in Vietnam, we supported a series of cynical dictators without wondering whether the Vietnamese thought our ideals worthwhile. An American field commander in Vietnam supplies us with a flawless statement of the philosophy of aggressive individualism: "It was necessary to destroy the village in order to save it."[44]

A Step to Extremism.   Islamic states feel an equal obligation to spread their faith through nationalism. When God is on your side, nationalism can easily become a holy war. The current monopoly on such wars is held by the Islamic nations, adopting the model of Iranian nationalism. Nationalism blessed by divinity invites extremism, and the willingness of Islamic terrorists to do harm has proved to be a major obstacle to negotiation. International terrorism is, however, peaceful by comparison with the behavior of Iranian children in the war against Iraq. Suicide missions—the creation of human chains over Iraqi mine fields—have been encouraged as tickets to heaven.[45] Similarly, Irish Catholics in Northern Ireland, blending religion and nationalism in a lethal mixture, have been willing to die, either in hopeless assaults against British troops or slowly in prison by starvation. The example the martyrs is not lost on the young who, given the opportunity, emulate their behavior.

South Africa: Zenophobic Nationalism.   The historically common connection of religion—mainly fundamentalism and Roman Catholicism—with nationalism is surely as powerful as the mixture of ideology and nationalism (Marxism and the Soviet Union) and race and nationalism (Nazi Germany, South Africa). The entanglement of nationalism with other loyalties gives it added strength. Nazi nationalism fed off racism, as does modern South Africa. White South Africans—60 percent of them Afrikaners, the descendants of Dutch settlers—comprise only about 19 percent of the total population but control the government by means of a system of strict segregation *(apartheid)* and an efficient and ruthless state security service. The 40 percent of the white population that is of English descent is widely regarded as less intransigent about apartheid but largely ineffective in challenging the policies of the Afrikaners. Years of isolation from Anglo-European society created a sense of defensive disconnection on the part of the ruling Afrikaners; their defeat in the Boer War with England at the turn of the 20th century is as much a part of lore as is their titanic struggles with the Zulus. There is an England for the English, but there is no homeland for the Afrikaners. They feel no sense of identity with Holland, a land from which they migrated many generations ago and do not look on as a refuge; their language, Afrikaans (a combination of English, Dutch, German, and various tribal dialects) is unique. Near-universal condemnation of South Africa's apartheid policy has contributed even more to a sense of "going it alone" and of preparing for apocalypse. Thus, as in Germany, a strong strain of racial fear is imbedded into a nationalistic collective culture. The Jews, the theory went, if not eliminated, would turn Germany into a decadent society; the blacks, the theory goes, if not strictly segregated, will turn South Africa into a nightmare of multitribal conflicts and declining economic and military power and, ultimately, will destroy of white culture.

As in Germany, the specter of communism is frequently invoked against the faint-hearted. A young Afrikaner offers this justification:

> We must never have a second battle of Blood River [in which a handful of Boers killed more than a thousand Zulus, or so Petrus had been taught]. You know, our people made an agreement [a "covenant" it is called in many South African textbooks] that the day

would be holy, if they won that battle, and they did. God was with us. . . . All those tribes, the Zulu and the Bantu and the Xhosa, they'd swamp us; they'd bury us; they'd push us into the Atlantic Ocean and the Indian Ocean. . . . Look what's happening in Rhodesia (he doesn't know, he says, the new name, Zimbabwe). Without white people, there'd be grass on the streets of Salisbury.[46]

Each defense of nationalism seems quite similar: a superior culture must be defended or exported, irrespective of the unsavory measures required. Nationalists invariably believe that history will prove them right.

National Cultures

An important ingredient of a culture is the ability to transmit its properties from one generation to the next, an example of which is the socialization process described in Chapter 1. National cultures depend on such subgroups for intergenerational transmission of values. Schools, families, organizations, churches, and the media are directly involved not only in the transmission of their own cultures, norms, and informal rules, but they are also needed by governments to instill a sense of identification, pride, and loyalty in the nation. In many cases, the transmission of cultural values is not an overtly political process. Children's stories are not overtly political, but they are nevertheless an agent of transmission. The intent of such stories is to provide something interesting so that children will learn to read quickly. But they are projective and tend to reflect the motives and values of the culture in the way they are told or in their themes or plots. "They represent therefore 'popular culture'—what is considered appropriate for children to read, not just those from a special social class."[47]

When subnational organizations do not transmit a common culture because they are poorly integrated into the national culture or when they overtly or tacitly oppose the national government, the ultimate result may be revolution, often through assertions of regional autonomy. The American Confederacy, the Canadian province of Quebec, and the Spanish Basque territories in the Pyrenees are examples of subcultural (regional) identification and national cultural identification in conflict.

Nations (as opposed to *states*) are not deliberately created. Rather, they evolve gradually from familiar ways of thinking, racial or ethnic or linguistic ties, economic interdependence, or shared history. The more homogeneous these experiences, the more cohesive the nation.

An Example: The Chinese Nation.   China, perhaps the oldest continuously identified country in the world, has gone through bloody turmoil for centuries but has never endured separatist wars of independence. It has experienced brutal conflict, the most recent of which was the Nationalist-Communist war of 1945–1949, and its internal wars are arguably the bloodiest known to scholars. Yet the idea of a Chinese nation has gone unchallenged for 2,000 years.

The continuity of Chinese culture is well illustrated by the period between 1911 and the establishment of the Communist government in 1949 (see page 49). Lacking effective national government, the country was ruled by warlords, each with an army and a territory to protect. The warlords collected taxes (pork, fish, opium, a licence fee for prostitutes, and a household protection tax),[48] provided defense against other warlords, and generally operated as independent, authoritarian governments. The warlords were a modern incarnation of the feudalism of early medieval Europe. In both its modern and medieval form, private armies and private governments challenged central authority. Regional feudal governments triggered a series of confrontations with the nation builders, such as Bismarck; he established a central German government in the 1870s almost two millennia after the creation of a central Chinese government. In the case of both the Chinese and the Germans, common cultures, languages, and traditions enabled the centralizers to prevail. In contrast, when nations are artificially spawned, nation building generally requires violence and repression.

States may, of course, be carved out of nations as a result of the fortunes of war. In time, they may develop national unity and a national culture. Some created since World War II are still in the throes of finding their identities.

Year of Independence or Creation	Nation
1946	Jordan, Mongolia, Philippines
1947	Bhutan, India,* Pakistan
1948	Burma, Israel,* South Korea, North Korea, Sri Lanka (Ceylon)†
1949	East Germany, West Germany,* Indonesia (Dutch East Indies), Laos, Taiwan (Formosa), Vietnam
1951	Libya
1956	Morocco, Sudan, Tunisia
1957	Ghana (Gold Coast), Malaysia (Malaya)
1958	Central African Republic (Ubangi-Shari), Guinea (French Guinea)
1960	Benin (Dahomey), Burkina Faso (Upper Volta), Cameroon, Chad, Congo (French Equatorial Africa), Cyprus,* Gabon, Ivory Coast, Madagascar, Mali (French Sudan), Mauritania, Niger, Nigeria, Senegal, Somalia (Somaliland), Togo, Zaire (Belgian Congo)
1961	Kuwait, Sierra Leone, Tanzania (Tanganyika, Zanzibar)
1962	Algeria, Burundi, Jamaica,* Rwanda, Trinidad and Tobago,* Uganda, Western Samoa
1963	Kenya
1964	Malawi (Nyasaland), Malta,* Zambia (Northern Rhodesia)
1965	Gambia, Maldives, Singapore
1966	Barbados,* Botswana (Bechuanaland), Guyana (British Guiana), Lesotho (Basutoland)
1967	South Yemen (Aden)
1968	Equational Guinea (Fernando Po, Rio Muni), Mauritius, Nauru, Swaziland

*Polyarchy or near-polyarchy.
†Colonial name, if different from current name, is given in parentheses.

1970	Fiji
1971	Bahrain, Qatar, United Arab Emirates
1972	Bangladesh (East Pakistan)
1973	Bahamas*
1974	Grenada,* Guinea-Bissau (Portuguese Guinea)
1975	Angola, Cape Verde, Comoros, Mozambique, Papua New Guinea,* São Tomé and Principe, Suriname (Dutch Guiana)
1976	Seychelles
1977	Djibouti (Somali Coast, Afars and Issas)
1978	Dominica,* Solomon Islands*
1979	Kiribati (Gilbert Islands),* St. Lucia,* St. Vincent*
1980	Tuvalu (Ellice Islands),* Vanuatu (New Hebrides), Zimbabwe (Rhodesia)
1981	Antiqua,* Belize (British Honduras),* Bermuda*
1983	Nevis,* St. Kitts*
1984	Brunei

FEDERALISM: THE ATTEMPT
TO CONTROL CENTRIFUGAL FORCES

Federalism is an attempt to balance the forces of regional, tribal, or ethnic cultures against the need for a consistent and reliable central government. It is an institutional response to cultural heterogeneity.

Federalism is the legal division of responsibility between a national government and *states* (as in the United States and Australia), *Länder* (as in West Germany), *cantons* (as in Switzerland), or *provinces* (as in Canada). These are the major federal systems. Mexico, the Soviet Union, India, and Brazil have some of the appurtenances of federalism but have so clearly encouraged the dominance of the central government that little real authority rests with subnational governments. The opposite of federalism is a *unitary* government, in which all powers are reserved for the central government. Most democracies are unitary; among the most durable are the United Kingdom, France, and the Scandinavian democracies of northern Europe.

Federalism and Nationalism

Carl Friedrich, a political scientist who participated in the preparation of Germany's postwar federal constitution, believes that federalism and nationalism are inextricably intertwined:

> Federal relationships may be utilized to provide a political order for a nation to be united out of separate and distinct entities, as was the case in Germany in the nineteenth century, that of India in the twentieth. Or federalism may serve as a means of combining several nations or nationalities into one political order, as is the case in Switzerland and Belgium.[49]

The logic is clear: if one can have a strong sense of place, nationalism, one can just as easily be loyal to "subnational territorial communities."[50] The question "Who am I?" may be answered with the nation listed behind other regional or ethnic identifications (I am a black American; I am a white southerner, etc.).

When faced with potential disintegration, the choices a nation can make are limited: allow the subnational loyalties to win (secession), eliminate the subnational loyalties (genocide), or live with them (federalism). Secession has occurred: Bangladesh was part of Pakistan. But Pakistan, for a series of reasons related to the internal disputes between Hindus and Muslims, was actually a bizarre country divided in half by about 3,000 miles of territory (East and West Pakistan were two Muslim enclaves separated by the Hindu Indian continent). With the help of the Indian army during a brutal war, East Pakistan won independence as Bangladesh. When what is now Norway wished to secede from Sweden in 1905, there was not a murmur of protest. More typical is the American Civil War, which preserved the Union at the highest battle-death cost in the history of warfare (a per capita death rate nine times that of World War II). Replacing a unitary with a federal system is less extreme than secession and is occurring under nationalist pressure in some democratic, authoritarian, and totalitarian regimes.

Belgium.   After debates going back into the 19th century, the Dutch-speaking Flemings in the north of Belgium (Flanders), who comprise about 60 percent of the population, sought in 1963 to elevate their language to official status, giving it equal footing with French, spoken in the Wallonia region in the south. The "language border" divided Belgium officially into Dutch- and French-speaking parts, and Brussels, the capital, (formerly Dutch-speaking) was declared bilingual. Several municipalities along the language border were exchanged between regions. One, Voeren-Fourons, became the center of demands for regional autonomy. At every local election since the creation of the language border, people demanded a "Retour à Liège" (Liège is the Walloon province to which Voeren-Fourons formerly belonged). The small city, with a French-speaking majority, never accepted a transfer about which it had not been consulted, and continued to object to its transfer to a Dutch-speaking region with which it felt no linguistic identity. Tensions reached crisis proportions when a French-speaking elected mayor, who refused to learn Dutch, was removed from office by the *Conseil d'Etat* (Supreme Court). Mayors are technically appointed by the Crown, so the action was legally possible, but the political consequences were formidable. The "mayor" continued as if nothing had happened, his recalcitrance leading to the resignation of the government and the dissolution of parliament. Inconclusive elections in 1987 resulted in a political impasse, finally resolved by the formation of a government (with three regions: Flanders, Wallonia, and Brussels). The agreement—denounced by the mayor of Voeren-Fourons since it would require municipal officials in mixed language areas to speak the language of the region—provided for continued devolution of power from the national to the regional governments.[51]

The Soviet Union.   Although little noticed in the years before Gorbachev, subnational ethnic loyalties in the USSR have long posed a major threat to regime stability. There are at least 90 different ethnic groups in the USSR, and many of them resent the dominance of Russian culture and Russian interests. Nationalistic yearnings are especially evident in the republics at the geographic edge of the USSR, some of which (Estonia, Latvia, Lithuania) were independent nations until absorbed by the Soviet Union in 1939. According to the Soviet constitutions, the republics are "sovereign." In fact, they are completely subordinate to the Kremlin. But this is among the facts being challenged by a new faction, the Interregional Group, which is calling for a new constitution and a recognition of "pluralism" (the code word for the end of party monopoly). The traditional language of instruction (officially Russian) in individual republics has become a symbolic issue. In Georgia and Armenia, local languages have long predominated, regardless of the official rules. The Baltic republics would almost certainly return to their independent status if given the opportunity. Aware of this, the KGB has traditionally maintained a higher degree of observation and intervention in the Baltics than in Moscow or Leningrad. However, in the late 1980s, with glasnost in full cry, demands for independence were raised to a previously unimaginable level, with demonstrations becoming routine and previously harassed pro-independence leaders surfacing. The Estonian Popular Front, one of the most daring of the groups seeking autonomy, was able to meet on several occasions with top advisers to Gorbachev; he does not welcome secession any more than Lincoln could; but concessions are being announced as this book goes to press.

Yugoslavia.   Whereas the republics of the USSR have had little autonomy, this has not been the case in Yugoslavia. The problem here is not with the suppression of local identification, but rather the reverse: the six Yugoslav republics have sufficient autonomy to threaten the unity of the country. Yugoslavia is more ethnically diverse than the Soviet Union; indeed, it is the most diverse of all European countries. The largest ethnic group, the Serbs, comprises only 36 percent of the population. Unlike the USSR, there is no national Communist party organization to gain a monopoly on political power. The League of Communists of Yugoslavia is exactly that—a coalition of the organizations of the six republics. The republic party organization is, of course, the dominant actor in each region, and much of the country's political talent never makes the trip to Belgrade.

In a socialist economy with a heavy state component, about the only economic functions performed by the *central* government are printing money and distributing funds to the less developed republics.[52] For republics such as Slovenia—which shares borders with Austria and Italy—a more unitary system would be unacceptable: Slovenes, the wealthiest ethnic group in Yugoslavia, identify economically, socially, and culturally more with their capitalist neighbors than with the Serb-dominated hard-line national government. Were Yugoslavia to become a multiparty democracy, it would disappear. Slovenia, with a free press, tolerates "alternative movements" (interest groups not affiliated with the party) and wants the slide toward capitalism to continue.

Whether the Yugoslav federation can stand the strain of tensions similar to those in the North and South before the U.S. Civil War is unclear. Although its constitution guarantees the right of secession, any attempts to secede would certainly bring a military response (the same right exists under the USSR's constitution). And unlike Belgium, Yugoslavia does have the ability to use the traditional weapons of authoritarian governments, the secret police and the military, to repress secessionist longings. Subnationalist enthusiasms, too vigorously asserted, have resulted in imprisonment and torture.

Federalism and Heterogeneity

Federalism is closely related to the degree of heterogeneity in a society. Using an index of homogeneity developed initially in the Soviet Union and modified by George Kurian, the index of homogeneity for the major federal systems is 58, while that of the major unitary democracies is 88.7 (100 indicates perfect homogeneity).[53] The federal systems have in common a strong sense of regional autonomy or a diverse society.

West Germany, the outlier among federal systems, did not become a nation until the last years of 19th century. Its current constitution dates from 1949. Australia, more homogeneous than its federal brethren, was a confederation of independent states from its initial founding as an English colony, shortly after England lost the United States, until 1906. Switzerland's cantons were completely independent for 500 years. In the United States, the issue of federalism was not resolved until 1865.

Canadian federalism is even more recently defined. Canada became bilingual in 1969; the *Parti Québécois* tried—with the encouragement of French president Charles de Gaule—to declare Quebec's independence shortly thereafter (it failed); and the Canadian constitution, outlining federal-provincial relations, was adopted in 1982. Though they differ in details, the federal systems try to strike a balance between central and subnational governments. The legal balance is specified in a constitution that is continually being interpreted and applied to current disputes. Policy disagreements between central and subnational governments are unending, with the central government gradually assuming the dominant position.

In practice, virtually all democracies and a substantial number of authoritarian and totalitarian governments are mixtures of both federal and unitary schemes, and when unitary governments employ federalism, it is in reality *administrative federalism*. In administrative federalism, certain functions may be allocated to a subnational unit because decentralization is regarded as a reasonable method of policy implementation or because certain policies are best administered when they can respond to ethnic or local eccentricities.

The United States and the Federal Republic of Germany: Systems in Delicate Balance

The constitutions of these federal systems were ratified by the states (or *Länder*). In neither country can national officials remove those elected in states, and in neither case can states withdraw from the federation. The constitution of both countries provides for specified responsibilities and "residual" ones (powers not specifically allocated). The states have residual power, but the national government has equally strong claims. For example, states in the United States and in the Federal Republic are responsible for education, but the national government in both countries has increased its funding, participation, and control of education. The issue of withdrawal from the federation has not arisen in the Federal Republic. The units created by the Allies after World War II— which became the *Länder*—bore virtually no resemblance to the independent states of the 19th century, with the exception of Bavaria, which has strong regional identity. Bonn, the capital, famous as John Le Carré's "small town in Germany," is a dull, uninteresting, intellectual backwater, compared to Munich, Hamburg, and West Berlin.

It is in these cities that the intellectual, cultural, political, and industrial elites gather. Thus the *Länder* quickly developed their own agendas.

In the United States, the problem of the permanence of the Union proved more intractable. Southern states developed strong regional cultures. The southern economy, an agrarian one mostly dependent on slave labor and free international trade, developed without major influence from the free, industrial north, with its determination to protect infant industries. Southerners such as Thomas Jefferson and John C. Calhoun wrote elaborate defenses of *nullification* and *interposition*, which claimed that the state could interpose itself between the federal government and its citizens when it judged a federal law to be unconstitutional and thus nullify such a law. Initially evoked against the Alien and Sedition Acts—which, since they provided for the suppression of seditious newspapers, Jefferson (correctly) believed to be unconstitutional—the doctrines became more concerned with tariffs and slavery in the 19th century. Since the alien and sedition laws were repealed before the doctrines of nullification and interposition could be tested, it remained for the Civil War to bring the matter to a head. The bloodiest war in our history established the indestructibility of the Union. Had the South not been culturally distinct, it would have surrendered in a year or less, rather than dragging on for four years.

In the Federal Republic of Germany, the *Länder* have a modified right of nullification. They are charged with the administration of federal laws, a responsibility conspicuously absent from American federalism. In some cases, a *Land* has refused to administer an unpopular law without triggering a constitutional confrontation. For instance, the laws approved in the 1970s to counter the threat of terrorism were not uniformly enforced. In Bavaria, a conservative southern *Land,* they were more scrupulously adhered to than in Baden-Württemberg, on the Swiss border. Delegating implementation of federal laws to the *Länder* makes them more powerful than American states. The U.S. Constitution was not ratified by state legislatures but by state conventions, whereas the West German ratification was by the *Land* parliaments. Thus from the beginning, the West German federal system gave subnational units a more prominent role than the United States did. In neither system is there a serious threat of the collapse of the union.

Federalism and Equality.   More troublesome are the problems of equality, uniformity, and response to local preferences. Federal systems are unequal by design. Since most expenditures for education are borne by states, per-pupil expenditures in poor states is less than in rich states. Students in Mississippi are not as well educated as those in Massachusetts. State universities in Texas receive a higher proportion of the state budget than those in Oregon; welfare payments per capita are higher in Oregon than in Texas. Is the existence of such inequalities a tolerable cost, in exchange for state budgets more in keeping with the local cultures they reflect? These are the issues of modern federalism: equal distribution of resources versus local accountability. The West German *Land* that winked at repressive federal legislation has its counterpart in the southern American state that resisted the implementation of federal civil rights legislation.

The conflict between equality and responsiveness is built into federal systems and is linked to the preference for individual and collective solutions, for liberal and conservative understandings of government. Liberals, generally seeking equality at the cost of responsiveness, believe that state governments cannot be trusted to take the lead in civil rights, equal employment, and the like. They believe that change is more difficult when separate state governments must be persuaded and thus prefer a single dominant government. And since states contribute to inequality by setting different spending priorities, only a strong central government can achieve a reasonable level of equality. Conservatives, seeking responsiveness at the expense of equality, argue that subnational governments can better adapt public programs to citizen expectations.

The Equal Rights Amendment.   The defeat of the Equal Rights Amendment illustrates those tensions. Easily approved by Congress and consistently supported by majorities of men and women, the ERA failed only because of the existence of a federal system. Whether this is a good or a bad outcome depends on whether you advocate equality or responsiveness. The two expectations really are in conflict; liberty and equality do not coexist well, and the cruel antagonism between these two noble ideals is one of the most vexing problems of politics.

WHEN NATIONS COLLAPSE: REGIONAL REVOLUTIONS

The American Civil War is an example of a *regional* revolution: centrifugal cultural forces are so strong as to lead to a choice between suppression by force or fragmentation of the nation. Regional revolutions are different from those based on class or ideology. The French, Russian, Cuban, and Nicaraguan revolutions were based on class and ideology. The American and Algerian revolutions were prompted by anticolonial impulse rather than regional subculture. The best laboratories for an examination of regional revolution are Asia and Africa. Of these regions, Kurian writes:

> Because the primary loyalty of an individual in traditional societies is to his race, language and religion, ethnicity becomes the basis for factional and separatist tendencies. More civil wars have been fought in Asia and Africa in modern times on the issues of race, language or religion than on that of political ideology.[54]

In support of his thesis, Kurian notes that the 10 most heterogeneous societies in the world (Chad, Kenya, Ivory Coast, Nigeria, South Africa, India, Cameroon, Zaire, Uganda, and Tanzania) are in Asia and Africa. The most heterogeneous countries on other continents are Canada and Yugoslavia, both of which have had major problems with regional loyalties; but they are less heterogeneous than the Asian and African countries and have been able to hold together as nations.

  Chapter 7 includes a study of the virulence of tribalism in Nigeria and its impact on authoritarian government there. India illustrates well the perils of nation building in heterogeneous societies. It aspires to democracy and seeks federalism as a solution to its problems. India's homogeneity index is 11, making it among the most varied nations in the world. India is destitute, with a per capita income of about $300. That it persists with its efforts to be democratic under such unfavorable circumstances is remarkable.

India's Unstable Balance

India's population is a collection of territorially dissimilar peoples, united by some cultural similarities. The preponderant religion is Hinduism, itself a diverse collection of beliefs and traditions. At the time of independence from England (1947), there was a major confrontation between Hindus and Muslims, resulting in massive slaughter and the secession of the Muslims into the new country of Pakistan (initially a self-governing member of the British Commonwealth, Pakistan became independent in 1950 and broke into two states, Pakistan and Bangladesh, in 1971). Some 11 million Muslims still live in India.

The diversity of India is illustrated by the fact that Hindi, the principal language, is spoken by only one-third of the population, in the north. The languages of the south come from a completely different linguistic tradition. The Mizos of the south are vociferous in asserting independence. Among the Hindu sects, the Sikhs, whose population is concentrated in the northern state of Punjab, developed major cultural differences (based on opposition to the caste system, a preference for monotheism, and a rejection of traditional Hindu passivity). The Bengalis, Kashmiris, and Assamese have strong regional loyalties of their own. Coupled with this bewildering diversity is the development of independent monarchies, much as in late medieval Germany. At the time of the British acquisition (1857), there was no true Indian nation; indeed, one of the major achievements of British rule was the ending of the seemingly endless wars between various monarchies. Hence the first independent, legally sovereign India came into being only in 1947.

The Indian federal system was created by the British parliament in 1935. It is consequently not really a federal system in the commonly understood sense of the term but rather a modification of the traditional British unitary government. State boundaries can be altered, and states can be abolished by the central government. States do not have separate constitutions, as is the case in the United States; they have virtually no independent revenue sources, and their governors are appointed by the central government. The states, however, have the advantage of cultural homogeneity. Initially, Indian states were artificially drawn, but under intense pressure from various separatist movements, boundaries were redrawn in 1956 to make them congruent with culturally distinct populations.

Because of this decision, states garner more loyalty than the central government. State elections in India are more interesting to residents than state elections in the United States, and turnout is as high as for national elections. Given the immense linguistic problems of trying to administer public policy centrally, the Indian government has (as is the case in West Germany) relied on state bureaucracies to implement its laws. Perhaps this quasi-federal system is all that India could tolerate.

Separatism is the central issue of domestic Indian politics. It led directly to the death in 1985 of Premier Indira Gandhi, daughter of independent India's first premier, Jawaharlal Nehru. The Hindu state of Assam, located on the Burmese border, was enraged by the immigration of Muslims. Assam blamed the central government and accused it of appropriating the profits earned by Assamese tea. In 1983, during local elections, massacres of immigrants by Assamese reached into the thousands, with axes and machetes being the preferred instruments of destruction. These primitive weapons were no match for the Indian army, which occupied Assam and supervised the election. The unpopularity of the central government was revealed in the fact that calls to boycott the election resulted in a turnout of 10 percent, far below normal.

While the Assam situation was stabilized for the moment, the Sikhs in Punjab began a separatist uprising. Unlike Assam, the Punjabi revolt was led by a martially oriented sect. The Sikhs have always enjoyed a reputation for aggressive behavior. Their religion is closely tied to military prowess and is similar to Hinduism in language only. Sikh males are required to carry a dagger at all times. The British made good use of the Sikhs, who constituted about one-fourth of the British army. Achievement-oriented, the Sikhs ignore the caste designations that debilitate traditional Hindu culture. The Punjab is one of the wealthiest states in impoverished India, with a per capita income 50 percent higher than the national average. Resented by other Hindi speakers, the Sikhs have demanded constitutional amendments allowing greater political and financial autonomy. After vigorous repression of their separatist demands, Sikh radicals killed Premier Gandhi. She was replaced by her son, who vowed to end the separatist crisis by granting Punjab more autonomy, a promise yet to be kept because of suspicion in his party that ultimately, India's richest state may be lost. Yet the Punjab is so culturally distinct that its allegiance can be preserved only by suppression. There is very little in the national consciousness to counteract the spirit of separatism.

The Continued Vigor of Regionalism

Regional rebellions are frequently linked to irreconcilable lifestyle differences. Unlike ideological revolutions, the regional movements are demands for an autonomous, compatible way of going about life. They occasionally acquire a semblance of political ideology, but they are really the consequence of the wish to continue a way of life, a way of getting married, worshiping, committing crimes and being punished, getting ahead or falling behind. They are expressions of cultural longings and hence attract more mass support, at least initially, than ideological revolutions do. There is a clearly perceived threat to the patterns of everyday life. Because people are more anxious to die for a way of living than for an ideology, suppression of regional rebellions is usually brutal. The treatment of India's Sikhs and Nigeria's Ibos, the wholesale slaughter of Armenians in Turkey after World War I, and, of course, the Holocaust of World War II are chilling testimony to the urge for cultural homogeneity. In 1988, the Iraqi air force used poison gas to kill thousands of Kurds, thus keeping the technology as well as the ideology of the repression of regionalism intact.

Democracies have ''managed'' the problems of regionalism, a goal that has eluded authoritarian governments. Regionalism can be tolerated and even nurtured only in cultures that accept diversity. When federal solutions are attempted in less open political systems, they can lead to incendiary consequences unlikely in systems built on compromise.

FOR FURTHER CONSIDERATION

1. What are the five elements of culture? Can you think of anything else?
2. Based on your readings from this book, compare the cultures of Germany, England, Japan, China, and the United States. What common elements exist that link the five?

3. Is the United States becoming more collectivist or more individualist? Support your opinion.
4. Define nationalism. Is a federalist or unitary government best suited for a strongly nationalist culture? Why?
5. Could the "Rambo mentality" exist in Japan? West Germany? Or is it unique to societies with a level of individualism like that of the United States?
6. The United States Government often complains that other countries (usually the Soviet Union, Cuba, or Nicaragua) are forcing their belief systems onto weaker countries and denying them the right to rule themselves. In your opinion, is that a hypocritical stance? Why or why not?

For the More Adventurous

1. Is the United States really a classless society? Compare it to the United Kingdom. To do so, read the most recent *World Development Report* (published for the World Bank by Oxford University Press). Table 24 in the 1988 edition gives income distribution for the industrial democracies. What percentage of household income goes to the *top* 20 percent in the United Kingdom? In the United States? What percentage goes to the *bottom* 20 percent?
2. How does regionalism affect federalism in polyarchic societies? In authoritarian systems? Read accounts of the Estonian independence movement; compare it with the polemics of John C. Calhoun and Thomas Jefferson concerning the Alien and Sedition Acts before the American Civil War. What can one deduce?
3. Watch the movie *Apocalypse Now;* read Joseph Conrad's *Heart of Darkness;* read Gabrielle D'Annunzio's *Triofono della Morte;* listen to Richard Wagner's *Die Walküre.* What kind of political leadership appeals to you after having done so?

NOTES

1. Romuald J. Misiunas and Rein Taagepera, *The Baltic States* (Berkeley: University of California Press, 1983), p. 13.
2. Clyde Kluckhorn and William Kelly, "The Concept of Culture," in *The Science of Man,* ed. Ralph Linton (New York: Columbia University Press, 1945), p. 97.
3. Terrence E. Deal and Allan A. Kennedy, *The Culture of the Corporation* (Reading, Mass.: Addison-Wesley, 1982), p. 15.
4. Jose Luis Llovio-Mendendez, *Insider* (New York: Bantam, 1988), p. 260.
5. Richard Grunberger, *The 12-Year Reich* (New York: Holt, Rinehart and Winston, 1971), p. 121. However, not until 1943 did homosexuality become a capital offense.
6. Llovio-Mendendez, *Insider,* p. 201.
7. Ibid., p. 172.
8. Fox Butterfield, *Alive in the Bitter Sea* (New York: Times Books, 1982), pp. 203–204.
9. Fox Butterfield, "Why Asians Are Going to the Head of the Class," *New York Times Educational Life,* August 3, 1986, Section 12, p. 20.
10. Alan Roland, quoted in Enz Schmitt, "Growing up Asian in America," *New York Times,* March 7, 1989, p. C8.
11. *Education Digest,* 1988, p. 333 (mimeograph).
12. Florence Rockwood Kluckhohn and Fred L. Strodbeck, *Variations in Value Orientations* (Westport, Conn.: Greenwood Press, 1961), p. 13.
13. V. N. Datta, *Sati* (Riverdale, Md.: Riverdale, 1988), p.219. See also Alan Roland, *In Search of Self in India and Japan* (Princeton, N.J.: Princeton University Press, 1988).

14. Reported in *The New York Times* in a series of articles.
15. Quoted in Chris Hedges, "Arab Concept of Honor May Be Hurdle to Mideast Peace," *Seattle Times/Post Intelligencer,* March 19, 1989, p. A17.
16. Gordon Craig, *The Germans* (New York: Putnam, 1982), p. 22.
17. Joseph Eichendorf, "Ahnung und Gegenwart." Translation by the author.
18. Craig, *The Germans,* p. 210.
19. Jonathan Gathorne-Hardy, *The Old School Tie* (New York: Viking Penguin, 1977), p. 51.
20. William Trevor, *The Old Boys* (New York: Viking Penguin, 1966), p. 20.
21. A. N. Wilson, *Incline Our Hearts* (New York: Viking Penguin, 1988), p. 28.
22. Margaret Drabble, *The Ice Age* (New York: Knopf, 1977), p. 16.
23. Anthony Sampson, *The Changing Anatomy of Britain* (New York: Random House, 1981), pp. 327–328.
24. World Bank, *World Development Report, 1984* (New York: Oxford University Press, 1984), p. 221.
25. Peter Hall, "Decline and Fall," *New Society,* January 1987, pp. 9–12.
26. Ibid., p. 12.
27. Robert Bellah, Richard Madsden, William M. Sullivan, Ann Swidler, and Steven M. Tipton, *Habits of the Heart* (Berkeley: University of California Press, 1985), p. 336.
28. See Aaron Wildavsky, "Choosing Preferences by Constructing Institutions: A Cultural Theory of Preference Formation," *American Political Science Review 81* (March 1987): 17.
29. Ronald Inglehart, "The Renaissance of Political Culture," *American Political Science Review 82* (December 1988): 1213.
30. Michael Paul Rogin, *Ronald Reagan, the Movie* (Berkeley: University of California Press, 1987), p. 7.
31. Francis FitzGerald, "Reagan's Band of True Believers," *New York Times Magazine,* May 10, 1987, p. 38.
32. Ibid.
33. Herbert Gans, *Middle American Individualism* (New York: Free Press, 1988), p. 39.
34. Samuel Huntington, *American Politics: The Promise of Disharmony* (Cambridge, Mass.: Harvard University Press, 1981), p. 42–60.
35. For a thorough and excellent discussion of cultural differences, see Samuel Huntington, *American Politics: The Promise of Disharmony* (Cambridge, Mass.: Harvard University Press, 1981), pp. 42–60.
36. World Bank, *Development Report, 1984,* p. 16.
37. Hugh Heclo, *The Welfare State in Hard Times* (Washington, D.C.: American Political Science Association, 1985), p. 16.
38. Arnold J. Heidenheimer, Hugh Heclo, and Carolyn Teich-Adams, *Comparative Public Policy* (New York: St. Martin's Press, 1983), p. 321.
39. Robert Coles, *The Political Life of Children* (Boston: Atlantic Monthly Press, 1986), pp. 142–143.
40. Ibid., p. 60.
41. Richard F. Hamilton, *Who Voted for Hitler?* (Princeton, N.J.: Princeton University Press, 1982).
42. Coles, *Political Life of Children,* p. 192.
43. Glen C. Dealy, "Pipe Dreams: The Pluralistic Latins," *Foreign Policy 57* (Winter 1984–1985): 108.
44. David Halbertstam, *The Best and the Brightest* (New York: Random House, 1973), p. 33.
45. Roy Mottahedeh, *The Mantle of the Prophet* (New York: Simon & Schuster, 1985), p. 376.
46. Coles, *Political Life of Children,* p. 192.
47. David McClellan, *The Achieving Society* (New York: Van Nostrand, 1961), p. 71.

48. James E. Sheridan, *Chinese Warlord* (Stanford, Calif.: Stanford University Press, 1966), p. 25.

49. Carl Friedrich, *Trends of Federalism in Theory and Practice* (New York: Praeger, 1968), p. 30.

50. Ivo D. Duchacek, *Comparative Federalism: The Territorial Dimension of Politics* (New York: Holt, Rinehart and Winston, 1970), p. 57.

51. Kris Deschouwer, "The 1987 Belgian Election: The Voter Did Not Decide," *West European Politics 11* (July 1988): 141–145.

52. Pedro Ramet, *Nationalism and Federalism in Yugoslavia, 1963–1983* (Bloomington: Indiana University Press, 1981), p. 79.

53. George Kurian, *The New Book of World Rankings* (New York: Facts on File, 1984), pp. 47–49.

54. Ibid., p. 48.

FOR FURTHER READING

Coles, Robert. *The Political Life of Children*. Boston: Atlantic Monthly Press, 1986. Anecdotal accounts of childhood, especially noteworthy for its treatment of Nicaragua and South Africa.

Crapanzano, Vincent. *Waiting: The Whites of South Africa*. New York: Vintage, 1986.

Darnton, Robert. *The Great Cat Massacre and Other Episodes in French Cultural History*. New York: Vintage, 1985. Do you want to know why the apprentices in a Paris printing shop in the 1730s held a mock trial and hanged all the cats they could find? Why, in the original "Little Red Riding Hood," did the wolf eat the child?

Duchacek, Ivo D. *Comparative Federalism: The Territorial Dimension of Politics*. New York: Rinehart and Winston, 1970.

Gans, Herbert J. *Middle American Individualism*. New York: Free Press, 1988. America's "silent majority" dissected.

Gathorne-Hardy, Jonathan. *The Old School Tie*. New York: Viking Penguin, 1977. British public schools ruthlessly but fairly scrutinized.

Grunberger, Richard. *The 12-Year Reich*. New York: Holt, Rinehart and Winston, 1971.

Hinz, Berthold. *Art in the Third Reich*. New York: Pantheon, 1979.

Huntington, Samuel. *American Politics: The Promise of Disharmony*. Cambridge, Mass.: Harvard University Press, 1981. Arguably the finest existing interpretation of the American experience.

Kluegel, James R., and Eliot R. Smith. *Beliefs about Inequality*. Hawthorne, N.Y.: Aldine, 1986. How the Americans view their lot, with good accounts of class differences.

Le Roy Ladurie, Emmanuel. *The Peasants of Languedoc*. Urbana: University of Illinois Press, 1974; *Carnival in Romans*. New York: Braziller, 1980. Le Roy Ladurie's work blends geography, demography, economic history, folk culture, and political life into a masterful account of his epoch of expertise, from the Renaissance to the Enlightenment.

McClellan, David. *The Achieving Society*. New York: Van Nostrand, 1961. A seminal work on the cultural imperatives of achievement.

Orwell, George. "Such, Such Were the Joys," in *A Collection of Essays*. Garden City, N.Y.: Anchor/Doubleday, 1954. Orwell reflects on his years at "Crossgates" (actually St. Cyprians) public school.

Rather, L. J. *The Dream of Self-destruction: Wagner's Ring and the Modern World*. Baton Rouge: Louisiana State University Press, 1979. A profound study of Wagner, German culture, and European literature.

Rogin, Michael Paul. *Ronald Reagan, the Movie*. Berkeley: University of California Press, 1987.

Rogin lives with demons, one of whom is Reagan; but his analysis of the Reagan style is timeless.

Roland, Alan. *In Search of Self in India and Japan.* Princeton, N.J.: Princeton University Press, 1988. The cultural varieties of psychiatry, with a useful collectivist-individualist emphasis.

Schorske, Carl E. *Fin-de-Siècle Vienna: Politics and Culture.* New York: Knopf, 1979. The sordid culture of Vienna produces Freud, Schönberg, Mahler, Kokoschka, Berg—and Hitler.

Shills, Edward. *Tradition.* Chicago: University of Chicago Press, 1981. Those things handed down from one generation to the next, the weight of the past, carefully explained.

Shostakovich, Dimitri. *Testimony.* New York: Harper & Row, 1979. The Russian composer discusses his relationship with Stalin.

Thompson, William Irwin. *The Time Falling Bodies Take to Light: Mythology, Sexuality, and the Origins of Culture.* New York: St. Martin's Press, 1981. People who believe that Marx and alienation are synonymous should read the chapter titled "Civilization and Alienation in Ancient Sumer."

Tilly, Charles, ed. *The Formation of National States in Western Europe.* Princeton, N.J.: Princeton University Press, 1975. See especially "Reflections on the History of European State-making."

Trevor, William. *The Old Boys.* New York: Viking Penguin, 1966. A novel by one of Ireland's finest writers, about the lifelong impact of public schools.

Wiener, Martin J. *English Culture and the Decline of the Industrial Spirit, 1850–1980.* Cambridge: Cambridge University Press, 1981. Can England come back? No, says Wiener, unless it changes its social structure and mental climate.

Wilson, A. N. *Incline Our Hearts.* New York: Viking Penguin, 1988. A fictional account of life in public schools by a modern Dickens.

CHAPTER 3
Democracy and Its Variants

Surely no word—except perhaps *revolution*—can attract such passion as *democracy*. Even countries without the most remotely democratic process or institution will assert that democracy prevails. East Germany, one of the strictest of the eastern European communist countries, for instance, is officially named the German Democratic Republic.

Communists can be quite serious in claiming "real" democracy. Soviet scholars believe that a nominally democratic process can result in demonstrably nondemocratic decisions. Any government that exploits workers is not democratic, irrespective of its institutions; any government that does not do so is democratic, irrespective of its institutions. A decision by a tiny elite, untrammeled by any mechanisms of accountability, can make a democratic decision; a popularly elected legislature can make an undemocratic one.

Westerners are interested in *process;* Russians are more concerned about the *content* of policy. A majority vote to deny shelter to the homeless is not democratic, according to this notion. Exploitative decisions are not democratic ones. A Western view would argue that even "good" decisions can be undemocratic. The process whereby the USSR is engineering *perestroika* (the privatization of the economy) is being undertaken, presumably out of necessity, by concentrating authority even more severely (reducing "democracy").

What is democracy, then? The lines are not firmly drawn, but there are 37 democracies in the world today (listed in Table 5.14). This chapter and the three that follow it will trace the evolution of the varieties of democratic polities and their functions. As we saw in Chapter 2, the structure of government will either be in rough conformity to culture and tradition or will ultimately be replaced by one that is. The different emphases in Western and communist thinking are not accidental.

DEMOCRACY: TOWARD A DEFINITION

Democracy is not a slippery idea to grasp. Democracies are political systems in which *plurality* votes determine the composition of governments. The opportunity to replace the majority, which must occur at regular intervals, must allow unconstrained competition among or between office seekers. That is, *any* party or faction can propose *any* alternative platform in order to persuade the voters to abandon the existing coalition and form another one. "The majority rules" is nice in the abstract, but in many clearly democratic systems (the United States and the United Kingdom, for example), the person with the most votes, majority or not, wins.

The definition just given is consciously minimal and procedural in order to avoid the emotional baggage that makes democracy both a symbol for good and an impossible dream. No one can top Pericles when it comes to muddled overstatement; he wrote this ode to democracy in 443 B.C.:

> [Our constitution] favors the many instead of the few; this is why it is called democracy. If we look to the laws, they afford equal justice to all in their private differences; if to social standing, advancement in public life falls to reputation for capacity, class considerations not being allowed to interfere with merit. . . . The freedom which we enjoy

in government extends also to our ordinary life. But while the law secures equal justice to all alike in their private disputes, the claim of excellence is also recognized; and when a citizen is in any way distinguished, he is preferred to the public service, not as a matter of privilege, but as the reward of merit. Neither is poverty a bar, but a man may benefit his country whatever be the obscurity of his condition.[1]

If Pericles was serious, as opposed to merely exultant, there are no democracies. *No* government, including Pericles' Athens, has achieved such a lofty goal. The reality of his world differed greatly from Pericles' romantic portrayal of it. It never occurred to him, nor to the dramatists or theorists of his age, that the institution of slavery and the denial of the vote to resident aliens and women reduced the claims to political democracy to a small proportion of the population of Athens.[2] In the United States, how many of us believe that public service is the reward of merit and that poverty is no bar to political advancement?

We can, of course, impose a less stringent standard, a set of procedural expectations, that serve also as a minimum. Robert Dahl believes that democracies must have the following guarantees:[3]

1. Freedom to form and join organizations
2. Freedom of expression
3. Right to vote
4. Eligibility for public office
5. Right of political leaders to compete for support
6. Alternative sources of information
7. Free and fair elections
8. Institutions for making government policies that depend on votes and other expressions of preferences

With the exception of the last, these are purely legal matters that any nation, should it wish to do so, could easily create. It is sensible to adopt Dahl's limited requirements, which he calls *polyarchy,* because it allows a start. All systems that assign positions of formal authority in response to a routinized indication of citizens' wishes—that is, an election—and do so in a manner that ensures that each vote counts equally are polyarchies, and since that term is unfamiliar, we call them democracies.

Both Pericles' and Dahl's definitions are as important for what they do *not* say as for what they do say. No mention is made of the institutional structures and processes by which the needs and expectation of the many are to be ascertained; nor is a system of redress proposed, in the event that the many are being ill served. Nothing is said about the content of laws. Democracies may, by majority vote, support a petition requiring that Jews abandon their property or that blacks be required to live in designated areas. Democracies may not, however, deny Jews or blacks the right to organize to restore the status quo.

Dahl's definition does not guarantee citizens anything more than a regularly scheduled opportunity to vote. The eligible citizens may be too weak from hunger to seize the opportunity or unable to read the names on the ballot, but tending to physical well-being is not the responsibility of a democratically elected government (unless it decides, by democratic means, to provide for health and welfare).

Nor is there any provision for organizing the economy, which may or may not be democratic. For example, majorities may outlaw the private ownership of means of production or of property in general. But majorities in a democracy cannot prohibit citizens with whom the majority disagrees from seeking to become the new majority. If the means of production are already nationalized, people who wish to return them to private hands must be able to say so and to seek a mandate. (In England in 1979, Conservative party leader Margaret Thatcher did just that: she promised to denationalize, won the election, denationalized, and won again.) To repeat, the regularly scheduled elections must be free to anyone who wishes to compete, irrespective of the unpopularity or even (in the eyes of the existing government) seditious nature of that person's beliefs.

It soon becomes clear that there is more to democracy than plurality. The realization of democracy in practice involves the far more complex issues of *equality, representation,* and *responsiveness.* To understand these terms, we must take close looks at specific democracies at work; we shall focus on ancient Greece, modern England, and the United States.

THE FIRST DEMOCRACY: ATHENS

Between the sixth and fourth centuries B.C., Athenian philosophers, artists, dramatists, and politicians debated the merits of democracy even as they installed it. The first written evidence that the Athenians were experimenting with democracy dates from 522 B.C., when Herodotus, on the occasion of a Persian uprising, cataloged the forms of government then extant and included rudimentary explanations of the Athenian mode of governance. It began with the governorship of Solon (594 B.C.) and ended with defeat by Sparta (401 B.C.) and gradual domination by Macedon through the conquests of Alexander the Great (356–323 B.C.). The beginning of the decline can be dated more precisely to the execution of Socrates in 399 B.C. Socrates, a rebel against democracy and an open admirer of Sparta, a military oligarchy, seemed to have sought death in order to expose the hypocrisy of the democracy he hated.[4]

Initially, *direct democracy,* in which a polity could be no larger than the number beyond which sustained and direct participation could occur, was the presumed mode for the genre upon its origination by Greek philosophers, notably Aristotle (384–322 B.C.), a moderate proponent of democracy, and Plato (428–348 B.C.), an equally brilliant, if extreme, opponent. Their ideas had very little to do with *representation,* the heart of modern democratic theory, because their "laboratory" (Athens) was so small. The participants needed to know each other, to understand strengths and weaknesses, biases and idiosyncrasies, peculiarities and preferences. The *Assembly* was the first body that attempted to reflect their vision of government.

The Assembly

The Assembly was open to any male over 18 years of age whose mother and father were Athenians. All who met this restriction could show up and talk for as long as they wished on any topic they desired. Only a tiny fraction of the eligible population made a regular habit of attending meetings of the assembly. But in answer to the cry "Who among the Athenians wishes to speak?" there was apparently no shortage of volunteers. The Assembly, naturally, was more in the nature of a popular sounding board with all the appropriate pageantry for hortatory speeches and none of the requisite privacy for deliberation and compromise:

> The meeting took place soon after dawn, and was held in a sort of rude open-air theatre built upon a sloping hill-side called the Pnyx. A herald ordained silence. Prayers were offered by a priest and a black pig was sacrificed.[5]

Without the adhesive bindings of political parties or interest groups, the Assembly could respond in almost unpredictable fashion to harangues. Pericles was fully aware of the extent to which political careers were made or broken because of a single speech. Later, Cleon and other demagogues who appealed to emotion rather than reason rose rapidly, more because of oratorical skill than of political experience. One could hardly expect a democracy that survived for two centuries to rely solely on a come-one, come-all town meeting for more than the more perfunctory guides to policy. Although it remained the final authority, power and the real work of the city-state passed to a smaller *Council of 500*. It was to this council that seekers of the antecedents of democracy turn.

Representative Democracy: The Council of 500

The earliest viable example of democracy is of *representative democracy*, not because Athenians were scheming to deprive the population of its legitimate rights but because like any full-time occupation, running a city-state is hard work. To share the burden, Council members were selected by a lottery for a term of duty, limited to a maximum of two terms (the length of a term was not fixed).

The Council was indeed needed to interpret the broad mandates of the Assembly. But as we will soon realize, the lottery did not encourage the Council to develop any sense of corporate accountability or institutional responsibility (without elections, no politician needed to look anxiously over his shoulder at his constituency). Furthermore, as is true of all political processes, the wealthy had more of the time and skills to engage in political activities (and the machinations of the political clubs before the drawing of the lottery reduced the egalitarian aims of the lottery substantially). Standing for office was, even as the Athenian democracy was in its last days, largely a province of the elite. This does not make Athens unique, of course. For example, attendance at New England town meetings—the closest approximation of the Athenian Assembly (albeit on a smaller scale—is strongly associated with length of time in the town, age, and socio-economic status.

Athens's politically active citizens had the time for indulgence of pastimes because slavery fueled the Athenian economy. Greater Athens's slave population was about 125,000, half the total population. The Periclean ideal of equal participation excluded slaves, as well as women and *metics* (resident aliens). Slaves were forcibly imported barbarians, while metics entered freely, acquiring economic rights but no rights of political participation. Between the metics and the slaves, the economy was kept running, albeit with substantial problems of income distribution.

The life of Greece was a more public life than that to which we are accustomed: the Athenian view of the ideal citizen included a full agenda of public service. Many avoided all but the most compulsory duties, but some—especially those from the established families with roots in *deme* (local) politics—made political life an avocation.

So eager were Athenians to free citizens from the messier public responsibilities that they even imported their police force, deeming it inappropriate for citizens to apprehend one another. So arrests were made by archers from barbarian tribes, who, clad in their native pants and high-peaked tight hats, were immediately recognized. They lived in tents outside the city and, of course, had no political rights.[6] Free Athenians were encouraged to be conscious of their exclusivity, even though they were exploiting slaves and resident aliens.

Clearly, it is not the dominance of the political process by the wealthy that made the Athenian democratic experiment unique; it is the extent to which, in spite of this natural tendency, popular participation was institutionalized. Aristotle believed man to be a political animal. If ever this were true, it was in Athens.

The Selection Process and Decision Making

Selection to the Council was by lot (much like people are drawn for jury duty in the United States). Just as in voter surveys, where researchers select a random sample of voters as representative of the universe of the total electorate, so the Athenian system was intended to prevent bias. Because Athens was small, with a population of about 30,000, and it excluded slaves and women from the lottery, its politically eligible population, possibly 14,500 adult males, was easily rotated through the legislature, which met 10 times annually.[7] One could argue that the method of selection to the Council of 500 was pure representation because it was, in theory, random. Yet the lot method of selection was not pure. The lots were drawn from citizens over 30 who presented themselves as candidates. Imagine from your own experiences the kinds of people willing to take a year or more from their private affairs to serve as legislators. Is it likely that citizens whose wages were determined by the hours or weeks of their service would have been able to compete for the job of councillor?

Athenians hoped that the lottery would assure them of a representative body, but since it was composed of the politically active and mobilized segment of the population, it was probably no more successful in speaking for the people than modern legislatures are. The problem of representation—the substitution of a small body for a larger population—has been present from the beginnings of the idea of democracy. However, as we shall see, the Athenian solution suspended serious examination of the idea.

Athenian democracy merits attention not only because it sought to be direct (the Assembly) and avoid elections (the Council of 500) but also because it was, in spite of the much vaunted lot system, a fine example of the politics of legislative elites. Ten tribes or *demes* were allocated 50 seats, irrespective of population, in a manner similar to that by which the American states are represented in the Senate. As occurred with the English Parliament, one did not have to live in a particular *deme* in order to represent it, and fraud was as widespread in ancient Athens as in Boston.

Various political clubs, organized largely to influence the prelottery machinations, were the chief participants in the creation of the list of candidates the *demes* presented for the lottery.[8] Skullduggery was as common in Athens as in Boston: "Rich and influential metics had no difficulty in hunting out a suitable little deme where, at not too excessive a price, their names would be enrolled without questions being asked."[9] People sought public office for the same reasons they do so today: they were ambitious, they sought to achieve their own version of the public interest, and they wanted the perks. Toward the end of the fifth century B.C., the problem of income distribution had become acute: about 55 percent of the population was living in poverty, and the opportunity for public service was also the opportunity for money. The lot system took on the desperation of games of chance.

The lottery kept those who served from being held accountable for what they did. They could not be defeated, since the lot was theoretically random (we have seen, of course, that lotteries were fixed). As a result, there was no "loyal opposition," no political party determined to expose the evils of the incumbents in order to gain control of the government.

Dahl and Tufte "imagine" that caucuses developed spontaneously in order to select the most qualified speaker to present a point of view.[10] Quite possibly they did. However, the difference between a temporary *coalition* and a permanent *faction* is substantial. Floating coalitions, specific to the issue of the moment, dissolve and are reconstituted with different participants. The opportunities for stable, responsive leadership are not very great. Factions did exist but they were concerned more with individual interests, such as votes for ostracism, than with policy.[11]

This was so because the Assembly and the Council, even with the inevitable delegation of power to smaller bodies, were not constituted by election. Of the Council, M. I. Finley writes:

> [It] was not a "government" in our sense. Nor was there any official opposition. Alternative policies were formulated within a small political class for which there was no technical term because it had no structured existence. . . . There were no formal party line-ups, no whips, no machinery to predetermine the final vote irrespective of speech-making.[12]

In other words, such informal ways of achieving a majority do not lend themselves well to political organization, as we know it through a party system. Everyone could easily see how the balloting was going, and the open balloting contributed to the predominance of unanimous votes. Consensus built on bandwagon effects was common because of the inherent nature of Athenian democracy.

Unstable factions are quite acceptable if the decision rules of a political institution are unitary (that is, if they assume the existence of a public interest),[13] and Athenian democracy was more unitary in its assumptions than modern representative democracies are. Although the formal decision rule in both the Assembly and the Council was majority rule, because it implied acceptance of the legitimacy of conflict,[14] most assembly decisions were actually by *consensus*.[15] And using the most exhaustive evidence imaginable, Mansbridge concludes that there was beyond that a "strong preference for unanimity."[16] There is a difference between *consensus* decision rules and *unanimity,* as Mansbridge explains:

Although the formal logic of consensus may be technically the same as that of a "unanimity rule," the two terms conjure up quite different processes. In a consensual process, as under a strict unanimity rule, the determined opposition of one member can usually prevent collective action, and if the group acts in spite of that opposition, the dissenter will not be obligated by the group decision. But the consensual process differs in form from a strict unanimity rule in that no vote is taken.[17]

Elections in the Athenian System

The irony of Athenian democracy is well expressed in the *election* of citizens to positions that are normally, even in the most radical of democracies, made by appointment. There was no bureaucracy, no civil service. The Council designated a rotating subcommittee as its voice in matters of everyday governance and never employed the equivalent of a professional staff. Since only two Council terms were allowed, about one-third of the total eligible population would have served on the Council in any decade and, during a portion of their service, on a smaller subcommittee. Affairs of state were truly in the hands either of the Assembly or the Council; it was government by amateurs.

The responsibility for making decisions, carrying them out, and living with the consequences was so much a part of Athenian social ideology that it would have been incomprehensible to delegate authority to a bureaucracy. *Magistrates,* whose service required professional knowledge, were elected by a show a hands or by acclamation. Also elected in this way were military leaders, archons, administrators of various financial accounts, and temporary commissions (as needed for, say, the construction of a public building). A seemingly bizarre reversal of priorities was at work: legislators were chosen by lot, but generals and civil servants were elected! The notion of a professional was abhorrent to the Athenian ideals; generals in one campaign, losing a bid for reelection, returned to the field as enlisted men. The final defeat by Sparta was due as much to the amateurism of Athenian warmaking as to Spartan brilliance.

The Problem of Accountability

The lack of accountability was serious. There was no point at which citizens or public officials could challenge the fundamental course of public policy. Pericles himself lost his command because of an unwise tactical decision in the Peloponnesian War (he was reinstated a year later). But there was no idea of how to hold policymakers, the Assembly and Council, responsible for the decisions that generals tried to implement. As the list of exiled generals grew, the demagogues became bolder since the blame for their loony schemes never trickled up. The essence of democracy in an imperfect world is the existence of *choice.* Whether the choice is between political parties or between factions of a dominant party is less important than the existence of a structured choice.

There is substantial evidence that Athens was rendered helpless by severe internal conflict, and as its twilight approached, there are clear indications that the promulgations of the Assembly encountered either active or passive resistance. Athens's decline was a consequence of both the inability to compete with professional armies and inefficient government. Its inefficiency was in turn the result of the inability to balance a passion for democracy with a commonsense understanding of what is required to maintain the routines of government. The limits of deliberation were quickly reached. How large can a deliberative body be without eliminating the probability of reasoned debate? Surely, 500 is too large. The sheer logistics of conducting such a large forum with even a modicum of attention to detail proved to be insurmountable. Dahl and Tufte estimate that, allowing 15 minutes' debate from a bare minimum quorum, five months' deliberation at a rate of 10 hours a day would be required to reach one decision![18]

The Assembly could hardly have been very influential in policy initiation; its agenda was set by the Council. But unlike other "rubber stamp" assemblies of comparable size, the Assembly, especially toward the end of the democratic city-state, became caught up in important debates, generally seeking the overthrow of commanders in the field:

> A mass meeting of several thousand men who chose to be present on that occasion listened to speakers—to men who opted to take the floor, without holding any office, without any formal duty or obligation—and then voted by show of hands, all in one day or less than a day.[19]

The Assembly ended its years as the promulgator of ideas regarded by Athenian citizens as radical and by the Council as dangerous. Council consent was required before a proposal could become a law, but the Assembly's power to amend made the modest safeguard not very effective. As a decision-making body, the Assembly resembled a mob.

As Athens became less able to compete militarily, corruption threatened its internal political process, to the extent that finally, all income from public service was abolished. Even so, various debtors' revolutions continued to plague Athens, and the brutality with which they were repressed is evidence of the continued deterioration of Athenian democracy. As the military killed seditious debtors at a rate of 1,000 per day, Athens got its first real taste of demagoguery: seizing the opportunity brought about by fear of violence, politicians began promising the abolition of all debts, the redistribution of all land, and the public seizure of all means of production.

Dissent and Decline

After the beginning of the Peloponnesian War (450 B.C.), the Assembly faced a relentless series of *coups d'état*. Freedom of speech became less absolute even as Athenian literature was flourishing. Often, brilliant artistic accomplishments accompany political degeneration, as though the artistic temperament needs anguish. There was anguish aplenty in Athens as the Assembly became even more impotent, confining itself to petty graft, systematic corruption, and the meting out of an occasional death sentence, such as that given to Socrates. Against this background emerged the mordant satire of Aristophanes, the ghastly tragedies of Euripides and Sophocles, and Plato's elegant account of the condemnation of Socrates.

In Euripides' *Medea*, produced in 431 B.C. (the same year in which Pericles' funeral oration glorified Greek democracy), Medea dispatches her children to kill a rival (which they do) and then kills them while the chorus chants, "Those who are childless have the best fortune." These authors ridiculed all political institutions as venal and

corrupt. Pompous public officials, obsessed military leaders, and cruel seekers of revenge populate their works.

Even comedies were at best bittersweet. Aristophanes, whose plays were produced
during the Peloponnesian War, wrote pacifist dramas against the war, his most re-
nowned being *Lysistrata*. (The plot involves women withholding sexual favors until the
war is over.) In *The Knights*, he attacked Cleon the demagogue; in *The Wasps*, he
lampooned Athenian juries.

Sophocles' *Oedipus the King*, a tale of almost unbearable brutality, stands as the
model for tragedy (a term first used in describing Greek drama). The emotions we use
to describe the dilemmas of modern life, such as alienation, angst, and anomie, were
felt in Sophocles' time. But there has since been no equal to Socrates in description of
horror. Walter Kaufman writes of the era:

> The popular notion that alienation is a distinctively modern phenomenon is untenable;
> Sophocles' Oedipus is a paradigm of alienation from nature, from himself, and from
> society. After having been thrown into a world into which he was never supposed to
> have been born, he is literally cast out into hostile nature. He is a stranger to himself,
> and so far from being at home with himself when he finally discovers his identity that
> his first impulse is to mutilate and blind himself; indeed, he wishes he could have
> destroyed his hearing, too, severing himself altogether from the world and from his
> fellow men.[20]

The fact that many people spent so much time attacking or defending democracy
is evidence of its decline. The intellectuals of degenerating Athens were like the American literary establishment in the 1960s and 1970s, bearing up through the assassination
of a president and other leaders, the commitment of troops to the quagmire of Vietnam,
the resignation of a vice-president for bribery and of a president for obstruction of
justice. Athenian intellectuals saw the sacrifice of a generation of youth in the Peloponnesian War and the betrayal of Athenian military efforts by generals. Upon defecting
to the Spartans and spilling all the Athenian military secrets he possessed, Alcibiades,
the most notorious traitor, so loathed his city that he called its governing process ''an
acknowledged madness.'' Its most influential politicians were those who proposed brutal
revenge on captured adversaries, satisfying the rage of the Assembly. Amateur generals
led mercenaries to the slaughter of noncombatants on the island of Melos, an act of
barbarity that provoked only the gentlest of protests. Pericles, whose brilliant defense
of democracy set the tone for the high point of Athenian government, died (of the
plague), and Cleon, a shameless rogue who provided us with the clearest example of
the demagogue and who had argued that it is better to have bad laws than to be changing
them continually, persuaded the Council to kill all male prisoners and sell the women
and children as slaves, an act of brutality that permanently alienated Athenian intellectuals and contributed to the decision to execute Socrates.

Coping with apparent flaws in the workings of democracy did not allow Athenian
theorists to spend much time thinking of alternatives, and in any event the military
conquest of Athens interrupted the development of democratic theory. The most energetic condemnation of democracy was by Plato, with a lukewarm defense by Aristotle.
Plato, in *The Republic*, divided all government according to the size and predilections

of its ruling class. Rule by a single person was either monarchy (good) or tyranny (bad); minority rule was either aristocracy (good) or oligarchy (bad); rule by the many was either polity (good) or democracy (bad).[21] Democracy was for him the distortion of a preferred mode of governance. Bitter about the strength of the demagogues, he complained:

> A democracy tramples all such notions [as respect for truth and beauty] under foot: with a magnificent indifference to the sort of life a man has led before he enters politics, it will promote to honor anyone who merely calls himself the people's friend.[22]

Besides providing the first data about democratic governance, the Athenians also offer the opportunity to reflect on the destruction of a democratic political system. As the system began to unravel, the Assembly became the focus of a series of close votes, unusual and indicative of the decline of the *polis*. The polis had been "a kind of super family. This attitude . . . explains why the Greeks never . . . 'invented' representative government. Why should [they] 'invent' something which most Greeks struggled to abolish, namely being governed by someone else?"[23] But now the feeling of community was ending, along with the ideal of the leisured amateur (which was resurrected in the American South and in the English public schools). All in all, the pressures on the Athenian democracy were too great, the built-in problems and limitations too large. Had Sparta not extinguished it, the Athenian system would have died anyway. Leslie Lipson argues that by the time of its humiliation, Athens got no more than it deserved.[24]

REPRESENTATION AND CHOICE: THE ENGLISH PARLIAMENT

About 1,700 years after the demise of Greek democracy, the idea of a responsive government reappeared. The Norman conquest of England in 1066 brought with it a vast and efficient administrative state, a bureaucracy. In 1215, the Magna Charta required consultation between the king and nobles. In 1240, a Great Council made this consultation formal. Simultaneously, the decendants of the Norman conquerors sought, sporadically but frequently, the advice of knights and nobles who, while not members of the Great Council, were thought to have a feel for sentiment in the provinces (beyond London).

These two bodies evolved into the House of Commons and the House of Lords, the first representative institutions serving as precursors to a democratic political system. The tension between Parliament, a term first used in the 13th century, and the crown was intense: Parliament was especially powerful during the reign of Elizabeth I (1558–1603), a position challenged by the Stuart kings of the 17th century and culminating in the execution of Charles I. The tension continued unabated until 1688, when James II, seeking to assert the doctrine of the divine right of kings, was forced to flee the country. Parliament invited James's son William, and his wife, Mary, to occupy the throne, which they did, knowing exactly where their authority came from. Hence they readily agreed to the Bill of Rights, asserting the authority of Parliament to be equal to that of the crown.

During the latter half of the 17th century, due possibly to a series of unusually stupid monarchs, the crown's ministers began meeting without the crown or its representative. This body gradually drifted away from the orbit of the crown and by the 18th century was popularly known as the cabinet. Since the cabinet consisted of the crown's ministers, the cabinet minister who assumed responsibility for convening meetings was called the *prime minister*.

The unsuccessful fight against the North American colonies, the ferment of the French Revolution, the rapidity with which the industrial revolution created masses of exploited and impoverished classes, led irrevocably to the institutionalization of elections. The Reform Act of 1832, although it enfranchised only a small portion of the electorate, shifted the balance of power in the direction of Commons. A series of reform acts followed the original one, until the shape of the present British system appeared. By the 20th century, the House of Commons, elected by a completely enfranchised population, had developed.

The development of Parliament was not only slow and evolutionary, it was also a movement of democracy downward from nobles to commoners, a process that took until the Representation of the People Act of 1918. It should be apparent, then, that theories of representation, absent from the Greek democratic experiment, were the heart of the British experience.

Units of Representation

The English monarchy, beginning with the Norman conquest in 1066, had displayed an unusual (for the times) interest in keeping accurate records of births, deaths, populations, debts, and taxes. The *Domesday Book,* the first such compendium, required an efficient central administration and a cooperative group of local governments. As the gathering of data became more routinized, local units were organized.

The earliest mention of the idea of representation in England was in 1100, a century before the Magna Charta.[25] Presumably the first allusion to representation in the Middle Ages, it discussed the *vill* (township) as needing a voice for pleading with the crown. Thus even before the Magna Charta, English custom included the germ of the idea of representation. The influence of administrative routines on the development of ideas of representative government cannot be overstated. The concept of a representative, decision-making body grew naturally out of the everyday needs of an efficient national bureaucracy.

Since so many of the administrative routines involved work and income, local communities contained guildlike *estates*. The various occupational groupings became associations that the king's assessors and census takers could rely on for the collection of data.

The *shire* replaced the vill as the building block of English representation. With parallels in most feudal societies, the shire was the geographic holding company for the *functional* representation of the estates: people who fight, people who work, and people who pray. Remnants of the estates can be found in the feudal guild system and later in European corporatism.[26]

Norman kings relied on the tenants of the shires, the barons, earls, and churchmen, to tell them when laws were flagrantly violated, when taxes were being ignored, or when opposition to wars was becoming serious. Local noblemen, becoming accustomed to providing information, also expected to be consulted before any major shifts in public policy were contemplated. The Magna Charta formalized these expectations and created the Great Council, the direct antecedent of England's Parliament and hence the first "democratic" institution since Athens.

By the late 13th century, the gentry, squires, and knights selected the representative of the *borough* (successor to the shire) to the Great Council, which now met regularly. Occasionally, when no knights or squires were available, a "freeman" would substitute. Gradually, the proportion of freemen increased, and their designation as representatives became more than just an occasional substitution. By the 14th century, regional assemblies that included nonnobles were called *commons*.[27]

The Great Council, now called *Parliament* (derived from the French *parler*, "to talk"), met at the summons of the crown; the commons was "indirectly summoned" by the sheriff at the request of the crown:

> To every sheriff in England went a writ ordering him to cause to be chosen two knights of his county, two citizens from every city, and two burgesses from every borough from the most discreet and hard-working and to cause them to come to the parliament provided with full and sufficient power to do and to consent to whatever may be ordained.[28]

Like the Great Council, the commons was an advisory body summoned either by the crown or its representative. Delegates sent to the two advisory bodies were not always the obedient and devoted servants that the crown sought. For example, Bedfordshire sent

> John Morteyn: Nine times M.O., 1307–1330; large landowner, several times summoned for military service; friend of Edward II . . . a strong partisan in politics with so many enemies that the king gave him permission to ride always armed. . . . Thomas Frembaud: . . . Constantly in debt; fined 2,000 pounds for various acts of violence . . . fought at Crecy; sheriff, escheator [imprisoned for arrears of accounts].[29]

The two separate meetings became a single Parliament by the middle of the 14th century. A typical Parliament originally consisted of 52 "spiritual lords," 77 "temporal lords," 10 councillors, 160 citizens and burgesses, and 141 minor members of the clergy. When the two groups merged, the knights of the commons joined the citizens, burgesses, and minor clergy of the Parliament to form the House of Commons. The House of Lords remained the province of the titled, and summonses were the right of the crown. Sheriffs retained responsibility for selecting the members of commons.[30]

The county court fixed qualifications for members of Parliament that remained unchanged until the Reform Act of 1832: members had to be knights or squires who were qualified to become knights with landholdings valued at 40 shillings or more.[31] One change, in 1430, defined the Parliament until the 19th century; the county court lost the right to nominate potential members of parliament to the sheriff, and the 40-shilling rule was applied to qualifications for voters as well as nominees.[32]

Emerging Theories of Representation

Theories of appropriate modes of representation developed spontaneously out of the day-to-day business of Parliament. Justifications for parliamentary consultation with the crown were likely to take the form of claims that Parliament "represents the body of all the realm."[33] In practice, less time was spent thinking about representation than in coping with individual claims and petitions. The Parliament, especially Commons, viewed its role as granting taxes and hearing grievances, representing collectively the views of individuals. The principle of linking taxation with the right to be heard, the belief that taxes had to be justified by those who spoke for the realm, had existed since the Magna Charta.

As private petitions became more numerous, they so clogged the agenda of Commons that it began to refer them to committees named by the Crown and the House of Lords. Commons began turning its attention to developing its own petitions. Rather than hearing individual grievances, Commons began to act for the community; to represent the needs of their constituents to the crown. No thought was given to modes of representation or responsiveness. Should members of Parliament snoot around in their districts, picking up suggestions and promising solutions? Could Commons' members act in the best interest of the community if no demands were apparent? In practice, Commons accepted the idea that it should channel community opinion to the crown. Often the legislation represented came from communities, groups (the guilds and associations), and individuals. The substance of the legislation shows well the nature of medieval politics: Commons drafted legislation about livery and maintenance, the term of office for sheriffs, uniform weights and measures, and trade regulation.[34]

The industrial revolution created a new class of potential constituents: the urban working classes. Beginning during the middle years of the 18th century and continuing through the First World War (which gave the world the opportunity to see what havoc could be wrought with the products of industrialization: on the first day of the battle of the Somme, 60,000 British soldiers were killed or wounded), the development of mass production emptied the rural areas and swelled the population of London, Manchester, Birmingham, and Liverpool to the exploding point with unskilled and semiskilled workers.

The extraordinary social change triggered by the "machine age" was exceeded first by the revolution in the American colonies and later by the French Revolution. These events created an atmosphere much like that in the United States during the Vietnam War. The colonial war was expensive in life, money, and prestige; the most powerful army in Europe was being beaten by a gang of irregulars. The American and French revolutions, though quite different in origin and intent, combined with the seething unrest of the urban poor to beget and strengthen the role of political parties in seeking out parliamentary candidates, with the Labour party later arguing for the rapid institutionalization of change, the expansion of the franchise, and "more democracy."

Paine versus Burke.   One of the most prominent radicals, Tom Paine, argued in *The Rights of Man* that as there had never been a formal or explicit ratification of the relationship of Parliament, the crown, and the "common folk," the government had no legitimacy. He was answered by Edmund Burke, speaking for the conservative factions (he was a Whig member of Parliament from Bristol). The dialogue between Burke and Paine brought back the same arguments that Aristotle and Plato had confronted in Athens: is "representative democracy" an oxymoron, a contradiction in terms? As the two were stating their arguments, the crown prosecuted a shoemaker, Thomas Hardy, for high treason, on the grounds that he advocated "representative government."

Burke, reflecting on the fact that he had been elected by a tiny fraction of the population (an allocation that had not changed appreciably for 300 years), argued that the system was just:

> Parliament is not a *congress* of ambassadors from different and hostile interests, which interests each must maintain, as an agent or advocate, against other agents and advocates; but parliament is a *deliberative* assembly *of* one nation, with *one* interest, that of the whole—where, not local purposes, not local prejudices, ought to guide, but the general good, resulting from the general reason of the whole.[35]

Since Burke believed that representatives should be free to act in the best interest of the country first and the constituency second (a belief encouraged by the absence of a residency requirement for members of Parliament), the size and composition of Parliament was of little concern. Representatives do not represent the views of their constituents, nor should they. Furthermore, Burke maintained that the "true" interests of constituents could not be discovered by any type of poll, survey, or election since people often do not know what is best for them:

> Such a representation I think to be, in many cases, even better than the actual. It possesses most of its advantages, and is free from many of its inconveniences; it corrects the irregularities in the literal representation, when the shifting current of human affairs or the act of public interest in different ways, carry it obliquely from its first line of direction.[36]

Burke conceded that there should be some relation to the constituent, but not one that binds the representative through elections.

Burke's theory of appropriate representation is similar to Rousseau's; both believed in a general will that could not be revealed by election, and both valued the community more than the individual. The banner of the enlightened community was grasped by Rousseau, who quite naturally gravitated toward utopian schemes for achieving the harmony promised by the general will. But by Rousseau's time, nation-states had become quite a bit larger than was true during the Grecian period. Rousseau believed that each increase in size resulted in a corresponding loss in the opportunities for individual participation and control.

Because Burke wrote on representation, he has occasionally been misunderstood. He had no patience with majority rule:

> But if we could suppose that such a ratification [of a law contrary to the public interest] was made, not virtually, but actually, by the people, not representatively, but even collectively, still it would be null and void. . . . It would be hard to point out an error more truly subversive of all the order and beauty, of all the peace and happiness, of human society, than the position that a body of men have a right to make what laws they please.[37]

The well-being of the collectivity is discovered by deliberation, meditation, and prayer, not by a crass head count.

Recognizing the inevitability of representative democracy, Burke nevertheless bemoaned the demise of the utopian collectivist view of representative democracy, feeling that since it is a surrogate for the unfeasible direct democracy that it replaced, representative democracy should mirror as closely as possible the views of the represented—what all would have proposed or opposed had they been present.

The romantic and unrealistic notion of representative government—that it existed solely as a convenience—confronts a more cautious, conservative view of representative democracy; it allows people who are interested in politics (a small minority) to govern while those who are not interested go about their lives, making money, getting married, finding jobs, acquiring hobbies, saving and investing, getting divorced, watching television, listening to music, taking vacations, and so on. Many of these activities involve the political system, but one can still do all of them without thinking much about politics.

Expansion of the Electorate

Burke's ideas were not, however, incompatible with the expansion of the franchise in England. His party, the Whigs, engineered the 1832 Reform Act. A modest adjustment of a centuries-old scheme, the Reform Act, while still retaining the wealth requirements for electors, made allowances for those whose wealth was tied up in real estate; a quarter of a million voters were added. Additional franchise expansions took place in 1867 (enfranchising householders paying £12 a year in rent, ministers, university graduates, men with £50 to their name, and men paying £1 a year in direct taxes; if these men also met the property requirements, they could cast two votes).

In 1884, the electorate was doubled (to 59 percent of adult males) by the enfranchisement of agricultural laborers and miners. In 1918, all men over 21 (who met residential requirements) and their wives (if over 30) were added to the voting lists. In 1928, the lowering of the voting age for women to 21 gave the United Kingdom universal suffrage.

The theory of representation guiding this second experiment in democracy differed greatly from that of the Greeks. Athenian democracy was based on the conviction that representation of one person by another was not democracy, that any dilution of the principle of direct democracy was reluctantly accepted as a practical matter. For the English, representation of the adult population began from the opposite end of the continuum of democracy: the crown granted nobles the right to be heard, and nobles extended the franchise to a small portion of the population. Each reform added a few more, in a process that began in 1205 and ended in 1928. This process was culturally and ideologically built on a quite different set of beliefs and assumptions. Burke's argument that representative government was a preferred alternative to direct democracy, rather than a necessary and inferior substitute for it, stands in stark contrast to the populism of the Athenians. The well-being of the people is the yardstick of successful government; government by the people is another matter entirely.

"WE THE PEOPLE": THE AMERICAN SYSTEM

The two main antagonists, direct democracy and representative democracy, continue to pose problems for democracies. Examine the extent to which the authors of the U.S. Constitution sought to buffer government: only the House of Representatives was elected directly; the Senate was chosen by state legislatures, the president by the electoral college, and the federal courts by the president and the Senate. Power was widely diffused because of the fear of unconstrained elites and also because of a deeply suspicious view of the populace. The House of Representatives was to reflect popular passions and whims, while the other branches of government provided balance.

The adoption of a federal system (with power divided between national and state governments) provided additional protection against an unwise public. To achieve hegemony, the people would have had to gain control of three separate branches of government and at least a majority of state governments, an unlikely occurrence.

These elaborate precautions were undertaken to defend the political system against factions. Few theorists are so naive as to assume the existence of the people as an amorphous mass; rather, they think of people as black or white, rich or poor, entrepreneur or laborer, physician or farmer, and so forth. The concept of "the people" is replaced by *groups of people*. This important transformation is a major contribution to democratic theory. The U.S. Constitution was a unique reaction against both the tyranny of government (against which the Revolution had been waged) and the tyranny of the masses; it reflected a fear of popular unrest as well as of elite tyranny. The rampant inflation in state currencies, the growing restiveness of debtors (as illustrated by Shays's Rebellion in Massachusetts), and the fear of economic and social disintegration were among the major factors impelling the construction of a new constitution.

Because of its origins, the American system remains uniquely "incremental": it changes slowly, as it was intended to do, in response to "demands." It is the only presidential federal system of government extant. There are other federal systems (Australia, Canada, West Germany, Switzerland), and there are other systems providing for direct election of president and hence some separation of powers (France). But only the United States combines the two methods of diffusing power. A more responsive method of governmental decision structure is the parliamentary, unitary mode adapted by most industrial democracies.

Democracy and Pluralism

Implied in theories of democracy and representation is the notion of *political equality*. Resources are not distributed equally—some groups win more often than others—but the *opportunity* for influence should not be withheld. But what of England? Since the franchise was extended only gradually, could it be said that a knight (who could vote) and a landless peasant (who could not) were politically equal? The escape from this dilemma is to define a citizen. Women, slaves, and resident aliens were excluded in Athens; women were excluded in the United States until 1920 and in Switzerland until 1970. But at least among the eligible, equality is presumed. If it does not exist in fact, say proponents of pluralism, it is because of failure to use existing opportunities.

In stark contrast are the theories of *economic determinism,* such as Marxism, which assert that political inequality is caused by economic inequality, which, in turn, is inherent in any market economy. James Madison, an author of the U.S. Constitution, set forth the idea that the cause of political inequality is economic inequality but the cure for this inequality was too severe; better then to channel and redirect factions (interest groups). In any event, Madison's link between economic and political inequality did not last, and modern pluralism rejects this notion.

But the social contract theories of the 17th and 18th centuries were precursors of pluralism. Hobbes, Locke, and Madison believed that individuals were both rational and selfish: they tried to maximize their own positions and were capable of recognizing and acting in their own self-interest. It was rational for people to contract to create a government because otherwise, as we saw earlier, life would be "solitary, poor, nasty, brutish and short."[38] Rationality became integral to pluralism.

Pluralism contains elements of normative (what should be) as well as empirical (what is) theory. The most frequently derived normative variant of individualism is the doctrine of *limited government.* If government exists because it serves a purely utilitarian function, its intrusion into personal life must be carefully constrained. The building block of society is the individual. The assessment of government could be undertaken in individualist terms: is a proposed course of action likely to enhance or impede the individual's ability to achieve personal goals?

The Problem with Democracy

To assert that democracy is government "of the people, by the people, and for the people" is to give it no definition at all. Can you imagine such a government? At what point would a government of and by the people become so cumbersome that it becomes impossible? How do we decide when a law is "for" the people? Even the most populist of democrats understands that size is the enemy of democracy.

Ideally, democracy brings individual participation to the decisions that affect one's life. In 1937, John Dewey wrote, "The keynote of democracy as a way of life may be expressed as the necessity for the participation of every mature human being in formation of the values that regulate the living of men together."[39] As we have seen, democratic theory in Athens valued popular participation not only as theoretically essential but also as a device for enhancing *individual* self-development. People given responsibility for the regulation of their own conduct are believed to develop character, self-reliance, intelligence, and moral judgment—in a word, dignity.

This mode of democratic theory is solidly in the individualist tradition. In using the collective term *society,* individualist democratic theorists intend to describe only an aggregation of free persons bound together by some common characteristic. There is no abstract notion of the collective will, no will or purpose other than that assigned to it by each person. With individuals as the building blocks of the polity, any aggregation that implies an overarching, Rousseau-like public interest is unacceptable. The existence of a public good and the development of a political process to understand, adopt, and implement it is at the center of the debates surrounding modern democratic theory.

Individualists hold with writers such as John C. Calhoun, who, in defending states' rights in the American South before the Civil War, wrote:

Instead of being the united opinion of the whole community [the public good] is usually nothing more than the voice of the strongest interest or combination of interests; and not infrequently a small but energetic and active portion of the people.[40]

Calhoun's ideas were later incorporated into pluralism, which has been the dominant trend in American political thought. A leading proponent of pluralism, David Truman, writes, "In developing a group interpretation of politics . . . we do not need to account for a totally inclusive interest because one does not exist."[41]

Pluralism reaffirms democracy in its various assertions:

1. Although citizens do not directly participate in decision making, their many leaders make decisions through a process of bargaining, accommodation, and compromise.
2. Competition among leadership groups helps protect individuals' interests. Countervailing centers of power—competition among business groups, labor organizations, civil rights groups, pro- and antiabortion associations, and so on—can check one another and keep each interest from abusing its power. Organization breeds counterorganization.
3. Individuals can influence public policy indirectly by choosing among competing elites in elections. Elections and political parties allow individuals to hold leaders accountable for their actions.
4. Although individuals do not participate directly in decision making, they can exert influence participating in organized groups that reflect their interests.
5. Such groups are open; new groups can form and gain access to the centers of influence of the political system.
6. Although political influence is distributed unequally, power is widely dispersed. Access to decision making is often determined by how much interest people have in a particular decision; and because leadership is fluid and mobile, power depends on one's interest in public affairs, skills in leadership, information about issues, knowledge of democratic processes, and skill in organization and public relations.
7. Numerous leadership groups operate within society. Those that exercise power in one kind of decision do not necessarily exercise power in others. No single faction dominates decision making in all areas of public policy.
8. Policy does not necessarily reflect majority preference but rather an equilibrium of interest-group interaction; that is, competing interest-group influences tend to balance out, and the resultant policy is therefore a reasonable approximation of the preferences of all the people.

Pluralism is not the same as traditional democracy, as it does not expect individuals to participate in many decisions. Voting and joining an interest group are the extent of individual participation required for effective pluralism. Pluralist thinkers recognize that individual decision making is not possible in complex, industrial, urban societies and that it must give way to interaction—bargaining, accommodation, and compromise—among society's institutions and organizations. The political system represents individuals through surrogate groups, as we shall see in Chapter 6.

Philip Green, a passionate partisan of political equality, nevertheless believes as follows:

> We do live in a real world of representation. It governs our lives, and usually we are the better off for this. . . . Our pseudorepresentative world is populated, as by movie actors on the giant silver screen, by presidents, senators, congressmen, mayors, agency heads, union delegates, holders of proxy shares, etc., who flicker by us, larger than life, and then are gone. . . . What is nondemocratic about all forms of pseudorepresentative government . . . is that it turns political access and influence into an episodic and occasional or even nonexistent event in the lives of most people. It makes experts at political action of people who have had something visibly important to gain or to protect from that action, and apathetic incompetents of the rest.[42]

In pluralist theory, political leaders, not individual citizens, hold government responsible. The principal actors are leaders of corporations; leaders of large organizations in labor, business, and agriculture; appointed government officials; and the military and governmental bureaucracies. (Yet decision making by active elites, whether it succeeds in protecting the individual or not, fails to contribute to *individual* growth and development, an important canon of Grecian democracy.)

Pluralism emphasizes that power is *balanced*. But balance of power is different from the ideal of political equality. Pluralists believe that the people who rule come from "different small groups of interested and active citizens in different areas and some overlap . . . by public officials, and occasional intervention by some people at the polls."[43] Individual influence is achieved through leaders who anticipate the reaction of citizens. Pluralism is thus best understood as the belief that advanced industrial democracies, especially the United States, *generate* a system of multiple, competing elites (including interest groups) that determine public policy through bargaining and compromise.[44]

According to the pluralist conviction, people join groups because they believe it is to their political advantage to do so, just as was the case with the abstract social contract (between people and government) of Hobbes and Locke. If individualists believe that the purpose of government is to shield individual liberty, the pluralist modification furnished the means for the accomplishment of this purpose. Individualism leaves to our imagination means whereby citizens participate in decision making. Pluralism specifies that most (some theorists would argue all) participation is made by active leaders, who represent the interests of passive followers.

Elite competition, generally expressed by organized interest groups, helps to safeguard individual nonparticipants from governmental abuse, since no set of interests is likely to be ascendant indefinitely. A particular interest will win in some years, lose in others, win in some arenas, lose in others, win on some issues, lose on others.

There is no "they." For instance, "business" was not united on President Reagan's commitment to free international trade. West Coast businesses, principally exporters and importers to the Pacific Rim, were enthusiastic. But Frost Belt midwestern heavy industry sought tariff protection against Japanese cars. The Frost Belt case was pressed in Congress, since the president was committed, and bargains were struck. Another good example is the American civil rights movement. Black leaders, long excluded from influence in the states, turned to the Supreme Court and to Congress, with considerable success. Proponents of the Equal Rights Amendment suffered the same fate: national victory but state defeat.

Pluralism does not argue that political resources and political influence are equally distributed. Yet the ability to influence a decision is often not a result of other resources such as economic influence but rather a consequence of how much stake a given group has in a decision. If a group regards the decision as a matter of life or death for its members, it will attempt—and generally succeed at—participation and influence. The resources of pluralism are interest, skill in organization and leadership, information, and commitment.

Public policy is thus not necessarily a majority preference but a reasonable approximation of the preference of the passive, and it is the best estimate we can hope for. It is at worst an equilibrium struck between the competing interest groups. We will see these groups in operation when we study nongovernmental organizations in Chapter 6.

CORPORATISM

Governments are active on occasion in encouraging the formation of groups and may play a major role in facilitating their effectiveness, but the process is not officially or formally institutionalized. However, many countries have gone far in assisting the creation of organizations and accord access selectively to those that they favor. These countries are said to practice corporatism. According to Philippe Schmitter, a lifelong student of the phenomenon:

> Corporatism . . . is a system of interest representation in which the constituent units are organized into a limited number of singular, compulsory, noncompetitive, hierarchically ordered and functionally differentiated categories, recognized or licensed [if not created] by the state and granted a deliberate representational monopoly within their respective categories in exchange for observing certain controls on their selection of leaders and articulation of demands and supporters.[45]

The essence of corporatism is its control or monopolization of the demand-making process. Although the exact classification of countries is disputed, the following list reflects a scholarly consensus of corporatism in democracies:

Low	Medium	High
Canada	Australia	Austria
France	Belgium	Japan
Ireland	Denmark	Norway
Italy	Finland	Sweden
United Kingdom	Iceland	Switzerland
United States	Israel	
	Luxembourg	
	Netherlands	
	New Zealand	
	West Germany	

We need to make a distinction between *social corporatism* (the democratic variety with regular elections and clear legal limits on the bureaucracy) and *state corporatism* (a single-party system with vague constraints on bureaucracy). Social corporatism, as in Austria, Norway, Sweden, and Switzerland, is also democratic. State corporatism, as in Taiwan and South Korea, is typically authoritarian.[46]

Interest Intermediation

In their representation functions, the role of interest groups under corporatism is almost entirely opposite their role in pluralist theory. Of paramount importance, in corporatism they are likely to have legitimate monopolies on the representation of *functional* interests. Corporatism applies the same representative monopoly to functional interests as pluralism does to geographic ones. The rules of the game accord the winners of elections the right of exclusive representation for a geographic area. Corporatism gives this same franchise to an interest group. A single organization is accorded the right to speak for, say, pharmaceutical manufacturers.

Unlike the American pluralist interest-group system, with fierce competition for the same clientele and substantial membership turnover, organizations are almost like guilds.[47] The strong corporatism of European countries and weak corporatism of the United States and Canada are sometimes ascribed to the enduring tradition of the guilds of the Middle Ages, which in England and France were either formally represented or consulted even as geographic representation was taking hold.[48]

We must distinguish corporatism from Marxism. In classical Marxist thought, the state is an instrument of oppression, initially at the bidding of the ruling class and, in its transitional phase, of the proletariat. In corporatism, the state is not necessarily oppressive; on the contrary, the state is liberating, in the tradition of Rousseau and the collectivist romantics. Corporatism is therefore compatible with authoritarian or even totalitarian regimes but need not be limited to them. Fascist governments can be corporatist; so can democratic ones. The seminal idea of corporatism is that geographic representation is inadequate and functional representation should replace or augment it. Governments create and sanction occupational associations—groups of farmers, electricians, computer programmers, and so on. In some forms of corporatism, such organizations have been given authority for policy implementation; in others, they are legitimately influential in policy formation. In Japan, Austria, and Switzerland, for example, the distinction between public and private is blurred. Austrian labor unions and Japanese manufacturers are as much a part of the governing process as are legislators and bureaucrats.

In every case, corporatist systems confer quasi-public, often monopolistic status on interest groups. Generally, corporatist governments recognize peak associations, organizations that represent a large population of smaller groups. For example, a peak labor organization would include the building trades, teamsters, electricians, and so on. A business peak association would include computer manufacturers, textile manufacturers, and the like. The smaller groups do not engage in political activities in defiance of, or even in augmentation of, the peak association.

What about groups that are unable to become part of a peak association because peak associations are solely occupational? In pluralist countries, the most successful groups are likely to be occupational, but ideological groups are also very active. This latter kind of group, in the United States called a single-issue organization, is excluded from access in corporatist systems. People who have a cause—for or against abortion, gun control, preservation of the environment, elimination of pornography, and so on— do not find the sort of congruence between cause and occupation corporatism requires. For instance, a physician might be more concerned about the wilderness than the American Medical Association is. Whereas the AMA would be part of a corporatist policy network for, say, the regulation of Medicare services, it would not be invited to participate in environmental legislation. But since environmental concerns are not occupational, neither would any other organizations. Those outside the system must find other avenues, as the environmental parties in Europe have. In the United States, the insider-outsider distinction is hazy, and representational monopolies rare.

Corporatism and Democracy

Corporatism creates major incentives by granting quasi-official status to economic interest groups and by connecting these peak associations directly to the appropriate government bureaucracies. The justification for corporatism is precisely its ability to remove policy from groups, such as parliaments or legislatures, that lack the ability to comprehend complexity and to transfer it to bureaucracies with specialized expertise. Corporatism is designed to make policy immune from ideological passion, partisan preference, or shifting public opinion. The adoption of corporatist mechanisms and processes was a conscious effort to ensure continuity in economic policy:

> What permitted stability . . . was a shift in the focal point of decision making. Fragmented parliamentary majorities yielded to ministerial bureaucracies, or sometimes directly to party councils, where interest group representatives could more easily work out social burdens and rewards.[49]

We will return to these modes and theories of representation, equality, and responsiveness as we examine the structures and functions of democracies in Chapter 4. Before we do, ponder the following two questions, which begin to reveal the complexities and fragility of democracy.

FUNDAMENTAL QUESTIONS OF DEMOCRACY

Can Democracy Commit Suicide?

If, by democratic means, a polity creates a dictatorship, we can speak of the suicide of democracy. Democracies may fail because of external pressures or internal stress, but they can also fail because majorities wish them ill. The theoretical idea of democratic suicide is called *totalitarian democracy*.[50] Rousseau was one of the more ardent proponents of totalitarian democracy. Recall his scorn for representative institutions and for voting as keys to the discovery of the general will. In Rousseau's thinking, the tangible reality of the general will made its discovery not negotiable: since it was real, the general will needed no votes to affirm it. Unanimity was the decision rule, and institutions (such as elected legislatures), with their bargaining and coalitions, were actually impediments to the unveiling of the elusive general will.

As a result of the urge for unanimity, various messianic political movements have eliminated any vestiges of elections, political parties, or legislatures, since their existence thwarts the location and implementation of the general will. The creation of a totalitarian government can be accomplished quite legally.

The most apparent example of the suicide of democracy is Germany in the 1930s. The electoral success of the National Socialist (Nazi) party is a rarely noticed but important aspect of the suicide of German democracy. The Nazis' share of the Reichstag vote increased from 3 to 18 percent between 1928 and 1930; it soared to 37 percent in 1932 (second place went to the ruling Social Democrats, with 22 percent), declined slightly to 33 percent in another 1932 election, and finished with 44 percent in 1933. Hitler was appointed chancellor by Reich President von Hindenburg. Thus Hitler's rule was legal, and his abolition of democratic institutions was not widely contested. In the three elections before the implementation of the totalitarian government we remember today, Hitler's party legitimately received the greatest number of votes.[51]

Can Democracies Be "Constructed"?

Many politicians are good and generous people, and many are scoundrels. Every now and again, a wise and forward-looking person gains control of a nondemocratic society, one with a single party and no meaningful competition. Such people, in such societies, can work wonders: we need look no further than Taiwan, South Korea, Singapore, and Spain for examples of such rule. In Taiwan and South Korea, standards of living have edged gradually into the "developed" range, and their once authoritarian leaders began guiding them toward democracy. Singapore is more politically regressive, but with a per capita income almost the equal of Japan's, few people notice. In Taiwan, Chiang Ching-kuo, son of the autocratic Chiang Kai-shek, legalized oppositon parties and revoked martial law, making competitive politics ultimately possible. In South Korea, Roh Tae Woo, long an active member of an authoritarian regime, quelled a potentially ruinous round of protest by promising and conducting open elections. In Spain, with the death of dictator Francisco Franco in 1975, there was no necessary reason for the young monarch, Juan Carlos, and a member of the Franco government, Adolfo Suarez, to choose to convert the country into a genuine democracy. Presumably, they did so because they felt it to be right.

Portugal and Greece also returned to democracy, and steps toward democratization have been undertaken in Argentina, Brazil, Turkey, and Peru. Although much attention has been given to countries slipping into authoritarian rule, those moving the other way have only recently been subject to systematic analysis.

Democratizing countries share one common trait: an active elite wishing to create a democracy. There is no "natural" progression from totalitarian to authoritarian to democratic polities; rather, there is deliberate intervention. Without such intervention, the transition would not have taken place. Donald Share's analysis of the Spanish transition highlights "the role of strategy and skill" and the essential participation of political elites. Nothing was inevitable. The Spanish elites "were not compelled to democratize by pressure from below, the international environment, or the economic crisis."[52]

Why and how was the successful transition achieved? The most powerful members of the former authoritarian regime agreed that a change was essential. In Spain, the powerful military had to be assuaged.

> [Suarez] worked methodically and diligently. . . . He initiated a series of contacts with virtually all the representatives of regime factions and oppositon groups. . . . Suarez reassured the military of limits to the reform. . . . By adhering to institutional rules of authoritarianism, Suarez and the king were able to win the initial support of most of the Franquist elite.[53]

Finally, the Spanish leadership "had to maintain enough control over the political situation to allow for an incremental and orderly transition."[54] As Share points out, the basic rules of the authoritarian regime were adhered to even as the structure of authoritarianism was discarded. Share's essential conclusion is that moderate, incremental, consistent movement from authoritarian to democratic modes of decision will succeed more often than will rapid, violent change. Indeed, revolutions, irrespective of their ideology, usually do not yield a more democratic regime in place of an authoritarian one.

The slower transition in Taiwan from a strict authoritarian to a democratic regime is not yet completed, but, like Spain, it would not have begun had not there been elite commitment. When Taiwan was occupied in 1949 by the defeated Nationalist armies, the repression of the native population was brutal. But land reform was very successful—arguably the most successful in the world—and with the death of the elder Chiang, his son began a slow process of relaxation of repression. Opposition parties were outlawed, but oppositon candidates were not, and many won local elections. The native Taiwanese population, enjoying the benefits of an economic miracle, were enlisted into the ranks of the Kuomintang, the vessel of authoritarian rule. Next, martial law was removed and opposition parties legalized. As in Spain, elites took each step with care, consulting with both opponents and supporters of change and striking a middle course.

These examples support the view that there is no natural progression toward democratic government; the masses are not hungering to be liberated. Without elite intervention, the transition would not have occurred. Without Juan Carlos, Suarez, or Chiang, the process would probably either not have taken place or would have been less consistent.

But what happens when authoritarian rulers are less enlightened? How do you get rid of a Marcos, a Duvalier, a Somoza? Even though such despots are more easily dislodged than Marxist ones, probably because their chief goal while in office is to rob the country blind rather than to create a true police state, there is no orderly procedure for elite replacement. Political parties make regular transfer of power possible. When the people want to throw the rascals out, the most convenient way to do so is through an open election contested by political parties.

Political parties seek to place their adherents on governmental bodies and select candidates to compete in elections in their name. There are many kinds of party systems, as we will see in Chapter 5; however, at a minimum, there must be at least two parties, and each should stand a reasonable chance of winning, if not in this election, then perhaps in the next. These conditions are imperfectly met. Some democracies (such as ours) regard political parties so lightly that it has removed them from the process of selecting nominees, preferring instead to rely on primary elections. In other democracies, the same party wins all or nearly all the time, but the opposition can muster at least a respectable showing and may place enough of its members in office to make its approval of majority policy desirable. Until recently, Japan fit the mold perfectly: the Liberal Democratic party had won every election since 1955, albeit with a plurality rather than a majority. In Sweden, the Social Democrats have earned a plurality in every election since 1948.

Many single-party authoritarian governments allow major factions to compete *within that single party*. But competing factions are not the same as competing parties, because there is no necessary relationship between the ideology of the factions and policy divisions among the followers. In the USSR, the Communist Party tolerates factions, and, in March, 1989, the Soviet Union held the most open election in its history. Heralded as "true democracy," the Soviet election was certainly the closest thing to political competition *ever* seen either in imperial Russia or in the USSR. But, for all its advances, it was *not* democratic.

The election—for a large assembly to nominate a smaller legislature—was, to the surprise and chagrin of party leaders, rather more open than they had intended. Most seats in the assembly were reserved for Communist Party candidates. In many cases, these candidates ran unopposed. But, as the electoral law (unlike the plurality rules in, say the United States and in the United Kingdom where the highest number of votes— even if they do not constitute a majority—wins) required a majority, Soviet voters defeated nine *unopposed* party candidates by destroying enough ballots so as to deny them a majority! Major party leaders—the military commander in Afghanistan, the party leader in the Ukraine—were denied seats.

Clearly the election demonstrated substantial popular dissatisfaction with the ruling party. But, *no opposition party* competed. You were either a Communist Party candidate or you were not. No inter-party competition occurred. Boris Yeltsin—a party maverick who (through an embarrassing exposure of the luxurious life style of party leaders) garnered nearly 90 percent of the vote and became a media hero in the West. But he specifically, and carefully, disavowed any commitment to "pluralism" (that is, to two or more political parties). He had originally professed such a belief but backed away, confining himself to the privilege and corruption issue and, when asked, speaking of the need to "study the problem" of two or more parties. The USSR in 1989 have thus progressed to the level, say, of authoritarian Taiwan until 1987, when an opposition party was allowed, and when there were plenty of "independents" but no legal opposition to the ruling Kuomintang party. Now, with an opposition party in the field, the ruling *party* can be replaced, a circumstance not possible in the USSR.

But unless a party can be electorally compelled to leave office, the system is not democratic. Authoritarian and totalitarian parties are not monoliths, but neither are they agents of responsiveness.

Remember that one of the primary characteristics of a democracy is that it is supposed to be responsive; that responsiveness can, however, lead to the suicide of democracy, since the democratic impulse is not widespread. In the United Kingdom, where representative democracy received its most sustained theoretical and institutional defense, pressure from continued harassment by the Irish Revolutionary Army has led the government to take the unprecedented step of limiting free speech. In 1988, the government, by administrative order, prohibited live or recorded interviews with members or supporters of the IRA. The British Official Secrets Act prohibits civil servants from revealing and media from publishing ''unauthorized'' information. *Spycatcher*, a kiss-and-tell memoir by a retired British intelligence official, published in Australia, might never have seen the light of day had its author tried for U.K. publication (the courts ruled that newspaper articles about the book could not be prohibited). In the same spirit, the government recently legislated away the right of defendants to remain silent (judges could interpret silence as an admission of guilt). Can countries that restrict freedom of speech still be considered polyarchies?

A simple remedy is the throw-the-rascals-out solution. But many, if not most, Britons either do not know or do not care about civil rights abuses, and economic recovery—the government's strong suit—is proceeding at full blast. Does this bring to mind the revelations made in the first pages of this book? Theoretical issues do not often trickle down to the populace.

FOR FURTHER CONSIDERATION

1. Differentiate between representative democracy and direct democracy. Is direct democracy best suited to public or private politics?
2. Explain the role of the public in the classical Greek democracy. How has that been forced to change in modern polyarchies?
3. What is political equality? Can any government reach political equality?
4. What is a corporatist government? List several examples of corporatist governments.
5. In Athens, the lottery system created a legislature which could not be held accountable for its actions. List several arguments for and against legislative accountability. Was the Athenian system in the control of a ''fickle and irrational mob hounding its chosen leaders out of envy, temper, and blindness to political and military necessity''?[55]

For the More Adventurous

1. The Athenian Democracy failed, in part because of the lack of a permanent bureaucracy. What changes were made in England to prevent this from reoccurring? Can a permanent bureaucracy (''nonresponsive'') augment democracy? Or are bureaucracy and democracy incompatible? Of Athenian leaders, Finley writes:

   . . . lacking that quality of support, that buttressing or cushioning effect, which is provided by a bureaucracy and political party . . . there was no government in the modern sense . . . a man was a leader solely as a function of his personal status . . .[56]

   Does he mean that government without bureaucracy is impossible?
2. Classify and describe the United States government in terms of the belief systems explained in this chapter. Compare your description to the belief system implied by the Constitution.
3. Reexamine the Social Contract theory discussed in Chapter 1 based on the topics presented in this chapter. England, home of Hobbes and Locke, has no written constitution. Would this omission efface the legitimacy of the English ''social contract?''

NOTES

1. Quoted in Thucydides, *The Peloponnesian War* (New York: Bantam, 1960), p. 116.

2. We do not want to impose modern values, however. The Greeks were not alone in their use of slaves, and the idea of women's suffrage did not appear until the middle of the 19th century. Lest we become too didactic, when did women and blacks earn the franchise in the United States? When were women given the vote in Switzerland?

3. Robert A. Dahl, *Polyarchy, Participation and Opposition* (New Haven, Conn.: Yale University Press, 1971), p. 3.

4. I. F. Stone, *The Trial of Socrates* (Boston: Little, Brown, 1988).

5. C. E. Robinson, *Everyday Life in Ancient Greece* (Oxford University Press, 1934), p. 53.

6. Ibid., p. 56.

7. The population of ancient Athens is subject to much misunderstanding, generally because of confusion of the politically enfranchised population with the total population. Estimates of citizens (that is, excluding slaves and women) range between 20,000 and 50,000. See M. T. W. Arnheim, *Aristocracy in Greek Society* (London: Thames & Hudson, 1977), p. 99; and Victor Ehrenberg, *The Greek State* (New York: Norton, 1960), p. 32.

8. Warren Breed and Sally M. Seaman, "Indirect Democracy and the Social Process in Periclean Athens," *Social Science Quarterly* 52 (1971): 634.

9. Gustave Glotz, *The Greek City and Its Institutions* (New York: Knopf, 1929), p. 357.

10. Robert A. Dahl and Edward R. Tufte, *Size and Democracy* (Stanford, Calif.: Stanford University Press, 1973), p. 69.

11. The best discussion of the Athenian political factions concludes that "it is not clear whether their organization was established on a permanent or a stand-by basis for emergencies." W. Robert Connor, *The New Politicians of Fifth-Century Athens* (Princeton, N.J.: Princeton University Press, 1971), p. 44.

12. M. I. Finley, *Politics in the Ancient World* (Cambridge: Cambridge University Press, 1983), p. 76.

13. See Jane Mansbridge, *Beyond Adversary Democracy* (New York: Basic Books, 1980), pp. 13–15.

14. Ibid., p. 13.

15. The only extant recorded vote shows a tally of 3,461 to 155. See Alfred Zimmern, *The Greek Commonwealth* (Oxford: Oxford University Press, 1961), p. 169.

16. The detective work is so impressive that it deserves more than a footnote in Mansbridge's book. She notes that virtually all contemporary accounts refer to unanimous votes and that popular Athenian theories of democracy indicated a distaste for split decisions. See Mansbridge, *Beyond Adversary Democracy*, pp. 336–337.

17. Ibid., p. 32.

18. Dahl and Tufte, *Size and Democracy*, p. 69.

19. Warren Breed and Sally M. Seaman, "Indirect Democracy and the Social Process in Periclean Athens," *Social Science Quarterly* 52 (1971), p. 634.

20. Walter Kaufman, *Tradgedy and Philosophy* (Princeton, N.J.: Princeton University Press, 1968), p. 145.

21. Antiquarians will note that the original Platonic categorization did not include a "good" form for rule by the many; only later was democracy accorded legitimacy.

22. Plato, *The Republic,* ed. Francis Cornford (Oxford: Oxford University Press, 1960), p. 263.

23. D. F. Kitto, *The Greeks* (Harmondsworth, England: Penguin, 1951), p. 129.

24. Leslie Lipson, *The Democratic Civilization* (New York: Oxford University Press, 1964), p. 26.

25. H. M. Cam, "Representation in Medieval England," in *Historical Studies of the English*

Parliament, ed. E. B. Fryde and Edward Miller (Cambridge: Cambridge University Press, 1970), p. 270.

26. Antonio Marongiu, *Medieval Parliaments: A Comparative Study* (London: Eyre & Spottiswoode, 1968), pp. 53–56.

27. T. F. T. Plucknett, "Parliament," in Fryde and Miller, *Historical Studies,* p. 199.

28. Ibid., p. 214.

29. Ibid., p. 216.

30. See Edward Miller, *The Origins of Parliament* (London: Routledge & Kegan Paul, 1960), p. 20.

31. J. R. Madicott, "Parliament and the Constituencies," in *The English Parliament in the Middle Ages,* ed. R. G. Davies and J. H. Denton (Philadelphia: University of Pennsylvania Press, 1981), pp. 61–87.

32. Cecil Lane, *The Coming of Parliament* (New York: Putnam, 1905), pp. 97–109.

33. A. L. Brown, "Parliament, c. 1377–1422," in Davies and Denton, *English Parliament,* p. 117.

34. Ibid., p. 127.

35. Edmund Burke, "Address to the Electors of Bristol," in *Works* (Boston: Little, Brown, 1871) vol. 7, 9.21, pp. 94–96.

36. Ibid., p. 154.

37. Edmund Burke, "The Tracts on the Popery Laws," in *Works,* p. 233.

38. Thomas Hobbes, *Leviathan* (New York: Collier, 1961), p. 100. (Originally published 1651.)

39. John Dewey, "Democracy and Educational Administration," *School and Society,* April 3, 1937, p. 144.

40. John C. Calhoun, "A Disquisition on Government," in *Source Book of American Political Theory,* ed. Benjamin F. Wright (New York: Macmillan, 1929), p. 537.

41. David Truman, *The Governmental Process* (New York: Knopf, 1951), p. 50.

42. Philip Green, *Retrieving Democracy: In Search of Civic Equality* (Totowa, N.J.: Rowman & Allanheld, 1985), pp. 175–179 passim.

43. Aaron Wildavsky, *Leadership in a Small Town* (Totowa, N.J.: Bedminster Press, 1964), p. 20.

44. In its normative version, pluralism means that elite competition is responsive to passive masses through elections. See Thomas R. Dye and Harmon Zeigler, *The Irony of Democracy,* 7th ed. (Pacific Grove, Calif.: Brooks/Cole, 1987).

45. Philippe C. Schmitter, "Still the Century of Corporatism?" in *The New Corporatism: The Social-Political Structures in the Iberian World,* ed. Frederick B. Pike and Thomas Stritch (Notre Dame, Ind.: Notre Dame University Press, 1974), pp. 93–94.

46. Ibid., pp. 102–103.

47. See Robert Salisbury, "Why Is There No Corporatism in America?" in Philippe C. Schmitter and Gerhard Lehmbruch, eds., in *Trends toward Corporatist Intermediation* (Beverly Hills, Calif.: Sage), p. 38. pp. 213–230; and Graham K. Wilson, "Why Is There No Corporatism in the United States?" in Gerhard Lehmbruch and Philippe C. Schmitter, eds., pp. 219–236. Both essays, published eight years apart, reach the same conclusion: the United States has no peak associations, a declining labor movement, and little inclination to engage in sophisticated economic planning.

48. Marongiu, *Medieval Parliaments,* pp. 53–56.

49. Charles S. Meier, *Transforming Bourgeois Europe* (Princeton, N.J.: Princeton University Press, 1975), p. 593.

50. J. L. Talmon, *The Rise of Totalitarian Democracy* (Boston: Beacon Press, 1982).

51. We should note, however, that the National Socialists never obtained an actual majority. Even in March 1933, after the Nazis had gained control of the government, they still fell

short of a majority. See Richard Hamilton, *Who Voted for Hitler?* (Princeton, N.J.: Princeton University Press, 1982), p. 4.

52. Donald Share, *The Making of Spanish Democracy* (New York: Praeger, 1986), p. 206.

53. Ibid., pp. 208–209.

54. Ibid., p. 211.

55. Jennifer Tolbert Roberts, *Accountability in Athenian Government* (Madison: University of Wisconsin Press, 1982), p. 29.

56. M. I. Finley, "Athenian Demagogues," *Past and Present 21* (1962):15–16.

FOR FURTHER READING

Connor, W. Robert. *The New Politicians of Fifth-Century Athens.* Princeton, N.J.: Princeton University Press, 1971. Factions, coalitions, and agenda setting in Athens. The demagogues examined through the plays of Aristophanes and Euripides (and from other contemporary sources).

Davies, R. G., and J. H. Denton, eds. *The English Parliament in the Middle Ages.* Philadelphia: University of Pennsylvania Press, 1981.

Finley, M. I. *Economy and Society in Ancient Greece.* New York: Viking Penguin, 1982. The best chapters are those comparing Sparta with Athens.

Finley, M. I. *Politics in the Ancient World.* Cambridge: Cambridge University Press, 1983.

Held, David. *Models of Democracy.* Stanford, Calif.: Stanford University Press, 1987. The great strength of this book is cogent and sensible comparison of Athenian and modern democratic theories, with abundant attention given to Rousseau, Hobbes, and Marx.

Jones, A. H. M. *Athenian Democracy.* Baltimore: Johns Hopkins University Press, 1986. If you want to understand "mobocracy," listen to Jones: "The conclusion seems inevitable that Athenian policy was really determined by mass meetings of citizens on the advice of anyone who could win the people's ear" (p. 19).

Mansbridge, Jane. *Beyond Adversary Democracy.* New York: Basic Books, 1980.

Marongiu, Antonio. *Medieval Parliaments: A Comparative Study.* London: Eyre & Spottiswoode, 1968.

Plato. *The Republic,* ed. Francis Cornford. Oxford: Oxford University Press, 1960.

Roberts, Jennifer. *Accountability in Athenian Government.* Madison: University of Wisconsin Press, 1982. An account of the impeachment of Greek officials, in many cases for political reasons.

Robinson, C. E. *Everyday Life in Ancient Greece.* Oxford: Oxford University Press, 1954. Especially strong on the treatment of women and slaves.

Sartori, Giovanni. *The Theory of Democracy Revisited. Part 2: The Classical Issues.* Chatham, N.J.: Chatham House, 1987.

Spitz, Elaine. *Majority Rule.* Chatham, N.J.: Chatham House, 1984.

Stone, I. F. *The Trial of Socrates.* Boston: Little, Brown, 1988. The noted American muckraker turns his scandal-hardened eyes to Athens, with surprising results.

CHAPTER 4

The Structures of Democracy

Reprinted by permission of NEA, Inc.

PRESIDENTIAL AND PARLIAMENTARY GOVERNMENT

All democracies are structured as either presidential or parliamentary governments. The essential difference is that the executive in parliamentary systems is not elected directly but rather is named by the party or coalition of parties that commands a majority in the legislature. In presidential systems, the chief executive is elected directly, independent of the legislature. Although the difference might seem minor, the consequences for government are profound.

To illustrate, in the United States, voters select a president by voting directly for a candidate (popular votes are translated into *electoral votes,* and the majority of electoral votes determines the election). Voters also select senators and representatives. Thus the president's election is independent of congressional elections. He may be (and usually is) a member of a different political party. Since the Republican party has won the presidency four of the last five times and the Democrats have controlled the House for this entire period and the Senate for all but one session, a government divided along partisan lines seems a permanent fixture.

The parliamentary equivalent of the American president, the prime minister, is elected indirectly. Voters select a *party* to govern the legislature. The leader of that party (or, in the event there is no majority, the person able to patch together a coalition) becomes prime minister by virtue of party position. Prime ministers may come and go without direct electoral victory or defeat. It is therefore technically impossible to have divided government. Margaret Thatcher, prime minister of Great Britain, was directly elected by the voters only to the House of Commons. The Conservative party, which she heads (having been elected by the party's members of Parliament), could remove her.

Among the most important countries that have parliamentary governments with no separation of powers and thus a chief executive selected from the parliamentary party with no independent authority are Australia, Austria, Belgium, Canada, Denmark, Finland, West Germany, Greece, Iceland, Ireland, Israel, Italy, Japan, Luxembourg, the Netherlands, New Zealand, Norway, Portugal, Spain, Sweden, Switzerland, and the United Kingdom (see Chapter 3). Of course, the party's leader, and hence the person to become prime minister, is known by voters in parliamentary systems with electoral rules (pluralities) that minimize the clout of third parties. But in other parliamentary systems, the prime minister's selection often depends on parliamentary bargaining; hence voters do not know who will be selected when they vote.

Among the most prominent of the presidential systems, with a chief executive elected directly, are the United States, Colombia, Costa Rica, Cyprus, the Dominican Republic, Ecuador, South Korea, and Venezuela. France has a mixed system, with a directly elected president who can dissolve the Chamber of Deputies and thus call a new election, as in parliamentary systems; the president also appoints a prime minister (see Chapter 5).

Most industrial democracies, including the two nations whose constitutions the United States was influential in writing, postwar Japan and West Germany, do not have presidential systems. Does this mean that there are flaws in presidential systems? Why did the Americans write parliamentary constitutions for other countries? Perhaps the answer is that ours it the only industrial democracy that does not have a parliamentary system; thus there is no tradition for such a form as ours in Europe or Asia.

WHY A SEPARATION OF POWERS?

Separation of powers is a rare, and generally unpopular, way of governing. One expert has observed that "most of the world's democracies have neither accepted the doctrine of separation of powers nor installed the American style of checks and balances." [1] Others concur:

> The separation of powers is distinctly American. Other Western democracies do not separate the legislature and the executive in our fashion, achieving a much closer coordination of the two, and with little apparent loss of liberty for their people. . . . The underlying analysis is the same, that separation of powers works too well, to the detriment of effective government. [2]

As we have pointed out earlier, the authors of the U.S. Constitution were profoundly worried about tyranny, either from an ill-informed mob or from a self-seeking tyrant, and sought a system of checks and balances:

> Mixed government [checks and balances] theorists were unconcerned about concentrating power as long as the interests of the different estates were in balance; separation of power theorists did not object to the domination of government by a single social class as long as different persons wielded the functionally distinct governmental powers. [3]

Taken together with federalism (see Chapter 2), separation of powers and checks and balances must be seen to be extraordinary reactions to the possibility of governmental or popular tyranny. The founders were seeking bulwarks against majoritarianism (government by popular majorities). They were not interested in creating a responsive government. (In our examination in Chapter 10 of how revolutionary the American Revolution really was we will see the impact of colonial culture on the protection of freedoms.) "Mixed government" theories abounded in 17th-century England and reached full fruition with Montesquieu's *Spirit of the Laws* (1748). [4] Montesquieu's ideas were based on the same gloomy view of human nature that typified the social contract theorists, especially Hobbes. Like Hobbes, Montesquieu believed people to be evil, prideful, envious, and power-hungry. Driven by passion more than reason, tendencies toward immoderate behavior and extremism were irresistible. But Montesquieu made no distinction between the rulers and the ruled: both were cut from the same mold. Hence no leviathan could be trusted to make life less "solitary, poor, nasty, brutish and short." Indeed, the government could, if it chose, make a major contribution toward that unhappy state: "Every man invested with power is apt to abuse it, and to carry his authority as far as it will go."

Pessimism pervades the writings of James Madison, whose *Federalist No. 51* is a superb defense of fragmented government:

> Ambition must be made to counteract ambition. . . . It may be a reflection of human nature that such devices should be necessary to control the abuses of government. But what is government itself but the greatest of all reflections on human nature? If men were angels, no government would be necessary. If angels were to govern men, neither external nor internal controls on government would be necessary. In framing a government which is to be administered by men over men, the great difficulty lies in this: you must first enable the government to control the governed; and in the next place oblige it to control itself.

The echoes of Hobbes are unmistakable, and social contract theory was given its clearest statement in the U.S. Constitution. It specifies that "all legislative power herein granted shall be vested in a Congress" (Article 1), "the executive power shall be vested in a President" (Article 2), and the "judicial power shall be vested in one Supreme Court, and in such inferior courts as Congress may from time to time ordain and establish" (Article 3).

Moreover, each of these institutions has an important check on the decisions of others. No bill can become a law without the approval of both the House and the Senate. The president shares in the legislative power through the veto and the responsibility to "give to the Congress information on the state of the Union, and recommend to their consideration such measures as he shall judge necessary and expedient." But the appointing power of the president is shared by the Senate; so is the power to make treaties. Congress can also override executive vetoes. The president must execute the laws but cannot do so without relying on executive departments, which Congress must create. The executive branch can only spend money appropriated by Congress. The Supreme Court is appointed by the president with the consent of the Senate.

Insofar as this system divides responsibility and makes it difficult for the people to hold government accountable, it achieves one of the authors' most basic goals. Each branch of government is chosen by different constituencies. Because the terms of these bodies are of varying length, a complete renewal of government at one stroke is impossible. Thus the people cannot wreak havoc quickly through direct elections. To make their will felt in all the decision-making bodies of the national government, they must wait years. These cumbersome arrangements were deliberately built into the U.S. Constitution to insulate government from popular passions.

If the system handcuffs government, it is working as intended. Majority rule is impossible. There was a clear exchange to be made: the authors of the Constitution were willing to sacrifice efficiency for protection against tyranny. Parliamentary governments are not, of course, tyrannical; but at the time of the writing of the Constitution, parliamentary democracy was unknown (monarchs still ruled England and France). As the American Revolution was fought, among other reasons, to be free of a tyrant, institutional devices to impede tyranny were natural. Factions—interest groups or political parties—would naturally seek to advance their private ambitions. Therefore, if government authority were divided, it would be difficult for the same misguided faction to gain control, since this would require an apparatus sufficient to seize control of three branches of government (the legislature, the executive, and the judiciary).

The Theory in Practice

Separation of powers and checks and balances in the United States have had a fluctuating history and became sources of even greater fragmentation because of reforms in the 1960s. The American republic was not very old before the separation of powers was diminished. In 1800 and 1824, the House of Representatives chose the president because of inconclusive results in the electoral college, and in the intervening years, congressional caucuses nominated presidential candidates. Thus the early years of the new nation's government were informally semiparliamentary: Congress selected the executive. Andrew Jackson, unable to persuade the caucuses of the merits of his cause, took his case to state-based parties, leading ultimately to *national conventions* of state party leaders. With the president nominated without the participation of Congress, separation of powers was given its first test.

The Jacksonian shift to the state parties insulated the presidency from Congress. From 1832 until the turn of the 20th century, all delegates to the national nominating conventions were chosen by state party "machines" (caucuses, executive committees, and the like). Party activists, local leaders, mayors, and state legislative leaders were the key players in the game of presidential nominations.

The turn-of-the-century reform movement generated the notion of the *presidential primary*. Rather than being selected by machine leaders, some states required that delegates be selected by the party membership (defined invariably as simply all who professed loyalty) in a primary election. Although quite popular during the Progressive era, the primary system lapsed into ill repute. About one-third of the delegates were chosen by primaries, but of this portion, not all were pledged to a particular candidate. In 1968, Hubert Humphrey received the Democratic party nomination without having entered a single primary election.

The nomination process became even more remote after the 1968 election. Between 1968 and 1972, the primaries were resuscitated; indeed, they became the single path to the nomination. Two-thirds of the delegates to nominating conventions were selected in primary elections and were pledged. Henceforth, the nominating convention merely ratified the choice of voters in primary elections. Thus the role of party *organizations* was destroyed. The electoral process and the political party will be discussed in detail in Chapter 5.

In Congress, authority was shifted away from party leadership toward subcommittees, creating the "subgovernments" that make the expression of congressional will so difficult to achieve. A "subcommittee bill of rights," approved in 1974, decentralized power. The number of subcommittees was increased substantially, and each was given a staff. Since elections to the House and Senate are not funded by the political parties but rather by political action committees (PACs, to be discussed in Chapter 6), party leaders had no control over the votes of individual members. There is little party discipline. In more than half of the votes in a given congressional session, a majority of votes in one party is *not* cast in opposition to a majority in the other party. According to John L. Sundquist:

> Members are likely to have won their seats . . . mainly by their own efforts. No party leaders handed them the nomination in the first place; they were self-selected, and they

put together their own organizations, raised their own money, and ran their own campaigns. . . . The party leadership can influence them, all other things being equal, but it cannot control or command them.[5]

In the electoral process, political action committees assumed more of a role in financing campaigns and even in recruiting candidates. The influence of parties, financially and organizationally, diminished. In the electorate, the strength of partisan identification eroded.[6] Political parties could generally provide enough cement to keep the system functioning fairly well. Voters normally did not "split" their tickets (a practice impossible in parliamentary systems); hence the same party could control the White House, the House of Representatives, and the Senate. Only John Quincy Adams, Zachary Taylor, and Rutherford B. Hayes experienced what has now become the rule: a president from one party facing a different party in control of all or part of Congress.

This non-divided government will rarely occur in the future. Presidential elections are unconnected to legislative ones; about 45 percent of the members of the House of Representatives represent districts that gave a majority to the presidential candidate of the other party. Republicans usually win the presidency; they occupied the White House for 16 of the 20 years from 1969 to 1989. During this period, the Democrats enjoyed an unbroken majority in the House. Power is indeed separated.

Iron Triangles

Traditionally, it was assumed that when Congress passed a law and then created a bureaucracy and appropriated money to carry out the intent of the law, that was the end of the political process. Political process preceded the administrative process. But neutrality in public administration is difficult in a presidential system. Political battles do not end with victory or defeat in Congress. Organized interests do not abandon the fight and return home simply because the site of the battle shifts from the political arena to an administrative one. Political and administrative questions do not differ in content, only in who decides them.

Once the bureaucracy takes over an issue, three major power bases—the iron triangles—come together to decide its outcome: the executive agency administering the program, the congressional subcommittee charged with its oversight, and the interest groups directly affected by the agency. Interest groups will be discussed in Chapter 6. Suffice it here to note that interest groups develop close relationships with the bureaucratic policymakers, and both the interest groups and the bureaucrats develop close relationships with the congressional subcommittees that oversee their activities. Thus agency–subcommittee–interest group relationships become established; even the individuals involved remain the same over fairly long periods of time, as senior members of Congress retain their subcommittee memberships.

When bureaucracies enter iron triangles, the tradition of an independent civil service is ill served. As Kenneth Meier observes:

> Together Congress, interest groups, and bureaus all have the necessary resources to satisfy each other's needs. Bureaus supply services or goods to organized groups but need resources to do so. Congressional committees supply the bureaus with resources

but need electoral support to remain in office. . . . The interest group provides the political support that the member of Congress needs, but the interest group needs government goods and services to satisfy members' demands. The result is a tripartite relationship that has all of the resources necessary to operate in isolation.[7]

In our system, about 3,000 administrative appointments are made by the Executive Office of the President. In parliamentary systems, a hundred or so are appointed; the remainder are career bureaucrats. Since our presidents tend not to have had much experience in governing, their staffs are usually made up of people with whom they agree. Each president brings in his cronies: Carter and the "Georgia Mafia" showed just how little effort is needed to fail when you know or care nothing about coalitions; Reagan's two terms were marred by the most egregious excesses of graft and corruption since Harding, and trusted aides who dreamed up the Iran-contra scheme concealed their efforts from career bureaucrats because they knew that their plans would not be approved.

The White House staff, not the cabinet, is the heart of the decision-making process. Cabinet officers often find it frustrating to be denied access to the president because of staff opposition. The actual structure of the White House staff varies with each president. Presidents begin their job with the assumption that their aides and various assistants will simply help organize their time, with no assumption of decision-making authority. It seldom works this way. The temptation to rely heavily on the staff is irresistible.

Reagan relied heavily on three members of the White House staff: Edwin Meese, counselor to the president; James Baker, chief of staff; and Michael Deaver, deputy chief of staff. Each of these officers had numerous deputies, assistants, and deputy assistants, named because they had proved themselves to be completely loyal to the president. In his second term, only Meese remained, and Reagan's staff became the haven for zealots.

Each administration also juggles the influence of various offices in the White House. The National Security Council has been a major factor in presidential decision making, spawning such influential men as Henry Kissinger and Zbigniew Brzezinski. Each of them powerful in his own right, they were often able to outfight the secretaries of state and defense. The NSC's original purpose was to coordinate policy from these two departments, but the personalities of national security advisers overshadowed those of the cabinet officers.

Reagan pledged to reduce NSC influence. However, the NSC was responsible for the Iran-contra debacle. Not only did Reagan not curb its influence, but he allowed it to become self-sustaining. The NSC staff carried out a covert operation in order to keep the contras "together body and soul" and to divert to them money earned in arms sales. We do not know if the direct exchange was accompanied by presidential approval. We do know that the NSC participants were obsessed with secrecy, and we also know they believed they were acting in accordance with the president's policy. Thus, rather than adhering to its original purpose, the NSC combined intelligence and policy functions. The struggle for power goes on.

All White House staff members have one thing in common: their sole responsibility to the president. They have no large governmental bureaucracy on which to depend for information. There are no alliances to be formed with organized groups.

Presidents sometimes fall victim to groupthink; nobody wants to be the bearer of bad news. Groupthink is fostered when the decision-making group is bound together by a strong set of interpersonal ties, as is the case with the White House staff and personal advisers. Reagan's advisers were personal friends who had known each other for many years socially and in their business activities. They were insulated from the public at large and held a fairly uniform view of appropriate policy. The result of this process is that the president can be misinformed, and criticism can be regarded as disloyalty.

Some presidents fall victim to groupthink even before they unpack their baggage. Early in his presidency, George Bush proved unapproachable on the subject of John Tower—doomed from the beginning—as his nominee for secretary of defense. Bush reportedly would brook no objection to his nominee, and his advisers soon began to construct a more tolerable reality. Tower was being condemned to private life not because he was the recipient of about $750 million in defense contractor consulting fees but because of "hypocrisy," "partisan politics," and "McCarthyism." There is some truth here. Tower did indeed drink and "womanize." But, as the bitter nominee pointed out, had only senators who had done neither been allowed to vote, a quorum would have been impossible. But he lost because he was on the take, not because he liked booze and women; and although a majority of the Senate is on the take, a majority is *not* on the take from defense contractors.

Groupthink was pervasive during the contra resupply missions. Cabinet officers, mainly Secretary of State George Shultz and Secretary of Defense Caspar Weinberger, were, in the jargon of the insider, "out of the loop." That is, once they expressed opposition, they were excluded from any part in the operation. Secrecy became an obsession; all who were not directly involved were enemies to be duped:

> To preserve itself, the group projects its hostility onto outsiders, and a we-they relationship develops in which group members come to believe they are entirely good—indeed superior—beings, while all outsiders are entirely bad, inferior, and untrustworthy. Now the group cannot accept outside advice or criticism; its members at the same time lose all normal skepticism about those who profess to support their cause. . . . At some point, the inner circle, sensing hostility from the outer members, withdraws into itself (North once told [former national security adviser Robert McFarlane that [McFarlane's successor John] Poindexter's job was much harder than his since 'I only have to deal with our enemies. He has to deal with the cabinet.')[8]

Groupthink makes seemingly inexplicable events clear.

Other Modes of Power Fragmentation

An insulated presidency at loggerheads with a decentralized Congress needs a referee: the Supreme Court and other lower courts have established the right of *judicial review* (the right to declare laws passed by Congress and signed by the president unconstitutional). Most parliamentary governments do not provide for judicial review; Canada, Australia, and West Germany do. Those governments have also adopted federalism as the mode of geographic fragmentation of power. Made necessary by either vast geographic distances (the United States and Australia) or by fundamental cultural or linguistic differences (Switzerland, West Germany) or both (Canada), federalism introduces yet another grid in the division of authority.

Only Switzerland provides for federalism without judicial review. And only the United States has mandated separation of powers, federalism, and judicial review. Ours is the most institutionally fragmented government extant. It is constructed to frustrate majorities.

Comparative analysis will place our governmental form and process in greater perspective.

PARLIAMENTARY DEMOCRACIES WITH A MAJORITY PARTY: ENGLAND

Parliamentary democracy may be neat and tidy, but only if there is a clear parliamentary majority (as in England) or a stable coalition (as in West Germany). Much of the admiration for parliamentary systems among American political scientists is for these, rather than the multiparty ones, which go through periodic losses of confidence.

Parliamentary democracies are governed by a directly elected parliament. The parliament cedes authority to a cabinet and a prime minister and can withdraw support by a vote of no confidence. Such a vote requires a dissolution of the government and a new election. If a dissolution does not occur within a specified period, elections are automatically held. Ruling parties can also call elections when they think they have the chance to increase support or when they want to display to doubting party members the durability and popularity of their programs. Margaret Thatcher called an election shortly after England defeated Argentina in the Falkland Islands skirmish in 1983.

Normally, the cabinet is composed of members of the majority party or the majority coalition, and the head of that party becomes prime minister. Despite the situation in the United States, cabinets really do play a major role in governing. Parliamentary democracies allow for graceful exits. Since a losing cabinet and prime minister will return to parliament—this time as the loyal opposition—their departure is not as harsh as that occurring when an American president loses. If the Conservative party in England loses an election, it is unlikely that Thatcher will lose her parliamentary seat. She and the shadow cabinet (members of Parliament expected to form the government the next time the party wins) sit in Commons rather than retiring in disgrace and bitterness. The opposition party and its shadow cabinet sit in Commons awaiting the opportunity to seize power.

Although prime ministers have a good deal more actual power than the American president, they do not enjoy much of the pomp and circumstance accorded presidents: their staff is small, no more than a handful, as opposed to the thousands in the Executive Office of the President. Cabinet ministers and the prime minister are in charge. There is little of the helicopter-assisted escape from the media, the frantic retreat to a weekend hideaway, the ruminating about the ''awesome burden,'' or the hushed reverence that accompanies American presidents; after all, the prime minister is only a member of Parliament. Less hyperbole and bombast would, of themselves, be sufficient to recommend cabinet government to a nation drenched in presidential obsession.

In comparison to presidential government, parliamentary democracies are likely to be able to make decisions quickly. The cabinet proposes a law; the party approves, and that is that: no bargaining, no compromise, no lobbying, no "access peddling," and no judicial review. Parliamentary democracies are also likely to establish clear lines of accountability. Voters know whom to blame—the ruling party. No excuses are offered, and no buck is passed.

The Role of Political Parties

Political parties in a country like Great Britain are highly disciplined. Deviation from a party position is rare; if more than a few members buck the party, a vote of no confidence may be in the offing. Junior party members—"back benchers"—get to the top by voting with the party; their campaign money comes from the party.

But it is a mistake to believe, as some people do, that a parliamentary system with a single majority party is a plebiscitary dictatorship. Prime ministers are strong-willed, or they would not have spent the years toiling in the trenches of the party required of prime ministers. They do not pop into government from the outside, like Reagan, Carter, Pat Robertson, or Jesse Jackson. They consequently know that their power is on loan. They can punish disobedient party members, but they can also lose a vote of confidence or be replaced as party leader during the out-of-power years. Thatcher has faced rebellion from the "wets," a derisive term she uses for the left wing of her party. In 1985, a former cabinet secretary and 30 Conservative party members formed an opposition group, called the Conservative Center Forward. They announced their intention to oppose Thatcher on her unemployment policy, as British unemployment has remained higher than the European average. But her decision to call an election in 1987, a year earlier than required, and the resounding victory of her party silenced the wets. In 1988, she faced a back-bencher revolt over her alleged reluctance to deal with Britain's outdated Official Secrets Act, forcing her to advance the matter to the top of her agenda.

However, unlike the United States, legislative committees are of little consequence, as they cannot bottle up legislation or even revise its substance. Although British committees, like American ones, maintain scrutiny over various executive departments and policy arenas, they do not consider legislation. They may provide information based on their efforts, but at best on a hit-or-miss basis. There are 14 committees in Commons, compared with over 250 Committees and subcommittees in the U.S. Congress. A good indication of their unimportance is the fact that six of them are not chaired by members of the ruling Conservative party! Giving a committee chair to an opposition party member would be unheard of in the United States.

Interest Groups

Lobbying the legislature is, of course, a rarity. Interest groups lobby the cabinet. When Labour is in power, unions have the built-in access that accompanies their dominance of the party. Like labor in corporatist countries, British unions are amalgamated into a peak association, the Trades Union Congress. But the TUC has little access to bureaucracies and relies instead on its ties to the Labour party, which in recent years has meant little.

The TUC is a more inclusive organization than the American AFL-CIO, representing 95 percent of all trade unionists. But unlike the iron-clad rule of corporatism, the TUC is decentralized. Individual unions can do as they please, and most strikes take place without TUC sanction (90 percent of British strikes are wildcat strikes).[9]

Thus even when Labour forms a cabinet, there is no reason to assume that work stoppages would decline; indeed, the "British disease," unmanageable labor disputes, only began to recede when the Conservatives broke a major strike and passed legislation mandating more union democracy (Labour had tried the same idea in the late 1960s; it led to antagonizing the unions and abandonment of the scheme).

Nor is business any more centrally organized. The nearest thing to a peak association is the Confederation of Business Industry; but financial institutions and retailers have their own separate organizations. The CBI, like the American National Association of Manufacturers, represents industrial rather than service businesses. Like the NAM, it is dominated by large firms, and, as in America, small businesses have their own interest groups. Unlike Labour, the CBI has no formal ties to a political party—in this case the Conservatives—but obviously, its individual members provide sympathy and money to the party.

By a plethora of advisory bodies and committees, British interest groups are functionally represented in the bowels of government. The British Medical Association, for instance, is intimately involved in the delivery of health services. Recognition of the legitimacy of interest groups is more formal than in the United States. Since much policy does not percolate up to the cabinet, lower-level bureaucratic accommodation of interest groups is substantial.

However, the British civil service, unlike the American, is more professionally accountable. Interest groups have institutionalized relations, in many cases as equals, with British bureaucracies. In the United States, about 20 percent of administrative personnel is politically appointed; in Britain, only a hundred or so ministers come and go with the ebbs and flows of party fortunes. British civil servants have a more firmly grounded tradition of neutrality and commitment to cabinet goals, thus making them marginally less open to co-optation by interest groups.

A cabinet secretary is less likely to be as well versed as the *permanent secretary,* a civil servant who is the highest-ranking permanent member of a department. In the United States, the analogous position is undersecretary, a political appointment. Even a cabinet minister's personal staff is composed of "young, promising civil servants who are aware not only of the need to be loyal to the minister but also of the cost to their careers of antagonizing the permanent secretary."[10]

Interest groups thus need the respect of the civil service. The civil service trusts groups with long histories of service to their members and with demonstrated expertise in the area of mutual concern. These are not the PACS or single-interest groups of the United States but rather the more professionally accountable occupational or professional associations with a small but persistent interest in policy: "All such groups perform a very important representative function, supplementing or even replacing Parliament and political parties as channels through which individuals can make their views known to the executive and thus affect policy."[11]

For example, the National Farmers Union and the Ministry of Agriculture and Fisheries share a quasi-official relationship:

[Meetings] are confidential, cordial, based on technical not party arguments, and above all frequent. . . . Officials of the NFU and the ministry were constantly in touch: there was no aspect of agricultural policy on which their views were not known to each other. Such contacts are almost hourly, in fact, and are reinforced by social contacts (at least at the highest levels) through membership of the same London clubs.[12]

Even though the United Kingdom's interest groups are more institutionally imbedded and hence less visible, they still fall short of the corporatist model of hierarchical, compulsory groups with true equality with the bureaucracy. No peak associations can speak for their members with any degree of assurance that their words will be taken seriously, and no British interest groups can claim a monopoly on representation. Agreements struck between government and the TUC do not stop strikes, and the major employers' association is far from cohesive.

The cozy relationship between British interest groups and bureaucracies does approximate the American iron triangles, with a good deal less iron and only two participants (legislative committees are rarely involved). This concord can decentralize what appears on the surface to be a rock-solid concentration of power in the cabinet.

PARLIAMENTARY SYSTEMS: THE "CONSOCIATIONAL" TRADITION

The power game changes in parliamentary systems when, by means of proportional representation, a coalition rather than a parliamentary majority is necessary. In some nations, such as Italy, the appearance of chaos is hard to conceal. In others, such as Switzerland, the inability of a party to achieve a majority makes little difference.

Switzerland's Corporatism

Switzerland is a federal republic whose presidency rotates annually among the seven members of the Bundesrat (Federal Council). The members of the Bundesrat are chosen by the two houses of parliament at the beginning of each term. The government is a semipermanent coalition of the four largest parties: the Radical Democratic party, the Social Democrats, the Christian Democrats (each with two members, with about one-fourth of the votes), and the People's party, with about 11 percent of the vote and one Bundesrat member. Permanent power sharing is also called *consociational democracy* (governing is by an inclusive coalition of the major segments or interests of the society, and each has a tacit right of veto).[13]

Swiss interest groups pervade economic life: about 68 percent of the Swiss belong to an occupational interest group, a number far higher than in the United States, whereas fewer than 25 percent belong to a political party:

Swiss democracy is geared to pressure groups; it is a form of government calculated to call such groups into existence and give them power. The system could conceivably continue for a time without parties, but without pressure groups it would not work at all.[14]

The most important, given the weakness of unions, is the Vorut, the peak association representing business. Although the Swiss business community has been divided over sensitive questions such as foreign workers or European integration, business relations are excellent due to the Vorut's ceaseless search for a workable consensus: geographically diverse groups and different economic interests come to adhere to a common political position through frequent consultations within a centralized peak association.[15]

The seven members of the Bundesrat are senior civil servants rather than party politicians. They speak publicly only with a collective voice, and disagreements are kept confidential. Since the Swiss civil service is small, it relies on the expertise and manpower of interest groups to conduct research and to develop policy. Switzerland is federal, rather than unitary, with local traditions and power stronger in the cantons than in the American states. The Swiss national government is thus by European standards impoverished: it receives only 29 percent of all tax revenues, compared to the European average of 58 percent.

The role of interest groups is so prominent that the Swiss constitution confers formal status on them. This, combined with the power of the cantons, has necessitated the Swiss style of government: bargaining among interests until a consensus is reached and then ratification by the government. Unlike other parliamentary democracies, there is no provision for a no confidence vote, and even though there is extensive direct democracy through referenda, no referendum mechanism can voice no confidence either. The extraordinary nature of Swiss corporatism is revealed by the fact that members of parliament, who are of little consequence in policy, nevertheless sit as representatives of interest groups, working either full-time or part-time for their groups. Like the U.S. Congress, interest-group caucuses cut across party lines. Like the Japanese, the Swiss are capitalist—hence economically competitive—to the core. Like the Japanese, the political process softens the conflictual tendencies of capitalism.

Japan

The comparison with Japan is apt. Even though Japan's parliamentary government is more orthodox, it is more consociational than it need be. Japan too seeks consensus, and opposition members of parliament were able to delay the Liberal Democratic party's plan for a national sales tax not because they had any parliamentary means for doing so but because the ruling party preferred to seek a consensus; since none was forthcoming, the plan was shelved. Japanese interest groups, too, encompass peak associations, and Japanese labor is, virtually impotent. The *Keidanren,* the most respected business organization, in tight coordination with the Ministry of International Trade and Industry, Japan's preeminent bureaucracy, has blurred the line between public and private. But while interest groups have been able to defy MITI simply by refusing to comply with its directives, the Japanese bureaucracy is more powerful than the Swiss. Its prestige is enormous:

> The contemporary bureaucracy is clearly the inheritor of the high levels of honesty, efficiency, and prestige established by the prewar bureaucracy. The higher civil service is truly an elite corps, which is the cream of the Japanese educational system, drawn from the most prestigious universities, especially Tokyo University, by a selection pro-

cess of rigorous examinations. Professionally very competent and enjoying security in their positions, these higher civil servants display a self-confidence in their dealings with politicians that would rarely be found in the United States.[16]

Private organizations are designated as enforcers of state-initiated policies, but state control places management under government supervision.[17]

IS ANY SYSTEM "BEST"?

Since Japan's economic miracle, and since Switzerland had the highest standard of living in the world, and since American politics has been cursed with deadlocks between the executive and Congress (a major cause of the Iran-contra scandal), parliamentary systems have been attracting attention. In the United States, the 200th anniversary of the ratification of the Constitution focused attention on the inherent problem of separation of powers: stalemate.[18]

Separation of powers and checks and balances are sometimes said to be outmoded. We know that they are unique, that in fact the United States is the only democracy that combines separation of powers and checks and balances with federalism. For better or worse, our system only rarely, as in the case of war, responds as rapidly as parliamentary governments, especially unitary ones, can.

Why is this so? One good reason is that when the Constitution was framed two centuries ago, only a few crucial tasks (defense and the establishment of a common market among the states) required a national government. Madison and his coauthors believed that the legislative branch could handle these jobs well.

But 200 years later, having fought three major wars and a variety of smaller ones, the balance of power has shifted to the presidency. It is clear that this development is not what Madison and the framers intended. Donald Robinson asks the essential question:

> Does the system still serve the constitutional values to which the framers were and we are committed? . . . I think not. . . . The framers would have been appalled at the extent to which the spirit of the legislative process now infects the administrative process.[19]

He refers to the decline of a singly accountable Congress and the rise of subcommittees, each of which develops its own "subgovernment," consisting of the administrative unit that it oversees and the interest groups that have a stake in the policy that the subcommittee and the bureaucracy undertake—the cozy relationship of the iron triangle. Robinson concludes that "From a constitutional standpoint, the important thing about these policy subgroups is that they operate virtually without reference to the separation of powers."[20]

Robinson also believes that separation of powers "violates enduring constitutional values."[21] He refers to the deliberate effort by the authors of the Constitution to make the legislative process tedious so that only well-considered proposals would be approved. It was a conservative strategy to allow careful scrutiny and avoid hasty decisions. However, Robinson remarks,

> the irony is that this structure now operates to protect a bloated government. Just as it was extremely difficult to pass a program of federal aid for health care, it is now virtually impossible to enact reforms to "contain" the cost of hospitalization. Just as it was perilously difficult to get Congress to prepare for World War II and to agree in 1950 to build military bases to back up our commitments to oppose Communist aggression, it is now almost impossible to impose rationality and efficiency on defense procurement.[22]

As the budget deficits grow, as the trade imbalance increases, as the United States continues to be outperformed by the Japanese to the point of the loss of our once international dominant economic position, Robinson thinks separation of powers is the culprit. The United States has not been able to persuade its allies of its ability to cut the budget. Its inability to do so is because of the numerous iron triangles protecting their special-interest groups:

> Thus, in important respects, the constitutional system no longer operates as the framers intended. It prevents elected officials from framing coherent policy, and it hinders executives from enforcing and implementing the law vigorously and steadily. It deflects the electorate from rendering a coherent judgment on the performance of the government and the promises of the opposition. It encourages administrative and judicial confusion by dividing the will that appoints people as administrators and judges. It induces candidates, the press, and the public to give excessive and inappropriate attention to electoral politics, at the expense of attention that needs to be given to the process of governing.[23]

> We badly need a united government that can act steadily and comprehensively on the macroeconomic problems inherent in a modern industrial giant like the United States. In foreign and military policy, the need is even more imperative. That government should be a constitutional democracy, not through the retention of the same system that has proved inept in economic policy, but through a change to vest control in periodic elections animated by a continuous, vigilant, opposition [parliamentary democracy].[24]

In January 1987, the Committee on the Constitutional System, a prestigious group of former cabinet officials from four administrations, former and current senators and members of Congress, scholars, and private citizens (the joint chairs are Lloyd Cutler, White House counsel to President Carter, Republican Senator Nancy Kassebaum of Kansas, and Republican C. Douglas Dillon, President Kennedy's treasury secretary), after five years of work, concluded that "the separation of powers between branches, especially the legislative and the executive, now produces confrontation, indecision, and deadlock."[25] The committee proposed putting the president, vice-president, senator, and House member on a single slate requiring a straight party ticket vote. This proposal involves radical surgery to make our system "more like the British and other European parliamentary systems."[26]

Where did the committee get its ideas? Woodrow Wilson was among the American presidents adamantly opposed to separation of powers:

It is quite safe to say that were it possible to call together again the members of that wonderful Convention to view the work of their hands in light of the century that has tested it, they would be the first to admit that the only fruit of dividing power had been to make it irresponsible.[27]

A good illustration of the problems Wilson anticipated is the Iran-*contra* scandal of 1987. Robert McFarlane, National Security Council director from 1983 to 1985, writes:

What brings this to mind is the Iran-Contra affair and, specifically, the way it has come and almost gone, with scarcely any recognition of the fact that its occurrence represents a serious malfunction in our system of government—one that can, and very likely will, happen again and again unless corrective measures are taken.[28]

General Brent Scowcroft, National Security Council director during the Bush administration, told the American Bar Association:

The Contra controversy is really a constitutional confrontation between an executive who has a foreign policy which he believes deeply is important to the United States and a Congress which is ambivalent or negative about it and wants to do something else. What the hearings did not do was to examine how to make the system work when there is this kind of impasse.[29]

As the eminent presidential scholar Richard Neustadt concludes, the Constitution provides for "separated institutions sharing powers."[30] Presidents are continually being frustrated by the expectations of what they should do, and when they are thwarted by the system of checks and balances and separation of powers, they circle the wagons and try to operate from the White House. The frustration leads to Watergates and Irangates and hence to more checks and balances. Mitch Daniels, White House political director at the end of the Reagan administration, confirms that frustration over Congress's growing role in foreign policy may have led to the Iran-*contra* affair. He speaks of the "constant intrusion of Congress in foreign policy, which was a main executive branch function."[31] Journalist Hedrick Smith concludes that "by now it must be apparent that something is seriously out of kilter in our political system."[32]

Parliamentary government can get "out of kilter" too. The French Fourth Republic, after World War II, suffered an average cabinet life of about six months, and Italy displays the same instability today. Yet in both nations, one can hardly argue that the consequence of instability was poor government. France, governed by an elite civil service trained at *L'Ecole Nationale d'Administration* (ENA), made France a leader in the European Economic Community and presided over an economic miracle, as France's per capita income grew at a brisk 3.5 percent a year. In Italy, the civil service is even more politicized than in the United States and a good deal more corrupt. Yet Italy too is enjoying an economic renaissance, edging ahead of the United Kingdom in per capita income. In this case, the political parties, operating in the manner of the 19th-century American urban machines, provide continuity even as they contribute to political instability.

Further, correcting political instability does not necessarily improve government performance. In Charles de Gaulle's Fifth Republic, the presidency was given far more authority than the American president had, yet in the 1981–1983 years of Socialist François Mitterand's presidency, the French economy, suffering like the rest in a world-wide recession, abandoned many of its socialist ideals to temper the stagnant economy but was not as successful as the other European industrial democracies.

One explanation for success during instability and failure during stability is that government and the economy, on the one hand, and everyday life, on the other, are not as connected in these democracies as in centrally planned socialist economies. Since economies tend to work best when the market rather than the state is the engine of decision, there is no reason why things cannot go along swimmingly while the government labors futilely to become stable. The United States, with floating coalitions, still enjoyed steady economic growth and reduced unemployment from 1982 into 1989. But in this case, the absence of any central authority meant that the budget deficit grew exponentially; ultimately, the economic bubble must burst. Without central authority, no hard economic choices could be made, leading to economic hard times.

Looking at other countries with systems like ours—Costa Rica, Venezuela, Colombia, the Dominican Republic—does not shed light on our problems, as these are not industrial democracies. But we can say that what America lacks is accountability and the ability to make and implement decisions. In the past, we have been less decentralized and more fortunate. We came out of World War II the most economically powerful nation in the world. But we are no longer in a league by ourselves, and managing decline might prove too difficult for government by floating coalition.

FOR FURTHER CONSIDERATION

1. Among industrial democracies, how many provide for separation of powers?
2. Explain what an "iron triangle" is.
3. Are American interest groups becoming more powerful or less powerful? What about interest groups in other countries?
4. Compare the advantages and disadvantages of a presidential government with the advantages and disadvantages of a parliamentary government. In what circumstances is each best? Which government did most recently adopt a presidential system? Which government did most recently adopt a parliamentary system?
5. Justify the separation of powers in the United States government. Now examine the industrial democracies: How many of the characteristics you use to defend separation of powers exist in parliamentary governments? How many can be found "only in America?"
6. How did the verdict in the Oliver North trial affect your view of separation of powers?

For the More Adventurous

1. Does having independent legislative, executive, and judicial branches of government guarantee a separation of powers? Use both historical and modern examples. Read Joel Brinkley and Stephen Engelbert, eds., *Report of the Congressional Committee Investigating the Iran-Contra Affair* (New York: Times Books, 1988).
2. List several benefits of majority rule. Then list several benefits of consensus. Compare the two on the basis of their "ultimate" good and of their utility. Aristotle believed that major-

ities *should* rule because the combined knowledge and experience of 51 percent exceeded the combined knowledge and experience of a lesser number. Do you agree with him or do you agree with a more pessimistic assessment that majority rule is preferable because ''a state of affairs where two human beings are subordinated to the arbitrary will of a third is twice as bad as a state of affairs where only one is so subordinated.''[33] Which view supports consensus, if procedurally feasible?

NOTES

1. Austin Ranney, *The Governing of Men* (New York: Holt, Rinehart and Winston, 1966), p. 398.
2. Robert A. Goldman and Art Kaufman, ''Preface,'' in *Separation of Powers: Does It Still Work?* (Washington, D.C.: American Enterprise Institute, 1986), p. iv.
3. H. Jefferson Powell, ''How Does the Constitution Structure Government?'' in *A Workable Government?* ed. Burke Marshall (New York: Norton, 1987), p. 22.
4. See J. Dedieu, *Montesquieu et la tradition politique anglaise en France* (Geneva: Slatkine Reprints, 1970).
5. James L. Sundquist, ''The New Era of Coalition Government in the United States,'' *Political Science Quarterly* (Winter 1988–1989):6–19.
6. Nelson W. Polsby and Aaron Wildavsky, *Presidential Elections* (New York: Free Press, 1988), p. 13.
7. Kenneth J. Meier, *Politics and the Bureaucracy* (North Scituate, Mass.: Duxbury, 1979), p. 51.
8. Frances Fitzgerald, ''Reagan's Band of True Believers,'' *New York Times Magazine*, October 4, 1987, p. 11.
9. Philip Norton, *The British Polity* (White Plains, N.Y.: Longman, 1984), p. 155.
10. Ian Budge and David McKay, *The New British Political System* (White Plains, N.Y.: Longman, 1983), p. 25.
11. Ibid., p. 27.
12. Ibid., p. 28.
13. Arend Lijphart, *Democracy in Plural Societies* (New Haven, Conn.: Yale University Press, 1977), p. 25.
14. Peter Katzenstein, *Corporatism and Change: Austria, Switzerland and the Politics of Industry* (Ithaca, N.Y.: Cornell University Press, 1984), p. 112.
15. Ibid., p. 114.
16. Edwin O. Reischauer, *The Japanese Today* (Cambridge, Mass.: Belknap Press of Harvard University, 1988), p. 254.
17. Chalmers Johnson, *MITI and the Japanese Miracle* (Stanford, Calif.: Stanford University Press, 1982), pp. 309–312.
18. Raymond A. Moore, ''The Constitution, the Presidency, and 1988,'' *Presidential Studies Quarterly 18* (Winter 1988): 56.
19. Donald A. Robinson, ''The Renewal of American Constitutionalism,'' in Goldman and Kaufman, *Separation of Powers*, p. 49.
20. Ibid., p. 50.
21. Ibid. Note that Robinson argues that separation of powers operates to the detriment of more fundamental constitutional values.
22. Ibid., p. 51.
23. Ibid.
24. Charles Hardin, ''Separation of Powers Needs Major Revision,'' in Goldwin and Kaufman,

Separation of Powers, p. 114.

25. Moore, "The Constitution, the Presidency, and 1988", p. 56.
26. Hedrick Smith, *The Power Game* (New York: Ballantine, 1988), p. 701.
27. Woodrow Wilson, *Congressional Government* (Boston: Houghton Mifflin, 1895), p. 285.
28. Robert McFarlane, "Iran-Contra Affair Points to Mediocrity in High Places," *New Tribune*, April 11, 1988, p. A11.
29. Quoted in William Robbins, "Iran-Contra Ambiguities," *New York Times*, January 14, 1988, p. A4.
30. Richard Neustadt, *Presidential Power* (New York: Wiley, 1986), p. 101.
31. Quoted in Charlotte Saikowski, "Is the Country's Top Political Office Structurally Flawed?," *Seattle Post Intelligencer*, March 17, 1987, pp. A2–A3.
32. Hedrick Smith, *The Power Game* (New York: Random House, 1988), p. 671.
33. Willmoore Kendall, "Is Violence a Human Necessity," in Nellie D. Kendall, ed., *Willmoore Kendall Contra Mundam* (New Rochelle, N.Y.: Arlington House, 1971), pp. 588– 593.

FOR FURTHER READING

Mansbridge, Jane. *Why We Lost the ERA*. Chicago: University of Chicago Press, 1986. How causes become cults, with more concern for preservation of the flame than for political success.

Neustadt, Richard. *Presidential Power*. New York: Wiley, 1986.

Polsby, Nelson W., and Aaron Wildavsky. *Presidential Elections*. New York: Free Press, 1988. A deservedly honored description of the American "noble experiment."

Rossiter, Clinton, ed. *The Federalist Papers*. New York: Mentor, 1961.

Sartori, Giovanni. *The Theory of Democracy Revisited. Part 1: The Contemporary Debate*. Chatham, England: Chatham House, 1987.

Smith, Hedrick. *The Power Game*. New York: Random House, 1988. Surprisingly sophisticated (for a journalist) analysis of who rules America; sure to displease conspiracy theorists since Smith concludes that no one does.

CHAPTER 5

Demand and Response: Political Parties and the Election Process

'WE BELIEVE THE LIL' FELLAS LONG FOR A CHANCE TO EXPERIENCE DEMOCRACY AND THE ELECTORAL PROCESS AS WE KNOW IT.'

Can government do what "the people" want? *Should* government do what "the people" want? Most respondents will probably say yes to both questions. Democracies, however, do not necessarily assume this answer. In the United States, for example, the Supreme Court exists precisely because the government need not do what "the people" want.

But it is fair to say that most democracies feel some sense of obligation to be *responsive*. Even though democracies may construct institutional barriers to responsiveness—like the Supreme Court—the dominant mode of justification is responsiveness. Political parties are justified as linkages between elites and masses, not as preceptors or teachers. They may not in reality link, but they are supposed to. In the USSR, by contrast, which in March 1985 provided for the first time a modicum of choice in its electoral process, all the competition was within the Communist party. Intraparty groups, sanctioned by the party, may compete, but a multiparty system is not a realistic possibility (Boris Yeltsin, the most radical of the antiestablishment candidates, stopped short of demanding more parties). The Communist party is still constitutionally, symbolically, theoretically, and emotionally the "vanguard of the proletarian." However, in 1989, a small quasi-opposition group, the "Left-Radicals," appeared.

Even the most ardent proponents of responsive government do not believe that each person need only speak in order to be heard. Where impassioned mobs cry out, "Power to the people," they generally mean "power to the people with whom I agree and am associated with politically." Other than hastily assembled mobs, there are two modes of political organization: political parties, the focus of this chapter, and interest groups, the subject of Chapter 6. Political scientists attach great importance to political organizations, especially political parties, because if government is every going to do what the people want, political parties will be the agents of responsiveness. A noted scholar writes:

> Political parties, with all their well-known human and structural shortcomings, are the only devices . . . which with some effectiveness can generate countervailing collective power on behalf of the many individually powerless against the relatively few who are individually or organizationally powerful.[1]

A more compelling task could hardly be imagined; is it really true that political parties are the only organizations between us and autocracy? Perhaps not, but they are surely necessary if politicians are to "look over their shoulders."

Elections are expected to provide voters with "meaningful choice," and the instruments by which such choice is accomplished are political parties. Unlike interest groups, political parties direct themselves initially to placing adherents to their principles in public office. Interest groups have begun to play a more active role in elections, but the distinction stands. Political parties are organizations whose primary purpose is to nominate and elect its candidates in order to control the personnel and policies of government. This description is abstract; in practice, the functions of political parties are much less clearly defined.

Among the democracies, there are two main types of party systems: two-party and multiparty. In two-party systems, such as that in the United States, the same two parties contest state and national elections. (There are occasional flurries from third parties, but the Democrats and Republicans are the only serious competitors.) Multiparty systems are those in which three or more political parties routinely contest elections, with each having a reasonable expectation of winning at least a significant proportion of the vote.

THE MEANING OF "MEANINGFUL"

How do parties provide "meaningful choice," and how do we define *meaningful?* Traditionally, students of parties have examined the difference between the stated *ideologies* of the political parties; the greater the difference, the greater the probability of voters' believing that their choice was meaningful.

Meaningful choice thus implies that the victory of a given party would result in policies that would not have occurred had the opposition won. Had the Conservatives rather than Labour won in England after World War II, would industry have been nationalized? Had Labour been able to defeat Margaret Thatcher and the Conservatives in the 1980s, would denationalization have been undertaken?

We might suspect that multiparty systems would offer clear alternatives, since each presumably felt that differences with similar parties were severe enough as to prohibit merger. This suspicion is true up to a point. The ability of multiparty systems to provide a more accurate representation of diverse interests depends on whether the culture is primarily *bipolar,* with most issues finding a natural either-or resolution, or *fragmented,* with many shades of opinion. Charles de Gaulle, frustrated by the bewildering array of parties and opinions in France, lamented, "How can you govern a country where there are more than 200 kinds of cheese?"[2] The popular essays collected as *The Notebooks of Major Thompson,* used for generations to teach the subtleties of French language and culture to Americans, have students learning about the "neo-anti-Gaullists," whose sworn enemies are the "anti-Gaullist" parties.[3] To blend these strongly felt, if marginal, differences into a whole like the American Democratic or Republican party would be impossible. Arend Lijphart (Table 5.1) has shown that as the number of issue dimensions (socioeconomic, religious, cultural-ethnic, urban-rural, and the like) increases, so does the number of political parties.

Two-party systems might paper over important differences to capture a majority of the vote, quite a serious problem if there are fragmented issue dimensions. But in practice, the number of parties and the number of issue dimensions seems congruent. In two-party systems, parties try to "aggregate" (that is, they try to form a holding company for various narrow interests), but in multiparty systems, parties and interests groups are sometimes one and the same thing. Parties "articulate" rather than aggregate.[4]

The American two-party system mutes differences partly by minimizing the costs of "belonging." How do you become a Democrat? Do you pay dues, carry a card,

TABLE 5.1 Number of Parties and Number of Issue Dimensions, 1945–1980

Number of Issue Dimensions	Number of Parties		
	1 to 3	3 to 4	More than 4
1.0 or 1.5	Canada Ireland New Zealand United Kingdom United States		
2.0 or 2.5	Australia Austria West Germany	Luxembourg Sweden	Denmark
3.0 or more		Belgium France Iceland Italy Japan Norway	Finland Israel Netherlands Switzerland

SOURCE: Arend Lijphart, *Democracies* (New Haven, Conn.: Yale University Press, 1984), p. 149. Reprinted with permission.

attend meetings, work for party nominees? In most countries, you must at least make an application; approval is routine (except, of course, in Communist countries), but dues are assessed. The only requirement in the United States is a declaration, usually at registration. The declaration is meaningless. "Closed" primary elections are held in which only registered party affiliates are allowed to vote, but court challenges have generally disallowed closed primaries. The primary election system itself dismantles political parties as organizations. Partly leaders cannot control either who votes in primary elections or, more critically, who competes in them. They cannot control who the nominees will be, since they have no jurisdiction over the use of the party name.

European political parties do not nominate by primaries but by intraorganizational agreement; hence their nominees are usually party loyalists with long histories of service to the party. In Europe, ideological positions have not softened much. In France, Italy, West Germany, and England, the competition among the elite between left and right has remained intense. Traditionally, *left* has meant supportive of domestic social and educational programs, the welfare state, working class values, and reform. *Right* has encapsulated belief in limited government, defense of individual liberties, and support for business. But each voter may define the terms in a different way. Younger voters are inclined to regard left ideology as commitment to nuclear disarmament, sexual and racial equality, and tolerance for countercultural lifestyles. In practice, however, "left" parties moderate their grandiose schemes. The French and Spanish socialists preside over vigorous market economies.

Intense competition does not necessarily mean a clear choice unless the competition assures some rotation in office. If you are a Communist party voter in Italy, you can expect your party to gain around one-fourth to one-third of the vote but not to win enough votes to govern.

Is the choice necessarily greater in nations with competitive systems, in which elections cause regular changes in personnel? The answer depends on perception. Consider American political parties. They are quite competitive; neither party enjoys an electoral monopoly for very long. The election of Democrat Franklin Roosevelt in 1932 and his three subsequent reelections gave rise to fears about the demise of the Republican party. But the Republicans maintained roots in state government, recovered with the election of Eisenhower in 1952, and with three consecutive presidential victories in the 1980s has provoked similar misgivings about the Democratic party. But the Democrats have maintained a base in the House of Representatives, regained control of the Senate in 1986, and were able to challenge the Republicans forcefully in presidential elections. Still, only one-third of post–World War II presidential elections have been won by the Democratic nominee.

Obviously, American elections provide for a change of governing personnel, but what about changes in policy? Both parties share the same fundamental ideology to a greater degree than occurs in European parliamentary democracies. Both parties believe in the sanctity of private property. A Democratic victory does not result in the nationalization of major industry, nor does a Republican defeat mean the dismantling of the Tennessee Valley Authority and the United States Postal Service. Both parties are committed to a free enterprise economy, individual liberty, limited government, majority rule, and due process of law. Moreover, since the 1930s, both parties have endorsed the public-oriented, mass domestic welfare programs such as social security, fair labor standards, unemployment compensation, a gradated income tax, countercyclical fiscal and monetary policies, and government regulation of utilities.

Both parties support the basic outlines of American foreign policy since World War II: anticommunism, military preparedness, the North Atlantic Treaty Organization, even the Korean and Vietnam wars. Rather than promoting competition about national goals and programs, the parties reinforce social consensus and limit legitimate political conflict. The two major parties are not identical in ideology; their positions show nuances of differences. Republican leaders are ''conservative'' on domestic policy, whereas Democratic leaders are ''liberal.'' Moreover, the social bases of the parties are slightly different. Both parties draw support from all social groups, but the Democrats draw disproportionately from labor, Jews, Catholics, and blacks, and the Republicans draw disproportionately from rural, small-town, and suburban Protestants, business interests, and professionals.

Active partisans feel more passionately about their beliefs than most other people; hence Democratic and Republican activists describe themselves in much more ideologically combative terms than the rest of us. With the help of media exaggeration they sometimes create the impression that the election of, say, a Republican is ''revolutionary,'' but this is not so.

The American people are actually decidedly neutral about our political parties; most have neither strong likes nor dislikes. We just do not think about them very much.[5] This is apparent as soon as we look at the underlying process of election; you may be surprised to learn that the view from the street varies greatly according to where that street is located.

SELECTING CANDIDATES

There are two ways for a party to name its standard-bearers. They can be *elected*, as in the United States' *primary elections*. Or they can be selected by some smaller body, a party caucus or leadership cadre, as is done everywhere *except* the United States.

A question—not by any means rhetorical—is, Are American political parties worthy of the name? They have surrendered their most important function to others, principally the media and primary election voters. Presumably, the surrender was made in the name of democracy. But can it be possible to allow "nondemocratic" political groups a role in democratic polities? That is, can linkage agents—organizations charged with fostering responsiveness—themselves be autocracies? The Europeans think so:

> Among Western nations, the American method of choosing candidates differs from all the others. . . . The United States is alone in so regulating parties as . . . to give those who are not formally organized in a party the opportunity to determine party candidates. . . . Everywhere else the selection of party candidates is basically a private affair. . . . Except in the United States, the organized party in some form is conceded the legal power to name candidates.[6]

Can *private* organizations be the agents of *public* democracy? Before considering some other ways political parties nominate candidates, consider first the proposition that all organizations, public or private, whatever their stated purpose, are oligarchies rather than participatory democracies. Roberto Michels, examining the European socialist parties and their auxiliary unions, believed that even when the professed goal of an organization is equality, "organization implies the tendency to oligarchy. In every organization, whether it be a political party, a professional union, or any other association of the kind, the aristocratic tendency manifests itself very clearly."[7] The argument against strong party organizations is thus that irrespective of their good intentions, they become instruments of the elite, and therefore *no* organization is better than an autocratic one.

Outside the United States, parties select candidates in the three following ways:

1. *Local committee:* Australia, Belgium, Canada, Denmark, Finland, France, Ireland, Norway, Sri Lanka, Sweden, Switzerland, Turkey, United Kingdom, West Germany
2. *Regional committee:* Italy
3. *National committee:* Austria, Colombia, India, Israel, Japan, Netherlands, New Zealand, Venezuela

We shall examine each system in turn.

CANDIDATE SELECTION BY LOCAL COMMITTEE: UNITED KINGDOM

The most popular way to select candidates is by local committee. The United Kingdom serves as an illustration.

As is true in the other European democracies, party membership in the United Kingdom requires a bit more than showing up at elections. Annual dues are assessed, and party membership cards are issued. Since, as is usual in European democracies, voter registration is designed to encompass the entire adult population, the additional steps of selecting a party and paying annual dues tend to eliminate most of the weak identifiers. In the United States, fewer people are registered—about 66 percent, compared with 99 percent in Europe—because registration requires a trip to the courthouse or auxiliary substation. At registration time, Americans declare their party allegiance. In the other democracies, since registration is automatic, one cannot register with a partisan tag, so in England, party membership comprises all Britons who have paid their annual dues and received their cards.

The two major parties, the Conservative party and the Labour party, differ organizationally as well as ideologically.

The Conservatives

England's Conservative party has about 2 million dues-paying members. These members are organized into *constituency associations,* based on the constituencies of Parliament. The constituency associations raise money and recruit members, and about half of them employ a full-time staff. Each local association is given a quota, a minimum level of funds to be contributed to the national party organization. Of course, not all the Conservative party's national funds come from constituency associations; it receives direct individual contributions and contributions from businesses or trade associations. Even so, perhaps a quarter of all Conservative party money comes from the constituency associations.

Meeting at annual conferences, the constituency associations offer advice and suggestions to the Conservative members of Parliament. The British system, especially among the Conservatives, illustrates a process fundamentally at odds with the United States'. Although the local constituency associations select parliamentary candidates who select a leader, the constituency associations' choice is constrained by national lists of acceptable candidates. Members of Parliament, then, are the most powerful component of the Conservative party.

The Conservative members of Parliament elect a *party leader*. The party leader will become prime minister if the party wins. If the Conservatives do not win a majority or cannot form a coalition with another party, the party leader is the leader of the opposition. In 1974, the Conservatives lost the general election. The former prime minister and still party leader, Edward Heath, was replaced by Margaret Thatcher. She led the Conservatives in opposition until 1979, when the Labour party lost a vote of confidence, thus requiring a general election. The Conservative party won, making Thatcher

England's first female prime minister. Like all British prime ministers, Thatcher was elected only as a member of Parliament, not as prime minister; she won the *party*'s election to become party leader, which made her prime minister. The Conservatives have won twice since 1979, and Thatcher has remained prime minister longer than anyone else in the 20th century. But the Conservative party could, if it wished, replace her as leader. She would still be a member of parliament.

Labour

Britain's Labour party gives less freedom to its party leader than the Conservatives do. The party conference, meeting annually, sets policy by a two-thirds vote. Between conferences, the National Executive Committee is responsible for party policy and organization. The Labour party's members of Parliament are more active in policy development than the Conservatives, and the party leader is more constrained. At party conferences, trade unions, which provide the bulk of the party's money, cast the most votes. The Labour party, unlike the Conservatives, enjoys a large indirect membership (union members pay through their organizations rather than directly). Labour has about 5 million affiliated members but only a handful of direct members. Constituency associations are less important than they are with the Conservatives, since unions can sponsor candidates for Parliament.

Until 1980, the Labour party leader was elected more or less as the Conservative one was, by the Labour members of Parliament (MPs). But a series of intraparty democracy demands, especially from the constituency associations, resulted in an electoral college system that gives unions 40 percent of the votes and the constituency associations and MPs 30 percent each. As in the Conservative party, the Labour party's leader will become prime minister if the party wins a plurality of seats in the House of Commons.

Labour divides authority among the Labour MPs, the constituency associations, and the unions, giving more voice to rank and file than the Conservatives do. But neither party has a process even remotely similar to our primary elections. All candidates, including those for Parliament, are chosen by the party organization.

CANDIDATE SELECTION BY REGIONAL COMMITTEE: ITALY

Although Italy's government appears chaotic, with resignations occurring more often than in other parliamentary democracies, its political parties are very strong. Between 1944 and 1987, the nation had 46 governments, the longest lasting just over two years. But the illusion of instability is mitigated by the powerful political parties. Emerging from the rubble of World War II, political parties preceded the government; by the time of the first postwar election, political parties had actually run the government for four years, and they retained much of the authority normally given to governments. *Partitocrazìa* (rule by party) has remained in place.

The point here is not that parties are more important than in the United States, for that is true of parties in all industrial democracies. Rather, the Italian ones, almost in the fashion of the Marxist one-party polities, link directly with the government. Most prime ministers, although they owe their job to the party, do not seek party approval for policy initiatives. But in Italy, little distance separates party and government: "The prime minister is normally little more than a figurehead who serves at the pleasure of party leaders, a fact explaining why many ambitious politicians prefer to be party secretary rather than prime minister."[8]

Parties have members, people who pay dues, but fraud in issuing membership cards is widespread, and in any case, individual party members count for nothing. Unlike parties in other formerly fascist countries, such as West Germany, those in Italy have not abandoned the autocratic structure used by Mussolini's Fascist party. Power effectively rests in executive committees; the chairman of this body is also secretary of the party. Executive committees are accountable to larger bodies—regional conferences of various sorts—and ultimately to a more broadly based constituent assembly. But the leaders select members of the larger committees, and hence accountability is sheer formality. So even though Italian politics often appears out of control, the major parties are very much in charge.

> *Partitocrazia* is not simply a matter of party control of the levers of governmental power. It extends well beyond to embrace most of the entire social, economic, and cultural life of the country. One of Italy's unique features is the existence of a vast sector of public and semipublic bodies that dominate virtually every area of national life: organizations as disparate as giant industries and banks, welfare and charitable agencies, radio and television, scientific and other research institutes, La Scala and other opera houses, the Venice Biennale and other cultural festivals, sport and recreational associations, hospitals and universities. . . . Controlled completely or in part by the state, they are subject to government influence, which in practice means party influence.[9]

Parties also distribute the spoils of office: jobs, building contracts, pensions, loans, franchises, and subsidies. Party constituent associations are thus more than agents of candidate recruitment; they are the instruments of the disposition of rewards, much like the now defunct American urban political machines.

The Christian Democrats

The Christian Democrats, the approximate analogue to the British Conservative party, has been the leading vote getter since the war, but never by an absolute majority. Christian Democratic pluralities declined incrementally, and in 1976, the party had to enter into an informal alliance with the Communists, who had received just about as many votes, in order to continue in government. In 1983, the Socialist party leader formed a governing coalition, which was disbanded in 1986. A similar fate befell a Christian Democratic Coalition in 1989. But the composition of the governing coalition is not as important as the party factions. During the raucous annual conventions, faction leaders—meeting, appropriately enough, in smoke-filled rooms—reach agreements on the composition of a cabinet should they continue in the coalition, which, of course, they will. The party's secretary and leader is chosen at these meetings, and the choice is ratified by the annual congress.

Between conventions, the National Council runs the party. This body, half of which is from the legislature, is elected by the annual congress. There are 30 ex-officio members, mainly faction leaders and regional secretaries, who augment the regular 160-person council. Day-to-day party affairs are managed by a 45-member executive committee, elected by the congress.

Parliamentary candidates are normally selected at the regional or provincial level. The parliamentary constituencies often contain several provinces, making intraconstituency party bargaining a complex affair. Each party will produce a constituency list, containing one name for each parliamentary seat to be filled. Since no party will win all the seats, the *preference vote,* a form of proportional representation is used. The voter chooses a party, then three or four members of that party. If a party wins, say, six seats, they will go to the top six vote getters. Candidates need not only party support for nomination but also—more important—party help in winning or placing well in the preference vote. The party is the most important source of this help, less so in the Christian Democratic party than the parties of the left, especially the Communist party.

The Italian Communists

The Communists can count on the votes of about one-third of the electorate, putting them in second place behind the Christian Democrats. Such strength may appear incongruous in a Catholic country with open elections and a prosperous economy, albeit one in which major institutions are managed by the government. The Italian Communist party is, however, genuinely independent of Moscow and not very fierce in its Marxism. It enjoys a reputation, unusual in such a traditionally corrupt and inefficient government, for good management of the many cities with Communist elected leaders and is generally believed to be the party most antagonistic to the Mafia. It has nevertheless not been invited to join in a formal coalition. Its greatest chance for inclusion was destroyed when terrorists killed Christian Democratic leader Aldo Moro in 1978 at the very moment when his party was interested in incorporating the Communists into the mainstream. The Red Brigades, denounced by the Communists, sought to repudiate the Communist strategy of compromise. Moro was not really the target; rather, the moderate Communists were to be exposed as frauds. Nonetheless, the party has sought to associate itself with the various Social Democratic parties in Europe and to eschew Leninism as dogma.

Curiously, given its moderation, it remains Leninist in organization, adhering to the principles of *democratic centralism* (prohibiting open dissent once a policy decision is made). Like the other Italian parties, the Communists are not democratic. Candidate selection, party platforms, and the like are routinely rubber-stamped by a compliant party congress, as true power rests with a seven-member secretariat, headed by the party secretary. Centralization and autocracy do not distinguish it from the other parties, however. But the strong sense of discipline is exceptional. Its candidates can count on much more help in gaining preference votes: whereas one-third of Christian Democratic candidates believed their party did nothing to help them, only 4 percent of the Communist candidates thought the party ignored them.[10]

In government, the strength of the parties is even more apparent. When a coalition collapses, an election is not automatically called. The old coalition stays on as a caretaker until a new coalition is put together. Failing this, an election will be called.

The *partitocrazia* is widely covered by Italian television. Joseph La Palombara recalls:

> One has the impression of a continuing "summit meeting" among men who may or may not be cabinet members but who nevertheless exercise powers of life and death over them, and over public policies as well. What kind of democracy is this, [reformers] ask, where those who head political parties, including parties that are supposed to be in opposition, get together outside parliament, or away from the cabinet, and decide by themselves which laws will or will not pass, which government will or will not survive?[11]

CANDIDATE SELECTION BY NATIONAL COMMITTEE: JAPAN

Japan's Liberal Democratic party (LDP), a center-right party, has been the dominant political force since the late 1950s, so we will confine our explanation of party organization to that party. In Japan, except for the Communists, party membership is available to anyone who wishes to join and pay dues. Since, like most people, Japanese find other activities more rewarding, their parties are dominated by professional politicians, mainly members of the Diet (parliament).

Parties maintain headquarters in Tokyo, with branch offices in prefectures (voting districts) and cities. In theory, annual party conventions determine policy. Membership at the annual gathering is limited to two Diet members and two delegates from each prefecture. Every second year, this assembly selects a president and vice-president. If the LDP wins, the party president becomes prime minister. Party leaders and prime ministers do not invariably change in harmony with an electoral cycle. In 1988, the party replaced Prime Minister Nakasone with Prime Minister Takeshita simply because the party thought it was time for a change and it wished to keep party traditions alive. Eighteen months later, ruined in a bribery scandal, he resigned and was replaced by Sosuke Uno, still with no election. (A few months later he resigned, to be replaced via LDP ballot by Toshiki Kaifu.)

The Executive Committee is the most powerful LDP organization, consisting of 15 members of the House of Representatives, seven from the House of Councillors (the other house in the Diet), and eight appointed by the prime minister as party leader. The selection of Diet candidates is undertaken by the Executive Committee, in cooperation with other national policy committees, mainly the National Organization Committee, the Diet Policy Committee, and the Party Discipline Committee. The chairs of these boards, together with the president, vice-president, and chair of the Executive Committee, constitute the overarching ruling body. Decisions about LDP Diet candidates take local preferences into account, but they are made nationally. This process sounds boring, but it is not; intraparty factions are as intensely competitive as Italy's. When the factions resolve their differences, the Japanese government can change executives without an election, as also happens in Italy.

These three examples show that in comparison with the United States, other industrial democracies treat political parties as private associations with public responsibilities. The only participants are an active elite, self-selected or anointed from above, but in no case can a casual participant have a say in the selection of the party's nominees. We turn now to a more detailed examination of the most bizarre of the lot: ours.

Although on paper, American political parties look similar to European ones, they are not. They have committees, rules, by-laws, and so on, but they have no control over the use of their names. Whoever wins the primaries is the party's choice. Candidates nominate themselves. Also, once candidates have nominated themselves, the qualification of the voters is virtually unconstrained. In many states, Democrats and Republicans are people who, on the day of the primary election, determine party affiliation on which party's primary seems more interesting. Each party's passing adherents are less reliable than Boston Celtic fans. The mode of declaration of loyalty is identical: One simply *becomes* a Celtic fan or a Democrat. But *maintenance* of loyalty is another matter entirely. If Celtic fans were as fickle as Democrats, tickets for the Boston Garden would not be sold out for every game.

The most important function of political parties is candidate selection. As one expert explains, "Candidate selection by political parties will determine both the choices set before the voters in elections and the composition of the governing and opposition parties, whose interactions in parliaments and congresses is the very essence of modern democratic government."[12] American parties ignore this function.

PRIMARY ELECTIONS

In the United States today, primaries are the dominant mode of selecting delegates who will, at national conventions, nominate a presidential candidate. It would be inconceivable for a person to be nominated without having contested and won the primary elections. For those of us coming of political age in the era of television, any alternative to primary elections seems downright undemocratic. But as recently as 1968, the Democratic party nominated a candidate who had not entered, much less won, a single primary election. In that year, the national convention was held hostage by retiring President Lyndon Johnson's obsession that his vice-president, Hubert H. Humphrey, be nominated, thus avoiding a repudiation of his Vietnam policy. From 1840 until the ill-fated Humphrey nomination, conventions selected nominees; delegates to conventions were selected by state party caucuses or comparable organizations. There was no *intraparty* democracy. This is the period now regarded with derision as the era of the "smoke-filled room."

Between 1912 and 1968, reformers began to propose an alternative method: the presidential primary. The reform movement reached its zenith with Woodrow Wilson's presidency. Wilson proposed a national primary to replace the haphazard collection of caucuses, machines, and state primary elections. But after Wilson, the nation lost its enthusiasm for reform. By the year in which Humphrey was nominated, only about one-third of the delegates to either party's convention were selected in a primary, and many of these were chosen in nonbinding primaries.

The Trauma of 1968

The year 1968 is permanently seared in the memory of Americans who watched in horror as the Democratic national convention deteriorated into a police-led assault on youthful protesters. Eugene McCarthy, a Democrat opposed to Johnson's prosecution of the war in Vietnam, entered the New Hampshire primary and earned 42 percent of the vote, a shockingly strong showing against an incumbent president (actually, Johnson had not bothered to enter and thus could amass only write-in votes). This was widely interpreted as a repudiation of Johnson. McCarthy ultimately gave way to another anti-war Democrat, Robert Kennedy, but not before compelling Johnson to announce that he would not seek renomination. But what he *did* seek was the nomination of Humphrey. As thousands of antiwar protesters descended on Chicago, Humphrey was cast in the unlikely role as defender of an unpopular war. When the protesters learned that irrespective of their efforts, Humphrey *was* to be nominated, they rioted. The Chicago police responded zealously, and the nation watched the carnage.

The Democratic party took Humphrey's razor-thin loss to Richard Nixon as evidence that the havoc of Chicago could not be repeated. To this end, a party commission, the McGovern-Fraser Commission, headed by George McGovern, proposed an *open caucus* mode of nomination. They resisted the then radical proposal that caucuses be replaced by direct primaries. One prominent political scientist believed that if caucuses were made more accessible, "the demand for primaries would fade away."[13]

As is often the case when moderates try to stem the tide of radical reform, the hope was futile. "Both Democratic and Republican legislators reflected on the general post-1968 reform ethos that supported a more participatory democracy, and what nomination method could be more broadly participatory than a primary?"[14] For the next election, a majority of delegates were chosen by primary election, and by 1988, more than two-thirds were chosen in primaries (see Table 5.2). Even states that have retained caucuses have found them transformed by television into de facto primaries.

TABLE 5.2 Delegates to National Conventions Selected in Primaries, 1968–1988

		Democrats			Republicans	
Year	Primaries	Delegates	Share of Votes (%)	Primaries	Delegates	Share of Votes (%)
1968	17	983	38	16	458	34
1972	23	1,862	61	22	710	53
1976	29	2,183	73	28	1,533	68
1980	35	2,378	72	34	1,516	76
1984	25	2,431	62	34	1,551	71
1988	34	2,842	68	36	1,771	78

Once the nominating process was made more visible, it was a natural target for the media. Although controversy has been taken out of conventions, it is very much alive in the primary election system. Primaries mean media exposure, money pouring into the state, and the horse race aspect of politics, which is of more interest than issues to the media and the voters.

As New Hampshire Goes . . . ?

If there were a national primary, that is, one held in all states simultaneously, no candidate would spend much time or money in New Hampshire. But New Hampshire, because it has the earliest primary, is more important to the media than New York, and New York's primary in April is more important than California's in June. This is because primaries generate media attention and momentum. As experiments in the democratization of politics, primaries are failures, and only one-third of the eligible voters participate. As opportunities for media participation in politics, however, they are superb.

When New Hampshire's legislature established the primary, it was held in May. The date was changed a few years later to March, to coincide with Town Meeting Day. But the spring thaw impeded drivers on unpaved roads, so the date was set back again, this time to February. Implausible as it may be, these perfectly sensible decisions cast New Hampshire in the media glare as the first test of strength. Until 1972, many candidates bypassed New Hampshire or announced their candidacies after its primary had taken place. But with the post-1968 reform, it became, along with Iowa, the most critical step. In 1984, Iowa and New Hampshire received 32 percent of the media coverage of the primaries, even though they contained only 3 percent of the nation's population and 3 percent of the delegates selected to either convention. Moreover, New Hampshire captures what there is to capture of public attentiveness. Before the event, 28 percent of national samples claim to be following the campaign on television; immediately thereafter, 45 percent begin to follow the campaigns, and although there is some backsliding, interest does not return to its pre–New Hampshire low. (However, the proportion following the campaign in newspapers, after a modest spurt, returns to about 17 percent; thus about half as many people follow the news by reading newspapers as do so by watching the tube.)[15]

It hardly needs to be said that voters make decisions on less than ideal criteria; it would be incredible that they would do otherwise. Besides keeping attention on "candidate issues" (questions about personality, integrity, and character rather than policy or ideas), the media spend most of their time speculating about the horse race components of the campaign. These are the questions posed in New Hampshire.

Contrary to myth, winning this primary does not guarantee nomination. Since the reform, among Democrats who won in New Hampshire, only Jimmy Carter became president. Since Republicans have had a near hegemony on the presidency, this circumstance is no surprise. Among Republicans, four New Hampshire winners—Nixon, Reagan (twice), and Bush—have won the presidency. Put another way, every president since reform has won New Hampshire. Doing well here gets you into the next phase of the primary season.

Intimate Dinner Parties Replace the Smoke-filled Room

Although the primary season officially begins in February, long before that the candidates are raising money, organizing staffs, and planning alternative strategies. These are the times for the political junkies, the small portion of the population that finds politics interesting and primaries irresistible. When the season begins, these people select the candidate they wish to work for and start the process of meeting legal requirements and organizing local staffs, getting ready for the combat. Few understand the extent to which this preprimary season is the functional equivalent of the smoke-filled room. In the 1980s, candidates were scrounging around for money, consultants, volunteers, and media support three to four years before the first test of strength, the Iowa caucuses in February.

This demeaning behavior enhances the media-encouraged trivialization of the electoral process. Television, always uneasy with abstract ideas, had the dream election in 1988: major candidates of both parties were making fools of themselves. Besides exploiting these insubstantial occurrences, the media expended substantial time and energy in probing popular reactions to the behavior and ethics of *reporters,* rather than explaining the ideas or preferences of candidates (admittedly difficult, since few offered any). Does the public have the right to know that a candidate:[16]

Drinks heavily	90%
Used cocaine in past year	88%
Has a serious medical problem	87%
Ever cheated on income taxes	80%
Used marijuana in past year	76%
Ever undergone psychiatric treatment	74%
Is a homosexual	62%

TYPES OF ELECTORAL SYSTEMS

Once nominated, whether by the usual method or by the American aberration, parties want to defeat their opponents and organize a government. This contest occurs in two-party or multiparty systems alike. But political party systems are not always easily categorized. How many "real" parties are there? Do we wish to impose some minimum level of electoral success? Although most observers would agree that the United Kingdom is a two-party system, with either the Conservatives or Labour organizing a government, there are also the Social Democrats (disgruntled ex-Labourites) and Liberals (who enjoyed considerable success in the 19th century and still elect a smattering of MPs). The *World Atlas of Elections* lists 13 parties in the United Kingdom.

Scholars have been able to categorize systems on the criterion of effectiveness in a way that makes sense. Common sense tells us that there are only two major parties in the United Kingdom. Blondel's categorization, for example, defines two-party systems as those with two dominant parties but some other small ones in parliament on occasion.

If, in addition to the two major parties, a third may be occasionally required to participate in coalitions, he speaks of a 2½-party system. Systems with more than 2½ parties
are true multiparty ones and can be divided once again into systems with a dominant
party (like Italy's Christian Democrats) and those without such a party (Switzerland,
Finland, the Netherlands). By means of a simple computation, Lijphart has developed
an intuitively pleasing way of measuring political party systems: Multiply the number
of parties by the proportion of seats held by these parties, divide into 1, and the result
gives the effective number of parties: [17]

Average Number of Effective Parties, 1945–1980

United States	1.9	France	3.3
New Zealand	2.0	Luxembourg	3.3
United Kingdom	2.1	Iceland	3.5
Austria	2.2	Italy	3.5
Canada	2.4	Belgium	3.7
Australia	2.5	Denmark	4.3
Germany	2.6	Israel	4.7
Ireland	2.8	Netherlands	4.9
Japan	3.1	Finland	5.0
Norway	3.2	Switzerland	5.0
Sweden	3.2		

Still there are problems: Sweden's Social Democrats ruled for 40 years, and Japan's
Liberal Democrats for three decades. Although in both these cases, opposition parties
were able to maintain a respectable showing in the legislature, effectiveness is a relative
thing.

THE POLITICAL CONSEQUENCES
OF ELECTION LAWS

Of the many complex explanations of the "cause" of two-party and multiparty systems,
one of the most appealing involves the political consequences of electoral laws. Electoral systems are of three essential kinds: the *plurality system,* the *majoritarian system,*
and *proportional representation.*

The Plurality System

The candidate with the most votes wins, even without an absolute majority. Often plurality systems are accompanied by *single-member constituencies.* The "first past the
post" system, when combined with laws allowing only one representative per district,
virtually mandate two parties. In a winner-take-all competition, with only one prize, the
odds of a small party winning are remote. Countries that use a pure plurality system—
the United Kingdom, the United States, Canada, and New Zealand—have two effective
parties. The plurality rule is applied in a special way in Japan: voters can support only

TABLE 5.3 Voting Pluralities

Country	Average Winning Margin (%)	Party Changes
Canada	11.4	3/14
Japan	20.8	0/10
New Zealand	3.8	4/14
United Kingdom	3.8	5/12
United States	10.8	5/10

one candidate, even though the constituency is assigned more than one member. The top three, four, or five vote getters win. (See Table 5.3.)

The Japanese modification of the usual plurality rule may be an explanation of its remarkable stability. If we compare the countries using plurality rules, the impact of Japanese law is apparent. The winning margin in Japan is huge, about twice its nearest competitor, and the same party has won consistently. Yet with this huge margin of success, the Liberal Democrats have not won an *absolute majority* since 1963! Here is how the law gives a major advantage to the incumbent party:

> The system makes it extremely difficult to "throw the rascals out" if and when a high degree of national dissatisfaction develops with the government in power. . . . In a single-member-district system such as prevails in the United States or Britain, a vote *against* an incumbent and his party automatically becomes a vote *for* the challenger and his. Hence, a shift of a few percentage points within a district can easily alter the electoral result and the party of the representative. In Japan, however, since most candidates receive somewhere between 12 percent and 25 percent of the district's vote, even a 10 percent shift in a major party's support usually means only a 3–4 percent shift in the support level of each individual candidate from that party. In some cases, this is sufficient to ensure defeat for one of them, but the potential for the individual elector to vote effectively against the party as a whole is almost nil. . . . Drastic shifts in the balance of party forces is extremely rare.[18]

The Majoritarian System

In this system, candidates must win a majority. This can be done in two ways: either a run-off between the top two candidates is held after the initial vote, or (in Australia and Ireland) voters *rank* candidates. If no candidate receives a majority, the last candidate is eliminated and the votes are redistributed to second choices. The process is repeated until a candidate earns a majority. The principal use of this system is in the Australian lower house; the upper house uses the single transferable vote.[19] The consequences are intriguing (see Table 5.4): in 1949, 1955, 1958, 1963, 1966, 1974, 1975, 1977, and 1980 the Liberal Party received *fewer* first *preference* votes than Labor yet was allocated *more* seats in the legislature. In 1975 and 1977, for example, the Liberals received a scant 40 percent of the first preference vote and a majority of seats.

TABLE 5.4 Australian Parliamentary Election Results, 1946–1984 (%)

	Labor		Liberal	
	Votes	Seats	Votes	Seats
1946	49.7	58	32.3	23
1949	46	39	39	45
1951	40.6	39	47.6	43
1954	50	47	38.6	39
1955	44.6	39	39.7	47
1958	42.8	37	37.2	48
1961	47.9	49	33.6	37
1963	45	41	37.1	43
1966	40.1	33	40.1	49
1969	47	47	34.8	37
1972	49.6	54	32	30
1974	49.3	52	41	54
1975	47.8	28	41.8	54
1977	39.6	30	38.1	54
1980	45.1	41	37.5	43
1983	49.5	52	34.4	26
1984	49.5	51	34.4	22

Proportional Representation

Proportional representation usually means the "list" system. While it can be made to appear formidably complex, the gist of the plan is that parties present a list of candidates in multimember districts. Voters chose a *party list*. Seats are allocated to each party according to the *proportion* of votes each receives.[20]

The intent—usually achieved—is to insure the health of smaller parties. Not only do proportional representation countries have more effective parties, but the shrinkage between electoral success and seats earned is less (see Table 5.5). The more equitable transfer of popular support to legislative representation means that voters who support third parties or even fourth parties have every reason to assume not only that their vote will not be wasted but also that the vote will be more faithfully reflected in legislative power. Lijphart has calculated an *index of disproportionality,* the difference between electoral and legislative strength, averaged for each election, for the two largest parties. For plurality systems, the index is 6.08, while for proportional representation systems it is only 2.03.[21]

As we saw, the Australian majority system is especially prone to distort party representation by using second-place finishes. But in the United Kingdom, the Conservative party has won the last three elections with pluralities, usually earning about 42 percent of the popular vote; nevertheless, the Conservatives have managed absolute majorities in Parliament. In the first two of three Conservative victories, the party won over 60 percent of the seats with about 42 percent of the vote. The majority was reduced

TABLE 5.5 Voting with Proportional Representation or Pluralities

	Legislative Parties	Electoral Parties	Shrinkage
Plurality Systems			
Canada	2.4	3.1	0.7
Japan	3.1	3.8	0.7
New Zealand	2.0	2.4	0.4
United Kingdom	2.1	2.6	0.5
United States	1.9	2.1	0.2
Average	**2.3**	**2.8**	**0.5**
Proportional Representation			
Austria	2.2	2.4	0.2
Belgium	3.7	4.1	0.4
Denmark	4.3	4.5	0.2
Finland	5.0	5.4	0.4
Iceland	3.5	3.7	0.2
Ireland	2.8	3.1	0.3
Israel	4.7	5.0	0.3
Italy	3.5	3.9	0.4
Luxembourg	3.3	3.6	0.3
Netherlands	4.9	5.2	0.3
Norway	3.2	3.9	0.7
Sweden	3.2	3.4	0.2
Switzerland	5.0	5.4	0.4
West Germany	2.6	2.9	0.3
Average	**3.4**	**3.1**	**0.3**

SOURCE: After Arend Lijphart, *Democracies* (New Haven, Conn.: Yale University Press, 1984), p. 160. Reprinted with permission.

in 1987, but it was nonetheless a majority. The reasons for this persistent pattern are simple: the Labour party can count on only a third or so of the electorate, but its geographic base is good enough for it to have seats in approximate proportion to its share of the popular vote. But the smaller parties, especially the Liberals and the Social Democrats (they ran together in 1987, calling themselves the Alliance), usually get one-fourth of the popular votes but only a tiny smattering of seats, since their support is not great enough in enough constituencies to win the proper amount of seats.

Now consider Denmark, which uses a proportional representation system. The results of its 1984 election are shown in Table 5.6. The obvious consequences of Denmark's exceptionally accurate rendering of voter preferences is the continued necessity for coalition governments. While Margaret Thatcher reigned unhindered, responsible only to her parliamentary majority, Denmark was ruled by a coalition of the Conservative, Liberal, Christian People's, and Center Democratic parties. We shall return to the role of the party in government, but first, let us examine how voters react.

France provides an excellent example of the political consequences of election laws.

TABLE 5.6 Election Returns in Denmark, 1984

	Popular Vote (%)	Seats (%)
Social Democrats	31.4	31.3
Conservatives	23.3	23.5
Liberals	12.0	12.3
Socialist People's party	11.4	11.7
Radical Liberals	5.5	5.6
Center Democrats	4.6	4.5
Progress party	3.6	3.4
Christian People's party	2.7	2.8
Left Socialists	2.6	2.8

Until 1985, France used a majoritarian scheme to elect its legislature. The Socialist president, François Mitterand, rammed a proportional representation system through parliament, assuming that the system would increase the number of parties in the National Assembly. His surveys told him that in the 1986 parliamentary elections, his Socialist party would lose its control of the legislature. Under the majoritarian scheme, the right-wing opposition would probably earn a majority of seats in the Chamber of Deputies; under a proportional representation plan, more and smaller parties would win seats, reducing the severity of the Socialist loss. Mitterand was right. In 1986, small right-wing parties siphoned off enough voters to make it impossible for the two large right-wing parties, running in tandem, to receive a majority. Thus, even though the Socialist vote declined from 38 to 33 percent in 1981, the Socialist party remained the largest in the legislature. In 1986, the Conservatives, with a working majority and a prime minister from their coalition, changed back to single-member districts with no proportional representation.

Plurality electoral laws facilitate two-party political systems; proportional representation encourages multiparty systems. Consider the imaginary situation outlined in Table 5.7: A parliament consists of 10 electoral districts. Three parties compete for these 10 seats. Under the single-member plurality rule, party A, which won a plurality of votes in 8 of 10 districts, would win 8 seats, even though its total vote was less than party B's. Party B, which won in two districts, would earn two seats, and Party C would earn none. But abolishing the single-member plurality rule in favor of proportional representation means that all three parties would be represented, based on their *proportion* of the total vote. Party A would lose a seat, party B would double its representation, and party C, which earned no seats under single-member plurality rules, would have three seats.

It does not always work out this way in practice, of course. Much depends on the performances of the least successful parties, the stability and durability of the vote of the most successful ones, and the gap between success and failure. There is a vast difference between a system with two competitive parties and two that win rarely and a

TABLE 5.7 Representation under Single-Member Plurality and Proportional Schemes

District	Party A	Party B	Party C
1	4,000	3,600	2,200
2	3,800	3,700	2,200
3	1,500	4,600	1,700
4	3,600	3,300	3,500
5	4,200	3,300	3,500
6	2,000	4,000	3,700
7	3,700	3,600	1,200
8	3,500	3,400	2,800
9	3,300	3,200	3,100
10	3,900	3,500	3,700
Total	33,500	36,800	27,000
Percentage	34	38	28
Seats won (single-member plurality)	8	2	0
Seats won (proportional representation, one district)	3	4	3

SOURCE: Fred Wilhoite, *Power and Governments* (Pacific Grove, Calif.: Brooks/Cole, 1987), p. 139. Reprinted with permission.

system with four genuinely competitive parties. And about five competitive parties is all that most political systems can endure.[22]

Consider the U.S. House of Representatives. Table 5.8 shows the percentages of votes and seats won by each major party between 1976 and 1986. Winners gain and losers lose from single-member plurality rules. Under proportional representation rules,

TABLE 5.8 U.S. House of Representatives Election Results, 1976–1986 (%)

	Democrats		Republicans	
	Votes	Seats	Votes	Seats
1976	56	67	43	33
1978	53	64	45	36
1980	50	56	48	44
1982	55	62	43	38
1984	52	58	47	42
1986	55	59	45	41
Average	**54**	**61**	**45**	**39**

the Republicans would enjoy a 6 percent gain and the Democrats suffer a 7 percent loss in seats.

WHAT MOTIVATES THE VOTERS

Voters facing these confusing choices are governed by the structure of choice. In the United States, primary elections feature different candidates, different rules, and confusing and contradictory information. Candidates for the presidency may enter primaries in states where they believe they will do well and eschew others. Candidates who run out of steam may concede, eliminating themselves from primaries held late in the season.

Election laws are the property of state legislatures, which structure primary elections as they please. Even though party headquarters tries to make them conform to national standards, they do not. Thus some primaries are "open" (requiring no proof of party registration) and others are "closed" (allowing only party registrants to vote in a party's primary).

Since most candidates in a party's primary election agree with each others, they must create "themes." The themes may be inaccurate. In 1988, Richard Gephart concealed his years of experience in Congress, where he is a widely admired establishmentarian, in order to sound like a crazed populist. Media coverage does not provide information about candidates' "report cards," only their success or failure.

But once the primaries are over, most people can figure out what to do. There are two parties, and single-member plurality rules prevail. In parliamentary systems, elections "compress" choice. Assume a rational voter, with gradations of opinion on a variety of matters. If one party is genuinely conservative and the other is truly radical, what does a voter who favors a moderate position between the two extremes do? In a presidential system, such a voter might decide to vote for a conservative chief executive but balance that choice with a vote for a liberal member of Congress.[23] Generally, however, voters are not so calculating and respond well to reduced information. "Rational ignorance" may sound oxymoronic, but it is sensible. In Chapter 1, we set forth the premise that most people care more about their daily lives than about politics. It follows that they know a good deal more about matters of immediate concern; someone who does not know where Nicaragua is may be able to tell you how to disassemble a fuel injection system. A tax accountant is paid to know IRS regulations, so that accountancy clients can concentrate on other things. Such divisions of labor are natural, and politics has them too. Political parties should be like tax accountants. They should reduce information costs and thus encourage participation. It is easier to figure out which party generally represents one's own interest and to stick with it, a task made easy by parliamentary systems and difficult by presidential ones, than to watch the news, read the papers, listen to speeches, go to meetings, and so on.

But voters in proportional representation systems, with no voice in candidate nomination (unless they are party activists), must sort through bewildering and complex decision rules that vex even careful students of politics. The Australian lower house is elected on a majoritarian basis, while the upper house is chosen by proportional representation. Perhaps compulsory voting, which Australia uses (along with Belgium, the Netherlands, Venezuela, and Greece), *is* required to maintain high turnout.

Voter Turnout

There are substantial, permanent differences in rates of voter turnout:[24]

Average Percentage Voter Turnout in National Elections, 1945–1984

1.	Australia*	95	14.	Norway	81
2.	Venezuela*	94	15.	France	79
3.	Austria	94	16.	Greece*	79
4.	Italy	93	17.	Finland	79
5.	Belgium*	93	18.	United Kingdom	77
6.	New Zealand	88	19.	Canada	76
7.	Portugal	88	20.	Ireland	75
8.	West Germany	87	21.	Japan	73
9.	Denmark	86	22.	Spain	73
10.	Sweden	85	23.	Turkey	67
11.	Netherlands	84	24.	Switzerland	65
12.	Sri Lanka	82	25.	India	59
13.	Israel	81	26.	United States	59
			27.	Colombia	47

The pitiful performance of the United States is striking. Explanations abound. We hear of the "happy nonvoter" theme often from people who believe that voting is an act of protest; low voting reflects a low level of dissatisfaction. Others reach the opposite conclusion: people do not vote because they believe that the existing political structure is insensitive to their needs or perhaps that it controls elections, allowing only compliant candidates to run (this view is especially popular among Marxist, conspiratorial theorists). All these explanations are hard to prove.

European politics usually involves parties with a more ideological thrust than American politics. The difference between Labour and the Conservatives in England, for instance, is greater than that between Democrats and Republicans. Also, parliamentary systems, especially if two-party, allow victors to implement their platforms.

Parties are more class-linked in Europe. Social Democrats and Labour are more closely connected to unions and express more class-derived rhetoric than the American Democrats. Class-based voting is in decline in Europe as well as in the United States,[25] but not so markedly. This undoubtedly makes elections in Europe more harsh, more polarized than American ones, where television has made them trivial affairs, with more attention given to makeup and "high negatives" (media jargon for a bad image) than to party or ideology.

Class voting is exceptionally low in the United States; G. Bingham Powell, Jr., believes that this fact alone reduces American turnout by 10 percent.[26]

---

*Voting is compulsory.

Percentage by Which Support of Working-Class-oriented Parties by Manual Laborers Exceeds Support by Other Workers[27]

Belgium	51	Norway	37
Netherlands	45	West Germany	34
Finland	48	United Kingdom	33
Denmark	43	France	33
Switzerland	43	Australia	33
Spain	42	Japan	30
Sweden	42	Canada	29
Austria	42	Ireland	25
New Zealand	40	United States	13
Italy	40		

If party-class linkages were as obvious as in Europe, American turnout would be about 69 percent, still quite low.

Rather than seeking one cause of American lethargy, common sense and reason suggest that a variety of factors are at work. One of the simplest and therefore most appealing explanations is that Americans are inundated by elections:

> No country can approach the United State in the frequency and variety of elections, and thus in the amount of electoral participation to which citizens have a right. No other country elects its lower house . . . every two years, or its president . . . every four years. No other country popularly elects its state governments and town mayors; no other has as wide a variety of nonrepresentative offices [treasurers, attorneys general, judges]. Only one other country (Switzerland) can compete in the number and variety of local referendums; only two (Belgium and Turkey) hold party "primaries" in most parts of the country.[28]

Americans vote less because, ironically, there are more opportunities to be "democratic." Our plebiscitary obsession makes us less "democratic" than countries where elections, occurring less often, have more meaning. People who work at ice-cream stores lose their taste for the product in a month or so; rather than trying to control munching, employers encourage it, knowing that the ultimate result will be less eating of profits. Americans live in an electoral ice-cream shop. A voter in Cambridge, England, has four opportunities in five years to vote; someone living Tallahassee, Florida, could have trudged to the polls 165 times in the same period![29]

Other institutional factors are at work to cripple democracy through excess. One of the most crucial, depressing turnout by about 14 percent, are cumbersome registration requirements.[30] In most other democracies, voter registration is as automatic as a utility bill, and at least 99 percent of voters are registered automatically. In the United States, as pointed out earlier, it requires at least a trip to a courthouse or other public facility.

Voter Decision Making

Voters learn about politics and elections via television. In the United States, this means that they rely largely on one of the three networks' evening news. American news is much more entertaining than television in Europe, where news programs are conversational, straightforward, and without much personality. European television is either administered by public corporations, as in Germany, or provided by a mixture of private and public interests. The United Kingdom's government-owned BBC is the best example. There are private channels, but BBC is invariably the leader.

Overt government participation in television programming has meant that, generally, European electoral coverage is less trivial than in the United States. For example, in West Germany, neither major party—the Christian Democrats and the Social Democrats—wants to privatize television, a course on which France recently embarked. The Germans fear excessive commercialization and believe that television should inform as well as entertain, a premise not apparent in American television.[31]

Given the rather silly American way of conveying information, turning what should be a serious business into just another game show, it is not surprising that Americans—although they watch at about the same rate as Europeans—trust television more (see Table 5.9).

Also, since European elections are parliamentary, with no direct election of the president (except for France), less attention is paid to personalities. Elections are shorter, generally lasting about two months, whereas in the United States, elections are in reality nonstop affairs, with serious presidential candidates preparing for an election four years ahead of time.

France: A System in Flux.   The French constitution, written by Charles de Gaulle in 1958, gives more power to the president than the U.S. Constitution. The president is elected by popular vote to a seven-year term, in a two-stage process that in some ways resembles an American primary election, although it is much shorter. If no candidate receives a majority in the first round of voting, a runoff between the leading two candidates is held. Since de Gaulle intended the constitution to remedy the coalition-dependent parliamentary governments that preceded him and since he was a megalomaniac of stupendous proportions, it is only natural that he designed a magisterial presence for the position. Following de Gaulle's examples, French presidents have been austere and aristocratic in bearing. Further, French parties are more chaotic than is normal in Europe, and elections, much as in the United States, stress personality.

TABLE 5.9 Confidence in the Media (%)

	France	Germany	United Kingdom	Spain	United States
How much confidence do you have in the media?					
A great deal, some	48	41	38	46	69
Hardly any, none	49	59	60	51	30
What areas do the media influence to a large extent?					
Judiciary	46	29	40	32	69
Legislature	37	44	48	38	78
Executive	48	46	44	41	81
Public opinion	77	71	80	70	88

SOURCE: Data from Laurence Parisot, "Attitude about the Media: A Five-Country Study," *Public Opinion*, January-February, 1988, pp. 18, 60. Reprinted with permission, of the American Enterprise Institute for Public Policy.

Partisan Loyalty

In Europe, ''candidates are elected because of their party label and not because of their personal attributes.''[32] This is less so in France and decidedly less so in the United States:

> [American] presidential elections attract great public interest, and candidate image exerts an important influence on voting choice. . . . . A similar situation exists in France. The two-candidate runoff in French presidential elections is decided by the size of the vote the candidates can attract from parties other than their own.[33]

In the United States, the proportion of voters claiming to be free of any partisan identification is increasing. About one-third are independents, up from 22 percent in the late 1960s and more than currently claim to be Republicans. If Americans voted along party lines, Republicans would always lose. Since Republicans have won the presidency in 6 out of 10 elections since World War II, their party's candidate has been able to find votes among independents and Democrats. One-third of the Democrats voted for Nixon in 1972; in the last two Reagan elections, Democrats gave the Republican candidates one-fourth of their votes, a rate equaled by Bush in 1988. Independent voters have invariably given the Republican candidate either a plurality or a majority.

In France, while the parties of the right continue to enjoy support among Catholics, and parties of the left attract a disproportionate share of the working-class vote, defections are becoming common, and the personality of the president is emerging as a more significant factor than in other European countries. Though hardly as inane as American elections, French ones nevertheless are among the more ''Americanized.'' Like American parties, French ones have become increasingly ambiguous about their programs: right-wing parties have become more tolerant of the welfare state, and the Socialists are now less rigidly in favor of massive nationalization of industry. As a consequence, ''French voters tend increasingly to make electoral choices on the basis of personality and other nonprogrammatic . . . criteria.''[34]

Even in countries with strong party traditions, partisan loyalties are eroding. In England, Margaret Thatcher's rejuvenated Tories regularly capture about one-third of the votes of trade unionists, even though their dues finance the Labour party. In West Germany, two-thirds of the voters stick with their party choice, but three-fourths did so two decades ago.

The Role of Ideology

Ordering events and circumstances into a coherent view of reality, into an ideology, is not a characteristic of most voters. Voters generally do not think abstractly, although more understand the differences between left and right than use them. And fewer people in the United States recognize and understand the difference than anywhere else. Perhaps because our parties are so pragmatic, our voters are less ideological than European ones. Americans score just slightly below the Europeans in the active use of an ideology—that is, the use of an ideology in reaching a decision in general—but as voters,

TABLE 5.10 Levels of Ideological Awareness (%)

	Active Use of Ideology	Recognize and Understand "Left" and "Right"	Self-Placement on Left-Right Continuum
Austria	19	39	75
France	—	—	81
Italy	55	54	74
Netherlands	36	56	90
Switzerland	9	39	79
United Kingdom	21	23	82
United States	21	34	67
West Germany	34	56	92

SOURCE: Russell J. Dalton, *Citizen Politics in Western Democracies* (Chatham, N.J.: Chatham House, 1988), p. 25. Reprinted with permission.

they score lower in the understanding and placement of themselves on a left-right continuum, as shown in Table 5.10.

In the table, "active use of ideology" means that the respondent mentioned an ideological concern at least once during the interview. Surely this is a most permissive research methodology. If one asks a different question, the percentage of ideological utterances to remarks about other factors (the nature of the times, the personality of party leaders, and so on), a different image of voters emerges: voters in the Netherlands use ideology 21 percent of the time, those in Britain 8 percent, in the United States 7 percent, in Germany 9 percent, and in Austria 8 percent of the time.[35] Voters are not very ideological, relying instead on the "nature of the times" as a guide to voting.

In addition to finding out how ideologically motivated the various electorates are, we need to know the nature of their ideologies. Keeping the same left-right distinction for the countries in Table 5.11, we see in Table 5.11 that the United States' electorate is less extreme than European electorates.

Notice that the United States has the fewest number of left ideologues in its "left-wing" party, the Democrats (which is not, by European standards, left at all); it also has the fewest number of right ideologues in its "right-wing" party, the Republicans. Not only are American parties centrist, but so are their actual and potential customers. To put the matter into better perspective, examine the differences between American Democrats and Republicans among left and right ideologies. There is approximately 17 percentage points difference between them. Now do the same calculation for any European country. The *smallest* differences are in Switzerland, and even there they are about three times as great as in the United States! In the two countries with active Communist parties, the differences are the most substantial. But even if we exclude them, the differences between the Socialists and the conservative parties is still quite large.

Do not forget that as the definitions of *left* and *right* vary from person to person, they also vary from country to country. The American left is to the right of the European left, because Americans are more individualistic. Table 5.12 shows the results when people were asked about governmental responsibility for various problems. Americans want to restrict government: Europeans see a more active role.

TABLE 5.11 Categorization of Ideology (% of voters)

	Left	Center	Right
Austria			
Socialists	48	31	21
Catholics	4	24	72
France			
Communists	95	4	—
Socialists	72	24	4
Center	7	65	28
Independent Republicans	2	40	58
UDR	1	25	74
Italy			
Communists	90	10	—
Socialists	76	22	2
Social Democrats	37	53	10
Christian Democrats	11	64	25
Liberals	3	57	40
Neo-Fascists	2	14	84
Netherlands			
Labor	59	28	13
Catholic	8	39	53
Liberal	9	32	51
Anti-Revolutionary Party	11	22	67
Christian Historical Union	11	22	67
Switzerland			
Social Democrat	52	33	15
Independent	24	55	21
Farmers	8	47	45
Radical Democrats	7	47	46
Catholics	10	31	59
United Kingdom			
Labour	52	36	12
Liberal	20	60	20
Conservative	6	29	65
United States			
Democrats	22	49	29
Republicans	5	48	47
West Germany			
Social Democrats	51	39	10
Free Democrats	19	58	23
Christian Democrats	4	37	59

SOURCE: Giacomo Sani and Giovanni Sartori, in *Western European Party Systems,* ed., Hans Dadler (Beverly Hills, Calif.: Sage Publications, 1983), pp. 322–333. Reprinted with permission.

Changing Values?   Europeans, Japanese, and Americans live in rich countries. There is poverty, to be sure, but European and American standards of living far outstrip those of other regions of the globe. This abundance has led some people to speculate that if we tend to want most whatever is in short supply, we are entering the ''postmaterialist''

TABLE 5.12 Rating Governmental Responsibility (%)

	United States	United Kingdom	West Germany
Fighting pollution	56	69	73
Fighting crime	53	56	78
Providing good medical care	42	74	63
Providing good education	47	68	55
Looking after old people	41	58	51
Guaranteeing jobs	34	55	60
Providing adequate housing	25	60	39
Equal rights for minorities	33	24	20
Reducing income inequality	13	19	27
Equal rights for sexes	24	19	27
Average	**37**	**51**	**49**

SOURCE: Copyright © 1983 by St. Martin's Press, Inc. From *Comparative Public Policy* by Arnold Heidenheimer, Hugh Heclo and Carolyn Teich Adams. Reprinted by permission of St. Martin's Press, Incorporated.

age, in which self-actualization (beautiful cities, environmental concern, control of work conditions, appreciation of community) is replacing concern about meeting material needs.[35]

The "new politics," an expression used in a similar way, connotes the same sort of commitment, as in the Greens of West Germany. There is some evidence that the material-postmaterial split is increasing in importance, but the "age of Aquarius" is not yet upon us (see Table 5.13). As an example of what these somewhat abstract categories mean, materialists are less likely than postmaterialists to believe that it is very important for the government to reduce income inequalities, to be inclined toward political protest, and to be highly ideological in their thinking about politics.[37]

Postmaterialists select the most left-leaning party; materialists opt for the right. Since most people accept some notions from each value system and are thus in the middle, it is unlikely that political parties will do very well running on a pure postmaterialist theme. In proportional representation countries, such as in West Germany, where the Greens have won a handful of seats, the postmaterialist parties can be expected to take their places among the fringes and thus to have a modicum of political influence. Nevertheless, in all countries, the center is where the votes are, and that is where parties concentrate their efforts.

Rhetoric and Policy

If European political parties are more ideologically distinguishable than American ones, does it follow that there is a more clearly discernible change in policy? Arguments can be made both for and against this proposition. Margaret Thatcher's election in England and François Mitterand's election in France seem to prove that changing parties mean changing policies.

Thatcher, a staunch Tory (Conservative), wanted to reverse the course of British economic history by denationalizing most of the industries that the Labour party had

TABLE 5.13 Trends in Material and Postmaterial Values (percentage of the population)

	1970	1984
France		
Material	38	36
Mixed	51	51
Postmaterial	11	12
United Kingdom		
Material	36	24
Mixed	56	59
Postmaterial	8	17
United States		
Material	35	21
Mixed	55	63
Postmaterial	10	16
West Germany		
Material	46	23
Mixed	44	58
Postmaterial	11	20

SOURCE: Russell J. Dalton, *Citizen Politics in Western Democracies* (Chatham, N.J.: Chatham House Publishers, 1988), pp. 84–85. Reprinted with permission.

nationalized after World War II. Mitterand wanted to extend nationalization to private industry in France. Both accomplished a portion of their goals; both compromised and backed away from more extreme policy changes. Given their less disparate policymaking apparatus (neither has much of the American notion of separation of power), it would be unusual if little happened.

Richard Rose observes that in England, while parties could deliver on their promises, the parties were narrowing their differences. By the time Prime Minister Thatcher stood for her second election, even with her strongly conservative rhetoric, she chose a moderate course. Rose notes:

> Forced to choose between reasserting her earlier Adversary convictions or defending the government's Consensus record in maintaining welfare state expenditure, she chose the latter. . . . Faced with a choice between reasserting free market rhetoric, consistent with her convictions but unpopular with the electorate, or embracing welfare state programmes that were popular with the electorate and sustained by the Conservative government expenditure, Mrs. Thatcher went for the electoral Consensus.[38]

Proponents of democracy as a *responsive* system will applaud Thatcher's decision to accept a moderate rather than a radical program, especially since her decision to do so was based on her perceptions of popular belief.

Mitterand's Socialist government was equally pragmatic. After a blazing start during which the new Socialist government nationalized 11 industrial sectors and the banks, unemployment and inflation forced new austerity, a more pragmatic policy, and a shift in priorities away from central planning or regulation. Although Mitterand himself was not very interested in ideology, the Socialist party manifesto was developed largely by the Marxist faction within the party. The Socialists prided themselves as being a genuine party of the left, as opposed to the other Social Democratic parties in Europe, which are decidedly more centrist.

But after several years, Mitterand's government allowed the market to destroy inefficient businesses, continued to sell arms around the world, minimizing the portions of its manifesto giving aid to revolutionary movements in Latin America and Africa. "Nationalized" businesses were told to make a profit or go under, and their management was unchanged. Even so, by 1983, French socialism embarked on an austerity plan that eliminated unnecessary jobs in both the public and private sector, reduced budgets, ignored the once sacred commitment to the 35-hour workweek, and embarked on a program to stimulate private investment and to provide more incentives for economic expansion. The exposure of the French government's deep involvement in sinking a Greenpeace ship off New Zealand, the failed efforts to reign in church-run schools (regarded as too inegalitarian by the Socialists), and other examples of ineptitude probably contributed to the return of an anti-Socialist majority to the Chamber of Deputies in 1985.

Are any choices meaningful? These two examples do not suggest that all partisan rhetoric is consciously designed to deceive. Rather, they imply that all politics in open systems is the art of the possible. From both the right (United Kingdom, United States) and the left (France), the lesson of compromise—especially when politicians believe voters have strong preferences—is apparent.

We conclude with a summary of the modes of government for the 38 democracies in the world in 1989 (Table 5.14). In the 1990s, the list may come to include these countries, which have installed but not yet solidified democratic rule or have only recently become independent:

Argentina	Nauru
Bolivia	Peru
Brazil	St. Christopher & Nevis
Dominica	St. Lucia
Honduras	St. Vincent & the Grenadines
Kiribati	Tuvalu
Mauritius	

It may also lose a few: Fiji was a functioning democracy until a 1987 coup.

FOR FURTHER CONSIDERATION

1. Compare and contrast how candidates are selected in England, Japan, Italy, and the United States?
2. Why should you care about New Hampshire?
3. Does the majority elect the American president? Why or why not?
4. Explain the role of the media in American elections. How is that different from the role of the media in countries such as West Germany and Great Britain?

TABLE 5.14 Democracies of the World, 1989

| | | Lower House Members† | | | |
	Head of Government*	Election	Term	System of Government‡	Economy§
Australia	PM selected by parl.	By majority	Diss.	Federal	Capitalist
Austria	PM selected by parl.	By prop. rep.	Diss.	Unitary	Mixed capitalist
Bahamas	PM selected by parl.	By plurality	Diss.	Unitary	Capitalist-statist
Barbados	PM selected by parl.	By plurality	Diss.	Unitary	Capitalist
Belgium	PM selected by parl.	By prop. rep.	Fixed	Unitary	Capitalist
Botswana	PM selected by parl.	By plurality	Diss.	Unitary	Capitalist
Canada	PM selected by parl.	By plurality	Fixed	Federal	Capitalist
Colombia	Pres. elected by plurality	By prop. rep.	Fixed	Unitary	Capitalist
Costa Rica	Pres. elected by plurality	By prop. rep.	Fixed	Unitary	Capitalist
Cyprus	Pres. elected by majority	By prop. rep.	Diss.	Unitary	Capitalist
Denmark	PM selected by parl.	By prop. rep.	Diss.	Unitary	Mixed capitalist
Dominican Republic	Pres. elected by plurality	By prop. rep.	Fixed	Unitary	Capitalist
Ecuador	Pres. elected by majority	By prop. rep.	Fixed	Unitary	Capitalist
Finland	PM selected by parl.	By prop. rep.	Diss.	Unitary	Mixed capitalist
France	Pres. elected by majority and PM selected by parl.	By majority	Diss.	Unitary	Mixed capitalist
Greece	PM selected by parl.	By prop. rep.	Diss.	Unitary	Mixed capitalist
Iceland	PM selected by parl.	By prop. rep.	Diss.	Unitary	Capitalist
India	PM selected by parl.	By plurality	Diss.	Federal and unitary	Capitalist-statist
Ireland	PM selected by parl.	By prop. rep.	Diss.	Unitary	Capitalist
Israel	PM selected by parl.	By prop. rep.	Diss.	Unitary	Mixed capitalist
Italy	PM selected by parl.	By prop. rep.	Diss.	Unitary	Capitalist-statist
Jamaica	PM selected by parl.	By plurality	Diss.	Unitary	Capitalist-statist
Japan	PM selected by parl.	By plurality	Diss.	Unitary	Capitalist
Luxembourg	PM selected by parl.	By prop. rep.	Diss.	Unitary	Capitalist
Netherlands	PM selected by parl.	By prop. rep.	Diss.	Unitary	Mixed capitalist
New Zealand	PM selected by parl.	By plurality	Diss.	Unitary	Mixed capitalist
Norway	PM selected by parl.	By prop. rep.	Fixed	Unitary	Mixed capitalist
Papua New Guinea	PM selected by parl.	By plurality	Diss.	Unitary	Capitalist
Portugal	PM selected by parl.	By prop. rep.	Diss.	Unitary	Mixed capitalist
Solomon Islands	PM selected by parl.	By prop. rep.	Diss.	Unitary	Capitalist
Spain	PM selected by parl.	By prop. rep.	Diss.	Unitary	Capitalist
Sweden	PM selected by parl.	By prop. rep.	Diss.	Unitary	Mixed capitalist
Switzerland	PM selected by parl.	By prop. rep.	Fixed	Federal	Capitalist
Trinidad & Tobago	PM selected by parl.	By plurality	Diss.	Unitary	Capitalist-statist
United Kingdom	PM selected by parl.	By plurality	Diss.	Unitary	Mixed capitalist
United States	Pres. elected by plurality	By plurality	Fixed	Federal	Capitalist
Venezuela	Pres. elected by plurality	By prop. rep.	Fixed	Unitary	Capitalist-statist
West Germany	PM selected by parl.	By prop. rep. and majority	Diss.	Federal	Capitalist

*PM = prime minister; parl. = parliament; pres. = president.

†Prop. rep. = proportional representation; diss. = can be dissolved and elections held at any time.

‡Federal = power divided between state and national government; unitary = power concentrated in national government.

§Capitalist-statist = substantial government ownership of production; mixed capitalist = substantial government intervention, especially in the provision of welfare and social services.

For the More Adventurous

1. Outline the major characteristics of the Italian party system. What are the advantages and disadvantages of such a system? Is it "democratic"? Is Italy "really" a polyarchy? Or do you agree that, as one sympathetic observer maintains, "If Italy is a strong democracy but nevertheless fails to conform to what our theories specify as the requisite conditions of democracy . . . it may mean . . . that we need to revise or expand our theories of the democratic state."?[39]

2. List the steps a candidate must take to become a party's presidential nominee in the United States. Repeat the process for the British Labour or Conservative party's rules for becoming party leader, and hence prime minister or leader of the opposition. Work up a brief biography of Ronald Reagan, George Bush, Margaret Thatcher, and Neil Kinnock.

3. Compare a multiparty system to a two-party system. Does a multiparty system necessarily mean that more diverse views are represented? Why or why not? Now compare a *government* formed by multiparty coalition with that formed by a majority (a two-party system). In which, if either, does "the majority" (or a plurality at least) rule? Compare legislative coalitions in Israel and Denmark.

4. Suggest possible changes in the United States party system to change the location of party responsiveness. List the groups toward which parties are *currently* responsive. Explain how your proposals would shift responsiveness. Is responsiveness a goal toward which the parties should strive?

NOTES

1. Walter Dean Burnham, "The Onward March of Party Decomposition," in *Controversies in American Voting Behavior,* ed. Richard G. Niemi and Herbert F. Weisberg (New York: Freeman, 1976), p. 431.

2. Quoted in Simone Oudot and David L. Gobert, *La France: Culture, Economie, Commerce* (Boston: Houghton Mifflin, 1984), p. 1.

3. Pierre Daninos, *Les carnets du major Thompson* (Paris: Livre de Poche, 1973).

4. Leon Epstein, *Political Parties in Western Democracies* (New York: Praeger, 1980), p. 72.

5. See Thomas R. Dye and Harmon Zeigler, *The Irony of Democracy,* 7th ed. (Pacific Grove, Calif.: Brooks/Cole, 1987), p. 176.

6. Epstein, *Political Parties,* p. 201–202.

7. Roberto Michels, *Political Parties* (New York: Free Press, 1962), p. 70.

8. Frederic Spotts and Theodore Wieser, *Italy: A Difficult Democracy* (Cambridge: Cambridge University Press, 1986), p. 5.

9. Ibid., p. 6.

10. Samuel H. Barnes, *Representation in Italy* (Chicago: University of Chicago Press, 1977), p. 148.

11. Joseph La Palombara, *Democracy, Italian-Style* (New Haven, Conn.: Yale University Press, 1987), p. 216.

12. Austin Ranney, "Candidate Selection," in David Butler, Howard R. Penniman, and Austin Ranney, *Democracy at the Polls* (Washington, D.C.: American Enterprise Institute, 1981), p. 105.

13. Austin Ranney, *Curing the Mischiefs of Faction* (Berkeley: University of California Press, 1975), p. 206.

14. Leon Epstein, *Political Parties in the American Mold* (Madison: University of Wisconsin Press, 1986), p. 99.

15. William C. Adams "As New Hampshire Goes . . .," in Gary R. Orren and Nelson W. Polsby, eds., *Media and Momentum* (Chatham N.J.: Chatham House, 1988), p. 55.

16. Michael J. Lipton, "Executive TV Guide Poll: Campaign 1988 and TV," *TV Guide,* January 23, 1988, pp. 3–7.

17. Arend Lijphart, *Democracies* (New Haven, Conn.: Yale University Press, 1984), p. 120.

18. T. J. Pempel, *Policy and Politics in Japan* (Philadelphia: Temple University Press, 1982), pp. 38–39.

19. In Ireland, it is used for parliamentary by-elections (to fill vacancies) and for the election of the president, a ceremonial position.

20. The *D'Hondt formula* is used in Europe except for Scandinavia and Italy; the *Saint-Lague* method is used in Scandinavia; and the *single transferable vote* is used in Ireland and in the Australian Senate. Voters rank individual candidates; votes not needed for candidates who have already made the quota are transferred to the next candidate until the seats are filled. The *largest remainder* scheme assigns a quota of votes, which party lists must achieve in order to be guaranteed a seat. The number of votes cast is divided into the number of seats to fill; parties failing to meet the quota are assigned "remainders." For example, if the quota is 5,000 and party A gets 8,200 votes, its remainder is 3,200 votes. If party B gets 6,100 votes, its remainder is 1,100. If party C gets only 3,000 votes, its remainder is 3,000; if party D gets 2,700, it too keeps all the votes as a remainder. Since two seats were won without remainders, two seats must still be allocated. Party A gets another one, since it has the largest remainder. But party B, which finished second, does not, since its remainder is less than that of party C. Party C, which finished third (with only about half as many votes as party B), gets the other vote. Italy uses this system.

21. Lijphart, *Democracies,* pp. 160–163.

22. Epstein, *Political Parties in the American Mold* p. 70.

23. R. Kent Weaver, "Are Parliamentary Systems Better?" in *Comparative Politics, 87/88,* ed. Christian Soe (Guildford, Conn.: Dushkin, 1987), p. 130.

24. Thomas R. Dye and Harmon Ziegler, *American Politics in the Media Age* (Belmont, Calif.: Brooks/Cole, 1981), p. 162.

25. Russell J. Dalton, *Citizen Politics in Western Democracies* (Chatham, N.J.: Chatham House, 1988), p. 167.

26. G. Bingham Powell, Jr., "American Turnout in Comparative Perspective," *American Political Science Review 80* (March 1986): 26.

27. Ibid., 38.

28. Ivor Crewe, "Electoral Participation," in *Democracy at the Polls,* ed. David Butler (Washington, D.C.: American Enterprise Association, 1981), p. 232.

29. Dalton, *Citizen Politics,* p. 40.

30. Powell, "American Turnout," p. 36.

31. David P. Conradt, *The German Polity* (White Plains, N.Y.: Longman, 1986), p. 42.

32. Dalton, *Citizen Politics,* p. 5.

33. Ibid., p. 187.

34. William Safran, *The French Polity* (White Plains, N.Y.: Longman, 1985), p. 86.

35. Samuel H. Barnes and Max Kaase, eds., *Political Action* (Newbury Park, Calif.: Sage, 1979), p. 220.

36. Ronald Inglehart and Hans D. Klingemann, "Ideological Conceptualization and Value Priorities," in ibid., pp. 203–214.

37. Hans D. Klingemann, "Ideological Conceptualization and Political Action," and Ronald Inglehart, "Value Priorities and Socioeconomic Change," in ibid., pp. 279–342.

38. Richard Rose, *Do Parties Make a Difference?* (Chatham, N.J.: Chatham House, 1984), p. 167.
39. Joseph La Palombara, *Democracy Italian Style,* p. 3.

FOR FURTHER READING

Aberbach, Joel D., and Bert A. Rockman. *The Administrative State in Industrialized Democracies.* Washington, D.C.: American Political Science Association, 1985.

Ambler, John S., ed. *The French Socialist Experiment.* Philadelphia: Institute for the Study of Human Issues, 1985.

Conradt, David P. *The German Polity.* White Plains, N.Y.: Longman, 1986.

Cooper, Barry, Allan Kornberg, and William Mishler, eds. *The Resurgence of Conservatism in Anglo-American Democracies.* Durham, N.C.: Duke University Press, 1988. The 1980s in Canada, the United States, and the United Kingdom.

Crotty, William. *Comparative Political Parties.* Washington, D.C.: American Political Science Association, 1985.

Dalton, Russell J. *Citizen Politics in Western Democracies.* Chatham, N.J.: Chatham House, 1988.

Dodd, Lawrence C. *Coalitions in Parliamentary Government.* Princeton, N.J.: Princeton University Press, 1976.

Epstein, Leon. *Political Parties in the American Mold.* Madison: University of Wisconsin Press, 1986.

————. *Political Parties in Western Democracies.* New York: Praeger, 1980. The best book comparing parties in various industrial democracies.

Hall, Peter. *Governing the Economy.* Oxford: Polity Press, 1986. England and France compared, brilliantly.

Heidenheimer, Arnold J., Hugh Heclo, and Carolyn Teich Adams. *Comparative Public Policy.* New York: St. Martin's Press, 1983.

Kavanagh, Dennis. *Thatcherism and British Politics.* Oxford: Oxford University Press, 1987.

La Palombara, Joseph. *Democracy, Italian-Style.* New Haven, Conn.: Yale University Press, 1987. Well received by the "intelligent layman" (notably Gore Vidal), but less so by the *American Political Science Review,* La Palombara writes with economy and the benefit of experience.

Lynn, Jonathan, and Anthony Jay. *Yes, Prime Minister.* Boston: Salem House, 1986. The companion to the popular BBC television series, which, while explaining why British government cannot work, persuaded Margaret Thatcher to appear. (Her solution: "Fire all economists!") Sir Humphrey Gordon, cabinet secretary, expressed the civil service's contempt for politicians: "Lunched with [Permanent Treasury Secretary] Appelby. Appelby was concerned because our new Prime Minister wishes to cut either taxes or public expenditure. This should be resisted. Politicians are like children—you can't just give them what they want, it only encourages them."

Pempel, T. J. *Policy and Politics in Japan.* Philadelphia: Temple University Press, 1982.

Reischauer, Edwin O. *The Japanese Today.* Cambridge: Belknap Press of Harvard University, 1988. Wise reflections on the Japanese culture.

Rose, Richard. *Do Parties Make a Difference?* Chatham, N.J.: Chatham House, 1984.

Safran, William. *The French Polity.* White Plains, N.Y.: Longman, 1985.

CHAPTER 6

Interest Groups:
Threats to Democracy?

Reprinted by permission: Tribune Media Services.

Although many European political parties are based organizationally on a surrogate for class (as when labor or socialist parties are supported financially by unions), political parties are technically a form of geographic representation. To augment a somewhat artificial basis of representation, interest groups have become a major party of the policy process in democracies, especially the complex industrial democracies. This mode of representation is sometimes called *functional representation* because it is based on a function (occupation) rather than a locality.

Any group that tries to exert influence on government is an interest group. The interest represented may be relatively narrow, as is the case with occupational and single-issue groups, or it may be more expansively conceived, as is true of Common Cause or the European "Green" political organizations.

Less narrowly focused interest groups are often described as *public interest groups*. The distinction between public and private interest groups is an arbitrary one most often used in the United States, where interest groups suffer a stigma, rather in Europe or Japan, where interest groups are often incorporated into the policymaking process. A public interest group is one that seeks a public good, the achievement of which will not selectively and materially benefit the members or activists of the organization. This definition leaves substantial room for interpretation by the group's members. A collective good is a policy that presumably benefits all people, whether or not they are in the group. Obvious examples are clean air and world peace. The problem is that while everybody wants these things, not everybody is willing to pay the cost. Clean air may be a high priority, but so is industrial development. Manufacturers who oppose stringent air pollution standards argue that their position is based on a different concept of the public interest from that held by clean-air activists. What is a public good to one group may be a private good to another.

BENEFITS THROUGH GROUPS

Economists have long employed the distinction between collective and *selective* goods. When a city purifies its water, it is providing a collective good, for all who use the city water supply benefit equally. It makes no difference whether a group is merely "categoric" (with little of significance in common) or has common interests or shared attitudes; there can be no discrimination among water users. By contrast, if a city distributed home purification devices to some but not all water users, those devices would be *selective*. Not all members of the water-using public would benefit equally from the good in question.

Whenever we differentiate collective from selective goods, it is essential to identify the group to which we refer, for the universality of benefit is determined by the particular set of people in question. Assume that a categoric group is all college students in the United States. Suppose that, taking its cue from most industrial democracies, Congress enacted a law providing a $300-per-month cost-of-living allowance to all college students. Such a stipend would be a collective good for students as a categoric group. However, if one were to define the categoric group as all persons of college age, the monthly allowance would become a selective benefit. Furthermore, when a collective good is made available in equal amounts to all persons, it is not necessarily valued equally by all recipients. The $300 stipend may be of less value to students from wealthy families than to those who are less well off.

The mere existence of a joint interest in a collective good (shared attitudes) is not a sufficient condition for rational people to unite in organized group activity or for an individual to join an existing group unless the potential group is very small. The argument rests squarely on the same rationality assumptions so critical for individualist social contract theory. The rational person who does pool resources in the pluralist scheme to gain an advantage in policy choice will be a "free rider." Such a person will realize that if others organize, the value added to the group by his or her membership will be insignificant. Moreover, since the good in question is collective (since policy choices ratified by public bodies are collective), this person will benefit from an organized group's acquisition of the good regardless of participation in the process by which it was obtained.

Since group membership is never without a price for the individual, no rational person will incur the costs of organizational participation unless the anticipated payoff resulting from such participation is appreciably higher than the probable payoff resulting from nonparticipation and that payoff exceeds the costs of group membership.

These arguments are in keeping with what we know about people's interest in politics. Beyond the stratum of the politically active and aware, most people are less interested in politics than in their everyday life; when the two coalesce, political activity may occur, only to cease when the problem recedes.

THE PUBLIC VIEW

When asked whether particular interest groups have too much power, American respondents revealed as much about themselves as about interest groups (see Table 6.1). Your belief as to whether a group is "too powerful" is a pretty good indicator of your feel-

TABLE 6.1 Percentage of People Saying a Group Has "Too Much" or "Too Little" Power

	Too Much	Too Little
Labor unions	57	9
Business and industry organizations	51	4
Doctors' organizations	44	6
Real estate operators	31	4
Military groups	30	11
Women's rights organizations	23	25
Church groups	22	29
Environmental groups	15	37
College organizations	14	16
Consumer groups	12	34
Veterans' groups	7	38
Farmers' groups	6	60
Senior citizens' groups	4	58

SOURCE: Thomas R. Dye and Harmon Zeigler, *American Politics in the Media Age,* second edition (Monterey, Calif.: Brooks/Cole, 1986), p. 117. Reprinted with permission.

ings about the group. People dislike labor unions but are crazy about senior citizens' groups. Labor's political decline is matched by the growing influence of lobbies for the elderly.

THE POLITICAL SCIENCE VIEW

The founders of America believed that interest groups were evil but unavoidable. James Madison condemned organized groups most severely. He described factions as actuated by some common impulse of passion, interest adverse to the rights of citizens, or the permanent and aggregate interests of the community.[1] Madison believed that the impulse to organize such groups, bad as they were, was rooted in human nature. It was to cure the mischiefs of faction that Madison constructed the system of checks and balances in national government as well as a federal relationship between national and state governments.

Despite the hazards Madison pointed out, the First Amendment guaranteed the rights of citizens to assemble peaceably and to petition the government for redress of grievances. The founders believed that groups could be dangerous but that the benefits of freedom of association overrode that danger.

Madison's belief that interest groups are inevitable is now the prevailing view of political scientists. However, rather than a necessary evil to be controlled, organized groups are today often regarded as an essential component of a healthy democracy: voluntary associations are the prime means by which the individual is able to relate effectively and meaningfully to the political system. As we saw, the pluralist (generally American) and corporatist (generally European) modes of anti-Madisonian thought are quite different. Americans usually regard groups as part of a demand-making process, a sort of Darwinian survival of the fittest, with public policy reflecting the balance of group strength; Europeans carry the notion of groups as healthy for democracy one step further and, in corporatist theory, include them in both the making and implementation of policy.

INTEREST GROUPS AND PLURALISM

Interest groups serve as the linchpin of pluralist theory. They are agents of connection: at the very core of pluralist theory is belief that individuals can best convey their needs and desires to the government through concerted group activity. In a large, complex society, one stands little chance of being heard, much less being able to affect the governmental decision-making process, but interest groups are channels through which people realize the democratic ideal of legitimate and satisfying interaction with government.

Proponents see three intertwined ideas as the bedrock of interest group pluralism:

1. Membership in organizations is widespread and thus broadly represents all individual interests.
2. Organized groups efficiently translate members' expectations into political de-

mands; nothing is lost in the translation, and members gain a great deal by presenting demands through a representative association.

3. Although interest groups are not always and uniformly successful, each group, whatever its demands, has equal access to the political resources necessary for success.

THE BIAS OF THE CLASS–INTEREST GROUP SYSTEM

Although some interest groups are more powerful than others, a more fundamental inequality exists between members of groups and nonmembers. The idea that groups are the primary means by which people relate to government implies that this opportunity is open to everyone. Although a majority of people belong to at least one organization, membership is in fact greatest among the professional and managerial classes and among college-educated, high-income people. This class bias is also expressed by the types of organizations people join. Unions (membership in which is frequently not voluntary) recruit members from among the more prosperous workers, whereas business associations recruit from among the more successful members of the business community.

Many poor people and members of minority groups do not have the time, money, interest, or skills to benefit from the organized interest group system. Sociologist Anthony Oberschall, writing of black organizations, reached a conclusion that applies equally well to other organizations that attempt to speak for the downtrodden:

> The main support within the black community, in terms of staff, membership, and resources . . . , came from the black middle class. . . . The single most important failure of the middle-class black and civil rights organizations was their failure to mobilize the lower-class black community. . . . The lower-class segment of the black population remained by and large unorganized and unmobilized.[2]

Given the propensity of the well-to-do to join organizations, it is only natural that much of the representing done by interest groups is for business interests, illustrated in Table 6.2. Schlozman concludes:

> When we consider the substantial portion of the pressure system consisting of groups organized about economic roles, the class bias of the Washington pressure system is unambiguous. The professionals and managers . . . constitute at most 16 percent of American adults; they are represented by 88 percent of the economic organizations.[3]

Still, lobbying victories do not always go to the haves. The federal government has traditionally tried to protect the downtrodden and underrepresented. Since such people are represented by lobbyists and organizations of social status equal to that of the business organizations, the task is eased. Also, business and professional associations do not necessarily oppose benevolence toward the less fortunate: large corporations, for example, support affirmative action. In many other cases, however, business associations are so busy fighting among themselves that they hardly notice the plight of others.

The corporatist systems of other countries are more deliberately exclusive. Since

TABLE 6.2 The Washington Lobbying Community

	Groups Having Their Own Washington Offices (%)	All Groups Having Washington Representation (%)
Corporations	20.7	45.7
Trade associations	30.6	17.8
Foreign commerce and corporations	0.6	6.5
Professional associations	14.8	6.8
Labor unions	3.3	1.7
Public interest	8.7	4.1
Civil rights/minority	1.7	1.3
Elderly/gays/women	2.5	1.1
Governments	1.4	4.2
Foreign groups	1.2	2.0
Other/unknown	13.2	8.2

SOURCE: Kay Lehman Scholzman, "What Accent for the Heavenly Chorus? Political Equality and the American Pressure Systems," *Journal of Politics, 46,* 4, November 1984, p. 1102. Reprinted with permission.

the primary interest of corporatist decision making is economic wages or income policies, international trade balances, deficits, and the like, only groups that might influence such policies are invited to participate. For example, in Austria, an informal collaboration between unions and business was institutionalized in 1957 as the Joint Commission on Prices and Wages. Labor representation to the commission is from the Austrian Federation of Trade Unions and from the Chambers of Labor. The Federal Chamber of Business and the Conference of Presidents of Chambers of Agriculture represent business. The Austrian government merely provides the structure for interest group bargaining and ratifies the decisions reached by the participating interest groups.

The bias of the interest group system in the United States is seen in political action committees (PACs), whose rapid growth is due largely to an increase in corporate PACs and trade associations.

POLITICAL ACTION COMMITTEES

The American political action committees, still relatively new, have created an international sensation by spending seemingly unlimited amounts of money for innumerable causes. Like primary elections, they are the United States' special contribution to political life.

Organized interest groups swarm all over Capitol Hill. Many national organizations have state or local chapters (such as the major labor and business lobbies, the National Rifle Association, and Common Cause), but their focus is on national policy.

As parties have declined in their ability to organize and finance campaigns, interest groups have moved rapidly to fill the gap. Interest group spending increased especially after the passage of the Federal Election Campaign Act in 1974. This act permitted

TABLE 6.3 PAC Funds, 1986 (millions of dollars)

	Money Raised	Money Spent	Contributions to Candidates
Business/corporate	82	79	49 (59%)
Labor	66	58	31 (47%)
Ideological	115	115	19 (29%)
Trade associations	76	73	34 (45%)

SOURCE: Federal Election Commission, Washington, D.C., December 1987 (mimeograph).

groups to form political action committees to collect contributions from people, industries, and unions and make campaign contributions to candidates (see Table 6.3). As parties have declined in their ability to organize and finance campaigns, interest groups have moved rapidly to fill the gap. Political action committees (PACs) are organizations formed under the 1974 election law to collect campaign contributions in the name of some group or cause for disbursement to political candidates.

PACs are growing in both number and influence. The first PACs were created by organized labor in response to a prohibition on union treasury money being used in elections. Unions, to escape the restriction, established separate accounting schemes, the most prominent being the AFL-CIO Committee on Political Education. Legally separate, it routinely contributed to Democratic candidates. Corporations, like labor unions prohibited from making direct contributions, held back from following labor's lead. Corporations had not been able to give money since 1907, whereas the legislation barring unions from contributing was not passed until 1947. But the various reform acts of the 1970s created identical opportunities for corporations, and they took them. Once begun, the PACs could not be turned back. The campaign reform laws themselves have made PACs a rational option.

In 1974, there were about 600 PACs, of which 89 were corporate PACs and 201 labor PACs. The "ideological PACs," the various right- and left-wing coalitions, had not yet appeared. By 1986, the number of PACs had surpassed 4,000. Since labor was already organized around PACs, the increase of labor PACs was modest, to 386. However, corporate PACs burgeoned to more than 1,700, and over 1,000 ideological PACs had been born. Labor, once the dominant participant, had been reduced to a minor influence.

Business PACs are sometimes formed by a single corporation, such as Boeing or American Telephone and Telegraph. Many corporations also cooperate in industrywide trade associations, such as the National Association of Manufacturers. Corporate PACs contribute smaller amounts than associations do. But since corporations can both establish their own PAC and simultaneously give to an association PAC, the impact is substantial. In 1986, corporate PACs were the biggest spenders, with $49 million going to the congressional campaign. However, the biggest spender among corporate PACs, AT&T, gave only $799,760. Although labor gave less, $31 million, its most generous contributor, the National Education Association, gave $2 million.

But nobody really believes that all expenses are reported. The true figure, about $1.8 billion, exceeds the sum of all reported expenses. Also, there are ways of getting money to legislators without listing them as contributions. One of the easiest is honoraria. In 1985–1986, the 10 leading defense contractors paid about $200,000 in honoraria for speeches, much of it to representatives serving on defense-related committees.

Some of the PACs operate almost exclusively at the broadest level, specializing in mass mailings. One of the most conspicuous of these is the National Conservative Political Action Committee, which was catapulted into the headlines by its claim to have defeated a half dozen liberal Democrats with its extensive negative advertising campaign. Others operate as the financial arm of established organizations, such as the American Medical Association's AMPAC.

PACs are the leading source of campaign money after individual contributions; however, since individual contributions are small and tend to get lost in the shuffle, the PAC contributions have more visibility. In 1986, PAC contributions were up about one-third from election year of 1984. PAC contributions accounted for one-third of the money spent in elections to the House and 21 percent of the money spent in Senate elections. The march of the PACs seems irreversible (see Table 6.4).

But the overall statistics do not reveal the real magnitude of PAC influence. In 1986, fully 194 members of the House of Representatives received at least half of their campaign funds from PACs; in 1978, only 63 did so. The flow of cash is so munificent that House candidates finished the campaign with a surplus of about $49 million. The money can be salted away for future campaigns, and if a representative was in office on January 8, 1980, the money can be legally converted to personal use. Just how big this slush fund can be is shown by the list of senators who have received more than $1 million from PACs since 1972 (see Table 6.5). Also, congressional incumbents have found PACs a ready source of money for campaign fund-raising dinners, generally at about $500 a plate. Although lobbyists feel they are being exploited, they fear reprisal if they decline. Thus another source of money becomes the captive of the PACs.

Where the Money Goes

Labor raises and spends less for its PACs than business does, and virtually all of its money goes to Democrats. Business and corporate PACs give about half of their contributions to Democrats and half to Republicans, realizing that since incumbents can be

TABLE 6.4 Growth among PACs

	Percent of Total Receipts from PACs	Number of PACs
1972	14	
1974	16	608
1976	20	1,146
1978	20	1,653
1980	26	2,551
1982	27	3,371
1984	29	4,009
1986	28	4,092

Federal Election Commission, Washington, D.C., 1987 (mimeograph).

TABLE 6.5 Top 10 Recipients of PAC Money

	Total Received	Percent from PACs
Senate		
1. Cranston (D.-Calif.)	$1,373,466	12
2. Symms (D.-Idaho)	$1,371,618	37
3. Bond (R.-Mo.)	$1,334,222	25
4. Specter (R.-Pa.)	$1,313,222	21
5. Daschle (D.-S.Dak.)	$1,205,400	35
House		
1. Wright (D.-Tex.)	$667,620	40
2. Gibbons (D.-Fla.)	$571,019	62
3. Gray (R.-Pa.)	$457,131	69
4. Michel (R.-Ill.)	$463,111	66
5. Gephardt (D.-Mo.)	$455,073	50

SOURCE: Federal Election Commission, Washington, D.C., December 1987 (mimeograph).

expected to win about 90 percent of the time, contributing to challengers is often point-less. Since the Democrats have held a majority of the seats in the House of Represen-tatives and since 80 percent of PAC money goes to incumbents, Democrats do rather well. Given the certainty of almost all of the labor PAC money and about half of the business and corporate PAC money, Democratic campaigns are not lacking in financial support. Most PACs are purely pragmatic: incumbents win, and Democrats have domi-nated Congress. Hence those who run under the banner of the ''party of the little man'' do quite well. The Senate PAC ''millionaires' club'' is half Democratic (see Table 6.5).

Ideological PACs spend most of their money in the congressional elections. They prefer to develop candidate training and recruitment schools, media consulting, polling, and advertising by themselves rather than giving the money to candidates, who would then presumably perform some of these functions. The National Conservative Political Action Committee is far more active in these efforts than any of its liberal counterparts.

One would expect the top money raisers (Table 6.6) to be also the top money spenders. This is not true, however, of the ideological PACs. None of the top five ideological raisers is among the top spenders. As we have noted, these PACs are more ambitious than the others; they engage in long-range activities, doing many of the things that parties once did. So even though they spend some money during an election, they spend more in programs addressed to long-range change.

What the Money Buys

What does the money buy? Money is more important for challengers than for incum-bents. Challengers lack name familiarity and, of course, have not been able to build a record of personal service and favors. Money rarely guarantees that an incumbent will be defeated, and PACs cannot therefore claim to have been instruments in a particular electoral outcome, although they do. Box scores are regularly distributed through PAC

TABLE 6.6 Top Money Raisers, 1986

Corporate PACs	
1. American Telephone and Telegraph (AT&TPAC)	$1,820,939
2. Philip Morris Political Action Committee (PHIL-PAC)	$688,453
3. AMOCO PAC	$647,594
4. Bear, Stearns and Co.	$612,899
5. United Parcel Service (UPSPAC)	$567,328
Labor PACs	
1. Democratic Republican Independent Voter Education Committee (DRIVE) (Teamsters)	$4,389,458
2. National Education Association PAC	$3,196,697
3. United Auto Workers (UAW-PAC)	$3,054,003
4. Committee on Letter Carriers Political Education	$2,070,897
5. Machinist Nonpartisan Political League	$2,053,075
Ideological PACs	
1. National Congressional Club (Sen. Jessie Helms)	$15,364,881
2. Fund for America's Future	$9,373,056
3. National Conservative Political Action Committee	$9,319,550
4. National Committee to Preserve Social Security	$6,201,412
5. Campaign America	$3,347,312
Trade Associations	
1. Realtors Political Action Committee	$5,680,699
2. American Medical Association (AMPAC)	$4,961,408
3. National Rifle Association Political Victory Fund	$4,692,544
4. League of Conservative Voters	$3,776,005
5. Association of Trial Lawyers (ATLA)	$2,970,762

SOURCE: Federal Election Committee, Washington, D.C., December 1987 (mimeograph).

newsletters with impressive records of victory. In 1985, the National Rifle Association lay claim to a victory record of 95 percent.

But money does not buy elections. Although a certain minimum amount is needed to contest an election, large expeditures do not ensure success. Even in an age of media dominance and image making, shoddy merchandise cannot be prettily packaged and sold. Money can be spent on adjusting a candidate's image; consultants, pollsters, and makeup artists can be hired; but if the image is beyond salvation, money won't help. Two-thirds of all campaign money is spent on television, buying airtime.

For the PACs themselves, their money buys access. PACs purchase the right to a serious hearing. Washington politicians believe PACs are more powerful than they are, and in a city where image and reality are scrambled beyond recognition, the appearance of power is just about as good as the real thing. Thus money does buy the right to present a case—if not to a senator or to a representative, then to an influential staff member (regarded by many lobbyists to be a better bet anyway).

In a frantic and complex legislative agenda, PACs gain an advantage simply by being able to demand and get time to argue; if the argument can be presented on a first-name basis, so much the better. The money thus does not buy elections. However, since it does buy access, and since PACs are the largest source of money (individual contributions, taken together, exceed PAC contributions, but few individual contributions match a single PAC contribution), they are major players in the game of influence.

If money cannot buy elections, neither can it buy votes. PACs are usually auxiliary to the founding interest group. Lobbyists for the organization's cause have little if anything to do with decisions about the allocation of money. The PAC money comes from a variety of sources, most of them local, and in many cases decisions about who gets what are made by the parent group, not the PAC. PAC and interest group staffs do not work closely together. We do not suggest that PACs are being robbed by legislators who take their money and ignore their interests, merely that as in all things political, the reality is more complex than common sense might dictate.[4]

The Military–Industrial Complex

In his last speech as president, Dwight Eisenhower warned of the growing power of the military-industrial complex, the industries dependent on arms manufacturing and sales. Since Eisenhower's warning, the complex has grown to include not only defense contractors but also universities conducting defense-related research, private consulting firms, the aerospace industry, subcontractors who depend on larger contracts to filter down, labor unions, government bureaucracies, and veterans' organizations.

The Pentagon is the largest single purchaser of goods and services in the nation. Defense industries account for 10 percent of all U.S. manufacturing. In some states, such as California, defense-related employment is the largest single source of personal income. More than 25 percent of the nation's scientists and engineers are employed in defense-related industries.

President Reagan's target was for 8 percent of the gross national product to be spent on defense, a figure higher than during the Carter or Nixon administrations but just about the same as during Eisenhower's second term. In fact, the trend toward more military spending was begun before Reagan's election, and the most precipitous decline occurred while Nixon was president. Obviously, the military-industrial complex is indeed more complex than is described during election campaigns. Senator William Proxmire (D.-Wis.) expanded the definition to a "military-industrial-bureaucratic-trade association-labor union-intellectual-technical service club-political complex." Defense contractors occasionally reach the status of virtually a government-owned corporation. Of the top dozen defense contractors, General Electric and Boeing receive slightly less than half of their income from defense contracts, while others are totally dependent on them: 87 percent of the sales of General Dynamics, 81 percent of the sales of Lockheed, 79 percent of the sales of McDonnell-Douglas, and 92 percent of the sales of Grumman were to the Department of Defense.

The defense industry has climbed aboard the PAC bandwagon, with each company maintaining a Washington staff of 12 to 40 people. Their job is to win contracts. They do so both by being persuasive about the merits of the case and by spending money to support the election of those who are in a position to influence the awarding of contracts. More than 50 percent of the PAC contributions of defense contractors go to legislators, such as those on the House and Senate Armed Services Committees, who decide about B-2 bombers and MX missiles. Table 6.7 shows how serious defense contractors are about PACs. The impact of interest group–political party configuration

TABLE 6.7 PAC Expenditures by the Defense Industry

Company	Department of Defense Contract Rank	1986 Campaign Spending ($)
General Dynamics	1	363,408
General Electric	2	243,100
McDonnell-Douglas	3	223,500
Rockwell International	4	407,225
GM-Hughes	5	229,545
Lockheed	6	425,621
Raytheon	7	228,668
Boeing	8	255,725
United Technology	9	244,825
Grumman	10	252,889

SOURCE: Philip J. Simon, *Top Guns* (Washington: Common Cause, 1987), pp. 53–111. Reprinted with permission.

on public policy and the role of parties and groups in governing as well as electing will show variations as great as those seen here.

THE PROBLEM OF MISREPRESENTATION

Critics of pluralism assert that the very organizations said to provide a linkage between rulers and the ruled are themselves undemocratic. One such critic writes that "the voluntary associations or organizations which the early theorists of pluralism relied upon to sustain the individual against a unified omnipotent government have themselves become oligarchically governed hierarchies."[5] Individuals may provide the numerical strength for organizations, but what influence does each have on the leadership? Rarely do interest groups have any internal mechanisms for ensuring the accuracy with which they assess members' expectations. They are usually run by a small elite of officers and activists. Very few people attend meetings, vote in organizational elections, or make their influence felt within the organization.

We saw in Chapter 4 the role that iron triangles play in the political process. A key ingredient in the operation of iron triangles is compromise—adjusting group goals so that a consensus is achieved. Compromise is most easily accomplished when interest groups are willing to bargain. This happens when their goals do not involve fundamental values and emotions. Economic interest groups can give a little to get a little because their membership is rarely concerned about the details of legislation. When the membership is called on to support or oppose legislation—through letters, for example—this is done to set the stage for negotiation. Membership in such organizations is rarely based solely on commitment to the policy activities of the lobbyists. Since the selective benefits of these interest groups (technical information, conferences, social activities, charter flights, cheap insurance) are frequently the reasons for joining a group, lobbyists can wheel and deal without membership interference. The system is well understood by legislators, who find it valuable. Interestingly, media coverage of this arrangement is virtually nonexistent.

Interest group leaders argue that 1,000 voices have more impact than one. But suppose if, in the combining of voices, the message is so garbled that it is unintelligible? Misrepresentation is the clear message of Michels's "iron law of oligarchy," which states that even the most democratically inclined organizations gradually evolve into oligarchies. The very fact of organization implies oligarchy.[6]

Entrepreneurs, those hardy souls who are committed to a cause and willing to invest their own time and money in the creation of an interest group, have different interests and skills from people who join later. As entrepreneurs are replaced—as the organization develops a bureaucracy—the members in leadership positions will inevitably be more politically sensitive and attuned to the nuances of political dialogue.[7]

Since organizational leadership, like all political leadership, imputes attitudes to passive followers, it is likely to be inaccurate. Erroneous perception of members' values is not necessarily ameliorated by many of the devices used by interest groups to convey a democratic image. Most organizations recognize the need for some form of communication between leaders and followers. The largest and most affluent hold national conventions, supplemented by member surveys, some of which are haphazard but others of which are quite carefully undertaken. There are examples of organizational leadership abandoning a proposed plan of lobbying activity because of negative response to organizationally conducted member surveys. Such examples are rare and tend to occur in organizations lacking any sort of "selective" benefits.[8]

LEADERS AND FOLLOWERS

People join organizations for a variety of reasons, many of which are unrelated to political goals or lobbying. Since politics is not very important to most people, many organizations find that they can attract and maintain members by providing selective benefits—that is, benefits that can be obtained only through membership in the organization. Some doctors join the American Medical Association only to receive the *AMA Journal* and other technical publications; some veterans join the American Legion to gain access to a friendly place to drink; some retired people join the American Association of Retired Persons (AARP) to be eligible for discount prescriptions at pharmacies; and some people join the Sierra Club to qualify for wilderness expeditions it organizes. People also join organizations—from fraternal orders to chambers of commerce—for friendship, prestige, or connections. Of course, some joiners have a genuine political commitment; women, for example, may join the National Organization for Women because they wish to support its program.

People who join an organization for selective benefits are largely unconcerned with lobbying by their organization. Lobbyists are left relatively free to pursue their goals in the name of the organization. So, can AARP members who joined to get discounts on prescriptions be regarded as a political constitutency when "their" lobbyist testifies on a complex social security problem? If their lobbyist took a position contrary to that of a majority of members, would they instruct that lobbyist to stop? If the lobbyist did not stop, would they resign from the organization?

In the following examples, the disconnected quality of leadership is shown to be true even in groups where ideology predisposes members toward mass participation.

Leaders do not consciously exclude others from their decision; rather, the gap between leaders and followers is a natural consequence of the dynamics of organizations.

THE AMERICAN ASSOCIATION OF RETIRED PERSONS: HOW TO WIN THE BATTLE OF ORGANIZATIONS

The American Association of Retired Person's membership is at 27 million and growing. It expanded by 75 percent between 1984 and 1989 and now accounts for perhaps 15 percent of the adult population. By the turn of the 21st century, the elderly will make up half the population. At its present rate of growth, the AARP will represent half of them, or close to one-fourth of all adults.

It is not really an association of retired people, since the minimum age for membership is now 50. It should have a very hard time maintaining itself, since so many people cannot have much in common aside from age:

> In an increasingly fragmented political environment, big isn't necessarily better. . . .
> The AARP can't afford the stridency of smaller groups for fear of public backlash.
> Internally, the political and ideological diversity of its members has circumscribed its
> agenda.[9]

It thrives because it is a major marketing and service organization, providing its members with immediate, tangible, personal, desirable services. For a small annual membership fee, members are offered a full-service insurance company (it teams with Hartford Insurance to offer automobile, home, and life insurance and with Prudential for health insurance at very competitive rates; it ranks just behind Blue Cross as a supplement to Medicare). It operates the world's largest mail order pharmacy, with prices a fraction of retail at even chain discount drugstores. It operates a travel bureau with discounts on hotel rooms, rental cars, and so on. *Modern Maturity,* its semimonthly magazine, is catching up with *TV Guide* as the nation's highest-circulation periodical. With investments yielding about $2 billion a year, it plans to begin a credit union and offer a credit card to its members.

Like many organizations, AARP is the creation of a few people trying to make money. It was begun in 1958 but was moribund and tainted with the questionable linkage between its founders and various insurance plans, none of which was very good. In a storm of horrible publicity, it severed its relations with all existing insurance carriers and offered the right to market insurance up for bids. By 1983, it was in solid shape and began a massive membership drive.

Its approach to lobbying remains delicate. It has established a public policy institute and hired well-trained and experienced researchers to prepare analyses. Its agenda is still of greatest importance to retired persons. However, it has succeeded at forming coalitions with other organizations with similar agendas: it has opposed cuts in food stamps and has joined with public interest or consumer groups on matters of more general concern. But the AARP sometimes lobbies even when it strains relations with its business partners. For example, it fights for expanding Medicare coverage to catastrophic illnesses even though its insurance partners may lose money and hence oppose expansion.

Whether or not its members agree with AARP lobbying is hardly the point. In James Whitmore's TV commercials for the AARP, nothing is mentioned about legislation or public policy. It stays away from PACs and campaign contributions. But imagine what its membership would be if it did nothing but lobby and contribute to campaigns, like many less affluent organizations.

You may well wonder why anyone would spend so much time worrying about why people join organizations. But the implications of personal motives in joining an organization for pluralism are substantial. How can organizations be the link between members and government if people join to get selective benefits?

> We can see that a group's formal membership is not a valid indicator of its political support. . . . Formal membership indicates that the group is successful at selling selective incentives, not that it is politically popular. Indeed, since selective benefits have nothing whatever to do with the group's goals, there is no guarantee that any dues-payers even agree with those goals. What could be farther from pluralist preconceptions?[10]

THE MYTH OF THE MONOLITH

Interests are frequently at odds, especially when the economic focus of an organization is wide, as is true of, say, the Chamber of Commerce in the United States. The chamber might be biased toward smaller businesses, since it builds its organizational muscle around local chapters, whose membership is recruited by salaried salespeople (many organizations pay commissions to recruiters).

A classic area of internal squabbling is tax reform. In 1985, President Reagan and House Ways and Means chairman Daniel Rostenkowsi announced agreement on a tax reform program that would reduce taxes and close loopholes. Capital-intensive businesses liked the old laws just fine; they provided for investment tax credit, accelerated depreciation, and foreign tax credits. The Reagan-Rostenkowski plan would repeal investment credit and reduce the generosity of depreciation and foreign tax credit allowances.

Small businesses and labor-intesive firms in the retail, service, food and entertainment, and high-technology sectors, which did not benefit from the existing tax codes, supported the new plan.

The bill's proposal to lower the maximum corporate tax rate from 46 to 36 percent was not much of an incentive for industries that under the existing tax codes could deduct enough to be virtually tax-free. Among the more formidable opponents was the United States Chamber of Commerce. While conceding that small businesses would benefit by reform, it believed that the purpose of the proposed law was the "deindustrialization" of America, a process already begun by the decline of heavy industry, the erosion of the work force belonging to unions (17 percent, half what it was at the end

of World War II), and the shift of employment to the service sectors. The National
Association of Manufacturers and the prestigious Business Roundtable allied themselves
with the Chamber of Commerce.

The pro-reform lobbyists were sponsored by the Tax Reform Action Coalition
(TRAC), whose most prestigious members were IBM and General Motors. A trade
association, the National Associations of Wholesaler-Distributors, also threw in its lot
with the reformers. Associations representing small businesses, principally the National
Federation of Independent Business, did not join the coalition because most of its members were individual entrepreneurs who would be hurt by the bill's tough minimum
individual tax rate. Another coalition, the CEO (chief executive officers') Tax Group,
was led by J. C. Penney and General Foods. Organized labor, assured of the preservation of tax-free fringe benefits, joined the reformers. One might have doubts about the
simplistic "business versus labor" misconception, observing IBM and the AFL-CIO
planning strategy.

Once the lines of battle were drawn, the lobbying and bargaining commenced.

> The Coalition Against Regressive Taxation (CART), initiated by the American
> Trucking Association, complained about a proposal to terminate the right to
> deduct excise taxes and tariffs from income taxes (truckers pay about $7
> billion a year in excise taxes and wanted to keep the deduction). The truck-
> ers were joined by the Distilled Spirits Council of the United States (DIS-
> CUS) and the Tobacco Institute. The Archery Manufacturers Association,
> one of the more exotic members of CART, wanted to keep its 11 percent
> excise tax on bows and arrows as a deduction.
> The National Federation of Independent Business, pacified by a plan to allow
> immediate write-off of $50,000 in investment, rejoined TRAC (Tax Re-
> form Action Coalition).
> The League of Women Voters, a liberal organization, joined with Phyllis
> Schlafly's conservative Eagle Forum to form a pro-reform partnership.

The bill passed easily and became law, 1987 being the first year of implementation.
There were enough payoffs to keep the pro-reform coalition alive to the end. For example, General Motors, one of the few heavy manufacturing companies that supported
the bill, was permitted retroactive use of the investment tax credit for its new plant in
Tennessee. GM worked another loophole to maximum advantage. As originally intended, the new tax law would provide advantages to manufacturers who sold to dealers
on installment. The law was written with financially strapped John Deere, a tractor
manufacturer, in mind. The old law allowed taxes to be deferred until full payment was
received. The new law required full tax payment during the year in which the first
payment was received. The loophole allowed the tax deferral to continue if the contract
was for full payment in nine months, a practice Deere had used for years. But it did
not say "Deere," so the auto manufacturers quickly rewrote their contracts with dealers.
Since the tax can be deferred every year indefinitely, the loophole is a permanent
tax cut.

THE POLITICS OF EXCLUSION:
LABOR AND MANAGEMENT

Organized labor in Washington traditionally supports liberal causes and Democratic candidates. Unions also lobby for civil rights legislation, even though their memberships do not always support such legislation. About 95 percent of the money contributed by unions to political candidates goes to the Democrats. In the 1984 presidential election, in spite of labor leaders' support of Walter Mondale, he won only 53 percent of union families' votes. Ronald Reagan won 45 percent.

As we have noted, in the European corporatist governments, labor's governmental role is firmly set, and no need to show its muscle is required. Indeed, Marxist critics of corporatism allege that its fundamental goal was to deradicalize labor unions: "It is primarily the labor movement . . . extracting concessions from the state."[11] By entering into these agreements, labor is said to act contrary to the intentions that guided their origins; that is, they cooperate in the preservation of a stable rather than an inflationary economy by not pursuing excessive wage demands.

In Austria, for example, a decision to strike cannot be made by an individual union acting unilaterally, but only after a protracted and complex set of negotiations between peak associations. The unions eschew the ideologically loaded subject of inequality in exchange for maximum influence "at the very highest levels in the arenas of economic and social policy most critical to Austria's strategy in the world economy; labor as a force for conservatism is of course not unique to Austria."[12]

Spain did not develop a powerful interest group system, even during the Second Republic (just before the Spanish civil war). Labor unions were weak, paralyzed by factional disputes. Other potential interest groups were undeveloped due to the delayed development in Spain of a capitalist economy, possibly because the alliance among the aristocracy, the church, and the middle classes was intolerant of independent interest groups. Unlike the European corporatist states, the Spanish work force is ununionized and conservative, somewhat like Japan's.

The Spanish church, which owned about one-third of Spanish national wealth, was the only clear example of a peak association. The Franco period (1939–1976), though authoritarian, did little to incorporate diverse segments of the economy into the implementation process, as is usually done in state corporatism. Spain's smooth transition to democracy quickly became the almost exclusive property of the Spanish Socialist Workers' party, which is apparently destined to establish a de facto one-party system like Japan's.

Japan's transition from authoritarianism to corporatism also resulted in a de facto one-party system. But Japan already had the bureaucratic-business link. During the Meiji revolution (1867–1868), capitalism replaced feudalism, and a market economy was the result. Although we are accustomed to thinking of the modern Japanese state rising from the ashes of World War II, the Meiji period was a forerunner, almost a duplicate, of the development of postwar Japanese corporatism. A massive industrialization effort was begun, culminating in the defeat of the Russians in the Russo-Japanese War in 1905. Interest groups were encouraged, sometimes created where none existed, by the state. Interest group leaders were usually former bureaucrats. As Takeshi Ishida explains, ''The conduct of their activities was very often governed by a need to help spread and develop the policies of the government, while the original function of interest articulation was more or less suppressed.'' [13]

Political parties then, as now, were not truly competitive. Between 1892 and 1937, the party in power was never replaced by election. Leadership replacement occurred when senior Japanese politicians, deciding it was time for a change, chose new prime ministers and used elections to ratify that choice. Japan's current political system, with leadership replacement almost the same as the before World War II, inherited the corporatism of the past and accepted a few of the occupying government's demands for more democracy but quickly reverted to the more comfortable, less confrontational style decreed by corporatism.

Thus whatever corporatism's merits, labor and business are the incorporated groups, not the various single-issue citizens' and protest groups that scatter themselves across the landscapes of pluralist democracies. Corporatism embraces only organizations that the economic division of labor creates; some students of corporatist societies virtually define corporatism in terms of the bargain struck with organized labor. It is primarily the labor movement that extracts concessions from the government or wins concessions by allying with other interest groups. Corporatism is an alliance between economic interest groups.

It is sometimes accused of providing a means of *co-optation*—buying off workers who might otherwise be attracted to Marxism. Unions in corporatist settings are the allies of industry in the cause of wage restraint. The notion requires either that workers are victims of ''false consciousness'' (operating, without knowing it, against their own best interests) or that their best interest lies in collaboration rather than confrontation. Workers enjoy a degree of material satisfaction in exchange for keeping to their place. In Europe, unions have direct access to the decision-making process: they are formally represented on policy boards and commissions. In Asia, ''corporatism without labor'' has shown that peak associations representing most workers are not necessary. The substitution of strong cultural expectations of loyalty and obedience or the willingness to oppress labor are efficient alternatives.

Labor has all too often been blamed for economic woes. One hears of the inability to compete in the Pacific Rim because of low wages and because of our inability to integrate labor into a decision-making consensus. The argument against unregulated unions, and hence for pluralist economies, is often made about interest groups generally. The argument is that when interest groups become active in the policy process in advanced industrial societies, their legitimate desire to protect their members' interest often creates a stagnant, impotent government. ''Interest group liberalism,'' a euphemism for corporatism, has been blamed for Congress's inability to balance the budget, for example. Each member of Congress wants to be reelected; a good strategy to ensure reelection is plenty of ''pork'' in the barrel. Representatives and senators honor the tradition of allowing each to include the odd post office, mass transit grant, or Small Business Administration grant in the budget. As each adds a share of the pork barrel, the total budget gets out of balance. But unless each agreed to stop pork barrel legislation, the one or two who refused to go along would probably not be reelected.

INTEREST GROUPS AND THE GOOD SOCIETY: A REVISIONIST VIEW

Some theories hold that powerful interest groups also impede a nation's economic growth. Mancur Olson writes that "on balance, special-interest organizations and collusions reduce efficiency and aggregate income in the societies in which they operate and make political life more divisive."[14] Interest groups, in pressing their clientele's claims, if they are successful, reduce the economic performance of a nation and hence, indirectly, its members' well-being.

Labor unions, should they go on strike protesting the installation of computing equipment in mass communications because it costs jobs, cause their country to slip behind other nations that have kept their communication system up to date. If an interest group persuades Congress that it needs tariffs to protect it against unfair international competition, the tariffs will reduce incentives to become cost-effective.

These theories imply that the absence of narrowly focused interest groups, such as those found in the United States, is an economic advantage: South Korea and Taiwan were Japanese colonies and did not develop any independent economic groups; Japan, a consensual society, folds conflict in and co-opts labor organizations; and the corporatist countries cope with potentially divisive groups by giving them a piece of the action.

Sweden is often cited, along with Austria, as an example of corporatist decision making at its purist. But as is usually the case, the reality is somewhat out of step with the theory. Sweden has the highest proportion of workers in unions (90 percent) in the world. But there is no single peak association to blend these workers into the policy process. The Swedish Employers' Association, the major business organization, employs only one-third of the Swedish work force. The Swedish Trade Union Federation does not represent public service employees, the fastest-growing employment category in the country. Add to this the growth of the white-collar workers and the great increase in the number of women working (largely in the public sector), and the ability of any organization to stake a claim for being encompassing is doubtful: "The Swedish labour markets are in a process of fragmentation [that] will lead to a long-term devolution of Swedish industrial relations."[15]

Peddling Access

Lobbying, representing a group to a legislature or bureaucracy, is usually inappropriate or unneeded when the group has members on various legislative and bureaucratic decision-making or supervisory bodies. Members of unions, for example, may serve in parliament and serve on the boards of agencies dealing with wages or working conditions.

In corporatist systems, access is automatic, and claims to have developed access through personal contacts and reciprocal relations are not taken seriously. There is, however, a difference between the more institutionally rigid and circumscribed European regulation of interest groups and the more personally reciprocal regulation in Asia. Even though Asian bureaucracies are institutionally powerful, there is still an element of interpersonal reciprocity, as in the United States.

The bargain is struck: certain groups are given a monopoly in exchange for compliance. Hence access is an ill-used concept. Why should people struggle for access when the government has granted it to them? Of course, only a few organizations—the peak associations that represent large confederations of members—are incorporated. Groups not included—and certainly most are not—are out of luck. Earlier we used corporatism to explain economic policy and outputs. Now we need the idea to understand the accommodation of governments to interest groups.

Groups and parties interact in both complementary and antagonistic ways (see Table 6.8). Corporatist countries, which, with multiparty systems, could be unstable, are not: Switzerland is the best example. Noncorporatist states with strong two-party systems are also rather coherent: the United Kingdom is a good example. Noncorporatist countries with weak or multiparty systems are, however, often chaotic: Italy, which has gone through one government about every nine months on an average since the end of World War II, and the United States, whose government is often paralyzed by group intransigence, are good examples.

Unlike citizens of other countries, where access is institutionalized, Americans have a deep suspicion of interest groups, especially economic ones; they are reluctant to accord them any collective responsibility. Americans have become all too aware of the enormous importance—and abuse—of influence peddling. Indeed,

> among the yardsticks that Washington has for measuring power, access is primary. That is the law of organizational politics everywhere, more important in Washington than elsewhere because influence and persuasion are the currency of the Washington power game. . . . It is a privilege to be treasured or a right to be jealously protected.[16]

Tangible symbols of access are priceless; Michael Deaver, a Reagan aide who left the White House staff to lobby, was given the president's daily appointment schedule. Other tangible evidence of access is where you ride and where you eat. Lobbyists who

TABLE 6.8 Relationship between Corporatism and Political Parties

	Corporatism	Party System (number of effective parties)
Austria	High	2.2
Japan	High	3.1
Norway	High	3.2
Sweden	High	3.2
Switzerland	High	5.0
Canada	Low	2.4
France	Low	3.3
Ireland	Low	2.8
Italy	Low	3.5
United Kingdom	Low	2.1
United States	Low	1.9

ride on *Air Force One*, the president's airplane, rate far above the madding crowd of everyday influentials.

In a comparatively unorganized interest group system, with little institutional access accorded to private organizations, one needs to know with whom to lobby. The difficulty of access is exacerbated by our uniquely fragmented decision-making structure. Separation of powers, a weak party system, a decentralized Congress, and a federal scheme (dividing authority between states and the national government) make the maze of decision making unusually complicated. There is no real sense of an encompassing authority; rather, numerous floating coalitions come and go with the rise and fall of issues. People interested in lobbying for an end to aid to the Nicaraguan contras would have been better off trying to gain access to the speaker of the House, Jim Wright of Texas, than to the secretary of state. Wright was in close communication with the Nicaraguan government and was, as cease-fires were signed, the most important person in Washington. On other issues, he was powerless. To know no more than who was really making a decision, interest groups and foreign governments were willing to pay Deaver retaining fees that ran into the millions of dollars.

American lobbyists place great faith in know-how and "know-who"; they portray themselves a phone call away from a Senate staff member, who can in turn connect him with an insider on the National Security Commission staff, who can get him an appointment with an assistant secretary of state for Latin American affairs. Some boast of having access to the holy of holies, the Oval Office. An extreme example are Michael Deaver and Lyn Nofziger, who also opened a lobbying business upon leaving the White House. Deaver was adept at selling his services to foreign governments, especially those from Asia, where personal reciprocity and contacts are basic to political processes. Both were convicted of violating ethics laws passed after Watergate that prohibit lobbying for a year after departure from government. They were selling themselves on the basis of having the ear of the president. Clients believed they could intervene where no one else could. Edwin Meese, attorney general during the second Reagan administration, spent a lot of time with his ex-colleagues, helping to grease the skids for grants and contracts and reinforcing their claim that they were princes of access.

We need to distinguish between consultants like Deaver and Nofziger, who accept clients as attorneys or physicians do, and lobbyists, who are employed by a single organization. A majority of them have had previous experience in government, but only a few have worked at the White House.[17]

Consultants, well-connected ones like Deaver and Nofziger, command retainers of about $250,000 a year from each client. They may have been worth it, or it might have been yet another scam, another hawking of contrived influence. They certainly convinced their clients. As Deaver explains, "There's no question I've got as good access as anybody in town."[18] He was permitted to keep his White House pass; he chatted regularly with Nancy Reagan. What did he actually do? "Strategic planning [for] . . . where they want to be vis-à-vis Washington in three to five years, and I help them to get there."[19]

> In a city where perception is often reality, Deaver is known as a master imagemaker. . . . It is not hard to see why the government of South Korea, under fire for unfair trade practices abroad and repression of political dissidents at home, would want to hire Deaver, even at Deaver's asking price of $1.2 million for a three-year contract.[20]

Not only do consultants charge more, but they tend to take on foreign governments as clients, knowing that even the most debt-ridden Third World autocracy can come up with lots of money, and they neither want nor need a PAC. Japan, among the world's developed industrial democracies, spends a fortune annually to try to cut back on Japan bashing and the imposition of protective tariffs; Angola, a Marxist country which faced a serious anticommunist revolt, hired former attorney general Elliot Richardson; South Africa employs former Reagan campaign manager John Sears. The list goes on: Brazil, Canada, Taiwan, Turkey—they all pay top dollar to buy access.

"UNELECTED REPRESENTATIVES"

As the number of subcommittees of standing committees grows ever larger, the complexity of the legislative process is increased. Legislators, even though most of them stay in office as long as they wish, have been slipping in their grasp of the details of legislation. The impact of the deterioration of authority on interest groups has been substantial, especially in iron triangles, which are developed and survive because everybody wins. Admittedly, iron triangles may be expensive, but the expense is borne by the least organized interest group—taxpayers.

Much of the day-to-day negotiations among iron triangles is managed or filtered by congressional staffs. This has the added benefit of freeing congressmen for other things, such as running for election, which is becoming more a *raison d'être* than a means to achieve a policy goal. Even though incumbents are rarely defeated, they do not wish to take chances: the defeat of seven Republican incumbents in 1986 caused shock waves that will not subside for years.

As legislators leave legislation to their staffs, those staffs grow astronomically. Since the 1960s, staff personnel has more than doubled. In 1967, there were 6,884 congressional employees; in 1986, there were 24,714. These are not clerks. They are well-educated, well-paid professionals—economists, lawyers, environmental impact specialists, defense experts, and so on—who have a major influence on public policy:

> The staff's role is vital in many respects. [Staff members] are the grease that makes the committees' wheels turn. From researching issues and organizing hearings to drafting coalitions and forming coalitions with other members' offices and interest groups, they are intimately involved every step of the way. And though staff members don't vote, they advise their bosses on which way to go. They also help round up proxy votes from absent members for committee votes and help negotiate deals that may obviate the need for other votes.[21]

If this sounds like what you thought senators or representatives do, think again. Staff personnel are also entrepreneurs. They seek interest group support for ideas that appeal to them, usually because of their training and professional commitments.[22]

They create demands to which they can respond:

> The impetus of staff . . . is to build coalitions by having programs respond, at least symbolically, to more demands rather than to let them die a natural death. The result is increasingly inclusive, increasingly complex legislation that can only be understood by

an expert. Needless to say, this increases the power of permanent Washingtonians with the necessary expertise, such as former staffers [lobbyists].[23]

The complex problems with which staff grapple are not known to the media. Since television reporters shortchange Congress anyway, they are even less likely to spend any time with staff. Staff members do not object: they of course want their boss to be reelected. It is to their advantage to make their boss look good when he or she does make it to the tube. In creating the illusion that elected representatives usually know what they are talking about, staff cements another myth. Staff networks do not include media people, since they have no need for each other. Thus possibly the most powerful bloc in Washington remains invisible, along with the interest groups that take part in iron triangles.

Iron triangles define power in Washington. In a microcosmic sort of way, they are small, self-contained corporatist systems. Consequently, a president—even a popular and energetic one—cannot hope to gain more than a fraction of a favored program, much of it in the first 100 days or so of the first term. Presidential failure is endemic to the system: Kennedy was assassinated and replaced by Lyndon Johnson, who, floundering on the shoals of his failed war in Vietnam, did not seek reelection; he was replaced by Richard Nixon, who, ruined by the Watergate scandal, resigned and was replaced by Gerald Ford, whose premature pardoning of Nixon contributed to his defeat by Jimmy Carter, who, unable to respond to massive inflation, oil shortages, and the kidnapping of American hostages during the Iranian revolution, lost to Ronald Reagan, who, unable to secure the release of American hostages held in Iran and elsewhere in the Middle East, authorized the sale of American weapons to Iran in an unsuccessful attempt to obtain the hostages' freedom.

With parties dead and interest groups ruling—in floating coalitions with iron triangle partners—even if a president wanted to do what was promised, as most presidents probably do (even though campaigns in the United States are more hyperbolic than in Europe), he or she could not. Power is divided, and no person or institution can be held accountable. The president deliberately misleading Congress, as in the Iran-*contra* affair, is almost an institutional necessity: Lincoln, Franklin Roosevelt, and Eisenhower, among others, have found it necessary to lie. Whether they were justified is the wrong question; the right ones are these: Are public officials *ever* justified in lying? Does the end *ever* justify the means? These are tough questions, made tougher by a system that for fear of tyranny has impeded accountability.

FOR FURTHER CONSIDERATION

1. Distinguish between collective and selective goods.
2. What is the relationship between *individual* motives for joining interest groups and pluralist theories about the *representative* functions of groups?
3. Compare the activities and goals of political action committees with those of political parties in the United States.
4. Contrast the role of interest groups in highly corporatist political systems with their role in pluralist ones.

For the More Adventurous

1. What *interest* do interest groups *represent?* Suggest possible changes in the organization of interest groups to better serve the representative function. How many of your suggestions would be compatible with the American culture?
2. Why do some governments encourage the development of interest groups, while others discourage their formation? What is it about each country that causes these reactions?
3. Devise a method to distinguish "weak claims from weak claimants." How would a PAC respond to your plan?
4. List several characteristics of iron triangles. Do iron triangles serve the collective good? Why or why not? David Stockman, director of the Office of Management and Budget during the first Reagan administration, lamented that

   Interest groups appropriated [state] authority, and the uses of state power were defined not by the Constitution, but by whatever claims the organized interest groups could successfully impose on the system. . . . Power . . . shifted form the institutions of central government to a plethora of mini-governments, made up of the "iron triangles" of bureaucracy, client, and congressional subcommittee.[24]

   Is Stockman describing corporatism?

NOTES

1. James Madison, *The Federalist Papers,* Federalist No. 10. (Originally published 1788.)
2. Anthony Oberschall, *Social Conflict and Social Movements* (Englewood Cliffs, N.J.: Prentice-Hall, 1973), p. 155.
3. Kay Lehman Schlozman, "What Accent for the Heavenly Chorus? Political Equality and the American Pressure System," *Journal of Politics 46* (1984): 1115.
4. John R. Wright, "PACs, Contributions, and Roll Calls: An Organizational Perspective," *American Political Science Review 79* (1985): 400–414.
5. Henry Kariel, *The Decline of American Pluralism* (Stanford, Calif.: Stanford University Press, 1961), p. 74.
6. Roberto Michels, *Political Parties: A Sociological Study of the Oligarchical Tendencies of Modern Democracies* (New York: Free Press, 1962), p 377. (Originally published 1917.)
7. Ibid., p. 610.
8. Andrew McFarland believes that a 20 percent negative response to a Common Cause survey is enough to kill a leadership-proposed initiative. See McFarland, *Common Cause* (Chatham, N.J.: Chatham House, 1984), p. 98.
9. Julie Kosterlizt, "Test of Strength," *National Journal,* October 24, 1987, p. 2562.
10. Terry Moe, *The Organization of Interests* (Chicago: University of Chicago Press, 1980), p. 30.
11. Gabriel A. Almond and Sidney Verba, *The Civic Cultures: Political Attitudes and Democracy in Five Nations,* Boston: Little Brown, 1965. p. 245.
12. Peter Katzenstein, *Small States in World Markets* (Ithaca, N.Y.: Cornell University Press, 1985), p. 247.
13. Takeshi Ishida, "The Development of Interest Groups and the Pattern of Political Modernization in Japan," in *Political Development in Modern Japan,* ed. Robert E. Ward (Princeton, N.J.: Princeton University Press, 1968), p. 302.

14. Mancur Olson, *The Logic of Collective Action* (Cambridge, Mass.: Harvard University Press, 1971), p. 34.

15. Scott Lash, "The End of Neocorporation? The Breakdown of Centralized Bargaining in Sweden," *British Journal of Industrial Relations 23* (July 1985): 225–253.

16. Hedrick Smith, *The Power Game* (New York: Random House, 1988), p. 71.

17. Kay Lehman Schlozman and John T. Tierney, *Organized Interests and American Democracy* (New York: Harper & Row, 1986), p. 269.

18. "Peddling Influence," *Time,* March 3, 1986, p. 28.

19. Ibid.

20. Ibid.

21. "The Hill People," *National Review,* May 16, 1987, p. 1171.

22. Michael Malbin, *Unelected Representatives* (New York: Basic Books, 1980), p. 249.

23. Ibid., p. 250.

24. David Stockman, *The Triumph of Politics* (New York: Avon, 1987), p. 36.

FOR FURTHER READING

Ball, Alan R., and Frances Millard. *Pressure Politics in Industrial Societies: A Comparative Introduction.* Atlantic Highlands, N.J.: Humanities Press, 1987.

Berry, Jeffrey M. *The Interest Group Society.* Boston: Little, Brown, 1984.

———. *Lobbying for the People.* Princeton, N.J.: Princeton University Press, 1977. Public interest groups explained. See McFarland (below) for an example of such a group.

Greider, William. *The Education of David Stockman and Other Americans.* New York: New American Library, 1986. Do "they" make American economic policy? There is no "they" there, according to Greider.

Katzenstein, Peter. *Corporatism and Change: Austria, Switzerland, and the Politics of Industry.* Ithaca, N.Y.: Cornell University Press, 1984.

———. *Small States in World Markets.* Ithaca, N.Y.: Cornell University Press, 1985. Austria and Switzerland, two corporatist regimes, are explained.

Lamare, James W. *What Rules America.* St. Paul: West, 1988. Lamare finds—and loathes—the "they."

Lowi, Theodore. *The End of Liberalism: Ideology, Policy, and the Crisis of Public Authority.* New York: Norton, 1969. Read in conjunction with Greider.

Malbin, Michael. *Unelected Representatives.* New York: Basic Books, 1980. The growing role of congressional staffs.

McFarland, Andrew. *Common Cause.* Chatham, N.J.: Chatham House, 1984. One of the few analyses of the internal dynamics of an interest group.

Moe, Terry. *The Organization of Interests.* Chicago: University of Chicago Press, 1980. Tough going, but well worth the effort. It answers the question, "Why do people join organizations?"

Olson, Mancur. *The Logic of Collective Action.* Cambridge, Mass.: Harvard University Press, 1971. The book that started the antipluralist revolution in America.

———. *The Rise and Decline of Nations.* New Haven, Conn.: Yale University Press, 1982. Nations that become creatures of interest groups decline.

Sabato, Larry J. *PAC Power.* New York: Norton, 1985.

Schlozman, Kay Lehman, and John T. Tierney. *Organized Interests and American Democracy.* New York: Harper & Row, 1986.

Wilson, Graham K. *Business and Politics: A Comparative Introduction.* Chatham, N.J.: Chatham House, 1986.

Wilson, James Q. *Political Organizations*. New York: Basic Books, 1973. The best overview of the subject.

Zeigler, Harmon. *Pluralism, Corporatism, and Confucianism: Political Association and Conflict Regulation in the United States, Europe, and Taiwan*. Philadelphia: Temple University Press, 1988.

CHAPTER 7

Authoritarian Government: The Predominant Form

Reprinted by permission, Mike Luckovich.

Between the two extremes—the democratic governments at one end of the contin-uum and the totalitarian ones at the other—the *authoritarian* governments are located. A good definition of authoritarian government is by Nisbet:

> Repressiveness is habitual, the role of the military is commonly great, and use is made of such practices as torture, imprisonment without due process, and summary, anony-mous execution. But at the same time, government in authoritarian as opposed to total-itarian societies is naturally checked in its power by the continued existence of largely free institutions—family, clan and kindred, church, social class, village and town, co-operative and confederation, all claiming and in large measure receiving corporate rights of autonomy. The values of tradition tend to be very strong in authoritarian societies, particularly the values of kinship, religion, and regional culture. Spain under Franco (1939–1975), Portugal under Salazar (1933–1968), Argentina under Perón (1945–1955) and Saudi Arabia are all examples of authoritarian states in the twentieth century.[1]

Democratic government, with the exception of the failed Greek experiment, is a relatively new idea. Totalitarian government is a thoroughly modern invention. But authoritarian governments have been here from the start. The first recorded organized government was authoritarian. Thus one might call authoritarian government the "nor-mal" form of government.

One can get into trouble easily by arguing that until the American Revolution in 1776, no democracies existed. The statement is not entirely accurate. Venice and Flor-ence during the Renaissance flirted—tangentially—with some forms of limited partici-pation, and certainly their constitutions restrained rulers, as did the Magna Charta.[2] The word *pòpolo* became voguish among Italian political theorists. Even Machiavelli (from whom the word *Machiavellian*—crafty, deceitful—was derived), claimed that "govern-ment by the people is better than government by princes." But " 'popular' government did not imply democratic government. . . . When Italian chroniclers refer to the *pòpolo* of a particular city, they merely mean that it has a republican as opposed to a tyrannical form of government."[3]

Of the 13 cantons in the pre-1798 Swiss Confederation, six were true democracies, at least theoretically, in which sovereign power was exercised by the *Landsgemeinde,* an annual assembly of all free citizens. And most of the "free cities" of Germany provided for full political participation by all male citizens. Again, however, although much romanticized (especially by American Antifederalists, who opposed adoption of the U.S. Constitution because of the loss of state sovereignty and claimed that in Swit-zerland, "the people *personally* exercise the powers of government"),[4] these cities and cantons were "oligarchic rather than democratic in their political system." The coun-cils, not popularly elected or accountable, enjoyed "almost complete authority" over citizens.[5]

One cannot disagree with Michael Novak:

> Consider the world at the beginning of the democratic capitalist era. The watershed year was 1776 . . . [when] the first democratic capitalist republic came into existence in the United States. . . . In 1800 . . . nearly all states were authoritarian.[6]

Novak specifies democratic and capitalistic, but the point is academic. Democracies are not only comparatively new; they are also fragile and scarce. Until the 18th century, the history of government was a history of authoritarianism. Today, most governments (67 in 1989) remain authoritarian:

COUNTRY	POLITY
Algeria	Socialist one-party
Bahrain	Traditional nonparty
Bangladesh	Military dominant party
Bhutan	Traditional nonparty
Brunei	Monarchy
Burkina Faso	Military nonparty
Burundi	Socialist one-party
Cameroon	Nationalist one-party
Cape Verde Islands	Socialist one-party
Central African Republic	Nationalist one-party
Chad	Military nonparty
Chile*	Military dominant party
China (Taiwan)*	Centralized dominant party
Congo	Socialist one-party
Egypt	Military dominant party
El Salvador	Centralized multiparty
Fiji	Military nonparty
Gambia	Dominant party
Guatemala	Centralized multiparty
Guinea	Military nonparty
Guyana	Centralized multiparty
Haiti	Military nonparty
Hungary	Communist one-party
Indonesia	Military dominant party
Iran	Quasi-dominant party
Ivory Coast	Nationalist one-party
Jordan	Limited monarchy
Kuwait	Traditional nonparty
Lebanon	Decentralized multiparty
Lesotho	Military nonparty
Liberia	Military dominant party
Madagascar	Military dominant party
Malawi	Nationalist one-party
Malaysia	Decentralized dominant party
Maldives	Traditional nonparty
Mexico	Decentralized dominant party
Morocco	Centralized multiparty
Nepal	Traditional nonparty
Nicaragua	Dominant party
Nigeria	Military nonparty

*Significant movement toward democracy.

COUNTRY	POLITY
Pakistan*	Quasi-multiparty
Panama	Military dominant party
Paraguay	Military dominant party
Poland*	centralized multiparty
Qatar	Traditional nonparty
Senegal	Centralized dominant party
South Korea*	Centralized multiparty
South Africa	Centralized multiparty
Sierra Leone	Socialist one-party
Singapore	Centralized dominant party
Sri Lanka	Centralized multiparty
Sudan	Multiparty
Suriname	Multiparty
Swaziland	Traditional nonparty
Syria	Centralized dominant party
Thailand	Centralized multiparty
Tonga	Traditional nonparty
Tunisia	Dominant party
Turkey*	Multiparty
Uganda	Traditional military
United Arab Emirates	Decentralized nonparty
Vanuatu	Decentralized multiparty
Western Samoa	Centralized multiparty
North Yemen	Military nonparty
Yugoslavia	Communist one-party
Zambia	Socialist one-party
Zimbabwe	Centralized dominant party

The total population of these countries, about 1.6 billion, represents 23 percent of the world's population. It is difficult to get a grip on the varieties of authoritarian government. There are traditional monarchies, countries ruled by military juntas, those governed by a powerful family or personality. The problem is, of course, that every government between the democracies and the few remaining totalitarian governments qualifies as authoritarian. If one adds the 1.6 billion people living in the "backslid" totalitarian countries, the variety is even more impressive (see Chapter 8). The description of the party system accompanying the list of authoritarian governments is meant to be bewildering rather than enlightening. Totalitarian governments are communist one-party systems. Democracies are either presidential or parliamentary, two-party or multiparty, federal or unitary. But authoritarian governments defy logical categorization. Because there are so many political systems and so much idiosyncrasy among the authoritarian governments, it is not as productive to give lengthy analyses of form, structure, and process per se as for democracy and totalitarianism. We will, however, take somewhat longer looks at a few, such as Nicaragua, Chile, and the Pacific Rim nations.

---

*Significant movement toward democracy.

A Typology of Authoritarian Governments

   I. Conservative Regimes
   - **A.** Traditional monarchies with family-based ruling groups and no significant political infrastructure. Examples: Morocco, Nepal, Kuwait.
   - **B.** Dictatorships dependent on the personality of a leader. Example: Malawi.

   II. Radical Regimes
   - **A.** Theocracies that seek to generate mass support. Example: Iran.
   - **B.** Military regimes that seek to install an ideology. Example: Algeria.

   III. Regimes with superficially democratic elections and some choice of parties but with limitations favoring the established elite. Examples: Taiwan, South Africa, Nicaragua.

   IV. Military regimes without a dominant ideology.
   - **A.** Direct military rule based on a *coup*. Example: Nigeria.
   - **B.** Civilian-military regimes, with power alternating between the military and civilian leadership. Examples: Chile, Egypt.

   V. Kleptocracies, ruled by thieves whose primary motivation is personal enrichment. Example: Haiti (under Duvalier), Philippines (under Marcos).

Citizens of authoritarian countries have limited political and civil rights. They frequently have more economic freedom, depending on the ideology of the autocratic regime. However, the real key to the definition is the line between public and private behavior. The line is not absolute; some autocratic governments aspire to tighter control, and their authoritarianism is due more to lack of resources than willingness to live and let live. Many left-wing authoritarian governments espouse a collectivist ideology and, given a firmer grasp on the machinery of government, would move into the totalitarian camp. The propensity of certain forms of autocratic regimes for a more thoroughly collectivist society is a point of considerable controversy.

TRADITIONAL MONARCHIES

Morocco, a former French and Spanish protectorate in North Africa, is governed by a constitutional monarch with genuine executive authority.[7] The king is recognized in Islam as the spiritual leader of the nation and is believed by more devout practitioners to have magical powers. The dynasty from which the present king springs has ruled Morocco since 1664 (except for the half century of the protectorate, when the monarchy became associated with nationalism and independence). Beyond tradition, religion, and association with popular causes, the monarchy has engineered some spectacular symbolic successes, the most important being persuading Spain to return disputed territory in the Western Sahara. But most important for the maintenance of royal authority are *clientelist* politics, the ability to appoint or control the appointment of almost all public jobs, and the willingness and means to suppress opposition.

Clientelism.   Morocco's active political and economic elite is small and cohesive, with few ideological pretensions and a firm understanding of what it takes to get ahead. State participation in the economy is substantial, creating even more opportunities for patronage. Although political parties—a frequent source of patronage in other systems—exist, their power has waned as the monarchy's has grown. Beyond the monarchy, Morocco's elite consists of no more than several thousand well-connected people:

> Interconnections among the elite are based on common bourgeois origins, shared educational experiences, joint involvement in the nationalist movement, and intermarriage among prominent families. Most elites are also known to one another and interaction among them is frequent and extensive, being based on far more than shared participation in formal political institutions.[8]

The major commandment required of the elite is to eschew ideology and to keep out of leftist or fundamentalist movements.

Repression.   Troublemakers have been exiled, arrested, and tortured. Criticism of the monarchy is prohibited, and publications that do so are closed down. There are political prisoners, but they are dwindling in number. Although the parliamentary parties are politically impotent, lively discussions of government policy are common, especially since the Moroccan economy has been declining precipitously. Serious military revolts were quashed in 1971 and 1972, and a fundamentalist critic of the monarchy was detained without trial for 3½ years. In 1983, another possible coup attempt was averted with the "accidental" death of its leader, an Islamic fundamentalist with strong Libyan connections. However, Islamic fundamentalism is far less pervasive than in Iran. But the survival of the monarchy could be threatened by apparently intractable economic problems. Its gross national product per capita ($590) is considerably less than that of neighboring Tunisia and Algeria, as is its economic rate of growth. Declines in the price of its major export, phosphate, and the continued expense of its Sahara expeditions have plunged Morocco into debt. Its ratio of debt to GNP, 104 percent, is far higher than Tunisia's (59 percent) or Algeria's (25 percent). These pressures, coupled with the continued insularity of the elite and occasional strikes (unions are free and independent), have lead the American CIA to worry about the stability of the regime. Comparisons with Iran are inevitable. Like Morocco, Iran once had a monarch allied with the West against Islamic fundamentalism in league with a small elite. After the end of his regime in Iran, the shah was welcomed in Morocco. But there is no institutionally viable opposition infrastructure; clientelism has seen to that.

PERSONAL DICTATORSHIPS

Malawi's dictator, Dr. Hastings Kamuzu Banda, is president for life, ruling without even the token institutionalization of a political party. At independence (1964), Malawi had a parliamentary government; a 1966 constitution established a presidential system, with the president chosen by the country's only party. In 1970, even this pretense was abandoned. In addition to his life term, Banda also appoints the other members of the government (including the National Assembly, which, although elected, allows the election results to be published in advance). The president is personally the minister of major government departments, defense, agriculture, and so on, and is head of the only party, the Malawi Congress party, to which all adults must belong. The party's youth brigades roam the country and, with the cooperation of the small but efficient army, help the president run the country with an iron hand. Dissent is not permitted; harassment and arbitrary arrest are widespread. If Malawi's ruling authority had an ideology, it could move up a notch to the near-totalitarian. But, curiously, Banda is content to leave the economy in private hands and has worked for some noble causes, raising the status of women, for example. Mired in poverty ($160 GNP per capita), Malawi is one of South Africa's few supporters, mainly because many of its workers earn money in South African mines. With the support of powerful South Africa, Malawi's dictatorship is secure.

THEOCRACIES

The shah of Iran, agent of brutal repression of political protests, left the country, dying with cancer, in 1979. Demonstrations continued, demanding that the Ayatollah Ruhollah Khomeini, the leader of fundamental Islamic political ideology, return from exile and assume the reigns of government, much as Lenin had done in 1917 in Russia. An interim government lasted only a few weeks and, again like the Russian experience, was replaced with a revolutionary Islamic government led by Khomeini.

Although, as in all governments, factions exist, the fundamentalist sect of Shiites, personified by Khomeini, has been dominant. Shiite ideology describes the Imam as a divinely inspired, infallible spiritual leader. There have been theocracies before, but even the most extreme, Calvinism, for example (which established blasphemy as a civil crime), allowed for some institutional separation of church and state. Not so with the Shiites, whose Imam is certainly not a *caliph*. Caliphs—the institutional center of Sunni Islam—are primarily temporal authorities whose religious duties are limited. The Imam is

> both sinless and absolutely infallible in his supposed pronouncements on the dogma and indeed on all matters. In fact, whereas in classical and medieval Sunni Islam the office of the caliph is recognized only as a practical necessity, belief in the Imam and submission to him is . . . the third cardinal article of faith, after a belief in God and his apostle.[9]

Given the fervor of Islam as an ideology, the wonder is that Iran did not become a totalitarian society rather than an authoritarian one. There is plenty of evidence that the Islamic Revolutionary Party (IRP) and Khomeini gave totalitarianism a good try but left the economy with a good deal of private choice. But certainly the IRP's approach to politics was totalistic. It wanted the politicization of social and private spheres. Khomeini asserted, "There is not a single topic in human life for which Islam has not provided instruction and established norms."[10]

Khomeini's "cultural revolution," while not as brutal as Mao's, was almost as ambitious. The Headquarters of Culture was established to coordinate "Islamization" of schools, universities, food habits, clothing, architecture, city planning, manners, art, the media, entertainment, and the family. All were regulated by the IRP. Iranian women, forbidden coeducation, comply with the *hijab* (Islamic code of dress); dancing is prohibited, and so are ''anti-Islamic ideas.''

The IRP, dominated by fundamentalist clerics, controls the office of the Faquih (occupied by Khomenini). Unwilling to concede Khomeini the title Imam, all rights and authority of the Imamate are exercised by the Faquih. The Faquih is not selected by the party but serves as the earthly representative of the Imam. Curiously, the Iranian parliament is openly disputatious, antifundamentalist critics having their say with impunity. But terror is very much a part of the scheme of things. Students are called on to spy on teachers, children to betray parents. The Revolutionary Guards, sanctioned by the constitution, grew to about 250,000 in order to attack—with modern military equipment— anyone who threatens Islamic unanimity. Internally, they have killed thousands of ethnic opponents to the regime and, in the war with Iraq, organized ''human wave'' attacks and the use of children to detonate mines, tactics that kept Iran in the war with Iraq well beyond the estimates of military experts.

Economic Policy.   Fundamentalist Islam favors collective over individual choice and speaks of the classless society central to Marxism (Marxists are nevertheless persecuted). The IRP's economic program is leftist but not Marxist. Private property is allowed as long as it is ''nonexploitative'' (government loans for start-up capital are interest-free). Irrespective of the rhetoric, Iranian economic life is still characterized by a good deal of diversity and choice: ''The regime has been careful not to alienate the middle class with excessive radicalism in regard to private property and profit.''[11]

With the Iranians finally losing the war with Iraq, much of the steam went out of fundamental Islamic ideology: the government of God was not, after all, invincible. With the death of Khomeini, Iran will presumably become more traditionally (that is less ideologically) authoritarian.

IDEOLOGICAL MILITARY REGIMES

Algerian's hard-won independence from France left it with a tough, implacable military elite with a commitment to Islamic socialism. Indeed, the National Charter specifies the National Liberation Front (FLN) as the promulgator of the ideology. Ideology aside, the Algerians have also been incorporating technically competent military men into the party elite.

Since independence, Algeria's leadership has been transferred from flamboyant revolutionaries to competent managers. Notwithstanding the resurgence of various regional and local assemblies and the opening of the FLN to a more heterogenous membership, the real power is secure in the hands of

> a technocratic elite whose claim to authority is based on the modern skills that they possess and for which there is a high value in the society. This technocratic system is made of up three major units that . . . are united in an overriding new allegiance to the state and to its developmental objectives. The military, party, and administrative technocrats . . . monopolize the state's critical military, mobilization, and managerial

affairs . . . ; however, the military remains the decisive elite group in Algerian politics today.[12]

You might wonder why this military elite cares much about Islamic socialism, but its origins in the war of independence against France give it the same sort of mystique that revolutionary parties frequently claim: the military elite is the guardian of the revolution and the FLN has effectively atrophied. Consequently, there is far more nationalism than socialism in the "official" ideology. The Islamic component to socialism has meant that although the economy is still subject to central planning, much of the ideology can be contained in personal, religious, or moral dicta. One consequence is that Algeria, in dramatic contrast to the truly ideological country in the region, Libya, spends very little on defense: Libya has about 25 soldiers per 1,000 inhabitants; Algeria has 8.

It spends far more on education than its neighbors and has enjoyed one of the few successful socialist economies. In the 1980s, its GNP per capita roughly doubled, to $3,000. Algerian socialism is less class-linked than traditional Marxism and has encouraged private ownership of small and medium-sized businesses. Even the public corporations are less subject to the central planning of even the most relaxed eastern European socialist economies, such as Yugoslavia.

Repression.   Anti-FLN teachings are not allowed, nor are associations or assemblies that espouse opposition to Islamic socialism. Some subversives have been held for long periods without formal charges or trials. The press is censored and in any case is not in private hands. Mail is routinely examined, and socialist revolutionary courses are mandatory (although more ritualistic, somewhat like the "evils of communism, joys of the American way" courses required in American high schools).

SUPERFICIALLY DEMOCRATIC REGIMES

Nicaragua

That the United States distinguishes between types of authoritarian government is well illustrated by the government's response to the Nicaraguan revolution. Between 1933 and 1979, Nicaragua was ruled by a family, the Somozas. The official head of state was Anastasio Somoza, the scion of the family installed by United States military intervention. Nicaragua was governed in traditional autocratic manner. Corruption was pervasive, the enrichment of the ruling elite being a generally accepted *droit du seigneur.* Limited opposition was left alone, but as fears of insurrection mounted, Somoza, as is the custom in authoritarian governments, increased torture, imprisonment without trial, execution by death squads, and exile, in an effort to hang on. He relied on the support of the military and the police, which were personally, rather than institutionally, loyal. Not much ideology was at stake. Like most autocratic governments initially dependent on the United States, this one took a ritualistic anticommunist posture. But anticommunism, even in its most passionate form, is not an ideology in the sense that Marxism is. Like Chile and Mexico, two authoritarian governments with strong links to the United States, Nicaragua was a reliable ally. Domestically, there was no forced collectivization, no land reform, no desire for radical change, and no need to create the "new man." Hence it was a right-wing authoritarian government content to keep things as they were. If you wanted to avoid getting your head broken, you stayed out of politics. The country was poor, with a gross national product per capita of about $800, and the wealth was unequally distributed, but no more so than that of other Central American governments.[13] In 1978, as the end of the Somoza dictatorship approached, the situation in Nicaragua was a combination of oppression and relative freedom. Elections were manipulated and fraudulent. But the media were privately owned and often highly critical of Somoza's leadership; censorship rose or declined with the mood of the governing elite. Union activity was free. Some 39 percent of the work force belonged to unions, but "the combination of economic and governmental power in the hands of one family reduces economic freedoms in a society without as much of the cushion of preindustrial forms as its comparative poverty and agricultural base might indicate."[14]

Partly as a consequence of such poverty and inequality (but also because Nicaragua was under United States military occupation during the years in which the Somozas were established as a puppet government), opposition was not confined to the radical Marxist Sandinistas (named in memory of Augusto César Sandino, who led an uprising against the occupying army from 1928 until 1933 and was murdered on the orders of the Somozas). Much like the Philippines a few years later, the opposition included "businessmen, landowners, labor, the peasantry, and the middle class."[15]

However, as the new government began the task of restructuring Nicaragua's economy and society, the Sandinistas gradually assumed the dominant position. Nevertheless, as late as 1982, the scope of Sandinista ideology was not apparent.[16] The American government began its long and tortured effort to destabilize the new government, painting it in pure Marxist revolutionary terms (and, as we learned in Chapter 2, funneling millions of dollars from arms sales and private contributions after Congress had denied the executive authority to continue aid to anti-Sandinista rebels), but its behavior was more complex. Although its base of support was more widespread than its predecessor's, its governing style was just about the same.[17] That is to say, the rhetoric was different, but the level of repression was unchanged.

Income growth after the revolution was not impressive; after a healthy spurt in 1981, Nicaragua began to register negative income growth (this was true of all Central American countries, having more to do with regional recession than with economic policy). Real GNP per capita declined consistently and today is less than before. However, the Sandinistas began an expansion of education, spending a great deal more money than the Somozas had, and sought to reduce illiteracy substantially. Health care conditions also improved; under Somoza they were dismal.

Land Reform.   But the real test of the revolution was land reform. Unlike such reforms in non-Marxist countries (Philippines, Taiwan), the initial thrust of the Sandinista effort was pure confiscation. Fully 20 percent of arable land was taken. Once taken, how was it to be distributed? Much to the surprise of its American tormentors, Nicaragua, after the initial harsh justice of confiscation, legislated guarantees of the right of private property for the new owners. Indeed, about 75 percent of seized land was privately owned, with the remainder owned by state cooperatives. The size of the individual holdings decreased dramatically.[18] It was a sound reform agenda, closely resembling (except for compensation) Taiwan's in the 1950s, and it certainly enhanced the loyalty of the farmers to the new regime (the farmers, in addition to the title to their plot of land, were each given a rifle with which to defend it).

However, unlike the brutal collectivism imposed by the USSR, Nicaragua was unwilling or unable to sacrifice much human life, and the result has been a chaotic agricultural sector. Rather than incurring our wrath because of its ruthlessness, reasoned assessors of things Nicaraguan fault the fledgling government for not really gaining control of the collective farms or reigning in the still economically dominant private ones. Confiscation was largely punitive, the goal being to punish Somoza's loyalists. Consequently, there is no logic to the land appropriation, either by region or by crop.[19]

The Urban Economy.   The same sort of indecisiveness characterized the Sandinistas' policy toward manufacturing. Of 400 firms employing more than 20 workers, only 80 were confiscated. As in agriculture, the decision to seize property was based largely on who owned it. Consequently, although there is a state planning commission, its responsibility is virtually random. It administers manufacturers producing about one-fourth of the total gross national product, hardly the stuff from which radical social or economic transformation is made. The Nicaraguan economy is best described as noninclusive mixed socialist. The state-owned companies account for 40 percent of GNP, private enterprise accounts for 36 percent, and the remainder is attributable to companies in which the state has a minority interest. As Weeks concludes (sympathetically if somewhat inaccurately), "The Nicaraguan economy . . . remained overwhelmingly a market economy."[20]

The prominence of the private sector does not mean that there was no change, just that Nicaragua has never contemplated a draconian, totalitarian government. Weeks sums up the changes well:

> It quickly became obvious to the wealthy families of Nicaragua that they did not hold dominant political power and had no prospect to do so in the foreseeable future. The new government clearly intended to change the balance of power between landlord and peasant and between capital and labor, as well as to institute limitations on private capital unheard of in Central America. . . . Before the revolution capital had a free reign and now the state intended, if possible, to assume leadership in the mixed economy.[21]

This agenda is a far cry from the obsession of totalitarian dictatorships. Nicaragua had, as the Sandinistas consolidated their power, the ability to have seized most private property but chose not to do so.

The Sandinistas Tighten Their Grip.   Nevertheless, Nicaragua's government was authoritarian in intent. As elsewhere in the region, the economy deteriorated; however, Nicaragua fared worse than most. Table 7.1 provides a measure of the quality of health care, a measure of the stability of the economy, and an index of the physical quality of life. The picture of Nicaragua that emerges is not that of a transformed society. Nicaragua's economy is effectively dead; its health index, in spite of is efforts, remains low; and its physical quality of life has not improved.[22] One solution is to tighten the screws, a course that the Sandinistas adopted. Their government, initially a coalition, became

TABLE 7.1 Comparison of Five Central American Countries

	Health Index*	Economic Stability†	Quality of Life‡
Costa Rica	44.25	10.50	85
El Salvador	28.00	6.15	64
Guatemala	24.13	13.40	54
Honduras	23.19	9.62	53
Nicaragua	24.48	3.26	55

*Life expectancy, number of physicians per capita.
†GNP growth, GNP per capita, inflation, foreign debt.
‡Estimate by *International Living*, January 1987, based on infant mortality, life expectancy, and literacy.

more oppressive. Members of the original coalition departed, leaving Sandinistas in charge of the implementation of policy. In a 1984 election that was, though not flawless, surely more open than in totalitarian regimes, the Sandinistas won with about two-thirds of the vote. This total is shockingly low by totalitarian standards, where 99.95 percent for the party is expected and achieved. Although major opposition groups did not participate, it is unlikely that the outcome would have been different had they done so. The election results were probably a good measure of the regime's support. To call the election a "Soviet-style sham," as President Reagan did, is surely a gross misstatement.

But the elections, although a reasonable mirror of popular sentiment, revealed a surprisingly strong, albeit unorganized, opposition. For comparison's sake, a 1987 election in Taiwan, with just about the same level of freedom, produced an 80 percent majority for the ruling Kuomintang party, and even then there was shock at the strength of the opposition. In the National Assembly, the Sandinistas have two-thirds of the seats, and parties of the right have most of the remainder. To strengthen the revolution, the Sandinistas have relied on education to socialize the youth in the proper ideology and on a growing internal security presence to monitor potentially threatening private associations.

Like the rulers of Cuba or China, the Sandinistas have come to rely on block or neighborhood committees to be their eyes and ears, to instill revolutionary ideology, and to track the movements of opponents or potential opponents. In addition, there are the *organizaciones populares:* the Sandinista Defense Committees, the Sandinista Workers Federation, the Rural Workers Association, the National Union of Farmers and Ranchers, the Luis Amada Espinosa Nicaraguan Women's Association, and the Sandinista Youth.[23] These organizations were auxiliaries to the FSLN (the Sandinistas). Other organizations were impeded in their attempts to criticize the regime by legislation suspending civil rights and by police harassment. In the schools, attention was turned to the creation of the "new man" who could "contribute to the transformation of the new society." The new man was to be "patriotic, disciplined, cooperative, modest, and able to understand that 'individual interest should coincide with social and national interest.' "[24] The campaign against illiteracy includes generous doses of Sandinista propaganda, as in "can you spell 'American imperialism'?" and the like.

This is clearly Marxist, but it is as much bluster as serious intent. There is no possible comparison between Nicaragua's political education and China's, the USSR's, or Cuba's. Nor is the governmental process as rigidly cohesive as in these totalitarian states. When Gorbachev announced glasnost, the vote in the Supreme Soviet (the legislative assembly) was unanimous, of course. The debate in the Nicaraguan Council of State is more sharply critical, and on occasion, the Sandinistas have yielded points to various coalitions of opposing parties. Nor is the judicial system as subservient as in totalitarian societies. The standard Marxist argument (all crime is institutionally induced) is rarely mentioned.[25]

If Nicaragua is not the Marxist demon portrayed by the American government, it is not the utopia portrayal by American academics either. Even though the 1984 election was not a complete fraud, major opposition parties (who would, as noted, probably have lost) did not participate because of the absence of free media and because of Sandinista harassment. Even though there is lively debate in the legislature, its deliberations are less important than the opinion of the partly. The party's dominance gives a Marxist cast to the governmental process.

The opposition's complaints are justified. Newspapers and radio stations are censored, all journalists are required to join a government-sponsored union, and there is no private television. The newspaper *La Prensa,* the center of the opposition, is routinely sanitized. *La Prensa* was also strong-armed by Somoza, and its editor was assassinated. The Sandinistas believe *La Prensa* conspires to overthrow their government and, especially in time of war, is justified in its behavior. As is frequently the case in autocratic systems, the information removed from *La Prensa* is often available in other newspapers, from the church, or on the Voice of America.[26]

The Roman Catholic church is locked in a bone-crunching conflict with the Sandinistas, who find it troublesome to tolerate but politically unfeasible to liquidate (which they, given their relatively benign form of government, are disinclined to do anyway). Church opposition was well formulated by Bishop Miguel Orbando y Bravo, speaking against compulsory military service:

> The absolute dictatorship of a political party which is constituted by force as the only arbiter and owners of the state, its institutions, and every type of social activity poses the problem of its legitimacy as well as the legitimacy of its institutions.[27]

These words, urging resistance, were published in *La Prensa,* an irony suggesting both by substance and medium of presentation that the Sandinistas are a long way from truly totalitarian repression.

The church speaks for Nicaragua's middle-class opposition. Originally in support of the Sandinistas' mixed socialism and its commitment to private property, middle-class conservatives were soon frozen out of any mode of participation, as the Sandinistas consolidated their power. Specifically, the Sandinistas had reshaped the formal structure of government: "Eliminating conservatives and asserting Sandinista control . . . , the Sandinistas diluted the representation of the bourgeois parties and private sector organizations . . . by increasing the representation of the mass organizations tied to the FSLN."[28] At the same time, nongovernment labor unions were prohibited. The coercion of the unions was followed by efforts to incorporate other previously independent groups into the government orbit of control and transform them into instruments of the state, a typically authoritarian (or even totalitarian) technique.

Even though the economy was not thoroughly nationalized, businesses were required to buy from and sell to the state. Further, the nationalization of financial institutions gave the state the critical role in international trade and limited the ability of the middle classes to take the money and run by moving capital out of the country. France did the same thing when François Mitterand, a Socialist, was chosen as premier. Nevertheless, the middle classes rightly concluded that the Sandinistas intended more economic control than they anticipated. The point was well made when leaders of middle-class business organizations were jailed.

There are possibly several thousand political prisoners, many not so fortunate as the businessmen whose connection with the church and international sympathy caused their early release. Many of these prisoners are turned in by the neighborhood watch committees, circumventing the more structured legal system. These excesses, coupled with the obvious admiration for Fidel Castro on the part of the Sandinista leadership, make a good case for arguing that Nicaragua is likely to become more authoritarian. The neighborhood committees sound very much like their totalitarian counterparts, and the rapidly growing secret police is Cuban-trained. The largest chunk of its foreign trade, aid packages, and military supplies is provided by the USSR, Cuba, and the eastern European centrally planned economies. Yet there is no Castro there, and Cuba was at a more advanced stage of autocratic control at the same point in its evolution.

In addition to fighting the contras (anti-Sandinista rebels funded by the United States), the government has been engaged in a protracted struggle with indigenous ethnic minorities, also the benefactors of American largess. How much of Nicaragua's autocratic behavior can be attributed to the United States' aggressive hostility? Perhaps some of the brutality, deaths, and mysterious disappearances would not have occurred, but the remainder of the authoritarian apparatus would in all likelihood have been the same.

Although much has been written about the unique status of Nicaragua, its leaders behave as typical authoritarians. Violent revolutions rarely evolve into democracy. Spain's autocratic government did so, but the revolution was in the 1930s, and the transition occurred four generations after the revolution. The Philippines might, with very generous definitions, qualify. But its revolution was virtually bloodless, brought on by the irresponsibility of the Marcos regime rather than by violence. The Philippine government is not yet democratic and faces a serious communist-led rebellion. Czechoslovakia, in 1968, looked as though it would allow genuine (that is, non-Communist) electoral competition, but the tentative opening (''Prague spring,'' so beautifully described in Milan Kundera's *Unbearable Lightness of Being),* ended with Soviet tanks rumbling into Prague. In any case, the Czech Communist party took power in a 1948 coup, not a revolution.

So the odds on Nicaragua's becoming more democratic are poor. In addition to the force of history, there is a long tradition of strong leadership in the area, and Sandinista leader Daniel Ortega quickly assumed the role of strong man, purging not only nonparty opponents but also weeding out competing intraparty factional leaders. Moreover, there is the heady rush of power; it is fun to run an authoritarian country, less fun to negotiate the rapids of group conflict in a democratic one. The perks of office are better, too. Although they layer their rhetoric with socialist phrasing, the Sandinista leaders are finding life at the top materially rewarding. They honor another Central American tradition, the treating of public funds as private property.[29] Party leaders' salaries are not revealed, they are given cars, pay no rent or utilities, and have access to U.S. currency with which to buy scarce imports at special stores. As the Sandinistas profess to be under the tutelage of Cuba's Castro, perhaps his immoderate personal lifestyle (a house in each of Cuba's 14 provinces, unparalleled opulence in his Havana residence) is also a guide.

If the Sandinistas will probably not reduce their political monopoly, what are the odds on Nicaragua's becoming more authoritarian, moving slightly toward totalitarianism? They are higher. Consider the overthrow of corrupt dictators between 1978 and 1987: Marcos in the Philippines, the shah of Iran, Duvalier in Haiti, Somoza in Nicaragua. Military governments were replaced by aspiring democratic regimes in Guatemala, Argentina, Brazil, and Ecuador. These were right-wing dictatorships with no serious ideology other than engorgement of the elite. In South Korea, Taiwan, and the People's Republic of China, movement in the direction of more political competition has begun. South Korea, responding to massive strikes and protests in 1987, scheduled open elections. Taiwan did likewise, without much protest before or fanfare afterward. On the mainland, one could argue that the party has retreated from Marxism and has relaxed its totalitarian control on the everyday life of the people (but there is little chance that intraparty competition, between the Communist party and a non-Communist one, will be allowed. Power purchased with lives is not easily relinquished. By establishing a monopoly over the economy, education, and communications, Marxists governments are more intractable than right-wing dictatorships. No one really knows how pervasive the legitimacy of the revolution is. Taking the 1984 election at face value, two-thirds of the people preferred the Sandinistas. But since then the economy has worsened and governmental vigilance has increased. One assessment concludes:

> Not many people doubt that the Sandinistas are running a nasty regime that is impoverishing their country. Most civil liberties have been suppressed, the last voice of an independent press was silenced this year, the church is harried and whole groups of Indians have been forced out of their homes [e.g., in 1986; conditions have improved since then]. Economic miseries have been piled on political ones. Nicaragua's foreign debt of $6 billion is far larger than the country's shrinking GNP, manufacturing industry has collapsed, even rice and beans are now rationed in peasant diets. The wisest policy towards such a regime is usually to let it self-destruct. The Sandinistas seem well on their way to that. The guess of some observers is that perhaps only a fifth of the city dwellers, and a slightly higher proportion of peasants, now back the government. But the worry about the Sandinistas is that they may be putting themselves in a position where no amount of unpopularity or incompetence will ever make any difference to their grip on power. Their 75,000-man army (Central America's largest by far) and 44,000-man reserve are there, very likely, not just to fight contras but also to impose a full-blooded communist government on the country.[30]

But the contras, survive only as the agent of the United States (and for how long?); surely popular support for them is no greater than for the Sandinistas. As the grim war continues, both sides commit horrible atrocities, alienating potential supporters. A European conference in 1987 heard a contingent of Nicaraguans who oppose both the government and the contras claim that 80 percent of the population supported them. Who knows? We can only be sure that the Sandinistas will not easily yield their power.

If you believe that false consciousness is a possibility, what is to be gained by, say, an open election? If a Marxist party loses, its defeat is attributable to the hoodwinking of the working classes. Thus in the 1984 election, the Sandinistas declared that the election was "not for the purpose of 'changing the government.' "[31]

Asian "Soft" Authoritarianism

The authoritarian governments of the Pacific—South Korea, Singapore, and Taiwan—have established a better record than their Central American counterparts. They have a more stable growth rate, their average individual income is higher, and the wealth is more equitably distributed. Although South Korea and Taiwan are becoming more "democratic," in that their governments are tolerating opposition parties, it is unlikely that they will move into the ranks of the competitive democracies.

Of the three major Asian authoritarian governments, South Korea comes the closest to fitting the "normal" assumptions concerning repression and exploitation. South Korea has not been able to establish the legitimacy of a ruling elite, a factor contributing to a spate of assassinations, military coups, protests, and finally, in 1987, an open election in which the opposition parties collectively won control of the legislature, a feat that put South Korea ahead of Taiwan in the race for democracy.

South Korean opposition groups have been more vociferous than those in either Singapore or Taiwan, and they have been more cruelly repressed. South Korea's human rights record is abominable in comparison with Singapore or Taiwan. Seriously enforced martial law was in effect in South Korea from 1972 until 1987. South Korea's work force too has been sorely tested. Although enjoying rapid economic growth, its income distribution is less favorable than Taiwan's or Singapore's. Its labor force, organized into compliant, semiofficial unions, was routinely denied the right to strike until 1987, when the dam broke. South Korean workers worked far longer hours than those in Taiwan and Singapore, and the rate of industrial accidents in South Korea is among the highest in the world.

In Taiwan, the opposition has been less violent, and government repression has been less harsh. Although until 1986 there were no legal opposition organizations, individual opposition candidates competed in local elections against the ruling Kuomintang party and won about 20 percent of the time. In 1986, the Democratic Progressive party was formed and won about the same proportion of votes. Here the comparison with South Korea is stark: after weeks of hard, confrontational, media-saturated demonstrations, an agreement allowing open elections was reached. In Taiwan, the exact same result occurred without more than an occasional demonstration.

Singapore's experience has been neither as confrontational as South Korea's nor as placid as Taiwan's. The People's Action party is invariably successful, and the election of a single opposition candidate is viewed as a serious crisis of legitimacy. Singapore's tough internal security laws are used against opposition candidates. Twelve were arrested in 1987 and held without bail or formal charges for several years for alleged sympathy with "Marxism." A few years earlier, when two opposition candidates were elected, PAP leaders spoke of "flaws" in the system, of democracy having gone too far.

TABLE 7.2 Economic Performance of Asian and Latin American Authoritarian Governments

	Inflation (1973–1984)	GNP per Capita ($, 1984)	GNP Growth (1968–1983)	Equality (Ward Index)*
Asian				
Taiwan	3.0	4,600	8.3	−15
South Korea	17.6	2,800	8.4	8
Singapore	3.1	7,260	7.4	−1
Latin America				
Chile	75.4	1,700	0.1	4
Mexico	31.5	2,040	2.9	23
Nicaragua	17.2	860	−1.5	41
El Salvador	11.3	710	−0.6	69

*The Ward index is a combination of infant mortality, doctors per 10,000 inhabitants, daily kilocalories consumed per capita, the Gini index, and a measure of social mobility. Negative numbers mean *more* equality; the higher the number, the greater the equality. Positive numbers mean *less* equality; the higher the number, the greater the inequality.
SOURCE: Reprinted by permission of the publisher from *The Political Economy of Distribution* by Michael Don Ward, p. 181. Copyright © 1977 by Elsevier Science Publishing Co., Inc.

But these governments, unlike those in Latin America, preside over economic miracles, as Table 7.2 makes clear. The abundant contrasts illustrate the futility of arguing that governments "cause" economic development; two groups of governments, each almost equally authoritarian, are incomparable. Life in Asian authoritarian systems is obviously more pleasant: inflation is low, per capita income is high and getting higher, and the gap between the rich and the poor is smaller.

If high-growth Asian authoritarian governments do not prove that authoritarian governments are preferable to democratic ones, are there aspects of their authoritarianism that might explain why they are so economically dominant? Chapter 2 offered one tempting theory made popular by the pop-scientific analyses of, especially, Japan; it may be, however, that Confucianism is a philosophical defense of authoritarianism, which, as a serendipitous side benefit, drives its adherents to high achievements. Observers since Marco Polo have sung the extravagant praise of the seemingly compliant, well-organized, and conflict-avoiding Asian countries. We saw that the above-average achievement of Asian children in American schools is credited to the Confucian respect for authority and stress on filial piety. Another often cited illustration is the savings rate: Asian save at least one-third of their income, leaving governments free of external debt and hence able to expand economically (the rate in Taiwan is about 44 percent, compared to 4 percent in the United States). The Philippines, a Christian country, is the most glaring example of an Asian government that has *not* grown economically and where the appeal of Confucianism is reinforced.

Whether the Asian countries prosper because they are Confucian is an impossible question to answer. What is beyond dispute is the similarity in their economic management. Their bureaucracies are well trained and generally limit corruption to "honest graft." Their decision-making style is consensual; there are "interlocking directorates" between government and business that have no counterparts in totalitarian or democratic societies. The symbiosis is uniquely Asian. There is usually a single, prestigious government department that serves as a "pilot light." Economic planning is centralized, and compliance by the private sector is easily obtained. Interest group conflict is minimized and contained.

There is more fine tuning in Asian authoritarian governments than in the industrial democracies, but governmental guidance generally takes the form of market manipulation (as opposed to state ownership, as in socialism):

> This cooperation is achieved through innumerable, continuously operating forums for coordinating views and investment plans, sharing international commercial intelligence, making adjustments to conform to the business cycle or other changes in the economic environment, deciding on the new industries needed in order to maintain international competitive ability, and spreading both the wealth and the burden equitably.[32]

DIRECT MILITARY RULE

Nigeria, a former British colony, is paralyzed by ethnic and regional loyalties. It has 250 ethnic groups speaking 100 different languages. Few countries better illustrate David Lamb's conclusion:

> Tribalism is the most potent force in everyday life in Africa. It often determines who gets jobs, who gets promoted, who gets accepted to a university, because by its very definition tribalism implies sharing among members of the extended family, making sure that your own are looked after first.[33]

In the north, a spare, desertlike area, the Muslim religion and culture and a traditional, hierarchic, authoritarian view of life are preeminent. Polygamy and the subordination of women—Muslim traditions—are still practiced. In the south, contact with Europeans and Christianity contributed to a more egalitarian world view. Southern tribes—especially the Yorubas and the Ibos—are more educated, wealthier, more individualistic, and more achievement-oriented. They are also a minority.

When the British arrived in the 19th century, they found that intertribal warfare and the selling of captives in tribal war as slaves had destroyed most of the Nigerian culture. As in India, British rule ended local wars but not tribal hostilities. The British treated the southern tribes, especially the Ibos, with more favor than tribes in the north, largely because the favored tribes were the most Western in culture. They were not autocratic, they honored individual achievement and disallowed most inherited wealth, making reputations a matter of individual accomplishment. They were eager to learn, and they looked toward England and Europe as havens of civilization. Like the Sikhs in India, the Ibos were detested. Unlike the Sikhs, the Ibos were placed at the controls of the country at independence in 1960. Arrogant, aloof, scornful of the primitive tribes of the north, the Ibos could not rule for long. Ibos and northerners traded coups, with the ferocity of the struggles illustrating well how severe regional disputes can be:

Northern soldiers chased Ibo troops from their barracks and murdered scores with bayonets. Screaming Moslem mobs descended on the Ibo headquarters of every northern city, killing their victims with clubs, poison arrows and shotguns. Tens of thousands of Ibos were murdered in the systematic massacres that followed.[34]

The short-lived republic of Biafra, created by Ibos, was the result of these outbreaks. Biafra lasted three years before Nigerian troops starved it into surrender.

The defeat of the Ibos led to optimistic hopes that nationalism could defeat regionalism, given a strong central government and a willingness to confront and defeat rebellions. The governmental system adopted after the defeat of Biafra was based on the federalism of the United States. However, in order to minimize the centrifugal forces of tribalism, the 19 states were given overlapping boundaries, dividing tribes into different political administrative units—the exact reverse of the Indian solution. The postwar Nigerian leadership, a military dictatorship, was surprisingly lenient toward the Ibos, and the war appeared to have ended the question of national versus regional loyalties. The military leadership stressed "one Nigeria." Nationalism became a required component of the political socialization process, with schools assuming major responsibilities for the creation of a Nigerian national consciousness and nation building.

Nigeria returned to civilian rule in 1979. Civilian rule was accompanied by a re-emergence of the old tribal loyalties. The United party was controlled by the Yorubas, the Nigerian People's party was the creation of the Ibos. The leader of the Ibo rebellion, Oxford-educated Chukweumeka Odumegwu Ojukwu, in exile, was not allowed to return. A northern Muslim, representing the pragmatic, business-oriented National party won. Another victory in 1983 suggested that the old regional tribalism had finally come to an end.

However, yet another coup replaced the civilian government with a military dictatorship in 1984. Among the numerous reasons for the coup were corruption and an economy declining because of the oil glut. But the continued tribal threat to stability looms large as an explanation. Ojukwu returned from exile in 1982 and breathed new life into the Ibo party; in the north, the People's Redemption party sought to impose a Muslim culture on the south, advocating, for example, Muslim legal codes rather than the Western ones preferred in the south. Fundamentalist riots were ruthlessly suppressed in 1982. Under such conditions, a military coup was unavoidable.

CIVILIAN–MILITARY REGIMES

Civilian–military regimes have generally no coherent ideology. Frequently, they rule for the single-minded purpose of taking all they can from the public treasury; those in Haiti and the Philippines are especially apt examples, but there are many more. Left dictatorships are just as corrupt but more self-righteous. The behavior of a right-wing dictatorship is well illustrated by Chile. In 1973, an elected Marxist government was overthrown (with substantial American help) and replaced by a military dictatorship. Although a plebiscite in 1978 affirmed the legitimacy of the dictatorship, no alternative was offered. The language of the plebiscite was outrageous:

> In the face of the international aggression unleashed against the government of the fatherland, I support [General Augusto] Pinochet in his defense of the dignity of Chile, and I reaffirm the legitimate right of the republic to conduct the process of institutionalization in a manner befitting its sovereignty.[35]

Even so, a no vote of 30 percent was reported. But Pinochet used the referendum to substitute a "state of emergency" for a "state of siege," thus partly restoring civil liberties. Further institutionalization was provided with a new constitution in 1981. Pinochet was to govern until 1989, unless another referendum turned him out of office (if not, he could govern until 1997).

President Pinochet developed repression to a degree equaled only by the totalitarian countries. Revenge for an attempt on his life was extracted in especially gruesome ways. The son of an exiled leftist was doused with flammable liquid and set afire by Chilean soldiers. Following the 1973 coup, nationalized industries were returned to the private sector, with the government intervening only in copper mining and petroleum. Unions, though restricted, have staged local strikes at the plant level with no repercussions. The media, though censored, reflect a wide variety of opinion.

Returning the economy to the private sector did produce the growth anticipated. Chile recorded a negative economic growth rate during the Marxist years, and it was anticipated that a vigorous dose of market economics would shake the economy out of its doldrums. Indeed, the influx of the "Chicago boys" (economists who espoused the laissez-faire economics of the University of Chicago's Economics Department) was intended to make Chile a showpiece for market economics. However, by 1982, Chile's economy was a genuine disaster, with GNP falling about 14 percent. But a turnaround of sorts occurred in 1985. The economy began to grow. This sudden upswing in Chile's economic fortunes coincided with growing dissatisfaction with Pinochet among his own supporters.

During the 1982–1983 recession, Pinochet's "natural constituency" turned against him:

> Groups which had railed vociferously against President Allende, and which had been closely associated with the *junta* in its early years, now called the Pinochet regime "the worst government in the country's history." Prominent leaders . . . verbally attacked General Pinochet in harsh, even insulting language.[36]

And therein lies the story of 1988: in that year, the plebiscite, with a turnout rate in the low 90 percent range, rejected (by a 55 percent majority) Pinochet's effort to remain on until 1997, requiring a new election (without Pinochet). Opposition leaders kept up their attacks. Labor unions, technically restricted, became one of the major focal points of resistance. Often they established alliances with the members of the old Christian Democratic party and other centrist remnants. The *Alianza Democrática*, an alliance of these center groups, called for Pinochet's resignation and a return to democracy. On the left, the technically illegal Marxist parties, though denied coalition with the center, operated openly.

By 1985, with the economic upswing showing no signs of abating, reliable surveys indicated that at best 20 percent of the population would support a continuation of the

Pinochet dictatorship. With newspapers declaring with once impossible irreverence, "If he doesn't want to leave, we'll have to throw him out," an opposition coalition issued a "national accord for transition to full democracy." Pinochet tried a return to repression, but the opposition was too highly placed. His hold on the military was precarious. In 1986, an assassination attempt cost the lives of several members of Pinochet's military escort, further disillusioning the military. Yet more urgency was created by the historic visit of Pope John Paul II of 1987, during which the pontiff pleaded for a peaceful and unified opposition. The violence that accompanied the papal visit further damaged the legitimacy of the Pinochet regime. But the ultimate damage was from the United States, long Pinochet's patron. Its various governmental programs for the encouragement of democracy, which have given money to Solidarity in Poland, contributed to Pinochet's opposition. With Pinochet's defeat, the stage was set for a return to open elections.

KLEPTOCRACIES

The unique characteristics of the kleptocracy is the apparent commitment of its ruling elite to self-aggrandizement, not as a deserved perk of government but as an end in itself. Ferdinand Marcos of the Philippines diverted for personal use most of the $2 billion annually given to his country by the World Bank. By diverting World Bank funds, U.S. aid programs, and other international sources of money, in addition to plain old-fashioned payoffs from international gangs, Marcos earned about $20 billion, making him the world's richest dictator. Marcos was in it for the money.

But crook though he was, his government never succeeded in diverting the majority of its resources into his personal accounts. That honor belongs to Mobutu Sese Seko of Zaire. About 60 percent of all government revenues in his country are "lost,"[37] and Mobutu controls about one-fourth of this revenue for his own personal use, without any even cursory accounting. Another 30 percent goes through the office of the presidency without any budgetary control. Because Zaire is poorer than the Philippines ($160 GNP per capita, compared with $560), the take is not as large: Mobutu is said to be worth about $10 billion. But the rate of robbery is the highest in the world; it is the "politics of appropriation," and Mobutu is unchallenged:

> [He] makes use of the country as his own private patrimony. He controls and distributes all the offices—all the posts, all the advantages linked to power. All revenue, all nominations, all promotions ultimately depend on presidential good will. No fortune, no enterprise, no position is sheltered from a decision by Mobutu.[38]

Mobutu's personal holding company—to manage the swag—employees 25,000 people. Although the figures are not, in themselves, conclusive, they are suggestive: from 1968 through 1986, GNP growth in the Philippines was an anemic 1.9 percent; in Zaire, GNP was −2.2 percent! (Only Uganda's was worse.) To what extent can Zaire's dismal performance be a attributed to Mobutu's compulsive stealing? Had he been a model ruler, Zaire would still be poor. But it is the world's purest kleptocracy.

ARE AUTHORITARIAN GOVERNMENTS "BAD"?

Remember that most people are not deeply interested in politics; in totalitarian regimes, the intersection of the personal and the political is apparent at every step through life, no matter how trivial. But in authoritarian governments, life need not be unpleasant. There are authoritarian governments that, while cracking down on dissent, have managed the economy quite well, so that their subjects are well off in comparison to those in Latin America and are, if not content, hardly marching to the barricades of revolution.

In sum, authoritarian governments are examples of both dazzling success and dismaying failure. Perhaps their most potentially dangerous flaw is the absence of an institutional device for ensuring a peaceful leadership transition. Although Mexico has solved this problem, since the president is limited to two terms and is invariably chosen from the ranks of the party faithful. But in El Salvador, Nicaragua, Taiwan, and South Korea, no clear process is in evidence. Indeed, in some authoritarian countries, such as Chile and South Korea, the process of leadership selection is itself a source of serious controversy.

In democratic societies, leadership change is institutionalized, and to a slightly lesser extent, totalitarian governments make provisions to ensure an orderly changing of the guard. Both the Soviet Union and the People's Republic of China appear to have solved the problem to the satisfaction of most participants. But the authoritarian governments, perhaps because they are dominated by neither a single charismatic leader nor a single source of authority, have not been as successful. What does one do when a Marcos or a Duvalier gains a foothold? However, some authoritarian governments—El Salvador, for example—appear to be at greater risk than others, such as Taiwan and Singapore. But unlike totalitarian societies, which one might judge "bad" generally, authoritarian ones depend on the benevolence of the elite—hardly reassuring but better than nothing.

FOR FURTHER CONSIDERATION

1. What is the essential difference between an authoritarian and a totalitarian government?
2. Attack or defend the assertion that Nicaragua is a totalitarian government rather than an authoritarian government.
3. Would a better name for the "radical regimes" be "ideological regimes"? Or is there some other common element they both share? Justify your position.
4. What does the adjective "soft" mean with regard to Asian authoritarian governments?
5. Why are most governments authoritarian?

For the More Adventurous

1. Are authoritarian governments "bad"? Why? Are they "bad" only because they are authoritarian or are they "bad" because of something they do (or do not) achieve? Examine India and Singapore. Compare: Gross National Product per capita, average life expectancy, caloric

intake, and political system. If you were forced to choose between living in India or in Singapore, which country would you choose?

2. Compare two conservative authoritarian regimes. Choose one that is a "traditional monarchy, with family-based ruling groups and no significant political infrastructure" and one that is a "dictatorship dependent upon the personality of a leader." Besides being authoritarian, what else do they have in common?

3. Observe how most news media describe the Sandinista regime in Nicaragua. In your opinion, is the picture that they present an accurate one? Look back at the coverage of the Somoza regime. Can you discern any significant change in how each authoritarian regime is described? If there is a difference, speculate as to the reason why. What does that say about the United States?

NOTES

1. Robert Nisbet, *Prejudices: A Philosophical Dictionary* (Cambridge, Mass.: Harvard University press, 1982), p. 18.

2. Quentin Skinner, *The Foundations of Modern Political Thought. Volume 1: The Renaissance* (Cambridge: Cambridge University Press, 1978), pp. 160–165.

3. Gordon Griffiths, "The Italian City-State," in *The City-State in Five Cultures,* ed. Robert Griffeth and Carol G. Thomas (Santa Barbara, Calif.: ABC-CLIO, 1981), p. 83.

4. Herbert J. Storing, ed., *The Anti-Federalists* (Chicago: University of Chicago Press, 1985), p. 267.

5. Christopher R. Friedrichs, "The Swiss and German City-States," in Griffeth and Thomas, *City-State,* pp. 130, 131.

6. Michael Novak, *The Spirit of Democratic Capitalism* (New York: Simon & Schuster, 1983), pp. 16–17.

7. This section draws heavily from Mark A. Tessler, "Morocco: Institutional Pluralism and Monarchical Dominance," in *Political Elites in Arab North Africa,* ed. William Zartman et al. (White Plains, N.Y.: Longman, 1982), pp. 35–91.

8. Ibid., p. 64.

9. Thomas W. Lippman, *Understanding Islam* (New York: Mentor, 1982), p. 144.

10. Quoted in Cheryl Benard and Zalmay Khalilzad, *The Government of God* (New York: Columbia University Press, 1984), p. 115.

11. Ibid., p. 131.

12. John P. Entelis, "Algeria: Technocratic Rule, Military Power," in Zartman, *Political Elites,* pp. 95–97.

13. The wealthiest 5 percent of Nicaragua's population received 28 percent of all income, compared to 25 percent in Costa Rica, 33 percent in Salvador, 30 percent in Guatemala, 28 percent in Honduras, and 30 percent in Panama. The poorest 10 percent in Nicaragua received 1.2 percent of the income, compared to 1.5 percent in Costa Rica, 0.8 percent in El Salvador, 1.3 percent in Guatemala, 2.1 percent in Honduras, and 0.6 percent in Panama. See Marcelo Alonso, *Central America in Crisis* (Washington, D.C.: Washington Institute for Values in Public Policy, 1984), p. 214.

14. Raymond D. Gastil, *Civil Rights in the World* (Boston: Hall, 1979), p. 287.

15. John Weeks, *The Economies of Central America* (New York: Holmes & Meier, 1985), p. 156.

16. John A. Booth, *The End and the Beginning: The Nicaraguan Revolution* (Boulder, Colo.: Westview Press, 1982), pp. 192–214.

17. To allege similarity between the behavior of a revolutionary government and the one it

replaced is to challenge a widely held belief among academics about the merits of the Sandinistas. I am not claiming they are uniquely evil, only that, as in all revolutions, the result is less liberating than originally anticipated. Twentieth-century Marxist revolutions (in Cuba, the USSR, and elsewhere) have not replaced authoritarianism with democracy and indeed did not intend to do so.

18. Joseph R. Thome and David Kaimowitz, "Agrarian Reform," in *Nicaragua: The First Five Years*, ed. Thomas W. Walker (New York: Praeger, 1984), pp. 297–298.
19. Weeks, *Economies*, p. 160.
20. John Weeks "The Industrial Sector," in Walker, *Nicaragua*, pp. 288–289.
21. Weeks, *Economies*, p. 171.
22. These data paint a picture of the entire region in economic disarray, not just Nicaragua. Conroy's data are less grim. He shows Nicaragua outperforming Central America in both GNP growth and GNP per capita growth. See Michael E. Conroy, "Economic Legacy and Policies," in Walker, *Nicaragua*, pp. 224–225.
23. Luis Hector Serra, "The Grass Roots Organizations," in Walker, *Nicaragua*, p. 65.
24. Deborah Barndt, "Popular Education," in Walker, *Nicaragua*, p. 320.
25. John A. Booth, "The National Governmental System," in Walker, *Nicaragua*, pp. 38–39.
26. John Spicer Nichols, "The Media," in Walker, *Nicaragua*, p. 187.
27. Quoted in Conor Cruise O'Brien, "God and Man in Nicaragua," *Atlantic Monthly*, August 1986, p. 51.
28. Dennis Gilbert, "The Bourgeoisie," in Walker, *Nicaragua*, p. 168.
29. See Barry Rubin, *Modern Dictatorship* (New York: McGraw-Hill, 1987), pp. 287–288.
30. "Why the Contras," *Economist*, September 6, 1986, p. 12.
31. "Nicaragua Is the Issue," *Economist*, February 2, 1985, p. 26.
32. Chalmers Johnson, "Introduction: The Taiwan Model," in *Contemporary Republic of China: The Taiwan Experience*, ed. James C. Hsuing (New York: American Association for Asian Studies, 1981), p. 5.
33. David Lamb, *The Africans* (New York: Random House, 1982), p. 9.
34. Ibid., p. 308.
35. Genaro Arriagada, *Pinochet: The Politics of Power* (Boston: Unwyn Hyman, 1988), p. 34.
36. Brian Loveman, *Chile*, 2d ed. (New York: Oxford University Press, 1988), p. 348.
37. Thomas M. Callaghy, *The State-Society Struggle* (New York: Columbia University Press, 1984), p. 189.
38. Ibid., pp. 178–179.

FOR FURTHER READING

Benard, Cheryl, and Zalmay Khalilzad. *The Government of God.* New York: Columbia University Press, 1984. An account of Iran's theocracy.

Callaghy, Thomas M. *The State-Society Struggle.* New York: Columbia University Press, 1984.

Dardness, John W. *Confucianism and Autocracy.* Berkeley: University of California Press, 1983.

Hawkes, Gary. *The Philippine State and the Marcos Regime.* Ithaca, N.Y.: Cornell University Press, 1987. Hawkes persuades us that "corruption, mismanagement, and violence . . . in defense of [his] own private interests" doomed Marcos.

Lippman, Thomas. *Understanding Islam.* New York: New American Library, 1982.

Llovio-Mendendez, Jose Luis. *Insider.* New York: Bantam Books, 1988. An ex–Cuban government minister tells all.

Loveman, Brian. *Chile,* 2d ed. New York: Oxford University Press, 1988.

Mottahedeh, Roy. *The Mantle of the Prophet*. New York: Simon & Schuster, 1985. The culture and politics of Iran explained cogently.

Omond, Roger. *The Apartheid Handbook*. New York: Viking Penguin, 1985. A clear guide to the labyrinthine racial regulations of South Africa.

Perlmutter, Amos. *Modern Authoritarianism*. New Haven, Conn.: Yale University Press, 1981.

Rubin, Barry. *Modern Dictators: Third World Coup Makers, Dictators, Strongmen, and Populist Tyrants*. New York: McGraw-Hill, 1987.

Seagrave, Sterling. *The Marcos Dynasty*. New York: Harper & Row, 1988. With questionable sources and a descernible bias, Seagrave nevertheless captures the flavor of decadence—tawdry and vulgar—that engulfed Marcos.

Weeks, John. *The Economies of Central America*. New York: Holmes & Meier, 1985.

Valladares, Armando. *Against All Hope*. New York: Knopf 1986. A grim, almost too grim, account of personal life in Cuba's prisons.

Zartman, William, et al. *Political Elites in Arab North Africa*. White Plains, N.Y.: Longman, 1982. A first-rate set of essays on a puzzling and intriguing region.

CHAPTER 8

Totalitarianism:
Polity over Diversity

Novosti Press Agency, Rome.

For those of us accustomed to living in the open society provided by democracies, the difference between totalitarian and authoritarian may be merely semantic. Both typically have one-party systems, and they both set limits on political activity, political discussions and writings, and political organizations, and neither type of government places as much value on the individual as democracies do.

But to lump all nondemocratic regimes in the same category is inaccurate. Common sense alone tells us that Mexico's one-party authoritarian government has very little in common with the Khmer Rouge dictatorship in Cambodia, the brutal dictatorship of Germany under the Third Reich, or the repressive governments in the Soviet Union and the People's Republic of China.

We know almost by instinct what the difference is, a difference illustrated by the following popular joke, current in Europe in the 1980s.

What's the difference between West Germany, Italy, Yugoslavia, and the Soviet Union? In West Germany, everything is allowed, except that which is prohibited; in Italy, everything is allowed, *especially* that which is prohibited; in Yugoslavia, everything is prohibited, except that which is allowed; in the Soviet Union, everything is prohibited, *especially* that which is allowed!

Authoritarian governments maintain the separation between public and private, whereas totalitarian regimes are dedicated to its elimination. The essence of totalitarian government is its willingness to commit the resources of the state to the destruction of the wall between public and private life. Such destruction is not easy or cheap, and totalitarian aspirations often fail. To commit the resources necessary to plan an economy down to the most minute detail, to eliminate racial, cultural, regional, and class diversity, to reeducate an entire population in the ways of the state ideology—this is not a task for the importune or the fainthearted. The very word *totalitarian* refers to the state's involvement in *all* aspects of society.

To show the differences, we can compare Stalin's industrialization scheme of the 1930s (see later in this chapter) to earlier examples of brutality with regard to death and destruction. The number killed was surely as great as those killed during the 13th-century Mongol conquest of Russia by Genghis Khan. But Stalin's goal was more comprehensive. The difference nicely underscores the contrast between ancient authoritarianism and modern totalitarianism:

When the Mongols conquered Russia in the thirteenth century, they slaughtered those who resisted them, laid waste the great cities of the land. But from those who submitted they exacted a tribute and allowed them to live in their own way, left them to their own institutions and faith. In the twentieth century the conquered were most of the nation, the bulk of the peasantry. Within a few years they were forced to change their entire manner of life, forsake their immemorial customs and rights.[1]

The Mongols and Stalin were equally contemptuous of life, and this superficial similarity sometimes encourages us to compare earlier authoritarian governments with modern totalitarian ones. When distinctions are made, the basis is usually the availability of advanced technology of repression (electronic surveillance, sophisticated computers, extraordinary weapons of destruction). True, sophisticated surveillance and torture are 20th-century innovations, as is totalitarianism, but the difference between authoritarian and totalitarian is not technical.

There is a greater contrast. Earlier authoritarians defended a *natural order*. The Chinese before the 1949 revolution, the medieval society sanctioned by the conservative Christianity of Aquinas, and the Franco government in Spain all illustrate this commitment. In Confucian China, the "mandate of heaven," although it allowed for absolutism, depended on mutual acceptance of reciprocal authority. In the Middle Ages, vassals gave obedience, but lords provided protection. And the key to the good polity is the establishment—or rather the discovery—and maintenance of a hierarchy, with each rung in the ladder rightfully and willingly occupied by the various designates. In Confucian China, the family was the model for the state; the father, the model for the emperor. In medieval society, education was left largely to the church. And in Franco's Spain, the church and the government were mutually supportive; the state did not destroy Catholicism, rather it exploited it. Such regimes are *conservative,* not revolutionary. When the order is disrupted, it needs immediate restoration by whatever means necessary; but there is no thought of changing human character.

In contrast, totalitarian government is made up of these components:

1. An official, revolutionary, ideology
2. A single, disciplined party
3. Terroristic police control
4. Party monopoly of the mass media
5. Party control of the armed forces
6. Central direction of the economy
7. Annihilation of all boundaries between public and private

Five countries have sustained *all* of these facets of totalitarianism:

Country	Polity
Albania	Communist one-party
Bulgaria*	Communist one-party
Mongolia	Communist one-party
North Korea	Communist one-party
Romania	Communist one-party

Life in these societies is unrelievedly grim. In North Korea, "no individual thoughts are advanced publicly or privately. Everyone is given a security rating that determines future success. . . . There are also reeducation centers and internal exile. There is no private business or agriculture."[2] In Albania, "media are characterized by incessant propaganda, and open expression of opinion in private conversation may lead to long prison sentences. . . . There are no private organizations independent of government or party."[3]

---

*Shows signs of losing its resolve.

To get an idea of the severity of these regimes, consider the list of "backslid" or unsuccessful totalitarian regimes, those that lost the resolve, could not afford the cost, or have not yet developed the technology:

Country	Polity
Afghanistan	Communist one-party
Angola	Socialist one-party
Benin	Socialist one-party
Burma	Socialist one-party
Cambodia	Communist one-party
China (ROC)	Communist one-party
Cuba	Communist one-party
Czechoslavakia	Communist one-party
Ethiopia	Communist one-party
East Germany	Communist one-party
Ginea-Bissau	Socialist one-party
Iraq	Socialist one-party
Kenya	Nationalist one-party
Laos	Communist one-party
Libya	Socialist quasi-one-party
Mozambique	Socialist one-party
Saudi Arabia	Traditional nonparty
Somalia	Socialist one-party
South Yemen	Socialist one-party
Tanzania	Socialist one-party
USSR	Communist one-party
Vietnam	Communist one-party
Zaire	Nationalist one-party

A WORLD VIEW: THROUGH A GLASS DARKLY?

The governments singled out in this chapter for more detailed attention—the Soviet Union, the People's Republic of China, and Cambodia—have been classic examples of the power of an ideology. But they no longer make the cut and are a notch down from the successful, sustained, totalitarian regimes just listed. Although they will certainly not become Western-style democracies, they have retreated irrevocably from the ideological obsession necessary to undergird totalitarianism. The ideological fervor is no longer there.

Both lists consist largely of communist or socialist regimes. Marxism, and its variants, is the only extant *total* ideology. In the 1930s, Mussolini's Italy and Hitler's Germany—obsessively anticommunist—would certainly be on the list (although Italy and, contrary to common perception, Germany would not survive the cut for the list of successes). Germany's failure is illustrative of the need for an inclusive ideology. Where were the stages of history, setting forth the inevitable triumph of the master race? Where was the detailed explanation of the irresistible logic of the cause? Compared with the sweep of Marxism, the ideological justification for Nazi Germany is a pastiche of crackpot prejudices.

Lacking an ideology, other than half-baked notions of racial supremacy, the Nazi party never established itself as the keeper of the faith, as did the Communist party in the USSR.[4] What is needed is a *vision:*

> Because they identify individual with collective goals and purposes, totalitarian ideologies are not only anti-individualist, [but] they promise an end to disharmony among individuals and within individuals. False consciousness, isolation, anomie, separation, loneliness, purposelessness—all are defined as subjective consequences of objective social ills, therefore as capable of being eradicated through social engineering. All twentieth-century radical critiques deplore the loss of individual identification with social roles and social purposes as a curse of modern society. All promise to ''solve'' man's isolation and to restore him to a full sense of social membership.[5]

The negation of the private life in exchange for redemption makes modern totalitarianism different both in kind and in purpose from authoritarian governments. The totalitarian ideology is a *world view.* It is not merely an economic or political ideology, and it is not confined to a narrow set of circumstances. Everything is explained, is of the same piece.

The classic totalitarian state eliminates or captures all potentially autonomous political, social, economic, and cultural organizations and employs ruthless measures to ensure subject compliance. The world's history is filled with tales of ghastly slaughter, much of it undertaken on dictatorial whim. But the modern totalitarian state kills, tortures, and indoctrinates because of a mission. Often such governments degenerate into slaughterhouses, but they begin with a purpose for which death is an acceptable cost.

The idea that power, in addition to being ''instrumental'' (a means to and end), can be an end in itself has spawned new inquiries into the behavior of political elites. The most promising theory, because it agrees with more general psychiatric theory, is that power for its own sake is a consequence of a need to dominate as a protection from ''low self-estimates.''[6]

In other words, some public politicians seek power to compensate for personal inadequacies. Low self-esteem is surely the most destructive of such inadequacies, and most of us would do almost anything to correct it. Low self-esteem is often linked to a negative personality—a person for whom life is simply not fun; it is sad and discouraging. Low self-esteem can be induced by families, and it is also genetically influenced. People with low self-esteem are suspicious and can become paranoid:

> Activity has a compulsive quality, as if the man were trying to make up for something or to escape from anxiety into hard work. He seems ambitious, striving upward, power-seeking. His stance toward the environment is aggressive and he has a persistent problem in managing his aggressive feelings. His self-image is vague and discontinuous. Life is a hard struggle to achieve and hold power.[7]

For such people, power is the goal. Once achieved, personal anxieties can be displaced, private demons can be publicly exorcised. Among American presidents, Wilson, Johnson, and Nixon are the clearest examples of such behavior. Among nondemocratic leaders, Hitler, Mao, and Stalin appear to have been the least balanced. Politicians generally believed to be instrumental (using power to achieve public goals, rather than to displace private anxieties) are Lenin, Thatcher, Gorbachev, and Deng.

In private politics, the consequences of low self-esteem can be tragic: homicide, suicide, broken families, and so on are all at least partly associated with personality disorder (and, of course, societal inequities).

But in public politics, the consequences may be more extreme. There are the seemingly trivial displacements: Castro of Cuba outlaws Christmas (this is the basis for the scene in Woody Allen's *Bananas,* in which the revolutionary leader of "San Marcos" declares the official language to be Swedish). But especially in societies with few constraints on leaders, displacement can be monumentally tragic: Hitler used the state to satiate his anti-Semitism (his prosecution of the war was secondary), Stalin eliminated an entire classes of rural peasants in the Soviet Union, and about one-seventh of the population of Cambodia was killed by Pol Pot. When personal instability is combined with a messianic ideology and an absolutist government structure, the havoc is almost beyond the imagination:

Politically Caused Deaths in the 20th Century (in millions)[8]

Source of intrasocietal deaths

Communist governments	99
Other totalitarian	25
Authoritarian	4
Democratic	1
Total	129

War deaths

International	33
Civil	8
Total	41

Public politics—the use of power publicly—can be deadly and not all that remote.

Totalitarian ideologies and movements find a nearly exact analogue in religious cults. Cult leaders have absolute authority over their flock, and they promise redemption in exchange for the surrendering of self. Cult members must devote all their energy to the cause, and cults actively suppress alternative or conflicting views of reality.[9]

Traditional religions can also be authoritarian, as is the Roman Catholic church; however, traditional religions do not require the sacrifice of the self. The difference between cults and the Roman Catholic church also provide a good analogue for the difference between a totalitarian and an authoritarian governmental system. People who are drawn to exotic cults have personalities comparable with those attracted to the initial stages of political totalitarianism: they are "marginal" (feel out of step with mainstream institutions and ideologies), have trouble with self-esteem, and are in search of a clarification of their identity; they want to know "who am I?"[10] But the appeals of totalitarianism cannot be easily dismissed as an aberration attractive only to the dispossessed. According to the totalitarian creed, the need for redemption is universal.

Jeane Kirkpatrick catalogs the religious nature of modern totalitarianism:[11]

1. The goals are universal; they do not involve individual aspirations.
2. They are teleological, and once in place are unalterable.
3. They are final; once they are achieved, a utopian state of being will be in place.
4. They are comprehensive, involving all aspects of life.
5. They are derived from a moral vision; they fulfill a vision of a perfect future.

PUBLIC AUTHORITY AND PRIVATE LIFE: THE MORALITY OF MARXISM

Totalitarian states are willing to invest enormous sums of money and energy into a most difficult task because they are governed by people driven to create a new set of individual values; they are uninterested in merely reforming political institutions. Totalitarian ideologies are *utopian*. They imagine a changed world that will be free of the conflict and tension of "normal" political, social, and economic life. Such extreme change values would never be adopted by less draconian measures, as they require a rethinking of the relationship between the individual and the group. The magnitude of the changes requires the imposition of more controls than any person, left alone, would tolerate. The key to totalitarian success is the ability to persuade or coerce people into doing things that they believe to be against their self-interest.

Marxism from Theory to Practice: The Russian Revolution

The Soviet Union is a good example of how far practice can stray from theory. Before proceeding, review the summary of Marxism under "The Collectivist Solution" in Chapter 1. As we saw there, its essential philosophy involves six aspects:

1. Economic determinism
2. Class struggle
3. Theory of surplus value
4. Inevitability of revolution
5. Dictatorship of the proletariat
6. Withering away of the state

Russia under the czars was fertile ground for a revolutionary ideology, for it had long lagged behind the West in social, economic, and political progress. Marx would have argued that Russia was so backward that it lacked the working class necessary for the transformation of society. But in the last decades of the 19th century, Russia began a desperate catch-up scheme, building railroads, borrowing Western capital to start factories, and encouraging a rich intellectual life. Politically, Russia was authoritarian. The political reforms of Europe—extension of the franchise in England, the rise of parliamentary democracy—passed Russia by.

Lenin and His Legacy

Economic progress and a slight relaxation of repression by the *Okhrana* (czarist secret police) were an irresistible combination for revolutionaries. One of the most precocious was Vladimir Ilyich Ulyanov (Lenin: 1870–1924) the son of a provincial education official, who lost his brother in a bomb plot against the czar. Thousands of students were attracted to revolution and terror, and in 1881, they actually succeeded in killing the czar. But Lenin's brother's attempt resulted in failure and his execution.

Exiled for subversion after a few months as an undergraduate, Lenin nevertheless taught himself enough law to pass the bar exams. But he was not a lawyer by disposition; he was a revolutionary. Possibly because of his brother's death, he hated the czars more obsessively than many of his fellow radicals. He converted to Marxism with his usual passion and wrote sophisticated Marxist analyses of the Russian economy. A brilliant intellectual with a charismatic, hypnotic personality, Lenin soon became the leader of the Russian revolutionary movements.

Among the various strands of Marxism then in vogue, the purists argued that Russia would have to become truly capitalist, as Marx believed capitalism was a natural phase in the evolution of the economy. These gradualists wanted to wait for a natural revolution. Others, less concerned with the exotica of Marxism, just wanted the life of the working class to become less grim and proposed nothing more than a welfare state.

But Lenin's factions wanted to "give history a shove." They were not content to watch the automatic evolution of socialism and wanted a revolution as soon as militarily feasible. It was not to be a natural revolution of the working classes; rather, the revolution was to be led by a small band of dedicated zealots. Once in power, this revolutionary elite could install socialism ahead of its time. Lenin's factions formed the Russian Social Democratic Labor party in 1898. Immediately subverted by the Okhrana, many of its leaders, including Lenin, went into exile. From Zurich, Lenin edited *Iskrana* ("The Spark") and expounded his modifications of Marxism.

In *What Is to Be Done?* (1902), Lenin asserted that a small, disciplined party of professional revolutionaries was necessary to counteract the tendency of the working classes to be bought off by modest reform. His reinterpretation of Marx was so profound that the original doctrine was virtually unrecognizable (in the USSR, the "official" ideology is "Marxism-Leninism"). Rather than allowing capitalism to drop like a piece of rotten fruit in the most advanced countries, it should be attacked where it was *weakest,* in the less developed countries, like Russia.

Marx placed his hopes on the urban proletariat, believing the rural peasants to be stupid ("wallowing in rural idiocy," he wrote). Lenin believed, to the contrary, that if the rural peasants were properly led by a revolutionary elite, they could become part of a massive revolutionary army. At the 1903 Social Democratic party conference in Brussels, Lenin's *Bolshevik* ("majority") faction seized control, committing the party to violent revolution.

1905: The Rehearsal.   In the Russo-Japanese War of 1905, Russia sought to shift attention away from internal troubles by starting a war with an "inferior" enemy. But the Japanese showed just how impotent czarist Russia had become by giving the czar's armies and navies a sound thrashing. Rather than rallying the population behind the flag, this disastrous war, in which several naval units muntinied, fanned the flames of revolution.[12] Workers seized factories in St. Petersburg, and the czar, seeking to abort a genuine revolution, decreed major reforms: freedom of speech and assembly, and an elected parliament (the *Duma*). But the Duma became too critical and was dissolved. At the Winter Palace in St. Petersburg, the czar's troops fired into an unarmed mob, providing an expressive symbol of the limits of reform.

World War I and the Return of Lenin.   Russia's performance in World War I was even more lamentable than in the Russo-Japanese War. Poorly led and poorly equipped, the Russian armies were slaughtered, and desertion was widespread.[13] The Russian economy disintegrated, and spontaneous peasant uprisings began anew.

The czar was overthrown in 1917 by a moderate faction led by Alexander Kerensky, who was determined to keep Russia in the war. But in 1917, the Germans arranged to transport Lenin back to Russia, assuming correctly that if Lenin were to gain power, he would end Russia's participation. Even though the Kerensky government controlled foreign policy, there was domestic chaos. Worker councils *(soviets)* governed St. Petersburg (now called Leningrad) and several other large cities. These soviets were affiliated neither with Kerensky nor with the Bolsheviks but were, at least temporarily, genuine and spontaneous workers' organizations. They were doing little more than keeping the cities running, albeit minimally, but they were governing.

Lenin used the soviets to seize power. First the Bolsheviks gained control of the soviets. Then, as the Kerensky government faltered, the soviets filled the vacuum. Lenin, now head of government, took Russia out of the war.

The Civil War.   From 1918 to 1920, Russia was plunged into a brutal civil war, with the White Army, aided by an Allied expeditionary force (including 20,000 U.S. troops), trying to crush the Red Army and, presumably, return Russia to a semblance of its prerevolutionary past. Curiously, the Red Army, faced with such a major challenge, chose this moment to invade Poland, seeking to spread the revolution. Not surprisingly, it was rebuffed. Ultimately, neither side won. Both just became too exhausted to continue, and by default, the Bolsheviks remained in power.

The New Economic Policy.   Millions of Russians had died in World War I and the 1918–1920 revolution. Lenin therefore gave up the romantic notion of exporting the revolution and began the unenviable task of rebuilding the Russian economy under an untried socialist model. A less propitious moment for economic radicalism could hardly be imagined. Although Lenin initially wanted a true centrally planned economy, the specter of millions more Russians starving while ponderous bureaucracies fiddled with production quotas persuaded Lenin to relax and, in effect, abandon socialism. Central planning just was not working, and the human toll was frightening. Only aid from the United States held deaths from starvation at several millions.

Stalin's Rise (1879–1953).   The New Economic Policy was at least a temporary abandonment of the goal of the revolution: a socialist economy. It left most of the urban
economy in private hands and did not tamper with the traditional rural market. Lenin
died in 1924, and in spite of his warnings, Stalin (1879–1953) assumed control. Born
in Georgia of impoverished parents, Stalin possessed not even a fraction of Lenin's
brilliance. He was also, technically, insane. Under his direction, the USSR became
socialist for the first time. Agriculture was collectivized, the fledgling industrial sector
was completely nationalized, and intellectual rigor mortis was enforced by the dreaded
NKVD (the heir of Okhrana and sire of the KGB).

The Revolution Spreads and Retreats.   The first Marxist revolution, and the first Marxist
political-economic system, was in the USSR. In 1949, the Chinese Communist party,
led by Mao Tse-tung and relying heavily on Lenin's theories of revolutionary organization, overthrew the Nationalist government of Chiang Kai-shek and established the
second Communist system. In eastern Europe, other Communist governments were established by the Red Army (except in Yugoslavia), but there were not genuine revolutions. Cuba's 1957 revolution did not embrace Marxism until after Castro assumed
power.

Other Communist governments have been installed, in Vietnam, after a genuine
Marxist movement led by Ho Chi Minh, and in Cambodia as a consequence of Pol Pot's
Lenin-inspired ideology. At about the same time, Laos accepted communism. In Chile,
Salvadore Allende became the first and only example of an elected Marxist government
but was overthrown in 1973 by a coup partly financed by the United States. Nicaragua's
1979 revolution, while containing many Marxists among its Sandinista leadership, has
yet to go all the way to a nonmarket economy (see Chapter 7).

By the 1980s, little of Marxist ideology remained. Both the USSR and China began
vigorous moves toward a market-driven economy. The movements came in fits and
starts, in part because there is no ready-made alternative ideology (capitalism's ideology
is not very coherent), partially because of conservative resistance, and also because of
economic upheavals precipitated by the introduction of market incentives. Each country
appeared poised for a radical departure by 1989, but each year brought new challenges.
In the USSR, considered by some experts as less likely to succeed since communism
had been in place longer, Gorbachev faced an intractable food crisis by proposing that
the collective farm system—the key to Stalin's agricultural collectivization—be largely
dismantled. This dispute touched at the heart of Soviet values: the nature of ownership,
economic security, and equality. Gorbachev's plan was approved—over the intense and
bitter opposition of party conservatives. In China, 1989 was the year of retrenchment
and renewed talk of centralization. In March, Prime Minister Li Peng's annual report
told the people to prepare for ''austerity'' and a heavier reliance on planning rather than
markets. Conspicuously absent during the presentation of the report was Deng, the in-
stigator of most of the post-Mao liberalization. The Chinese, with characteristic ambi-
guity, explained, ''We shall never return to the old economic mode characterized by
overcentralized, excessive, and rigid control. Nor shall we adopt private ownership,
negating the socialist system.''[14]

Among the later converts to communism, Cuba, Albania, Romania, Bulgaria, North
Korea, and East Germany are still ruled by true believers. But the communist ''threat,''

which drove the United States into fits of aberrant behavior for four decades, has abated. The ideology, once so potent, is effectively dead, and ''market socialism'' is the new rallying cry. Nor is there an apparent successor to Marxism; no genuine world views, no inclusive theories of life are currently extant. Is totalitarianism becoming extinct? For the moment, it appears so. But who knows? All-embracing ideologies are seductive. One might suppose that Islamic fundamentalism might fill the bill; it is inclusive, providing a clear world-view, delineating good and evil, setting forth the path to the good life, and so on. But Islam is limited, geographically, more than Marxism. It has little appeal in the West, the occasional Farrakhan and the raft of black athletes with new names notwithstanding. Marxism appealed more to those who did not want in this life than to the masses it set out to liberate:

> Socialism in general and the Marxist version of it in particular continue to have strong appeal among Western intellectuals. . . . Socialism and especially Marxism have *least* appeal in the countries within the Soviet orbit. . . . It is very difficult to find intellectuals in Eastern Europe who, once they are candid with an outsider, take Marxism in any of its forms seriously.[15]

Not so with Islam. When Salman Rushdie was condemned to death by Iran's Khomeini, Western intellectuals fought for the chance to stand by him, and celebrity reading of *The Satanic Verses* eclipsed being seen at Elaine's, or endorsing Jesse Jackson, temporarily.

ALIENATION AND THE TOTALITARIAN OPPORTUNITY

Alienation—a process of disillusionment resulting in a loss of identity, a sense of rootlessness, and the feeling of distance from society's primary and secondary groups[16]— is the modern world's malady for which a totalitarian solution is sometimes offered. ''Who am I?'' became the desperate question of 20th-century intellectuals. Increasingly, the answer was, ''I don't know.''

The notion of alienation goes back to the Middle Ages but was given its fullest expression by Hegel (1770–1831), Marx, and Freud (1856–1939). According to Hegel, alienation causes people to be seen as mere objects and can be overcome only by the transcendence of God. Marx, as we know, saw alienation as a consequence of capitalism. Private property compels a division of labor. The division of labor compels men to ''sell themselves'' (see the theory of surplus value, page 18). In so doing, people come to see themselves as means to an end, as objects, rather than as having any intrinsic worth.

Like Marx (and Rousseau), Freud and his followers understand alienation to be caused by civilization, but not necessarily capitalism. Civilization requires conformity; conformity demands repression; and repression causes alienation by separating us from our natural inclinations.

Systematic Analysis of Alienation

Many students of mass attitudes—not necessarily Marxists—agree that alienation appears simultaneously with the decline of the Middle Ages and the appearance of capitalism. Medieval society created a hierarchy of positions: each person (knights, serfs, lords, housewives, and so on) knew his or her place in the hierarchy and did not challenge it. Many were unhappy with their lives, but at least they knew who they were. There was a high degree of symmetry between self-image and society's image of the self.[17]

Modern life shatters this symmetry. The appearance of mercantile capitalism ended the unity of work and everyday life that medieval life had achieved. With capitalism came social-class conflict, as opposed to the hierarchy of earlier times. Social mobility, the growth of large cities, the development of efficient mass communication, the appearance in Europe of modern states with modern bureaucracies, and the decline of Catholicism made life even more uncertain:

> One major effect of the modernization of institutions has been the *pluralization* of the worlds of social experience. . . . Individuals are thrown back and forth between grossly discrepant social contexts. Consequently, what experiences of symmetry there are, are unclear and unreliable: The mirrors are constantly shifting. As a result, both image and reflection take on an aspect of vertigo, that is, of unreality. As the individual becomes more uncertain about the world, he necessarily becomes uncertain about his own self, since that self can be subjectively real only as it is continually confirmed by others. . . . As the social identification process becomes increasingly fragmented, the subjective experience of identity becomes increasingly precarious. . . . The old question, "Who am I?" . . . attains a new measure of urgency.[18]

The democratic and authoritarian response to anxiety has been to separate public and private; to regard private as just that: nobody's business. Alienation may drive people from job to job, work may be routinized and boring, but private life, especially the family, is supposed to provide relief. Voluntary associations—occupational, racial, and so on—provide a modicum of identity. But the essence of an open society is allowing each person to be

> free to a degree that, even in the most libertarian society, would be intolerable in the state and in the economy. He can marry whom he chooses . . . and he can have several consecutive choices. He can . . . organize his home as he sees fit, and raise his children by his own lights. He can exercise a choice of "religious preference" and similar choices within a broad and freely available spectrum of ideologies, moral and aesthetic practices, and therapeutic cults. Put simply, whatever may be the frustrations of the individual's experiences in the public sphere, in his private life he is free to a historically unprecedented degree.[19]

By excluding the state from the regulation of these choices, open and partially open societies allow each person to make choices and live with the consequences. By allowing a very large amount of individual control over such decisions, democracies and authoritarian countries assume that each person is the best judge of what works well.

Chroniclers of Despair

But, many say, *choice* spawns alienation. Choice, whatever its benevolent consequences, causes insecurity. Choice creates doubt. Doubt and the resolution of doubt are the central theme of alienation as described by the intellectuals.

There are no more stunning examples of alienation than Shakespeare's plays. The fatal flaw in Hamlet's character is a search for personal identity in a society that consistently alters "objective" reality. As his search becomes more hectic, he constantly tests reality: Hamlet examines each character in the play in turn according to the roles he is supposed to play, the feelings he is supposed to have toward them, and his real feelings toward them. Discontinuity ultimately drives him mad.

Shakespearean heroes and heroines are invariably multifaceted, with character changing according to circumstance. Yet when identity is resolved, the outcome is rarely a happy one. His characters ask, "Who am I?" and when they find out, they are doomed. Shakespeare's sort of alienation is due to flawed character. In Marxian thought, the culprit is capitalism, and the cure is the abolition of private property. But even writers who reject Marxism express alienation in social terms.

One of the most impressive of such writers was Albert Camus (1913–1960). In *The Stranger,* he created a protagonist, Mersault, who never expresses any opinion or any emotion: he is truly disconnected, as is shown by the following encounter:

> Marie came that evening and asked me if I'd marry her. I said I didn't mind; if she was keen on it we'd get married. Then she asked me again if I loved her. I replied, much as before, that her question meant nothing or next to nothing, but I supposed I didn't. "If that's how you feel," she said, "why marry me?" I explained that it had no importance really but if it would give her pleasure we could get married right away. . . .
>
> "Suppose another girl had asked you to marry her . . . would you have said 'yes' to her too?"
>
> "Naturally."[20]

Later, Mersault meets a neighbor who is a pimp. Mersault recalls:

> He slapped me on the shoulder and said: "So now we are pals, ain't we?" I kept silent and he said it again. I did not care one way or the other, but as he seemed so set on it, I nodded and said "yes."[21]

When the pimp complains of problems with one of his girls, Mersault agrees to write a letter requesting an assignation, a device to lure her into the pimp's room. Why did Mersault agree? Because he "had no reason not to." When the woman's cries of anguish and terror as she is beaten by the pimp fill the house, Mersault's wife, Marie, is upset and cannot eat, so Mersault recounts, "I ate it all myself. She left the house, and I had a nap." Ultimately, Mersault is executed for an absurd crime. In effect, he commits suicide because, according to Camus's *existentialism,* life without belief in absolute moral standards is absurd.

Camus insisted that Mersault was normal; he was simply adjusting his behavior to an absurd world. In much the same way, George Orwell allows George Winston, the protagonist in *Nineteen Eighty-four,* his grim novel of a future totalitarian England, to come upon a severed hand and kick it into the gutter "as though it had been a cabbage stalk." Rather than "curing" such individuals, we must "cure" society. Hence the totalitarian solution becomes attractive.

Is this assumption justified? Most of us do not write elaborate essays about our loss of identity. But what about other behavioral manifestations of alienation? Followers of Rousseau argue that many crimes—especially those that are especially brutal and irrational—are expressions of alienation by the common people. Child abuse, rape, senseless murder, refusal to intervene to assist people in distress, and alcohol and drug abuse are said to be consequences of a view of life as valueless: humans can be killed without remorse. Certainly suicide and homicide, crude measures though they may be, tell us something about the propensity to view humans as cabbage stalks. According to Marxists, these two modes of destruction should be low in totalitarian states and rampant in open, individualist ones.

These assumptions do not hold unwaveringly. The United States, international symbol of the anarchy of open societies, fulfills the theory as the homicide leader of the developed world. But suicide—which Camus and many of his followers regarded as the essential philosophical question of the age—is another matter. No open country, not even Austria or Finland, can approach Hungary. Indeed, both murder and suicide are higher in the countries for which reduction of individual choice was supposed to end anxiety. Ironically, among the relatively closed societies, Chile and Argentina, which make no such claims, have less "human cabbage" syndromes than those that promise deliverance. (See Table 1.3 in Chapter 1.)

Other evidence supports the conclusion that no matter how it is measured, anxiety is not reduced by decreasing or eliminating choice: property crimes are higher in open societies, as is drug abuse, but alcohol abuse is much more serious in the totalitarian or aspirant countries. In the USSR, reformers believe alcoholism to be a serious drag on the economy, and it became a major target of Gorbachev's economic policies.

Rousseau expressed well the contempt that totalitarians have for the modest tinkering of welfare-capitalist systems. Man in the state of nature was not alienated, but with modernity and capitalism came the "dissolution of the self."[22] According to Rousseau's beliefs, a benevolent welfare system, no matter how well intentioned and well administered, cannot overcome dissolution of self. Theoretically, the totalitarian argument makes sense. Empirically, it does not. Life with restricted choice appears as unnatural as the anarchy that totalitarians fear.

Camus, who came to believe that all revolution led to the "strange and terrifying growth of the modern state," concluded that Marx's noble dream had been subverted by the very process it despised: the growth of the democratic welfare state. The tinkering turned out not to be useless:

> Marx's fear is confirmed: reforms and trade unions brought about a rise in the standard of living and an amelioration of working conditions . . . . The miserable condition [of workers], far from becoming general and even deteriorating, as he would have liked, has been on the contrary alleviated."[23]

THE "NEW MAN"

One of the most enduring and extraordinary facets of totalitarian ideology is the aspiration to create a so-called new man. Fascist states (principally Germany and Italy) imagined the perfect man as enthusiastically obedient, with no intellectual independence apart from the state (Germany also intended for him to be Aryan).

The new man idea of the Nazis was derived from a long history of obsession with the "superman": the artistic and intellectual elite, the heroic superman of Nietzsche, Wagner, Stephan George, and a host of minor writers required a reaffirmation of natural laws of the survival of the fittest. Fascism—profoundly anti-intellectual, occasionally mystical, and ultimately anti-Semitic—appealed to the most sickening of human instincts. The Nazi new man was a "blond beast of prey," devouring inferior species with the joy of the kill. He was aggressive and obedient.

The excesses of the Nazi movement occurred with no serious attempt to justify them; on the contrary, some energy was spent in concealing them. And after all, the only clearly defined goal of the Nazi movement was the elimination of the Jews. Some selective breeding was done at various stud farms, with SS types plunging away at chunky Bavarian farm girls, and of course there were the ponderous racial purity laws. There was a lot of heiling and Hitler-youthing, but all one needed to do was appear vigorously enthusiastic. As mad scientists creating the new man, the Nazis were a bust.

A lot of romantic twaddle about the new German man nevertheless demanded only that Germans accept authority as passively as they had done in the past. The propaganda machines of Germany ground out round-the-clock advertisements for the Third Reich in the 1930s, persuading at least a plurality of Germans that dictatorship was preferable to democracy. (The task was surely aided by the absence of a democratic tradition in Germany.) Nazi propaganda may have been more emotional than old-fashioned German romanticism, but its appeal was similar.

While fascism attracted an odd collection of supporters in some artistic and literary circles (Ezra Pound and William Butler Yeats, for example), most intellectuals were instead drawn to Marxism. Communist totalitarian governments imagine quite a different utopia: the new man is enlightened, selfless, and politically active because of enhanced rationality. "Normal" means of building the new man are available. When the Nicaraguan Sandinistas, flushed with the success of their semi-Marxist revolution, talked of the "new Nicaraguan man," they had in mind nothing more than heavy-handed political education.

The education system, the mass media, and propaganda can be effective in promoting compliance, but not in creating the *unnatural* new man. Limited goals such as externally manifested loyalty—marching, chanting slogans, going to rallies, and the like—require little fundamental change in human nature. But to get blind obedience or selflessness, human nature must be basically altered. If successfully manufactured, the new Soviet woman, for examples, would be

> modest, firm, dedicated, sympathetic, courageous, bold, hard-working, energetic. . . . She gave no thought to her personal welfare. . . . She could put up with physical hardship, face combat and torture if captured, and even endure death, believing that her sacrifice had contributed to a better world.[24]

The goal of totalitarian persuasion is the creation of a new man who meets elite expectations not because of fear or loyalty but because he wants to: compliance is ultimately independent of external authority. The need for truly voluntary compliance lies behind totalitarian states' willingness to be genuinely "total," to exclude no aspect of life from scrutiny and change.

Without the creation of the new man, the revolution would be for naught. Why go through the horror of revolution merely to install one elite in place of another? The true totalitarian has no such incremental interest. Che Guevara, himself possibly one of the few Marxists who never became corrupted (possibly because he was killed before he found an institutional role in the Castro government), was a passionate devotee of the new man:

> Human beings must be stripped of egoism and individualism. You must develop to its maximum a man's revolutionary consciousness and make his materialistic appetites disappear. He should be satisfied with the absolute reward of doing his duty. In socialism there is no room for material incentives. They are the chief corruptors of consciousness. . . . The authentic revolutionary is generous, he owns nothing. He loves humanity. He dies for the revolution![25]

These are truly the dreams of "mad scientists," of Dr. Frankenstein, Dr. Jekyll, or Dr. Strangelove. And, as is the case with the various incarnations of the mad scientist, revolutionaries like Guevara are, beneath their willingness to do anything for the cause, good but misunderstood.

STALIN'S TERROR

As we have seen, Joseph Stalin, who seized the leadership of the Communist party of the USSR upon Lenin's death, was more brutal and violent than Lenin. He allowed his subordinates to develop and promulgate the first authentic new man ideology, but the extremes of his personality led to means that could not possibly be justified by the goal. Stalin's intent was to compress centuries of industrial development into a five-year span. Stalin consolidated his power and in 1928 began the transformation of Russian society. The process through which the industrialization would occur was ruthless, far more excessive than anything imagined by Lenin, much less Marx.

Agrarian Collectivism

In response to a minor political act, the withholding of a few million tons of grain, Stalin began the forced collectivization of Russian agriculture. The goal was to transfer all arable land from private to collective (state) ownership by confiscation and reassignment. Land was to be taken from its putative owners and given to collective farms, organized and managed by state agronomists. The rural market was to be destroyed, single-family farms were to be eliminated, and rural "factories"—believed to be more efficient than privately owned farms—were to become the centerpieces of the new collective agricultural economy.

Although he did not initially plan such an extreme transformation, Stalin became obsessed with substituting state-owned collective farming for private farming. The embryonic plans for collective farms assumed a slow pace of change, with improving foreign investment and an increased rate of domestic savings providing the capital. As the economy grew, the conservative agrarian way of life would be replaced by collective farms with modern equipment, thus showing the advantages of collective farming.

But the results of initial collectivization were discouraging. Ten years after the 1917 revolution, the economy was operating at its pre–World War I level. How could farmers be persuaded to abandon a centuries-old way of life for a higher standard of living when the country had no goods to buy and no equipment to demonstrate? Stalin saw only one way to interrupt the cycle: forced collectivization. Anyone who resisted would be killed. By the end of 1928, collective farms supplied about half the food requirements of the cities. However, subsequent famines negated much of these gains. After the initial flurry, which resulted in about 60 percent of all farming being collectivized, the movement lost its momentum and declined to about 25 percent within a few years. However, Stalin regrouped for another assault, and by 1932, most Soviet agricultural production was on collective farms. In that year, deaths from famine reached 5 million, but the program continued, and the extent of the famine was concealed. Inflated harvest reports, begun in 1933, continued for three decades. The only conclusion that makes any sense is that the goal was not to design an efficient agricultural system but to eradicate the *kulaks* (the rich peasants). The policy, viewed in this light, was a success. As one participant explained, "It took a famine to show them who is master here. It cost millions of lives, but the collective farm system is here to stay. We have won the war."[26]

The use of war as an analogue is appropriate. Surely Stalin's collectivization and dekulakization programs should be considered as parts of a larger process of class liquidation.[27] As is usually the case when classes or races of people are killed, the "enemy" loses both human qualities and individuality. Dekulakization became a slightly sanitized euphemism for mass murder.

Stalin as Mass Murderer.   For Stalin, the means and end—removing kulaks to collectives—had become confused. Just as the true goal of the Nazis was the destruction of the Jews (as it became apparent that the war was lost, devoted Nazis stepped up the death quotas for Jews, hoping to finish them off before the war was over), Stalin's real goal became destroying a subversive class.

The kulaks *as a group* were guilty of obstruction. Therefore, if a kulak or his family were enthusiastic about collectivization, it was of no matter:

> We must smash the *kulaks,* eliminate them as a class. . . . Unless we set ourselves these aims, an offensive would be mere declamation, bickering, empty noise. . . . We must strike at the *kulaks* so hard as to prevent them from rising to their feat again. . . . Can we permit the expropriation of *kulaks* . . . ? A ridiculous question. . . . You do not lament the loss of the hair of one who has been beheaded. . . . We must break down the resistance of that class in open battle.[28]

The Death of Marxism in the USSR.   How far from Marx had Stalin come? How far
from Lenin? There is nothing preceptorial about Stalin; he wanted and got genocide.
The severity with which the Soviet government waged its war is well illustrated by the
notion of dekulakization, or political rehabilitation. Government and party bureaucracies
devised a scheme for classification of kulaks: those actively engaged in resistance, non-
active opponents, and those who could be "reeducated." Active resisters were sent to
Siberia and the gulags, but passive opponents were usually only exiled from the village.
Local stores were prohibited from selling goods to individual farming families, who
were allowed to remain. Land was confiscated, and the owners were often expelled. In
some cases, kulaks were compelled to exchange their cultivated land for land of poor
quality, located far from the village. Taxation on private farms was triple that of collectives; and children of resisting kulaks were denied entrance to schools.

Initially, kulaks thought capable of being reeducated were to be allowed to enter
collective farms for a probationary period. But party leaders rejected this relatively
enlightened policy because it did not meet the stated goal of "eliminating the kulaks as
a class."[29]

Gradually the word *kulak* was becoming redefined to mean any peasant who did
not want to join a collective farm. Party publications were remarkably frank about what
was happening. A sinister 1930 party memo defined *kulak* to mean "the carrier of
certain political tendencies," while a local agricultural newsletter admonished: "The
peasant is beginning to associate with this idea [of mass collectivization] the possibility
that he too may find himself one day among the dekulakised, falling thus into the camp
of the enemies of Soviet power."[30] Thus to be dekulakized was no longer to be cleansed
of politically incorrect thoughts; rather, it described a process whereby one became an
"enemy of the people."

Sorting Out Who's Who

One problem in totalitarian genocide—a difficulty rarely encountered in mere authoritarian brutality—is the development of a reliable list of people to be exterminated or
reeducated. Kulaks, despised by Stalin, nevertheless sounded like no more than a line
or two in a statistical abstract by the time the bureaucracies got them defined as people
who

> (a) possess means of production valued at more than 1,600 rubles and let or lease means
> of production or hire labor for over 50 days during the year, or (b) possess means of
> production valued at more than 800 rubles and hire labor for over 75 days during the
> year, or (c) possess means of production valued at more than 400 rubles and hire labor
> for more than 150 days a year.[31]

These were "official" enemies of the regime, but the list went farther to include a great
many others:[32]

1. All former members of prerevolutionary bourgeois political parties
2. All former members of monarchical unions and organizations
3. All former members of the Union of Independent Grain Growers

4. All former members of the gentry or titled persons
5. All former members of the Boy Scouts and other youth organizations
6. All "nationalists"
7. Officials and employees in the active service of the Tsar (legal officials, members of the secret police, constables of all sorts, prosecutors, judges, commissioned and noncommissioned officers)
8. Commissioned and noncommissioned officers of the White Army
9. All civil employees in areas administered by the White Army
10. All servants of religious bodies
11. All former merchants, shopkeepers, and supporters of the New Economic Policy
12. Kulaks
13. Relatives of people in an "illegal position"
14. All foreigners
15. People with relatives or acquaintances abroad
16. All members of religious sects or communities, especially Baptists
17. All scholars and specialists of the "old school," especially those with undeclared political orientation
18. All persons previously convicted of espionage and similar crimes

Since they were denied political reeducation, opponents who were not exiled or shot just drifted around, were assigned poor-quality land, and were arrested if they did not meet procurement quotas. It need hardly be said that the incentives to volunteer for relocation on a collective farm were substantial. The "death trains" carrying kulaks to Siberia rolled around the clock, and many passengers died before reaching the concentration camps. If the father of a family had been arrested, his children often rode the death trains alone or were left behind to become beggars and prostitutes.

Besides death from executions and from concentration camps, millions died from starvation and exposure. Although the actual count may never be known, Stalin himself admitted that the toll was greater than during the first years of World War II, when German troops advanced to the outskirts of Moscow. He reckoned that 10 million were executed. With products confiscated, families broken up, farms destroyed, mass deportations, and periodic famines, the death toll was probably about 16 million.[33] This is not to be confused with the higher total of 20 million proposed by Soviet historian Roy Medvedev in 1989.[34] He included collectivization, forced labor camps, famine, and executions to get the higher total. His more inclusive list, which exceeds substantially the 20 million figure, is instructive:

> 1 million imprisoned or exiled from 1927 to 1929, accused of being saboteurs or members of opposition parties.
> Between 9 and 11 million peasants driven from the land during collectivization.
> 2 million arrested or exiled during collectivization.
> 6 to 7 million killed in the "punitive famine" of 1932–1933.
> 1 million exiled from Moscow and Leningrad in 1935 for belonging to families of nobility, merchants, capitalists, and officials.
> 1 million executed in the purges of 1937–1938.
> 4 to 6 million sent to labor camps during the purges.

2 to 3 million sent to camps for violating labor laws in 1940.

10 to 12 million forcibly relocated during World War II.

1 million arrested for political crimes from 1946 to Stalin's death in 1953.

250,000 Ukrainians and Poles thought until recently to have been killed by the Nazis.[35]

Stalin and Hitler.   Such staggering numbers bring Nazi atrocities to mind. There are some differences. Hitler tried but failed to kill all the Jews in Europe. There was no talk of reeducating them. Stalin did not necessarily intend to kill all the kulaks, and some were excluded from the slaughter. But there was enough talk of guilty *classes* to make the comparison valid.[36]

Both Stalin and Hitler had serious personality disorders, causing them to see conspiracies where none existed (in psychiatric parlance, they were paranoid). Stalin believed in class warfare. To him, collectivization was not an economic policy, although it probably began as one; it was a religion. Although the economic plans of the middle and late 1930s acknowledged mistakes, admitted to some overzealous implementation, and did not propose additional collectivization, Stalin believed he had no choice but to eradicate an enemy of socialism. He loved power, and he loved violent conflict, but he did what he did not only to satisfy these urges but also because of his intense commitment to the paramount morality of socialism. Until the collectivization crusade ran aground, Stalin was *consumed* by it.

Collectivization may have left the modern Soviet Union a legacy beyond its brutality; it has proved to be an agricultural disaster. During Stalin's time, the justification for collectivization was that it was brutal but necessary: it "helped to modernize agriculture, to secure a reliable food supply, to free capital for industrial production, and to release labor for heavy industry."[37]

But as recent information makes clear, grain production—the Achilles heel of Soviet agriculture—did not increase between 1912 and 1952; it was restored to the 1928 (precollectivization) level only in 1956.[38] In 1989, the key to the perestroika reforms became the dismantling of the collective farms. Soviet agricultural economists revealed some dismaying statistics:

In 9 of 12 five-year economic plans, the growth of agriculture was negative or insignificant.

There has not been a successful five-year period since the one ending in 1970.

One-third of Soviet produce rots before reaching the consumer.

Of 211 food products now monitored in Moscow, only 23 are readily available.

Nearly half of the country's 50,000 collective farms operate at a loss or at the margin, requiring annual subsidies of about $32 billion.[39]

As Medvedev concludes, "The myth that collectivization was harsh but effective does not withstand an examination of the performance of Soviet agriculture."[40]

The Purges

Stalin's extermination of enemies and perceived enemies within the party was only slightly less imposing than the annihilation of the kulaks. There were fewer deaths—about 1 million executions and 2 million deaths from exhaustion or brutality in the prison camps. About 12 million served time in the concentration camps during the purge, so its consequences were substantial.[41] Were the purge trials just another example of Stalin's seemingly endless appetite for inhuman behavior, we would move on. They are noteworthy because they reintroduced the importance of public confessions, in general disrepute since the Inquisition's *autos-da-fé,* and because the NKVD began to experiment with psychological cruelty in order to obtain these admissions.

The importance of the public recantation comes from the totalitarian need for absolute control. The collectivization was undertaken without any concern for the disposition of the kulaks. The purges and trials were another matter entirely, since they involved active party members.

In many cases—the majority, in fact—there was no evidence of disloyalty. The nature of the alleged crime was usually vague. The trials focused on the long-forgotten, numerous, byzantine factions within the party—Trotskyites, Zinovites, and Bukharinites, for example. Stalin feared them, especially Trotsky's followers, for good reason. Trotsky, with an intellect second only to Lenin's, made the crude Georgian Stalin appear even more loutish. A year before he died, Lenin dictated a testament condemning Stalin, who, Lenin believed, did not use his power with "sufficient caution" and was "too rude." Consequently, the revolution's father urged his successors to remove Stalin and install Nicolai Bukharin; Bukharin was executed but after a less than complete confession. Trotsky, who also competed with Stalin, was exiled in 1929 and murdered in 1940, in Mexico.

Vindictive, suspicious, and paranoid, Stalin wanted not just to kill his opponents but to destroy them emotionally. During Lenin's lifetime, physical abuse rarely occurred. Stalin's innovation, which he imposed over serious party opposition, was uniquely his, not Marxism-Leninism's. The trials were conducted without any regard for rules of evidence; therefore, the confession was an alternative to legitimate evidence. Some of the accused confessed in hopes of being spared, but most confessed because interrogation techniques made them genuinely repentant. Stalin's courts used the phrase "enemy of the people," making more detailed catalogs of guilt unnecessary and the confession even more central.[42]

Such confessions testify unmistakably to the power of the totalitarian state. In czarist Russia, the Okhrana was never satisfied without a confession, a practice derived from the close link between prerevolutionary Russian rulers and the Russian Orthodox church. Fyodor Dostoyevsky's *Crime and Punishment,* a novel of salvation through confession by a killer, details the relentless pursuit of the confession in Russian culture before the revolution. Whereas Dostoyevsky's protagonist is driven to confess by inner devils, the totalitarian confession is more pragmatic as well: "It is more in accordance with totalitarian ideologies that a defendant should confess, even under duress: it is better discipline and a good example to all ranks."[43]

In response to these needs, the Soviet political police amplified and expanded on techniques used in the revolution. Arrests were often random; people who had done or said nothing were arrested and immediately isolated. Interrogation and imposition of unbearable pain could last from a few days to a year. The incentive to find some plausible answer was therefore immense.

After the initial session, the torture became one of negotiation between confessor and victim. Confessors appeared at times deranged, almost manic, screaming, and at other times benevolent and caring. An extraordinary interview with an examiner shows the technique to full advantage:

> I told him that I was personally convinced that he was not a counterrevolutionist. I took from my desk confessions of his imprisoned comrades, and showed them to him as evidence of how low they had fallen in their opposition to the Soviet system. . . . For three full days we talked and argued. Mrachkovsky did not sleep a wink. . . . I brought him to the point where he began to weep. I wept with him and we arrived at the conclusion that all was lost, that there was nothing left in the way of hope or faith, that the only thing to do was to make a desperate effort to forestall a futile struggle on the part of the discontented masses. For this the government must have public "confessions" by the opposition leaders.[44]

Prisoners would be dragged from cell to cell, witnessing others in various stages of torture or humiliation. After about a month, all but a handful had confessed and were ready for the public trial. In almost all cases, the confessions were "genuine." Prisoners believed they had wronged the party, were persuaded that they had betrayed the revolution, and thus deserved what they got. Any show of clemency was gratefully accepted.

The most perplexing aspect of the purges was the sincerity of the confession. Prisoners came to regard an admission of guilt as a last service to the party they had betrayed. The defendants

> shared Stalin's contemptuous belief that the masses can only comprehend a very simple and quite extreme story. But . . . they felt that the fables they agreed to tell were in some special sense true; that is, they came to believe that there was some kind of equivalence between the opposition they had actually felt (and the small deeds that grew out of this) and the extreme offenses to which they admitted.[45]

They might have quarreled with the party's decision in their own case, but they did not—at least at the end of the trial—deny the legitimacy of the party's decision.

In *Darkness at Noon*, Arthur Koestler fashioned a novel of the trials based partly on his own experiences and partly on Bukhanin's. The protagonist, Rubashov (Bukhanin), makes a full disclosure of the crimes that made him an enemy of the people.

> I know that my aberration, if carried into effect, would have been a mortal danger to the Revolution. Every opposition, at the critical turning points of history, carries in itself the germ of a split in the Party, and hence the germ of civil war. Humanitarian weakness and liberal democracy, when the masses are not mature, is suicide for the Revolution. And yet my oppositional attitude was based on a craving for just these methods—in appearance so desirable, actually so deadly.[46]

Rubashov loves Big Brother and is genuinely repentant.

In comparison with the Nazi tortures, the Soviet lust for the confession was less psychopathological and more ideologically driven. Soviet torturers were true believers, loyal Marxists who tortured because they believed they were fulfilling a higher collective mission. Both the motives of the agents of the totalitarian state and the repentance of the accused are different in these two examples. Soviet confessions revealed a unity between the individual and the party and an acceptance of the doctrine of the unimportance of the individual. In Nazi Germany, the torturers and the tortured were enemies; in the Soviet Union, they were not. The distinction is not important if you are a victim, but it is nevertheless real.

ORWELL'S TERRIBLE VISION

The extremes to which the attempt to create the new man may go is illustrated in Orwell's *Nineteen Eighty-four*. Originally published in 1948, the story had begun to take shape in Orwell's mind in the early years of World War II. Orwell sought to identify the central motif of totalitarian government as it then existed. The centerpiece was the absence of objective truth. Orwell wrote:

> From the totalitarian point of view, history is something to be created rather than learned. . . . Totalitarianism demands . . . the continuous alteration of the past, and in the long run, probably demands a disbelief in the very existence of objective truth. . . . The implied objective . . . is a nightmare world in which the leader, or some ruling clique, controls not only the future but the past.[47]

Thought Control. Three major social groups exist in *Nineteen Eighty-four:* the inner party, the outer party, and the "proles" or masses. Orwell had in mind the rigid divisions between members of the party and the vast majority who are denied membership. In the Soviet Union, which provided much of the basis for Orwell's book, no more than 10 percent of the population was in the party, and the rewards of party membership were and are substantial. Somewhat like Orwell's fictitious party, the Russian Communist party acknowledged two classes: workers and peasants. But in fact, there are layers of class stratification as stultifying as in *Nineteen Eighty-four:*[48]

> The *top class,* 25,000 party chiefs, KGB elite, artists and entertainers. At the apex are Gorbachev and the Politburo.
> The *military officer class,* 800,000 or so military officers with good party histories.
> The *rising class,* 23 million urban professionals, middle- and lower-level party central committee functionaries, heads of research institutes (the "nomenklatura," dependent on superior classes for their privileges).

Orwell's plot revolves around the life of a member of the outer party, Winston Smith. Much of the surveillance that the inner party undertakes is directed toward the outer party, rather than the proles, who are regarded as unlikely to be sophisticated enough to recognize and reject reconstituted "truth." In an accurate and chilling portrayal of elite scorn, Orwell wrote that the proles "can be granted intellectual liberty because they have no intellect."

Winston works in the Ministry of Truth but is not a member of that ministry's Thought Police. His job is to alter, on direction from the inner party, any historical record of "unpersons" (those who have ceased to be and hence never were) or any differences between the present and past versions of truth that could cast the slightest doubt on the validity of the current party line. Any inner party policy or terminology that has become obsolete is removed from all records to make the current rendition appear to have always been the correct one.

After this is done, Winston must forget that he has done it. Should he admit, even to himself, that the inner party was altering history, he might come to the attention of the Thought Police. Winston's fear is justified: his neighbor's son turned in his father because he mumbled something disloyal in his sleep. The point here is quite important for understanding Orwell's image of life in the totalitarian society. You can keep quiet most of the time, but unless you genuinely harbor no seditious thoughts, your involuntary utterances might trip you up. To admit, even unconsciously, that rewritten history was not true or to suspect that the inner party was occasionally wrong was to commit "thoughtcrime."

Yet Winston occasionally had to remember old history, for the inner party sometimes resurrected an unperson when the circumstance required. Winston would then re-create the person and rewrite the current altered version of history. To survive, one had to train one's mind to engage in "doublethink":

> Winston sank his arms to his sides. . . . . His mind slid away into the labyrinthine world of doublethink. To know and not to know, to be conscious of complete truthfulness while telling carefully constructed lies, to hold simultaneously two opinions which cancelled out, knowing them to be contradictory and believing in both of them, to use logic against logic, to repudiate morality while laying claim to it, to believe that democracy was impossible and that the Party was the guardian of democracy, to forget, whatever it was necessary to forget, then to draw it back into memory again at the moment when it was needed, and above all, to apply the same process to the process itself—that was the ultimate subtlety: consciously to induce unconsciousness, and then, once again, to become unconscious of the act of hypnosis you had just performed. Even the word "doublethink" involved the use of doublethink.[49]

To accomplish this is no easy task, as it requires internalizing the language and ideology of the inner party.

To make authority more tangible, abstract authority is called "Big Brother." At one point, Winston is ensnared by a bogus conspiracy set up by the inner party, which routinely tests members of the outer party to isolate and eliminate weakness. Once snared, the task of rebuilding Winston's psyche begins. Orwell correctly anticipated the use of psychological as well as physical cruelty in brainwashing. The tormenters lead Winston through three steps: learning, understanding, and acceptance. The use of physical pain decreases as the process advances; it is used initially to dispel any notions of heroics.

Routine bullying, constant questioning, bright lights, lack of sleep, and the "third degree" were alternated with periods of tender, avuncular care by the inquisitors. The object of the rotation of kindness and cruelty was to establish a bond of affection and dependence. Positioned in an electronically wired rack, Winston endures incremental increases in what he believes to be life-threatening pain, until his interrogator held up his hand with four fingers extended. Upon being asked what he would say if the inner party insisted there were five, Winston for a brief interval insists there would still be only four. But as the pain intensifies, he responds "five." But the response is not good enough; he still believes there are four and is lying.[50] This is the point at which many authoritarian systems stop. But the totalitarian needs a washed brain, not a compliant one. More pain is administered, and Winston at least can honestly answer that he no longer knows. But Winston makes little progress in phase 2, understanding. He cannot understand *why* anyone should rule with such ruthlessness. The answer is too simple: to prove the totalitarian thesis.

Winston, compliant and desperate, still believes that there is "some spirit" in the universe that cannot be overcome. The inner party asserts:

> We control life, Winston, at all its levels. You are assuming that there is something called human nature which will be outraged by what we do and will turn against us. But we create human nature. Men are infinitely malleable . . .: you are a difficult case. But don't give up hope. Everything is cured sooner or later.[51]

Winston has professed love for a woman named Julia, and they agree not to betray one another. At the depths of his degradation, after having his two remaining teeth jerked out and wallowing in his own filth and vomit, he still takes pride in keeping this pledge. The final stage, acceptance, will occur when he renounces her.

Each of us has some fear, our own personal hell, that, once exposed, would end any minute thoughts of resistance. For Winston, it was rats. The inner party takes him to Room 101, which contains the "worst thing in the world." The worst thing in the world for Winston is to have a cage of rats attached to his face that they might devour it (a torment that Orwell gleaned from reports of the Soviet secret police, Cheka). Once so threatened, Winston, in the most famous passage in the novel, shouts frantically, "Do it to Julia! Do it to Julia! Not me! Tear her face off, strip her to the bones. Not me! Julia! Not me!"[52] The story ends with Winston idly doodling $2 + 2 = 5$ just before the public confession and execution.[53] As the bullet enters his brain, Winston has found inner peace: "It was all right. Everything was all right, the struggle was finished. He had won the victory over himself. He loved Big Brother."[54]

Orwell's prophetic novel asks more questions than it answers and is still subject to intense debate. Among the points worth considering is that the inner party has no ideology. It performs atrocities without any concern for the use of atrocity to build— granted, with pain and suffering—a new society. Winston was to be killed. Why bother with brainwashing? Here Orwell wanted to make the point that totalitarianism becomes its own justification. Whatever ideology may have once inspired the inner party, it had long since been forgotten.

Orwell wants us to understand that totalitarian governments lose their ideological *raison d'être* but not their will to survive. In the Soviet Union, notions of equality—so central to Marx—were quickly forgotten as the party elite engorged itself. The state not only did not "wither away," it quickly became so bureaucratically inert that the monarchy it replaced seemed almost innovative in comparison. In *Animal Farm,* Orwell's incisive description of Communist equality is imbedded in the allegory of a children's story, as in *Gulliver's Travels.* Animals carry out a revolution against human beings, but soon the pigs and guard dogs dominate. The other animals perform the most difficult tasks, as directed by the pigs, who explain that "all are equal but some are more equal than others."[55] Actually, Lenin's early commitment to a small band of professional revolutionaries that directs a larger party of soldiers (the "inner party" and "outer party" of *Nineteen Eighty-four*) raises the question of whether equality was ever intended.

Other Marxist governments seem Orwellianly inegalitarian. In Cuba, for example, there are the *mayimbes* (an Afro-Cuban term for "ruling class"), for whom special privileges are accorded. Because of their "great responsibilities," the *mayimbes* should not be "tormented by domestic worries." There are exclusive stores, modeled on the Soviet *beriozhka* (hard currency stores), private hospitals, luxury cars, and, above all, plenty of women (*mayimbes* are male).[56] The example was set by Castro who:

> . . . spent lavishly on himself and gave away as gifts luxury houses, cars, and . . . waterproof Rolexes, the preeminent emblem of personal power. . . . He indulged his every whim, ate well, and was known in leadership circles for his womanizing.[57]

We need only add, of course, that such behavior is not limited to leaders of revolutionary totalitarian movements but is alas, human nature:

> No matter what . . . the ideals with which they come to power, all elites facing a similar situation sooner or later behave in similar ways. When they have the opportunity to take a disproportionate share of the goods that make civilization bearable, they take it.[58]

BRAINWASHING IN CHINA

The extent to which totalitarian governments engage in thought control, as opposed to terror to induce compliance, is difficult to ascertain. If we generalize and consider those that have tortured on the way toward the creation of the new man, we can list Stalin's purges of the 1930s, the People's Republic of China from the Korean War through the death of Mao, the revolution in Cambodia from 1975, and the Soviet Union's use of psychiatry to induce conversion. (Perhaps you wonder about the exclusion of Nazi Germany; it is actually atypical, as its mass killings were intended as genocide, and although brutal abuses of mind and body were common, the Nazis' aims were a good deal less exalted than the examples selected for examination.)

China developed sophisticated means of thought "reform." Borrowed from the Russians was, among other things, the notions of sin and guilt, which are prominent in Christianity but rarely found in Chinese culture or philosophy. But the Chinese progressed well beyond the Russians and were more interested in individual salvation than in liquidation or imprisonment. The Confucian tradition of self-examination and "rectification of names" (changing a person to fit a certain category, such as scholar) was similar to communism in assuming that people can remake themselves by changing the environment and then adapting to it.

Confucianism stresses harmony, the absence of conflict, as does communism, and, perhaps most important, Confucianism is based on a hierarchy loyalties, son to father, subject to ruler, and so on. Communism substituted Mao for the familial father, and the devotion to him is frequently phrased in the language of the family. Though far gentler than communism, Confucianism likewise proposes a way of life for the whole person and makes no separation of public from private, the hallmark of totalitarianism. The Confucian influence, when combined with the Russian insistence on ideological purity, yielded a thought reform effort that demanded absolute submission. Chinese interrogators became "master psychologists" and were the subject of several motion pictures, the most memorable being *The Manchurian Candidate*.[59] These terrifying examples of brainwashing, however, were directed toward captured Westerners. Our concern here is with the Chinese population.

Mao's Genius

The Chinese Communists had experimented with thought control during the 1920s, when they were beginning the civil war. The collapse of the dynasty in 1911 had not resulted in a unified government, although Chiang Kai-shek's Nationalists (Kuomintang) were able to maintain a tenuous hold. Initially, the Kuomintang maintained a united front with the Mao's Communists, but by 1926 the split was irrevocable. During the late 1920s and 1930s, the few thousand remnants of the Communist party were ruthlessly hounded by Chiang, surviving in small towns and in the mountains. Mao (1893–1975), still a Confucian at heart, was a genius on the same level as Lenin and developed a Chinese brand of Marxism-Leninism even as his party was under the organizational control of the Russians.

In college, Mao had developed the theme that a phase of oppression would be followed by a phase of liberation, that China's weakness internationally would be followed by a period as one of the world's most powerful nations. In the *Hsiang River Review*, which he founded, Mao developed the belief that, unlike the Russian Revolution, the Chinese revolt could be a genuine mass movement with the rural peasants at its foundation.

He agreed with Lenin that the intellectual basis of a revolution must be a world movement against capitalism, but in China the party, rather than being the vanguard of the revolution, must become the teacher, the uplifter, of the masses. But his musings were interrupted by the necessity of yet another retreat from Chiang's relentless pursuit. In 1934, Mao and a few thousand loyalists began the Long March to Yenan. There, the theory and organizational implementation of the Chinese revolution was refined.

When the Japanese invaded, Mao and Chiang renewed their alliance, but the war went so badly for the Nationalists that the Communists were able to organize the Red Army into a militarily competitive force, capable for the first time of at least confronting the Nationalists. Even so, when the Japanese surrendered, the Nationalists had at least twice as many men under arms as the Communists. But in 1949, using the Red Army wisely and selectively, the Communists ran the Nationalists into the sea; they established a government in exile on Taiwan.

Besides capturing and converting their armed opponents, the Communists began to experiment with political education for the flood of intellectuals who were fleeing the corrupt rule of Chiang Kai-shek. During World War II, the Communists continued to develop thought control, stressing the similarities between the Communist new man and the Confucian ideal. Techniques were refined, using United Nations troops captured during the Korean War, and were applied domestically.

The Great Leap Forward

China became more brutal during the Great Leap Forward (1958–1960) and the Cultural Revolution (1966–1976) but initially avoided violence whenever possible. The avoidance of violence was feasible because immediately following the Communist victory in the civil war in 1949, mass executions of counterrevolutionaries eliminated the remnants of resistance to the revolution.

The architect of the revolution, Mao Tse-tung, consolidated his power during the Korean War and began land reform soon after. Like Stalin, Mao engaged in land reform with great ferocity. Executions ran at a rate of about 22,500 a month, more than Stalin achieved. However, since land reform in China did not last as long as Stalin's war against the kulaks, the total number of executions was probably only about 3 million.[60]

To cope with those not killed, Mao introduced the idea of thought reform. He regarded it as central to the success of the revolution and published several guidelines about its methods. His writings show that, unlike Stalin, Mao felt the right approach was that of physician removing a diseased limb: he would cure an ideological disease, thus saving the person.

Mao's commitment to thought reform embraced a series of reflections on the cause of counterrevolutionary thought, a subject that bored Stalin. Like Marx, Mao believed that people surrounded by corrupting institutions (capitalism) would respond rationally by adopting extreme individualism—dog eat dog—as their credo. In an insane world (capitalism), it would be mad not to devote one's entire attention to looking out for number one. But Mao did not believe that changing institutions (communism) was enough and wrote often about the "sociological roots" of crime (including counterrevolutionary thought) in terms of remaking personalities:

> The evil ideology and evil habits left behind by the old society, calling for the injuring of others for self-profit and seeking enjoyment without labor, still remain in the minds of some people to a marked degree. . . . Thus if we are to wipe all crimes from their root, in addition to inflicting on the criminal the punishment due, we must also carry out various effective measures to transform the various evil ideological conceptions in the minds of the people so that they may be educated and reformed into *new people*.[61]

Thought reform was also, in Mao's eyes, politically essential, for although the revolution had been won with the blood of peasants, the intellectual class must be won over. Initially, the winning of their minds and hearts was to be attempted by massive "study campaigns," begun with university faculty in Peking, which would then spread the new ideology to the other university faculties.

"Struggle Sessions"

But the campaign was more emotional than cerebral and featured thousands of intellectuals making hysterical public confessions, or "struggle sessions." All confessions contained the same ingredients: an avowal of past errors, a delineation of progress because of Communist counsel, and an accounting of remaining defects with a pledge to continue the job of cleansing. One important aspect of struggle sessions was humiliation.

Thus lifetimes of scholarly work were denounced as counterrevolutionary, often in the presence of students; students' suggestions for further improvement were invariably greeted with servile gratitude. A Harvard-trained professor of philosophy confessed:

> Born of a bureaucratic landlord family, I have always led a life of ease and comfort. . . . The principal source of my various pleasures lay in the decadent philosophy of the bourgeoisie. . . . In order to maintain my way of life I had to have special privileges. . . . Only now have I realized that . . . the old democracy is but the dictatorship of the bourgeois class, and the so-called individual freedom is but the dictatorship of the bourgeoisie to exploit and oppress the laboring people. My numerous criminal deeds in the past should thus be attributed to my acceptance of individual liberalism. . . . The miracles of the People's Liberation Army demanded my wholehearted respect . . . and they love the people so much. . . . I began to realize the scientific and truthful nature of Marxism-Leninism. . . . I shall eradicate the bourgeois ideologies which have for years dominated my life. . . . I shall strive to become a new man and a teacher of the people in substance as well as in name.[62]

Public humiliation and denunciation lent these episodes a bizarre cast:

> Targets might be required to stand on a platform, heads bowed respectfully to the masses, while acknowledging and repeating their ideological crimes. Typically they had to "airplane," stretching their arms out behind them like the wings of a jet.[63]

In some cases, the "airplane ride" was more brutal, as Red Guards tossed the ropes binding a victim over a bar at the top of the room and hoisted him up, allowing him to squirm in agony.

The process that culminated in the public confession began in most cases with the revolutionary university, a rather pleasant place despite austere conditions. The universities were expanded Communist party cells, with instruction from leaders. After periods of informal discussion, the curriculum became more formal, including Leninism, Maoism, the history of the Chinese revolution, and so on. But shortly thereafter, small groups began to assemble with less discussion of the courses and more insistence on a discussion of each person's own beliefs. Criticism became more intense and was now directed exclusively by party members rather than the participants themselves. Confessions (generally of Nationalist sympathies during the civil war) became quite common, as each participant tried to outconfess his colleagues and perhaps gain an early release.

As the process continued, the vilification became more intense and more personal. Attention shifted away from past mistakes toward the discovery of a new identity. The critical point was reached when the detainee denounced his father. The Confucian system stresses filial piety as the center of civilization; hence the renunciation of filial piety leaves a person without worth and in desperate need of another identity. The new identity will be the party, since all ties to traditional morality have been renounced, and the new man is a "filial Communist." Like his Russian counterpart, the Chinese new man is thought to be capable of "subordinating his own interest to those of the Party and the people in every conceivable manner, ready to make any sacrifice, and to be, in so doing, the happiest of men."[64]

Chinese thought control is based more on cultural dictates than on torture. Korean

POWs were given the "third degree," deprived of sleep, and subjected to other indignities and agonies developed by the Russians and refined to a science by the Chinese, but internal thought control relied on the well-established psychiatric principle of *transference:* old familial loyalties were transferred to the Communist party. Though the process was not pleasant, it was far less painful than the Russian practices.

The "Hundred Flowers" Campaign and Reaction to It

Mao was sufficiently confident about the loyalty of the intellectuals to begin the Hundred Flowers campaign, named for his pronouncement, "Let a hundred flowers bloom together, let the hundred schools of thought contend." But he had underestimated the failure of the various thought reform programs; he estimated that no more than 3 percent of the university graduates were hostile to Marxism, but he was wrong. Apparently, the confessions extracted during the struggle sessions were superficial. The litany of criticism shocked him. Intellectuals were not criticizing the party for being inefficient; rather, they were attacking its premises. After a month, the campaign was over and the reaction began. Mao had permanently lost confidence in the intellectual class; he also feared it. About 700,000 skilled people were removed from their jobs and branded with the old Soviet appellation "enemy of the people." Almost all were imprisoned. It was in this poisonous atmosphere that Mao embarked on the Great Leap Forward, an epic undertaking exceeding Stalin's collectivization in brutality.

Like Stalin, Mao wanted to push China into the ranks of the industrialized world as rapidly as possible. Like Stalin, Mao was aware of economists' painfully slow remedies. The "rational" solution would have been to divert the high rate of investment in heavy industry to light industry, producing more consumer goods and thus providing an incentive for improved productivity.[65] But besides taking too long, such plans relied too much on individualism. Mao (like Castro and Khadafy, among other radical leaders) had a strong ideological bias against rewarding individual greed. People should work hard for the good of the society, not to fill their own pockets.

And so it began. In a few months, 90 percent of the Chinese population had their economic life completely transformed. The goal of collectives was not solely economic. Comprising perhaps 50,000 people, collectives were to instill group identification, reduce family loyalty (by, for example, serving meals collectively), and diminish individualism by paying additional incentives to people who needed them, irrespective of their contribution.

The consequence of this madness was famine among the peasants and the virtually complete destruction of China's infant steel industry. The slogan "Overtake Britain in 15 years," with which the Great Leap Forward was launched, soon became a macabre joke as between 20 and 30 million people died from starvation or malnutrition.[66]

From the beginning, Mao had believed that political will could overcome economic difficulties, that Red agricultural experts would devise a uniquely Chinese way of compressing history. The engine was ideology, not expertise, and it failed. The Great Leap Forward ended in disaster in 1960, with Mao's influence severely tested. Mao conceded that like Castro, he knew or cared nothing about economics; the Great Leap Forward was truly a "Mao-made catastrophe."[67]

The Final Chapter: The Cultural Revolution

Openly and successfully challenged by factional opponents, Mao began to plan a more grandiose scheme for the elimination from China of the remnants of antisocialist thinking. In preparation for the Cultural Revolution (1966–1976), Mao launched a "socialist education" program, with the purpose of radicalizing the youth, to whom he increasingly turned in his struggles against more pragmatic opponents. The program had a strong anti-intellectual bias, as Mao became increasingly convinced that traditional Chinese Confucian education was an enemy of his vision for a classless society.

Mao's *Little Red Book,* so popular on American campuses a few years later, was distributed in massive quantities, especially to the army, which used it as an official training manual and, in keeping with its urging, abolished all rank and differences in uniforms and salary.

The Cultural Revolution began with the sympathies of the young, few of whom knew or cared anything about the byzantine struggles between leadership factions or Mao's urgent need to rid Chinese society of the vestiges of intellectual independence from socialism. Mao's instrument was the Red Guards, young gangs who set about the task of dismantling China's educational system and as much of its presocialist past as it could. The People's Liberation Army provided logistical support as the purges and destruction reached the stage of hysteria. Mao's opponents in the party were rooted out, and 400,000 of them were ruthlessly killed, usually by long-term maltreatment rather than swift execution.

But it was the stark anti-intellectualism of the movement that made it a precursor of the horror of Cambodia. Fairbank recalls:

> A "literature of the wounded" soon began to report individuals' disasters—the scholar whose manuscript of an unpublished lifework is burned before his eyes, the husband who tries in vain to save the class status of his children by divorcing his wife, who had been labeled a rightist, the famous novelist who is simply beaten to death, the old school principal who is set to cleaning latrines.[68]

People were also forced to move against their will; about 12 million urban youths (10 percent of the urban population) were evacuated to rural areas.[69] Of course, being in the Red Guards was fun, not necessarily because of the cruelty but because of the train rides to distant cities, the mass meetings, the opportunities to ridicule former agents of authority, especially educators, the long absences from school, and the elimination of academic standards when classes resumed.[70]

The Cultural Revolution finally lost its momentum; the Red Guards were often out of control, and the People's Liberation Army was used to restore order. With the death of Mao and the arrest of the Gang of Four (Mao's wife and three other factional leaders), China began to recover. How does the Cultural Revolution compare with other social disasters? It was different from the Russian collectivization and dekulakization carnage in that its murders were less systematic. At different times during the Cultural Revolution, different targets suffered different kinds of torture and humiliation. There was no clear scapegoat, no finger pointing at kulaks or Jews.[71]

But the uncertainty of who would be the next to go was unnerving and gave the Cultural Revolution a special kind of extremity:

> It was not just the sweeping nature of the losses or the depth of isolation that made the cultural revolution extreme. It was the apparent meaninglessness of the movement as well. And the inability of many to find meaning in their suffering led . . . to false confessions, suicide, and madness.[72]

Similar findings emerge from interviews with the survivors of Nazi concentration camps. If violence can be made absolutely random, resistance crumbles quickly.

How much change has occurred since Mao's death and the rise of Deng and the pragmatists? Data from Chinese news media indicate the following trend in arrests for political and ideological offenses:[73]

Period	Political and Ideological Arrests (% of total arrests)
1949–1951	66
1950–1952	66
1952	13
1957	93
1966–1976	99
1977–1978	59
1979–1984	21

The reversion to Maoism—the armed suffocation of rebellion in 1989—seemed inconsistent with the events of the last decade. Superficially, this was true. But China is a country which has dispatched robbers with a bullet to the back of the head. Also, while the regime was loosening its grip *economically,* it was not interested in human rights or political "pluralism" (the code word for the relaxation of the party's monopoly on political power). Certainly, legal reform did not occupy much of the regime's time. What Deng Xiaoping had hoped to accomplish was economic reform—a greater reliance upon the market—*without* political reform. The fact that Deng held only minor party positions but was still in charge is itself a telling commentary on the institutional weakness and primitive power structure of Chinese politics. Using political power to place one's family members in privileged positions has been the rule of the game in China long before the revolution and, indeed, the impulse to protect one's family was a strong motive for the suppressions of 1989. Scarcely noted in our exuberance over economic reforms was an *increase* in arrest for "economic" crimes, "public order" offenses, and prosecutions for violation of population policy during the Deng years.

THE KHMER ROUGE REVOLUTION

The Khmer Rouge overthrew an American backed government in Cambodia in 1975 and changed the name of the country to Kampuchea. In 1978, the Khmer Rouge were themselves defeated and replaced with a friendly government by Vietnam. In the three years in which they ruled, the Khmer Rouge proved themselves more ruthless than either the Russians or the Chinese.

Upon occupying the capital city, Phnom Penh, the Khmer Rouge began the following steps immediately:

1. All private property was abolished.
2. All urban dwellers were removed to rural areas.
3. All personal property was subject to seizure by the state.
4. All people were classified by class background (peasants, workers, soldiers). Those denied a classification were killed.

There were good military reasons for evacuating cities also. The Khmer Rouge, about 60,000 illiterate peasants, would have been unable to control the existing bureaucracy or to establish surveillance against clandestine opposition. Thus 3 million people were evacuated, leaving the city deserted.

The evacuation of Phnom Penh was a stunning example of revolutionary ideology. It had been planned two years earlier by *Angka Loeu*, the intellectual elite of the Khmer Rouge. This group of 20 intellectuals, living in Paris in the 1950s, developed a theory of "necessary violence" and ruralization. They planned a complete economic and social revolution. A leader among the Paris Cambodians was Saloth Sar, who, using the *nom de guerre* Pol Pot, led the Khmer Rouge. (However, unlike Lenin, Stalin, or Mao, he was unable to sustain himself in power once the revolution had succeeded. He lost effective power about a year after the capture of Phnom Penh and was replaced in 1979.) The chance to try out their theories occurred two decades later when the Khmer Rouge insurgency was successful and Phnom Penh fell.

The shock of the evacuation can hardly be overstated: an entire city was suddenly abandoned, virtually all personal possessions were left behind, and the city looked very much like a science fiction depiction of the desolation of a nuclear war:

> Komphot walked out into the hot night, and his head began to swim. Laid before him was a ravaged city, an anxious, empty city. It took Komphot some time to gain control of his emotions. *There were no people!* He stared at the litter on the streets, at the evidence of all he had not witnessed. There were no people![74]

Why did the Khmer Rouge undertake such a massive program, resulting in widespread death and the elimination of the remnants of urban civilization? The Russians did not evacuate Moscow, nor the Chinese Peking, though, as we have seen, they moved people around at will and killed millions in the process. But the Khmer Rouge wanted to eliminate all evidence of a former country called Cambodia. They wanted to withdraw not just from the international community but from the century.

They believed that only a return to the purity of rural labor, and hence the elimination of an urban economy, would allow Kampuchea to develop economically. The Khmer Rouge were the ultimate example of Rousseau's infatuation with the "state of nature." There were no telephones, no mail, no regular airline service. The borders were mined and patrolled, and the coast was carefully watched. No one came in, and no one went out. Kampuchea was completely isolated, and its revolution had begun. While Mao and Stalin struggled with the residue of capitalism, the Khmer Rouge had eliminated it. They (correctly) believed that private property was the essence of capitalism. No private property means no capitalism, and Phnom Penh was the symbol of private property:

If we had kept Phnom Penh [private property] would have had much strength. . . .
We were stronger, had more influence than the private sector when we were in the
countryside. But in Phnom Penh we would have become [private property owners']
satellite. However, we did not keep them in Phnom Penh and private property has no
power.[75]

The Khmer Rouge were incensed not just by private property but also by the special qualities of urban property and life, which they regarded as reminiscent of the old
colonial Cambodia. They believed that Phnom Penh's comparatively high standard of
living was a result of its servile status in the international economy. Most, if not all, of
the city's economy was dedicated to the production of luxury goods for the few who
could afford them (certainly none of the peasants could): "Virtually the entire urban
sector was labeled as unproductive because it was perceived as serving a small minority,
the . . . bourgeoisie, and its way of life was being paid for with agricultural exports
produced by peasant laborers."[76]

But there was more in the evacuation of the city than an economic theory that was
far from unique to this revolution. There was a genuine loathing for Western culture.
Like Mao's Cultural Revolution, which required women to wear sexless uniforms and
to eschew makeup, there was a strong puritanism in the Khmer Rouge image of decadent urban life. Even though their leaders spent years in Paris planning the revolution
and were influenced by European Marxist theory, they hated not only the economics of
dependency but also its cultural attributes. Upon entering Phnom Penh,

> sons and daughters of our workers and peasants were taken aback by the overwhelming
> unspeakable sight of long-haired men and youngsters in bizarre clothes making them-
> selves undistinguishable from the fair sex. . . . Our traditional mentality, mores, tra-
> ditions, literature and arts and culture and tradition were totally destroyed by U.S. im-
> perialism and its stooges. . . . Our people's traditionally clean, sound characteristics
> and essence were completely . . . replaced by imperialistic, pornographic, shameless,
> perverted and fanatic traits.[77]

The Khmer Rouge succeeded in acquiring all private property. Further, they had to
subvert primary groups: "The state had to usurp the authority of the family if it was to
survive. The family was the most potent, hence the most feared, of all relationships in
the former society."[78]

When the former urban dwellers were relocated in rural work camps (this took
about three months), the attacks on the family intensified. Sexual intercourse between
husband and wife was prohibited, as was any form of sexual activity. Married couples
could have only brief conversations, and a violation brought the death sentence. Other
minor offenses that cost a person's life were tardiness, criticism of economic plans, use
of alcohol and marrying without party permission. Black garments were compulsory.

The Execution of the Educated

Once the people were relocated and the cities abandoned, the Khmer Rouge created new
economic organizations. Workers slept in barracks, ate at common canteens, and worked
from sunup to sunset every day. While the work camps were being organized, the

Khmer Rouge began the task of killing "enemies of the revolution." They developed a plan for systematic killing, guessing that random violence would be less successful. Accordingly, their targets for liquidation were specified as follows:[79]

1. All officers, noncommissioned officers, and many enlisted men, in the defeated armies
2. Many bureaucrats of the defeated regime
3. All royalty (with the exception of the exiled Prince Sihanouk, who supported the revolution)
4. People engaged in commercial enterprise
5. Skilled factory laborers
6. Many Western-educated intellectuals
7. All Moslems
8. Many Buddhist monks

There is no way of assessing how many died, since not even the formal executions were reported accurately. The Khmer Rouge did, however, enjoy the ghoulish practice of taking snapshots before, during, and after the executions (there are even photographs of Khmer Rouge taking photographs of each other as they hacked and sawed at their victims). There were indeed "killing fields" (from which a motion picture derived its name). Each "sector" had many of them. Generally, they were located next to older buildings—schools, for example—and consisted of a field for torture and death and a pit for burial of the corpses. Of the 33 sectors, one reported 38,400 executions from 1975 to 1978, but it is likely that this figure is only a fraction of the actual total. In any case, if this report is typical, there were about 1.25 million executions. This total represented about one-seventh of Cambodia's population.[80]

There were surely many more, and the deaths from abuse, overwork, exposure, and malnutrition were not, of course, included in the various sector reports. "Work and murder, work and murder were the two certainties of Democratic Kampuchea."[81] Making the final count even more difficult to assess was the inability of the Khmer Rouge to generate an economy or to feed the people; famine followed the collapse of food production.

Kampuchea Compared

We see in the Khmer revolution several ideas common to the Great Leap Forward, the Cultural Revolution, and Stalin's war against the kulaks.[82] These movements regarded political attitudes as more important than technical skills. They believed that such skills were easily acquired and vastly overrated. Moreover, well-educated people were likely to be counterrevolutionary because the old society had rewarded them well. Since educated classes were not legally classified (they were neither peasants, workers, nor soldiers), they were ipso facto enemies and were to be killed.

But the Khmer revolution was more extreme than earlier ones. Even Mao and Stalin had not tried to eliminate inequalities in wealth, especially in such a short period of time. The Khmer Rouge achieved equity because they believed in absolute equality more fervently than the other revolutionary leaders; they believed in it so passionately that they let nothing stand in their way. They were "willing to liquidate the traditional ruling class, empty the cities, abolish markets, money, and private property all in the name of egalitarian collectivism, rapid economic development, and the dictatorship of the proletariat."[83] In their obsession with liquidation, the Khmer Rouge most closely approximated the dekulakization program, but even this comparison makes the Khmer Rouge more extreme. The glorification of violence, the absolute rigidity of their extermination schedule, and their complete lack of mercy make them most comparable to the Nazis. There is no "preceptorial vision" class or race extermination.[84]

Once potential enemies were killed, the Khmer Rouge began to focus on members of the party who were suspected as being unenthusiastic. These new targets required more carefully developed means of torture. During the first phase of the killings, torture was an indulgence since people with improper class backgrounds were killed irrespective of their contrition. During the second phase, confessions were extracted. Torture had to be prolonged. Among its practitioners, the most highly regarded skill was to be able to create unbearable pain just below the threshold of loss of consciousness and premature death. But the Khmer Rouge, given their obsession with self-sufficiency, had little contact with their professional colleagues in other countries. As a result, their techniques lacked the sophistication of those the Chinese developed during the Korean War. Even though the Chinese maintained an embassy and provided advisers of various kinds, the Khmer Rouge did not trust them to provide technical help in the techniques of torture.

Consequently, the Khmer Rouge's interrogations were no more successful than their economic schemes. Nevertheless, there are similarities with Chinese and Russian torture, mainly the need for the confession. The routine was as follows:

> "We place them in irons and chains. We check what they have on them and when we are interrogating we place no objects near them for fear that they might take these objects and use them as weapons. . . . It is important to do torture by hand." However, women were beaten with whips and the party insisted that interrogators "absolutely not beat them with our hands. . . . Once we have pounded on the enemies for a long time they are in pain even when not beaten. They are in pain and get so skinny that it is no longer possible to beat them. . . . If the enemies are in pain to the point they are unable to open their mouths, [it] would be annoying to the party. . . . The purpose of torture is to get answers. . . ; it's not something we do for the fun of it."[85]

The beatings were interrupted by political propaganda sessions, culminating with the confession. Khmer Rouge torturers were taught to get a confession in the prisoners' own words, written by hand. They are told to promise freedom in exchange for the confession, to "do whatever is necessary to make them uncertain about the question of life and death so that they will still hope that they may survive."[86]

The turning inward of the Khmer Rouge, the concentration on disloyal members of the party, occurred because the revolution had become a demonstrable failure. Without propping up from China, Kampuchea would have simply ceased to exist. So the Khmer Rouge needed scapegoats and found them within their own ranks as Kampuchea deteriorated even further into total madness. As Mao had done, the Khmer Rouge recruited replacements for the purges among the youth. But the revolution never got beyond the stage of purging and killing. The intent was to strip away traditional bases and then rebuild with new values.

Due possibly to the brevity of their rule, however, the Khmer Rouge never got around to the phase of building the new man, and since they executed almost everyone they tortured, it is doubtful that they had any notion of the psychiatric reconstruction championed by the Chinese or even the political education of the Soviet revolution. They closed the schools rather than use them as instruments of political indoctrination; even use of radios was prohibited.

One explanation for the speed and ferocity of the Khmer revolution is the belief that a quick and thorough revolution would make it impossible for a new class of masters to appear, as was true, they believed, of other communist revolutions. But as the years failed to reduce the violence, it is hard to escape the conclusion that the Khmer Rouge were interested primarily in death: "Whenever the Khmer Rouge were faced with lack of comprehension or passive resistance, they chose to exterminate rather than reeducate."[87]

In the late 1980s, Khmer Rouge guerrillas in camps in Thailand, awaiting the opportunity to return, displayed the xenophobic obsessions that characterized their rule. The camps were harshly run, with military conscription common, defection punished by death, and contact with foreigners proscribed. Lavishly funded by the Chinese, the Khmer Rouge await the chance for a second coming.

THE POLITICAL USES OF PSYCHIATRY

Perhaps, given their primitive society, the Khmer Rouge had no choice. But the Soviet Union, emerging from the crude brutality of the purges, became at least as sophisticated, technically, as the Chinese. The psychiatric confinement of dissenters in the Soviet Union was widely practiced in the 1950s, drifted into disuse, and reemerged in the mid-1960s. In the late 1980s, under relentless international pressure and in response to Mikhail Gorbachev's need for more legitimacy, the practice was for the most part discontinued.

Enforced hospitalization did not require a court order or a legal review. A person could be confined on the authority of a single psychiatrist, later confirmed by a panel of three additional psychiatrists. Psychiatrists followed a loose and broadly defined notion of mental illness. For example, prisoners were classified as schizophrenic with no symptoms of the disease. One psychiatrist explained rather paradoxically that "the absence of symptoms of an illness cannot prove the absence of the illness itself." When symptoms were alleged, the diagnosis was unrelated to any generally accepted canon of psychiatry. Prisoners were said to suffer from "nervous exhaustion brought on by her search for justice, reformist delusions, and a mania for reconstructing society."[88]

The logic of the argument is flawless: since the Soviet Union is without major problems, anyone who dissents is mentally or emotionally disturbed and needs treatment. The Soviet psychiatrists made no real distinction between some commonly understood classifications of mental illness—depression, anxiety, compulsions, schizophrenia, and so on—and political dissent. Although even the "accepted" mental problems were curable by heavy doses of Marxism, political dissent required more persuasive techniques. This view is very much in the tradition of the new man. Orwell, whose *Nineteen Eighty-four* was drafted before the development of mind-altering drugs, nevertheless could have had Big Brother puzzling over those poor souls who persisted in dissent.

Among the more noteworthy "madmen" of the USSR are Anatoly Koryagin, a psychiatrist who was imprisoned after he refused to issue a diagnosis saying a labor union activist was insane, and Zhores Medvedev, who was forcibly committed in 1970 for writing articles debunking Trofim Lysenko's bogus genetic theories. Lysenko, you will recall from Chapter 1, was an agronomist held in high repute during the Stalin era in the Soviet Union, who claimed that he could change organisms by altering the environment and that the changes could be genetically transmitted. Hence human beings could induce evolutionary changes in human nature by changing institutions. The new Soviet man could be created by changing the environment, and the desired characteristics, once in place, could be transmitted to the next generation. Medvedev, after release from the psychiatric hospital, was exiled in 1973. He went to London, where he was a senior research scientist at the National Institute for Medical Research. Medvedev is the author of *Soviet Agriculture, The Rise and Fall of T. D. Lysenko, Soviet Science,* and several books written with his twin brother, Roy, a dissident historian living in Moscow.

The main administrative instrument for the treatment of dissenters is the Serbsky Institute of Forensic Psychiatry, officially part of the Ministry of Health but in fact a branch of the KGB, the Soviet secret police. The institute conducts an investigation of the prisoner's past for any signs of instability, questions friends about unusual behavior, and assigns the prisoner to a "special psychiatric hospital." At such hospitals, the use of drugs to induce pain is well established.

Much of the treatment of dissidents is derived from the behavior modification theories of Ivan Pavlov who in the 1940s established that mental illness was a consequence of chemical imbalance and thus could be corrected chemically. He had earlier introduced the idea of the *conditioned response*. With a proper combination of punishment and reward, dogs could be made to salivate when they heard a bell previously associated with food. After a time, they salivated whenever they heard the bell and continued to do so even when the bell was not followed by food.

As the special psychiatric hospitals were being revived, Pavlov's theories became very much in vogue. Freudian notions of curing the patient by discovering the meaning of the symptoms were rejected in favor of behavior modification, which asked not why a behavior occurred but only how it could be modified. Since collectivist ideology disregards individual needs or aspirations, collectivist psychiatry embraced Pavlov rather than Freud: it does not matter why a person is behaving improperly, whether because of an overextended Oedipus complex or an inability to move beyond the early (anal-compulsive) stages of emotional development. If the symptoms of the distress can be eliminated, the affliction will be of no consequence.

Pavlov himself is well regarded among legitimate advocates of behavior modification, and his belief in the efficacy of treating mental illness as a chemical problem is widely accepted. Behavior modification has relieved some of the symptoms of autism among children and has enabled people to give up harmful habits (aversion therapy for heavy smokers, for instance). However, Pavlov's legitimate research objectives were politicized. Soviet medical students preparing for psychiatry spend about one-fourth of their time studying Marxism, Leninism, Marxist economics, dialectic materialism, and scientific atheism. If they encounter somebody who professes religious beliefs or who rejects Marxist theories of economic development, they would regard that person as mentally ill. Medical texts define schizophrenia as a deranged desire to reform Soviet society.

Drugs in the special psychiatric hospitals are used to induce pain and hence are derivative from Pavlov's emphasis on behavior modification; they are not used to relieve symptoms of mental unbalance (as is, for example, lithium carbonate in the treatment of manic-depressives). The drugs of choice are aminazine, a major tranquilizer (equivalent to Thorazine) that, used in excessive amounts, causes severe depression and sensory distortions; haloperidol, another tranquilizer that produces convulsions and epileptic symptoms, and sulfazine.

Sulfazine has gradually become the standard pharmacological tool because it creates unbearable pain of several varieties quickly. Originally developed to treat malaria by inducing a rapid increase in body temperature, sulfazine was used occasionally in the 1920s to treat extreme schizophrenia (it was the chemical equivalent of shock therapy). Because it caused fever, nausea, mental disorientation, and severe muscle spasms, most Western psychiatrists found sulfazine to be of no value and stopped its use. The side effects that made sulfazine too extreme for general use were the very qualities that made it so attractive in the Soviet Union. Sulfazine is generally used over a two-month period, with the strength of the injections increased weekly. Since the initial injection exceeded the normal strength, it caused a violent, long-term reaction at the point of injection, usually the buttocks. After about an hour, the full effect of the drug could be felt:

> The pain was so excruciating that a victim could not sit down . . . could not lift his legs. . . . The pain is so intense that they cannot move from their beds for three days. Sulfazine is simply a way to destroy a man completely. If they torture you and break your arms, there is a certain specific pain and you can somehow stand it. But sulfazine is like a drill boring into your body that gets worse and worse until it's more than you can stand. It's impossible to endure. It is worse than torture, because, sometimes, torture may end. But this kind of torture may continue for years.[89]

Patients in the special psychiatric hospitals can have their cases reviewed and, if sufficient progress can be shown, can be released (even though the original sentence is open-ended). When they are not open-ended, terms range upward of 15 years. Patients are not required to make public confessions, merely to convince a review panel that their aberrant behavior has been modified. Political prisoners assigned to special psychiatric hospitals are legally not charged with a crime; rather, they are victims of a curable mental illness. (It would make as much sense to extract a confession from a person hospitalized with a physical ailment.) But the severity of the treatment, the abuse of drugs, and the length of the sentences make one wonder what purpose is being served. It is unlikely that a person could endure pharmacological torture for a decade or more and not be converted to the satisfaction of the examiners.

Proving progress is not an easy task, since the concept is just as vague and politicized as the initial diagnosis. Compared with the number of people confined in other institutions, those in special psychiatric hospitals are few. They number in the hundreds, not the thousands. But theirs is a special kind of hell, unmatched in cruelty and in the politicization of a profession. The use of science for political purposes is well established in totalitarian states. Like that of the Nazis, Soviet biology has been driven as much by ideology as science.

Old ways die hard. In 1989, Soviet psychiatrists, seeking readmission to the World Psychiatric Association, invited extensive foreign inspection of the USSR's psychiatric hospitals. Here is what they found:

> Many political prisoners have been freed from mental wards and the government has adopted standards to protect psychiatric rights. But one American specialist said the visiting psychiatrists concluded that some of the persons they interviewed were confined to mental wards for political reasons. . . . Soviet doctors still commonly use the broadbrush diagnosis "schizophrenic" to lock up people who would be considered healthy in the West, and . . . patients are still treated with massive doses of pain-causing psychotropic drugs that Western doctors consider to have no medical value.[90]

EPITAPH

Totalitarian ideologies are unnatural; they are so bizarre that they cannot be sustained very long. The destruction of the distinction between public and private is too expensive, the goals (remaking human nature) too expansive, and the economic consequences too extreme. However, while currently in serious flux, these states are very much with us. Chapter 9 examines the structures and institutions of totalitarianism and how they affect the daily lives of people we are beginning to know a little better.

We have seen that totalitarian regimes are often the extensions of the personality disorders of powerful leaders: Stalin, Hitler, Mao, Pol Pot. It is as though these leaders, unconstrained, use governments as private domains through which they act out their fantasies. They are not overthrown (who would dare?) but fall victim to inertia. When the person for whom the purity of ideology is a matter of personality preservation finally dies, the process of the reduction of state intrusion and the elimination of dogma can begin. When Chinese reformers seeking to recover from Mao's madness by reliance on the market tell their Marxist critics to "seek truth from facts," they are expressing the retreat from totalitarianism that has characterized the last decades of the 20th century. A sensible interpretation of the violence in China in 1989 is that it was the last temper tantrum of an aging elite.

FOR FURTHER CONSIDERATION

1. How has the role of the bureaucracy changed in the Soviet Union from the time of Lenin to now?
2. Can the ideology of Hitler and the Nazi party be considered a typical totalitarian ideology? Why or why not?
3. What is the role of the secret police in a totalitarian society?
4. Compare the totalitarian concept of crime with that of an open society.
5. Who was the most successful candidate in the 1989 Soviet elections? How did he answer the question, In whose interest is the state run?

6. What are "politically incorrect shoes?" Where and when was the phrase used? Could such a phrase be used in an open society?

For the More Adventurous

1. Outline Marxist theory in your own words. Choose several Marxist countries and trace their development according to the outline you just made. Are they truly Marxist governments? Where on the scale are these countries now? How long did it take them to get there? What lies ahead? Do you agree with Jean-François Revel that the belief that there exists some variety of Communism other than Stalinism is an "illusion."[91]
2. What countries do you know of that participated in mass extermination campaigns (they need not be of the same magnitude) that can be compared to those perpetrated by Stalin and Hitler? What type of government was in power at the time of such actions? What do these societies have in common?
3. A common factor in the establishment of many totalitarian governments is that the "revolution" begins with the most educated. Why do you believe this is true? Imagine an abstract model of political society whose suitability has been demonstrated once and for all. What would you do to achieve it?

NOTES

1. Adam B. Ulam, *Stalin: The Man and His Era* (New York: Viking Penguin, 1973), p. 289.
2. Raymond D. Gastil, *Freedom in the World* (New York: Freedom House, 1988), p. 338.
3. Ibid., p. 267.
4. Amos Perlmutter, *Modern Authoritarianism* (New Haven, Conn.: Yale University Press, 1981), p. 6.
5. Ibid.
6. Alan C. Elms, *Personality in Politics* (New York: Harcourt Brace Jovanovich, 1976), p. 66.
7. Ibid., p. 78.
8. Rudolph R. Rummel, "War Isn't the Century's Biggest Killer," *Wall Street Journal,* July 7, 1986, p. 5, and wire service estimates.
9. Andrew Pavlov, *The Cult Experience* (Westport, Conn.: Greenwood Press, 1982), p. 4.
10. G. W. Swope, "Kids and Cults: Who Joins and Why," *Media and Methods 49* (1980): 18–21.
11. Jeane Kirkpatrick, *Dictatorships and Double Standards* (New York: Simon & Schuster, 1982), pp. 117–118.
12. Sergei Eisenstein's film *The Battleship Potemkin* celebrates these events.
13. Alexander Solzhenitsyn'a *August 1914* (London: Bodley Head, 1971) describes Russian infantry, armed with wooden spears, advancing against German machine guns.
14. Ester B. Fern, "Chinese Government Taking Hardline Stance," *New York Times,* March 21, 1989, p. 1.
15. Peter L. Berger, *The Capitalist Revolution* (New York: Basic Books, 1986), p. 200.
16. The family is an example of a primary group; an occupational association is a secondary group.
17. Peter L. Berger, " 'Sincerity' and 'Authenticity' in Modern Society," *Public Interest,* Spring 1973, p. 85.
18. Ibid., p. 86.
19. Ibid., pp. 87–88.

20. Albert Camus, *The Stranger* (New York: Alfred Knopf, 1969), p. 34.
21. Ibid., p. 55.
22. Marshall Berman, *The Politics of Authenticity* (New York: Atheneum, 1970), p. 136.
23. Albert Camus, *The Rebel* (New York: Alfred Knopf, 1956), p. 213.
24. Barbara Evans Clements, "The Birth of the New Soviet Woman," in *Bolshevik Culture,* ed. Abbott Gleason, Peter Kenez, and Richard Stites (Bloomington: Indiana University Press, 1985), p. 220.
25. Jose Luis Llovio-Mendendez, *Insider* (New York: Bantam, 1988), pp. 81, 113.
26. Quoted in Robert Conquest, *The Great Terror* (Harmondsworth, England: Penguin, 1971), p. 47.
27. Robert Conquest, *Harvest of Sorrow* (New York: Oxford University Press, 1986), p. 144.
28. Isaac Deutscher, *Stalin* (New York: Oxford University Press, 1949), p. 324.
29. Charles Bettelheim, *Class Struggles in the USSR: Second Period, 1923–1930* (London: Monthly Review Press, 1978), p. 466.
30. Ibid., p. 468.
31. Conquest, *Harvest of Sorrow,* p. 74.
32. Based on ibid., p. 72.
33. Barrington Moore, Jr., *Authority and Inequality under Capitalism and Socialism: USA, USSR, and China* (New York: Oxford University Press, 1987), p. 52. This figure does not separate victims of dekulakization from victims of the purge. Moore estimates that 10 million died as a consequence of the collectivization of agriculture.
34. Roy A. Medvedev, "The Number of Victims of Stalinism Is about 40 Million People," *Moscow News,* February 13, 1989, p. 3.
35. Ibid., p. 3.
36. See Conquest, *Harvest of Sorrow,* pp. 117–143. The Nazi enemies list featured not only Jews but also gypsies, homosexuals, Jehovah's Witnesses, Communists, Social Democrats, the "work-shy," and the mentally or physically handicapped.
37. Zhores Medvedev, *Soviet Agriculture* (New York: Norton, 1987), p. 95.
38. Ibid.
39. Ibid., p. 97.
40. Ibid.
41. Combining deaths from collectivization and from the purge and subtracting deaths in World War II, the Soviet Union's population at the time of Stalin's death comes out about 20 million short. Stalin was probably responsible for virtually all these deaths, making him more bloodthirsty than Hitler.
42. Nikita Khrushchev, "Crimes of the Stalin Era," *New Leader,* January 21, 1956, p. 14.
43. Conquest, *Harvest of Sorrow,* p. 208.
44. W. G. Krivitsky, *In Stalin's Secret Service* (New York: Harper & Row, 1939), p. 203.
45. Nathan Leiltes and Elsa Bernaut, *Ritual of Liquidation: The Case of the Moscow Trials* (New York: Free Press, 1954), p. 111.
46. Arthur Koestler, *Darkness at Noon* (New York: Macmillan, 1941), p. 183.
47. George Orwell, "The Prevention of Literature," in *Shooting an Elephant* (Garden City, N.J.: Doubleday, 1954), pp. 120–121.
48. David K. Willis, *Class: How the Russians Really Live* (New York: St. Martin's Press, 1985), pp. 287–309.
49. George Orwell, *Nineteen Eighty-four* (New York: Signet, 1949), pp. 176–177.
50. Orwell used the 2 + 2 = 5 example in 1943: "If [the leader] says two and two are five, well, two and two are five." See "Looking Back on the Spanish Civil War," in *Shooting an Elephant,* pp. 163–165.
51. Orwell, *Nineteen Eighty-four,* p. 205.

52. Ibid., p. 236.
53. An odd error appears in British editions: Winston doodles 2 + 2 = , leaving a space where the answer should be. The answer 5 appeared in the first British edition and in all American editions; it was subsequently removed from the British books. Hence British students were taught that Winston still clung to a remnant of resistance. Orwell's intent was quite the opposite.
54. Orwell, *Nineteen Eighty-four,* p. 245.
55. George Orwell, *Animal Farm* (New York: Harcourt Brace Jovanovich, 1954), p. 97.
56. Llovio-Menéndez, *Insider,* (New York: Bantam Books, 1988), p. 128.
57. Ibid.
58. Moore, *Authority and Inequality,* p. 115.
59. See Robert Jay Lifton, *Thought Reform and the Psychology of Totalism* (New York: Norton, 1963), p. 233.
60. Paul Johnson, *Modern Times* (New York: Harper & Row, 1983), p. 548.
61. Quoted in Lifton, *Thought Reform,* p. 14.
62. Quoted in ibid., pp. 473–484.
63. Ibid., p. 336.
64. Ibid., p. 386.
65. John Fairbank, *The Great Chinese Revolution, 1800–1985* (New York: Harper & Row, 1986), p. 299.
66. Ibid., p. 296. Other estimates run as high as 50 million; see Simon Leys, *The Burning Forest: Essays on Chinese Culture and Politics* (New York: Holt, Rinehart and Winston, 1985), p. 131.
67. Fairbank, *Great Chinese Revolution,* p. 303.
68. Ibid., p. 135.
69. See Liang Heng and Judith Shapiro, *Son of the Revolution* (New York: Knopf, 1983).
70. Ibid.
71. Anne F. Thurston, *Enemies of the People* (New York: Knopf, 1987), p. 210.
72. Ibid., p. 221.
73. Yuan-li Wu, "A Statistical Analysis of Judicial Practice and Human Rights Conditions in the People's Republic of China," in Wu et al., *Human Rights in the People's Republic of China* (Boulder, Colo.: Westview Press, 1988), p. 300.
74. Elizabeth Becker, *When the War Was Over: The Voices of Cambodia's Revolution and Its People* (New York: Simon & Schuster, 1986), p. 38.
75. Quoted in ibid., p. 196. An alternative interpretation holds that as a result of American bombing during the final phases of the Vietnam War and the refusal of the Americans to send emergency food supplies, Phnom Penh was in immediate danger from famine and hence the evacuation was a medical necessity carried out with minimum loss of life; see George Hildebrand and Gareth Porter, *Cambodia: Starvation and Revolution* (London: Monthly Review Press, 1976), and William Shawcross, *Sideshow: Kissinger, Nixon, and the Destruction of Cambodia* (New York: Simon & Schuster, 1979). But since this is not the explanation offered by the Khmer Rouge and since the evacuation had been planned before the American bombing, this explanation seems about as credible as the denial of the Holocaust by modern-day anti-Semites. But even if it is true, the theory cannot explain why, after the bombing ended, the Khmer Rouge turned their hatred on their own people.
76. Karl D. Jackson, "The Ideology of Democratic Kampuchea: Motivations for Total Revolution" (typescript), p. 11.
77. Becker, *When the War Was Over,* p. 144.
78. Jackson, "Ideology of Democratic Kampuchea," p. 223.
79. Becker, *When the War Was Over,* p. 233.

80. The invading Vietnamese claimed 3 million deaths; see Lawrence Ziring and Eugene Kim, *The Asian Political Dictionary* (Santa Barbara, Calif.: ABC-CLIO, no date), p. 242.
81. Ibid., p. 297.
82. Michael Vickery, Kampuchea: Politics, Economics, and Society (London: Pinter, 1986), p. 144.
83. Jackson, "Ideology of Democratic Kampuchea," p. 60.
84. Charles E. Lindblom, *Politics and Markets* (New York: Basic Books, 1977), p. 276.
85. Jackson, "Ideology of Democratic Kampuchea," p. 295.
86. Ibid., p. 296.
87. Jackson, "Ideology of Democratic Kampuchea," p. 72.
88. Jonathan Power, *Amnesty International: The Human Rights Story* (New York: McGraw-Hill, 1981), p. 117.
89. Kevin Klose, *Russia and the Russians: Inside the Closed Society* (New York: Norton, 1984), p. 81.
90. Michael Gordon, "Soviet Psychiatric Hospitals Opened," *New York Times,* March 12, 1989, p. 19.
91. Jean-François Revel, *The Totalitarian Temptation* (New York: Penguin, 1977), p. 29.

FOR FURTHER READING

Arendt, Hannah. *The Origins of Totalitarianism.* Orlando, Fla.: Harcourt Brace Jovanovich, 1973. The most influential work in the genre.

Becker, Elizabeth. *When the War Was Over: The Voices of Cambodia's Revolution and Its People.* New York: Simon & Schuster, 1986. A brutal account of the implementation of the Khmer revolution.

Camus, Albert. *The Rebel.* New York: Vintage Books, 1951. The French novelist wants both radical change and political morality and finds that he cannot have them.

Crick, Bernard. *George Orwell.* Boston: Atlantic–Little, Brown, 1980.

Conquest, Robert. *Harvest of Sorrow.* New York: Oxford University Press, 1986. The horror and futility of Stalin's collectivization of agriculture, now available in the USSR.

Fairbank, John. *The Great Chinese Revolution, 1800–1985.* New York: Harper & Row, 1986.

Howe, Irving, ed. *1984 Revisited: Totalitarianism in Our Century.* New York: Harper & Row, 1983. The essays of Michael Walzer ("On 'Failed Totalitarianism' "), Robert Tucker ("Does Big Brother Really Exist?"), and James B. Rule ("1984: The Ingredients of Totalitarianism") are especially noteworthy.

Kirkpatrick, Jeane. *Dictatorships and Double Standards.* New York: Simon & Schuster, 1982. A much debated argument about authoritarian and totalitarian governments and the fundamental distinctions between them.

Koestler, Arthur, *Darkness at Noon.* New York: Macmillan, 1941. Koestler's fictional account of the Stalin purges.

Leys, Simon. *The Burning Forest: Essays on Chinese Culture and Politics.* New York: Holt, Rinehart and Winston, 1985.

Lifton, Robert Jay. *Thought Reform and the Psychology of Totalism.* New York: Norton, 1963. How to wash a brain.

Moore, Barrington, Jr. *Authority and Inequality under Capitalism and Socialism: USA, USSR, and China.* New York: Oxford University Press, 1987. Moore argues, persuasively, that differences are in the justification for inequality rather than its elimination or exacerbation.

Peters, Edward. *Torture.* New York: Basil Blackwell, 1985. The legal and political theory that justifies torture, from ancient to modern times.

Orwell, George. *Nineteen Eighty-four*. New York: Signet, 1949.

Rovere, Richard H., ed. *The Orwell Reader*. Orlando, Fla.: Harcourt Brace Jovanovich, 1956.

Sartre, Jean-Paul. *Anti-Semite and Jew*. New York: Schocken Books, 1948. How reasonable people can become anti-Semites.

Ulam, Adam B. *Stalin: The Man and His Era*. New York: Viking Penguin, 1973.

Waite, Robert. *The Psychopathic God: Adolph Hitler*. New York: Basic Books, 1977. Hitler was insane from the beginning. Was he crazier than Stalin? See Ulam.

CHAPTER 9

The Organization
of Totalitarianism

Like other governments, totalitarian ones are flawed in achieving their aspirations. Even if totalitarian governments were able, logistically, to eliminate the public-private distinction and regulate all aspects of life, the cost would be prohibitive.

We are accustomed to thinking of totalitarian governments as efficient monoliths, easily getting the better of their democratic rivals by avoiding the delays of negotiation and compromise. But totalitarian governments are plagued with conflict, just like democratic ones. This chapter will examine the main contestants in the competition for power: the *party ideologues,* the *bureaucracy* (which emphasizes technical skill in contrast to the party faithful), the *military,* and the *secret police.* None of these institutions represents the public at large because in totalitarian ideology, there is no need. Remember that totalitarian ideology eschews representation. As we saw in Chapter 8, theorists believed that one can act for the people without consulting them; indeed, since the people rarely understand their own best interests, it is better to ignore them. As one explanation has it:

> The task of the leaders is not to put into effect the wishes and will of the masses. . . .
> The task of the leaders is to accomplish the interests of the masses. Why do I differentiate between the will and the interests of the masses? In the recent past we have encountered the phenomenon of certain categories of workers acting against their interests.[1]

This assertion is very much in the tradition of Rousseau, who made a clear distinction between the *general will* (the correct policy) and the *will of all* (the expressed opinion of the people).

THE PARTY

We start by examining the institutions used by the powerful, before we switch perspectives to the view from the bottom. Although the details of totalitarian organization vary, power is, technically, monopolized by the party. The Soviet Union's formal structure was typical:

Party	Number	Government
Politburo, Secretariat, general secretary	1	Supreme Soviet president, Council of Ministers
CSPU Central Committee, All-Union Congress	1	USSR Supreme Soviet
Union republic central committees	15	Union republic supreme soviets, councils of ministers
Autonomous republic committees	20	Autonomous republic supreme soviets, councils of ministers
Provincial and regional committees	128	Provincial and regional soviets, executive committees

Autonomous regional and area committees	18	Autonomous regional and area soviets, executive committees
Large city committees	300	City soviets, executive committees
District (rural and urban) committees	3,600	District soviets, executive committees
Smaller city committees	500	City soviets, executive committees
	42,000	Village soviets, executive committees
Primary party organizations	420,000	Places of employment
Party members	18 million	
—	280 million	Citizens

The ultimate source of power, theoretically, in the party is the congress, which meets about every five years. It elects the Central Committee (307 voting and 170 nonvoting members) to handle all party affairs between congresses. It must meet at least twice a year. But biennial meetings are not the stuff of genuine power; the party elects the Politburo from its membership.

The Politburo

The *Politburo,* with 14 full members and 6 nonvoting members (as of the mid-1980s), is the most powerful unit of the party and hence of the government. There is no clear analogue to such institutional concentration of power in democratic regimes, for its power is limited largely by information overload. It simply cannot manage everything, but it nevertheless has

> all of the powers and duties of the president's cabinet, a good portion of congressional power, some judicial powers, and a portion of the power and responsibilities that in the United States are held by boards of directors of major corporations.[2]

It is led by the general secretary, currently Mikhail Gorbachev. It is a genuine cabinet and is not invariably dominated by the general secretary. In addition to the general secretary, the Central Committee elects secretaries (the Secretariat) to manage the party bureaucracy. But none of these elections is ever in doubt, since—as is common in such small groups—behind-the-scenes power brokers in the Politburo control entry into this most exclusive club. Within the Politburo, struggles over who is to be general secretary, who is to be admitted to membership, and who is to be removed generate as much tension and instability as real Western elections. For example, Khrushchev's demise in 1964 was precipitated by a hare-brained scheme to produce wheat in arid Kazakkhastan. Gorbachev's rise was partly a consequence of Politburo acceptance of the harsh realities of the Soviet economy and the belief that radical surgery was required. Had this opinion not commanded at least a majority, Gorbachev would have remained second secretary. The support for Gorbachev's reforms preceded him. Not since the death of Stalin, in 1953, has the Politburo been impotent.

Gorbachev's Irony

Widely regarded in the Western media as a more humane, more democratic Soviet leader, Gorbachev, in the late 1980s began to acquire more power than any general secretary since Stalin. The paradox is that to shake the system loose from the conservatism of the massive bureaucracies, Gorbachev needed to assume almost complete control *personally*. In 1988, a hastily called meeting of the Central Committee elected Gorbachev president of the Supreme Soviet (the Supreme Soviet promptly approved). Thus he became the leader of both the party and the government.

His intention was to give elected government legislative bodies—especially the local soviets—the authority they thought they had won in the revolution. Other general secretaries have also been president, but Gorbachev's more general reorganization scheme envisages a genuinely independent government legislature. The scheme calls for the abolition of the position of president and the creation of a chairman of the Supreme Soviet, with extensive power to set foreign and domestic policy. He intends that local party leaders also serve as chairs of the legislative bodies in their areas, maintaining party control even as he resuscitates the soviets. Here is the new Soviet government structure:

> *Congress of People's Deputies,* with 2,250 members, meets once a year to elect a president and a smaller Supreme Soviet (both by secret ballot). Composition:
> > 750 delegates elected from territories of equal population,
> > 750 delegates elected from republics, autonomous regions, and regions of various ethnic groups,
> > 750 delegates elected by the Communist party (100 seats), trade unions, and other organizations.
>
> *Supreme Soviet,* with 400 to 450 members, meets twice annually in three-month sessions. Its Presidium has the right to issue decrees, but the Supreme Soviet can veto them. It considers all legislative and administrative matters.
>
> *Presidium,* with a senior vice-president, 15 vice-presidents (one from each republic), and the chairs of the Supreme Soviet committees and commissions.
>
> *President* is much stronger, with broad powers to run the administration of the country, head the Defense Council, present proposals to the Supreme Soviet, conduct negotiations with foreign countries, and sign treaties. Serves two five-year terms.
>
> *Council of Ministers,* the actual government, is headed by a *prime minister* and includes a dozen ministers and deputy ministers, as well as the various ministers and agency chairs.

The scheme is designed to give Gorbachev relief from party conservatives by establishing the government as a legitimate competitor for influence. In the March 1989 elections, the 100 seats reserved for the party in the Congress of People's Deputies were filled by 100 nominees (one for each seat) of the party. One candidate spurned was Boris Yeltsin, a populist orator of considerable skill who, though an ardent champion of perestroika and glasnost, is feared by Gorbachev as unpredictable. He nevertheless took his candidacy to one of the territories (in Moscow) and was nominated. His most potent appeal is an open attack on the privileges (special stores and so on) enjoyed by the party elite. Amid investigation by the party (which he had petitioned for "rehabilitation"), Yeltsin (and scientist Andrei Sakharov, denied nomination by the Academy of Sciences), pushed Gorbachev to the limits of his patience. Gorbachev was, of course, named president.

Within the Politburo itself, Gorbachev was able to dispatch opponents with ease. His main enemy, Egor Ligachev (secretary of state for ideology) was placed in charge of a new commission on agriculture, a meaningless portfolio, and replaced by Vadim Medvedev, passionate supporter of the Gorbachev agenda of experiments with market economies. Thus at the end of the 1980s, Gorbachev was emerging as a strong man of the old totalitarian tradition, like Mao, Romania's Ceausescu, Cuba's Castro, and North Korea's Kim. The Stalinesque personality cult is, ironically, being revived in an effort to dismantle some of the more egregious excesses of totalitarian economics. Gorbachev seeks, at least temporarily, a totalitarian solution to the failure of the Soviet economy. From the point of view of the man on the street, nothing much has changed: the lines for food are as long as ever, possibly longer. As Simon Leys argues, "Totalitarianism . . . appears to be an extravagant luxury that no poor country can afford with impunity."[3] But to break the lock of orthodoxy and instill a modicum of common sense, Gorbachev is becoming the "good czar."

THE BUREAUCRACY AND THE PARTY

Government bureaucracies—the civil servants responsible for implementation of laws and the collection of data to inform policy choices—are major contestants for political power irrespective of the political system in which they operate. They compete for power on the basis of *expertise*. The extent to which they succeed varies with the times and the political system; all developed nations have strong bureaucracies. In democratic societies such as the United States', bureaucracies face genuine challenge from elected officials; in totalitarian nations, they do not but are confronted by fierce adversaries nonetheless. The point is illustrated by the party-government relationship in the USSR.

The adversarial relationship between party and bureaucracy is a source of constant tension. The system in theory has the party establishing general goals and the government implementing them, but this neat division of authority is no more realistic in the USSR than separation of powers in the United States. Since the party organization parallels the government structure, the party *apparatchiks,* who number only about 500,000—a fraction of the size of the government bureaucracy—are in a disproportionate position of strength. Although they were once regarded as keepers of the faith and hence were viewed with suspicion by the technically trained bureaucrats working for the various government ministries, nowadays the apparatchiks are just about as technically literate as their government counterparts. Those who work for the party's economic department are the most pragmatic of the lot.

But the apparatchiks are supervisory: they work for the party. And even though the party is supposed to be excluded from the operational side of the economy, it is not:

> The authority . . . left to government institutions is a residual composed of all the mundane details of economic administration . . . that the Politburo cannot or does not involve itself in. . . . Because the Politburo is the court of last resort in both the party and the government, the residual authorities of the government can change dramatically, and quickly, over time.[4]

The party decides what to decide. It can decide to push conveyor-rotor technology into manufacturing, and the relevant government bureaucracies lose control over what in most countries would be a middle-level decision. Also, the party, through the *nomenklatura* system (listed ranks of jobs filled directly by the party or with party approval), effectively appoints ministers and their chief deputies.[5]

Experts versus Ideologues

The single dominant party is the keeper of the ideological legacy. In the USSR and China, the party is linked to the overthrow of the previous regime and hence can claim legitimacy as the liberator of the oppressed. In both countries, admission to the party is by invitation to worthy initiates, not at the discretion of each person, as was true of the Nazi party in Germany. The use of the party to reward the allegiant and as a vessel for the carrying of the revolutionary tradition is important, for it distinguishes totalitarian government from the less extreme authoritarian ones such as those of Taiwan or Mexico, where the party is the curator of the revolutionary tradition but does not restrict membership. In the USSR, acceptance of party dogma is the necessary condition for admission:

> A party member is expected to be an activist but also a conformist. The first requirement of the Soviet citizens who seek to join the party is that they accept the program and the statutes. The procedure for admitting new members ensures that not many nonconformists find their way into the party. A person who wants to join the party must serve for a year as a candidate member. During this probationary period he is watched closely to determine if he deserves the title member of the party.[6]

Since it is in the interest of party members to preserve the revolutionary heritage (since it provides the basis for their legitimacy), they are generally conservative in the face of change. For example, in China, even as Marxist orthodoxy recedes in nonpolitical life, the party is still the keeper of the flame: "Party members—much more than ordinary citizens—are still required to maintain a commitment to basic Marxist principles and premises."[7]

Since virtually all people employed in the administrative agencies of totalitarian governments are party members, one might assume that administrative bureaucracies and the keepers of ideologic purity have similar interests. To a degree, this is true. In most modern totalitarian political systems, cohesion between party and bureaucracy is achieved by elevating party loyalty above technical skill. We saw in our discussion of terror that ideologues do not hold abstract knowledge in high esteem. If you believe that in building a dam, "correct thought" is more important than engineering skill, the revolt against intellectuals makes sense. Knowledge independent of ideology is a constant threat.

Bureaucrats in the Totalitarian Revolution

Leninist theories of bureaucracy run heavily in the direction of scorn for expertise. Lenin did not believe that civil servants in the employ of the former czarist government would be able to transfer their training to accommodate political masters with a radically different view of politics, society, and the economy. For Lenin, social class was an invariably reliable predictor of political values; administrators under the employ of the czar would never agree with the goals of the revolution because their class would be displaced. Upon achieving victory, totalitarian regimes generally purge the bureaucracy, either, as Lenin wrote, by dismissing them and replacing them with people with the ''right'' class background or (as was frequently done) killing them.

The oddity here is that revolutionary leaders are often brilliant theorists with powerful intellects, yet they turn on the educated classes with startling brutality. Lenin distrusted even the bureaucracy that replaced the royalist one because he suspected bureaucrats would use their power to create an inegalitarian society with the bureaucracy as the ''new class.'' During Lenin's time, no member of the party or government could earn more than the wage of a skilled worker, and men of the lower class were given ''affirmative action'' admission to the Communist party, to the universities, and to the major cities. Stalin abandoned this policy, replacing the idealistic Marxist slogan ''From each according to his ability, to each according to his needs'' with ''From each according to his ability, to each according to his work'' (1936 constitution, Article 12).

The privileges of party membership have grown even more important as the standard of living declined. Lenin's fears were fully justified, his ''worst-case scenario'' realized. In terms of income, social esteem, and quality of life, there is as great a distance between a Soviet party official and a farm laborer as there is between a Supreme Court justice and a ditchdigger in the United States. But—and here the role of the party becomes essential—Supreme Court justices, and politicians in general, are wealthy *irrespective* of their ''official'' position. Were they to be ''purged,'' not much in their personal lives would change. But

> a member of the Soviet elite is completely dependent on official position for access to the material goods of this world. If the official loses the post . . . [the] pleasant apartment, the second home in the country, the use of the government limousine, access to special stores and high-quality allotted medical services are all liable to vanish.[8]

Fears of elite privilege were shared by Mao, whose Cultural Revolution glorified primitive anti-intellectualism, and by the Khmer Rouge leadership. With Mao, any knowledge, irrespective of its complexity, must be subordinate to ideology. This is why, in China, those deemed salvageable were sent into the country to ''learn from the people.'' As Lenin phrased it, ''Any cook could rule the state.'' Ironically, in China, the gradual withdrawal of the party from economic life has meant that alternative channels of economic success are available and that party membership may be an unnecessary burden for the politically apathetic but entrepreneurially ambitious.

Whither the State? It Has Not Withered

Remember that the totalitarian parties are *preceptorial*, geared for political education, and in their communist manifestation are regarded as a temporary bridge to an egalitarian future when the state will "wither away." A bureaucracy's primary task is to enlighten the people, to teach them their true self-interest, and then to go away and let them live in peace and comfort:

> From the moment when all members of society . . . have learned how to govern the state *themselves,* have taken this business into their own hands, have "established control over the insignificant minority of capitalists . . . and the workers thoroughly demoralized by capitalism—from this moment the need for any government begins to disappear.[9]

It would be senseless to train for a career in the civil service in order to preside over its demise. Of course, nothing of the sort has occurred.

Most current Soviet authors, in discussing the role of the state in the economy, concentrate on capitalist economies and avoid confronting a major problem for Leninist theory: When do you expect the state to wither away? The answer, when it is offered, is, Not for a while yet. Realistic theoreticians do not discuss the withering away of the state; rather, they focus on the party as a mechanism for ensuring that government will be responsive to the legitimate needs of the masses. Hence Lenin's notion that any cook can run the state is replaced by refreshing candor. The question now is not who runs the state but in whose interest it is run. Gorbachev is among the first Soviet leaders to acknowledge that the people have been poorly served. He is routinely confronted by lines—the ubiquitous lines to buy *anything*—even longer than before. But he knows that access to food and drink, a decent standard of personal life, is more important to the workaday Russian than high-blown theory. Thus his theoreticians are backing away from the idea of the state as a temporary phenomenon to be run by cooks:

> State administration calls for professionally trained specialists. All things considered, even the socialist state of workers and peasants is run by specialists who are neither peasants nor workers in the textbook sense. But it is not their social conformation which defines the class nature of the state; quite the reverse—the class nature of the state determines their social function.[10]

In other words, the key to understanding a bureaucracy is in whose interests such decisions are made. (This formulation resembles pluralist theories of democracy as much as it resembles Leninist ideology.) This serves to justify the fact that communist governments have not withered away but rather have expanded to become more "total" than their predecessors.

China: "Serve the People."   Nowhere is the dilemma of the necessity of bureaucratic expertise and the primacy of fervor better illustrated than in the People's Republic of China, where technical skill has been branded as an agent of "bourgeois liberalism" in one generation and heralded as the savior of socialism in the next. As in the Soviet Union, China's government and its single party have parallel bureaucracies. Lenin believed the party should be a "parallel structure"; that is, not only should it serve as a recruitment organization, but it should also establish shadow ministries. For each state bureaucracy, there should be both a designated representative of the party and a party unit functioning simultaneously with the state bureaucracy. During the Cultural Revolution, both suffered indignities, but the state bureaucracies suffered more. Like all bureaucracies, the Chinese one was wedded to the idea of neutral competence, a notion totally foreign to the Cultural Revolution. Places in universities were allocated on the basis of class, with students who could prove a legitimate peasant background being given a leg up; local party organizations also scrutinized candidates to verify the correctness of their political ideas.

The tension between the ideologues and the bureaucrats was slow in developing. Initially, the Communist government allowed the bureaucrats who had been serving the defeated Kuomintang government to remain on. Those who did so were subjected to thought reform and brainwashing, as we have seen. After being certified as ideologically correct, which usually took about a year, the former Nationalist bureaucrats returned to their previous jobs and comprised a large segment of the middle-level bureaucracies, where political perfection was not required.[11]

Even during the early years of the Cultural Revolution, bureaucrats were not seriously threatened. But as the movement intensified, proposals for "the destruction of bureaucracy and its replacement with loosely structured, highly participatory administrative organizations" were given serious attention.[12] The aim was to replace *institutionalized* bureaucracies with informal "work groups," to be assembled and disbanded as the occasion required.

The rhetoric surrounding the fight between experts and ideologues set forth the dispute clearly. In explaining the replacement of an established bureaucracy with a revolutionary committee (the Shanghai People's Commune), party propagandists wrote:

> The new organ is basically different from the economic leading organ of the former Municipal People's Council. It *uses politics to run the economy and is not a purely professional department*. . . . Most of the workers in the Front Line Command have had no experience in leading economic work. But by taking Mao Tse-tung Thought for their guide, relying on the masses, and practicing criticism and self-criticism, they are doing it successfully.[13]

The object—successfully reached in most cases—was to subordinate state bureaucracies to the party. Gradually, the bureaucracy nevertheless resumed its position of influence, even though it became more politicized. With the rehabilitation of the leadership clique banned during the Cultural Revolution, the restoration of the bureaucracy was almost complete. But the bureaucracy accepts, indeed must accept, the characteristically Communist doctrine that party dominance and party orthodoxy are more important than neutral competence. The return of the bureaucracy after the Cultural Revolution was at the expense of the hastily constructed "people's committees" and not at the sacrifice of the party.

PARTY, GOVERNMENT, AND THE ECONOMY:
COMMUNISM AND FASCISM

Although the original theories of totalitarianism were promulgated in support of fascism rather than communism, the establishment of fascist governments in Italy and Germany in the 1920s and 1930s did not result in a party dominance as complete as in the current socialist states. The dominant role of the state in the economy enhances the role of the party. If the party can maintain control of the governmental administrative apparatus, it will have a powerful voice in managing the economy, since about 90 percent of the economy is state-owned.

These conditions were not matched in Germany or Italy. Much of the economy remained in private hands, even during World War II, and the Italian Fascist party and the Germany Nazi party were challenged by private business, the secret police, the military, and, occasionally, segments of the bureaucracy. In Germany, the SS moved quickly from an intraparty contestant to the dominant intraparty actor to virtual independence from the Nazi party.[14]

The Nazi party was from its beginning an organization of marginal men, lower-middle-class anti-Semites bitter about the loss of World War I, bitter about the depression, and bitter about their lives.[15] About one-third of the members were blue-collar workers. Other "overrepresented" groups were small businessmen and farmers, while bureaucrats, professional intelligentsia, and capital-possessing elements were underrepresented.[16] The working-class brutality of the Nazi movement was well represented in the infamous storm troopers (SA), which was two-thirds blue-collar.[17]

Hitler himself was attracted to mystical, pseudoscientific pamphleteers of an intellectual level comparable to that of supporters of the Ku Klux Klan in the United States. In comparison with Lenin, whose ideas were solidly grounded in a European intellectual tradition, Hitler's Nazi's heroes were long-forgotten authors of shoddy flyers ranting about Jews. Beyond anti-Semitism, there was not much to show for Nazi ideology. There were some semisocialist elements to appease the strong blue-collar constituency, but Hitler neither knew nor cared much about economics and, other than the *Führerprinzip* (dictatorship principle), there was no articulation of policy goals. It is fair to say that Hitler, like Stalin and Mao, did not believe that economists knew what they were doing and that a strong political will could easily mobilize the economy. It need hardly be added that he, and they, were wrong.

The Nazi party expanded from this base and won elections by appealing to a broader segment of the population. One suspects that its appeal among the German masses was substantially greater than that of the Soviet Communist party among its people. But it never acquired the admiration that the Russian Bolsheviks enjoyed among intellectuals, the military, or the bureaucracy. Although a substantial number of artists and musicians—Herbert von Karajan and Wilhelm Furtwangler among conductors—seemed at least acceptably enthusiastic, the Third Reich's most famous composer, Richard Strauss, remained aloof, and its most famous author, Thomas Mann, repudiated the regime. Even creative men initially identified with nationalism and German romanticism—Oswald Spengler, Ernst Jünger, Martin Heidegger—condemned the Nazis. Among the professional military, the old Prussian Junker elite thought the party to be crude plebeians and ultimately tried to assassinate the Führer. The government bureaucracy, recruited during the interwar years, had little interest in fanaticism. There was no major resistance, just apathy, among the intellectuals.

Once in power, Hitler lost interest in the party and did not establish a parallel organization (which would create a party agency for each corresponding one in the government). Both Lenin and Mao used the party both to seize power and to manage the affairs of state. For them, the party was an "organizational weapon" to reshape and control society.[18]

Contrasting the Nazis and the Communists.   The contrast between the Nazi party and the Bolsheviks is important, for it brings out the central role of a genuine ideology. The Russian Revolution was guided by truly brilliant theory; the Nazi seizure of power had only *Mein Kampf.* The Bolsheviks led a revolution; the Nazis' ascension was less dramatic and occurred legally, almost tamely. After a series of impressive showings in national elections, Hitler was invited to form a government in the established parliamentary manner. Germany's failure at achieving totalitarianism is possibly explained by the fact that unlike the Soviet Union or China, no revolution accompanied the seizure of power; an extant government, with its attendant bureaucracy, was in place. Out of governmental chaos the Soviet revolution built a more integrated totalitarian society. Hannah Arendt, a profound student of totalitarianism, concludes that

> Nazism, up to the outbreak of the war and its expansion over Europe, lagged behind its Russian counterpart in consistency and ruthlessness. . . . Only if Germany had won the war would she have known a fully developed totalitarian rulership.[19]

Whereas in the USSR, the Communist party, albeit with the usual intraorganizational squabbles, was the locus of authority, in Germany, the Nazi party was not. There were myriad competing centers of power: the SS, the SA, and so on. Initially, especially during the years before World War II, the Nazi party did indeed impose at least symbolic unity over the various governmental bodies, but Reich economic policy was nevertheless confusing and, if not incoherent, certainly not ideologically driven. But after the war began, and as the goal of the state turned inexorably toward the eradication of Jews, the SS, not the Nazi party, became the central administrative structure of the state, and its loyalty was to Hitler, not to an ideology. Even Hitler's charisma proved incapable of achieving coordination:

> The National Socialist party . . . experienced continual fluctuations once Hitler had attained power. The bureaucracy and the military . . . grew stronger. . . . The military and the *Beamten* (civil servants), allied with industrialists, posed a serious challenge to the authority of the party. An even more serious threat was posed by the secret police. . . . Headed by Himmler, it had its own power base and the potential to threaten the Führer's own power. . . . The propaganda ministry under Joseph Goebbels was also certainly beyond state and party control.[20]

Whereas Lenin and his followers relied heavily on ideology, Hitler and his followers were soon wallowing in mass murder and exotic romanticism. In retrospect, we have stressed the military and racial components of German fascism to the detriment of its administrative and ideological ingredients:

No completely coherent model of political economy was ever introduced in Nazi Germany. Hitler's basic position was that National Socialism meant the subordination of the economy to the national interest. . . . He boasted that there was no need to nationalize the economy since he had nationalized the entire population. Under Hitler the German economic system remained a compound of primarily private ownership of property and capital operating under an ever increasing and rigid structure of state regulations and controls.[21]

Despite the talk of revolution when Hitler came to power, the civil service was never purged, and party members did not automatically assume positions of responsibility. Only about half of the bureaucracy consisted of members of the Nazi party, and in the most powerful organization in the Third Reich, members were accepted on the basis of professional criteria first and party membership second. There is no denying the horror the SS inflicted on Europe, but it was not the work of party hacks.

Nazi Economics

Initially, Nazi rule took the aspirations of its constituents into account. As in the American New Deal, the Nazis sought to protect small businesses from chain store competition. Department stores, for example, were excessively taxed in comparison to small competitors, licencing for crafts and skilled labor became more rigorous, and in early public works schemes, an advantage was given to small contractors. Of course, independent associations—interest groups—were reorganized, and their functions were coordinated by the bureaucracy (not unlike corporatism). Trade unions were abolished. Coordination and modest reform came at a terrible cost. Even before the war, the Nazis showed a taste for violence. The consequence was not as extreme as in the Soviet collectivization program, but the liquidation of labor union leaders and the increasingly severe restrictions imposed on Jews were portents of things to come.[22]

Germany's success at totalitarian control was more dependent on a single charismatic leader than on a party bureaucracy. A strong case can be made for Germany's realization of totalitarian direction being directly dependent on the war effort. As preparations became more intense, the economy was virtually strip-mined to convert it to war production. By 1939, the economy was clearly subordinated to the war effort, and business interest groups were replaced by party-coordinated auxiliary associations. But even then, there was little overt nationalization, and the conversion to a war economy was engineered by business cartels and monopolies.[23]

As the war intensified, so did the efforts toward total mobilization. But gradually, Nazi war aims shifted; the destruction of the Jews, the infamous "final solution," assumed more prominence than strategic or tactical problems. The technology of war was not abandoned, but the technology of mass murder was raised to equal status. The unique contribution of the Nazis to totalitarianism was the development of efficient genocide.

Corporatist Fascism

Nor was the Italian Fascist party any more successful at centralizing command. Mussolini sought a corporatist decision-making structure partly because he could not rely on his party. But he never achieved much more than the superficial trappings of corporatism. Mussolini sought compulsory *cartels* (combinations of businesses) but was forced to settle for voluntary ones. The cartels were not totalitarian in the sense that they "disciplined private power in the public interest."[24]

Furthermore, many of Italy's intellectuals were genuinely enthusiastic about Fascism and wrote rather compelling defenses of its economic and social philosophy. Italian Fascism thus did not acquire the overtones of hysterical lunacy so prominent in Germany.

The *Partito Nazionale Fascista,* like its German counterpart, did not enter office with a clear-cut set of ideological tasks to achieve. But it did propose a more coherent economic program. When the Italian government was converted into a one-party structure in 1927, the PNF was brought directly under state bureaucratic control and became "a bureaucratic instrument at the service of the state."[25] As in Germany, the party was unable to harness the energy of the economy and, like Germany, found the established military difficult to control. Italy was a failure at totalitarianism.

Totalitarianism and Socialism

Thus throughout history, only socialist or communist countries have achieved true totalitarian government. Socialism need not be totalitarian, but totalitarianism must be socialist, since even a modicum of private initiative defeats the purpose of the totalitarian state. We can well imagine an open, democratic socialist country; however, the evidence is not encouraging. With rare exceptions, genuine socialism is imposed by force. Orthodox Marxist theorists agree that there must be a transitional dictatorship.

The problem occurs when the time comes for power to be relinquished. More recent Marxism argues that Marx did not understand the nature of the modern state, the necessity for stable forms of power to resist, for example, multinational corporations. As we realized earlier, modern Marxists do not take seriously the notion of the state withering away. A planned economy and a repressive political regime seem to have a natural affinity, leading some observers to believe that authoritarianism and probably totalitarianism find a natural proclivity in the managed economy. As Peter Berger concludes, "Central planning of the economy and despotic politics are intrinsically linked phenomena."[26]

The Planned Economy and Mode of Governance

The close connection between central economic planning and despotic governance is well illustrated by such disparate governments as Libya and Iran, both ruled by fundamentalist Islamic theocracies.

Although both countries are strongly committed to Islamic fundamentalism, Iran is marginally more open. Libya is a one-party dictatorship, while Iran allows (carefully constrained) opposition. Media are marginally under less control in Iran than in Libya. Both countries are tenacious in their dedication to totalitarian rule, but Libya is more successful.

Like most mergers of religion and politics (the Crusades and the Inquisition come readily to mind), fundamentalist Islamic governments believe that their mission is to implant the truth, but Libya's fundamentalism is more closely directed toward the economy. Muammar Khadafy's image of the state and the market is more akin to that of the USSR than was that of Khomeini of Iran. In both countries, economic stagnation followed the coup, and in both countries, oil exports are the major source of income. Although data are not regularly collected and are suspect, Libya s government has played a more commanding role in the economy.

Until the 1970s, Libya had a mixed economy, with the private sector remaining active in the retail and wholesale trade. In 1978, Khadafy professed his unique brand of socialism in *The Green Book*. He proposed a society without private property, employees, or money and nationalized about 200 private corporations (many of which were controlled by foreign capital). The wholesale and retail trade was transformed into state enterprises, and even small merchants and shopkeepers were put out of business as Libyans were required to shop at state-owned supermarkets. Arguing that all private commerce must cease, Khadafy argued that the only solution to the problem of poverty is

> to abolish the wage system, emancipate man from its bondage and return to the natural law which defined relationships before the emergence of classes, forms of government, and man-made laws. . . . The exploitation of man by man and the possession of some individuals of more of the general wealth than they need is a manifest departure from natural law and the beginning of the distortion and corruption in the life of the human community.[27]

Notice the similarity—no doubt unconscious—to Rousseau's collectivism. There is the reference to a state of natural goodness before the emergence of government, Rousseau's state of nature. Because of departure from ''natural law,'' exploitation began, and only by a return to nature can this abuse be ended.

In Iran, similar rhetoric accompanied the overthrow of the shah, but economic policy was cast aside as the war with Iraq consumed most energy and resources. Iran's ruling elite subscribes to the collectivism typical of extremist movements. Unlike Libya, private property has not been confiscated. The prevailing view is that private property is acceptable as long as it is not ''exploitative.'' And even though radical factions favor it, nationalization of external trade, banks, and insurance companies has not occurred.[28]

THE MILITARY

The military's influence varies according to time and regime. In totalitarian countries in which control was wrenched from the previous ruling elite by long and bloody conflict, episodes glorifying the party and those exalting the performance of the army are intermingled. In the Soviet Union, and especially China (where the People's Liberation Army, though outmanned, defeated the Western-backed Kuomintang), the army has been traditionally ''politicized.'' In both countries, the military has been usually well constrained by civilian authority.

In some cases, the military's ability to execute its functions has been impeded. In World War II, the Red Army got off to a disastrous start, due in part to the purges in the 1930s, which took a heavy toll among the ranks of the professional military. Similarly, the People's Liberation Army in China suffered embarrassing losses to North

Vietnam in 1979 because its officers owed their status more to political faith than to military skill. During the closing stages of the Cultural Revolution, the PLA intervened to restrain the Red Guards and thus plunged itself into the kind of political squabble it had scrupulously avoided until then. While the PLA was functioning as a civil guard loyal to Mao, its professionalism suffered. While the military in these two societies has fallen victim to civilian meddling, it has not launched a "power grab." The closest we come to such an effort is the PLA's role in restraining the chaos of the Cultural Revolution. Mao clearly asked for the PLA's support with great reluctance, and once it had done its work, Mao sought successfully to lower its profile. Lin Piao, head of the PLA, who stood to profit from the army's role as savior of the revolution, was killed (the official version is that Lin Piao, then minister of defense, was killed en route to Russia after planning a failed coup against Mao).

In both countries, with the rise of pragmatic political elites, the military is resuming its role as professional defender of the realm, with little evidence that the excesses of Russia's collectivization during the 1930s or China's during the Cultural Revolution will be repeated. Neither Gorbachev nor Deng owes his position to the military's support; to the contrary, the evidence suggests that in the byzantine maneuvering for power that accompanies death or disgrace, the military has been left out in the cold.[29] China's PLA after its role in the brutal murders of 1989 will presumably never regain its mystic symbolism.

Socialist success in controlling the military was not matched in Nazi Germany or Italy. In Germany, the professional military establishment was always scornful of Hitler, although his early and unorthodox success temporarily silenced it. As the war aims shifted from defeating the allies to killing the Jews, Prussian plots to kill Hitler multiplied but failed. The SS assumed more responsibility for the war effort, and Heinrich Himmler, SS director with no previous military experience, became the most influential policymaker during the war. In Italy, the halfhearted effort at mobilization for war made the military almost a joke. Mussolini continually blustered about "permanent war" but invested very little in military production, with the predictable result that the Italian armies were humiliated and in no position to engage in any power brokerage.

THE SECRET POLICE

The secret police are another matter entirely. Totalitarian regimes must establish successful internal surveillance systems if they are to succeed. After all, the size of the task of total control makes relentless surveillance the *raison d'être* of the state. Consequently, people with the skills required to establish and maintain a reliable secret police are in demand. In some situations, the secret police of the prerevolutionary regime assumes the same responsibility under the new revolutionary reign (the transfer of personnel occurs usually when the defeated regime has a well-developed system of oppression).

These situations were not present during the Nazi and Soviet seizures of power. The Okhrana, the Czar's secret police, was quite good in infiltration and informed the Czar of the seriousness of his situation but was ignored. The Okhrana's specialty was surveillance and information gathering; it was not especially skilled in torture or other forms of interrogation. Organized in the 1880s, the Okhrana also served frequently as an *agent provocateur*, creating work where none existed. But the Cheka, the first of a series of organizations assigned the responsibility of internal intelligence in the Soviet Union, was faced with an immediately threatening situation. In addition to the externally funded counterrevolutionary armies, which were capable of waging serious campaigns against the new government, there were major disagreements within and among the various segments of the revolutionary party. As it evolved through numerous and complex bureaucratic reorganizations, the KGB (Committee for State Security), or Soviet secret police, has developed into a major participant in the struggle for power, a status never achieved by the Okhrana. Cheka's early success in exposing and eliminating anti-Bolshevik factions has stood it in good stead.

Similarly, the Nazi secret police were unable to recruit from the ranks of their predecessors, for Germany between the wars had only the traditional intelligence operations assigned to the military, and the severity of the peace treaty ending World War I had reduced intelligence to a shell of its wartime organization. The Social Democrats, a party traditionally opposed to secret police, were in power during the immediate postwar years, further inhibiting the development of internal security. In Berlin, a section of the municipal police tried but failed to coordinate intelligence gathering among the several Germany states. However, to keep secret the production of arms prohibited by the Versailles Treaty (at the end of World War I), a central state police was created. There were various local and state police forces, but none was capable of providing the kind of intelligence needed by a totalitarian party.

In a curious footnote to a grim history, German records note than Heinrich Himmler, whose name is synonymous with unspeakable horror, was initially appointed as commissar for the Munich Metropolitan Police! Upon creation, the Bavarian Political Police, the institutional forerunner of the Gestapo, relied heavily on the staff of the Munich Metropolitan Police, but the new bureau's duties were largely confined to compiling lists of various groups of enemies of the state, most of whom were not yet driven underground. Once Dachau was opened (in 1933), it became apparent that no conventional police department could do the job. From this base the SS developed. Simultaneously, in Berlin, the Gestapo (*Geheime Staatspoliizei*, or secret state police) was established. The SS, Nazi to the core, and the Gestapo, more dependent on the remnants of military intelligence, remained locked in a bureaucratic power struggle until 1936, when Himmler consolidated his SS empire.

The more leisurely pace at which the Nazi secret police evolved is due to the absence of any serious domestic opposition. Unlike the Cheka, which faced a serious possibility that the regime would not endure, there was no doubt that the Nazis, especially after the consolidation of power in 1933, would be in control. The Soviet victory was not secure until 1921, and Lenin died in 1924. The Nazi administrative apparatus was in place within three years of the naming of Hitler as chancellor.

As the Nazi regime began mobilization, the political influence of the security establishment increased proportionately, and at the regime's end, as the dying government turned even more viciously on its own, the SS operated without noticeable interference from anyone, including Hitler. But in the Soviet Union, popular spy novels to the contrary, the political importance of the KGB has been in decline. Obviously, the KGB is a significant player in a regime that restricts the marketplace of ideas, but the KGB has not been able to parlay its value to the government and the party into the role of kingmaker. Of the recent party leaders, Andropov had a KGB background, but Chernenko and Gorbachev did not. Mikhail Gorbachev, who shows signs of developing a long-lasting position at the apex of party power, spent his formative years in the provinces, with a specialization in agricultural administration. Even the most obsessed devil theorists would be hard pressed to find any connection between Gorbachev and the internal security apparatus. His rise to power supports the argument that ''there has been since Stalin's death a deep-seated consensus within the civilian party organs against any pronounced upgrading of KGB or military power, and nothing has happened to crack that consensus.''[30]

A similar inability to convert a valued resource into unchallenged political power is found in less developed totalitarian regimes such as China or Cuba. In the Chinese model, people associated with internal security do not have much of a political advantage. In China, none of the leadership struggles since the death of Mao have resulted in the elevation of a member of the Public Security Bureau to a position of substantial influence. There are factional politics galore in China, but the internal security apparatus has little edge. Deng was well connected and survived the purges to return to political power, but he owes little to the Public Security Bureau.

In China, few people could name the bureaucracy analogous to the KGB. It is called the Public Security Bureau and is as pervasive as the KGB in the Soviet Union, but in a fundamentally different way. Unlike the KGB, some of its personnel is uniformed and performs relatively routine security jobs, crowd control, verifying internal travel passports, and the like. But it also censors mail and telephone calls and, most significantly, organizes and trains the *danwei,* the street committees, which do the bulk of intelligence gathering. Possibly because of its relatively primitive economy, China— and Cuba too—relies less on sophisticated electronic snooping than on the diligence of the block committees. The pervasive room and telephone bugging of Moscow or Leningrad is largely absent from Beijing. Instead, telephones are allowed only within easy hearing of the committees. Government officials have private telephones, but the only ones available for personal use are in shops, offices, or other places where conversations can be overheard easily. Fox Butterfield concludes that telephone restriction is ''one of the most basic mechanisms of government control.''[31]

The use of citizens' committees as informants is not exclusively related to shortage of funds, however. The Nazis used informants and encouraged children to report on suspicious activities by their parents. In the United States, the Internal Revenue Service rewards people who report tax cheaters with a portion of the recovered money. But the use of auxiliaries in these circumstances has not produced the pervasive system of control found in China. While the names Gestapo, SS, and KGB are inextricably intertwined with notions of unspeakable terror, much of the internal violence in China was not undertaken by the Public Security Bureau but by Red Guards or even poorly organized mass movements operating with the approval of the party. The fundamental difference between the Chinese experience and that of more developed economies cannot be overstated:

> Where the Stalinist terror was executed by a professional elite—the secret police, elements of the judiciary and the party *apparat*—Mao's terror was the product of a mass movement. . . . The torture and killing were [in the USSR] carried out by a small group, probably comprising fewer than 100,000 men, within the NKVD. In China tens

of millions took part in the struggle meetings and street battles. . . . Stalin's use of terror was . . . nonetheless controlled and highly centralized. In 1937–38 alone, he and Molotov signed some 400 execution lists drawn up by the NKVD, each containing the names of several hundred senior officials. But at least there were lists: the scale of the purge was precisely defined. In the Cultural Revolution this was not so. The terror that Mao unleashed was general and uncontrolled.[32]

Although we cannot be sure, impressionistic accounts suggest that the Chinese way is more thorough. Consider this description of a comparable committee in Cuba, noticing that intelligence gathering and more socially useful activities are combined, as in China:

As important in organizing the country and stimulating the public have been the neighborhood "Committees for the Defense of the Revolution." Every street has one and everyone may join. . . . The CDRs report on suspicious counterrevolutionaries, list possessions of those who have asked to leave Cuba, organize everything from fiestas to volunteers to work in the country, and interfere in all private life for the public good. . . . These committees are really the core of the new Cuban society, creating a new culture of propaganda, participation, conformity, and labor.[33]

These committees perform a unique service to the state and to the citizens. They integrate internal security with genuinely helpful services. For the communities they serve, the committees are marriage counselors, birth control information centers, and ombudsmen (for pothole fixing, sanitation, and the like). Much like the less organized neighborhood crime groups in the United States, committee members patrol the streets at night and cooperate with local police in apprehending criminals. The committees are the crucial link for domestic security investigations. In China, each committee serves no more than 800 households. There are usually electoral contrivances, but they are generally meaningless. Committee members know more about the private lives of citizens than Americans could imagine or Russians hope to achieve with their more centralized secret police. The blending of two functions, intelligence and help, is becoming more evenly balanced in China, thus establishing a more community-based and legitimate image of intelligence. A clue to the ubiquitous nature of the committees is this remark by a committee member in Beijing about the citizens the committee serves: "If they have not yet committed a crime, but we think they are going to, we try to educate them."[34]

Obvious differences between the subtle incursion of the Chinese and the bluntness of the Soviet methods are found in going through the routines of life. There are almost no private automobiles in China, for example, and they would be of limited use since the cities are so swollen with people that there is nowhere to drive them. But in the Soviet Union, private automobiles are beginning to crop up. With their appearance, the Soviet police installed checkpoints for every 20 miles of highway. If you fail to arrive at your stated destination, it is a simple matter to discover at which point in your journey you missed a checkpoint. No more telling illustration of intrusion can be found than on the two-lane highways of the Soviet Union.

IMPLEMENTATION: THE VIEW FROM THE BOTTOM

Just as many countries fail to remain stable democracies, many totalitarian ones must tolerate "slippage." People can be doggedly persistent about their individualism and are ingenious in inventing ways to fool the system, to get along better than we might think. In the throes of obsessive repression, as in German-occupied countries during World War II or in Kampuchea during the terror, though many are killed, many others are clever enough to slip through the cracks. This is especially true when the violence is predictable. In Kampuchea, people learned to conceal their class origins and never to complain, and they lived. Only when a totalitarian state kills without reason, as in the final stages in Kampuchea and in the Nazi concentration camps, does the ability to survive disappear.

Survival in abnormal times is a subject of continual fascination; but we are less interested in heroism and guile than in the routines of life in normal times. Does the Soviet government maintain order only with a heel on the neck of a public seething with lust for Western goods? A Russian might very well respond by wondering how much longer the black population can be exploited before it turns to its natural savior, the American Communist party; or perhaps the Russian might wonder how many times each of us has been mugged. There are many such stereotypes, most of them distorted. Life is different in totalitarian than in open societies, but governments govern and people obey in all systems. People are preoccupied in all societies with satisfaction of their personal needs and longings. Is getting a driver's licence less important to each person than replacing an unpopular leader? The impact of politics and economics on the people will be thoroughly explored in Chapter 11. We touch on a few representative areas here.

Education

Education is far more selective in authoritarian than in open societies. The United States has seriously attempted mass education. European universities are accessible to perhaps one-third of the potential student population, but in totalitarian societies, higher education is more constrained, not only by difficult admissions policy but also by pernicious use of the spoils system. Offspring of party leaders manage to get into the most prestigious universities even though their credentials are dubious. But once in, they find the course of study more difficult than that of European universities and more regimented than that of American ones. Political education is ubiquitous, from elementary schools through undergraduate and postgraduate education. Medical students take compulsory Marxism-Leninism in the Soviet Union and equally irrelevant (from an individualist point of view) courses in China.

In addition to heavy doses of ideology, totalitarian schools stress conformity and compliance, the collectivism that is the foundation of the society. Youth societies, which find their antecedents in the successful *Hitlerjugend* organizations in Germany in the 1930s, are closely linked to schools, far more so than, say, the Boy Scouts. In the USSR, the Octobrist, Young Pioneers, and Komsomol party youth organizations are closely keyed in to the school year, providing the appropriate fervor for various patriotic holidays and making nonconformity even more costly.

These are, after all, preceptorial societies. It would be foolish to expect them not to use schools—an obvious agent for the transmission of political values—to achieve the goals of the state. Like the larger society, the schools are institutions with an addiction to fervid propaganda. But they have high academic standards, since life chances are rigidly linked to them. School days and school calendars are long. Achievement is high, but creativity is low. On any measure of achievement, students in the advanced totalitarian societies would perform better than American ones but not better than European ones. Possibly because American schools are among the industrialized world's worst, the achievements of totalitarian education seem awesome.

We do not know whether an equally important goal of totalitarian education—collectivism and loyalty—is well served by schools. A USSR teacher training manual dated 1982 asserts:

> The objective of educational work in socialist society is the formation of a convinced collectivist, a person who does not think of himself outside society. . . . The formation of Communist morals is the unifying foundation of the requirements for teaching children.[35]

It is probable that Soviet children are as adept at "giving them what they want" as are American ones and that there is as much giggling and making of obscene gestures during the playing of "The Internationale" as during the playing of "The Star-spangled Banner."

There are really no Russian equivalents of the American ghetto education, nor can you find sympathy with the "if it feels good, do it" educational theories so popular here a few years ago. School is not supposed to be fun, and few fret about the "well-rounded person" so essential to our more relaxed and markedly inferior educational system. But the children of the elite have access to schools that specialize in foreign languages and international trade or politics, subjects that would be of no use to most Soviet citizens. Certain universities or institutes are pretty well set aside as reservations for the offspring of the *nomenklatura* class:

> At Moscow State University, [those are] the faculties of journalism and law, since they are largely "political" fields, and the Foreign Languages Institute and the Moscow Institute of International Relations, because they lean toward foreign travel and foreign careers. These are known as the places where some of the highest ranking Party and government people place their sons and daughters or grandsons and granddaughters, quite frequently by using *blat* [favors] to get flunking grades on entrance examinations falsely changed to A's.[36]

Work

As we would expect from our look at Hitler's economics, in Nazi Germany, no effort was made to allocate workers or jobs by central planning; inducements and incentives were used often. In the USSR, a system of internal passports has been used to restrict intercity movement and hence career choices, but explicit allocation of jobs is rare. Only in China has the central planning apparatus relied on compulsory job assignments, although the introduction of limited capitalism in the late 1970s modified the job assignment program slightly. There are no independent labor unions, and workers generally cannot change jobs without government permission. Strikes are prohibited.

Socialist governments occasionally experiment with limited private enterprise. In both China and the Soviet Union, small firms, once prohibited, are now permitted provided they do not exceed a certain number of employees. Especially in rural China, private ownership of property is flourishing. However, Cuba's experiment with similar market incentives was terminated, and in the other developed totalitarian systems, there is very little private enterprise.

The upshot is that socialist economies still have a long way to go in delivering an acceptable standard of living. The total private consumption in the USSR, expressed as a percentage of consumption in other countries, portrays a depressed standard of living:[37]

United States	34%
West Germany	46%
France	46%
Austria	50%
United Kingdom	54%
Spain	57%
Japan	59%
Italy	65%
Hungary	74%
Poland	80%
Yugoslavia	101%
Romania	119%

Thus Soviet citizens consume (food, entertainment, housing, and so on) about one-third as much as do Americans; the Russians are even worse off than several other Communist nations.

Women and Work.   Provisions for working women, day-care centers, and the like are more prevalent than they are in Western societies.[38] Most women work, but attitudes toward gender equality are less egalitarian than in the West, even though the official gospel insists that there is no inequality. Strong Old World traditions discourage unconventional views. Matriarchy is more persistent than in market-oriented polities. Aleksandra Biryukova, one of the two women in the history of the USSR to serve on the Politburo (the other was dropped and disciplined for using government funds to build a country home for her daughter), says that she dislikes the "angry" books of Alexander Solzhenitsyn (still officially banned) and believes that women's "natural inclination toward children and family," rather than discrimination, is the cause of women's inability to rise to the top.[39]

In some places, such as the USSR, feminist organizations are banned (so are most voluntary associations); in others, they are incorporated into the bureaucracy, as has occurred with the Federation of Cuban Women. Constitutional guarantees of sex equity are found more often in totalitarian constitutions than in open societies. In the USSR, abortions, paid maternity leaves, and subsidized day care are taken for granted. But the quality of care is, if not primitive, certainly not likely to warm the cockles of Gloria Steinem's heart. State abortions rarely use adequate anesthetic. About 700 deaths from abortions occur annually in the Russian Republic (the largest of the 15 Republics). A Soviet woman complains, "Our medicine is very cruel—it has a stone heart and Stone Age equipment." [40]

As is usually the case, law and reality conflict. Just as in the United States, there are "ghettos" into which employed Soviet women drift. For every American female bank teller, there is a Russian female physician (medicine is less prestigious in the USSR). Although reliable information is hard to find, it is likely that women's wages in some totalitarian states are equal to those of Western Europe (where day care and maternity leaves are provided) and are better than in the United States. Women's wages in the USSR are about 75 percent of men's, compared with 70 percent in the United States. However, women are better off in Norway, Italy, and West Germany than they are in the USSR, so generalizations are pointless.

The status of women is more precarious in the fundamentalist Islamic states than in European socialist ones. Seclusion and restriction of women make them dependent on their husbands. Veiling is compulsory in the most conspicuously fundamentalist state, Iran, and in Saudi Arabia, and most women are veiled in Libya, Algeria, and Morocco. Genital mutilation (to lessen sexual desire and hence guarantee the delivery of a virgin bride) is practiced extensively in some Islamic states, but abortion is prohibited (except to save the mother's life). In such polities, women make up less than 15 percent of the labor force and spend their lives in traditional roles. Women are rarely enrolled in colleges and universities, and over 75 percent of them are illiterate. Since these countries are no more or less totalitarian than the European ones, it is likely that the dismal status of women is cultural rather than political. Neither totalitarian nor open governments necessarily exploit women, but when totalitarian ones do, the opportunities for the redress of grievances are slight.

Making Ends Meet

In centrally planned economies, preceptorial urging against individualism take the form of formal prohibitions against private enrichment. Most government leaders sincerely believe Marx's predictions that capitalism contains the seeds of its own destruction and that capitalist countries will ultimately unravel because of their fundamental contradictions. Consequently, an underground economy, estimated to be at least one-third of the gross national product, thrives. Moonlighting, illegal since the 1920s until a recent relaxation, is a way of life. Plumbers, carpenters, electricians, mechanics, ticket agents, university admissions officers, and shopworkers engage in an unending conspiracy to escape central planning by trading their services. While moonlighting occurs in all countries, it is more pervasive in totalitarian ones because the "official" economy, while solving macroeconomic problems (such as unemployment or illiteracy), does not cater to the all-too-fragile human desire to lead a comfortable daily life.

Called *blat* in the Soviet Union, trading favors is equally prevalent in China (but less so in Cuba). In a typical transaction, a new faucet is installed in exchange for a pair of ballet tickets; a car is repaired for an appointment with a leading physician, or a scholarly article is published after its author helps arrange for the editor to meet an important party official. Reciprocity raises seemingly powerless institutions to the pinnacle of influence. A worker in a state-owned shop can humble anyone, irrespective of influence, if he or she can provide a rare and highly prized can of instant coffee.

Shortages in consumer goods are unavoidable in centrally planned economies, and long lines or rationing schemes have been the norm for years. The most strategic position is a job in a retail or wholesale distribution center. A shortage of hard currency makes cash exchange a risky adventure, rather than a routine job, and there are harsh penalties for surreptitious currency trading. Many foreigners, noting the prevalence of scowling men in trench coats, wonder why they (without a clue to any secrets, military or otherwise) are so carefully watched. Currency violations are troublesome, and the surveillance is heavy. In a typical deal, you can sell a pair of jeans to a Soviet citizen for about $150 and exchange the rubles you receive at the official rate of $1.13 apiece. But these rubles are practically worthless to the Russian. He can sell the jeans, however, for hard currency to, say, a returning member of an athletic team who has smuggled in a few deutschmarks. With this hard currency, the original seller can get into a *beriozhka* shop (which accepts only hard currency) and buy commodities unavailable in stores that accept Soviet currency.

Private cars used as taxis (without identification) will scoop you up when no legitimate means of transportation is available, in the hope that you will tip in hard currency. Waiters will improve their service if you make clear your intention to leave a hard currency tip. One such example concerns the never-ending problem of apartment repairs. Although rent is very low because of subsidies, repairs can take years. However, you can use your hard currency to buy a case of vodka (the high-quality brands available only at *beriozhka* shops) and exchange it for speedy repairs. Since lines of consumers waiting to buy vodka—even the inferior types sold domestically—are long, such an offer would not be refused. Gifts to automobile mechanics have the same result; vodka means that when you retrieve your car, your radio has not been removed, nor has an older battery been substituted for the original one. Vodka has become the standard currency of the underground economy.

Without *blat,* life would be grim; with *blat,* life can be pleasant. As a result, it is virtually impossible to eliminate. Even though no country spends more on internal security than the Soviet Union (the KGB even has a special "economic crimes" division), it has recently bowed, however slightly, to the inevitable. In 1986, Mikhail Gorbachev's pragmatic regime legitimated private bartering of services and commodities that do not compete directly with state-owned enterprises and do not involve the employment of outside labor. Private enterprise can exist, but it cannot grow. It is improbable that these reforms will hinder the underground economy in services or goods that are in competition with the state.

A Comparison with the United States

In the United States, income is distributed somewhat more equitably than in the Soviet Union.[41] U.S. income distribution is fairly constant. The lowest 20 percent of income earners receive 4.7 percent of available income, while the highest 20 percent receive

42.7 percent. The income earned by the top group has been gradually decreasing since the Great Depression began in 1929 (it was 54.4 percent then). However, in the 1980s, the income proportion earned by this group has been inching upward. The economic situation of the bottom group rarely changes. The greatest increase is among those who are in the middle-income groups; they now receive about 52 percent of all income, compared with 33 percent in 1929. Another dramatic change is the income of the top 5 percent; their share has declined from 30 percent to 15.8 percent. In terms of real dollars, the lowest quintile earns about $11,000, while the highest quintile earns about $33,000; the top 5 percent earns about $76,000.[42]

The best predictors of individual wealth are family background, education, and inheritance.[43] The policy preferences of various administrations appear to have little to do with income distribution. For example, progressive taxation has not redistributed income. Although we feed ourselves on the rags-to-riches myth, very few people escape the social class in which they are raised. Middle-upper- to upper-class families value education; education raises incomes. As more people get better jobs, inequality is diminished. But as long as social class predicts who will graduate, economic rewards will be unequal and linked to social status.

Much the same is true in the Soviet Union. The offspring of the *nomenklatura* class have access to education, better jobs, and more money. Social mobility is not appreciably different in the Soviet Union and the United States. Class-linked advantages are greater in the Soviet Union. The accouterments of status are well illustrated by traffic flows. When *nomenklatura* class members go for a spin, traffic cops receive word of the route and clear the center strip. Once the strip is clear, all traffic from the approaching direction is halted in the event the car wants to turn left. This symbolism would be unlikely in the United States. Although the actual distribution of money income is comparable, the symbolism of inequality is more prevalent in the Soviet Union.

Available evidence suggests that the advantages enjoyed by the Soviet *nomenklatura* class are approximately those of a lower-middle-class American family. The major difference is that money talks in the United States. "The essential feature of capitalist society is not privilege, but money; in real socialist society, it is not money but privilege."[44]

What about the collective good? In the Soviet Union, medical care is readily available to all who need it, but its quality is medieval; in the United States, about 37 million people have no medical insurance and receive about the same kind of care as the average Soviet citizen. In the Soviet Union, the number of homeless is rising; in the United States, the "street people" phenomenon shows just how insensitive capitalism can be. But for the average American, housing is vastly superior to that in the USSR. In the Soviet Union, travel abroad is permitted only to entertainers, athletes, and government or party officials; in the United States, foreign travel is permitted by anyone who can afford it. In the Soviet Union, inequality is bitterly resented; in the United States, it is defended. We adhere to the belief that

> economic advancement based on hard work is plentiful. From this premise two deductions follow. Individuals are personally responsible for their economic fate: Where one ends up in the distribution of economic rewards depends upon the effort one puts into acquiring the necessary skills and attitudes and upon the native talent with which one

TABLE 9.1 Generational Comparison of Occupational Status in the United States

Father's Occupation	Son's Current Occupation				
	Upper White Collar	Lower White Collar	Upper Manual	Lower Manual	Farm
Upper white collar	52	16	13	15	1
Lower white collar	42	20	15	22	1
Upper manual	29	13	27	29	1
Lower manual	23	12	24	41	1
Farm	18	8	23	37	15

SOURCE: Thomas R. Dye, *Power and Society* (Pacific Grove, Calif.: Brooks/Cole, 1987), p. 74. Reprinted with permission.

begins. As a consequence, since individual outcomes are proportional to individual inputs (talent and effort), the resulting unequal distribution of economic rewards is, in the aggregate, equitable and fair.[45]

What about reality? Do people who work hard and delay gratification get ahead? Or is upward mobility a rarity? If we compare the occupational status of fathers and sons, we can see how much mobility actually exists. Table 9.1 shows that a majority of the sons of upper-white-collar fathers were themselves in upper-white-collar occupations, but the rest of those sons descended to less prestigious occupations than their fathers' (downward mobility). At the other end of the scale, only 41 percent of the sons of lower manual workers ended up in the same kind of job. This means that nearly 60 percent of those sons rose to more prestigious occupations than their fathers' (upward mobility). Overall, there appears to be more upward than downward mobility in the United States. This seems to be typical of many industrial democracies: Upward mobility exceeds downward mobility in the United States, West Germany, Sweden, Japan, France, and Switzerland. But downward mobility exceeds upward mobility in Denmark, the United Kingdom, and Italy.[46]

It is generally believed that there is more upward mobility in centrally planned economies than in market economies because of the opportunity to move up within the manual labor class by acquiring new skills. In command economies without the freedom to change jobs, there is less risk in investing in on-the-job training. In market economies, labor turnover makes the investment risky and hence relatively rare. Substantial majorities of highly skilled workers in Yugoslavia, for example, received their training through in factory training or part-time attendance at trade schools or "workers' universities."[47]

Consequently, unlike the United States, skilled manual positions are more prestigious than lower-white-collar ones. The reversal of the relative status of these job categories makes comparison of mobility precarious, however. In any case, the relatively fluid mobility within the segments of a class has been "bought at a considerable cost to human liberties, and is dependent upon a high degree of centralized political control over economic life."[48] Yet there are no affirmative action programs (guidelines for the recruitment of previously disadvantages classes) in centrally planned economies. Soviet exiles, obviously not representative of the USSR's most enthusiastic supporters, provide an interesting comparison:

> Equality [in the USSR] is static. It squelches all hope for a new and different life. In the Soviet Union you are doomed to the life of a state employee, and unless you turn thief, nothing in your life will change. After all, everything is equal (except of course for those who are more equal). In America, the land of inequality, your chance—the chance for you to change your life—is waiting for you somewhere in the chaos of economic freedom. You may never find it, but the fact that it is there gives your life an entirely different perspective.[49]

Even though Americans accept the doctrine of the survival of the fittest, there are occupations that Americans believe to be overpaid. Majorities believe that government officials, owners and executives of large corporations, professional athletes, medical doctors, and movie stars and other top entertainers earn too much. Majorities also believe that lower-level white-collar workers, elementary and high school teachers, non-unionized factory workers, and university professors are underpaid.[50] This seemingly contradictory belief system is not hard to understand. Americans believe that inequality is necessary and desirable in principle, but they believe that some groups of people are treated unfairly.

Commitment to inequality as a consequence of effort elevates those who succeed to a position of deference that approaches that of the Soviet *nomenklatura* class. Business leaders are the object of adoration in aggressively free market, individualist societies, just as party officials are, at least officially, held in high regard in collectivist ones:

> Businessmen generally and corporate executives in particular take on a privileged role in government that is, it seems reasonable to say, unmatched by any other leadership group other than government. . . . Because public functions in the market system rest in the hands of businessmen, it follows that jobs, prices, production, growth, the standard of living, and the economic security of everyone all rest in their hands. . . . In the eyes of government officials, therefore, businessmen do not appear simply as the representatives of a special interest. . . . They appear as functionaries performing functions that government officials regard as indispensable.[51]

Leisure

Leisure activities point up the more politicized complexion of totalitarian life. Whatever you enjoy—athletics, music, theater, television—will be infused with political overtones. Politicization distinguishes totalitarian governments not only from modern authoritarian or open ones but also from the dictatorships of the past. It began in Germany, with the "Strength through Joy" program to organize leisure. Strength through Joy booked inexpensive vacations and organized various camping or skiing trips at greatly reduced cost, since the programs were heavily subsidized. Taking work and sleep into account, the German administrators estimated that about 42 percent of a year was available for leisure, far too much time uncontrolled by the party, and hence the Strength through Joy program. An example, from Berlin in 1940, shows Strength through Joy to be the major administrative organization involved with state direction of leisure. Some 38 million Germans took part in the following activities:[52]

21,146 theater performances
988 concerts
20,527 after-hours "cultural enrichment" programs
93 exhibits
273 factory exhibits
61,503 guided tours of museums
19,060 adult education courses
388 sports events
178,278 gymnastics courses in factories
1,196 vacation trips and sea voyages
3,499 short excursions and weekend trips
5,896 hikes
1,889 intra-Reich train trips

The war ended Strength through Joy, but when we ask, "how could it happen?" one possible answer is that is seemed like a good idea at the time. For the government, the investment is a good one because it harnesses those troublesome free hours and converts them into state-supportive, and state supported, activities.

Modern totalitarian governments are as aware as the Nazis were that control of leisure strengthens the regime. The idea is that excellence in, say, athletics, is a skill to be dedicated to the state. The most apparent example of the politicization of sport is the Olympics, where Eastern-bloc countries display athletes who have been trained from early youth at full state expense. Similarly, Eastern-bloc musicians are recognized and trained early, producing some of the finest ballet, opera, and symphonic performers in the world. The Bolshoi Ballet makes its personnel decisions when a child is 7 years old. Technically, Soviet classical music is almost flawless. However, the repertoire is so conservative that Soviet artists occasionally defect in order to perform a more varied program.

But since leisure, culture, and art serve the state, the menu of available books, motion pictures, magazines, trips, and music is carefully regulated. One of the most enjoyable games played by Kremlinologists (students of Soviet politics) is the appearance, disappearance, and reappearance in photographs (in history texts and the like) of various leaders whose fortunes rise, fall, and rise. In a perfect replica of Orwell's Ministry of Truth, Soviet censors remove photographs of disgraced leaders, along with the accompanying text. A year or so later, the material may be reinserted.

Newspapers, magazines, and television hold a monopoly on information; competing sources are rarely allowed. One of the great shocks to Westerners upon entry into a totalitarian society has been the absence of *Time, Newsweek, U.S. News and World Report, USA Today,* and the *International Herald-Tribune,* all routinely devoured by Americans trooping through Europe. One sure way to guarantee a difficult time at customs is to load up your bags with American periodicals; if you really want to experience the terror of everyday oppression, try packing *Playboy*. However, by the end of the 1980s, Western newsmagazines were being removed from the proscribed list, and the *International Herald-Tribune* announced plans for a Moscow edition.

The result of this relentless pursuit of politically harmless mass communications is a stultifying, relentless sameness. *Pravda* on Sunday, October 7, 1984, featured a photograph of workers inviting its readers to

> take a look at your comrades at work, at your family members, at your friends. You will see: there are no useless people in our country. Everyone lives by the work and deed of the Soviet Constitution. Yes, we ourselves—with the labor of our own hands, minds and talents—give birth daily to that great wonder, unknown before socialism— the unifying and elevating creative might of free labor. It is precisely to it that we owe everything we now have, everything we take pride in: the might and prosperity of the motherland, her position of high authority in world affairs, the full-blooded peaceful living of our people. It is labor that gives each of us the opportunity not only to manage our own destiny, but the destiny of the state as well.

In the "international information" section of the paper, under the subheading "The World of Capitalism," the reader learned that in Paris, unemployment remained serious because of the "clear profit of private enterprise, which grew by one-third." From Stockholm, the news is as grim: food prices have increased by 100 percent, while the level of real wages is declining; from Ottawa, "average Canadians learned that they would lose a major portion of their disposable income because of rampant inflation. The poor are getting poorer and the rich? Profits earned by industrial corporations have never been higher."

Pravda also published the day's television schedules. Here are the listing for Channel 1:

> 8:00 News
> 8:35 Work with Us, Work Better
> 9:35 Cartoons
> 10:05 Don't Fear, I'm with You
> 11:15–2:30 (no programming)
> 2:30 News
> 2:50 Documentary: A Farmer and His Land
> 3:40 What and How We Study at PTU
> 4:15 Film: "The Amazing Adventures of Dennis Korbalev"
> 5:25 Song and Dance Ensemble from Mordovskaya, ASSR
> 6:05 Gardening
> 6:35 Cartoons
> 6:45 Our World Today
> 7:00 "Things and People" (a speech by the first secretary of the Dnepropetrovsk combine factory)
> 7:35 Jubilee Night for the People's Artists of the USSR
> 9:00 News

Cynical Soviet citizens call television "the party's sleeping pill." The glasnost policy of First Secretary Gorbachev in 1986 and 1987 lightened TV up a bit. Most of the news still used slow, encompassing shots of new hydroelectric plants and the like, but viewers were occasionally stunned to see war footage shot in Afghanistan. Totalitarian mass communications will always remain an instrument of indoctrination. As Gorbachev's new chairman of state television explained, "Our TV and radio must be wholly a political TV and a political radio. All TV and radio programs must be subjected to one aim—to the propaganda, explanation and implementation of party aims." [53] Soviet TV is becoming less heavy-handed because it suits the policy goals of the current leadership.

Movies, music, and art are viewed as instruments of state policy, and they too enjoy periodic lapses in surveillance. Even during the periodic thaws, about three-fourths of the programs of the major ballet, symphony, and opera companies will be Russian: Tchaikovsky, Glinka, and Borodin more than Prokofiev or Shostakovich. If your tastes run more to rock or jazz, there are a different set of problems. My first introduction to Soviet views of popular music occurred during dinner at a large Leningrad hotel. After the meal, a waiter asked my young children to excuse themselves because of the nature of the postdinner entertainment, whereupon a combo dressed in typically Russian baggy, ugly suits played, "Yes, We Have No Bananas." Western popular music is beginning to penetrate in markets other than the black, and some Soviet rock bands have sprung up.

Jazz and rock musicians, especially those not given to "Yes, We Have No Bananas," live on the edge of legitimacy. Members of jazz societies have been sentenced to jail in Czechoslovakia and Bulgaria, but rarely in the Soviet Union. The problem is that preventing illicit commerce in smuggled videotapes is proving to be very difficult. Even music prohibited in urban nightclubs pops up in pirated videos. The video players themselves are part of an illegal underground trade. To prevent smuggling of videos, government stores sell VCRs that are made incompatible with Western tapes, but the compatible ones spring up anyway. Recognizing the futility of such efforts, the Soviets reversed themselves and mass-produced compatible VCRs, simultaneously establishing stores authorized to rent ideologically acceptable films, such as the Eisenstein classics (*Ivan the Terrible*), the ubiquitous World War II movies, and tapes of current opera performances.

Movies, too, are becoming less bombastic. Beginning with *Moscow Does Not Believe in Tears* (1986), Soviet directors no longer go through censors before production. Completed films are also free of central constraints, although regional associations of cinematographers, elected from local unions, can block distribution. But *Little Vera* (1988), with its relentlessly depressing portrayal of urban Russia—drugs, prostitution, suicide, pollution—contained the first explicit sex in the history of Soviet cinema. It drew more than 45 million viewers, a record. But there are limits; no film even remotely critical of Gorbachev or Lenin has made it to general release.

Totalitarian governments hope to use popular music as they had previously used other forms of expression: to serve the state. Therefore, they are reluctant to prohibit it entirely and hope instead to co-opt the performers. The Young Communist League, failing to lure youngsters away from rock, was allowed to sponsor concerts at which the performers agreed to moderate their lyrics. Rock music is, unlike classical music, rebellious if it is good. The availability of recordings of Western rock depends on the efficiency of the black market and the attitude of the censors. Cassettes, once unobtainable legally in China, now flourish (especially in the provinces closest to Hong Kong and Taiwan), but periodic efforts to purge the country of "bourgeois liberalism" make their continued availability difficult to estimate. In the USSR, decisions about recordings are made centrally without much market guidance. Soviet composers are well represented, but rock is not. Much depends on style. Soviet censors cannot catch every suggestive lyric, but they can try. They would be at home with American fundamentalism, united in the belief that gullible youngsters will be seduced into drug use, promiscuity, and rebellion by the primitive savagery of rock.

Rock symbolizes a larger problem: how can a totalitarian society control information in an era of rapid technological advance? If the underground commerce in *Rambo* cannot be stopped, what of computer networks and the rapid duplication and transformation associated with them? Photocopiers or personal computers are strictly prohibited, with severe penalties for violators. Direct telephone dialing was eliminated, after a brief trial, in 1980. If totalitarian states inhibit the development of communications technology, they will fall behind; if they leave it alone, they will lose their monopoly over communication. It is a difficult problem.

Sex

The most immediately apparent aspect of life in totalitarian society that stuns Westerners is the absence of privacy. Americans, with their obsessive concern about being left alone by the government, cannot come to grips with a society in which there are no such guarantees. The government does not invariably snoop around into your sex life, but it can, and few people would protest. Of course, the degree of intrusion varies enormously from country: China, the Soviet Union, Rumania, and Cuba are very nosy, East Germany and Czechoslovakia less so. Poland and Yugoslavia, though part of the Warsaw Pact, are not totalitarian at all. Of other totalitarian nations, such as North Korea and Albania, very little is known.

Modern totalitarian societies are surprisingly prudish about sex, possibly because they view sex as an act in the creation of young Nazis or young Communists or (as in China) as an urge likely to upset the delicate balance of the economy. Irrespective of the specifics of their views, sex is never regarded as an essentially private act to be enjoyed without regard for social and political consequences. In China, abortions are compulsory. In Romania, they are illegal unless the mother's life is threatened and even then only in the presence of a party official; birth control devices are banned; and childless couples are burdened with excessive taxes. Even mild or soft-core pornography is illegal, and the few Western films available are carefully edited. Homosexuality is a crime, as is prostitution. Obviously, people in totalitarian societies enjoy sex; they just enjoy it with more of a sense of the illicit. When the occasional suggestive line slips by the censors, the giggling and hooting by adults sounds just like that of American children, and when Muscovites heard about *Little Vera*, the lines outside the cinemas exceeded in length those outside the liquor stores.

Crime and Punishment

Totalitarian societies do not always assume that a person is innocent until proved guilty (the presumption exists in the Soviet Union but not in China), nor do they necessarily believe in extenuating circumstances. Recall that Marx believed that capitalism caused crime. The removal of capitalism has therefore meant the end of crime. Since crime has not ended, the criminal must be regarded as deviant. Poverty, greed, lust, and immorality are caused by capitalism. The irony is that economic crimes (speculation in currency or in prohibited items) is so pervasive that if all speculators were arrested, totalitarian economies would halt. Much like America's Prohibition of the 1920s or the 55-mile-per-hour speed limit, the decision to pluck one from among the millions of violators probably means that the detainee had no ability to bargain with the police since single entrepreneurs were rarely arrested.

Most ordinary crime is prosecuted through "people's courts" elected or appointed by the party. Defense councils may be appointed by the people's courts. A major problem is that of a competent defense. Since an accused is a living violation of Marxism, the profession of attorney has not prospered. Courts are unquestionably subordinate to the party because the law, like athletics, art, and sex, serves the state. Party members cannot be arrested without the approval of a party committee, which will, unless the crime is flagrant, withhold it. "Nonpolitical" crime is not as serious a problem in most totalitarian countries as it is in the United States, but we, not they, are the exception. Although it is less lenient than our criminal justice system (which is judged excessive even by European standards), totalitarian justice does not require the execution of shoplifters.

The problem is with Marxism. Marxist legal scholars accept the idea that crime is socially caused and consequently have an ambivalent attitude toward criminals. On the one hand, criminals cannot exist; on the other hand, they are evidence of injustice. Nevertheless, criminal codes do exist and are generally honored. The blending of the political element into apparently nonpolitical crimes adds an element of risk. In Cuba "many delinquent acts are considered counterrevolutionary activities directed by the enemy, [and] it is difficult to differentiate between political and common criminal acts."[54]

Especially in China, the legal system is a politicized component of the party machine. Even in this inferior position, the legal system

> can be bypassed altogether: under administrative detention regulations, the police are empowered to send a person to do forced labour, to confiscate his goods or sentence him to up to four years in a re-education camp (compared with the maximum fifteen-day prison term in the equivalent Soviet law)—all without reference to any court. The regulations are used for petty criminals and "troublemakers" and those who commit "minor counter-revolutionary or anti-socialist reactionary offenses and whose criminal responsibilities have not been investigated and affixed.[55]

Large-scale embezzling in any totalitarian society can mean the death penalty, since it is a conspicuously political crime, but in China, pornographers, robbers, and smuggles have also been executed. During the drive for a pragmatic economic policy, a rising crime rate undermined the leadership's policy and supported the conservatives, who believed that "Western ideas" invariably raise the crime rate. To combat the problem, the leadership launched an anticrime campaign complete with mass rallies. Although the rate of executions is unknown, a reliable estimate is about 5,000 per year. Dispatched with the traditional bullet in the back of the neck, the detained were tried, sentenced, and executed in two hours under the direct supervision of the central party leadership. Crimes left unpunished before the crackdown resulted in death.

Most people are not "really" criminals; that is, they are not rapists or murderers. The problem in totalitarian society is that the list of offenses includes most of everyday life. When a crackdown occurs, institutional safeguards cannot protect a person against a politically motivated arrest. In the Soviet Union, however, the participation by criminologists and legal experts has reduced the capriciousness of criminal law.

Seen from the perspective of everyday life—a life not involving political dissent as much as complaints over stale bread, dull music, or bad vodka—totalitarian regimes are foreboding but not demonic. During periods of deep substantive change, they are brutal. During periods of comparative calm, life becomes less a battle for political freedom than a quarrel over long lines. In the Soviet Union, while Gorbachev's pragmatic politics and intrabureaucratic squabbles have captured the media's eye, much of the street talk in Moscow was about the crackdown on alcoholism, making vodka even more valuable as a medium of exchange. Life goes on, and totalitarian governments, like democratic ones, fail at least as often as they succeed in fulfilling their objectives. *Blat* befuddled Soviet authorities until they bent policies a little toward human nature.

FOR FURTHER CONSIDERATION

1. Explain the difference between an authoritarian and a totalitarian government. What, if any, assumptions do they share?
2. What are the essentials of Marxism? How has that theory been forced to change in order to survive?
3. Briefly outline Lenin's time as the leader of the Soviet Union. Do the same for Stalin and Mao in China. What similarities can you find? In what ways do they differ?
4. Was the Khmer Rouge regime in Cambodia typical or atypical of a totalitarian takeover? Why?
5. List several characteristics common to authoritarian governments, then list several characteristics common to totalitarian governments. How similar (or how different) are the two? Compare their reliance on a charismatic leader. What does this say about both systems?

For the More Adventurous

1. Compare the American Federal Bureau of Investigation, the Central Intelligence Agency, and the West German Office for the Defense of the Constitution with their counterparts in the USSR and in China.
2. When USSR exiles speak of the "chaos of economic freedom" are they using a phrase of approbation or condemnation?

NOTES

1. János Kádár, address to the Hungarian National Assembly, May 11, 1957.
2. Ed A. Hewett, *Reforming the Soviet Economy* (Washington, D.C.: Brookings Institution, 1988), p. 164.
3. Simon Leys, *The Burning Forest* (New York: Holt, Rinehart and Winston, 1985), p. 131.
4. Hewett, *Reforming the Soviet Economy*, p. 164.
5. Darrell P. Hammer, *The USSR* (Boulder, Colo.: Westview Press, 1986), p. 117.
6. Ibid., p. 82.

7. Harry Harding, *Reform after Mao* (Washington, D.C.: Brookings Institution, 1988), p. 222.

8. Barrington Moore, Jr., *Authority and Inequality under Capitalism and Socialism* (New York: Oxford University Press, 1987), pp. 62–63.

9. V. I. Lenin, "The Economic Base of the Withering Away of the State," in *State and Revolution*, ed. V. I. Lenin (Moscow: Foreign Languages Publishing House, 1968), p. 93. (Originally published 1932.)

10. Konstantin Zardof, *The Political Economy of Revolution* (Moscow: Progress Publishers, 1987), p. 133.

11. Harry Harding, *Organizing China: The Problem of Bureaucracy* (Stanford, Calif.: Stanford University Press, 1981), p. 37.

12. Ibid., p. 263.

13. Quoted in ibid., p. 293. (Originally published in 1932.)

14. Amos Perlmutter, *Modern Authoritarianism* (New Haven, Conn.: Yale University Press, 1981), p. 14.

15. Michael H. Kater, *The Nazi Party: A Social Profile of Members and Leaders, 1919–1955* (Cambridge, Mass.: Harvard University Press, 1983).

16. Stanley G. Payne, *Fascism* (Madison: University of Wisconsin Press, 1980), p. 60.

17. C. J. Fischer, "The Occupational Background of the SA's Rank and File Membership during the Depression Years, 1929 to Mid-1934," in *The Shaping of the Nazi State*, ed. Peter D. Stachura (London: Barnes and Noble Books, 1978), pp. 131–159.

18. Perlmutter, *Modern Authoritarianism*, p. 107.

19. Hannah Arendt, *The Origins of Totalitarianism* (Orlando, Fla.: Harcourt Brace Jovanovich, 1973), p. 310.

20. Perlmutter, *Modern Authoritarianism*, p. 29.

21. Payne, *Fascism*, p. 91.

22. A. J. Nichols, "Germany," in *Fascism in Europe*, ed. S. J. Woolf (London: Methuen, 1968), pp. 65–91.

23. Robert A. Brady, *The Spirit and Structure of German Fascism* (New York: Howard Fertig, 1969). Originally published in 1937, the book is a careful analysis of the administrative structure of Nazism.

24. Roland Sarti, "Fascist Reforms and the Industrial Leadership," in *The Ax Within: Italian Fascism in Action*, ed. Roland Sarti (New York: Franklin Watts, 1974), p. 136.

25. Payne, *Fascism*, p. 72.

26. Peter L. Berger, *The Capitalist Revolution* (New York: Basic Books, 1986), p. 181.

27. Muammar Khadafy, *The Green Book* (n.p., n.d.), pp. 55–56.

28. Cheryl Benard and Zalmay Khalizad, *The Government of God* (New York: Columbia University Press, 1984), p. 126.

29. See Timothy J. Colton, *Commissars, Commanders, and Civilian Authority: The Structure of Soviet Military Politics* (Cambridge, Mass.: Harvard University Press, 1981); and Timothy J. Colton, *The Dilemma of Reform in the Soviet Union* (New York: Council on Foreign Relations, 1986).

30. Colton, *Dilemma of Reform*, p. 99.

31. Fox Butterfield, *Alive in the Bitter Sea* (New York: Times Books, 1982), p. 308.

32. Philip Short, *The Dragon and the Bear: Inside China and Russia Today* (New York: Morrow, 1982), p. 153.

33. Hugh Thomas, *The Cuban Revolution* (New York: Harper & Row, 1977), p. 681.

34. Suzanne Steinthal, "Chinese Government Remains Hardline," *Seattle Times*, March 22, 1987, p. A19.

35. Susan Jacoby, *Inside Soviet Schools* (New York: Schocken, 1975), p. 91.

36. Hedrick Smith, *The Russians* (New York: Times Books, 1983), p. 33.

37. Horst Herlemann, ed., *Quality of Life in the Soviet Union* (Boulder, Colo.: Westview Press, 1987), pp. 15–20.
38. See Joni Seager and Ann Olson, *Women in the World: An International Atlas* (London: Pan Books, 1986), a useful compendium of statistics on the status of women.
39. Michael Gordon, "Old World Views Remain in Soviet Society," *New York Times*, January 24, 1989, p. A6.
40. Jane Perlez, "Soviet Medicine Still Lacking," *New York Times*, February 28, 1989, p. A3.
41. Michael Don Ward, in *The Political Economy of Distribution* (New York: Elsevier, 1977), uses various indices to permit comparison of aspects of economic well-being. Large negative scores indicate more equality; large positive scores, less equality. On his equality scale, the United States scores − 138, the Soviet Union − 102.
42. Ibid.
43. Christopher Jenks, *Who Gets Ahead?* (New York: Basic Books, 1977), pp. 290–311.
44. Boris Voslenskym, "Fulfilling the Leninist Plan," in *Foundations of Soviet Totalitarianism,* ed. Robert B. Daniel (Lexington, Mass.: D. C. Heath, 1972), p. 178.
45. James R. Kluegel and Eliot R. Smith, *Beliefs about Inequality* (Hawthorne, N.Y.: Aldine, 1986), p. 5.
46. Seymour Martin Lipset and Reinhard Bendix, *Social Mobility in Industrial Society* (London: Heinemann, 1959), p. 25.
47. Frank Parkin, *Class Inequality and Political Order* (New York: Praeger, 1971).
48. Anthony Giddens, *Power, Property, and the State* (Berkeley: University of California Press, 1981), p. 253.
49. Vassily Aksyonov, *In Search of Melancholy Baby* (New York: Random House, 1987), p. 78.
50. Ibid., p. 120.
51. Charles E. Lindblom, *Politics and Markets* (New York: Basic Books, 1977), pp. 172, 175.
52. Richard Grunberger, *The Twelve-Year Reich* (New York: Holt, Rinehart and Winston, 1971), p. 198
53. Alan Riding, "Gorbachev Appoints New TV Chair," *New York Times*, March 13, 1988, p. 1.
54. Luis P. Salas, "Juvenile Delinquency in Postrevolutionary Cuba: Characteristics and Cuban Explanations," in *Cuban Communism*, ed. Irving Louis Horowitz (New Brunswick, N.J.: Transaction Books, 1981), p. 251.
55. Short, *Dragon and the Bear,* p. 384.

FOR FURTHER READING

Aksyonov, Vassily. *In Search of Melancholy Baby*. New York: Random House, 1987. Russian cynicism at its best, by an exile who also finds much to lament about America.
Bessel, Richard. *Life in the Third Reich*. Oxford: Oxford University Press, 1987.
Colton, Timothy J. *The Dilemma of Reform in the Soviet Union*. New York: Council on Foreign Relations, 1986.
Gleason, Abbott, Peter Kenez, and Richard Stites. *Bolshevik Culture*. Bloomington: Indiana University Press, 1985.
Harding, Harry. *Reform after Mao*. Washington, D.C.: Brookings Institution, 1988.
Herlemann, Horst, ed. *Quality of Life in the Soviet Union*. Boulder, Colo.: Westview Press, 1987. Much information about everyday life, generally ignored by political scientists.
Hewett, Ed A. *Reforming the Soviet Economy*. Washington, D.C.: Brookings Institution, 1988.

Knight, Amy W. *The KGB: Police and Politics in the Soviet Union.* Boston: Unwin Hyman, 1988.

Koonz, Claudia. *Mothers in the Fatherland.* New York: St. Martin's Press, 1987.

Liang Heng and Judith Shapiro. *Son of the Revolution.* New York: Knopf, 1983.

Medvedev, Zhores. *Soviet Agriculture.* New York: Norton, 1987.

Peukert, Detlev J. K. *Inside Nazi Germany: Conformity, Opposition and Racism in Everyday Life.* New Haven, Conn.: Yale University Press, 1982. Among the best of the growing literature in the view from the streets in autocratic regimes.

Proctor, Robert N. *Racial Hygiene: Medicine under the Nazis.* Cambridge, Mass.: Harvard University Press, 1988. The chapter treating "political biology" and "Jewish psychology" should make my epilogue go down a bit easier.

Shue, Vivienne. *The Reach of the State: Sketches of the Chinese Body Politic.* Stanford, Calif.: Stanford University Press, 1988.

Voinivich, Vladimir. *The Anti-Soviet Union.* Orlando, Fla.: Harcourt Brace Jovanovich, 1985. One of the USSR's most visible exiles writes a bitter, sardonic set of essays about life in the USSR, his first book after exile.

———. *Moscow 2042.* Orlando, Fla.: Harcourt Brace Jovanovich, 1987. A novel of the future set in Moscow.

Voslensky, Michael. *Nomenklatura.* London: Bodley Head, 1983. A devastating description of privilege in the USSR.

CHAPTER 10

Revolution: The Rhetoric and the Reality

Sovfoto/Eastfoto.

Revolution conjures up the most vivid portrait of how a country abruptly and radically changes political elites. Elites are simply whoever has power. All government is government by elites; hence revolutions substitute one set of elites for another. Indeed, although there are as many definitions of revolution as there are of democracy, all agree that revolution must be sudden and extraordinary. Most often the antonym is *evolution* (development, growth, maturation).

High-sounding revolutionary slogans like "Liberté, égalité, fraternité" or "Power to the people" camouflage formidable human suffering and loss of life. The argument that the "end justifies the means" is the staple of revolutionary rhetoric. By comparing revolutionary rhetoric and ideology with economic and social reality, we can understand better what revolution accomplishes.

We should be clear about how revolutionary elites are established and succeed and the consequences of their actions for the people who, though few of them took part in the revolution, must live under its dictates.

WHAT IS REVOLUTION? AN OVERVIEW

Revolution has myriad definitions, which describe varieties of political violence and socioeconomic change. Scholars and writers define revolutions differently.

Brinton's Contribution

When used carelessly, revolution is employed to detail many kinds of political violence contrived for a variety of ends: military coups (both left-wing and right-wing), wars of independence, popular rebellions, short-term economic and social transformations, long-term social and economic change, and "traditional" revolutions like the French, Russian, Chinese, Cuban, Iranian, and Nicaraguan. Historian Crane Brinton, in his classic 1938 treatise *The Anatomy of Revolution,* admitted difficulty in finding a precise definition for the phenomenon of revolution. He pointed out that the term *revolution* had "come in common usage to be hardly more than and emphatic synonym for 'change,' perhaps with a suggestion of sudden or striking change."[1] He understood that revolution was a very serious matter—one of the most important historical experiences involving the most widespread, national deployment of political violence. He suggested that

> we keep in the corners of our mind a much more definite meaning. . . . Our focus is on drastic, sudden substitution of one group in charge of the running of a territorial political entity for another group. There is one further implication: the revolutionary substitution of one group for another, if not made by actual violent uprising, is made by *coup d'état, Putsch,* or some other kind of skullduggery.[2]

Brinton believed that at least four major historical events could rightly be called revolutions:

1. The English Revolution of the 1640s
2. The American Revolution of 1776
3. The French Revolution of 1789
4. The Russian Revolution of 1917

Unfortunately, Brinton's description is limited. It does not, for instance, differentiate between a right-wing military takeover of a civilian government, which may have no aspiration for social or economic change, and a left-wing, popularly based revolutionary movement with a well-thought-out plan for social and economic change. For example, some of the putative revolutions in Africa were more concerned with tribal disputes than with revolutionary ideology, and many of those in Latin America were not serious about change other than the substitution of one ruling elite for another.

Consider Ethiopia, the African continent's most overtly Marxist government. Though Western scholars have suggested that Ethiopia's was the only "true" African revolution, there is more than Marx at work. Its origins were rooted in a millennial kingdom rather than a colonial territory, interrupted only by a five-year Italian occupation (1936–1941).[3] Its complex history includes virtually permanent insurrection by the Somalis, Eritreans, and Tigréan Christians. These groups were separatist during the rule of the emperor, Haile Selassie, and they continued in opposition after his overthrow in 1974: "For Somalis and most Eritreans . . . Ethiopia is a colonial power, and they are engaged in a people's war to bring national liberation."[4]

The revolution was not a consequence of an organized socialist movement; rather, it was a virtually assured consequence of a regime decomposing, ruined by incompetence, corruption, and tribal imperialism. A military coup easily toppled Selassie. As in Cuba, the new regime declared its Marxism after the coup. Eritrea, bordering Sudan and the Red Sea, by 1989—with external help from the Arab countries—had just about brought the Marxist government to its knees; but the most serious challenge to the Marxist regime came from two Marxist groups, the Eritrean People's Liberation Front and the Tigré People's Liberation Front! The United States supports the "territorial integrity" of Ethiopia.

In Mexico, the 1911 revolution, sometimes said to be "the first of the world's great twentieth-century revolutions,"[5] seems illusory. Its more radical leaders, Emiliano Zapata and Pancho Villa, though populist, were not "ideological." Once they were dispatched, the revolutionary presidents—Carranz and Obregon—were at best traditional liberals. Not until 1934, under Lazaro Cárdenas, did even modest land reform begin. Postwar presidents have shown no disposition toward either left or right: Gustavo Días Ordas (1964–1970), a symbolic "rightist," was followed by Echeverría (1970–1976), a symbolic "leftist," who was replaced by three successive centrists: López-Portillo (1976–1982), de la Madrid (1982–1988), and Salinas (1988–). In an election marred by widespread allegations of fraud, the son of Lazaro Cárdenas (who had begun land reform) ran an opposition campaign, claiming to be the true inheritor of the spirit of the revolution.

More Systematic Attempts at Definition

Fred Willhoite defines revolution as

> an ambiguous word that refers to some kind of sudden and significant change in government accomplished by extralegal or illegal means. . . . [It] usually denotes one or more of these developments: sudden downfall or overthrow of a government; emergence of a new government from an all-out struggle for ruling power; efforts by leaders of the new regime to bring about great changes in society.[6]

Willhoite goes on to distinguish between many related phenomena, which lead to a rapid change in political leadership through violence. A coup d'état (literally: "stroke of state") only involves a military takeover of the civilian government, but since usually no economic or social changes follow, Willhoite does not consider coups and violent rebellions true revolutions.[7]

Willhoite also makes a useful distinction between *political, social,* and *great* revolutions. A political revolution essentially involves a change in governmental leadership, with no real economic or social change intended (for example, the American Revolution). In contrast, a social revolution also involves some attempt to effect real social change (as in the French Revolution). But the focus, as with the political variety, is relatively short-term. Willhoite argues that the so-called great revolutions are not only political and social but also include successful, long-term efforts to make major economic and social changes, in some cases over decades (as in the Russian, Chinese, and French revolutions).[8]

If, adding the dimension of time, we include the concept of long-term change in our definition of revolution, at what point does *revolution* become indistinguishable from *evolution?* This consideration of the "timespan" of revolutionary change will be significant later when we examine major historical revolutions.

Another way to conceptualize Willhoite's typology is to view revolutions in terms of three main variables:

1. Kind or scope of change (quality)
2. Amount of change (quantity)
3. Length of time (duration)

intended to accomplish these changes. In the case of the so-called great revolutions, the dimension of economic change is usually included as well.

The American Revolution, for example, was not a social or great revolution, its effect on the history of the world notwithstanding. The American experience was a war of independence from England's monarchical rule. The internal power structure of the American political system did not change during or after the revolution, nor were any sweeping economic or social changes imposed on the general populace.

The American colonists simply wanted to be free of England's rule, essentially to be left alone to pursue their own economic and political future. No one was interested in promising any great changes for the people or for empowering any disenfranchised groups, like the slaves, for example.[9] It now seems ironic that Crane Brinton identified the American Revolution as one of the four archetypes when many theorists now do not regard it as a true revolution.

Peter Calvert defines revolution as a political process having four characteristics, which he argues are observable and partly measurable. According to Calvert, revolutions have the following characteristics:

1. A *process* where the political policies of the current ruling government become discredited to the general populace or key groups in society
2. An *event* happening at an identifiable point in time resulting in a change of government through the use armed force (or the threat of force)

3. A general more-or-less coherent *programme* for political and/or social change by the new revolutionary leadership after attaining power
4. A political *myth* that gives the new leadership short-term status as the legitimate government[10]

These four factors closely parallel Willhoite's definition of a great revolution. In addition, as we will see shortly, the loss of credibility of the existing government was originally noted by Brinton as a crucial precondition for a successful revolution.

Scholars have been working to measure the impact of revolution, which pits group against group in a death-lock struggle. Potentially, the outcomes of revolution can illustrate the most profound differences between old (prerevolutionary) and new (postrevolutionary) regimes and their respective governing elites. Theoretically, the sweep of revolution can provide a historical "before and after" picture of how a country's political, economic, and social system changes. In practice, however, broad and accurate comparisons of society before and after revolution are not so easy to achieve. The task of measuring change is complex, involving many economic, social, and political variables. There have been many revolutions, each containing many idiosyncratic characteristics and unique variables.

Because of the emotional zeal with which proponents and opponents of revolution speak, it is sometimes difficult to separate rhetoric from reality, fiction from fact. Moreover, the longer span of time that passes between the revolution and present day, the more difficult it is to attribute current economic, social, and political realities solely to the revolution. How does one know if today's conditions are due to a prior revolution? Perhaps current conditions are merely a result of industrial evolution and modernization. Perhaps certain countries would be better off today if they had not experienced revolution. How does one know if the country might have arrived at more or less the same point in a more peaceful fashion?

We will point out evidence to suggest that the long-term differences in economic and social conditions in several socialist and capitalist countries that have experienced revolution may not be as profound as some social scientists have previously suggested. In conclusion, we will speculate on the lasting change produced by revolution. The topic will be addressed in more detail in Chapter 12, which addresses the question "so what?"

WHAT "CAUSES" REVOLUTION?

Speculation about what causes revolution is rife, with many theories competing for attention. Brinton said that internal divisiveness is a precondition for revolution, and he observed that the "ruling class . . . the people who run things" seemed to be divided and inept in all four societies experiencing revolution that he studied (England, America, France, and Russia).[11] Thomas H. Greene also argued that "revolution frequently begins with 'divisions among members of the ruling class.' "[12] He also cited modern examples, which included dissension within the czarist regime in Russia prior to 1917, increasing internal conflict in Batista's ruling coalition in Cuba after 1956, and divisions within the ruling elites of 16 Latin American countries between 1948 and 1962.[13]

But surely there is more, and revolutionary theorists like Marx, Lenin, and Mao saw the real cause of revolution as the inevitable result of an absolute "historical and economic determinism.'' These theorists highlight the importance of class antagonisms between the ruling elite and working (and later peasant) classes. In addition, conflicts within the ruling class (such as divisiveness and dissension) serve to exacerbate the onset of revolution.

The Revolution of Rising Expectations

Historically, ineptitude of the elite is demonstrated in the tendency for government officials, under fire in prerevolutionary societies, to attempt to placate dissatisfied citizens by initiating minor economic and social improvements. Ironically, this flaccid attempt at reform increases their chances of downfall, because later when they renege on these small efforts at change, they inadvertently fuel the fire of potential civil violence by unwittingly creating rising expectations in the general populace.

Traditionally, writers on revolution have made the assumption that revolutions occur when people are at their lowest ebb, economically and socially. Such conjectural reasoning makes common sense, and for years it was never challenged. But James C. Davies, developing his J-curve theory of rebellion and revolution, argued differently. He wrote that the real cause of revolution was people's psychological attitudes, their states of mind or expectations. Davies believed subjective perception to be a more crucial determinant of revolution that economic and social conditions. According to Davies, the inclination for men to engage in revolutionary behavior is strongest not when people's deprivation is most severe but rather when things begin to get a little better and people get their hopes up about further improvement. If then people are confronted with reversal or a setback, they are more likely to become violent.[14]

Davies explained the process:

> Revolutions are most likely to occur when a prolonged period of objective economic and social development is followed by a short period of short reversal. The all-important effect on the minds of people in a particular society is to produce, during the former period, an expectation of continued ability to satisfy needs—which continue to rise— and, during the latter, a mental state of anxiety and frustration when manifest reality breaks away from anticipated reality. The actual state of socioeconomic development is less significant than the expectation that past progress, now blocked, can and must continue in the future.[15]

In short, the primary cause of revolution is a ''subjective perception,'' an attitudinal crisis of expectations. Fred Willhoite, in describing Davies's theory, says that raised expectations lead to more intense frustration and eventually to violence because the gap between people's ''actual need satisfaction'' and their ''expected need satisfaction'' widens.[16]

This distinction between the actual (objective) economic and social conditions and the (subjective) perception of conditions is crucial. For example, concerning the Russian Revolution of 1917, historian Peter Gatrell argues that the economy was growing from 1850 to 1917 and that many characteristics of so-called backwardness were changing in prerevolutionary Russia. He argues that the actual economic conditions for the people were not particularly bad.[17] But what really counted was the people's perception of economic and social conditions (that is, subjective reality), which Lenin and the Bolshevik Communist party elite were able to manipulate to their advantage.

The same theory about human behavior has been advanced in the social-psychological literature on violence toward self and others. Researchers who study suicidal and homicidal behavior argue that people are not inclined to kill themselves or their loved ones when their objective circumstances are at their worst. They are most likely to do so shortly after things start getting better. Confronting a disappointment after experiencing some minor improvement apparently destroys the optimism of future improvement. This development, researchers say, drives people to violent behavior—against themselves, their loved ones, or people in general, whom they may perceive as their source of pain.

THE GOALS OF REVOLUTION
AND THE ROLE OF ELITE LEADERS

Are there really any significant or lasting differences between old and new governing elites who struggle for power during revolution? Or are the distinctions more apparent than real, more transient than permanent?

Often revolutionary rhetoric publicly justifies "throwing the rascals out" and frequently redefines government's fundamental role in promoting the most salient values embraced by the new governing elites. Often this rhetoric, as Willhoite points out, is simply "manipulative persuasion designed to camouflage . . . [the] leader's ultimate objectives."[18]

Castro and Ortega

Two contemporary examples—Fidel Castro in Cuba and Daniel Ortega in Nicaragua—demonstrate that revolutionaries (especially Marxist-Leninists) were very careful not to disclose their true ideology and goals while they were amassing popular support to attain absolute power. Both revolutions were fortunate in having a corrupt and loathsome dictator to assault—Batista in Cuba and Somoza in Nicaragua; both were equally fortunate in having a genuine national hero around whom to focus their revolutionary efforts: José Martí in Cuba and Augusto Sandino in Nicaragua.

Castro either disguised his Marxist beliefs to get popular support and avoid U.S. interference or was uncertain about his ideology. Sympathetic accounts describe him as

> not . . . much influenced by Marx's writings . . . more revolutionary, genuinely nationalistic, unconventional, audacious. . . . His ambition . . . [was] too great, his temperament too quixotic to enable him to submit to the discipline and higher authority such as Communism regards as necessary.[19]

Others, less inclined to take Castro at face value, are more dubious about the evolutionary nature of his thinking:

> Until the proper moment, when the revolution was strong enough, it was expedient for
> Fidel not to alienate potential supporters or prematurely to alarm world opinion, espe-
> cially in the United States, with professions of Marxist affinities.[20]

In any case, only a handful of his followers were Marxists, and the opposition to Batista
was not exclusively, as was the case in Russia and China, of a dominant ideological
motif. Some of the most passionate anti-Batista intellectuals were devoutly anticommunist also. However, two years after the overthrow of Batista—and seven months after
the disastrous Bay of Pigs invasion by U.S.-backed Cuban exiles—Castro declared, "I
am a Marxist-Leninist and I shall be a Marxist-Leninist to the end of my life." In 1965,
The Communist party became "official," and the United Party of the Cuban Socialist
Revolution, whose leaders had been compromised by persistent sexual scandals, was
dissolved.

In Nicaragua, the Sandinistas consented to a prerevolutionary agreement allowing
for political pluralism. The Sandinistas, during the fight against Somoza, contained three
factions: the *proletarios,* a traditional Marxist wing; the *Guerra Popular Prolongada,* a
Maoist-Castro bloc; and the *Terceristas.* This latter group, which included Daniel Ortega and his brother Humberto, became the most durable because it attracted social
democratic, bourgeois, and social Christian followers. However, its leaders, the Orte-
gas, were Marxists.

Only after attaining full political power did the Sandinistas impose the Marxist-
Leninist doctrine of monopoly rule.[21] Humberto Ortega wrote, in 1979, "The dialectical
development of human society leads through capitalism to communism" and that the
Sandinistas will ensure that Nicaragua adheres to this view "as long as we have our
Marxist-Leninist cause and a solid vanguard to provide leadership in the struggle."[22] In
1981, in a speech to Sandinista Army officers, Ortega proclaimed the Sandinista revolution to be Marxist-Leninist and said that any alliance with the "bourgeoisie" (for the
purpose of holding elections, for example) was "temporary and exclusively tactical."
The elections, he assured his audience, would "in no way decide who is going to hold
power. For this power belongs to the FSLN [Sandinista party], to our Directorate."[23]
Bayardo Arce, member of the Sandinista Joint National Directorate, was even more
explicit in 1984:

> What a revolution really needs is the power to act. The power to act is precisely what
> constitutes the essence of the dictatorship of the proletariat—the ability of the [working]
> class to impose its will by using any means at hand [without bourgeois formalities]. For
> us, then, the elections . . . are a nuisance. . . . Those things become weapons of the
> revolution to move forward the cause of socialism. . . . It is useful, for example, to
> display an entrepreneurial class and private production. . . . The important thing is that
> the entrepreneurial class no longer controls all the means to reproduce itself. . . . We
> are using an instrument claimed by the bourgeois [elections] . . . in order to move
> ahead on matters that are strategic. . . . Bourgeois democracy has an element which
> we can manage and even derive advantages from for the construction of socialism in
> Nicaragua.[24]

"Sandismo," more a set of opaque anti-Yankee nationalistic symbols than an ideology,
is of little importance and rarely appears in speeches by Sandinista leaders, any more
than José Martí's speeches or writings are cited in Cuba.

Typically during revolution, the public function of the new governing elite is to redress some perceived major economic and social injustices. The new regime generally justifies transferring power and privileges from one group to another, usually from the perceived haves to the supposed have nots—or at least to leaders ostensibly representing this latter group of disenfranchised people.

The Revolutionary Core

As revolutionary fervor grows, a crucial ingredient for success is the concentrated effort of effective organizational leaders, often a party or political faction. This leadership usually consists of a small group of dedicated political activists, an elite. Even in the earliest stages of revolution, sometimes months or years in advance, some small elite group of dedicated political activists is busy organizing, proselytizing, and giving political expression to certain discontented groups in society. In addition, even when economic and social preconditions for revolution are ripe, this elite must orchestrate the political actions that result in the overthrow of the old regime and the creation of a new governing elite.

The classic prototype of revolutionary leadership is, of course, the Marxist-Leninist model. The Communist party, acting as the "vanguard of the proletariat," engineers the actual revolution by claiming to act on behalf of the disenfranchised economic and social group. The Communist party promises eventually to turn power over to the workers, peasants, or some other popular group. Unfortunately, this final stage—the so-called withering of the state and the move from socialism to true communism, which theoretically involves transferring power to the people—has never happened historically, making Marxist-Leninist models very risky at best.

As many political theorists have noted, the general citizenry (the masses) are generally disinclined to participate in the political system unless the issues are made relevant to their day-to-day lives. In fact, Willhoite contends, historically, the masses often have failed to take arms against their governments, even when experts predicted that they should.[25]

Describing the role of the revolutionary leader in his comparative study of revolutions, Greene asserts:

> The successful revolutionary leader, by definition, is able to interpret these greater events and more general conditions into terms that have meaning for the everyday life of rank-and-file citizens. He does this in an especially coherent and appealing way; he simplifies complexity.[26]

Revolutionary ideology is the stuff of political elites, not of the masses or general citizens. As Robert E. Scott, in his essay on Latin American political elites, so aptly phrased it: "Pie in the sky is nowhere as attractive as bread in the hand."[27]

The Legitimacy of Revolutions: The People

Every revolution has claimed that its ultimate authority rests with the people (or at least that it was undertaken on their behalf). The people form a rarely defined symbol, sometimes incorporated into written constitutions. The 1987 Cuban constitution, for example, declares Marxism-Leninism as the state ideology, the Communist party as the sole representative of this ideology, and the dictatorship of the proletariat as the operative principle of state power, and it creates "organs of people's power" to facilitate the dictatorship.[28] Scholars with revolutionary daydreams write of "the people in the vanguard," creating the impression that those not in the vanguard are not of the people.[29]

Revolutionary elites are not typically peasants or working-class members, nor are they even usually from the class they purport to represent. Although revolutionary elites justify their legitimacy by claiming to represent the interests of the people, those leaders come from very different worlds. Of Lenin's childhood we learn that

> summers were like paradise. Everything that could possibly enchant the children was theirs for the asking. The large white house with the columns and the two verandas looked down on the river Ushna. There were woods and coppices near the riverbank and the wheatfields stretched into the distance. . . . There was a boathouse with three boats. Stables, carriage house, farmyard, a long avenue of lime trees, another of birches, and a small village for the peasants who worked on the estate.[30]

Fidel Castro, primary architect of the Cuban Revolution, was

> the son of a very rich peasant, receiving the superb education denied to his father. . . . Fidel's childhood appears to have been very pleasant and basically happy, certainly a privileged childhood even by the standards of the affluent landowners of the day.[31]

Mao too came from a family that was "better off than most. . . . [His] upbringing was secure. Other boys of the same era could expect less."[32] Moreover, in Cambodia, under the communist Khmer Rouge regime, which ruled from 1975 to 1979, three of the highest-ranking government officials had earned Ph.D.'s from the University of Paris. The most recent revolution, Nicaragua's, was the creation of those of "predominately middle- and upper-class origins. . . . Peasants and proletarians, although represented, were relatively scarce."[33]

Why should this surprise us? Revolution takes a great deal of time, money, and sophistication. Like more routine politics, revolution attracts those with the skills required to do well.

The American Founding Fathers: Power to Some People

The American Founding Fathers—an elite class who emerged from the American Revolution—paid homage to the interests of the people as they forged a new nation. As William Domhoff states:

> Even the Founding Fathers, as the leadership group in the fledgling ruling class of that era, with its members far removed from the general population in their wealth, income, education, and political experience, did not consider promulgating their new constitution designed to better protect and enhance private property and commerce without asking for the consent of the governed.[34]

Piven and Cloward have argued that the U.S. Constitution itself, with its intricate checks and balances, was really an effective legal device for protecting the property of the "revolutionary elite against the appetites of the general populace."[35] This view was strongly expressed by Alexander Hamilton and the Federalists, who urged caution against "the imprudence of democracy."[36]

Some American constitutional scholars, historians, and political scientists, have argued that the mechanism of checks and balances makes changing laws and altering public policy very difficult. This favors the interest of the elite in power, who were in early America primarily the property owners. The general populace and those without power in the society were effectively denied access into the circle of elite political and public policy decision making.

In revolutionary America, the people and the elites (founders) had a mutual interest against being dominated by an external force, such as the British crown. Checks and balances not only assured that America would not be dominated externally but also rather conveniently kept rival groups within the system from gaining any political advantage over the landowning elite internally.[37]

The Paradox of Revolutionary Elites

In her classic essay on revolution, Hannah Arendt, though lamenting the fact that "revolutionary parties" are always dominated by elites, concludes that elitist rule is unavoidable. She writes, "That political 'elites' have always determined the political destinies of the many and have, in most instances, exerted a domination over them, indicates . . . the bitter need of the few to protect themselves against the many."[38]

Some revolutions, while invoking the people as the object of their intent to alter social and economic relations, do not pretend that the people know what is best. Others—the American, for example—place great faith in procedures to provide some symbolic representation to the people while assuring themselves that populist yearnings are institutionally repressed. But irrespective of intentions, "the people" is no more than a meaningless phrase that will nevertheless remain forever in vogue.

THE STAGES AND PROCESS OF REVOLUTION

Most of the early notions about how revolutions progress were described by Brinton. He put together a three-stage model: the first stage was the rule of the moderates, the second was radical rule, and the third was the reaction against radicalism, which ended radical rule.[39] Other scholars have analyzed revolutionary processes and stages in a similar fashion. Willhoite cites several recent historical examples, which more or less illustrate Brinton's stages. He notes that the rule of moderates took place in the French (1789), Russian (1917), Portuguese (1974), and Iranian (1979) revolutions. However, he qualifies this by saying that in most Marxist-Leninist-inspired revolutions, as in China (1974), North Vietnam (1954), and Cambodia (1975), the rule of moderates (in Brinton's classic sense) is very short-lived, if it exists at all. He also qualifies including the Cuban and Nicaraguan revolutions because, he argues, moderates never really were in control, but in both cases, Castro and Ortega had to give the "appearance of moderation" to form coalitions that would draw popular support.

He cites examples of the second stage of revolution, the rule of the radicals, by describing the ascendancy of the Jacobin faction in France, the dominance of the Bolsheviks in Russia, and rule by the radical clergy in Iran, led by the Ayatollah Khomeini.

Willhoite illustrates the third stage of revolution, the end of radical rule, by citing the end of Jacobin terror in France. However, regarding Russia, he agrees with Michael Walzer that perhaps terror never really ends as long as the revolution is dominated by a small, active, and powerful elite group, as has characterized the Soviet Union.[40]

As an aside, if the Russian Revolution was born in 1917, when did (or does) it reach maturity? Is it still living, or did it expire? If one interprets events like Stalin's crackdown in the 1930s and China's Cultural Revolution in the late 1960s under direction of the radical Red Guard, perhaps the process of revolution in totalitarian countries represents a long-term, protracted process. If so, perhaps Mikhail Gorbachev's glasnost in the Soviet Union is merely an intermission, not the final act of the process of revolution.

Although studies of revolutionary stages and processes are academically interesting and perhaps historically valuable, the long and short of it is that revolutionary factions, led by elites, compete for power, eventually ending in one group totally monopolizing political power.[41]

Of course, the elites may compromise to a degree and may even distort their true intentions until after they reign supreme. Moreover, some periods of the revolution are very violent, but some are more moderate. Coalitions come and go, and compromises go by the wayside. The more vital question, however, is, What does it all really mean? Does the revolution really benefit the general public in the end? It is to this question that we now turn.

DO REVOLUTIONS PRODUCE REAL AND LASTING CHANGE?

Writers on revolution, especially contemporary revolutions, have occasionally heralded the wondrous accomplishments of a favored set of revolutionary elites to the point of absurdity, thus making the task of assessment more emotional than it should be. Like the study of religion—of which revolution is almost a secular counterpart—separating myth from reality, belief from truth, and fact from fiction is difficult. Unfortunately, some scholars on revolution distort facts (albeit sometimes unwittingly), and many revolutionary writers and elites simply lie about what revolutions accomplish. There is a progressive bias in much of the literature on revolution:

> Revolution has become a magic word in modern politics, even though there is little agreement on precisely how and when it ought to be used. Over the course of two centuries it has come to be virtually identified with "progress," despite the fact that experience casts doubt on their connection.[42]

"Yes, people are always much better off because of revolution, because the greedy rich have to share their wealth with the people, resulting in a more equal distribution of wealth'' and ''No, revolutions never make conditions better for people, because all revolutions are evil communist conspiracies'' are tempting global generalizations to make. But, of course, such broad statements are patently absurd. We generally recognize them as absurd when they are made by revolutionary elites. For example, nobody believes that North Korea ''caught up with the advanced industrial countries in the per capita output of major industrial products and surpassed them in some items.''[43]

We get caught up in the spirit of revolutions partly because revolutionary leaders—Castro, Ortega, Mao, Lenin—are captivating. We learn, for instance, that the Nicaraguan economy

> grew steadily under Sandinista rule. . . . [The Sandinistas] succeeded in carrying out innovative and highly successful social programs without inordinately straining the national budget. . . . Any attempt to impose a dogmatic Marxist-Leninist system would certainly have generated a mass exodus of population.[44]

Yet in 1988, inflation in Nicaragua topped 10,000 percent, with salaries worth one-tenth of their 1980 value; the nation was an armed camp, with 120,000 armed soldiers policing a population of 3.4 million; and thanks in part to the emigration of one-third of the country's professional class, the economy was in ruins. The 1984 election was alleged to be ''scrupulously conducted,'' even though two of the parties were in fact fronts for the Sandinistas and two others were part of the preelection ruling junta. Finally, international pressure may ''force the Sandinistas to become what they did not wish to be—more socialist, less politically open, more repressive, more militaristic, and more reliant upon the socialist bloc and isolated from the West.''[45] (Sandinista leadership, as we have seen, does not need to be forced to become more socialist.)

Such misleading statements are not unusual. During the Lenin years, much the same was written about the Soviet Union; then Mao stole our hearts with his communal emphases. Next, the genuinely charismatic Castro became an American media hero (especially to Barbara Walters). Each revolution is different. *This one* will not result in just another oligarchy; *this one* will redistribute wealth. Cuba is ''unique because it does not use terror, except in isolated instances.''[46] Then Armando Valladares's prison memoirs appeared:

> Every night there were firing squads. . . . The recruits who made up the platoons of the firing squads received five pesos and three days' leave for each man executed. . . . Added to that terror of death came another—the terror inspired in us by early-morning ''inspections.'' [The official executioner] would order the garrison to form up in full military gear and attack the prisoners. He called the prison his ''private hunting reserve.'' . . . The authorities did not bother to notify the families of the men they had executed, so that quite often the mothers, wives, and children of executed men appeared at visiting time asking to see them.[47]

We read that

> Nicaragua's ability to grapple with seemingly impossible trade-offs, to learn from previous revolutions, and to stay on course in the face of threats from more powerful

neighbors, especially the United States, shows [that] this revolution is different from many of the revolutionary movements.[48]

But no revolution is really different. If one could demonstrate that people's general economic and social conditions were not better (or even worse) after revolution or that conditions before the revolution were not all that bad, it might be reasonable to question the desirability and accomplishments of that particular revolution. Two observers reveal that wealth in both capitalist and socialist postrevolutionary societies is equally maldistributed. In spite of the tenets of socialist revolutionary ideology, the consequence of revolution is inequality. It is as though the revolution had never occurred! They conclude that neither socialist nor capitalist nations can claim greater equality:

> The prevailing view in academic circles that socialism fosters equality rests upon ideology rather than empirical observations of capitalist and socialist nations. . . . There is no reason to believe that socialist systems are more egalitarian than capitalist systems at the same level of economic development.[49]

Barrington Moore, who addressed the issue of the consequences of revolution in the major examples of capitalism and socialism, concluded:

> Though the determinants of position on the ladder are different, mainly economic in the USA and mainly political in the USSR, the distance from the bottom rung to the top one turns out to be about the same in both cases. In other words, there is as much inequality in the Soviet Union as the United States. . . . The same holds true for China. Looking now at the bottom of the social pyramid we find large numbers of people who are forced to make do at the margin of subsistence. . . . Thus the range of inequality is essentially the same under socialism and liberal capitalism.[50]

Should we not compare the United States with the two major examples of Marxist revolution? We tend to forget that the United States too is founded in revolution. The relative wealth of the United States, then, is less important than the conclusion that irrespective of the nature and intentions of the revolution, economic and social relations are not significantly different.

But there *is* a choice between revolution and inflexibility. Nations that attempt, without challenging the market, to make it less harsh can improve the distribution of material rewards:[51]

Policy Correlates of Income Distribution*

Public Policy		Quality of Life	
Welfare effort	.74	Urbanization	.65
Defense effort	− .26	Life expectancy	.75
Armed forces	.02	Infant mortality	− .73
Education effort	.38		

---

*The correlations range from −1 to 1, with 1 representing a perfect relationship and 0 representing no relationship.

The following list shows that countries that try harder—that is, spend less for defense and more for health and welfare—have a more equitable distribution of material rewards than those that do not. The strong correlation (.74) between welfare spending and income equality shows that the best way to achieve equity is to direct resources in that direction. In Chapter 2 we discussed cultures and budgets, noting the greater commitment of European people and governments to welfare. But of greater importance here is the relative success of incremental (that is, modest) policy commitments as opposed to violent revolution as a means of achieving fairness. A better quality of life and more equitable income distribution are inextricably intertwined. Consider this index of social progress, developed to summarize a nation's commitment to health, welfare, and education:[52]

Index of Social Progress

Centrally Planned Economies

Hungary	166
Bulgaria	163
Poland	163
Romania	158
Czechoslovakia	147
Albania	134
USSR	132
Average	**151**

Market Economies

Sweden	201
Denmark	191
Norway	189
Austria	184
Netherlands	182
West Germany	175
Finland	173
Belgium	171
Australia	168
France	168
United Kingdom	165
Canada	161
Switzerland	159
Japan	157
Italy	155
United States	121
Average	**170**

As you can see, the centrally planned (revolutionary) governments are no better than the market economies at spending their money for the people—indeed, they are a little worse. Statically, the greater impact of spending priorities is expressed as a proportion of variance explained. A country's budget preference is 11 times more reliable a predictor of income distribution than form of government.

Some changes, however, augur poorly for revolutionary zeal. Life is getting shorter in the eastern European socialist countries. In Hobbesian terms, life is beconming more "brutish and short." Cuba and North Korea are major exceptions. Still, the decline of life spans in the USSR is dramatic, the most severe decline recorded for all nations. In 1981, Americans lived an average of four years longer than Russians; in 1984, they lived eight years longer.

One dimension of revolutions does make them different: there is considerably less freedom after the revolution than before. The average person, caring more for comfort than intellectual development, nevertheless gets tired of political bombast and compulsory enthusiasm. For a Cuban factory worker, for example, "at 5:00 P.M. his workday ends, but it isn't always easy for him to go home. There may be a production assembly where his work record is examined or his acts of revolutionary consciousness are reviewed."[53] Is this any way to end the day?

One can never be sure about the legitimacy of closed regimes. If given an option, presumably few people would select them. That is, after all, the point of revolution. Tourists from Eastern bloc nations interviewed by Radio Free Europe would prefer western European Social Democratic parties, if given the choice (see Table 10.1). The antipathy toward the Communist parties of these eastern Europeans is both uniform and stable; it has not changed in several decades.

THE FUTURE OF IDEOLOGY

Nicaragua is Cuba's client. Cuba's ambassador has "direct input on Sandinista decisions."[54] In 1987, peace proposals for the region included the demand that Nicaragua encourage an "authentic process of democratic pluralism." Implementation of this plan would forever alter the nature of the Nicaraguan revolution. The Sandinistas, rather than

TABLE 10.1 Party Preferences of Eastern Tourists in Western Europe (%)

	Czech	Hungarian	Polish
Communist	3	7	4
Social Democrat	43	42	35
Christian Democrat	29	26	34
Other right	11	21	22

SOURCE: Henry C. Hart, "The Tables Turned: If East Europeans Could Vote," *Public Opinion*, October–November 1983, p. 55–56. Reprinted with permission of the American Enterprise Institute for Public Policy Research.

continuing as the vanguard of the revolution, would become just another political party. If the party agrees, this would indeed make Nicaragua different, for no Marxist-oriented party that has lead a revolution has *ever* given up power.

This is not to say that the voluntary relinquishing of power is out of the question. After all, in Czechoslovakia in 1968, the party intended to do just that: to allow free and open elections. It was prevented from doing so only by a USSR-led invasion. Control disintegrated swiftly in Hungary in 1956 and in Poland in 1981. But in none of these cases had the party leadership been installed by an actual revolution; rather, Soviet engineered coups had installed them soon after the end of World War II. The Sandinistas, like the Bolsheviks and the Chinese People's Liberation Army, won a costly revolutionary war. So the stakes are higher. A more likely option is to abandon the ideology and keep the power, as is being tried in China and the USSR. In 1989, the Sandinistas, declaring their socialism to be adjusted to the "context of Central American reality," proposed massive reductions in government spending, including military spending, and made the first tentative gestures toward privatization. Whether or not the proposals amounted to a "textbook lesson in capitalist economics," they were certainly a step in that direction.[55]

Giving up an ideology is not the same, at least at first, as giving up power. Since free markets and free politics are movements in a similar direction, the economic reformers in Marxist states are taking a risk. Much depends on the mind-sets of the elites and the economic conditions of the country. Cuba's Castro, a Jesuit-trained ideologue who merely substituted one religion for another, would rather have a failed economy than an impure doctrine. It was, after all, his revolution. Perhaps the same thing can be said about Ethiopia's Marxist government; their coup replaced the emperor with a Marxist government. But Ethiopia is the world's poorest country, debilitated by drought, famine, and civil war. It acquired its Marxism before the major Marxist models began their recantation.

Nicaragua poses a different opportunity; among its major role models, only Cuba remains pure. Both the USSR and China are in the midst of change. Although Nicaragua's economy is in total disarray, it is not nearly as prostrate as Ethiopia's. The Sandinistas have won a reasonably fair election but have not been tested since the collapse of the economy.

But what of future revolutions? Where will a new ideology arise? Marxism is a spent force, much like Christianity. In the Middle Ages, Christianity was revolutionary, as the Crusades attest. In the 20th century, Marxism became the religion of revolution, but it no longer packs much punch. Today, Islam is the only serious contender for an ideology with the passions of its predecessors, and Muslim radicals are as willing to resort to extremes as were the Khmer Rouge or Stalin. But Islam—even fundamentalist Islam—is more ideologically fragmented than Marxism, akin more to Christianity during its secular decline. The sole revolutionary Islamic regime—Iran—does not present a clear picture of how the religion translates into politics. Iran more closely resembles, say, Yugoslavia, a curious Marxist country with an uncertain identity, than the USSR of the 1930s. Nonetheless, estimates of political stability are inversely related to the presence of a strong fundamentalist Islamic presence. But there is even more of an economic cause of instability, and evidence to support the J-curve, than there is with regard to Islam. Political stability and good economic performance are linked, but not perfectly (that is, they are not linear):[56]

Nations (Grouped from Most Stable to Least Stable)	Economic Performance Index
Brazil	17
China	56
Portugal	16
Singapore	41
South Korea	24
Taiwan	45
Venezuela	12
Group average	**30**
Algeria	18
Argentina	7
Ecuador	16
India	12
Malaysia	22
Poland	11
Saudi Arabia	31
Sri Lanka	14
Thailand	19
Turkey	13
Uruguay	11
Yugoslavia	18
Zimbabwe	34
Group average	**17**
Bangladesh	25
Bolivia	6
Ghana	1
Indonesia	18
Kenya	12
South Africa	12
Tanzania	9
Group average	**12**
Chile	6
Nigeria	15
Salvador	6
Uganda	12
Vietnam	14
Zaire	2
Zambia	5
Group average	**8**

Ethiopia	12
Iran	14
Iraq	17
Sudan	9
Group average	**13**

The most unstable group, though economically in bad shape, is not as close to collapse as the group of nations slightly less stable than they. Far more likely are coups. Since Ethiopia and Iraq are near totalitarian, they may provide the next opportunities for revolution and its consequences.

FOR FURTHER CONSIDERATION

1. Distinguish between a Revolution and a *coup d' état.*
2. Compare the American Revolution with the French Revolution and the Russian revolution.
3. Compare Brinton's and Davies's explanations of the causes of revolutions. Which do you find more compelling?
4. Compare everyday life before and after revolutions.

For the More Adventurous

1. In 1989, Soviet leader Gorbachev visited Cuba and Great Britain. Read accounts of his meetings with Castro and the United Kingdom's Margaret Thatcher. Which seemed the more cordial?
2. Imagine the circumstances under which a revolution would *not* result in the substitution of one privileged class for another.
3. Suppose Marxists parties, in power, are defeated in a fair election. If they abide by this decision, are they still Marxist?
4. Marx regarded the French Revolution as the paradigm of a revolution. In 1989, the French celebrated the 200th anniversary of their revolution. Look at the goals of the French Revolution, compare them with current French political and economic society. Read French historians' accounts of the revolution, timed to accompany the anniversary. Can French historians and Marx be reconciled?

NOTES

1. Crane Brinton, *The Anatomy of Revolution,* rev. ed. (Englewood Cliffs, N.J.: Prentice-Hall, 1952), p. 1
2. Ibid., pp. 1–2.
3. Richard Greenfield, *Ethiopia: A New Political History* (New York: Praeger, 1965), p. 189; See also Crawford Young, *Ideology and Development in Africa* (New Haven, Conn.: Yale University Press, 1982), p. 69. Around 450 B.C., the Greek historian Herodotus first used the term *Aethiopia* to refer to the country immediately to the south of Egypt. The word meant ''Land of Burnt Faces'' and represented for the Greeks the beginning of exotic Africa. Verdi's opera *Aïda,* set in ancient Egypt, identifies Aïda as an Ethiopian slave.
4. Colin Legum and Bill Lee, *The Horn of Africa in Continuing Crisis* (New York: Africana, 1979), p. 88.

5. Thomas E. Skidmore and Peter H. Smith, *Modern Latin America* (New York: Oxford University Press, 1984), p. 225.
6. Fred H. Willhoite, *Power and Governments: An Introduction to Politics* (Pacific Grove, Calif.: Brooks/Cole, 1988), p. 381.
7. Ibid., pp. 300–302.
8. Ibid., pp. 299–302.
9. Charles A. Beard, *The Supreme Court and the Constitution* (Englewood Cliffs, N.J.: Prentice-Hall, 1962), pp. 134–144; and Howard Zinn, *A People's History of the United States* (New York: Harper & Row, 1980), pp. 233–235.
10. Peter Calvert, *Revolution* (New York: Praeger, 1970), p. 8.
11. Brinton, *Anatomy of Revolution*, p. 55.
12. Thomas H. Greene, *Comparative Revolutionary Movements* (Englewood Cliffs, N.J.: Prentice-Hall, 1974), pp. 113–114.
13. Ibid., p. 114.
14. J. C. Davies "The J-Curve of Rising and Declining Satisfaction as a Cause of Some Great Revolutions and a Contained Rebellion," in *Violence in America*, ed. Hugh Davis Greyham and Ted Robert Gurr (New York: New American Library, 1971) pp. 671–709.
15. Ibid., p. 69.
16. Willhoite, *Power and Governments*, p. 299–302.
17. Peter Gatrell, *The Tsarist Economy, 1850–1917* (New York: St. Martin's Press, 1986), pp. 231–234.
18. Willhoite, *Power and Governments*, p. 317.
19. Hugh Thomas, *The Cuban Revolution* (New York: Harper & Row, 1977), p. 273.
20. Jose Luis Llovio-Mendendez, *Insider* (New York: Bantam, 1988), p. 208.
21. Willhoite, *Power and Governments*, p. 318.
22. Lindsey Gruson, "Nicaragua Addresses Its Ideology," *New York Times*, March 9, 1981, p. A4.
23. Ibid.
24. Ibid.
25. Willhoite, *Power and Governments*, pp. 313–314.
26. Greene, *Comparative Revolutionary Movements*, p. 27.
27. Robert E. Scott, "Political Elites and Political Modernization: The Crisis of Transition," in *Elites in Latin America*, ed. Seymour Martin Lipset and Aldo Solari (Oxford: Oxford University Press, 1967), pp. 228–233.
28. Max Azicri, *Cuba* (London: Pinter, 1988), p. 98.
29. John A. Booth, *The End and the Beginning: The Nicaraguan Revolution* (Boulder, Colo.: Westview Press, 1985), p. 159.
30. Robert Payne, *Lenin* (New York: Avon, 1964), p. 63.
31. Tad Szulc, *Fidel* (New York: Morrow, 1986), p. 107.
32. Ross Terrill, *Mao* (New York: Harper & Row, 1980), p. 5.
33. Booth, *End and the Beginning*, p. 271.
34. G. William Domhoff, *Who Rules America Now? A View for the '80s* (Englewood Cliffs, N.J.: Prentice-Hall, 1983), p. 8.
35. Francis Fox Piven and Richard A. Cloward, *The New Class War: Reagan's Attack on the Welfare State and Its Consequences,* rev. ed. (New York: Pantheon, 1985), pp. 71–72.
36. Alexander Hamilton, *Federalist No. 51*.
37. For a more detailed account of how the American founding elite viewed their revolutionary war of independence and fashioned the U.S. Constitution to protect their interests, read Thomas R. Dye and Harmon Zeigler, *The Irony of Democracy: An Uncommon Introduction to American Politics,* 7th ed. (Pacific Grove, Calif.: Brooks/Cole, 1970), pp. 24–64. A good contrast between the American and Russian revolutions can be found in Karl W.

Deutsch, *Politics and Government: How People Decide Their Fates*, 3d ed. (Boston: Houghton Mifflin, 1974), pp. 315–331.

38. Hannah Arendt, *On Revolution* (New York: Viking Penguin, 1963), p. 280.
39. For a serious discussion of revolution, see Brinton, *Anatomy of a Revolution*, pp. 72–263.
40. Michael Walzer, A Theory of Revolution, *"Marxist Perspectives"* 2 Spring 1979, pp. 31–37."
41. For an excellent overview of revolution, see Willhoite, *Power and Governments*, pp. 297–350.
42. Ibid., pp. 319–320.
43. Genaro Carnero Cheka, *Korea: Rice and Steel* (Pyongyang, North Korea: Foreign Language Publishing House, 1972), p. 97.
44. Thomas Walker, *Nicaragua: The Land of Sandino* (Boulder, Colo.: Westview Press, 1985), p. 43.
45. Booth, *End of the Beginning*, p. 290.
46. Amos Perlmutter, *Modern Authoritarianism* (New Haven, Conn.: Yale University Press, 1981), p. 19.
47. Armando Valladares, *Against All Hope* (New York: Knopf, 1986), pp. 19–21.
48. Thomas Walker, *Nicaragua: The Land of Sandino* (Boulder, Colo.: Westview, 1981), p. 89.
49. Thomas R. Dye and Harmon Zeigler, "Socialism and Equality in Cross-national Perspective," *PS: Political Science and Politics 21* (Winter 1988): 45–56.
50. Barrington Moore, Jr., *Authority and Inequality under Capitalism and Socialism: USA, USSR, and China* (New York: Oxford University Press, 1987), p. 118.
51. Dye and Zeigler, "Socialism and Equality," p. 13.
52. Richard J. Estes, *The Social Progress of Nations* (New York: Praeger, 1984), p. 94.
53. Llovio-Mendendez, *Insider*, p. 283.
54. Juan M. del Aguila, "Cuba's Declining Fortunes," *Current History*, December 1987, p. 425.
55. Nancy Kreisler, "Sandinistas Advance Economic Reforms," *New York Times*, January 31, 1989, p. 4.
56. Stability groupings from *The Economist*, December 20, 1986, pp. 69–72. Index developed independently.

FOR FURTHER READING

Aguila, Juan D. del. *Cuba: Dilemmas of a Revolution*. Boulder, Colo.: Westview Press, 1988.
Arendt, Hannah. *On Revolution*. New York: Viking Penguin, 1963.
Brinton, Crane. *The Anatomy of Revolution*, rev. ed. Englewood Cliffs, N.J.: Prentice-Hall, 1952.
Gatrell, Peter. *The Tsarist Economy, 1850–1917*. New York: St. Martin's Press, 1986. Believe it or not, life was better for the average person before the revolution.
Gilbert, Dennis. *Sandinistas*. New York: Basil Blackwell, 1988. The Sandinistas are said to be neither as black as U.S. policy depicts them nor as white as American supporters prefer to imagine.
Greene, Thomas H. *Comparative Revolutionary Movements*. Englewood Cliffs, N.J.: Prentice-Hall, 1974.
Johnson, Chalmers. *Revolutionary Change*. Boston: Little, Brown, 1966.
Loomis, Stanley. *Paris in the Terror*. New York: Lippincott, 1964. Portraits of the French Revolutionary leaders.
Rude, George. *The Crowd in the French Revolution*. New York: Oxford University Press, 1959.

Terrill, Ross. *Mao*. New York: Harper & Row, 1980.

————.*The White-boned Demon*. New York: Morrow, 1984. The demon is Madame Mao.

Thomas, Hugh. *The Cuban Revolution*. New York: Harper & Row, 1977.

Von Laue, Theodore H. *The World Revolution of Westernization: The Twentieth Century in Global Perspective*. New York: Oxford University Press, 1987. Twentieth-century totalitarianism explained as a reaction to the expansion of Western power.

CHAPTER 11

So What?: What Difference Does the Polity Make?

Reprinted by permission of UFS, Inc.

Why are some countries able to lift themselves from poverty while others are not? Why are the wealthy countries primarily in Europe, Asia, and North America? What control does a government have over a nation's economy? Is one form of government better equipped to manage than others?

In 1987, the Population Crisis Committee, a research organization concerned with population control, published its Human Suffering Index, a composite index based on such factors as literacy, infant mortality, income, and caloric intake. It rated Switzerland as having the world's best quality of life; it rated Mozambique as having the worst.[1]

Human Suffering Index

Group 1: Extreme Human Suffering

Mozambique	Nepal
Angola	Mauritania
Chad	Nigeria
Mali	Kampuchea
Ghana	Rwanda
Somalia	Bhutan
Niger	Bangladesh
Burkina Faso	North Yemen
Central African Republic	Cameroon
Zaire	Sudan
Benin	Burundi
Malawi	Kenya
Guinea	Sierra Leone
Ethiopia	Tanzania
Togo	

Group 2: High Human Suffering

Congo	Iran
Haiti	Indonesia
South Yemen	Syria
Zambia	Burma
Ivory Coast	Peru
Pakistan	India
Liberia	Botswana
Uganda	Sri Lanka
Senegal	Tunisia
Lesotho	Saudi Arabia
Vietnam	Turkey
Madagascar	Egypt
Papua New Guinea	Philippines
Algeria	Ecuador
Nicaragua	Dominican Republic
Bolivia	Paraquay
Morocco	Oman

Jordan	Iraq
South Africa	Honduras
El Salvador	Brazil
Guatemala	China

Group 3: Moderate Human Suffering

Malaysia	Costa Rica
Thailand	Mauritius
Mexico	Argentina
Mongolia	Uruquay
Albania	Kuwait
Panama	Portugal
Lebanon	Isreal
Chile	Yugoslavia
South Korea	Cuba
Venezuela	Hong Kong
Colombia	Greece
Guyana	Spain
Jamaica	Romania
United Arab Emirates	Poland
North Korea	

Group 4: Minimal Human Suffering

Ireland	France
Trinidad and Tobago	United Kingdom
Czechoslovakia	Sweden
Bulgaria	Japan
USSR	Denmark
Singapore	Austria
Hungary	Canada
Iceland	Belgium
Italy	United States
Finland	Netherlands
Australia	Luxembourg
New Zealand	West Germany
East Germany	Switzerland
Norway	

International Living, a magazine for travelers, reached a similar conclusion with slightly different data: Among the best, Switzerland was second to the United States, and among the worst, Ethiopia was exceed by Chad, Angola, and the Central African Republic.[2] *The Economist*, using slightly different criteria (including, for example, cultural opportunities, which, one need hardly add, are of minimal interest in Chad or Mozambique), concluded that the most livable countries are, in order, France, West Germany, Australia, Japan, Canada, Sweden, the United States, the United Kingdom, and Switzerland.[3] However you measure, the results are comparable: living in industrial democracies is better than living in African authoritarian countries.

Average personal income in Switzerland is about 120 times greater than in Ethiopia. This ratio between the world's poorest and richest countries exceeds the comparable distribution of income within any country.[4]

Between these two extremes are the *developing* countries, whose economic performance is steadily improving. But for the Ethiopias of the world, little headway has been made. Living in Ethiopia is agony; living in Switzerland is bliss. About the only good aspect of life in Ethiopia is that it is short: life expectancy is 46 years, a little more than half what it is in Switzerland. Ethiopia is ravaged by famines; it cannot feed its population and depends on ineffective international contributions to stave off utter catastrophe.

In another similar country, Chad, people are either succumbing to a myriad of diseases that resist cure or falling victim to massacres, reprisals, and counterreprisals by warring tribal groups that the government, one of the world's most brutal, cannot control but can only abet by mass killing on its own. Much of the violent death is caused by incessant fighting between the Christian and animist south against the Muslim north.

Chad, Ethiopia, and the others in the group have suffered stagnant economies (about 0.38 percent annual growth), while the well-off countries enjoyed 3 percent annual economic growth. The rich are getting richer and the poor are getting poorer.

POLITICS AND ECONOMICS

Who is to blame for such inequities? It is time to return to the question with which we ended the first chapter of this book: What can government do? The question is not new; it has been asked repeatedly, with answers varying according to predisposition. Marxists believe that as long as the means of production are in private hands, there can be no genuine growth, no growth that does not enhance the fortunes of the rich and drive the poor deeper into desperate poverty. Supporters of capitalism argue that the profit motive—greed—encourages individuals to acquire wealth, and as a natural consequence, individual greed leads to collective economic growth and stability.

The major proponents of these disparate philosophies travel the globe preaching to the poor, and African countries are urged to accept capitalism or socialism as a condition for economic aid. The International Bank for Reconstruction and Development, a United Nations affiliate, is a leading propagandist for free enterprise, while the Soviet Union is the most active proponent of socialism. The USSR has decided to renounce its role in the promotion of socialism internationally, and China's economic establishment has declared that "Marxism does not require public ownership," ("market socialism" has become the slogan of the new Marxists) but Cuba's Castro has declared the promulgation of Marxist ideology a "sacred" obligation. And if Marxism is no longer a serious alternative to market economies, the message has not penetrated into Latin America. Irrespective of their solutions to the problem of the production and distribution of wealth, the two competing philosophies agree with Marx: politics and economics are inextricably intertwined.

As we saw in Chapter 1, the nations of the world are not easily placed into categories. There are several ways of classifying governments, using different taxonomies. Earlier we used this classification:

Polyarchies
Near polyarchies
Authoritarian governments
Near totalitarian governments
Totalitarian governments

Governments can also be arrayed on a continuum from those with the greatest reliance on the free market to those with the least:

Inclusive capitalist
Noninclusive capitalist
Noninclusive capitalist-statist
Inclusive capitalist-statist
Noninclusive mixed capitalist
Inclusive mixed capitalist
Noninclusive socialist
Inclusive socialist

A brief definition of each is in order before proceeding.

Inclusive Capitalist Systems.   The economic system of these countries is driven by the market and private enterprise, with government participation limited to subsidy and regulation, as opposed to ownership. Taxes are designed for the sustenance of government, rather than for the achievement of a social or political goal, such as an equitable income distribution. Examples are Switzerland, the United States, Costa Rica, Canada, and Japan.

Noninclusive Capitalist Systems.   These countries encourage free markets, but at least half of the population engages in "traditional" economic activity, generally feudal or communal. Examples are Thailand, Fiji, Chad, and Haiti.

Inclusive Capitalist-Statist Systems.   The economy is these countries is guided by the government, by both large-scale ownership and investment. Regulation is intense, but there is little commitment to broad welfare programs, and citizens who fall by the wayside have little recourse. Examples are Taiwan, Argentina, Italy, South Africa, and Saudi Arabia.

Noninclusive Capitalist-Statist Systems.   The ambitions of these countries is the same as in inclusive capitalist-statist ones, but they lack the resources to achieve their goals. Consequently, at least half of their economic production is only marginally constrained by government. Examples are Bolivia, India, the Philippines, Uganda, and Oman.

Inclusive Mixed Capitalist Systems.   A major purpose of these governments is to use control of the economy to achieve social and political objectives. A large portion of their budgets goes into education, welfare, and health care. Taxation is used for reasons not clearly related to the raising of revenue. Examples are Denmark, Israel, Nicaragua,

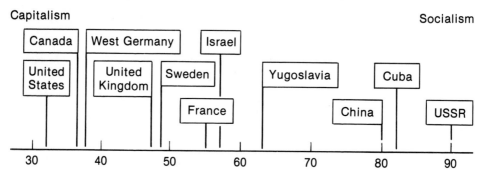

Fig. 11.1. Proportion of the Economy under Central Control

Poland, and Yugoslavia. An interesting addition to the list is China, which until the post-Mao reforms was an inclusive socialist economic system.

Noninclusive Mixed Capitalist Systems.   These countries have been forced to lower their expectations because they cannot afford large-scale welfare programs. Burma, the Congo, and Zambia are examples.

Noninclusive Socialist Systems.   The only difference between these countries and the inclusive socialist ones is their degree of success. Because their economies are primitive, they are not easily assembled into a collectivist mode. Kampuchea, Afghanistan, and Angola are examples.

Inclusive Socialist Systems.   In these countries, the national economy is under direct government control. Some private property and enterprise are allowed, but only as exceptions to the general rule of state control. Cases are the USSR, East Germany, North Korea, and Vietnam.

   Figure 11.1 illustrates the continuum. At the risk of oversimplification, I group the countries of the world according to the dominant modes of political and economic organization (see Table 11.1).

TABLE 11.1 Percentage of Countries in Each Combination

Political System	Economic System		
	Most Capitalist	**Mixed**	**Most Socialist**
Near-polyarchical	70	30	0
Authoritarian	21	54	25
Near-totalitarian	40	42	18
Totalitarian	0	38	62

Which Is "Best"?

These economic and political systems have meaning both in themselves and as devices to achieve other goals. Suppose we believe that collective control of an economy is just, because our morality rejects the ethics of individualism. If we believe in an equal (not necessarily equitable) distribution of income and think capitalism is poorly equipped for redistribution, does it necessarily matter that socialism may not do a better job? Suppose we believe in individual economic freedom and are convinced that those who fail do so because they are lazy. Does it really matter that evidence of systemic failure refutes our belief? In both these cases, we believe in the intrinsic worth of a process. Sometimes we should ask a question even if the answer disappoints us. When we ask, "So what?" or "What difference does the government I live under make to me?" several answers may surface.

Governments generally assume or reject responsibility for two components of an economy: *income distribution* and *income growth and stability*.[5] Wealth—measured by gross national product (the sum of all the goods and services produced in a country in a year) per capita—is the essential ingredient for any economic policy: a country cannot redistribute what it does not have. Another important indication of economic health is GNP growth. What kinds of political and economic systems encourage growth? In the United States, we have become fascinated by the consistent growth of the Asian countries, principally Japan, Singapore, South Korea, and Taiwan. At the end of World War II, Japan lay in ruins, and personal wealth in South Korea and Taiwan was roughly the same as Ethiopia's or Chad's. Since then, these Asian countries have experienced more growth than any others. To get an idea of the rate of growth, in the last decade, Ethiopia's personal income has increased from $100 to $120, while Taiwan's increased from $1,000 to $5,000! (In 1950, Taiwan's was $150, Ethiopia's $100).

All governments strive for economies that enjoy steady growth, are able to withstand shocks such an international recessions or shortages in key resources (usually petroleum), and can keep inflation low and employment high.

EQUALITY OF INCOME DISTRIBUTION

In 1983, John Kenneth Galbraith rightly identified income distribution as "one of the major debates in the nonsocialist world."[6] He argued that since the principal component of socialism is public ownership to eliminate inequality, the goal was beyond debate. However, since he wrote, the traditions of Marxism have been seriously challenged. Although many Marxist countries are denationalizing or in other ways encouraging private ownership, only the Chinese have explicitly rejected the central tenet of traditional Marxism, the abolition of private property. We learn from a leading Chinese economist that

> a new definition of socialism is needed, focusing on broad issues of social justice like equality of opportunity, instead of public ownership of means of production. . . . While Marx was generally correct in the field of politics, he erred in economics by opposing private property.[7]

The statement is notable on a variety of counts. First, there is the usual gobbledygook of authoritarian language: Marx is correct in politics but wrong in economics? To Marx, they are one and the same. Socialism should focus on ''equality of opportunity''? No country is more legally committed to equality of opportunity than the United States: it, alone among industrial democracies, has *affirmative action*—discrimination *in favor of* designated groups (women, minorities) in hiring and academic admissions.

But in rejecting equality of results in favor of equality of opportunity, the Chinese, while making mincemeat of Marx, pay homage to a central concern of all political theory: fairness, or ''distributive justice'': ''*who* distributes what to whom in virtue of what *critical characteristics,* by what *procedures,* with what distributive *outcomes.*''[8] Few people argue against justice; at stake is the who, what, why, and how. Even if we are cynically Machiavellian, caring not a whit about abstract justice, pragmatic politics compels rulers to try to prevent insurrections. People who believe inequality is a fundamental cause of violence argue that fair or not, extremes of wealth contribute to instability.

Much of this debate assumes that socialism, initially designed to guarantee the populace against extremes of wealth, has done so. Lindblom writes:

> It is in the communist [socialist] provision of . . . some degree of equality in the distribution of income and wealth that the communist [socialist] claim to approximate the humanitarian vision . . . seems undeniable. On those fronts the communist [socialist] systems have to be credited with great accomplishments, on the whole probably greater than those of the polyarchies (capitalist democracies).[9]

Unfortunately, the world is more complicated than we would prefer if we are to make claims for the ability of different kinds of political or economic systems to deliver on their promises. One of the most obvious complications is wealth. Rich countries can do more than poor ones irrespective of intentions. At the most minimal level, there is not much point in distributing wealth more equitably in Ethiopia or Chad. But how much better off is the average person living in the United Arab Emirates, bloated with oil revenues? If they chose to do so, the oil-rich countries could raise the standard of living of citizens not directly engaged in oil production, but Ethiopia cannot.

Freedom is most frequently cited as a goal competitive with equality.[10] Since few of us, given maximum individual freedom, would voluntarily part with our wealth, state-imposed redistribution is required. Leaders of states that intervene directly do so in the belief that they are trading liberty for equality. Although revolutions claim to be able to deliver both, a choice of one would appear to be inevitable. Lindblom writes:

> [Equality has been a] communist [socialist] aspiration since the nineteenth century, when the pursuit of liberty and equality, which had been taken up during the Enlightenment, went separate ways. Democrats went to the right, seeking liberty. Communists [socialists] went to the left, seeking equality.[11]

If we must select one and not the other, socialism (until the Chinese revisions) selects equality, and capitalism chooses freedom. Much of what we read about politics and the economy assumes that this trade-off is a realistic one. Industrial democracies guarantee

TABLE 11.2 Political Systems, Economic Systems, and the Economy*

	Equality	Growth
Polyarchy-totalitarianism	0.73	−2.86
Capitalism-socialism	−0.466	−2.76
GNP per capita	8.5	−5.29

*Scores are Student's *t*. Any score larger than 2.00 is "significant" (that is, not accidental). Negative scores mean an inverse relationship.

much more individual freedom than socialist ones. While they occasionally mumble a few phrases about freedom, the leaders of communist nations usually concede that they constrain behavior to a degree unthinkable in industrial democracies. Tass, the Soviet information agency, did not intend a parody when it quoted Gorbachev as saying, "Quite a lot has been said about the Communist Party's role as the political vanguard of society in conditions of perestroika," and added, "The process of preliminary selection of candidates was really democratic. Wide support has been given to those party members who proved by their deeds their commitment to the policy of restructuring."[12]

If we put these "variables" into an explanatory table (see Table 11.2), we reach two conclusions: (1) Equality of income distribution is unrelated to either political or economic system, as the only significant relationship is between wealth and equality. Wealthy countries are more equal than poor countries, irrespective of their political or economic system. (2) Economic growth is associated with political system, economic system, and wealth. The more a political system moves in the direction of totalitarianism, the less robust becomes its economic growth; the more an economic system moves in the direction of socialism, the less robust becomes its economic growth, but as countries become wealthy, their economic growth slows.

Rich countries are more equal than poor countries (see Table 11.3). Countries that deliberately set about the task of reducing extremes of wealth and poverty are no more successful than those that leave it alone. The failure of governmental systems to influence income distribution is important, because economic growth is not identical to economic development. Rather than growth just for growth's sake, most people look to economic advancement as an opportunity to improve the quality of life. Hence wealth concentrated in the hands of a tiny elite does little good. A country may have a per capita income of $20,000 but an unfair income distribution, so that the benefits of capital are lost. This is rarely the case. Brunei, an oil-rich nation on the Borneo coast, enjoys a GNP per capita of about $22,000. However, virtually all of this money is controlled by the ruling family, leaving most residents as impoverished as those in countries with a per capita income less than one-fourth of Brunei's. It is especially important that countries approaching or passing the takeoff stage include as many people as possible in their ascent.

The takeoff stage—that magic moment when economies shift from stagnant to expanding, when they move, say, from "developing" to "newly industrialized"—is difficult to isolate. Some theorists believe that a certain minimum standard of living must be obtained before growth can even be contemplated. Others believe that the rate of

TABLE 11.3 Patterns of Growth and Equity

These are countries with the most equitable distribution of income:

Country	Economic System	Political System
1. Switzerland	Inclusive capitalist	Polyarchy
2. United States	Inclusive capitalist	Polyarchy
3. Italy	Capitalist-statist	Polyarchy
4. Czechoslovakia	Inclusive socialist	Near totalitarian
5. Austria	Mixed capitalist	Polyarchy
6. Belgium	Inclusive socialist	Polyarchy
7. Hungary	Inclusive socialist	Authoritarian
8. USSR	Inclusive socialist	Near totalitarian
9. United Kingdom	Inclusive mixed capitalist	Polyarchy
10. Poland	Inclusive mixed socialist	Authoritarian

These are the countries with the least equality in incomes:

Country	Economic System	Political System
1. Liberia	Noninclusive capitalist	Authoritarian
2. Burkina Faso	Noninclusive mixed socialist	Authoritarian
3. Bolivia	Noninclusive capitalist-statist	Near polyarchy
4. Algeria	Inclusive socialist	Authoritarian
5. Ecuador	Noninclusive capitalist	Polyarchy
6. Zaire	Noninclusive capitalist-statist	Near totalitarian
7. Indonesia	Noninclusive capitalist-statist	Authoritarian
8. Somalia	Noninclusive mixed socialist	Near totalitarian
9. South Yemen	Noninclusive socialist	Near totalitarian
10. Cameroon	Noninclusive capitalist	Authoritarian

growth must be sustained over a long period of time. Still others believe that a minimum level of income equity must be achieved.

As Table 11.3 shows, nothing distinguishes the least equal nations except their poverty. While all manner of political and economic systems are represented in the list of the most unequal, their GNP per capita is about *one-eighth* that of the most equal nations.

The View from the Streets

Many of the restrictions that socialist governments impose on freedom are done so in the name of equality. According to Marxist theory, with the socialist revolution, the state collectivizes all means of production, transforming "surplus value" (private profit) into surplus product controlled by the state. Part of the surplus is used to pay wages, the other to pay a "social wage" (services provided by the state). Although the final stage in the evolution of communism, "from each according to his abilities, to each according to his needs," implies an absence of any but the most insignificant differential, socialist governments have not applied the theorem as strictly as they might. There are wage differentials, but they are not as great as in market economies, and there are minimum guaranteed incomes. An opera star or top party leader might earn 40 times as much as an unskilled worker, a ratio less excessive than in capitalist countries. With all income paid by the government, there is little opportunity for anybody to strike it rich. Salaries for major entertainers are about 5,000 rubles a month ($5,600 at the official exchange rate of $1.12 per ruble).

The salary of a Russian entertainer, like the salary of any other employee, is fixed by a formula. There are few Beatles or Rolling Stones; no Reggie Jacksons, almost no self-made people such as Microsoft's Bill Gates, who at 31 became America's youngest billionaire. The absence of conspicuous consumption because of a universal salary structure does not mean, however, that the problem of poverty has been overcome. Although statistics have only recently become available (since poverty was "officially" caused by capitalism), and hence we do not know much about changes in rates of poverty, at least 20 percent of the Soviet population lives below the "minimum material security level" (about $124 a month). Around 14 percent of the American population lives below the poverty line ($464 per month).

One of the most exhaustive plans for income distribution occurred in Cuba. Workers were placed into five major occupational groups:

"Productive workers" (blue-collar workers, both skilled and unskilled)
White-collar service employees
Administrative and clerical workers
Technicians and professionals with university training
Executives (administrators)

Within each category are grades from 1 to 9. This categorization is much like that of any public civil service, and since the state was managing the economy, an expanded civil service seemed an appropriate way to go about income distribution. All would not be paid equally, but all would be paid according to a schedule. Extra effort (as in overtime), extra risk (hazardous jobs), or a high rate of success (exceeding quotas) carried bonuses. Cuba has tried to eliminate material incentives for moral ones, especially during the years in which Che Guevara was a dominant force, but has largely given up. Wage scales were reintroduced, and even authors' royalties, abolished during the heady days of ideological obsession, were once again allowed (the government pays by the page according to the author's prestige).[13]

However, in an abrupt double about-face in 1986, Castro first toyed with privatization and within-rank incentives, allowing farmers to sell produce on private markets. But just as Castro's patron (the USSR) was moving seriously in the direction of a mixed economy, Cuba's modest experiment was canceled. The stress between the conservative client state and the suddenly reformist patron will make Cuba an interesting target of research. The Soviet economy, though not as impressive as those of the industrial democracies, nevertheless delivers "minimal human suffering;" whether it can persuade its client to march in step toward less central control remains to be seen.

Like Cuba, the Soviet bureaucracy establishes categories of workers. But the origins of Soviet income policy are more clearly associated with economic chaos. Though the Cuban revolution was harsh, there was no international intervention.

In the USSR, tales of deprivation exceed simple shortages; they touch on dignity.

Soviet housing policy makes no allowances for human foibles. For instance, a single woman and her ex-husband, forced to live in the same apartment, do not speak, making daily life quite unpleasant. The single woman was able to gain some access to trade union housing and swap her two rooms for one room in a union cooperative for herself and her mother and for two more rooms farther out of town for her two sons and daughter-in-law. She could never have swung the deal by using "official" channels, since apartment changes are given first to families with less than 9 square meters allocated per person, and even then the waiting lists are long. The less fortunate adjust. A divorced couple still share an apartment, each sleeping in a separate locked room, because they could not match their arrangement by living singly; the inhabitants of a 27-square-meter room, suddenly deprived of their children (who married and moved), are forced to accept another family, unknown to them, because they have now exceeded 18 square meters (9 per person).

The standard of living in the Soviet Union is bad and getting worse. The key is shortages, a victim of central planning. Roy Medvedev, who believes that Marx or Lenin would disown the USSR, explains:

> Privileges tend to arise where there are shortages. Certain products are . . . available for practically the whole population while others are produced in limited quantity which can satisfy only a small part of the demand. Under the Soviet price system, shortages either mean enormous queues or else distribution takes place via some other channel—personal contacts, *nomenklatura* privilege, or, worst of all, bribery. . . . New kinds of goods and services are constantly appearing but inevitably become scarce almost at once, which means that only a few people can enjoy them.[14]

The actual price of goods in the Soviet Union is quite low, since prices are controlled and subsidized. But the average Russian works about three times as long for the same goods as Americans do. The comparisons are in minutes of work time to purchase goods or services:[15]

	Washington	**Moscow**
One loaf of rye bread	18	11
One chicken	18	189
One grapefruit	6	112
1 liter of milk	4	20
1 liter of red wine	37	257
One head of cabbage	7	7
3 ounces of tea	10	36
Car wash	40	139
Bar of soap	3	17
Bus fare, 2 miles	7	3
Baby-sitter, per hour	44	279
First-class postage stamp	2	3
Men's haircut	62	34
Pair of jeans	240	3,360
Pair of men's shoes	360	2,220
Washing machine	2,760	10,620

The average Soviet wage is about $3,800 a year (since rubles are nonconvertible, no one is really sure; some estimate that in purchasing power, it is about half the "official" level). The average compact car there costs about $12,700, and a color television set costs about $1,100. An apt comparison is with the German Democratic Republic (East Germany) and Czechoslovakia, major socialist allies of the Soviet Union. Their overall economic performance is inferior to the Soviet Union's, but their GNP per capita is about $2,000 more. They are willing to spend more for consumer goods, so lacking in the USSR.

Privilege in the Classless Society

The orthodox Marxist view holds that class divisions are rooted in private property. Since private property exists at best as a minor component of the economy, there can be no classes. Obviously there are. The solution to the problem of privilege in the classless society is the notion of "positional differentiation." This arcane phrase is meant to describe inequalities based on one's status with respect to the resources of production. The intelligentsia, a formally acknowledged status, can legitimately earn more than manual laborers, especially since their relationship is "nonantagonistic," as compared with the deadly contest between bourgeoisie and workers in capitalist society. Even the distinction according to one's position in production is a transitional phase on the way to pure socialism.

In any case, no amount of personal wealth is equal to the status attained by party membership in most socialist countries. The "new class" has appropriated for itself as much of the amenities of life as possible in stagnant economies. Irrespective of any differences in earning capacity based on an occupational hierarchy, there is such a sharp cleavage between the minority in the party and the majority on the outside looking in that this basic distinction partly eradicates all other potential divisions:

> The coercive activities of the party apparatus and the secret police permeate all spheres of life to such a degree that fear of the Party becomes the central fact of existence for most men and their families. Under these conditions, when people are continually threatened with the possibility of arrest, sentiments of a class character do not emerge. Differences in social background, income, occupation and the like, have a greatly reduced influence on behavior and outlook in the face of more pressing anxieties and concerns.[16]

Ironically, a Marxist interpretation is compatible with the powerful, monopolistic role of the party. Marxism teaches that control of the means of production is the essential ingredient for economic and political power. In capitalist societies, the owners are private sector firms and corporations. But in a socialist economy, ownership of the means of production is vested in the party. Therefore, whereas the actual composition of the ruling class may vary, there is a ruling class and it is *not* the proletariat. The party, the "vanguard of the proletariat," is becoming less representative of the class over which it assumed guardianship.

TABLE 11.4 Education of Members of the Soviet Communist Party (%)

	Nongraduates	High School Graduates	Some College	College Graduates
1927	90	9	1	0
1937	81	12	2	5
1947	68	22	2	8
1957	62	33	4	12
1967	49	32	3	16
1977	34	39	2	25

SOURCE: After Jerry F. Hough, *Soviet Leadership in Transition* (Washington, D.C.: Brookings Institution, 1980), p. 28. Reprinted with permission.

The party is transforming itself from an instrument for the recruitment of peasants and workers into an agency for the retention of the more educated strata. One-fourth of the party membership consists of college graduates, as compared with only about 15 percent of the total population. The highly educated are significantly overrepresented (see Table 11.4).

The irony is that the Marxist requirement that the emergence of a classless society depends on the subjection of market forces to political control means that control of the means of production enhances the power of the party and the bureaucracy. Centrally planned economies have merely substituted one elite for another.

The party *nomenklatura* is the framework through which privilege is dispensed. A continuation of old czarist table of ranks, the *nomenklatura*, a list of ranks, consists of positions filled directly by the party or with party approval. About 23 million people in the USSR have *nomenklatura* jobs (about 9 percent of the total population). There are three levels of *nomenklatura* employees, the most privileged being those directly appointed by the Politburo and Central Committee of the party.[17]

Perhaps a million people (2 million including families and relatives) hold these much sought plums. The cabinet ministers, directors of the various parts of the Academy of Sciences, editors of the party publications, party bosses in the republics, deputy ministers, high-ranking military leaders, and key ambassadors are the most visible examples of the privileged class. The *nomenklatura* system makes distributions of real wealth, as opposed to reported income, more tentative than in the West. The ways in which *nomenklatura* employees can rise above many of the shortages, lines, and frustrations that make life onerous are numerous and varied.

The Conspicuous Consumer

Private stores for the *nomenklatura* are at three levels of opulence. The Bureau of Passes, on Granovsky Street in Moscow, is the most infamous example of "members only" shopping opportunities for the elite. The Central Committee, the staff, and families of members and staff can shop there. Although few outsiders have been inside the Bureau of Passes, it is said to be an all-purpose shopping center, with clothes comparable to those in European department stores and food or wine comparable to those in American supermarkets. For the privileged few, this opportunity is worth a fortune. One can find "Russian delicacies like caviar, smoked salmon, the best canned sturgeon, export brands of vodka or unusual vintages of Georgian and Moldavian wines, choice meat, [and] fresh fruits and vegetables in winter that are rarely available elsewhere."[18]

The Granovsky Street shop is duplicated by those for deputy ministers at Government House; those who joined the party before 1930 have their shop on Komsomol Lane; marshals (generals or admirals), scientists, authors, athletes, Heroes of Socialist Labor, and entertainers have their own shops. The availability of and prices for goods vary inversely with their status in the hierarchy. At the very top are unlimited supplies at or below cost. Also, the "Kremlin ration" (about $800 a month) is tacked on to officially listed salaries of the party elite, meaning that they can feed their families luxuriously without touching their income. Even excluding the opportunities for getting ahead without using money, the income of a member of the Central Committee is about 10 times that of the average Soviet citizen.[19] Since the maximum tax rate is 13 percent of income over 200 rubles, little equality is gained here. Not only is the tax regressive, but the *nomenklatura* pay tax only on their "official" salary (excluding the Kremlin ration).

The restricted outlet or restricted-distribution stores are a step down. These are either special sections of public stores, such as GUM, the large department store on Red Square, or home delivery services. They service the staff of major cabinet ministries, the KGB, and directors of various state-owned industries. There are about 100 such restricted-distribution stores. Normally, no money changes hands. Shoppers have a specified quota marked on their identification cards.

Finally, the *beriozhka* shops are open to anyone with hard (Western) currency. They are popular with tourists who have these currencies and are frequented by artists, musicians, athletes, members of diplomatic staffs, and others likely to travel. Also, "certificate rubles" are issued to Soviet citizens who have earned money abroad. They are supposed to be changed back into rubles but are generally traded at 8 to 1 for regular rubles on the black market; they are also accepted in the *beriozhkas*.

Housing

Given the chronic shortage of housing, decent accommodation is almost as important as access to consumer goods. Although the official living space guides specify 9 square meters, the actual allocation is about half that. The higher the rank, the better the quality is the rule for urban dwellers. The desire to live in comfortable surroundings is so great that the Soviet leadership has used the loss of a good apartment as a threat, not only against citizens who are toying with dissent but also against unsuccessful participants in international competitions. Olympic losers and defeated chess masters have found their Moscow apartments reallocated upon their return.

For the most desirable flats, money is not enough. Middle-rank professionals could not afford them if it were. But cooperatives may be formed, paying the state 40 percent of construction costs and the remainder at a very low interest rate paid back monthly. The monthly payments are about 50 rubles. One step up the hierarchy are apartments built for those just below the top; they are not on the Central Committee but are likely to be marshals or internationally known entertainers or authors. Their apartments are provided either free or for nominal rent.

But for those who can shop at Granovsky Street, there is an additional opportunity: the dacha, the second vacation home outside the city. There are two kinds of dachas: the state-owned ones, which are free, and the privately owned ones. The private ones are better, but neither can be purchased unless official approval is given, and they can be reclaimed at any time.

Medical Care

Medical attention is free, and prescription drugs are very cheap. However, the quality of medical attention is not very good. The hospitals are overcrowded and dirty, and the level of skill is inadequate. Much is made of the fact that most Russian physicians are women; less is said about their level of payment, about 100 rubles a month, less than factory workers. It is not surprising that high-level *nomenklatura* employees do not frequent public hospitals. The Ministry of Health maintains the Fourth Directorate, a private network of clinics. The right to register with these hospitals comes with the job. At the apex is the Central Committee's own hospital, which rivals Western ones in the technology of treatment and in the physical environment.

Money

Many of these valuable resources do not involve money; indeed, the Soviet system continues to discourage people from enhancing their financial status. Efforts to legalize small-scale private enterprise have been frustrated. To enter the small open market, an entrepreneur must also have a state job and may not employ anyone beyond the immediate family. All earned income must be deposited in a state-owned bank, and a modest increase is likely to bring a visit by the KGB.

Even though money is not as important as in capitalist societies, Soviet officials have been engaging in graft, some serious, some not, since the overthrow of the czar. Leonid Brezhnev, the party leader throughout the 1970s, was tolerant of graft, but Mikhail Gorbachev has made a serious effort to reign in the bureaucracy. Central planning, as we have seen, encourages corruption. The Soviet bureaucracy is not as corrupt as those in Latin America or Africa, but its systemic graft is greater than that of the industrial democracies. In the central Asian Soviet republics, bribery arrests have been increasing, and executions are becoming less rare, if not actually routine. A typical scam is the overreporting of crops, billing Moscow for nonexistent cotton or grain, and upon receiving the money for the fictitious crop, using it to buy dachas or Zils (the huge black limousines favored by high-ranking party officials). Smuggling caviar is also popular.

But only people with the right connections can build private wealth, and only those with access to more interesting arrays of consumer goods can use it. As Hedrick Smith observed, "Money in the Soviet system is nothing. You have to be able to spend it. A Central Committee member does not get much pay but he gets all kinds of things free."[20]

The existence of privilege in the world's first communist society should not be taken to mean that the USSR is much different from the capitalist countries. The very fact that income distribution in the USSR is similar to that of industrial democracies is the more important point. As we have seen, the Soviet Union has pursued elite advantage with vigor, while simultaneously promulgating an egalitarian ideology. Except for the elite, life is grim, but few die of starvation as is true of genuinely backward economies. Medical attention is usually available, although the quality is frequently appalling. *Nobody* is officially unemployed, although the number of people living in metro stops in Moscow seems about the same as in New York. Of course, the housing of most Russians is below the standard we would expect to find among the families living in poverty in the United States, and unemployment is eliminated by creating jobs for which there is no justification (attendants on every floor of a hotel, innumerable street sweepers, transportation conductors, and so on).

Conditions of work are better now than they were in the 1950s, and the workweek, as in the West, is now five days. But alcoholism is rampant and worker safety is neglected. Unlike most of the European centrally planned economies and industrial democracies, life expectancy in the Soviet Union is declining. Inadequate medical care accounts for some of this decline, as do excessive smoking and drinking (both indications of increased alienation). Infant mortality is increasing because women have babies late (they are waiting for housing), and again medical care is inadequate.

What disturbs most Soviet citizens is the ability of the *nomenklatura* class to avoid the grim everyday life of the average person. In the United States, as in most capitalist countries, nobody makes much of a case for imposed equality. We generally agree that people who make more money deserve it. But in the worker's state, inequality is simply not justified:

> The resentment of wage and status inequality is by no means unique to the Soviet Union. It exists in every society, noncommunist as well as communist. But the unmitigated hypocrisy that pervades the Soviet ideology, and the effort to convey a sense that somehow the Soviet Union, because it is a "workers' state," has eliminated inequality, exacerbates the frustration.[21]

The Poor and Unequal

But what of the nations, generally poor, that have the least equitable income distribution? If the USSR and the United States are among the leaders, how must life be in less fortunate circumstances?

Liberia, with the worst inequality score, serves well as an example. Beginning in 1816, American philanthropic organizations began to raise money to return freed slaves to Africa. Refused admission to Sierra Leone, they settled nearby on the West African coast and, in 1847, became a republic. The Liberians became a grotesque parody of the American south by oppressing the indigenous population, which they called aborigines. The "Americo-Liberian" descendants became an aristocracy. The pre–Civil War South was reproduced as faithfully as possible:

> They controlled the commerce, ran the government and sent their sons abroad to be educated. The men wore morning coats and top hats, drank bourbon, joined the Masons and formed a secret society called Poro that acknowledged no African heritage.[22]

It was ruled peacefully with uneventful transfer of power until a violent coup in 1980, engineered by a semiliterate sergeant, Samuel K. Doe. But nothing much was done about the economy of a country that many people have regarded as a joke. It used United States currency and named its subdivisions after American states. The ruling class was firmly allied with the United States, especially to Firestone and other multi-national corporations, and it kept its aborigines firmly under foot. The great discrepancy in income between the ruling class and the aborigines explains Liberia's poor record in income distribution. The strong, possibly dominant position of the American multinationals has done nothing to alleviate the problem. The 1980 coup was ostensibly begun to give the aborigines more opportunity to participate in the economy and in government, but nothing has come of it. Most of the economy is owned by multinationals and the government, making the reduction of inequality difficult. Doe is really quite stupid and brutal. (An economic adviser, educated in the United States, tried to persuade Doe to raise the price of gasoline. When Doe balked, he explained, "You don't sign this paper, country go blooey." Doe understood.)

INCOME GROWTH AND STABILITY

The most growth is enjoyed by market economies and by polyarchies. Central planning and political repression do not produce economic well-being. In Table 11.2, we noted that as countries moved away from market economies and toward totalitarianism, their economic performance deteriorated. But within the market economies and polyarchies, there are variations in economic management. If one considers economic growth, economic stability (steady growth), rates of inflation, rates of unemployment, balances of trade, and economic diversification since 1950, the best-performing economies are these:

Country	Corporatism	Economic System
1. Japan	High	Inclusive capitalist
2. Switzerland	High	Inclusive capitalist
3. Norway	High	Inclusive mixed capitalist
4. West Germany	Medium	Inclusive capitalist
5. Austria	High	Inclusive mixed capitalist
6. United States	Low	Inclusive capitalist
7. Finland	Medium	Inclusive mixed capitalist
8. France	Low	Inclusive capitalist
9. Netherlands	Medium	Inclusive mixed capitalist
10. Sweden	High	Inclusive mixed capitalist

The countries with the worst economies are these:

Country	Economic system
1. Ghana	Inclusive capitalist-statist
2. Zaire	Noninclusive capitalist-statist
3. Nicaragua	Noninclusive mixed socialist
4. Niger	Noninclusive capitalist
5. Zambia	Noninclusive mixed socialist
6. Peru	Noninclusive capitalist-statist
7. Bolivia	Noninclusive capitalist-statist
8. Chile	Inclusive capitalist
9. El Salvador	Inclusive capitalist
10. Jamaica	Inclusive capitalist-statist

Characteristics of Successful Economies

We discussed *corporatism* as a means of regulating group conflict. Corporatism describes a governmental process whereby bureaucracies assist in the creation of private business and labor organizations and accord access selectively to the ones they favor. The essence of the system is the overt incorporation of private organizations into the economic planning process, a sort of functional representation. Economic policy and planning is characterized by cooperation between public bureaucracies and private organizations. The fact that Switzerland and Japan—by any standard the world's healthiest economies—are also corporatist suggests perhaps that a market economic system with substantial bureaucratic intervention is compatible with a healthy economy while a more extreme socialist planning model is not. Among the least corporatist governments, only France and the United States make the list. Corporatism need not require a heavy investment of government resources; Japan and Switzerland are both vigorously corporatist—in that their bureaucracies cooperate with interest group—but neither's government makes a major contribution to gross national product.

The top 10 countries are also thriving democracies, as evidenced by the positive relationship between political participation and a healthy economy. Democracy does not "cause" growth, but democracy requires a stable economy. As Diamond explains:

> Perhaps the most common generalization linking political systems to other aspects of society has been that democracy is related to the state of economic development. The more well-to-do a nation, the greater the chances that it will sustain democracy.[23]

Why is this the case? Do nations develop wealth, through capitalism, and democracy simultaneously? Does one "cause" the other, and if so, which came first? Is there a causal element common to both?

Economic Growth and Inequality

When economies improve, do all citizens benefit? Does a "rising tide lift all boats"? The problem of growth and equity (which is not the same as wealth and equity) was given its major focus by Simon Kuznets in the mid-1950s. He proposed a law of income growth and development; as economic growth continues, there is an initial rise in inequality and then a leveling off and ultimately a decline in inequality.[24]

Some of the capitalist societies of Europe and North America seem to have followed this pattern, as have the European centrally planned economies. But the evidence is mixed. What is not in dispute is the grim reality of everyday life as today's rich nations developed. The industrial revolution (from about 1790 to the end of the nineteenth century), harsh and cruel, produced a sharp and tenacious rise in inequality, especially in England, the leading developing nation. Unlike most of Europe, English industrial development did not occur around established cities; rather, tiny villages suddenly became swollen by massive migration from the country. Birmingham, Leeds, and Manchester, formerly bucolic villages, tripled in population and became instant industrial slums. Life was brutal. Karl Marx's theories about exploitation and capitalism were developed from his observations of the *English* working class. Charles Dickens's realistic novels *(Great Expectations, Little Dorrit, Oliver Twist)* captured the popular imagination by describing the brutal, almost unbelievable squalor of working-class life:

> Two rooms, seven inmates . . . dirty flock bedding in living-room placed on box and two chairs. Smell of room from dirt and bad air unbearable . . . there is no water supply in the house, the eight families having to share one water-tap . . . with eight other families who are living in the other houses. The grating under this water-tap is used for disposal of human excreta.[25]

Under such conditions, it is hardly surprising that infant mortality was half again as much in the north as in London. Conditions were comparable to those of Africa today. The only missing ingredient in Hobbes's dreaded state of nature was the solitary life—for working-class English families developed a sense of class loyalty in excess of the European working classes.

> By the 1830's the character of the British working class as a tribe apart, with its own values, had matured. These values were highly collectivist . . . with an intolerance towards the eccentric or individualist. . . . And this character was to endure down the generations, along with the bitter ancestral memories passed from father to son to grandson to great grandson.[26]

But the evidence that actual income was becoming more skewed toward the rich is, even with Kuznets's own data, unclear. In the United Kingdom, for example, the proportion of income received by the richest 5 percent consistently declined, both before and after taxes (from 48 percent in 1880 to 18 percent in 1957).[27] A similar pattern was found in the United States, Germany, Norway, Sweden, Denmark, and the Netherlands. But we do not know the pattern of income development before 1880, presumably the midpoint in development for these countries. It is probable that inequality did indeed increase until about 1880 and then began its decline.

But what of today's lesser developed countries? The evidence is far from clear, and the data are far from uniform. However, here is an approximation of what is taking place:[28]

Country	Economic Performance	Trends in Inequality
Argentina	Poor	Inequality rose
Bangladesh	Poor	Inequality rose
Brazil	Fair	Inequality rose
Costa Rica	Fair	Inequality fell
El Salvador	Poor	Inequality rose
India	Poor	Little change
Mexico	Fair	Inequality rose
Pakistan	Fair	Inequality fell
Philippines	Fair	Inequality rose
Singapore	Good	Inequality fell
Sri Lanka	Fair	Inequality fell
Taiwan	Good	Inequality fell

There really are no discernable trends, with the exception of the outstanding performance of the two Asian countries, Taiwan and Singapore. But inequality also fell in several less impressive economies, Pakistan and Costa Rica. We can say, however, that poor countries rarely reduce income inequalities. Further, the case of Taiwan does not support the "things will get worse before they get better" thesis. Inequality fell consistently as wealth increased and began to level off in the 1980s. Although not much more reduction of inequality can be expected, Taiwan is "in the admirable position of combining rapid economic growth, sharply reduced inequality, and widespread alleviation of poverty."[29] The same can be said for Singapore (but not South Korea).

Economy and Government

While planned economies are barriers to growth, this is probably more due to the incompetence of government officials than to any inherent flaws in planning. The rapidly expanding economies of Asia do not resemble Western capitalist countries; Japan, Taiwan, Singapore, and South Korea are *guided* capitalist systems. While they prefer, with some exceptions, not to nationalize, they are disinclined to allow private business to do whatever it chooses.

Guided Capitalism

Both European and Asian corporatist states stress public-private sector cooperation. There is more governmental guidance in Asia, more fine-tuning a capitalist economy largely run by the private sector. The intervention generally takes the form of *market manipulation*. There is more government tinkering with tax incentives for the development of new products, for example. Since Asian countries lagged behind European industrial democracies, there was more need for such incentives. Given the commitment to the use of the market, with implementation and compliance largely in private hands, Asian corporatist systems, much like their European counterparts, stress close coordination between public bureaucracy and private business. Chalmers Johnson writes:

> This cooperation is achieved through innumerable, continuously operating forums for coordinating views and investment plans, sharing international commercial intelligence, making adjustments to conform to the business cycle or other changes in the economic environment, deciding on the new industries needed in order to maintain international competitive ability, and spreading both the wealth and the burdens equitably.[30]

Asian corporatist systems differ from European ones not so much in the commitment to collaboration between bureaucracies and interest groups but in the diversity and range of groups given legitimacy and in the relationship between bureaucracies and political parties.

European corporatist systems are generally willing to grant legitimacy exclusively to business and labor, and then only to the peak associations (associations that represent all or most of a segment of the economy: auto manufacturers, for example) given quasi-official status in their governments. In Asia, only business has acquired legitimacy, and given the priorities of the time, various kinds of businesses drop in and out of favor. There are, as Johnson suggests, innumerable opportunities for collaboration. But we saw in Chapter 6 that only in Japan is there the institutional legitimacy, the creation of formal mechanisms of exchange, that is typical of European corporatist governments. In Japan, the most respected business organization, the *Keidanren,* is in such tight coordination with the Ministry of International Trade and Industry (MITI), that the line between public and private is indistinguishable.

There are just as many opportunities to avoid collusion in Taiwan, South Korea, or Singapore. In these Asian systems, peak associations are more beholden to the bureaucracy. In Taiwan and South Korea, they have not been able, given the more authoritarian nature of the state, to become as independent; they are not, however, as subservient as critics suggest.[31]

In all Asian systems, peak associations operate as auxiliary governments; in the authoritarian governments, they are agents of implementation. They are not, in the bureaucratically preferred perfect world, the source of "pressure." In reality, successful economic policy there depends on a compliant business community in much the same way that European corporate systems depend on a docile labor movement.

As these Asian nations continue their economic progress, they demonstrate the compatibility of rational planning and advancing economies. Among industrially developed nations, while the heavy-handed planning of the Eastern bloc has demonstrated that the days of its utility are passed, less severe forms of intervention are routine. In France, for example, the state, even when its elected leaders are in favor of "privatization," has always been a major player in the game of economics. France's most easily recognized product, Renault automobiles, is produced by a nationalized industry that receives direct government subsidies of about 1.5 billion francs annually. Airbus, the European corporation that manufactures commercial aircraft, receives direct government subsidies from three European countries.

CULTURE AND DEVELOPMENT

Among the many dimensions of culture discussed in Chapter 2 was the passive as opposed to the achievement-oriented culture. These distinctions are important for understanding why many nations cannot develop. Although many of the reasons for failure are institutional or historical, we have seen that a major roadblock is the attitudes and behavior of leaders. They can try, if they choose, to create a just and fair economic system, to allocate as many resources as possible toward the goal of universal education, to extend life by commitment to public health, and to offer incentives for achievement.[32]

Achieving cultures achieve. A particularly sensitive notion—the suggestion that people are not entirely helpless and not entirely blameless for their misfortune—conjures notions of racism. But cultural traditions are not genetically transmitted, and hence they can be changed. Carlos Rangel's work on Latin America explains how such traditions develop and places Latin American culture closer to the passive end of the continuum. He believes that colonization by Spain was an unfortunate circumstance, since Spanish culture emphasized

> antisocial individualism, an aversion to work, and an affinity for violence and authoritarianism. Slaves did much of the hard work in the colonies, leading to the infamous hacienda system, which continued the tradition of exploitation. Slavery is a dangerous institution for development, since it creates an "absurd prestige of idleness."[33]

Add to this institutional aberration the passivity encouraged by the Roman Catholic church (with the "afterlife" righting wrongs), and the ingredients for cultural deterioration are in place: "Unlike the traditional attitude of predominately Protestant societies, work is not thought to be a positive value; it is regarded as a necessary evil, something people must do to live, but something to be avoided."[34]

When we ask, as we do often, why Taiwan or South Korea but not Mexico, some cultural explanations merit our attention, especially since Mexico has far more natural resources than any of the Asian countries:

> Lack of both an advanced infrastructure and a supportive public policy does not fully explain why Mexico has yet to blossom into another Taiwan or Korea. The East Asian powerhouses all share a Confucian culture that emphasizes work, savings, education, social harmony and a positive view of the future. . . . In Mexico values and attitudes derive from traditional Hispanic culture, which nurtures authoritarianism, excessive individualism, mistrust, corruption, and a fatalistic world view, all of which work against economic progress. That culture also attaches a low value to work, particularly among the elite, and discourages entrepreneurship, thus further braking economic growth. Mexico is not going to develop into another Taiwan because cultural aspects of development do matter. The stereotype of a lazy Mexican is terribly wrong. But there is not the commitment to the work ethic that you find in Chinese culture.[35]

The lesson is that no economic or political system by itself, whether it is a market or a centrally planned one, is the key to success.[36] If the current vogue of market solutions to development problems neglects the fact than no system is better than the people who operate it, the results will be much the same as in the past. Nevertheless, the market no longer appears as the creature of oppression:

> The intellectual battle between the two broad schools of thought—call them state-activists and market-optimists—is more or less over. Most developing countries have tried state-activism and found it wanting. A dash for industrialization left them with lots of steel mills, hydro-electric plants, national airlines and multi-layered bureaucracies, but

far less economic growth than promised. South Korea, Taiwan, Hong Kong, and a few others which shunned that model and gave markets a chance to work have prospered beyond anybody's expectations.[37]

A market economy is not the same thing as an absolutely laissez-faire, survival-of-the-fittest economic system. The successful developers are guided market systems; the government intervenes to ensure a well-educated work force, paid for by the state, through college and graduate school. These governments strengthen market forces but do not subvert them.

Worldly Ascetics

Max Weber, one of the first to inquire into the causes of democracy, believed that both capitalism and democracy were consequences of the Protestant Reformation. He wrote of "rationalization," a process whereby the assumptions of one set of institutions (in this case, the Protestant stress on individual responsibility) is transferred to another. Within the domain of Protestantism, Weber believed that the doctrine of predestination was an especially apt example of rationalization. People who believed that God had predestined them for a fate either in heaven or hell would, ironically, work as hard as possible in order to come to terms with the unending anxiety about their afterlife. If they were successful, they took it to mean that they had been spared perdition: would God bless with success those whom he had condemned?[38]

A harsh doctrine, predestination contributed to the rigid rules of the Puritans, for whom life was a struggle, mercifully short, with no clergy to grant forgiveness. The removal of the clergy as the agent of man in pleading a case before God (carried to its extreme in the selling of indulgences) left man alone. There was no confession, no simple penance for sin; although his fate was predetermined, man had only himself to blame or praise for his worldly condition. Here, then, is Weber's paradox: solace can be found only in work, not for the acquisition of wealth, but for its own sake. Presumably, if the worker were indeed blessed, capital accumulation would be a consequence of unremitting labor. Thus wealth was an indication of God's pleasure and, so long as it was not used for personal self-indulgence, was to be judged by its fruits. Traditional Christianity's suspicion of wealth was transformed. It was no longer as hard for a rich person to enter the kingdom of heaven as for a camel to pass through the eye of a needle.

The "spirit of capitalism" was hard work. Those who accepted the spirit of capitalism were thought to be "worldly ascetics," a phrase Weber used to distinguish capitalism from traditional ascetic societies, which rejected worldly goods.

Weber never actually developed his notes into a precise theoretical formulation, and there is abundant evidence that he overestimated the uniqueness of Protestantism. He was especially wrong in his assessment of Eastern doctrines, principally Confucianism and Buddhism, as impediments to capitalism. But the question is a good one: What is the relationship between culture and economic life? Even though Weber erred in interpreting Confucianism, he was right in asserting that not all cultures are congenial to the spirit of capitalism.

Confucianism: Today's "Protestant Reformation"?

Just as Weber believed that the Protestant Reformation was a precursor of modern capitalism, many theorists believe that modern Confucianism is especially adept at fostering strong economies. When the linkage between Confucianism and capitalism is claimed, we generally think of the "four tigers" of Asia: Japan, Taiwan, South Korea, and Singapore. However, to speak of Asia as "Confucian" is not the same as to describe a country, say Austria, as Roman Catholic. Confucianism is not a religion (although it was made the "official state belief system" for the Han dynasty in 136 B.C.).[39]

The compatibility of Confucianism with formal religions and political philosophies is fundamental to understanding why Asian countries can be so shaped by it. Jesuit philosophers, proponents of the European Enlightenment, Voltaire, Montesquieu, and even Marx have owed a debt to Confucius, even though they have very little else in common. Confucianism is not a formal theory, like Marxism; rather, it is an abstract guide to a way of life. Roderick MacFarquhar explains Confucianism as a "cause" of industrial accomplishments:

> Confucianism has been the ideology par excellence of state cohesion, and it is that cohesion which makes post-Confucian states particularly formidable. . . . Comet-like, they trail an incandescent tail of post-Confucian East Asians: Koreans from South Korea, Chinese from Taiwan, Singapore, and Hong Kong. . . . The significant coincidence is culture, the shared heritage of centuries of inculcation with Confucianism. The tenets of Confucianism still provide an inner compass to most east Asians. . . . All east Asian peoples, however they met the challenge of the west, benefited from their Confucian heritage. Since Confucianism was essentially an agnostic ideology, concerned with the management of the visible world, the post-Confucians experienced little of the spiritual angst that afflicted Hindus, Moslems and indeed Christians in their collision with the "materialism" of the industrial revolution.[40]

Peter Berger explains that the type of Confucianism that permeates Asian politics

> is not that of the Mandarins of Imperial China, but Confucian derived (or at least Confucian legitimated) values motivating very ordinary and unlearned people—petty entrepreneurs in Taipei, say, or bank clerks in Manila (or for that matter, San Francisco).[41]

Nevertheless, Taiwanese education includes compulsory courses in Confucian ideology, and when Prime Minister Lee of Singapore felt that his country was slipping into degeneracy (the opposition had elected one legislator), he called for a reinstitution of Confucian values, the "rhetoric expected of a Confucian statesman."[42] Efforts to emulate Taiwan's curriculum ensued.

As a cultural tradition, Confucianism is as varied as the politics, economics, and history of Austria and Mexico, both Roman Catholic. The Asian countries had their "separate versions of Confucianism, which increasingly diverged as each country followed a different path to political modernization."[43] The description of the different paths depends on who is describing them. James Hsiung writes, "Compared with China, both Korea and Japan were incompletely Confucianized."[44] Pye concludes that "the evolution of Confucianism . . . produced . . . distinct political cultures."[45]

Confucianism, then, is a shorthand way of referring to the broader notion of political culture. Hung Chao-tai explains, "Confucianism as we now know it has absorbed ingredients of Taoism and Buddhism."[46] An apt analogy is the Protestant Reformation. Just as Protestantism revoked some of the more dogmatic aspects of Catholicism without renouncing Christianity, so did Japan develop substantial modifications in the doctrinal teachings of Confucianism without eliminating its essence.[47]

The economies of Confucian countries are less conflictual than those of more individualistic cultures. The proportion of the work force in unions is very low. Taiwan prohibited strikes, by force of martial law, until 1988, but there were scattered work stoppages before and after the change in legislation. Singapore also outlaws strikes, while Japan does not. Yet work stoppages rarely occur in these countries, because of prohibition or disinclination.[48] South Korea, an unusually combative country by Confucian standards (attributed by Pye to persistent problems of political legitimacy and the inability of a leader to earn much popular respect),[49] is the obvious exception. They all have low unemployment, low inflation, and high GNP growth.

Can the Pacific Rim's success, then, be credited to Confucianism? This conclusion seems hard to accept, unless we keep in mind its secular, cultural, informal nature. A way of political life dominated by a meritocracy seems an efficient way to govern, unless we are concerned with accountability (as Confucian scholars were not, except at the broadest level of a social contract). Thomas Gold identifies the cultural characteristics that contribute directly to a booming economy as "ambition for self and family; high value on education and learning by copying exemplars; frugality; the family as an economic unit; and entrepreneurship."[50] Ronald Inglehart asserts that

> the Confucian cultural tradition . . . is an important element underlying the economic dynamism of certain portions of Asia. During the period from 1965 to 1984, 5 of the 10 fastest-growing nations in the world were countries shaped by Confucian and Buddhist traditions: Singapore, South Korea, Hong Kong, Taiwan, and Japan. . . . Moreover, three more of the top 20 countries had significant Chinese minorities that in each case played disproportionately important economic roles: Malaysia, Thailand, and Indonesia. Finally, immigrants of East Asian origin have shown disproportionately high rates of economic achievement throughout Southeast Asia and in the United States, Canada, and Western Europe. It is difficult to avoid the conclusion that the Confucian cultural tradition is conducive to economic achievement today.[51]

However, once an economy is developed, it may become less conducive to materialist values. Inhabitants of the wealthiest countries tend to be the least concerned about physical or material well-being yet simultaneously express the greatest satisfaction with life; publics with the most materialist views of life are found in the high-growth, not-yet-rich countries.[52]

FOR FURTHER CONSIDERATION

1. Summarize the relationship between wealth, political systems, economic systems, and income distribution.
2. What is the *nomenklatura* in the USSR?

3. In what countries, as the economy grew, did inequality *decline*. What explanation can you offer for this ''counter-intuitive'' occurrence.
4. Why might money not be the best measure of well-being in the USSR?

For the More Adventurous

1. How does the recent shift in the Chinese concept of private property influence the world view of Marx's economic theory? Now, examine the proliferation of social welfare programs in Western industrial democracies. What does that signal for Adam Smith's argument? Can either man be said to be ''correct'' when his theory is viewed in operation?
2. What changes have the Soviets recently made to combat the problem of income inequality? What changes, if any, can the United States government leaders make to reduce inequality after viewing the Soviet attempts? What does this say about differences between the two countries?
3. Compare the Swiss political, governmental, and economic system with that of the United States. What do they have in common? In which areas are they most different? Repeat the process for Switzerland and Japan. Examine each country, for the past decade, on these dimensions: GNP per capital growth, GNP per capita, unemployment, public debt, and inflation rate. *International Living* (January, 1987) ranks—with regard to overall quality of life— The United States first, Switzerland second, and Japan seventh. Read figure 2, p. 1208 in Ronald Inglehart's ''Renaissance of Political Culture,'' *American Political Science Review, 82* (December, 1988). Can you reconcile some of the apparent contradictions that manifest themselves in that figure?
4. Do you believe the book's explanation for the difference between developing countries in Asia and developing countries throughout the rest of the world to be correct? What part do you find most persuasive? Least persuasive?

NOTES

1. Population Crisis Committee, *Human Suffering Index* (Washington, D.C., 1987).
2. *International Living,* January 1987, pp. 6–7.
3. *The Economist,* May 13, 1984, p. 13. The original ranking included climate, which, as it is presumably beyond government control, I omitted.
4. This analysis excludes the oil-exporting Middle Eastern countries.
5. For our discussion, we will use the data from World Bank, *World Development Report, 1988* (New York: Oxford University Press, 1988), and Robert E. Ward, *The Political Economy of Income distribution* (New York: Elsevier, 1978).
6. John Kenneth Galbraith, *The Anatomy of Power* (Boston: Houghton Mifflin, 1983), p. 87.
7. Quoted in Steven Weisnau, ''China Moderates Marxism,'' *New York Times,* December 9, 1988, p. A5.
8. Robert E. Lane, ''Market Justice, Political Justice,'' *American Political Science Review 80* (June 1986): 385.
9. Charles E. Lindblom, *Politics and Markets* (New York: Basic Books, 1979), p. 266.
10. Freedom is measured on the scale developed in Raymond D. Gastil, *Freedom in the World* (New York: Freedom House, 1988), pp. 30–34.
11. Lindblom, *Politics and Markets,* p. 266.
12. Scott Eagan, ''Gorbachev Announces Candidates for Soviet Offices,'' *New York Times,* January 9, 1989, p. 2.
13. Carmelo Mesa-Lago, *The Economy of Socialist Cuba* (Albuquerque: University of New Mexico Press, 1981), pp. 141–174.

14. Roy A. Medvedev, *On Socialist Democracy* (New York: Knopf, 1975), p. 229.
15. Esther Fern, "Everyday Life in the Soviet Union," *New York Times*, June 11, 1988, p. A4.
16. Frank Parkin, *Class Inequality and Political Order* (New York: Praeger, 1971), pp. 138–139.
17. Mervyn Matthews, *Privilege in the Soviet Union* (London: George Allen & Unwin, 1978), p. 34.
18. Hedrick Smith, *The Russians* (New York: Times Books, 1983), p. 30.
19. Michael Voslensky, *Nomenklatura* (London: Bodley Head, 1983), p. 184.
20. Smith, *The Russians*, p. 50.
21. Marshall Goldman, *The USSR in Crisis* (New York: Norton, 1983), p. 102–103.
22. David Lamb, *The Africans* (New York: Random House, 1982), p. 125.
23. Gary Diamond et al., "Democracy in Developing Countries: Facilitating and Obstructing Factors," in *Freedom in the World*, ed. Raymond Gestil (New York: Freedom House, 1988), p. 225.
24. Simon Kuznets, "Economic Growth and Income Inequality," *American Economic Review* (March 1955) vol. 2: 1–28. Actually, Kuznets's idea—"It's going to get worse before it gets better"—is only an assumption, not a firm conclusion.
25. Charles Dickens, *Dickens' Working Notes for His Novels* (Chicago: University of Chicago Press, 1987), p. 233.
26. Correlli Barnett, *The Pride and the Fall* (New York: Free Press, 1987), p. 190.
27. See Gary S. Fields, *Poverty, Inequality, and Development* (Cambridge: Cambridge University Press, 1980), p. 78.
28. Ibid., pp. 88–92.
29. Ibid., p. 228.
30. Chalmers Johnson, *MITI and the Japanese Miracle* (Stanford: Stanford University Press, 1982), pp. 309–312.
31. Alice H. Amsden, "The State and Taiwan's Economic Development," in *Bringing the State Back In,* ed. Peter B. Evans, Dietrich Rueschemeyer, and Theda Skocpol (Cambridge: Cambridge University Press, 1986), pp. 97–98.
32. Lawrence W. Harrison, *Underdevelopment Is a State of Mind* (Lanham, Md.: University Press of America, 1985), p. 3.
33. Carlos Rangel, *The Latin Americans* (Orlando, Fla.: Harcourt Brace Jovanovich, 1977), p. 193.
34. George Foster, *Culture and Conquest* (New York: Quadrangle, 1960), p. 4.
35. Bruce Stokes, "Mexican Momentum," *National Journal*, June 20, 1987, p. 1577.
36. Aaron Wildavsky makes the same point in regard to cultures: none is totally self-contained. See Wildavsky, "Choosing Preferences by Constructing Institutions: A Cultural Theory of Preference Formation," *American Political Science Review 81* (March 1987): 3–22.
37. "Trade Routes to Prosperity," *Economist*, July 4, 1987, p. 13.
38. Max Weber, *The Protestant Ethic and the Spirit of Capitalism* (New York: Scribner, 1958). The original essay appeared in 1904 and was reprinted in 1920. Weber was preparing a revision at the time of his death. I use the 1904 text.
39. James B. Hsiung, "East Asia," in *Human Rights in East Asia,* ed. James B. Hsiung (New York: Paragon House, 1985), p. 7.
40. Roderick MacFarquhar, "The Post-Confucian Challenge," *Economist,* February 9, 1980, pp. 67–72.
41. Peter L. Berger, *The Capitalist Revolution* (New York: Basic Books, 1986), p. 158. Berger echoes with approval Robert Bellah's term, *bourgeois Confucianism*.

42. Lucian Pye, *Asian Power and Politics* (Cambridge, Mass.: Harvard University Press, 1985), p. 254.
43. Ibid., p. 55.
44. Ibid., p. 59.
45. Hsiung, "East Asia," p. 8.
46. Hung Chao-tai, "Taiwan," in Hsiung, *Human Rights*, p. 90.
47. The analogy is in Michio Morishima, *Why Has Japan "Succeeded"?* (London: Cambridge University Press, 1985), pp. 7–14.
48. See Industrial Development and Investment Center, *Labor Laws and Regulations of the Republic of China*, October 1984.
49. Pye, *Asian Power and Politics*, p. 238.
50. Thomas Gold, *State and Society in the Taiwanese Miracle* (Armonk, N.Y.: M.E. Sharpe, 1986), p. 55.
51. Ronald Inglehart, "The Renaissance of Political Culture," *American Political Science Review 82* (December 1988): 1228.
52. Ibid., p. 1225.

FOR FURTHER READING

Brown, Michael K., ed. *Remaking the Welfare State*. Philadelphia: Temple University Press, 1988.

Das Gupta, A. K. *Growth, Development, and Welfare*. New York: Basil Blackwell, 1988.

Friedman, Robert, and Neil Moshe Sherer. *Modern Welfare States*. New York: New York University Press, 1987.

Goldman, Marshall. *The USSR in Crisis*. New York: Norton, 1983. A distinguished economist tells why Gorbachev will probably lose.

Green, Philip. *The Pursuit of Inequality*. New York: Pantheon, 1981. A refutation of arguments in support of inequality, whatever the source.

Horowitz, Irving Louis, ed. *Cuban Communism*, 6th ed. New Brunswick, N.J.: Transaction Books, 1988.

Heclo, Hugh. *The Welfare State in Hard Times*. Washington, D.C.: American Political Science Association, 1985.

Lash, Scott, and John Urry. *The End of Organized Capitalism*. Madison: University of Wisconsin Press, 1987.

Levy, Frank. *Dollars and Dreams: The Changing American Income Distribution*. New York: Russell Sage Foundation, 1987. Income distribution may be a consequence of changes in the structure of society rather than an outcome of politics or policy.

Lindblom, Charles E. *Politics and Markets*. New York: Basic Books, 1979.

Morishima, Michio. *Why Has Japan "Succeeded"?* London: Cambridge University Press, 1985. One of the few dispassionate accounts of why Japan is number one.

Novak, Michael. *The Spirit of Democratic Capitalism*. New York: Simon & Schuster, 1982. An attempt to give capitalism a coherent ideology.

Pye, Lucian. *Asian Power and Politics*. Cambridge, Mass.: Harvard University Press, 1985.

Rhoads, Steven E. *The Economist's View of the World: Government, Markets, and Public Policy*. Cambridge: Cambridge University Press, 1985. Can a book dedicated to "Bananaman, Pooman-chu, and the Birdman" amount to much? Yes!

Weber, Max. *The Protestant Ethic and the Spirit of Capitalism*. New York: Scribner, 1958. (Originally published 1904.)

CHAPTER 12

Why the Poor
Are Always with Us

Reprinted by permission of UFS, Inc.

Are there aspects of political, cultural, and economic organization that the poor countries share? The inability of the poor countries to improve their status has attracted even more attention than the sudden growth of the Pacific Rim. We turn now to a discussion of the explanations of why the poor seem, apparently, to be always with us.

Like many questions for which political scientists grope for answers, this one is freighted with emotion. On the one hand, if it can be shown that poor countries are kept that way by rich ones, that rich countries exploit poor ones, then the solution to poverty cannot be addressed without redressing the dependence of rich on poor. No efforts—military aid, education, loans, technical assistance, and so on—will change the structure of poverty because it is caused by exploitation by rich nations. Poor nations are not at fault. On the other hand, if the culture, history, economics, or governmental processes of poor countries can be shown to influence poverty, poor nations are not blameless (nor are they helpless).

Most responsible social scientists do not rely on pat, simple ideologies, and the world of wealth and poverty is far more complex than these two opposing views would have us believe. West Indian novelist V. S. Naipaul writes of "those who continue to simplify the world and reduce other men to a cause, the people who substitute doctrine for knowledge and irritation for concern, the revolutionaries who visit centres of revolution with return air tickets." [1] Let us avoid Naipaul's justifiable contempt.

HISTORY AND DEPENDENCE

Without exception, the countries with the worst economies were in a colonial relationship with a European nation. In contrast, the wealthy nations were generally the colonizers. Colonies were dependent on colonizers for government and for the development of an economic infrastructure. Colonizers could, if they wished, exploit colonies, using them largely as producers of raw materials rather than encouraging them to develop their own industry and preventing or discouraging universal education. Colonizers could, if they were inclined, use colonies as dumping grounds for the least competent members of the civil service. Or they could help colonies become self-sufficient, establishing an efficient bureaucracy and raising levels of literacy. Colonial powers adopted more enlightened policies not necessarily because they were altruistic but because they regarded colonies as potential markets as well as sources of raw material.

Colonialism has more forms than is commonly realized. There are formal colonial arrangements, such as those between Britain and the American colonies, the United States and the Philippines, or Japan with Korea and Taiwan. Less structured but equally dependent internation relationships exist, for example, between the USSR and Cuba or the United States and Nicaragua (before 1979). Perhaps the classic example of de facto colonialism was the behavior of Europe toward China. The currently popular name for this sort of dependency is *neocolonialism*.

Christians and the "Heathen Chinese." Irrespective of the nature of the colonial administration, colonial powers could not resist feelings of superiority, especially when the colonies were in Asia. The infamous missionaries who swarmed over China in the 19th century were fine examples of colonizers with the "Christian duty" to bring civilization to the "heathens." The fact that China had developed an advanced civilization, with the world's first professional civil service, at a time when Europe was populated by roving bands of savages lends irony to Western arrogance, of which the following is typical:

> Believing our civilization to be superior to theirs we should endeavor to elevate the Chinese to our standard. . . . Granted that China has shown unwillingness to accept foreign advice and act on foreign suggestions, to what is such unwillingness attributed? First of all, the Chinese are a very conceited people—they will hardly allow that their condition is to be improved upon; secondly, the Chinese are a very contented people.[2]

Such arrogance was a complete about-face from the opinions of the first, Jesuit, missionaries of the 18th century, who echoed the admiration, even awe, of the Chinese first expressed by Marco Polo. Perhaps the purest expression of European racism was the Opium Wars, begun when China objected to the sale of opium by Europeans. To preserve the market for opium, the British imposed the Treaty of Nanking, requiring indemnity for seized opium, the occupation of major cities by foreign armies that were exempt from Chinese law, and the prohibition of all but a nominal import duty. Thus China was flooded with opium, armies of occupation, and cheap Western merchandise (ultimately the Chinese lost control of customs duties). By the beginning of the 20th century, Germany, France, Britain, and Russia were carving up China at a rapacious rate. The Boxer Rebellion of 1901 resulted in yet another Chinese defeat and more occupation armies.

Obviously, China was exploited. Although technically China was not a colony, it was forced into a colonial posture. The argument for dependency is that there is no incentive for colonial powers *not* to exploit—that profit and exploitation are intertwined and that a rational colonial policy therefore precludes the development of an indigenous economy. The modern example of dependency is the exploitation of Third World countries by multinational corporations rather than governments (but government policy is believed to be guided by the corporations).

Is the Chinese example a common one? Peter Berger summarizes the argument nicely:

> Decisions on national economic policy are now made outside the country and for the benefit of others. The national economy is "distorted," because its course is dictated by external needs and not by its indigenous logic. National enterprise is smothered, often to the point of "industrial infanticide"—that is, domestic industrial development is arrested in the interest of the foreign enterprises dominating the national economy.[3]

Many poor nations are dependent on richer ones for foreign trade, in many cases for the importation of technologies of production that may be unsuitable for the recipient culture. The idea that advanced capitalist countries will *invariably* exploit underdeveloped ones is based on an analysis of institutions rather than motives. Leaders of capitalist nations might be well intended, but the "historical imperative" of capitalism compels abuse. Capitalism has an inherent need to gain control of the economies of poorer countries and, in so doing, to ruin them.

However, the colonial impulse does not seem to be a capitalist monopoly. Pseudocolonial relationships, as measured by the proportion of exports and imports that go to the "colonial" power, exist between the United States and these countries:[4]

Honduras (imports, 44 percent; exports, 58 percent)
Mexico (imports, 61 percent; exports, 55 percent)
Haiti (imports, 56 percent; exports, 78 percent)
Canada (imports, 68 percent; exports, 66 percent)

They also exist between the Soviet Union and these countries:

Cuba (imports, 70 percent; exports, 64 percent)
Czechoslovakia (imports, 48 percent; exports, 45 percent)
Bulgaria (imports, 66 percent; exports, 58 percent)

Thus both major bloc leaders, the United States and the USSR, have other nations in a dependent status.

Marx believed capitalism to be synonymous with exploitation of the colonial and underdeveloped world; Lenin provided a more cogent analysis of the dangers inherent in colonialism:

> All Communist parties must give active support to the revolutionary movements of liberation; above all we must strive as far as possible to give the peasant movement a revolutionary character, to organize the peasants and all the exploited classes into the soviets, and thus bring about the closest possible union between the Communist proletariat of Western Europe and the revolutionary peasant movements of the East and of the colonial and subject countries. . . . It is the duty of the Communist International to support the revolutionary movement in the colonies and in the backward countries.[5]

Lenin spoke when actual colonialism was still a bona fide relationship between countries; today, most former colonies are politically independent. However, their political independence has not enabled them to achieve the stable economy presumed by Lenin. Once the formal colonial relationship was ended, former colonies should have been able to act in their own best interest and raise the standards of living of their people. Continued poverty in the Third World has raised doubts about the validity of Leninism and has caused a new set of dependency theories to emerge, generally subsumed under the rubric of *neo-Marxism*.

NEO-MARXISM

Neo-Marxist theories argue, like Marx and Lenin, that there can be no "capitalist development." Orthodox Marxism proposes six stages of economic development:

1. Prehistory
2. Primitive culture
3. Feudalism

4. Capitalism
5. Dictatorship of the proletariat
6. Communism or socialism

Only the last three concern us. In the capitalistic phase of economic development, the industrial revolution and growth in commerce drove population into urban areas. These peasants owned nothing except their own labor, and their incomes were artificially repressed, leaving the owners of the means of production free to accumulate enormous wealth. They did so by expropriating ''surplus value'' (the difference between the total actual value of production and the subsistence wages paid to workers; all rents, interest payments, and profits are surplus values). The ever-growing disparities between the wealth of capitalists and the impoverishment of labor would generate excruciating class conflict and a workers' revolution.

As we have seen, this revolution led to the dictatorship of the proletariat. During this period, the means of production would be nationalized (seized from the capitalist class and held in trust for the workers). Once all material needs were satisfied, the socialist stage could be reached, and each person would be rewarded ''from each according to his ability to produce, to each according to need.'' Government would no longer be necessary.

Neo-Marxism accentuates the power of multinational corporations in influencing the governments of developed countries to defend their interests in the underdeveloped world—to protect them against efforts to nationalize them, for example. Other agents of oppression are international aid organizations that owe their funding and allegiance to the wealthy nations (the World Bank, for example). Developed nations are referred to as the ''center,'' the less developed ones as the ''periphery.'' Within the periphery, established elites (landlords, government officials, and union leaders, for example) profit from the continuation of an unequal relationship.

Because of the structural needs of the center and because of the greed of elites in dependent countries, the *necessary* relationship is one that transfers profit from the periphery to the center.[6] Theontonio Dos Santos argues:

> Underdevelopment, far from constituting a state of backwardness prior to capitalism, is rather a consequence and a particular form of capitalist development known as dependent capitalism. . . . Dependence is based upon an international division of labour which allows industrial development to take place in some countries while restricting it in others, whose growth is conditioned by and subjected to the power centres of the world.[7]

THE RESPONSE

Defenders of capitalism who do not believe that free market economies and development are incompatible argue that the socialist experiments of underdeveloped countries are themselves more a cause of poverty than any relationship with wealthy nations. The anti-Marxists further contend that even when the governments of poor countries are not lured into socialist schemes, they are often inefficient and corrupt. Former colonial powers left behind infrastructures, both economic (railroads, highways) and social (well-trained bureaucracies, well-funded schools), that help poorer countries to develop. Moreover, if capitalism is a ''cause'' of the poverty of the Third World, what of socialism? Eastern European countries are reliant, to various degrees, on the Soviet Union; their economies, while superior to those of the Third World, are inferior to those of western Europe. Finally, the emerging agreement, from such statist societies as China and the USSR, that market forces can enhance growth has cast doubt on the traditional dependency theorists.

THE PROBLEM OF CORRUPTION

As we saw in our discussion of ''kleptocracies,'' corruption exists in all governments. Sometimes it becomes an impediment to the proper functioning of a bureaucracy, and at other times it actually enhances performance. In the United States, George Washington Plunkitt, a Tammany Hall boss, called the latter ''honest graft.''[8] Robert Merton's examination of the American urban political machine demonstrated that corruption is, if not essential, certainly useful for economic development.[9]

Political machines were able to fuse legally separate governmental organizations into a functional whole through corruption; they also provided welfare (jobs, money, and so on) to immigrant families that in turn provided votes:

> In our prevailingly impersonal society, the machine, through its local agents, fulfills the important social function of humanizing and personalizing all manner of assistance to those in need. Foodbaskets and jobs, legal and extra-legal advice, setting to rights minor scrapes with the law, helping the bright poor boy to a political scholarship in a local college, looking after the bereaved—the whole range of crises when a feller needs a friend, and, above all, a friend who knows the score and who can do something about it—all these find the ever-helpful precinct captain available in the pinch.[10]

The money for these services came from payoffs: contractors kicking back a percentage of their profits from building projects, teachers kicking back a percentage of their salary, organized crime paying off politicians for protection (in exchange for which they controlled crime, confining it to a narrow corridor of the city and keeping middle-class areas relatively crime-free). The machine converted the money from corruption into services for the immigrants, who in turn provided votes for the reelection of the machine. Moral qualms aside, the system worked quite well.

Honest graft is the minor corruption that Asian governments practice to perfection. In a highly personalized culture, such as is found in Asia, reciprocity—the belief that one good turn deserves another—is a way of life. Americans who do business abroad simply figure in the cost of honest graft in their prices. But when corruption becomes the goal of government, as happened in the Philippines and Haiti, for example, its benefits disappear. When elites in developing countries use the power of the state primarily to enhance their personal wealth, the economy suffers greatly. One reason for

the precipitous decline of the Philippine economy was Marcos's determination to preserve economic monopolies to enrich himself and his friends.

Destructive graft is more pervasive in Africa than in Asia. Corruption at the highest
level (rather than honest graft) is accepted as a way of life by both elites and masses.[11]
A look at *The Economist*'s 1986 ratings of economic performance and corruption is
instructive (performance is rated according to GNP growth, GNP per capita, inflation,
and debt):[12]

	Group Average Performance Rating
Group 1 (least corrupt): Singapore, Hong Kong, Taiwan, South Korea, Sri Lanka, Portugal, Venezuela	27
Group 2: Algeria, Argentina, Brazil, China Morocco, South Africa, Turkey, Uruguay	19
Group 3: Chile, Ecuador, Malaysia, Poland, Saudi Arabia, Thailand, Vietnam, Yugoslavia, Zimbabwe	19
Group 4: Burma, Greece, Guatemala, Peru, Philippines, Tunisia	14
Group 5: Egypt, India, Mexico, Pakistan, El Salvador, Sudan, Zambia	12
Group 6 (most corrupt): Bangladesh, Bolivia, Colombia, Ethiopia, Ghana, Indonesia, Iran, Iraq, Kenya, Nigeria, Tanzania, Uganda, Zaire	12

There are several explanations for the proclivity of African governments for corruption.
One is that they are generally guided by revolutionary ideologies, and the state usually
plays a major economic role.[13]

Since African nations are tribally organized, with kinship groups commanding at
least as much loyalty as the central government, there is more of a natural inclination
toward corruption:

> The families of public bureaucrats will tend to view the official positions of their mem-
> bers as possessions of the corporate descent group, to be used for the group's benefit.
> . . . Giving aid and showing generosity to one's relatives and others to whom one has
> a personal tie is a primary social virtue. . . . From the vantage point of the civil
> servant, not only does his position within his extended family depend upon his full
> exploitation of the resources of his office, but how well he does for his family will also
> greatly affect his standing in the larger community.[14]

The problem is exacerbated by the colonial heritage. African bureaucrats are performing
tasks formerly performed by the European colonial civil service. The Europeans had
exalted status and were conspicuous consumers ruling over far less affluent subjects.
They drove Jaguars, lived in fancy Western-style houses, imported European clothing
and liquor. They had "big man" status. Africans who assumed these positions expected

to adopt the same lifestyle. High civil service positions are still called "European posts." A survey of Ghanian civil servants revealed that they believed their positions entitled them to a home, a car, imported suits—all the accouterments of the good European lifestyle.[15] Since a Jaguar, for example, cost about $10,000 at the time of the survey and the highest-paid civil servant was earning between $2,000 and $4,000 annually, the gap between expectations and reality was quite large. Because African nations are much more impoverished than Asian ones, the temptations to seize the good life are all the greater.

The essential component of any analysis of the social and economic costs of graft are to be found in its functions: Is corruption an agreeable way to achieve unity and economic growth, with a substantial enrichment of the active participants as a side benefit, or is the role of government that of providing opportunities for the active elite to enrich itself? In the Philippines,

> politics is a major industry; it is a way of life. Politics is the main route to power, which, in turn, is the main route to wealth. . . . More money can be made in a shorter time with the aid of political influence than by any other means.[16]

This is the case in Africa and, to a slightly lesser extent, in Latin America, but it is not true of most of Asia, where honest graft is the rule. There is more money to be made in private business. The essential requirement is to be left alone. There is status in public office, and the income gap between aspirations and realistic estimates is not so large. Corruption can help in overcoming bureaucratic regulations that might hinder economic expansion, just as 19th-century corruption in the United States (the railroads and utilities were buying state legislatures to keep out of their way) hastened the growth of the American economy:

> In terms of economic growth, the only thing worse than a society with a rigid, overcentralized, dishonest bureaucracy is one with a rigid, overcentralized, honest bureaucracy. A society which is relatively uncorrupt . . . may find a certain amount of corruption a welcome lubricant easing the path to modernization.[17]

Leland Stanford's bribes were nothing compared to the impact of railroads on the American economy. Bribery was acceptable because political capacity was not diminished. The quality of public officials might have been less pristine than many reformers wished, but the level of stupidity was not high. When corruption causes bright people to avoid government jobs or to make decisions that damage the economy, the line between honest graft and debilitating depravity has been crossed. An excellent example of crossing the line is Kenya. Jomo Kenyata, Kenya's liberator from British colonial rule, became rich like most other absolute rulers of underdeveloped countries, but his personal enrichment was not the sole purpose of his government. Since his death, however, corruption has gradually become far more serious:

> Though Kenyans were aware of the corruption that flourished under Kenyata, they know that corruption is different today. Kenyatta ran a vast patronage system like the Chicago political machine. The top officials skimmed the money but a lot of it was passed down.

Favors were given out. Politicians stayed in office by helping people with their problems. "Under Kenyatta everybody stole, and everybody was encouraged to get big," a Nairobi shopkeeper said, echoing a sentiment often heard in Nairobi. "Now people are afraid to get too big, because if they do the President will take their business."[18]

Crossing the Line: Mexico and Nigeria

Both Mexico and Nigeria are blessed with oil, and they both squandered their resources and were devastated by the oil glut of 1982. Nigerian oil, with a low sulfur content, is potentially more desirable than Middle Eastern oil because it is less likely to pollute. When the oil market boomed, Nigeria's income from oil soared from $400 million to $9 billion a year. Mexico's fortune was comparable. Thanks to their nationalized oil industry (Mexico owns 100 percent of Pemex; the Nigerian government owns 55 percent of that nations' refineries), both governments found themselves with vast sums of disposable income and no apparent means of holding themselves accountable. In Nigeria, the money was spent by the ruling class. A new class was born, the privileged upper middle class; massive development schemes were begun; new universities, new television stations, and a gleaming new airport were built. The minimum wage was doubled, and all civil servants were granted an immediate 60 percent salary increase. People abandoned the farms for the cities in search of the loot:

> Generals and civil servants grow rich on meager salaries and everyone has his price. You have to "dash" the receptionist to get a hotel room, the immigration official to get an entry permit at the airport, the doctor to get a bed at the hospital. Fifteen percent kickbacks on construction contracts are standard practice.[19]

In Mexico, the binge was comparable. The government embarked on unprecedented public spending and blatant nepotism. President López Portillo named his son, his sister, his cousin, his wife, and his mistress to major government positions where they too would have a chance at the *mordida* ("the bite," identical to the "dash" in Africa). His wife, in the grand tradition of Imelda Marcos, swooshed all over the globe for shopping in New York and Paris, meditation in India. Her husband bought a $2 million villa for his mistress; his wife took it over, so he bought his mistress another. His own five-mansion hilltop estate was begun at about the same time.

A major portion of the plunder is traditionally reserved for the last year in office, the "year of Hidalago." A picture of Miguel Hidalago, an independence hero, appears on Mexican money; Mexican presidents and their aides spend the last year in office grabbing as much money as they can. Comparative statistics are hard to come by; needless to say, the World Bank does not keep a running tab of the extent of corruption among its client nations. López Portillo is believed to have taken $3 billion. This puts him in a good strong second place to Ferdinand Marcos of the Philippines and well ahead of "Baby Doc" Duvalier of Haiti.

Both governments began to run out of money even as the oil revenues increased; they raised the price of oil, but by then demand had declined and the binge was over.

Both governments were bankrupt. The new Nigerian capital city, Abujah, lay half completed, a symbol of corruption and inefficiency. The 1985 coup was initiated out of frustration. Fully 44 percent of Nigeria's foreign exchange earnings was spent on debt service at a time when oil proceeds (95 percent of all export receipts) were spiraling downward; for three straight years, gross national product declined while severe shortages of food and medical supplies pushed up the rate of inflation. Combined with an increasingly repressive government, these hardships of everyday life became unbearable.

A government with democratic aspirations was installed, ironically, by a military coup in 1979. An elected government was in place until 1983 and failed to make a dent in the pervasive corruption; neither the coup that removed the elected government nor the military coup that removed the previous junta was able to do better.

In Mexico, yet another president from the totally dominant Institutional Revolutionary party, Miguel López de la Madrid, promised to address the issue of corruption but failed to stem the tide. There were some show trials of members of the preceding administration, but there always are. López Portillo himself, before settling into the routine of daily pillage, brought three officials from his predecessor's cabinet to trial. De la Madrid did not do as well, convicting one cabinet-level official, the director of Pemex, for corruption. But one of the most hated of the Portillo pirates, former Mexico City police chief Arturo Durazo, has not been brought to trial since 80 government witnesses recanted pretrial testimony. And of course López Portillo himself will not be tried.

Mexico's foreign debt, $80 billion, is among the highest in the world, having multiplied from $12 billion in a decade. Wealthy Mexicans rushed to get their money out of the country; in retaliation, the government devalued the peso by 40 percent, but the flow of capital continued. Next, banks were nationalized to assure unconstrained control. Still the crisis continued. The peso, pegged at 12.5 to the dollar in the late 1970s, plummeted to 2,400 to the dollar by 1989.

A decline in the value of a nation's currency should bolster exports by making imported goods more expensive, but in Mexico's case there was little opportunity for this to occur. With the rate of inflation soaring from 18 percent in 1975 to triple digits in the 1980s and with GNP growth declining from a respectable 5 percent to *minus* 5 percent, the domestic economy was in no position to do much more than hang on for dear life. At best, the Mexican economy will move to a zero growth rate, providing little opportunity for more jobs to match Mexico's high birthrate. The only solution for many is escape, and the flood of illegal immigrants to the United States has been rising substantially.

This tragedy was not caused by the traditional *mordida*, such as traffic cops extracting money from motorists under the guise of a traffic infraction, but rather by the flow of corruption upward, causing it to become less a glue for the system and more a racket. Cocaine traffic and gang wars between Mexican police and Colombian drug dealers can hardly be described as honest graft: "A system which had never worked smoothly without corruption was no longer working smoothly because of excessive corruption."[20]

The drug branch of the police illustrates well how excessive Mexican corruption has become. Mexico provides about one-third of the heroin and marijuana consumed in the United States, a traffic estimated at about $1.5 billion annually. The police operate as the drug dealers' enforcers, offering protection against rival gangs and killing the occasional American drug enforcement agent who gets too close.

The police are not "just following orders" but are clearly being protected by government officials at the highest level. The Mexican press avoids investigative journalism because reporters are routinely bribed each month (the funds are drawn against government accounts). Those who cover the oil industry do especially well, with Pemex providing an additional stipend. Preoccupied with enriching themselves, Mexican officials, given a great opportunity with the enormous quantities of oil, blew it. Mexico zoomed from rags to riches to rags. The World Bank found it "inconceivable" that a country that had earned $47 billion in oil revenues could have gone to seed so rapidly.[21] But it was not only conceivable, it was predictable. Neither Nigeria nor Mexico had the political will to manage wealth wisely; like *noveau riche* oil barons in the United States, they spent the money until it was gone. Writing about an equally misgoverned society, Uganda, *The Economist* concluded that Uganda's "wretched rulers showed that a perfectly good country really can be destroyed, possibly beyond the power of reasonable men to repair it."[22]

The Missing Ingredient

As became the custom when dealing with failed governments, the International Monetary Fund and the World Bank demanded and got agreement to dismantle the money-guzzling public corporations in Nigeria and Mexico. But these reforms, welcome though they may be, do not strike at one of the rarely discussed shortages in the underdeveloped world: competent and honest decision makers. No system can survive excessive corruption and administrative incompetence, irrespective of its mode of organization. We tend to neglect the human factor because it is distasteful to confront. But when a Duvalier ravages Haiti or a Marcos steals the Philippines blind, the problems of incompetence, self-interest, and corruption surface, only be dismissed when the "good guys" take over. But in most cases there are no good guys: Idi Amin is replaced in Uganda by Milton Obote, who proves to be even more of a brute. Economist Michael Todaro speaks of

> the very real and often binding constraint on economic progress that arises out of the shortage of public (and private) administrative capability. Many observers would argue that . . . managerial and administrative capability is the single scarcest resource in the developing world. . . . There has been much concern about incompetent and unqualified civil servants; cumbersome bureaucratic procedure; excessive caution and resistance to innovation and change; interministerial personal and departmental rivalries . . . ; lack of commitment to national goals as opposed to regional, departmental, or simply private objectives on the part of political leaders and government bureaucrats; and finally, in accordance with this lack of national as opposed to personal interest, the widespread phenomenon of political and bureaucratic corruption that is a pervasive problem of many third world governments.[23]

The absence of such debilitating problems in such insurmountable quantity separates Asia from Latin America and Africa. All governments in all of history have had incompetent, corrupt elected or appointed officials: Japan's Prime Minister Tanaka took bribes from Lockheed, and the United States' President Lyndon Johnson and Vice-President Spiro Agnew took envelopes filled with cash from just about anybody who reached across their desks. The post–Civil War administration of military hero Ulysses S. Grant was especially corrupt. In Taiwan, a major scandal involving unauthorized use of investors' money exposed governmentally supervised credit unions as reckless and forced the resignation of the minister of economic affairs. Graft is endemic to Soviet society. Deputy Trade Minister Vladimir N. Sushkov dealt regularly with large American corporations. About $2 million in presents from executives hoping to win contracts were found by police, and Sushkov was sentenced to 13 years in prison.

But in the less developed world, especially in undeveloped countries, incompetence and corruption are not exceptions; they are the rule. Economic development would operate to their disadvantage, because political development soon follows economic development (as South Korea learned in 1987). Corrupt politicians protecting the ill-gotten gain of the wealthy few are not inclined to encourage economic development, and they would be irrational to do so. When a wealthy country patronizes a poor one, usually because of some strategic or military interest, corruption is magnified as the dollars begin to flow in. Two good examples are South Vietnam before the final defeat and El Salvador today. South Vietnam's leaders were able to amass huge fortunes by selling American weapons before they could be used, buying heroin with the profits, selling the heroin to traders along the Thai-Cambodian border, and socking the money away in foreign bank accounts. As American commitment increased, so did the opportunity for corruption. South Vietnam's leaders had no reason to seek an early termination of the war, for the war was their opportunity to ravage. Much the same things goes on now in El Salvador, the United States' ally against Nicaragua. Facing a difficult, intractable revolution, Salvador's ruling elites are stealing at about the same rate as those in South Vietnam did. People excluded from the orgy are naturally bitter; the root cause of the defeat of American client states is not communism or even grinding poverty. The cause is the arrogant corruption that apparently inevitably accompanies American money:

> In a small society like Salvador, corruption is a visible, palpable thing that intrudes on everyone's life. If you are an average Salvadoran, you see the oversized Mercedes-Benzes of the military, the suddenly sprawling mansion of the recently appointed official and the wives dressed as goddesses, while you know that you yourself have nothing.[24]

Since the members of the middle class who cannot get in on the take are more likely to be resentful than the truly poor, who never get the chance no matter who is governing, the loss of middle-class support is a major blow to American client states. In South Vietnam, Vietcong and North Vietnamese political indoctrination officers reported that resentment rather than ideology was the spur. It makes little sense to assume that Marxism-Leninism became a cause worth dying for, since for most people, abstract systems of thought are unlikely. But it makes a great deal of sense to imagine widespread alienation as massive injections of American money gradually prostitutes an entire society and its institutions deteriorate before our eyes.

Controlling population growth is another political problem that attracts more interest than incompetence and corruption, even though it is not clear how direct an influence it has on economic development. Population increase is not directly associated with economic growth and stability, but it certainly adds to the problems of capital accumulation and saving. Yet only China has taken uncompromising action against this problem. The solutions are draconian and could only be undertaken by a near totalitarian state. Unless more nations are willing to become even more intrusive, the Chinese totalitarian solution is impractical. Forced sterilization in India contributed to the defeat of Indira Gandhi, suggesting that only nations without institutions of political accountability can act to prevent population increase. The spurt in population in Mexico following the oil boom is the more typical pattern. There is no denying the fact that some desperately poor countries (Uganda, Nicaragua, Zambia) have high rates of population increase. But some comparatively well-off ones (Ivory Coast, Zimbabwe) do also. And among the countries with the lowest increases in population are Austria, Bulgaria, and Hungary—hardly the economic heavyweights of Europe. Population increase and its control have great emotional appeal, but they are not by themselves key to understanding the problem of poverty.

GHANA: TEST CASE FOR FAILURE

When examples are sought for the worst case of an economy in decline, Ghana often comes to mind. Currently the world's weakest economy, Ghana at independence (1957) was the richest and most educated country in black Africa. Its 1960 GNP per capita of about $500 placed Ghana among the World Bank's middle-income countries. Known as the Gold Coast while a British colony, it was the first black African country to win independence. The name Gold Coast was derived from the money earned by slave traders, but the nation was blessed with immense natural wealth. At independence, Ghana's exports were more than 30 percent of GNP; it was the world's largest producer of cocoa and the largest exporter of manganese.

Its decline is almost impossible to imagine. In 1960, when Ghana's per capita GNP was $500, Taiwan's was $169. Today, Taiwan's is $5,300 and Ghana's is $420! Ghana's personal wealth has been steadily declining at a rate of about 0.7 percent a year. At the same time, rampant inflation brought about by simply printing money without increasing available goods made a tube of toothpaste cost about $7.00. Ghanaian laborers were earning about $1.50 a day, while the most basic ingredients for a meal for a family of four cost $11.00. How could such a tragedy have occurred?

There are two causes. First, the country's leaders were corrupt, and second, their economic schemes were illusory. Corruption was excessive, even by the more relaxed standards of the less developed countries:

> Ghana was brought to its knees after independence by its own leaders, men who pillaged with unabashed thoroughness. For many, what mattered was not that Ghana prospered and grew, but that they got their cut, deposited in European bank accounts. . . . The Cocoa Marketing Board was unable to account for half of its foreign exchange earnings between 1975 and 1979. The ruling soldiers flew scores of Mercedes-Benzes into Ghana for their own personal use (cost, $110,000 each plus shipping charges) and squandered so much money that soon there was no more foreign exchange. The transportation system broke down, the stores displayed little but empty shelves, [and] the legitimate econ-

omy was replaced by a black-market system known as *kalabule* (cheating and smuggling).[25]

Presiding over the corruption was Kwame Nkrumah, a longtime proponent of independence, who stole enough to make himself a multimillionaire.[26] Had he merely stolen, perhaps Ghana would not have suffered. But his view of the economy was inappropriate, based more on visionary theories than on a realistic assessment of resources. He wrote of the necessity of maintaining a strong political party organization "fortified with an African socialist ideology" and warned of the ever-present danger of "petit bourgeois elements."[27] His commitment to socialism never wavered.

His first mistake, the one from which all else seemed to develop, was his determination to move rapidly from an agrarian economy to one based on finished manufactured products. Within a socialist, centrally planned economy Nkrumah created a wall of protection around Ghanaian industry and began to squander money on unfeasible projects: $16 million on a conference hall for a single meeting of the Organization of African Unity, $9 million on a few miles of highway that were never used, $15 million on planning for a Volta River project to rival Egypt's Aswan Dam. By 1965, Ghana had lost foreign reserves of $481 million and had become a debtor nation.

With the economy being strip-mined into bankruptcy, Nkrumah turned more toward the eastern European model of the centrally planned economy and to the authoritarian-to-totalitarian mode of governance practiced by these countries. He established a tyrannical regime where bribery and corruption were rampant and freedom of speech a rarely afforded luxury. Opponents to Nkrumah's schemes were jailed, and he made himself president for life. A rubber stamp legislature passed laws allowing for imprisonment for five years without trial. Nationalization of the economy resumed without opposition. By 1965, there were 47 state corporations, all losing vast sums of money. Overseeing this operation was the National Development Corporation, the infamous "clearinghouse of bribery," into which state funds were channeled in order to maintain the single legal party, the Convention People's party. With jobs awarded only to party stalwarts, the NDC was able to fill more Ghanaian elite pockets while forcing the price of imported goods to increase.[28]

Ghana's good relations with European centrally planned economies, ironically, permitted them to exploit the African nation. In fact, Ghana's exploitation is one of the best dramatizations of the perils of dependency, but with Marxist states as the culprits. These countries increased Ghana's problems by requiring payment in sterling or dollars, creating a desperate hard-currency problem. Moreover, Ghana was sold machinery and other equipment at prices higher than Western firms operating without the intervention of a government would have charged. Often the products were useless, and nobody could figure out why they were shipped. The stories of white elephants became legend: a tannery in the south, 500 miles from the meat factory that would supply its leather; a tomato and mango canning plant with a projected output of 2,500 acres of crops constructed in an area that could grow neither tomatoes nor mangoes; tractors shipped by one eastern European country that turned out to be snowplows.

Confronting the flight of both capital and trained Ghanaians, Nkrumah began to borrow heavily and to require exit visas. He was removed by a coup in 1966, but no genuine progress was made. In such a chaotic environment, the first coup is rarely the last; the men who removed Nkrumah (and installed a democratically elected civilian government) were themselves removed in 1972; the new regime was in turn replaced in 1978. In 1979, a young air force lieutenant, Jerry Rawlings, led yet another coup. Rawlings handed over power to an elected civilian government. Not surprisingly, Ghana's situation worsened. Its debt had grown to $6 billion, and its inflation rate was running at 100 percent a year. It suffered from truly stupid economic policies, increased price distortion (which reduced incentives for production and increased them for smuggling), and severe drought. Real personal incomes dropped by 80 percent between 1970 and 1982, while GNP per capita declined by 30 percent. In 1981, Rawlings again seized power.

The lesson of Ghana is clear. The underlying causes of its decline into poverty are political: commitment to a planning mode that was obviously not working, a determination to make socialism work in Africa's showpiece nation, and pervasive corruption:

> Ghana's choice of economic strategy is severely constrained by its lack of trained and experienced policy managers. . . . Neither economic controls nor extensive dependence upon public enterprises . . . can be managed effectively under such manpower constraints. In these circumstances any government—whatever its ideological persuasion—must depend on the market as much as possible, and on intervention as little as possible, to manage its economy.[29]

The Turnaround. In 1983, Rawlings abandoned the ideology that has led to ruin, cutting government expenditures and shifting 30 of the 47 publicly owned corporations to the private sector. In the remaining state corporations, Rawlings tried to replace political appointees with professionally trained managers. Price controls have been largely eliminated, and serious consideration is being given to closing down publicly owned corporations that cannot show a profit even with better management. Inflation is now at 25 percent, alarming but far below the triple-digit figures to which Ghanaians had become accustomed. The civil service, which until the late 1970s was growing four times faster than the population, is being reduced at the rate of about 5 percent a year. Gross national product is increasing at the same rate. The turnaround was not entirely Ghanaian in origin. The World Bank made austerity and privatization conditions for its generous aid programs, causing a Ghanaian newspaper to lament that the country was reduced to "beggar status, subsisting on foreign aid and loans."[30] Still, since 1983, Ghana has enjoyed an average GNP growth rate of 6 percent, Africa's highest.

The West desperately wants an African success to justify its free market ideology, and Ghana has been selected as the model, just as it was, as the first independent African state, chosen to be a model for development three decades earlier. As one assessment concluded, "The only hope for Ghana is that the country may someday be blessed with a strong government that understands the need for economic liberalization."[31]

The new economic order is being imposed against the wishes of Ghana's most active interest groups, among them the unions and the leftist intellectuals. By accepting the free market reforms demanded by international lending agencies, Rawlings has become more vulnerable politically. Plots and attempted coups are a way of life, as are executions. Security—staying alive—has preoccupied Rawlings, and his regime has become increasingly authoritarian. The military has become excessively brutal as the use of detention without trial has increased. But "it is doubtful that any government could have launched economic reform programs like Rawlings' if there had been democratic rule; previous governments have shied away from devaluation and budget cuts in the face of popular dissent."[32] Ghana is the model for Western pride: a once state-dominated economy forced to adopt free market innovations, no longer hopeless. It is the third largest World Bank client (after India and China).

TAIWAN: TEST CASE FOR SUCCESS

Japan seized Taiwan from China during the Sino-Japanese War at the end of the 19th century and Taiwan remained a Japanese colony until Japan's defeat in World War II. Its population, excluding a few indigenous aboriginal peoples, migrated in the 50 years before the Japanese occupation, mostly from Fukien Province, on the South China coast. In 1949, the defeated Nationalist armies, retreating from the victorious People's Liberation Army, which had consolidated control of the Chinese mainland, retreated to Taiwan and set up a government in exile, which continues today.

The style of government, authoritarian and inclusive, capitalist-statist, was compatible with the traditions of China, from whence its current rulers sprang. To pacify a potentially rebellious native population, the "mainlanders" traded shares in future industrial enterprises for land, which they redistributed to the previous tenants. Although Taiwan was the beneficiary of a huge American investment (it was viewed as an anti-Communist outpost during the Korean War), its rate of development has continued unabated despite the decline of American investments. If dependency theory is accurate, Taiwan, once a Japanese colony and then a de facto American one, should be mired in poverty. Since it is not, we need to know why not. Why did Taiwan go from poverty to comparative wealth while Ghana declined from comparative wealth to poverty?

Taiwan's economic strategy makes good sense. Although a sizable portion of its total economic output was in publicly owned corporations, the private sector developed consistently. Bureaucratic control of the economy was much like that of France: a guided market system, with the state taking a major interest in growth and income distribution but a limited role in the actual management of the economy.

Initially, Taiwan adopted the traditional development strategy that led Ghana to ruin: it sheltered infant industry with high tariffs and kept interest rates artificially low. When these policies produced little economic growth, they were discarded. Here, then, is one fundamental difference between economic success and failure: successful countries are not wedded to an ideology that requires that failed schemes be continued beyond rationality. Taiwan abandoned low interest rates, shifted its emphasis from "import substitution" (becoming economically self-sufficient) to export promotion. The failed policy had kept Taiwan's exports to traditional colonial ones—sugar, rice, pineapples, and some minor consumer junk—sold largely to its prewar overlord, Japan. A small, highly protected, local industrial infrastructure produced shoddy goods for consumers with little money. Under the traditional development strategy, about 90 percent of Taiwan's exports were agricultural.

When the policy shifted and subsidies to farmers were discontinued, the proportion of agricultural exports began to shrink, and the proportion of industrial products began to increase. Taiwan concluded that its international competitive advantage lay in industries that are labor-intensive rather than capital-intensive. Thus the government provided incentives (usually tax breaks) to entrepreneurs who wished to produce textiles, clothing, shoes, and other light industrial products. Since it had little arable land, its agricultural exports, while becoming less important, became more exotic: mushrooms, asparagus, and snails for France.

Once these decisions were made, the economy entered a period of self-sustained growth. This initial spurt is most essential for success. There is a "poverty trap" from which a country must escape quickly. Low income levels and low levels of productivity are self-reinforcing, just as is a "culture of poverty" in any country. Gunnar Myrdal called the poverty trap a theory of "circular and cumulative causation," by which he merely meant that the rich get richer and the poor get poorer.[33] Taiwan broke out of the poverty trap by dropping failed policies, trying others, and using its resources to maximum competitive advantage.

Abandoning artificially low interest rates provided an incentive for savings, making money for investment available without the need for excessive dependence on foreign investors. Interest rates are now directly linked to inflation, money supply, and demand, as in the United States. By providing tax-free saving opportunities (individual income from interest is tax-exempt, as are corporate profits plowed back into the company for expansion), Taiwan became a nation of savers: domestic savings is about *one-third* of total gross national product (compared to 6 percent in the United States).

PRICE DISTORTION

An excellent example of the kinds of government intervention that seems to impede growth is *price distortion*. The World Bank had devised a method of "simulating" a perfectly free market (since none exists) and then estimating deviations from it. The World Bank's preferences are not based solely on its dependence on capitalist countries for funding.[34] It regularly conducts careful and reliable assessments of growth. It is now convinced that the Ghanaian lesson is that "countries with the worst distortions [that is, with the greatest amount of government control of the economy] experienced significantly lower domestic savings and lower output per unit of investment, thus leading to slower growth."[35]

In support of its theory, the Word Bank examined the price distortion and economic growth of 31 less developed and developing nations (including Ghana, which had the greatest distortion). In addition to price distortion, rate of savings was used as a control variable. The results support the bank's position. The correlation between distortion and growth is $-.48$, a very significant relationship: the greater the price distortion, the lower the growth. The reasons for the negative relationship between price distortion and growth are not hard to discern. Price controls to improve income distribution often hurt the poorest (as when low food prices, intended to benefit the urban poor, reduce the incomes of the urban poor). Controlled low interest rates intended to help investors and farmers often reduce the pool of savings available and force small investors and farmers to suffer high interest rates in black market loan shark operations. The case of the African droughts illuminates these problems. A major reason for the droughts is that governments appropriate their best land for cash crops, forcing local farmers to eke out a living in ill-suited areas. The plowing of these arid lands reduces their ability to respond to drought. Irrigation is reserved for cash crops, not food crops, and since most African governments keep the price of food artificially low, there is no private alternative to public irrigation. Irrigation schemes for cash crops, used to generate foreign exchange, prevent poor governments from buffering farmers against drought. The result is famine.

However, in Zambia, regarded a few years ago as an example of how free market principles could pull a country up by its bootstraps, the average person has lost two-thirds of his income due to a collapse in the price of copper, the country's main export. Zambia is now as cursed with debt, inflation, unemployment, and political unrest as Ghana was during the Nkrumah years.

In accounting for the negative relationship between price distortion and economic growth, savings rate, another good predictor of growth, does not seem to change the relationship. Price distortion is *independently associated* with poor economies. The same result can be obtained by examining the rate of savings as an independent contributor to economic growth, with the same results: savings and growth are independently related (at .24, not as strongly as economic performance and price distortion, but still significantly). Savings provides ready capital for investment. Savings provides an opportunity for a country to break out of the circular causal chain of poverty causing more poverty. There must, of course, be some money to save, making income growth the beginning of the upward spiral. A "takeoff point" must be reached, a time at which an underdeveloped nation overcomes and reverses the tendency for its standard of living to decline.[36] The trigger for development, the necessary but not sufficient condition, is high savings per worker. Early takeoffs, notably those in England and Japan in the 18th and 19th centuries, were typified by an active role for a strong, professionally competent bureaucracy. The governmental role was in the process of resource allocation—establishing goals and priorities—rather than in resource management.[37] The same style typified the Asian governments as they launched their successful takeoffs.

When do you know when the takeoff has begun? Experts disagree; some suggest that when domestic savings are at least 12 percent of gross national product, a takeoff can be expected, while others have developed a more complex formula. But all agree that Taiwan reached the takeoff stage between 1962 and 1963. Its savings as a ratio of GNP leaped from 8 to 13 percent, continuing to increase until the 1980s. Taiwan was therefore ready to maintain a healthy economy without the help of foreign capital.[38] The goal, the obsession, of developing countries, self-sufficiency, is achieved more efficiently by improving the rate of savings than by any other device, including tariff protection.

The contrast with Ghana cannot be more apparent. Both countries wished to break the poverty cycle to reach the takeoff point. Ghana chose a "big push" strategy of massive investment (without savings increases, the money for investment was borrowed), with import substitution (domestic manufacture of products previously imported) as the key generator of economic independence and local industry, protected by high tariffs, as the engineer. State ownership of the means of production was an article of faith. Taiwan chose a slower but more successful route to economic success, basing its program on the generation of domestic sources of capital for investment. Taiwan succeeded and Ghana failed.[39]

Ghana's approach, import substitution, has failed other nations in their attempt to develop. The idea is plausible: to encourage producers to make goods for domestic consumption rather than export. Import substitution normally requires high tariffs while the indigenous industry—usually heavy industry—is developed. Unfortunately, the consumer goods once imported are rarely replaced by domestic production, and prices soar. High tariffs bloat bureaucracies, encourage unnatural monopolies, and reduce incentives to compete. Red tape can smother business and require corruption to survive. In Brazil, for example, *despachantes,* who charge to guide businessmen through the maze of rules and regulations, have their own union and professional examinations. Consequently, countries that, like Ghana, try import substitution have poor records of growth. The following table compares the economic performance of import-substituting countries to those that look outward to a world market:[40]

Country	Growth Rate (percent change, 1973–1985)
Outward-oriented	
South Korea	6.5
Taiwan	6.4
Hong Kong	6.3
Singapore	6.3
Import-substituting	
Bangladesh	2.0
India	2.0
Burundi	1.2
Dominican Republic	0.5
Ethiopia	−0.4
Sudan	−0.4
Peru	−1.1
Tanzania	−1.6
Argentina	−2.0
Nigeria	−2.5
Zambia	−2.5
Bolivia	−3.1
Ghana	−3.2
Madagascar	−3.4

LESSONS FROM THE CASE STUDIES

The examples we have discussed encourage several generalizations:

1. A high rate of savings reduces the problem of "externalities." When trade shocks, oil gluts, or any sort of international financial crisis occurs, high rates of savings provide a cushion. But savings rates can be maintained only in an expanding economy. Subsidies on consumer goods and food, though emotionally satisfying, reduce the willingness to save.

2. Once domestic capital is generated, it must be invested wisely to obtain maximum return. Investment in state-owned enterprise has proved to be a poor investment.

3. Investment should be made in enterprises that will enable the country to expand its exports and restrain its imports. Countries prosper with above-average export growth. Slow industrial growth and tariff protection impede progress toward this goal. When developed nations impose high protective tariffs, less developed countries suffer. Thus when less developed countries try to impose high tariffs, the reaction of potential importers makes the cost exceed the benefits.

4. Cultural values that postulate hard work, savings, and patience are conducive to the achievement of successful strategies for an improved economy. Confucianism is such a culture. It emphasizes

    a highly developed sense of practicality or pragmatism, an active rather than a contemplative orientation to life, great interest in material things (emphatically including a positive valuation of wealth) and last but not least, a great capacity for delayed gratification (especially on behalf of one's family).[41]

5. Centrally planned economies tend to impede growth. Market economies may be insensitive to a plan for development, but they allow small entrepreneurs to make mistakes and to learn from them, whereas the same decision made collectively would spread the penalties of failure far and wide.

6. Although the institutional structure or processes of the political-economic system are not linked to economic success, political decisions are.

7. *Externalities* (events beyond the control of a government, such as an oil shortage or a price collapse) are always a threat to growth. Poor countries are less able to respond to externalities. The best defense against externalities is diversification: if the price of coffee or copper falls, part of the loss in revenue should be made up by other exports. This is impossible in many countries.

8. Colonial status has little impact on economic growth and stability. In the Ghanaian case, the decline and fall were due to bad decisions by politicians and to corruption. Neither of these faults can be traced to Britain, the former colonial overlord. Living conditions were better under the British than they have been since independence.

WHY SUCCESSFUL GOVERNMENTS
CANNOT BE EMULATED

Asian countries provide the single exception to the rule of the haves and the have nots. Most poor nations have always been and will always be poor. Some poor nations that were once more prosperous have become poor, and some that were once poor are no longer so. But in general, little change can be expected. Efforts to change the balance of poverty are always in vogue, since world poverty puts even the wealthy nations at risk.

The first wave of development theory was inclined toward socialism. Principally exported from European intellectuals, socialism is now no longer given serious consideration by development economists. As one disillusioned Tanzanian exclaimed, "Patronizing Europeans have tried out here the socialist experiments their electors would not let them try at home."[42] Socialism is, however, not merely a way of organizing an economy; it is also a secular religion, and "to the extent that socialism retains this mythic quality, it cannot be disconfirmed by empirical evidence in the minds of its adherents."[43]

Vladimir Voinivich, a Soviet writer exiled in 1980, in his Orwellian fantasy about Moscow in the 21st century, describes a deity consisting of Christ, Marx, and Lenin; he wishes to convey the necessity of accepting socialism as a religion.[44] An especially good example of the link between socialism and morality is the emergence of the New Jerusalem movement in England. At the turn of the 20th century, when the industrial revolution was creating unspeakable squalor, active religious leaders (especially Nonconformists and Unitarians) embraced socialism as a solution to the problem of poverty.

The initial experiments (during the post–World War II independence movements) bore the imprint of this religion. In Africa, the most self-conscious socialism was Tanzania's. Its leader to independence, Julius Nyerere, is a highly regarded statesman with an international reputation in the major proponents of both socialism and capitalism. His socialism was the first blueprint for development, and it failed ignominiously. Because Nyerere is a persuasive leader, his country enjoyed massive foreign aid, amounting to 14 percent of its gross national product. Without this aid, his government would have collapsed earlier than it did. American grain kept Tanzanians from starving, and Chinese engineers built a huge railroad from Dar es Salaam, the capital, to Zambia. The railroad survives only because Chinese engineers run it, with subsidies from the United States and West Germany.

Tanzanian socialism effectively eliminated individual incentive by taxing high incomes at confiscatory levels; the country grew poorer by the day, as the doctrine of *ujamaa* (Swahili for "familyhood") proved impracticable. Nationalized industry and collective farming attested to the futility of planning for an agrarian economy based on small plots of collectively owned land. By abolishing most private enterprise, Tanzania gave state corporations the job of supplying the newly centralized farms. It simply did not work, and only the most obsessed romantics believe that it could ever have worked. Tanzania declared education, in Swahili, the right of all, but most schools closed because they had no texts and teachers were not paid. When droughts came in 1984, Tanzania's government simply collapsed, and Nyerere resigned as chairman of the ruling party.

In Latin America, the economic stability of socialist states is not encouraging. Nicaragua has one of the world's worst economies, along with Peru, Bolivia, and Chile. It can be argued that Nicaragua has been so harassed by the United States that it has been unable to get its economy on track; but what then of Cuba, with an economy less stable than that of Brazil, Trinidad and Tobago, Mexico, Grenada, Haiti, Belize, or Costa Rica (but more stable than Argentina, El Salvador, or Jamaica)? Cuba's economic performance is less dismal than that of the African socialist states because it had, before the revolution, one of the most vibrant economies in the Caribbean. The Cuban economy is now virtually completely reliant on the USSR and is incapable of self-sustained economic growth.[45] Though not as poor as the African socialist countries, Cuba's economic failure is of the largest magnitude: "The Cuban leadership has been unable to significantly change the island's economic structure after 25 years of socialism." As we would anticipate from our discussion of equity, growth, and political system, Cuban income distribution has not changed dramatically, although it has improved somewhat.[46]

The relationship is one of economic dependence but occasional political spats. Even the economic relationship has its ups and downs. Cuba has been given trade credits of $3 billion through 1990. At the same time, subsidies have been reduced. Although Russia pays an artificially high price for sugar, Cuba's main export, it charges Cuba an artificially high price for oil. The result of this relationship is a feeble economy. Cuba's economy is about as healthy as is Tanzania's or Somalia's. In Latin America, Cuba's economy outperforms only those of Bolivia, Peru, and Nicaragua. Cuba's economy is outperformed by those of Costa Rica, Uruguay, Venezuela, Guatemala, Mexico, Colombia, Ecuador, the Dominican Republic, Panama, Brazil, and Paraguay. As the rest of the socialist world considers markets, Cuba's Castro, after a brief flirtation with economic incentives, has become one of the socialist bloc's most conservative leaders, rejecting the Soviet lead in experimentation.

CAN A CONTINENT DIE?

The problems in Africa are more severe than in Latin America. We can speak all we like about economic strength and weakness, worry about inflation rates and import substitution, but in very few places does the extent of poverty approach that of Africa. Of the 10 poorest countries (measured in terms of real per capita annual income), 6 are in Africa. Many Africans are poorer than they were under colonial rule, and the continent remains on the brink of an economic crisis so vast as to be almost beyond belief; entire countries may simply disappear, their governments disband, and their population become refugees or nomads. Hobbes's theories of a state of nature may be given their first empirical test. Life spans hover around the mid-thirties; daily caloric intakes fall short of the minimum daily requirements by at least 15 percent; infant mortality rates are almost too stunning to believe (259 per 1,000 in Zambia, compared to 7 per 1,000 in Sweden); and between 5 and 15 percent of the adult population can read. Year in, year out, irrespective of who does the ranking, Africa is a living nightmare. Many of the measures used to measure social or economic progress, budget priorities, and the like are simply meaningless. How important is the fact that the pupil-to-teacher ratio in

Burkina Faso is 608 (compared to 18 in Sweden) when the average life span is 31 years? One wonders if life might not remain about the same if there were no governments.

An International Responsibility?

Following the lead of its World Bank component, the United Nations committed itself in 1986 to a more coordinated rescue operation. At the urging of the African members, the UN increased its lending and aid in exchange for governmental reform and a more serious commitment to free markets. The program, involving about $130 billion, shows how politically sensitive economic development has become. From Western nations came the demand that the enabling documents stipulate that "the role of the private sector is . . . to be encouraged through well-defined and consistent policies." From the USSR came a demand for inclusion of a phrase claiming that Africa's problems were "deeply rooted" in its colonial past. The final statement was, in the grand tradition of international agreements, a compromise: "Some [or Africa's problems] lie in the colonial past. Some of these flow from the post-independence era; others are a combination of economic, political and endemic factors." Actually, the UN resolution went a bit beyond the usual twaddle by bemoaning "insufficient managerial/administrative capacities."

"Plus Ça Change?"

Actually, there is some reason to be just a bit more optimistic this time around. The two leading proponents of socialist planning as an economic savior are backing away from their hard-line ideology. The People's Republic of China has begun to move, in fits and starts, toward economic decentralization and monetary incentives and could conceivably move in the direction of a Yugoslavian or Hungarian-style system (that is, from an inclusive socialist to an inclusive mixed socialist system). The People's Republic has even cooked up a name for its new economic policy: the "socialist commodity economy." China's success, its suddenly diminished need to import food, and its dramatic improvement in rural incomes shocked even the Chinese leaders who slowed things down in 1987. But it is improbable that even with the death of the pragmatic leaders who started the economic reform, China could ever revert to its heavy-handed economic ways.

The key to whether the market will return to vogue is the behavior of the first socialist state, the Soviet Union. It's leader, Mikhail Gorbachev, moved further than most people thought he would in seeking to dismantle the world's most powerful economic bureaucracy. He called for a partial dismantling of the two linchpins of the Soviet economy, central planning and subsidized prices (previously he had followed China in allowing small private enterprise). If successful, these changes would equal those wrought by Stalin in the 1930s, when the rush to collectivization replaced the more moderate Lenin-authored New Economic Policy.

With respect to central planning, Gorbachev attacked the most visible symbol of socialism, the State Planning Committee (Gosplan). Gosplan prepared detailed production targets for every sector of the economy, carefully orchestrating the most minute nuances of supply and demand. Although central planning has finally run its course, the

Soviet economy did grow an average of about 5 percent annually from 1929 until 1970, a remarkable achievement when we consider the destruction of industry that occurred during World War II. Although most observers predicted that Gorbachev would propose only cosmetic changes, due to the entrenched power of the bureaucracy, he proposed dramatically that central planning be limited to the establishment of national economic goals, much like the Asian corporatist countries now provide. By proposing that the elaborate price control system, which requires that the government set prices for about a quarter of a million commodities (often at a fraction of their true cost and often greatly in excess) be abandoned, Gorbachev signaled a willingness to try the market. If his policies survive, the leading proponent of the idea that the market is evil will have changed its tune.

But encouraging poor countries to eschew central planning and trust the market does little about the fundamental problem of corruption. When the money begins to roll, why should we assume that elites who have stolen their countries blind in the past will suddenly stop doing so at the very moment when there is more to be stolen?

Can Poor Countries Be Released From the Poverty Trap?

The vicious cycle of poverty suggest that strong will is essential, but so is help from the richer nations. Growth requires capital, which requires savings, which requires high income. But these conditions can be met, as least theoretically. The notion of perpetual poverty is refuted by the existence of rich nations; they all started out poor, with low levels of capital. If the vicious cycle theory were infallible, there would be no wealthy nations. The rapid success of the Asian countries is a more modern refutation, as is, to a lesser extent, Australia.

Development is not a purely economic problem. As we have seen, culture is a strong factor in aiding or impeding growth. Max Weber's thesis is relevant here: the culture of Protestantism and the culture of Confucianism are belief systems that encourage economic growth. Unless we understand the cultural basis of an economy, the infusion of massive amounts of capital will not do any good. A cultural system that has not developed without external help is unlikely to do so with such help. So capital must be accompanied by the introduction of new and appropriate technology, the education and training of civil servants to use this technology, the education of the government and the population about the debilitating effects of corruption and incompetence, the persuasion of economically and politically powerful elites that development will not reduce their influence, and the commitment of national leaders to the need to think in terms of national, rather than subnational, interests. So far, the rich still get richer and the poor still get poorer.

FOR FURTHER CONSIDERATION

1.   Outline the main tenets of dependency theory.
2.   How does neo-Marxism differ from Marxism?
3.   What is the relationship between official corruption and economic growth?
4.   What is price distortion? What does it have to do with economic growth?

For the More Adventurous

1. According to Matthew's Gospel, Christ encountered a devoted follower who poured a valuable ointment on his head. Christ's disciples objected to the waste, saying the ointment should have been sold, and the proceeds given to the poor. Christ is said by Matthew to have responded "Why trouble ye the woman? For she has brought good work upon me. For ye have the poor always with you; but me ye have not always" (Matthew 26:11). Should Christians believe that poverty is a fixed and necessary condition of human affairs? Read the proceedings of the Second Vatican Council (Vatican 11, 1962–1965), *Gaudiem et Spes*. This encyclical is the source of "liberation theology" which says that the poor must be made aware of their political power and hence shed their poverty (see Leonardo Boff, *Jesus Christ Liberator*. Maryknoll, N.Y: Orbis Books, 1978). Can Vatican 11 and Matthew be reconciled? What is the relationship between liberation theology and Marxism? Can one be a Christian Marxist?

2. In the United States, Attorney General Edwin Meese (in office between 1980 and 1988), Vice-President Spiro Agnew (in office between 1968 and 1971), Defense Secretary designate John Tower (in 1989), and Speaker of the House Jim Wright (in 1989) were found to have been bribed (in effect). In Japan, Prime Minister Takeshita (1989) and other members of the ruling Liberal Democratic party, including former Prime Minister Nakasone, were exposed as the recipients of bribes (in effect) from businesses. How did this behavior impact upon the economies of the United States and Japan. Compare these episodes with comparable ones in poorer countries.

3. Do you believe that short-term political repression is necessary for the sake of economic development and hence democracy? Can you think of examples which prove and disconfirm this proposal? Must *all* economically successful countries endure a period of repression?

4. Assuming that each GNP grows at its current rate, what will be the GNP per capita for Singapore, Taiwan, and South Korea in 2020? What about Switzerland, West Germany, and Japan? Compare the ratio of each nation in the first group with each nation in the second as of today and according to your estimates for the future. Can you predict the political system likely to develop in each country?

NOTES

1. V. S. Naipaul, "The Killing of Trinidad," *Sunday Times* (London), May 19, 1974, p. 41.
2. J. R. Brown, "A Western View," in *China Yesterday and Today*, ed. Molly Joel Coyle, Jon Livingstone, and Jean Highland (New York: Bantam, 1982), p. 144.
3. Peter L. Berger, *The Capitalist Revolution* (New York: Basic Books, 1986), p. 122.
4. U.S. Bureau of the Census, *Statistical Abstract of the United States: 1988* (Washington, D.C., 1987).
5. Lenin, speech to the Third International, 1920, cited in Roy C. Macridis, *Contemporary Political Ideologies* (Boston: Little, Brown, 1986), pp. 276–277.
6. Theontonio Dos Santos, "The Crisis of Development Theory and the Problem of Dependence in Latin America," *Siglio 21* (1969): 89.
7. Ibid., p. 144.
8. On the distinction between honest graft (low-level corruption) and debilitating abuse of office (high-level corruption), see Susan Rose-Ackerman, *Corruption: A Study in Political Economy* (Orlando, Fla.: Academic Press, 1978).
9. Robert K. Merton, *Social Theory and Social Structure* (New York: Free Press, 1956), pp. 72–82.

10. Ibid., p. 74.
11. David H. Bayley, "The Effects of Corruption in a Developing Nation," *Western Political Quarterly 19* (December 1966): 719–732; see also Ronald Wraith and Edgar Simpkins, *Corruption in Developing Nations* (London: Allen & Unwin, 1963).
12. *The Economist*, December 20, 1986, pp. 69–72.
13. Samuel Huntington, *Political Order in Changing Societies* (New Haven, Conn.: Yale University Press, 1968), pp. 59–71.
14. Robert M. Price, *Society and Bureaucracy in Contemporary Ghana* (Berkeley: University of California Press, 1975), pp. 148–149.
15. Ibid., pp. 153–156.
16. George E. Taylor, *The Philippines and the United States: Problems of Partnership* (New York: Praeger, 1964).
17. Huntington, *Political Order*, p. 69.
18. Michael Paul Maren, "Kenya: The Dissolution of Democracy," *Current History*, May 1987, p. 228.
19. David Lamb, *The Africans* (New York: Random House, 1982).
20. Alan Riding, *Distant Neighbors* (New York: Vintage, 1986), p. 193.
21. Leopoldo S. Solis and Ernesto Zedillo, "The Foreign Debt of Mexico," in *International Debt and the Developing Countries*, ed. Gordon W. Smith and John T. Cuddington (Washington, D.C.: World Bank, 1985), p. 276.
22. *Economist*, June 20, 1987, p. 18.
23. Michael P. Todaro, *Economic Development in the Third World* (White Plains, N.Y.: Longman, 1981), pp. 483, 463.
24. Mitchell Seligson, *Authoritarians and Democrats: Regime Transition in Latin America* (Pittsburgh, Penn.: University of Pittsburgh Press, 1987) p. 203.
25. Lamb, *Africans*, pp. 284–285.
26. Henry Bretton, *The Rise and Fall of Kwame Nkrumah* (New York: Praeger, 1966), p. 66.
27. Kwame Nkrumah, *I Speak of Freedom* (London: Panaf Books, 1961), p. 162.
28. T. Peter Omari, *Kwame Nkrumah: The Anatomy of an African Dictatorship* (London: Hurst, 1970), pp. 105–106.
29. Michael Roemer, "Ghana, 1950–1980: Missed Opportunities," in *World Economic Growth: Case Studies of Developed and Developing Nations*, ed. Arnold C. Harberger (San Francisco: Institute for Contemporary Studies, 1985), p. 223.
30. James Brooke, "Ghana Embraces Change (e.g., a Stock Exchange)," *New York Times*, May 13, 1987, p. 4.
31. Roemer, "Ghana," p. 225.
32. Jon Kraus, "Ghana's Shift from Radical Populism," *Current History*, May 1987, p. 228.
33. Gunnar Myrdal, *Asian Drama* (New York: Pantheon, 1968), p. 233.
34. Unlike Latin America, where most debt is owed to private banks, in Africa 80 percent of the debt is owed to governments or to international organizations such as the World Bank.
35. World Bank, *World Development Report* (New York: Oxford University Press, 1984), p. 57. The case for removing distortions and relying on the market rests on the arguments that prices influence production decisions and that reform will increase production efficiency. The most prominent mechanisms of price distortions are government monopolies (or government-sanctioned private monopolies), control of foreign exchange, artificially inflated or deflated prices (such as artificially low rent and artificially high prices for farm products), unrealistic minimum wage laws, trade restructions, and holding interest rates well below inflation (which penalizes savers and creates excess demand for credit).
36. W. W. Rostow, *The Stages of Growth* (London: Cambridge University Press, 1960), pp. 1–12.

37. Robert T. Holt and John E. Turner, *The Political Basis of Economic Development* (New York: Van Nostrand, 1966), p. 283.

38. Foreign capital inflow as a source of capital formation declined from 40 percent in 1962 to 5 percent in 1966.

39. Ghana's rate of savings is about 9 percent.

40. World Bank, *World Development Report 1988* (New York: Oxford University Press, 1988), p. 193.

41. Berger, *Capitalist Revolution*, p. 163.

42. *Economist*, June 20, 1987, p. 15.

43. Berger, *Capitalist Revolution*, p. 204.

44. Vladimir Voinivich, *Moscow 2042* (Orlando, Fla.: Harcourt Brace Jovanovich, 1987).

45. Carmelo Mesa-Lago, "The Socioeconomic Performance of Cuba," in *Cuban Communism*, 6th ed., ed. Irving Louis Horowitz (New Brunswick, N.J.: Transaction Books, 1988), pp. 23–28.

46. Carmelo Mesa-Lago, "Cuba's Centrally Planned Economy: An Equity Tradeoff for Growth," in ibid., p. 180.

FOR FURTHER READING

Cardoso, Henrique Fernando, and Enzo Faletto. *Dependency and Development in Latin America*. Berkeley: University of California Press, 1979.

Chirot, Daniel. *Social Change in the Twentieth Century*. Orlando, Fla.: Harcourt Brace Jovanovich, 1977.

Clark, Robert P. *Power and Policy in the Third World*. New York: Macmillan, 1986.

Harberger, Arnold C., ed. *World Economic Growth: Case Studies of Developed and Developing Nations*. San Francisco: Institute for Contemporary Studies, 1985.

Harrison, Paul. *Inside the Third World*. New York: Viking Penguin, 1981. An English journalist describes in harrowing detail the realities of life in the world's poorest countries.

Huntington, Samuel, and Joan Nelson. *No Easy Choice*. Cambridge, Mass.: Harvard University Press, 1976.

Jenkins, Jerry, ed. *Beyond the Informal Sector*. San Francisco: Institute for Contemporary Studies, 1988. The "informal sector" is the underground economy.

Lamb, David. *The Africans*. New York: Random House, 1982.

Naipaul, Shiva. *North of South: An African Journey*. New York: Viking Penguin, 1980. Reflections by the late Caribbean novelist (brother of V. S.) on his travels through Kenya, Tanzania, and Zambia, with a Graham Greene–like eye for the sardonic.

Naipaul, V. S. *An Area of Darkness*. New York: Vintage, 1981. Shiva's older brother tours the country of his family's origin, India.

Nisbet, Robert A. *Social Change and History: Aspects of the Western Theory of Development*. London: Oxford University Press, 1969.

Riding, Alan. *Distant Neighbors*. New York: Vintage, 1986. Journalistic, impressionistic, but interesting account of the Mexicans.

Russet, Bruce, and Harvey Starr. *World Politics*. New York: Freeman, 1989. In a class by itself, much more than a standard international relations text.

Skidmore, Thomas E., and Peter H. Smith. *Modern Latin America*. New York: Oxford University Press, 1984. The authors predict "hybrid capitalism" for Latin America.

Spalding, Rose, J., ed. *The Political Economy of Revolutionary Nicaragua*. Boston: Allen Unwin, 1987.

Todaro, Michael P. *Economic Development in the Third World*. White Plains, N.Y.: Longman, 1981. 4th edition, 1989.

Young, Crawford. *Ideology and Development in Africa*. New Haven, Conn.: Yale University Press, 1982.

Epilogue

We are living at a propitious moment: the major ideologies of the 20th century are being rejected by their once most ardent proponents. Fascism died on the battlefield; communism is dying because economies using its principles have failed. Irrespective of the means of demise, we applaud the end of ideology; it has been delayed, but it does seem finally to be upon us:

> For the radical intellectual who has articulated the revolutionary impulses of the past century and a half, [a destructive war of a breadth and scale hitherto unknown and the bureaucratized murder of millions in concentration camps and death chambers have] meant an end to chiliastic hopes, to millennarianism, to apocalyptic thinking—and to ideology. For ideology, which once was a road to action, has become a dead end.[1]

Though blueprints for utopia are no longer taken seriously, one should not lose sight of the fact that it was not intellectuals who threw in the towel but rather leaders of failed economies: It was Deng who urged the Chinese to "seek truth from facts." It was Gorbachev who, in his 1988 speech to the United Nations, proclaimed it "is obvious that the use or threat of force no longer can or must be an instrument of foreign policy." (How different from traditional communism's harsh assertion, voiced by Lenin, "National wars against the imperial powers are not only possible and probable; they are inevitable, progressive, and revolutionary").[2]

CURING THE MISCHIEFS OF IDEOLOGY

Gorbachev and Deng have risen above ideology. Why is this necessary? Robert Nisbet observes, "The single most revealing and perhaps frightening thing about ideology is its immunity, once it has begun to grow on its own psychological nutrients, to the voice of experience and concrete reality.''[3] Psychologists call this ability to maintain belief in spite of continual, definite evidence to the contrary *cognitive dissonance*.[4] A belief system—an ideology—is personally very important; it pervades one's life, providing consistency, logic, and coherence. When evidence contradicts a belief system, one must either abandon the belief system or reject the evidence. Since abandoning the belief system means giving up a way of life, we tend to reject the evidence. Do you like to smoke? Does smoking kill you? Do you want to die? What is the easiest solution?

Often ideologies are *strengthened* in the face of disconfirming evidence. Seventh-Day Adventists from time to time proclaim the end of the world, fixing a precise date (March 21, 1844, was the first of them). The day comes, the world does not end. So they fix another date. The Seventh-Day Adventists fix dates every year or so, but the cult continues to flourish—its devotees give up their material possessions awaiting Armageddon.

Political ideologies—which can be as constraining as religious ones—are equally adept at immunizing one against information. Much of the turmoil of our century has been caused by ideologues obsessed with the pursuit of an unachievable goal. But now most of them are gone, and those that remain pose no genuine threat: one can hardly imagine Cuba rising to the class of world power, and Islam is culturally too limited to appeal to people not socialized into it since childhood. By 2030, 25 percent of the world's population will be Moslem. A small minority of it—perhaps ten percent—will be Shiite, the most ideologically obsessed sect. Fundamentalist Islam—although it is collectivist and anti-American and hence should be immensely popular among Western intellectuals—is too ascetic, too *personally* extreme to spread beyond the cultural boundaries of its incubation. Whereas Marxism remains popular in universities, and Castro and Ortega retain their symbolic attraction (Gorbachev, the new hero of the Chamber of Commerce, is another matter), fundamentalist Islam's leaders cannot (presumably they would not want to) get in the front door. One does not see those who wore ''be my comrade'' T-shirts and shouted ''no pasarán'' (a Sandinista slogan) whacking their heads on the ground as they pray to Allah. If fundamentalist Islam is the next ideology it is, mercifully, no more culturally exchangeable than, unfortunately, Confucianism. Of course it is dangerous. The Speaker of Iran's parliament urged Palestinians to ''kill Westerners wherever they find them.'' But Islam has nothing to do with *class,* and has no slogans or symbols of universal appeal. Try to imagine an Episcopalian Jihad and you get the idea.

Now that socialism has run its course and market economies are acknowledged as ''natural,'' there is little danger of another world view developing. Market capitalism, while based on the natural human inclination to get ahead, is a pallid alternative to the complex dogma of communism. And since ''capitalism evokes hatred'' and ''the word is associated with selfishness, exploitation, inequality, materialism, [and] war,''[5] much of its theoretical support is defensive, almost apologetic. Perhaps because it lacks moral vigor, capitalism contributes to international pacificism.

In fact, the petering out of socialism may contribute to world peace: socialist countries are more heavily armed and commit more of their resources to weapons than capitalist ones do.[6] The persistent militarism of socialist nations is driven by the bureaucratic imperatives of a society organizes on collective coercive principles. A centrally regulated socialist state organizes society for collective enterprises and relies on government coercion to carry on these enterprises. This is the characteristic organizational mode for economic activity as well as sports, education, entertainment, and recreation. (In contrast, capitalist states, whether authoritarian or democratic, rely mainly on markets to organize societal activity and on voluntary exchange to carry on these enterprises.) By elevating collective enterprise over private enterprise, socialist nations provide the bureaucratic impetus for the most basic of collective efforts, national defense. The military easily gains primacy in a centralized society devoted to collective enterprise. And by favoring coercion over voluntary exchange as the central form of societal interaction, the military assumes a legitimacy that it does not enjoy in voluntaristic societies.

Yet the sort of changes envisioned by the new breed of communist leaders might threaten the institutional basis of militarism. If market economies are less belligerent than socialist ones, the acceptance of market principles is a more significant guarantor of peace than the (albeit well-intentioned) statements of leaders. "Liberal regimes" (market economies; citizens who possess legal rights; "republican," representative governments) have created a "pacific union."[7] Like it or not, if economic imperatives guided the USSR and the People's Republic of China toward the market, these same urgent needs may guide socialist nations away from militarism. But merely because less collectively oriented societies are disinclined to impose their will militarily, and merely because they are not guided by a world view, do not assume that their elites are not vulnerable to the need to reduce cognitive dissonance.

THE DECLINE AND FALL
OF AMERICAN GOVERNMENT

In the United States, we have become specialists in selective perception. Our country is at the end of its tether; our military and economic hegemony is ending, and our standard of living is slipping. By the turn of the 21st century, the Japanese will be installed as the economic leader of industrial democracies and the European Common Market will be its major competition; standards of living in Germany will exceed ours (in Switzerland they already do). There is nothing wrong with being a second-rate power; other countries have had to adjust (England did rather well in letting its empire go). But we must emulate Gorbachev: when it is time for a change, get on with it.

However, we cannot because the American decision-making structure, marvelously evocative of an individualistic culture, is out of date. Presidential primaries produce candidates who do not know how to lead; their advisers conduct surveys, find out what sells, and tell their clients to say it. They do. George Bush proclaimed his campaign to be about "a thousand points of light" (does anyone know what that means?). During the campaign, the leading topic of the media was crime (never mind that American presidents, in a federal system, are not responsible for law enforcement). But once the election was over, the issue was forgotten.[8] Why raise it if it was of no substantive interest? Because it would sell. Presidential primaries are the worst leadership selection system imaginable. Only the luck of the draw allows us to elect an occasional president who is not a fool or a crook (at least simultaneously).

How Bad Is It?

Two observers summed it up pretty well:

> In fact no one dreamed up the Rube Goldberg system that now determines the nominees of each party; it evolved on its own, guided by the law of unintended consequences. And no, it is not good for democracy; successive attempts at reform have created the illusion of popular selection, not the reality. Most of the electorate is excluded from participation until a handful of voters in unrepresentative states winnows the field by at least half. If a Third World nation had devised such a nominating system and imposed it on its people, Americans might logically conclude that it had decided to forsake democracy.[9]

> Every institution in American politics has its share of critics who are convinced it does not work. . . . Most of the time the point is impossible to prove. The criticism can be met with an equally plausible claim that the institution under siege operates about as well as we have a right to expect in an imperfect, pluralistic society. In one case, though, it is not a close question. Common sense says that the way we nominate presidential candidates is silly. We have a system that is capable of producing good presidents only by accident, and we have a right to object to it. . . . There is something wrong with allowing candidates to select themselves and then try to secure nomination through one to four years of shallow, demeaning hucksterism.[10]

It is time for a change. Unless we find a way to escape the tyranny of the primaries, our leaders will continue talking about ''a thousand points of light'' as the decline becomes harsher.

Even if we could manage to wrest our politics away from the image makers, the very constitutional system we revere makes even the wisest leaders vulnerable to attacks of irrationality. Separation of powers is an idea whose time is past. No other industrial democracy would contemplate such an anomaly, and the two defeated powers of World War II—Germany and Japan—are equipped with constitutions that make coordination feasible. Paul Kennedy gets right at the American dilemma:

> A country needing to reformulate its grand strategy in the light of the larger, uncontrollable changes taking place in world affairs may not be well served by an electoral system which seems to paralyze . . . decision making. . . . It may not be helped by the extraordinary pressure applied by lobbyists, political action committees, and other interest groups, all of which, by definition, are prejudiced . . . and . . . through a mass media whose . . . *raison d'être* is chiefly to make money and secure audiences. . . . The country may not always be assisted by its division of constitutional and decision-making powers, deliberately created when it was geographically and strategically isolated from the rest of the world two centuries ago . . . but which might be harder to operate when it is . . . called upon to make swift decisions vis-à-vis countries which enjoy far fewer constraints.[11]

Can the Americans find their Gorbachev, someone who will tell them the truth? What would we substitute for what we've got? The Japanese or Swiss governmental systems—parliamentary governments with tight corporatist traditions—can hardly be transferred to the United States. There is the overwhelming dictate of culture. The American culture, even if its electoral and governmental system were to join the 20th century, is too individualistic to tolerate the strictures of corporatism.

We can certainly scrap primary elections, since they are really only a couple of decades old. Our institutional memory is so short that we presume that the primary method of nomination is embedded in our democratic culture. So immediately has the presidential primary become a way of life that any scheme to tamper with it provokes patriotic outrage. Senator Paul Simon, busily competing in Democratic primaries in an endeavor to be his party's nominee, wrote that suggestions to eliminate primary elections would "trash the democratic principles upon which our nation was founded."[12] If a United States senator and presidential aspirant can be so obtuse, what of the rest of us?

HOW TO REASON WITHOUT IDEOLOGY

What *should* government do? About what? I start with the assumption that government should give people the means to pursue their private aspirations. It is foolish to reject individual hopes, to try to remake human nature. Presumably, for example, we want to get ahead. But what good is individual wealth if a country is destablized by continuous violence because of serious discrepancies in the distribution of wealth? For that matter, what about the morality of extremes of wealth and poverty (both within and between nations)? We know that poverty cannot be eliminated (and politicians that tell us it can should be sent packing). But we also know that since the corporatist systems are ascendant, the old slogan "Government that governs least governs best" is as meaningless as the silly epithets of socialism. In an international market, governments can and should help their businesses compete. Markets and government are not incompatible concepts.

In thinking of government, economics, social problems, and so on, use a simple analogy. If you break your arm, any physician can fix it. The malady is easily diagnosed, and the cure is straightforward. But suppose you wake up with free-floating anxiety, depression, and strong suicidal urges. Depending on your choice of physicians, psychologists, naturopaths, faith healers, or medicine men, you will be told that you hated your father, that you have guilt because of repressed sexual longing for your mother, that you should exercise more, that you should drink tea rather than coffee, that you should take two tablets of Valium and Elavil and call in the morning, that you should learn to relax by meditation, that you must vomit out the evil spirits, or that you should give the guru all your money.

Governments can fix broken arms: they can explore space, build interstate highway systems, construct mass transit, and reduce pollution. Governments are less able to cure the political or economic equivalent of free-floating anxiety. Improvement in the quality of life, when it occurs, is incremental. Eschew utopianism. Also avoid the symbols of either-or ideology: Nicaraguan rebels are not "freedom fighters," and Sandinistas are not "idealistic reformers." Sidestep exploitation by ideologues of left or right. Look beyond slogans to reality. Developing your independent powers of analysis can help you resist the flood tide of rhetoric, the symbolic posturing of politicians and academics.

Be wary of those who promise to solve society's problems with the stroke of a pen: to end racism, eliminate poverty, cure the sick, prevent crime, clean the air and water, provide new energy, all without increasing governmental costs or restricting individual freedom. There are no simple solutions. Beware those who know who "they" (Jews, capitalists, socialists, the youth, the power structure) are and how to get rid of them. There is no "they".

Learn to think and analyze information systematically, not anecdotally. In fact, no mind frame is more difficult to eliminate or more of an impediment to understanding than the use of anecdotal information to generalize. Ronald Reagan was a great master at this. Are blacks trapped in poverty? His yard man was not. How many welfare recipients drive Cadillacs? Are the English sick of Margaret Thatcher? The person I met on the subway is. The propensity to build up generalizations from our own experiences is overcome by asking if they are typical. Of course, nobody's singular experiences are typical. For instance, the statement that blacks are three times more likely than whites to vote for Democrats can be met, wrongly, by the remark, "I know a black family that always votes Republican." We must examine the behavior of *representative samples* rather than generalizing on the basis of a few cases.

For example, if governments are obligated to defend us against violent death, should capital punishment be used as a deterrent to murder? We know that there is no evidence to support the conclusion that capital punishment deters murderers. But so what? Perhaps you want the death penalty because you think it is *morally* right. What is right for you is, irrespective of data, what is right for you. But learn to distinguish between what *is* (empirical theory) and what *ought to be* (normative theory). Normative theories cannot be disproved. There is no way to measure the legitimacy of normative theory. So on the subject of the death penalty, believe in it because you want to, not because it deters crime. Does pornography cause violent crime? Serial killer Ted Bundy said so, but he was wrong. Do you want to ban pornography because it is morally offensive? Get on with it, but ban it because you dislike it, not because it causes mayhem. Does abortion damage the psychological stability of those who undergo it? It may have upset your sister, but representative samples do not support this idea. Oppose abortion because it is morally wrong, if you believe this to be so.

Finally, listen to George McGovern, Democratic presidential nominee in 1972, temporary conscience of the people, and idol of Shirley MacLaine. He wrote: "No one living in a democracy should take himself or his special cause too seriously. The glory of America lies in its diversity and in its tolerance of competing convictions."[13] No one has said it better.

FOR FURTHER CONSIDERATION

1. What is selective perception. How does ideology relate to it?
2. Why does capitalism lack the emotional appeal of communism or socialism?
3. Why does the text argue that American political institutions are "outmoded?"
4. Why is anecdotal information inimical to rational political discourse?

For the More Adventurous

1. Return to the list of countries created since World War II (Chapter 2). Classify them according to the criteria presented in this book. What to you adduce? Aristotle believed the optimum form of government to be aristocracy, in which the "best" (the few) exercise power in the "interests of all." Would he approve?

2. In response to a suggestion for elections, the Cuban foreign minister retorted: "The Cuban People chose their destiny thirty years ago." An American political analyst claimed "The American people desire a foreign policy which is didactic and instructive." An interest group leader asserted ". . . women will never obey a law that says abortion is illegal." What do these three statements have in common?

3. The government of Poland has established new election rules which will allow 38 percent of the seats in the lower house to go to the Communist Party, 38 percent to the labor union, Solidarity, and the rest to be open. What assumptions about "political man" are best illustrated by this scheme?

4. Prepare a list of four statements of political relationships. These should be relationships between variables which you believe to be empirically correct (capital punishment deters homicide; abortion causes psychological damage to the mother; capitalist economies are more exploitative than socialist ones; traditional societies accept authority; young people vote like their parents; power corrupts, and so on).[14] Try to disprove each of them.

5. Is this book authored by: a philosopher (one who is concerned about what government *ought* to do, what its goals *should* be), an advocate (one who seeks to persuade others to adopt some course of action they have determined to be right and proper), or a researcher (one concerned with describing the workings of the political system, without caring who will gain or lose by this knowledge)?[15] Is this course *taught* by a philosopher, advocate, or researcher? Are *you* are philosopher, advocate, or researcher? Can these roles be mutually supportive? or are they incompatible?

NOTES

1. Daniel Bell, *The End of Ideology* (New York: Collier, 1961), p. 393.
2. V. I. Lenin, "The Economic Base of the Withering Away of the State," in *State and Revolution*; ed. V. I. Lenin (Moscow: Foreign Languages Publishing House, 1968), p. 233. (Originally published 1932.)
3. Robert Nisbet, *Prejudices* (Cambridge, Mass.: Harvard University Press, 1982), p. 183.
4. Leon Festinger, *A Theory of Cognitive Dissonance* (Stanford, Calif.: Stanford University Press, 1957).
5. Michael Novak, *The Spirit of Democratic Capitalism* (New York: Simon & Schuster), p. 31.
6. Thomas R. Dye and Harmon Zeigler, "Socialism and Militarism," in *Political Science and Politics* (forthcoming).
7. Michael W. Doyle, "Liberalism and World Politics," *American Political Science Review* 80 (December 1986): 1151–1170.
8. "The Issue Agenda," *Media Monitor*, February 1989, p. 2.
9. Laurence I. Barrett, "Oh What a Screwy System," *Time*, January 25, 1988, p. 20.
10. Alan Ehrenhalt, "Picking Presidents: A Nomination for Change," *Congressional Quarterly*, June 27, 1987, p. 1415.
11. Paul Kennedy, *The Rise and Fall of the Great Powers* (New York: Random House, 1987), p. 524.

12. Paul Simon, personal communication, January 11, 1988.
13. George McGovern, from his syndicated column of January 11, 1985.
14. See William Buchanan, *Understanding Political Variables*, fourth edition (New York: Macmillan, 1988), p.8.
15. The terms are Buchanan's, in ibid., p. 10.

FOR FURTHER READING

Aganbegyan, Abel, *Perestroika, 1989*. New York: Scribner, 1989. A good guess about the future of the USSR.

Bernstein, Robert A., and James A. Dyer. *An Introduction to Political Science Methods*. Englewood Cliffs, N.J.: Prentice-Hall, 1984. Bonehead statistics, probably about right for most of us. Very good on using more than two variables.

Brown, Robert. *Explanation in Social Science*. Hawthorne, N.Y.: Aldine, 1963.

Buchanan, William. *Understanding Political Variables*. New York: Macmillan, 1988. How to study and analyze politics and avoid the errors induced by common sense.

Buena de Mesquita, Bruce. *The War Trap*. New Haven, Conn.: Yale University Press, 1981; and "The War Trap Revisited," *American Political Science Review* 79 (1985): 157–176. "Rational" man and selective perception reconciled.

Connoly, William. *Political Science and Ideology*. New York: Atherton, 1967.

Doane, David P. *Exploring Statistics with the IBM PC*. Reading, Mass.: Addison-Wesley, 1988. If you buy the floppy disk, you will be a whiz in no time.

Eckstein, Arthur M. *Senate and General: Individual Decision Making and Roman Foreign Relations, 264–194* B.C. Berkeley: University of California Press, 1987. Rome lurches toward decline, unable to develop coherent policy because of the decline of political authority. Sound familiar?

Festinger, Leon. *A Theory of Cognitive Dissonance*. Stanford, Calif.: Stanford University Press, 1957. How strong beliefs make fools of us.

Finifter, Ada W. *Political Science: The State of the Discipline*. Washington, D.C.: American Political Science Association, 1983. These essays show political scientists at their best.

Kennedy, Paul. *The Rise and Fall of the Great Powers*. New York: Random House, 1987. If decline is inevitable, relax and enjoy it. If we seek to avoid or delay it, we have to mend our political ways.

Lodge, George C., and Ezra F. Vogel. *Ideology and National Competitiveness: An Analysis of Nine Countries*. Boston: Harvard Business School Press, 1987. A country's ideology shapes its ability to compete in an international market.

Ogilvy, G. Stanley, and John T. Anderson. *Excursions in Number Theory*. New York: Oxford University Press, 1966. An excellent exposition on the Fibonacci sequence and its applications to social science.

Oxford Analytica. *America in Perspective*. Boston: Houghton Mifflin, 1986. American Express, Bristol-Myers, and Sun Oil commissioned a group of Oxford scholars to project economic, political, and psychological trends for a decade. They show us the information they used and how they used it.

Tarbachnick, Barbara, and Linda S. Fidell. *Using Multivariate Statistics*. New York: Harper & Row, 1983. "But there are *so many* variables." True, and this book shows you how to account for them. Human behavior is, mercifully, not random.

Wolfe, Tom. *The Purple Decade*. New York: Farrar, Straus & Giroux, 1982. Contains "Those

Radical Chic Evenings,'' which mercilessly parodied Leonard Bernstein's fascination with Black Panthers and propelled Wolfe into popular fame but exile from the establishment.

Zajonic, R. B. ''Feeling and Thinking: Preferences Need No Inferences,'' *American Psychologist 39* (1980): 151–175.

Index

Terms and page numbers in bold indicate where in the book those terms are defined.